Joel Whitburn's MUSIC STARS

**Brief Bios of Every
Recording Artist Who Ever Charted**

Hal Leonard Corporation
New York

Copyright © 2009 by Joel Whitburn

All rights reserved. No part of this book may be reproduced in any form, without written permission, except by a newspaper or magazine reviewer who wishes to quote brief passages in connection with a review.

Published in 2009 by Hal Leonard Books
An Imprint of Hal Leonard Corporation
7777 West Bluemound Road
Milwaukee, WI 53213

Trade Book Division Editorial Offices
19 West 21st Street, New York, NY 10010

Printed in the United States of America

Book design by Jeanne Olynick

Library of Congress Cataloging-in-Publication Data is available upon request.

ISBN 978-0-89820-176-5

www.halleonard.com

A+
Born Andre Levins on 8/29/1982 in Hempstead, Long Island, New York. Teenage rapper.

AALIYAH
Born Aaliyah Dana Haughton on 1/16/1979 in Brooklyn, New York; raised in Detroit, Michigan. Died in a small Cessna plane crash in the Bahamas on 8/25/2001 (age 22). Female R&B singer/actress. Acted in the movies *Romeo Must Die* and *Queen Of The Damned*. Married R. Kelly at age 15 on 7/31/1994 (marriage later annulled).

ABBA
Pop group formed in Stockholm, Sweden: Anni-Frid "Frida" Lyngstad (born on 11/15/1945) and Agnetha Faltskog (born on 4/5/1950; vocals), Bjorn Ulvaeus (born on 4/24/1945; guitar) and Benny Andersson (born on 12/16/1946; keyboards). All members born in Sweden, except Frida who was born in Norway. ABBA is an acronym of members' first initials. Benny and Bjorn recorded together in 1966. Bjorn and Agnetha were married from 1971-79. Benny and Frida were married from 1978-81. Disbanded in 1982. Bjorn and Benny co-wrote the musical project *Chess* with Tim Rice (featuring "One Night In Bangkok"). The smash Broadway musical *Mamma Mia!* features the music of Abba.

ABBEY TAVERN SINGERS, The
Traditional Irish group that performed at The Abbey Tavern near Dublin, Ireland: Margaret Monks, Michael O'Connell, Mary Sheehan, Brian O'Rourke, John O'Brien, Bill Powers, Tommy Rick, Seamus Gallagher, Joe O'Leary and Paddy Downes.

ABBOTT, Billy, & The Jewels
Born William Vaughn in Camden, New Jersey (changed last name so as not to be confused with orchestra leader Billy Vaughn). First recorded on ABC-Paramount in 1962 with the R&B group The Corvells ("Take My Love"). The Jewels were actually Parkway Records vocal group The Tymes.

ABBOTT, Gregory
Born on 4/2/1954 in Harlem, New York. R&B singer/ songwriter (wrote and produced both of his hits). Formerly married to Freda Payne.

ABC
Electro-pop/dance group from Sheffield, Yorkshire, England: Martin Fry (vocals), Mark White (guitar), Stephen Singleton (sax), Mark Lickley (bass) and David Palmer (drums). At the end of 1983, the latter three left, leaving duo of Fry and White.

ABDUL, Paula
Born on 6/19/1962 in San Fernando, California. Pop-dance singer/choreographer. Former cheerleader for the NBA's Los Angeles Lakers. Choreographed Janet Jackson's *Control* videos and Tracey Ullman's TV show. Started own Captive label. Married to actor Emilio Estevez from 1992-94. Starred in the 1997 TV movie *Touched By Evil*. One of the judges on TV's *American Idol*.

AB LOGIC
Techno-rave studio group assembled by Belgian producers Jacko Bultinck and Peter Gillis, featuring singer Marianne and rapper K-Swing.

ABRAMS, Miss
Born Rita Abrams on 8/30/1943 in Cleveland, Ohio. Taught grade school in Mill Valley, California.

A.B. SKHY
Rock band from San Francisco, California: Dennis Geyer (vocals, guitar), Howard Wales (keyboards), Jim Marcotte (bass) and Terry Andersen (drums).

ABSTRAC'
Female dance trio from the Bronx, New York: Mary, Marsha and Topaz.

ACCENTS, The
R&B vocal group from Philadelphia, Pennsylvania: Robert Draper (lead), Robert Armstrong, Billy Hood, James Jackson, Arvid Garrett and Israel Goudeau. Garrett had been in the R&B vocal group Three Sharps & A Flat.

AC/DC
Hard-rock group from Sydney, Australia: brothers Angus and Malcolm Young (guitars), Ron Belford "Bon" Scott (vocals), Mark Evans (bass) and Phil Rudd (drums). Cliff Williams replaced Evans in 1977. Bon Scott died of alcohol abuse on 2/19/1980 (age 33) and was replaced by Brian Johnson. Simon Wright replaced Rudd in 1985. Wright joined Dio in 1989; replaced by Chris Slade of The Firm. Rudd returned in 1995. Angus and Malcolm are the younger brothers of George Young of The Easybeats and Flash & The Pan.

ACE
Pop-rock band formed in London, England: Paul Carrack (vocals), Phil Harris and Alan King (guitars), Terry Comer (bass) and Fran Byrne (drums). Disbanded in 1977. Carrack joined Squeeze in 1981, then Mike + The Mechanics in 1985.

ACE, Johnny
Born John Alexander on 6/9/1929 in Memphis, Tennessee. Shot himself playing Russian Roulette backstage at the City Auditorium in Houston, Texas, on 12/24/1954; died the following day (age 25). R&B singer/pianist/organist/songwriter. Worked with the B.B. King band, then formed The Beale Streeters with Bobby Bland and Earl Forest before going solo.

ACE HOOD
Born Antoine McColister in Deerfield Beach, Florida. Male rapper.

ACE OF BASE
Pop-dance group from Gothenburg, Sweden: vocalists/sisters Jenny (born on 5/19/1972) and Linn (born on 10/31/1970) Berggren with keyboardists Jonas "Joker" Berggren (born on 3/21/1967; their brother) and Ulf "Buddha" Ekberg (born on 12/6/1970).

ACE SPECTRUM
R&B vocal group from Harlem, New York: Ed Zant, Aubrey Johnson, Elliot Isaac and Rudy Gay.

ACKLIN, Barbara
Born on 2/28/1943 in Oakland, California; raised in Chicago, Illinois. Died of pneumonia on 11/27/1998 (age 55). R&B singer/songwriter. Cousin to Monk Higgins, who produced her first sessions for Special Agent in 1966 (as Barbara Allen). Backup vocalist at Chess Records in the mid-1960s. Formerly married to Eugene Record of The Chi-Lites.

ADAMS, Bryan
Born on 11/5/1959 in Kingston, Ontario, Canada. Rock singer/songwriter/guitarist. Lead singer of Sweeney Todd in 1976. Teamed with Jim Vallance in 1977 in songwriting partnership. Cameo appearance in the movie *Pink Cadillac.*

ADAMS, Faye
Born Faye Tuell in 1923 in Newark, New Jersey. Joined the Joe Morris Blues Cavalcade in late 1952. Recorded with Morris on Atlantic as "Fay Scruggs."

ADAMS, Johnny
Born Lathan John Adams on 1/5/1932 in New Orleans, Louisiana. Died of cancer on 9/14/1998 (age 66). R&B singer nicknamed "The Tan Canary." First recorded on the Ric label in 1959 with "I Won't Cry."

ADAMS, Oleta
Born on 5/4/1962 in Seattle, Washington; raised in Yakima, Washington. Female R&B singer/pianist. Backing singer on Tears For Fears' *Seeds Of Love* album and tour.

ADAMS, Yolanda
Born on 8/27/1962 in Houston, Texas. Black female gospel singer.

ADDERLEY, "Cannonball"
Born Julian Adderley on 9/15/1928 in Tampa, Florida. Died of a stroke on 8/8/1975 (age 46). Nickname derived from "cannibal," in tribute to his love of eating. Alto saxophonist/leader of jazz combo featuring brother Nat Adderley (cornet) and Joe Zawinul (piano; left in 1971 to form Weather Report; replaced by George Duke).

ADDRISI BROTHERS, The
Pop singing/songwriting duo from Boston, Massachusetts. Dick was born on 7/4/1941. Don was born on 12/14/1938; died on 11/11/1984 (age 45). Wrote The Association's "Never My Love."

ADKINS, Trace
Born Tracy Adkins on 1/13/1962 in Springhill, Louisiana; raised in Sarepta, Louisiana. Male country singer/songwriter/guitarist.

AD LIBS, The
Black doo-wop group from Newark, New Jersey: Mary Ann Thomas (lead), Hugh Harris, Danny Austin, Norman Donegan and Dave Watt. First recorded for T-Kay in 1962. Originally called the Creators.

ADVENTURES, The
Pop group from Belfast, Ireland: Terry Sharpe (vocals), husband-and-wife Patrick (guitar) and Eileen (vocals) Gribben, Gerard "Spud" Murphy (guitar), Tony Ayre (bass) and Paul Crowder (drums).

ADVENTURES OF STEVIE V
Black dance group from Bedfordshire, England. Assembled by producer Stevie Vincent. Includes singer Melodie Washington and multi-instrumentalist Mick Walsh.

AEROSMITH
Hard-rock band formed in Boston, Massachusetts: Steven Tyler (vocals; born Steven Tallarico on 3/26/1948), Joe Perry (guitar; born on 9/10/1950), Brad Whitford (guitar; born on 2/23/1952), Tom Hamilton (bass; born on 12/31/1951) and Joey Kramer (drums; born on 6/21/1950). Perry left for own Joe Perry Project in 1979; replaced by Jimmy Crespo. Whitford left in 1981; replaced by Rick Dufay. Original band reunited in April 1984. Tyler's daughter is actress/model Liv Tyler.

AFI
Hardcore punk-rock band formed in Ukiah, California: Davey "Havok" Marchand (vocals), Jade Puget (guitar), Hunter Burgan (bass) and Adam Carson (drums). AFI: A Fire Inside.

AFRIQUE
R&B-jazz studio group formed in Los Angeles, California: David T. Walker and Arthur Wright (guitars), Charles Kynard (organ), Joe Kelso, Paul Jeffery and Steve Kravitz (horns), King Errisson, Paul Humphrey, Wallace Snow, Charles Taggart and Chino Valdes (percussion), Chuck Rainey (bass) and Ray Pound (drums).

AFROMAN
Born Joseph Foreman on 7/28/1974 in Los Angeles, California; later based in Hattiesburg, Mississippi. Novelty rapper/songwriter.

AFTERNOON DELIGHTS, The
Female studio vocal group from Boston, Massachusetts: Rebecca Hall, Suzanne Boucher, Janet Powell and Robalee Barnes. Group named after Starland Vocal Band's #1 hit from 1976.

AFTERS, The
Christian pop-rock band from Mesquite, Texas: Josh Havens (vocals, guitar), Matt Fuqua (guitar), Brad Wigg (bass) and Marc Dodd (drums).

AFTER 7
R&B vocal trio from Indianapolis, Indiana: Keith Mitchell with brothers Melvin and Kevon Edmonds. Keith is the cousin of Mark "L.A. Reid" Rooney. Kevon and Melvin are the brothers of Babyface. Keith left in 1997.

AFTERSHOCK
Hip-hop duo from Staten Island, New York: rapper Guy Charles Routte and singer Jose Rivera.

AFTER THE FIRE
Rock group from England: Andy Piercy (vocals, bass), John Russell (guitar), Peter Banks (keyboards/guitar; Yes, Flash) and Pete King (drums).

AGUILERA, Christina
Born on 12/18/1980 in Staten Island, New York (Irish mother; Ecuadorian father); raised in Wexford, Pennsylvania. Pop-dance singer/songwriter. Regular on TV's *The Mickey Mouse Club* (1992-93).

A-HA
Pop trio from Oslo, Norway: Morten Harket (vocals), Pal Waaktaar (guitar) and Magne "Mags" Furuholmen (keyboards).

AHMAD
Born Ahmad Lewis on 10/12/1975 in Los Angeles, California. Male hip-hop artist. Member of 4th Avenue Jones'.

AIKEN, Clay
Born on 11/30/1978 in Chapel Hill, North Carolina. White male vocalist. Finished in second place on the 2003 season of TV's *American Idol.*

AIR SUPPLY
Pop vocal duo from Melbourne, Australia: Russell Hitchcock (born on 6/15/1949 in Melbourne) and Graham Russell (born on 6/1/1950 in Nottingham, England). Their regular backing band included David Moyse and Rex Goh (guitars), Frank Esler-Smith (keyboards), David Green (bass) and Ralph Cooper (drums).

AIRWAVES
Pop trio from Wales: Ray Martinez (vocals, guitar), John David (bass) and Dave Charles (drums).

AKENS, Jewel
Born on 9/12/1940 in Houston, Texas. Male R&B singer/producer.

AKON
Born Aliaune Thiam on 10/14/1981 in St. Louis, Missouri; raised in Dakar, Senegal; in 1988, moved with family to Jersey City, New Jersey. Male R&B singer/songwriter/producer.

ALABAMA
Country group from Fort Payne, Alabama: Randy Owen (vocals, guitar; born on 12/13/1949), Jeff Cook (keyboards, fiddle; born on 8/27/1949), Teddy Gentry (bass, vocals; born on 1/22/1952) and Mark Herndon (drums, vocals; born on 5/11/1955). Randy, Jeff and Teddy are cousins. Earlier incarnation of group known as Wildcountry, 1969-77.

ALAIMO, Chuck, Quartet
Rock and roll band from Rochester, New York: Chuck Alaimo (sax; died in November 1978, age 48), Tommy Rossi (drums), Pat Magnolia (bass) and Bill Irvine (piano).

ALAIMO, Steve
Born on 12/6/1939 in Omaha, Nebraska; raised in Rochester, New York. Star of TV's *Where The Action Is,* 1965-66. Member of The Unknowns. Appeared in the movies *Stanley* and *Wild Rebels.* President of Vision Records in Miami since 1987. Cousin of Jimmy Alaimo of The Mojo Men.

ALARM, The
Rock group from Rhyl, Wales: Mike Peters (vocals), Dave Sharp (guitar), Eddie MacDonald (bass) and Nigel Twist (drums).

ALBERT, Eddie
Born Edward Albert Heimberger on 4/22/1906 in Rock Island, Illinois. Died of pneumonia on 5/26/2005 (age 99). Played "Oliver Wendell Douglas" on TV's *Green Acres.*

ALBERT, Morris
Born Morris Albert Kaisermann on 9/7/1951 in Rio de Janeiro, Brazil. Adult Contemporary singer/songwriter.

ALBERTI, Willy
Born Carel Verbrugge on 10/14/1926 in Amsterdam, Netherlands. Died of cancer on 2/18/1985 (age 58).

AL B. SURE!
Born Albert Brown on 6/4/1969 in Boston, Massachusetts; raised in Mt. Vernon, New York. R&B singer/songwriter.

ALCHEMIST, The
Born Alan Maman in 1983 in Beverly Hills, California. White hip-hop singer/songwriter/producer.

ALDEAN, Jason
Born Jason Aldine Williams on 2/28/1977 in Macon, Georgia. Country singer/guitarist.

ALESSI
Pop duo of identical twin brothers Billy and Bobby Alessi. Born on 7/12/1953 in West Hempstead, New York.

ALEXANDER, Arthur
Born on 5/10/1940 in Florence, Alabama. Died of a heart attack on 6/9/1993 (age 53). R&B singer/songwriter. Teamed with Rick Hall in studio work at Muscle Shoals. First recorded for Judd in 1960. Only rock-era artist to have his compositions recorded by The Beatles, The Rolling Stones and Bob Dylan.

ALI, Tatyana
Born on 1/24/1979 in North Bellmore, Long Island, New York. R&B singer/actress. Played "Ashley Banks" on TV's *The Fresh Prince Of Bel-Air.*

ALIAS
Rock band formed in Los Angeles, California, by former Sheriff bandmates Freddy Curci (vocals) and Steve DeMarchi (guitar), with former Heart members Roger Fisher (guitar), Steve Fossen (bass) and Mike Derosier (drums).

ALICE DEEJAY
Techno-dance act from Amsterdam, Netherlands. Formed by producers Eelke Kalberg, Sebastiaan Molijn and DJ Jurgen. Fronted by female singer Judy with Gaby and Jane.

ALICE IN CHAINS
Male hard-rock band formed in Seattle, Washington: Layne Staley (vocals), Jerry Cantrell (guitar), Mike Starr (bass) and Sean Kinney (drums). Starr replaced by Mike Inez (former bassist for Ozzy Osbourne) by 1994. In 1995, Inez recorded with Slash's Snakepit and Staley recorded with Mad Season. Staley died of a drug overdose on 4/5/2002 (age 34).

ALICE WONDER LAND
Born Alice Faye Henderson. Discovered by songwriter Stephen Schlaks, the co-owner of Bardell Records (wrote Kenny Dino's "Your Ma Said You Cried In Your Sleep Last Night"). Alice was his neighbor's maid.

ALIEN ANT FARM
Rock band from Riverside, California: Dryden Mitchell (vocals), Terry Corso (guitar), Tye Zamora (bass) and Mike Cosgrove (drums).

ALISHA
Born in Brooklyn, New York. White female dance singer.

ALIVE AND KICKING
Pop-rock group from Brooklyn, New York: Pepe Cardona (male vocals) and Sandy Toder (female vocals), John Parisio (guitar), Bruce Sudano (organ), Thomas "Woody" Wilson (bass) and Vito Albano (drums). Sudano married Donna Summer on 7/16/1980 and was a member of Brooklyn Dreams.

ALKAHOLIKS, Tha
Rap trio from Los Angeles, California: James "J-Ro" Robinson, Rico "Tash" Smith and Eric "E-Swift" Brooks. Changed name to Tha Liks in 2001.

ALL-AMERICAN REJECTS, The
Punk-rock band from Stillwater, Oklahoma: Tyson Ritter (vocals, bass), Nick Wheeler (guitar), Mike Kennerty (guitar) and Chris Gaylor (drums).

ALLAN, Davie (And The Arrows)
Born in 1945 in Los Angeles, California. Began as a session guitarist for Mike Curb. While in high school at Van Nuys, California, Curb and Allan formed The Arrows, consisting of Allan (Fender lead guitar), Drew Bennett (bass), Mike Curb (keyboards; later replaced by Jared Hendler) and Larry Brown (drums).

ALLAN, Gary
Born Gary Allan Herzberg on 12/5/1967 in Montebello, California; raised in La Mirada, California. Country singer/songwriter/guitarist.

ALL CITY
Rap duo from Brooklyn, New York: J. Mega and Greg Valentine.

ALLEN, Deborah
Born Deborah Lynn Thurmond on 9/30/1953 in Memphis, Tennessee. Country singer/songwriter.

ALLEN, Donna
Born in Key West, Florida; raised in Tampa, Florida. R&B singer. Former cheerleader for the Tampa Bay Buccaneers.

ALLEN, Lee
Born on 7/2/1927 in Pittsburg, Kansas. Died of cancer on 10/18/1994 (age 67). Black saxophonist; played on hits by Fats Domino, Little Richard and others. Played tenor sax on The Blasters' first three albums.

ALLEN, Lily
Born on 5/2/1985 in Hammersmith, London, England. Female singer/songwriter.

ALLEN, Peter
Born Peter Allen Woolnough on 2/10/1944 in Tenterfield, Australia. Died of AIDS on 6/18/1992 (age 48). Cabaret-style performer/songwriter. Married to Liza Minnelli from 1967-73. Co-writer of "Arthur's Theme" and "I Honestly Love You."

ALLEN, Rex
Born on 12/31/1920 in Willcox, Arizona. Died after being struck by a car on 12/17/1999 (age 78). Western singer/guitarist/actor. Starred in numerous western movies in the 1950s. Narrator for numerous Walt Disney documentaries during the 1960s and 1970s. Own TV series, *Frontier Doctor*, in 1954.

ALLEN, Rex Jr.
Born on 8/23/1947 in Chicago, Illinois. Country singer/songwriter/guitarist. Son of Rex Allen. Traveled with his father from age six. Formed the groups the Townsmen and Saturday's Children. Hosted TNN's *Nashville On The Road* and worked as a regular performer on *The Statler Brothers Show*.

ALLEN, Richie
Born Richard Podolor in Los Angeles, California. Prolific record producer/songwriter. Also see The Hondells and The Pets.

ALLEN, Steve
Born on 12/26/1921 in Manhattan, New York; raised in Chicago, Illinois. Died of heart failure on 10/30/2000 (age 78). Comedian/actor/songwriter/author. In 1954, became the first host of TV's *The Tonight Show*. Played title role in the 1956 movie *The Benny Goodman Story*. Hosted own variety and talk shows, 1956-80. Married to actress Jayne Meadows.

ALLEY CATS, The
Black vocal group from Los Angeles, California: Bobby Sheen (of Bob B. Soxx & The Blue Jeans), Gary and Chester Pipkin, Sheridan Spencer, Brice Coefield and James Barker.

ALL-4-ONE
Male interracial vocal group from Los Angeles, California: Jamie Jones (born on 11/6/1974), Delious Kennedy (born on 12/21/1970), Alfred Nevarez (born on 5/17/1973) and Tony Borowiak (born on 10/12/1972).

ALLISON, Gene
Born on 8/29/1934 in Pegram, Tennessee; raised in Nashville, Tennessee. Died of liver failure on 2/28/2004 (age 69). R&B singer. First recorded for Calvert in 1956.

ALLISONS, The
American female group; not related to the British male duo.

ALLMAN, Gregg
Born on 12/8/1947 in Nashville, Tennessee; raised in Daytona Beach, Florida. Rock singer/organist. Founding member of The Allman Brothers Band. Married to Cher from 1975-77. Acted in the movie *Rush*.

ALLMAN BROTHERS BAND, The
Southern-rock group formed in Macon, Georgia: brothers Duane (lead guitar; born on 11/20/1946) and Gregg Allman (keyboards; born on 12/8/1947), Dickey Betts (guitar; born on 12/12/1943), Berry Oakley (bass; born on 4/4/1948), and the drum duo of Butch Trucks (born on 5/11/1947) and Jai Johnny Johanson (born on 7/8/1944). Duane and Gregg known earlier as the Allman Joys and Hour Glass.

ALLMAN BROTHERS BAND, The — cont'd
Duane was the top session guitarist at Muscle
Shoals studio; killed in a motorcycle crash on
10/29/1971 (age 24). Oakley died in another cycle
accident on 11/11/1972 (age 24); replaced by
Lamar Williams (died on 1/21/1983). Chuck Leavell
(keyboards) added in 1972. Group split up in 1976.
Gregg formed The Gregg Allman Band. Betts
formed Great Southern. Leavell, Williams and
Johanson formed the fusion-rock band Sea Level.
Allman and Betts reunited with a new Allman
Brothers lineup in 1978. Disbanded in 1981. Allman,
Betts, Trucks and Johanson regrouped with Warren
Haynes (guitar), Allen Woody (bass) and Johnny
Neel (keyboards) in 1989. Neel left in 1990;
replaced by Mark Quinones. Woody died on
8/26/2000 (age 44).

ALL SAINTS
Female interracial vocal group from London,
England: sisters Natalie and Nicky Appleton, with
Shaznay Lewis and Melanie Blatt.

ALL SPORTS BAND
Pop-rock group dressed up in various athletic
uniforms: Michael John Toste (vocals), Cy Sulack
(guitar), Chuck Kentis (keyboards), Alfonso Carey
(bass) and Jimmy "The Boxer" Clark (drums).

ALLURE
Female R&B vocal group from Long Island, New
York: Alia Davis, Akissa Mendez, Lalisha McLean
and Linnie Belcher.

ALMOND, Marc
Born Peter Mark Sinclair Almond on 7/9/1957 in
Southport, Lancashire, England. Male singer/song-
writer/multi-instrumentalist. One-half of Soft Cell duo.

ALPERT, Herb / The Tijuana Brass
Herb was born on 3/31/1935 in Los Angeles,
California. Trumpeter/bandleader/producer/
composer. Played trumpet since age eight. A&R for
Keen Records. Produced first Jan & Dean session.
Wrote "Wonderful World" hit for Sam Cooke.
Recorded as Dore Alpert in 1962. Formed A&M
Records with Jerry Moss in 1962. Used studio
musicians until early 1965, then formed own band.
Alpert and Moss formed the Almo Sounds label in
1994.

ALPHA TEAM
Electronic-rave duo from Chicago, Illinois: Dane
Roewade and D.J. Attack.

ALPHAVILLE
Male pop trio from Berlin, Germany: Marian Gold
(vocals), Frank Mertens (keyboards) and Bernhard
Lloyd (drums).

ALSTON, Gerald
Born on 11/8/1942 in North Carolina. Lead singer of
The Manhattans from 1971-88.

A.L.T. And The Lost Civilization
Born Al Trivette in Los Angeles, California. French-
Mexican rapper. Formerly with Latin Alliance.
A.L.T.: Another Latin Timebomb.

ALY & AJ
Teen pop vocal/songwriting duo from Torrance,
California: sisters Alyson "Aly" Michalka (born on
3/25/1989) and Amanda Joy "AJ" Michalka (born on
4/10/1991). Both are also actresses and appeared
in several TV shows.

AMANDA
Born Amanda Lameche in 1985 in France; raised in
Taby, Sweden. Female pop singer. Her sister, Anais
Lameche, is a member of Play.

AMAZING RHYTHM ACES, The
Country-rock group from Knoxville, Tennessee:
Howard Russell Smith (vocals, guitar), Barry "Byrd"
Burton (guitar), Billy Earhart III (keyboards), Jeff
Davis (bass) and David "Butch" McDade (drums).
Disbanded in 1980. McDade died of cancer on
11/29/1998 (age 52).

AMAZULU
Female reggae-styled trio formed in London,
England: Ann Marie Ruddock (vocals), Sharon
Bailey (percussion) and Lesley Beach (saxophone).

AMBER
Born Marie-Claire Cremers on 5/9/1969 in The
Netherlands; raised in Germany. Female dance
singer/songwriter.

AMBOY DUKES, The
Hard-rock band from Detroit, Michigan: John Drake
(vocals), Ted Nugent and Steve Farmer (guitars),
Rick Lober (keyboards), Bill White (bass) and Dave
Palmer (drums). Numerous personnel changes with
Nugent the only constant. Disbanded in 1975.

AMBROSIA
Pop group formed in Los Angeles, California: David
Pack (vocals, guitar), Joe Puerta (vocals, bass),
Christopher North (keyboards) and Burleigh
Drummond (drums). Group disbanded in 1984.
Puerta joined Bruce Hornsby & The Range.

AMERICA
Soft-rock trio formed in London, England: Dewey
Bunnell (born on 1/19/1952), Gerry Beckley (born
on 9/12/1952) and Dan Peek (born on 11/1/1950).
All played guitars and shared vocals. Met while in
school in England (all were sons of American
military personnel). Moved back to the U.S. in
February 1972. Continued as a duo after Peek left
in 1976 and became a popular Contemporary
Christian act.

AMERICAN BREED, The
Interracial pop-rock band from Chicago, Illinois:
Gary Loizzo (vocals, guitar), Al Ciner (guitar), Chuck
Colbert (bass) and Lee Graziano (drums). Later
members Kevin Murphy (keyboards) and Andre
Fischer (drums) went on to form Rufus.

AMERICAN COMEDY NETWORK, The
Group of former DJ's headed by Andy Goodman.
DJ Bob Rivers contributed song parodies to the
group.

AMERICAN FLYER
Soft-rock band formed in New York: Craig Fuller (Pure Prairie League), Eric Kaz (Blues Magoos), Steve Katz (Blood, Sweat & Tears) and Doug Yule (The Velvet Underground).

AMERICAN HI-FI
Male rock group from Boston, Massachusetts: Stacy Jones (vocals), Jaime Arentzen (guitar), Drew Parsons (bass) and Brian Nolan (drums). Jones was drummer with Letters To Cleo.

AMERIE
Born Amerie Rogers on 1/12/1980 in Fitchburg, Massachusetts (Korean mother; African-American father); raised in several different areas as miltary father traveled frequently, eventually settled in Washington DC. Female R&B singer/songwriter.

AMES, Ed
Born Edmund Urick on 7/9/1927 in Malden, Massachusetts. Lead singer of The Ames Brothers. Played the Native American "Mingo" on the TV series *Daniel Boone*.

AMES, Nancy
Born Nancy Alfaro in 1937 in Washington DC. Singer/actress. Her grandfather was president of Panama. Cast as the "TW3 Girl" on the American TV series *That Was The Week That Was*.

AMES BROTHERS, The
Pop vocal group from Malden, Massachusetts. Formed in 1947. Family name Urick. Consisted of lead singer Ed Ames (born on 7/9/1927) and his brothers Joe (born on 5/3/1921; died on 12/22/2007, age 86), Gene (born on 2/13/1923; died on 4/26/1997, age 74), and Vic (born on 5/20/1925; died in a car crash on 1/23/1978, age 52). Own TV series in 1955. Ed recorded solo and acted on Broadway and TV.

AMESBURY, Bill
Born in 1948 in Larder Lake, Ontario, Canada. Pop singer/songwriter/guitarist. Later had a sex change and known as Barbara Amesbury.

AMOS, Tori
Born Myra Ellen Amos on 8/22/1963 in Newton, North Carolina; raised in Baltimore, Maryland. Alternative pop-rock singer/songwriter/pianist.

ANA
Born Ana Rodriguez on 2/22/1972 in Cuba; raised in Orlando, Florida. Female dance singer.

ANAIS
Born Anais Martinez on 6/22/1984 in Santo Domingo, Dominican Republic; later based in the Bronx, New York. Female Latin singer. Winner on the second season of the Puerto Rican TV talent competition *Objetivo Fama*.

ANASTACIA
Born Anastacia Newkirk on 9/17/1973 in Brooklyn, New York; raised in Chicago, Illinois. Female pop-dance singer.

ANDERSON, Bill
Born James William Anderson III on 11/1/1937 in Columbia, South Carolina. Country singer/songwriter/actor. Hosted Nashville Network's TV game show *Fandango*. Known as "Whispering Bill."

ANDERSON, Elton
Born on 7/15/1928 in Lake Charles, Louisiana. Died on 10/25/2000 (age 72). Black singer who sang and played guitar with the Sid Lawrence Combo. Sid played bass guitar and was killed in a car crash in 1956.

ANDERSON, Ernestine
Born on 11/11/1928 in Houston, Texas. Jazz singer. Formerly with Eddie Heywood and Lionel Hampton.

ANDERSON, Jade
Born in 1981 in London, England. Female singer. Daughter of Jon Anderson (lead singer of Yes).

ANDERSON, Jesse
R&B singer/songwriter.

ANDERSON, John
Born on 12/13/1954 in Orlando, Florida; raised in Apopka, Florida. Country singer/songwriter/guitarist.

ANDERSON, Keith
Born on 1/12/1968 in Miami, Oklahoma. Country singer/songwriter/guitarist.

ANDERSON, Lale
Born on 3/23/1910 in Bremerhaven, Germany. Died on 8/29/1972 (age 62). Female singer.

ANDERSON, Lynn
Born on 9/26/1947 in Grand Forks, North Dakota; raised in Sacramento, California. Country singer. Daughter of country singer Liz Anderson. An accomplished equestrienne, Lynn was the California Horse Show Queen in 1966.

ANDERSON, Sunshine
Born on 10/26/1973 in Charlotte, North Carolina. Female R&B singer.

ANDREONE, Leah
Born on 5/24/1973 in San Diego, California. Female pop singer/pianist.

ANDRE 3000 OF OUTKAST
Born Andre Benjamin on 5/27/1975 in Atlanta, Georgia. Male rapper. One-half of OutKast duo.

ANDREWS, Chris
Born on 10/15/1938 in Romford, London, England. White male singer/songwriter.

ANDREWS, Jessica
Born on 12/29/1983 in Huntingdon, Tennessee. Country singer.

ANDREWS, Julie
Born Julia Wells on 10/1/1935 in Walton-on-Thames, England. Noted Broadway and movie actress. Starred in the acclaimed Broadway productions of *My Fair Lady* and *Camelot*. Won 1964's Best Actress Oscar for *Mary Poppins*.

ANDREWS, Lee (And The Hearts)
Born Arthur Lee Andrew Thompson in 1938 in Goldsboro, North Carolina; raised in Philadelphia, Pennsylvania. Formed vocal group The Hearts in 1952. First recorded for Rainbow in 1954. Group on Chess included Thomas "Butch" Curry, Ted Weems, Roy and Wendell Calhoun.

ANDREWS, Patty
Born on 2/26/1918 in Mound, Minnesota. Member of the Andrews Sisters. Appeared in 15 movies including *Private Buckaroo* (1942) and *Road To Rio* (1947).

ANDREWS, Ruby
Born Ruby Stackhouse on 3/12/1947 in Hollandale, Mississippi. R&B singer who sang backup with The C.O.D.'s in 1965.

ANGEL
Hard-rock group from Washington DC: Frank DiMino (vocals), Edwin "Punky" Meadows (guitar; The Cherry People), Gregg Giuffria (keyboards; Giuffria, House Of Lords), Mickey Jones (bass) and Barry Brandt (drums). Felix Robinson replaced Jones by 1978.

ANGEL, Ashley Parker
Born Ashley Ward Parker (stepfather's last name is Angel) on 8/1/1981 in Redding, California. Male pop singer/songwriter. Former member of O-Town.

ANGEL CITY
Dance studio trio: producers Bruce Elliot-Smith and Pete Hammond, with vocalist Lara McAllen.

ANGELICA
Born Angelica Garcia on 5/21/1972 in El Monte, California. Latin pop-dance singer.

ANGELINA
Born Angelina Camarillo in 1978 in Union City, California. Latin pop-dance singer/songwriter.

ANGELS, The
Female pop trio from Orange, New Jersey. Formed as The Starlets with sisters Phyllis "Jiggs" & Barbara Allbut, and Linda Jansen (lead singer). Jansen was replaced by Peggy Santiglia (later of Dusk) in 1962. Studio backing vocalists for Lou Christie and others in the mid-1960s. Barbara replaced by Lana Shaw, formerly of The Serendipity Singers. Peggy replaced by Debbie Swisher, formerly of The Pixies Three.

ANGELS & AIRWAVES
Alternative-rock band from San Diego, California: Tom DeLonge (vocals, guitar), David Kennedy (guitar), Ryan Sinn (bass) and Atom Willard (drums). DeLong is also a member of Blink-182. DeLong and Kennedy are also members of Box Car Racer. Sinn is also a member of The Distillers. Willard was a member of The Offspring from 2004-06.

ANIMALS, The
Rock band formed in Newcastle-upon-Tyne, England, as the Alan Price Combo. Consisted of Eric Burdon (vocals; born on 5/11/1941), Alan Price (keyboards; born on 4/19/1942), Bryan "Chas" Chandler (bass; born on 12/18/1938), Hilton Valentine (guitar; born on 5/21/1943) and John Steel (drums; born on 2/4/1941). Price left in May 1965; replaced by Dave Rowberry (died of heart failure on 6/6/2003, age 62). Chandler pursued a management career and discovered Jimi Hendrix in 1966; died in his sleep of an apparent heart attack on 7/17/1996 (age 57). Steel left in 1966; replaced by Barry Jenkins. Group disbanded in July 1968. After a period with War, Burdon and the other originals reunited in 1976 and again in 1983.

ANIMOTION
Techno-pop group formed in Los Angeles, California: Astrid Plane (female vocals), Bill Wadhams (male vocals, keyboards), Don Kirkpatrick (guitar), Charles Ottavio (bass) and Frency O'Brien (drums). Plane and Wadhams left by 1988, replaced by Cynthia Rhodes and Paul Engemann. Rhodes was an actress (in movies *Staying Alive* and *Dirty Dancing*). Engemann was formerly with Device. Rhodes married Richard Marx on 1/8/1989. Plane and Ottavio married on 10/13/1990.

ANKA, Paul
Born on 7/30/1941 in Ottawa, Ontario, Canada. Performer since age 12. Father financed first recording, "I Confess," on RPM 472 in 1956. Wrote "It Doesn't Matter Anymore" (Buddy Holly), "She's A Lady" (Tom Jones) and the English lyrics to "My Way" (Frank Sinatra). Also wrote theme for TV's *The Tonight Show*. Own TV variety show in 1973. Appeared in the 1959 movie *Girls Town*, the 1962 movie *The Longest Day* and the 1992 movie *Captain Ron*. Longtime popular entertainer in Las Vegas.

ANNETTE
Born Annette Funicello on 10/22/1942 in Utica, New York. Became America's most popular Mouseketeer after her debut on the TV series *The Mickey Mouse Club* in 1955. Acted in several teen movies in the early 1960s. Co-starred with Frankie Avalon in many movies, the last being *Back To The Beach* in 1987. Diagnosed with multiple sclerosis in 1987.

ANN-MARGRET
Born Ann-Margret Olsson on 4/28/1941 in Valsjöbyn, Jämtland, Sweden; raised in Wilmette, Illinois. Actress/dancer/singer. Starred in many movies (including *Viva Las Vegas* with Elvis Presley) and Broadway shows. Married Roger Smith on 5/8/1967.

ANOTHER BAD CREATION
Pre-teen R&B-rap vocal group from Atlanta, Georgia: Chris Sellers, Dave Shelton, Romell Chapman, with brothers Marliss and Demetrius Pugh. Appeared in the movie *The Meteor Man*.

ANT, Adam
Born Stuart Leslie Goddard on 11/3/1954 in London, England. Formed romantic-punk group Adam And The Ants in 1976. Three original Ants left to join Bow Wow Wow; Ant headed new lineup in 1980. Ant went solo in 1982. Acted in the movies *World Gone Wild* and *Slam Dance*, and several TV shows, including *The Equalizer*.

ANTELL, Pete
Born Peter Blaise Antonio in Queens, New York. Rock singer/songwriter. Later a composer for TV movies.

ANTHONY, Marc
Born Marco Antonio Muniz on 9/16/1968 in the Bronx, New York. Latin singer/actor. Starred in Paul Simon's Broadway musical *The Capeman* and in the movie *Bringing Out The Dead*. Married Jennifer Lopez on 6/5/2004.

ANTHONY, Ray
Born Raymond Antonini on 1/20/1922 in Bentleyville, Pennsylvania; raised in Cleveland, Ohio. Big band leader/trumpeter. Joined Al Donahue in 1939, then with Glenn Miller and Jimmy Dorsey from 1940-42. Led U.S. Army band. Own band in 1946. Own TV series in the 1950s. Appeared in the movie *Daddy Long Legs* with Fred Astaire in 1955. Wrote "Bunny Hop." Married to actress Mamie Van Doren from 1955-61.

ANYTHING BOX
Dance trio led by New Jersey native Claude Strilio (vocals) with Dania Morales and Paul Rijnders.

APACHE
Born Anthony Teaks in Jersey City, New Jersey. Male rapper.

APOLLONIA 6
Female R&B trio formed by Prince. Led by Patty "Apollonia" Kotero (co-star of movie *Purple Rain* and cast member of TV's *Falcon Crest*, 1985-86). With former Vanity 6 members Brenda Bennett and Susan Moonsie.

APOLLO 100
Studio group from England: Tom Parker, Clem Cattini, Vic Flick, Jim Lawless and Brian Odgers.

APPALACHIANS, The
Folk group. Included Priscilla Mitchell Hubbard (married to Jerry Reed) and Stan Robinson (father of Chris and Rich Robinson of The Black Crowes).

APPLE, Fiona
Born Fiona Apple Maggart on 9/13/1977 in Manhattan, New York. Adult Alternative pop-rock singer/songwriter/pianist. Daughter of singer Diane McAfee and actor Brandon Maggart.

APPLEJACKS, The
Studio band led by Dave Appell (born on 3/24/1922 in Philadelphia, Pennsylvania).

APRIL
Female dance singer April Kelly.

APRIL WINE
Rock band formed in Halifax, Nova Scotia, Canada: Myles Goodwyn (vocals, guitar), Brian Greenway and Gary Moffet (guitars), Steve Lang (bass) and Jerry Mercer (drums; Mashmakhan).

AQUA
Pop-dance group from Denmark: Lene Grawford Nystrom, Rene Dif, Claus Norreen and Soren Rasted.

AQUATONES, The
White doo-wop group formed in Valley Stream, Long Island, New York: Lynn Nixon and Larry Vannata (lead singers), David Goddard and Eugene McCarthy. Female lead Nixon trained as an operatic soprano; died in January 2001 (age 60).

ARBORS, The
Pop vocal group formed in Ann Arbor, Michigan, by two pairs of brothers: Edward and Fred Farran, and Scott and Tom Herrick. Edward Farran died of kidney failure on 1/2/2003 (age 64).

ARCADIA
Pop-rock trio from England: Duran Duran's Simon LeBon (vocals), Nick Rhodes (keyboards) and Roger Taylor (drums).

ARCHER, Tasmin
Born on 8/3/1963 in Bradford, Yorkshire, England (of Jamaican parentage). Black female singer.

ARCHIES, The
Studio group created by Don Kirshner; based on the Saturday morning cartoon television series. Lead vocalist Ron Dante (born Carmine Granito on 8/22/1945 in Staten Island, New York) was also the voice of The Cuff Links and co-producer of many of Barry Manilow's hits. All tunes written and produced by Jeff Barry, who was one-half of a prolific hit-writing partnership with his then-wife Ellie Greenwich. Other vocalists included Greenwich, Toni Wine, Tony Passalacqua and Andy Kim (who co-wrote four of their six hits). The cartoon characters' names are Archie, Betty, Veronica, Jughead and Reggie.

ARCHULETA, David
Born on 12/28/1990 in Miami, Florida; raised in Murray, Utah. Male singer. Finished in second place on the 2008 season of TV's *American Idol*.

ARDEN, Jann
Born Jann Arden Richards on 3/27/1962 in Calgary, Alberta, Canada. Female singer/songwriter.

ARDEN, Toni
Born Antoinette Aroizzone in Brooklyn, New York. Female vocalist. Sang with Al Trace in 1945 and Joe Reichman in 1946.

ARENA, Tina
Born Philopina Arena on 11/1/1967 in Melbourne, Australia. Female singer.

ARGENT
Rock group from England: Rod Argent (vocals, keyboards; The Zombies), Jim Rodford (bass; Argent's cousin), Robert Henrit (drums) and Russ Ballard (guitar; later a successful songwriter/producer). Henrit later joined Charlie. Rodford and Henrit were later with The Kinks.

ARKADE
Pop trio from Los Angeles, California: Michael Price, Dan Walsh and Austin Roberts (Buchanan Brothers).

ARMATRADING, Joan
Born on 12/9/1950 in St. Kitts, West Indies; raised in Birmingham, England. Black singer/songwriter/guitarist.

ARMEN, Kay
Born Armenuhi Manoogian on 11/2/1920 in Chicago, Illinois. Singer/actress. Appeared in the 1955 movie musical *Hit The Deck*.

ARMENIAN JAZZ SEXTET
New York-based group of Armenian descent: Aram Manoogian, Berge Minasian, Cory Tosoian, Eddie Arvanigian, Thomas Minasian and Arthur Melkonian.

ARMS, Russell
Born on 2/3/1922 in Berkeley, California. One of the regulars on TV's *Your Hit Parade*, 1952-57.

ARMSTRONG, Louis
Born Daniel Louis Armstrong on 8/4/1901 in New Orleans, Louisiana. Died of heart failure on 7/6/1971 (age 69). Nickname: "Satchmo." Joined the legendary band of Joe "King" Oliver in Chicago in 1922. By 1929, had become the most widely known black musician in the world. Influenced dozens of singers and trumpet players, both black and white. Numerous appearances on radio, TV and in movies.

ARNELL, Ginny
Born on 11/2/1942 in New Haven, Connecticut. Female singer.

ARNO, Audrey
Born Adrienne Medini on 3/7/1942 in Mannheim, West Germany. Female singer/actress. Bandleader Hazy Osterwald was born on 2/18/1922 in Bern, Switzerland. Both were German TV stars.

ARNOLD, Calvin
Born in Detroit, Michigan. R&B singer/songwriter.

ARNOLD, Eddy
Born Richard Edward Arnold on 5/15/1918 in Henderson, Tennessee. Died on 5/8/2008 (age 89). Became popular on Nashville's *Grand Ole Opry* as a singer with Pee Wee King (1940-43). Nicknamed "The Tennessee Plowboy."

AROUND THE WAY
R&B vocal trio from New York City, New York: Lena Fraticelli, Michael Bertot and Kashu Myles (from Jamaica). Also features rapper Kenny Diaz.

ARPEGGIO
Disco studio group assembled by producer Simon Soussan.

ARRESTED DEVELOPMENT
Hip-hop group from Atlanta, Georgia: Todd "Speech" Thomas, Dionne Farris, Aerle Taree, Tim Barnwell, Montsho Eshe, Rasa Don and Baba Oje.

ARRINGTON, Steve
R&B vocalist/drummer from Dayton, Ohio. Ex-member of Slave (1979-82).

ARTIE THE 1 MAN PARTY
Born Artie Yanez in Juarez, Mexico. Later moved to California. Dance DJ/producer/singer.

ARTISTICS, The
R&B vocal group formed in 1958 at Marshall High School in Chicago, Illinois. Backup work for Major Lance. First recorded for Okeh in 1963, with Curt Thomas, Larry Johnson, Jessie Bolian and Aaron Floyd. Lead singer Robert Dobyne added in 1963; replaced by Marvin Smith (ex-El Dorados) in 1964. Smith left in 1967, but sang on studio recordings. Other lead singers were Tommy Green and Fred Pettis. Disbanded in 1973. Bolian died on 8/24/1994 (age 53).

ARTISTS AGAINST AIDS
All-star group organized to benefit worldwide AIDS research. Featured performers include Christina Aguilera, Backstreet Boys, Mary J. Blige, Bono (U2), Destiny's Child, Eve, Nelly Furtado, Ja Rule, Alicia Keys, Jennifer Lopez, Nas, Nelly, *NSYNC, P. Diddy, Britney Spears and Gwen Stefani.

ARTISTS STAND UP TO CANCER
All-star female vocal gathering: Ashanti, Natasha Bedingfield, Beyoncé, Mary J. Blige, Mariah Carey, Ciara, Keyshia Cole, Sheryl Crow, Miley Cyrus, Melissa Etheridge, Fergie, Leona Lewis, Rihanna, LeAnn Rimes and Carrie Underwood.

ARTISTS UNITED AGAINST APARTHEID
Benefit group of 49 superstar artists formed to protest the South African apartheid government; proceeds went to political prisoners in South Africa. Organized by Little Steven and Arthur Baker. Featuring Pat Benatar, Bono (U2), Jackson Browne, Jimmy Cliff, Bob Dylan, Peter Gabriel, Bonnie Raitt, Lou Reed, Bruce Springsteen and many others.

ART N' SOUL
R&B trio from Oakland, California: Tracy (vocals, bass), Lattrel (keyboards) and Dion (drums).

ART OF NOISE, The
Techno-pop trio from England: Anne Dudley (keyboards), J.J. Jeczalik (keyboards, programmer) and Gary Langan (engineer). All three were part of Trevor Horn's production team in the early 1980s. Worked with ABC, Frankie Goes To Hollywood, Enigma and others. Disbanded in mid-1990.

ARVON, Bobby
Born Robert Arvonio on 9/13/1941 in Scranton, Pennsylvania. Singer/songwriter/pianist.

ASHANTI
Born Ashanti Douglas on 10/13/1980 in Glen Cove, Long Island, New York. Female hip-hop singer/songwriter.

ASHE, Clarence
Born in Memphis, Tennessee. R&B singer/songwriter.

ASHFORD & SIMPSON
Husband-and-wife R&B vocal/songwriting duo: Nickolas Ashford (born on 5/4/1942 in Fairfield, South Carolina) and Valerie Simpson (born on 8/26/1946 in Brooklyn, New York). Recorded as Valerie & Nick in 1964 ("Bubbled Under"). Team wrote for Chuck Jackson and Maxine Brown. Joined staff at Motown and wrote and produced many of the label's top stars. Valerie recorded solo in 1972. They married in 1974. Valerie sang female part on

ASHFORD & SIMPSON — cont'd
three Marvin Gaye/Tammi Terrell duets due to Terrell's ailing health.Valerie's brother, Ray Simpson, was the lead singer of Village People.

ASHTON, GARDNER & DYKE
Pop trio from England: Tony Ashton (vocals, keyboards), Kim Gardner (bass) and Roy Dyke (drums). Ashton died of cancer on 5/28/2001 (age 55). Gardner died of cancer on 10/24/2001 (age 53).

ASIA
All-star rock group from England: John Wetton (vocals, bass; King Crimson, Uriah Heep), Steve Howe (guitar; Yes), Geoff Downes (keyboards; Yes, The Buggles) and Carl Palmer (drums; Emerson, Lake & Palmer). Mandy Meyer (Krokus), replaced Howe in 1985. Pat Thrall (Automatic Man, Pat Travers Band, Hughes/Thrall) replaced Meyer in 1990.

ASSEMBLED MULTITUDE, The
Studio group from Philadelphia, Pennsylvania. Arranged by Tom Sellers (died on 3/9/1988 in a fire in his hometown of Wayne, Pennsylvania, age 39).

ASSOCIATION, The
Pop band from Los Angeles, California: Gary Alexander (born on 9/25/1943), Russ Giguere (born on 10/18/1943) and Jim Yester (born on 11/24/1939; guitars), Terry Kirkman (born on 12/12/1939; keyboards), Brian Cole (born on 9/8/1942; died of a drug overdose on 8/2/1972, age 29; bass) and Ted Bluechel (born on 12/2/1942; drums). All shared vocals. Larry Ramos (guitar) joined in 1967. Richard Thompson replaced Giguere in 1970.

ASTLEY, Jon
Born in Manchester, England. Noted rock producer (The Who, Eric Clapton and Corey Hart). No relation to Rick Astley.

ASTLEY, Rick
Born on 2/6/1966 in Newton-le-Willows, England. Pop singer/guitarist. No relation to Jon Astley.

ASTORS, The
R&B vocal group from Memphis, Tennessee: Curtis Johnson (lead), Eddie Stanback, Richard Harris and Sam Byrnes.

ASTRONAUTS, The
Surf-rock group from Boulder, Colorado. Guitarists Bob Demmon, Dennis Lindsey, Rich Fifield and Storm Patterson, with drummer Jim Gallagher. Fifield and Patterson share vocals. Lindsey died of heart failure in 1991.

ATARIS, The
Punk-rock band formed in Anderson, Indiana; later based in Santa Barbara, California: Kris Roe (vocals, guitar), John Collura (guitar), Mike Davenport (bass) and Chris Knapp (drums).

ATC
Pop vocal group: Joe (from New Zealand), Sarah (from Australia), Tracey (from England) and Livio (from Italy). ATC: A Touch of Class.

A*TEENS
Teen Abba tribute group from Stockholm, Sweden: Dhani Lennevald, Sara Lumholdt, Amit Paul and Marie Serenholt.

ATHENAEUM
Alternative-rock group from Greensboro, North Carolina: Mark Kano (vocals), Grey Brewster (guitar), Alex McKinney (bass) and Nic Brown (drums).

ATKINS, Chet
Born on 6/20/1924 in Luttrell, Tennessee. Died of cancer on 6/30/2001 (age 77). Revered guitarist. Began recording for RCA in 1947. Moved to Nashville in 1950 and became prolific studio musician/producer. RCA's A&R manager in Nashville from 1960-68; RCA Vice President from 1968-82.

ATKINS, Christopher
Born Christopher Atkins Bomann on 2/21/1961 in Rye, New York. Teen movie actor; starred in *The Blue Lagoon* and *The Pirate Movie*.

ATKINS, Rodney
Born on 3/28/1969 in Knoxville, Tennessee. Country singer/songwriter/guitarist.

ATLANTA DISCO BAND, The
Disco studio group from Atlanta, Georgia, assembled by producer Dave Crawford. Includes members of MFSB.

ATLANTA RHYTHM SECTION
Group formed by musicians from Studio One, Doraville, Georgia, in 1971. Consisted of Rodney Justo (vocals), Barry Bailey (born on 6/12/1948) and J.R. Cobb (guitars; born on 2/5/1944), Paul Goddard (bass; born on 6/23/1945), Dean Daughtry (keyboards; born on 9/8/1946) and Robert Nix (drums). Justo, Daughtry and Nix were with Roy Orbison's band, The Candymen. Cobb, Daughtry and band manager/producer Buddy Buie were with the Classics IV. Justo left after first album; replaced by Ronnie Hammond. Nix left in late 1979; replaced by Roy Yeager.

ATLANTIC STARR
Urban contemporary group from White Plains, New York: brothers David (guitar; born on 9/8/1958), Wayne (keyboards; born on 4/13/1957) and Jonathan (trumpet) Lewis, with Sharon Bryant (vocals; born on 8/14/1956), Cliff Archer (bass) and Porter Carroll (drums). Barbara Weathers replaced Bryant in 1984. Rachel Oliver replaced Weathers in 1991.

ATTITUDES
Group of top session musicians: David Foster (keyboards), Danny Kortchmar (guitar), Paul Stallworth (bass) and Jim Keltner (drums).

AUDIENCE
Rock group from London, England: Howard Werth (vocals, guitar), Keith Gemmell (sax), Trevor Williams (bass) and Tony Connor (drums).

AUDIOSLAVE
Rock band consisting of former Rage Against The Machine members Tom Morello (guitar), Tim Commerford (bass) and Brad Wilk (drums), with former Soundgarden leader Chris Cornell (vocals).

AUDREY
"Break-in" novelty production created by Plus label owner Samuel Kaufman (writer credit "C.B. Samuel" is actually Kaufman).

AUGER, Brian
Born on 7/18/1939 in London, England. Jazz-rock keyboardist.

AUGUSTANA
Alternative-rock band formed in Los Angeles, California: Dan Layus (vocals, guitar), Josiah Rosen (guitar), Jared Palomar (keyboards, bass) and Justin South (drums).

AURRA
R&B group from Ohio: Starleana Young and Curt Jones (vocals), Steve Washington and Tom Lockett, Jr. (saxophones), and Philip Fields (keyboards). All but Fields were members of Slave. Young and Jones later formed the duo Déja.

AUSTIN, Gene
Born on 6/24/1900 in Gainesville, Texas. Died on 1/24/1972 (age 71). Godfather of country singer David Houston.

AUSTIN, Johnta
Born on 6/28/1980 in Atlanta, Georgia. Male R&B singer/songwriter. Pronounced: john-TAY.

AUSTIN, Patti
Born on 8/10/1948 in Harlem, New York. R&B-jazz singer. Her father, Gordon, was a big band trombonist. Dinah Washington and Quincy Jones proclaimed themselves her godparents. Debuted at Harlem's Apollo Theatre at age four. Signed to a record contract with RCA at age five. By the late 1960s was a prolific session and commercial jingle singer. In the 1988 movie *Tucker*.

AUSTIN, Sherrie
Born on 8/28/1970 in Sydney, Australia; raised in Townsville, Australia. Country singer/actress. Played "Pippa McKenna" on TV's *The Facts Of Life* (1987-88). Former member of Colourhaus (as Sherrié Krenn).

AUSTIN, Sil
Born Sylvester Austin on 9/17/1929 in Dunnellon, Florida. Died of cancer on 9/1/2001 (age 71). R&B tenor saxophonist. Played with Tiny Bradshaw Band before forming own group.

AUTOGRAPH
Hard-rock band from Los Angeles, California: Steve Plunkett (vocals, guitar), Steve Lynch (guitar), Steven Isham (keyboards), Randy Rand (bass) and Keni Richards (drums).

AUTOMATIC MAN
Rock group formed in San Francisco, California, by Michael Shrieve (drums; Santana). Included Bayete (vocals, keyboards), Pat Thrall (guitar; Pat Travers Band,Hughes/Thrall, Asia) and Donni Harvey (bass).

AUTRY, Gene
Born Orvon Gene Autry on 9/29/1907 in Tioga, Texas. Died of respiratory failure on 10/2/1998 (age 91). The first cowboy singing star of the movies. Formed Challenge Records. Former owner of the California (Anaheim) Angels baseball team.

AVALON, Frankie
Born Francis Avallone on 9/18/1939 in Philadelphia, Pennsylvania. Teen idol managed by Bob Marcucci. Worked in bands in 1953 in Atlantic City, New Jersey. Performed on radio and TV with Paul Whiteman, mid-1950s. Singer/trumpet player with Rocco & His Saints in 1956, which included Bobby Rydell. Co-starred in many movies with Annette. Appeared in the movies *Jamboree!*, *Guns Of The Timberland*, and *The Alamo*. Owner of Frankie Avalon Products, a line of health supplement products.

AVANT
Born Myron Avant on 4/26/1976 in Cleveland, Ohio. Male R&B singer/songwriter. Played "Dexter" in the 2004 movie *Barbershop 2: Back In Business*.

AVANT-GARDE, The
Duo of Chuck Woolery and Elkin "Bubba" Fowler. Woolery was the original host of TV's *Wheel of Fortune* and *Love Connection*.

AVENGED SEVENFOLD
Hard-rock band from Huntington Beach, California: Matt "M. Shadows" Sanders (vocals), Brian "Synyster Gates" Haner (guitar), Zach "Zacky Vengeance" Baker (guitar), John "Johnny Christ" Seward (bass) and Jimmy "The Rev" Sullivan (drums).

AVENTURA
Latin group from the Bronx, New York (originally from the Dominican Republic): Anthony Santos, Lenny Santos, Max Santos and Henry Santos Jeter (none are related).

AVERAGE, Johnny, Band
Born Mick Hodgkinson on 9/17/1946 in Rainworth, Nottinghamshire, England. Died of cancer on 6/19/2007 (age 60). Rock guitarist. His wife, Nikki Wills, was the featured vocalist.

AVERAGE WHITE BAND (AWB)
White funk group from Scotland: Alan Gorrie (vocals, bass), Onnie McIntyre (guitar, vocals), Hamish Stuart (guitar, vocals), Malcolm Duncan (sax), Roger Ball (sax, keyboards) and Robbie McIntosh (drums). Gorrie and McIntyre were members of Forever More. McIntosh died of a drug overdose on 9/23/1974 (age 24); replaced by Steve Ferrone. McIntosh and Ferrone were members of Brian Auger's Oblivion Express. Stuart later joined Paul McCartney's touring band.

AVILA, Bobby Ross
Born on 3/7/1975 in San Bernardino, California. R&B singer/songwriter.

AXE
Rock band from Gainesville, Florida: Bobby Barth (vocals, guitar), Michael Osborne (guitar), Edgar Riley (keyboards), Wayne Haner (bass) and Ted Mueller (drums). Disbanded in 1984. Group made the Adult Contemporary chart in 1976 as Babyface. Osborne died in a car crash on 7/21/1984 (age 34).

AXTON, Hoyt
Born on 3/25/1938 in Duncan, Oklahoma. Died of a heart attack on 10/26/1999 (age 61). Son of songwriter Mae Axton ("Heartbreak Hotel"; died on 4/16/1997, age 82). Appeared in the movies *The Black Stallion* and *Gremlins*. Wrote hits "Greenback Dollar" for The Kingston Trio, "The Pusher" for Steppenwolf, and "Joy To The World" and "Never Been To Spain" for Three Dog Night. Started own Jeremiah label in 1978.

AYERS, Roy
Born on 9/10/1940 in Los Angeles, California. R&B-jazz vibraphone player/keyboardist/vocalist. With Herbie Mann from 1966-70. In 1970, formed Ubiquity whose guest players included drummer Billy Cobha, guitarist {George Benson, trombonist Wayne Henderson (The Crusaders) and vocalist Dee Dee Bridgewater.

AZ
Born Anthony Cruz in Brooklyn, New York. Male rapper. First pressings show artist as AZ The Visualiza.

AZAR, Steve
Born on 4/11/1964 in Greenville, Mississippi. Country singer/songwriter/guitarist.

AZUL AZUL
Latin group from Bolivia: Fabio Zambrana (vocals), Ricardo Fries (guitar), Ademar Villagomez (bass) and Boris Anzoategui (drums).

AZ YET
R&B vocal group from Philadelphia, Pennsylvania: Dion Allen, Darryl Anthony, Marc Nelson, Shawn Rivera and Kenny Terry.

BABY BASH
Born Ronald Bryant on 10/18/1975 in Vallejo, California; raised in Houston, Texas. Latin male rapper.

BABY / BIRDMAN
Born Bryan Williams on 2/15/1969 in New Orleans, Louisiana. Male rapper/songwriter. Co-founder of Cash Money Records. Member of Big Tymers and Cash Money Millionaires. Nicknamed "Da #1 Stunna." Also records as Birdman.

BABY BOY DA PRINCE
Born in 1986 in New Orleans, Louisiana. Male rapper.

BABYFACE
Born Kenneth Edmonds on 4/10/1959 in Indianapolis, Indiana. R&B vocalist/instrumentalist/songwriter. Formerly with Manchild and The Deele. Dubbed "Babyface" by Bootsy Collins. Brother of Melvin and Kevon Edmonds of After 7. Also did production work for Paula Abdul, Bobby Brown, The Boys, The Jacksons, Midnight Star and Karyn

White; co-founder of LaFace Records in Atlanta in 1989. Babyface's wife, Tracey, was president of Yab Yum Records. Also see Milestone.

BABY JANE & THE ROCKABYES
Black female vocal group from the Bronx, New York: Madelyn "Baby Jane" Moore, Yvonne DeMunn, Estelle McEwan and Yolanda Robinson. Name inspired by the movie *Whatever Happened To Baby Jane*. Also recorded as The Elektras (Bubbled Under in 1963 with "All I Want To Do Is Run").

BABY RAY
Born Raymond Eddlemon in New Orleans, Louisiana. Male R&B singer.

BABYS, The
Rock group from England: John Waite (vocals), Walt Stocker (guitar), Mike Corby (guitar, keyboards) and Tony Brock (drums). By 1980, keyboardist Jonathan Cain (later of Journey) had replaced Corby, and bassist Ricky Phillips joined group. In 1989, Waite formed Bad English with Phillips and Cain.

BABY TALK
Pop studio group assembled by producer David Hummer.

BACHARACH, Burt
Born on 5/12/1928 in Kansas City, Missouri. Conductor/arranger/composer. One of pop music's all-time great songwriters. Married to actress Angie Dickinson from 1966-80. Married to songwriter Carole Bayer Sager from 1982-90.

BACHELORS, The
Pop vocal trio from Dublin, Ireland: brothers Declan and Conleth Cluskey, with John Stokes. Formed in 1958 as a barbershop trio, The Harmony Chords.

BACHMAN, Tal
Born on 8/13/1968 in Winnipeg, Manitoba, Canada. Male rock singer/songwriter/guitarist. Son of Randy Bachman (of Bachman-Turner Overdrive).

BACHMAN-TURNER OVERDRIVE
Hard-rock group from Vancouver, British Columbia, Canada: brothers Randy (vocals, guitar; born on 9/27/1943) and Robbie (drums; born on 2/18/1953) Bachman, with C. Fred Turner (vocals, bass; born on 10/16/1943) and Blair Thornton (guitar; born on 7/23/1950). Originally known as Brave Belt. Randy had been in The Guess Who and recorded solo. Randy left in 1977 to form Ironhorse; regrouped with Turner in 1984. Randy is the father of Tal Bachman.

BACKSTREET BOYS
"Boy band" formed in Orlando, Florida: Nick Carter (born on 1/28/1980 in Jamestown, New York), Howie Dorough (born on 8/22/1973 in Orlando, Florida), Brian Littrell (born on 2/20/1975 in Lexington, Kentucky), A.J. McLean (born on 1/9/1978 in West Palm Beach, Florida) and Kevin Richardson (born on 10/3/1971 in Lexington, Kentucky). Carter is the older brother of singers Aaron Carter and Leslie Carter.

BACKUS, Jim
Born on 2/25/1913 in Cleveland, Ohio. Died of pneumonia on 7/3/1989 (age 76). Actor, starred in dozens of movies. Played "Thurston Howell III" on TV's *Gilligan's Island*. Also famous as the voice of "Mr. Magoo" in the cartoon series.

BAD BOYS BLUE
Pop-dance trio formed in Cologne, Germany: John McInerney (from Liverpool, lead vocals), Andrew Thomas (from Los Angeles) and Ova Standing (from Zaire).

BAD BOY'S DA BAND
Rap group assembled by P. Diddy for the reality TV series *Making The Band 2:* Dylan John, Sara Stokes, Lloyd "Ness" Mathis, Frederick Watson, Lynese "Babs" Wiley and Rodney "Young City" Hill.

BAD COMPANY
Rock band from England: Paul Rodgers (vocals; born on 12/17/1949), Mick Ralphs (guitar; born on 3/31/1944), Raymond "Boz" Burrell (bass; born on 8/1/1946; died on 9/21/2006, age 60) and Simon Kirke (drums; born on 7/28/1949). Rodgers and Kirke from Free; Ralphs from Mott The Hoople; and Burrell from King Crimson. Rodgers, who left group in late 1982, was a member of The Firm (1984-86) and The Law (in 1991). Vocalist Brian Howe joined in 1986. Burrell left in 1987. Dave "Bucket" Colwell (guitar) and Rick Wills (of Foreigner; bass) joined in late 1992. Howe left in early 1995; replaced by Robert Hart. Band named after a 1972 Jeff Bridges movie.

BAD ENGLISH
Rock supergroup: John Waite (vocals), Ricky Phillips (bass), Jonathan Cain (keyboards), Neal Schon (guitar) and Deen Castronovo (drums). Waite, Phillips and Cain were members of The Babys. Cain and Schon (ex-Santana) were members of Journey. Schon and Castronovo joined Hardline in 1992.

BADFINGER
Rock band from Swansea, Wales, originally known as The Iveys. Consisted of Pete Ham (guitar), Tom Evans (bass), Joey Molland (guitar; joined in 1969, after band recorded "Maybe Tomorrow") and Mike Gibbins (drums). All but Gibbins shared vocals. After Ham committed suicide on 4/23/1975 (age 27), group disbanded. Molland and Evans reunited in 1978 with Glen Sherba (guitar), Tony Kaye (keyboards, Yes) and Richard Bryan (drums). Evans committed suicide on 11/19/1983 (age 36).

BADLEES, The
Rock group from Philadelphia, Pennsylvania: Pete Palladino (vocals), Bret Alexander and Jeff Feltenberger (guitars), Paul Smith (bass) and Ron Simasek (drums).

BADU, Erykah
Born Erica Wright on 2/26/1971 in Dallas, Texas. R&B singer/songwriter/actress. Played "Rose Rose" in the movie *The Cider House Rules*.

BAEZ, Joan
Born Joan Chandos Baez on 1/9/1941 in Staten Island, New York (of British and Mexican parentage). Pre-eminent folk song stylist. Became a political activist while attending Boston University in the late 1950s. Made her professional debut in July 1959 at the first Newport Folk Festival. Orientation changed from traditional to popular folk songs in the early 1960s. Influential in fostering career of Bob Dylan.

BAGBY, Doc
Born Harold Bagby in Philadelphia, Pennsylvania. Black organist. Owner of the Red Top label.

BAHA MEN
Dance-junkanoo band from the Bahamas led by Isaiah Taylor, with Rick Carey and Omerit Hield (vocals), Marvin Prosper (rapper), Herschel Small and Patrick Carey (guitars), Tony Flowers (percussion), Jeff Cher (keyboards) and Colyn Grant (drums).

BAILEY, Philip
Born on 5/8/1951 in Denver, Colorado. Co-lead singer of Earth, Wind & Fire. Recorded Christian music from 1984-90.

BAILEY, Razzy
Born Erastus Bailey on 2/14/1939 in Hugley, Alabama; raised in Lafayette, Alabama. Country singer/songwriter.

BAILEY RAE, Corinne
Born on 2/26/1979 in Leeds, West Yorkshire, England. Black female neo-soul singer/songwriter.

BAINBRIDGE, Merril
Born on 6/2/1968 in Melbourne, Australia. Female singer/songwriter.

BAIRD, Dan
Born on 12/12/1953 in San Diego, California; raised in Atlanta, Georgia. Former lead singer of the Georgia Satellites.

BAJA MARIMBA BAND
Band led by marimbist Julius Wechter (born on 5/10/1935 in Chicago, Illinois; died of cancer on 2/1/1999, age 63). Band featured various studio musicians with Wechter the only constant. Wechter also played with Herb Alpert and Martin Denny.

BAKER, Anita
Born on 1/26/1958 in Toledo, Ohio; raised in Detroit, Michigan. R&B/jazz-styled singer. Female lead singer of Chapter 8 from 1976-83.

BAKER, Arthur
Born on 4/22/1955 in Boston, Massachusetts. Prolific producer. Since producing Afrika Bambaataa's "Planet Rock" in 1982, has produced or mixed for New Order, Bob Dylan, New Edition, Bruce Springsteen, Fine Young Cannibals, The Rolling Stones, U2, Paul McCartney and many others. Co-produced/co-wrote the Artists United Against Apartheid project. Formed own labels, Streetwise and Minimal.

BAKER, George, Selection
Baker is Johannes Bouwens (born on 12/8/1944), leader of pop group from the Netherlands that includes Jan Hop, Jacobus Anthonius Greuter, George The and Jan Gerbrand Visser. Female singer Lydia Bont joined in 1975 (heard on "Paloma Blanca").

BAKER('S), Ginger, Air Force
Born Peter Baker on 8/19/1939 in Lewisham, England. Drummer for Cream and Blind Faith. Got start as replacement for Charlie Watts (who left to join The Rolling Stones) in Alexis Korner's Blues Inc. (C.C.S.) in 1962. Then with the Graham Bond Organization. Air Force featured Steve Winwood, Denny Laine (Moody Blues, Wings) and Rick Grech (Family, Traffic, Blind Faith). Joined Masters Of Reality in 1992.

BAKER, LaVern
Born Delores Williams on 11/11/1929 in Chicago, Illinois. Died of heart failure on 3/10/1997 (age 67). Recorded as "Little Miss Share Cropper" and "Bea Baker." One of the most popular female R&B singers of the early rock era. After working with the Todd Rhodes Orchestra, 1952-53, toured Europe, solo. Signed with Atlantic Records in 1953. Backing group: The Gliders. Moved to the Philippines in 1969 and for 20 years worked as an entertainer and manager at a servicemen's club in Subic Bay.

BALANCE
Pop-rock trio from the Bronx, New York: Peppy Castro (vocals; Blues Magoos), Bob Kulick (guitar; brother of Bruce Kulick of Kiss) and Doug Katsaros (keyboards).

BALDRY, Long John
Born on 1/12/1941 in Haddon, Derbyshire, England. Died of a chest infection on 7/21/2005 (age 64). Influential blues rocker. Formed Steampacket with Rod Stewart, and Bluesology with Elton John.

BALIN, Marty
Born Martyn Buchwald on 1/30/1942 in Cincinnati, Ohio. Co-founder of Jefferson Airplane/Starship and KBC Band.

BALL, David
Born on 7/9/1953 in Rock Hill, South Carolina. Country singer/songwriter/guitarist.

BALL, Kenny
Born on 5/22/1931 in Ilford, Essex, England. Trumpet player. His Jazzmen: Diz Disley (banjo), Johnny Bennett (trombone), Dave Jones (clarinet), Colin Bates (piano), Vic Pitts (bass) and Ron Bowden (drums).

BALLADS, The
R&B vocal group from Oakland, California: Nathan Romerson, John Foster, Leslie LaPalmer and Rico Thompson. LaPalmer died on 2/8/2003 (age 60).

BALLARD, Hank, & The Midnighters
R&B vocal group from Detroit, Michigan. Formed in 1952 as The Royals: Henry Booth, Charles Sutton, Lawson Smith and Sonny Woods. In late 1953, Henry "Hank" Ballard (born John Kendricks on

11/18/1927 in Detroit; died of cancer on 3/2/2003, age 75) replaced Smith and became lead singer. Name changed to The Midnighters in 1954 when they scored three huge R&B hits. Had the original recording of "The Twist," written by Ballard. After group disbanded in 1965, re-formed with Frank Stadford, Walter Miller and Wesley Hargrove. Worked in the James Brown Revue.

BALLARD, Russ
Born on 10/31/1945 in Waltham Cross, Hertfordshire, England. Pop-rock singer/songwriter/producer. Guitarist of Argent, 1969-74.

BALLIN' JACK
Interracial jazz-rock group from San Francisco, California: Jim Walters (vocals, trumpet), Glenn Thomas (guitar), Jim Coile (sax), Tim McFarland (trombone), Luther Rabb (bass) and Ronnie Hammond (drums). Rabb and Hammond joined War in 1979.

BALLOON FARM, The
Psychedelic-rock band from New Jersey: Mike Appel, Ed Schnug, Don Henny and Jay Saks. Appel went on to manage Bruce Springsteen.

BALTIMORA
Born Jimmy McShane on 5/23/1957 in Londonderry, Northern Ireland. Died of AIDS on 3/28/1995 (age 37). Pop singer.

BALTIMORE, Charli
Born Tiffany Lane on 10/11/1973 in Philadelphia, Pennsylvania. Female rapper.

BALTIMORE AND OHIO MARCHING BAND, The
Studio group assembled by producers Joey Day and Alan Dischel.

BAMA
Session group from Muscle Shoals, Alabama. Headed by songwriters Terry Skinner and J.L. Wallace.

BAMBAATAA, Afrika
Born Kevin Donovan on 4/10/1960 in South Bronx, New York. Pioneering funk DJ/rapper. Also known as Khayan Aasim. The Soul Sonic Force is rappers M.C. G.L.O.B.E. (John B. Miller), Mr. Biggs (Ellis Williams) and Pow Wow (Robert Allen) with D.J. Jazzy Jay.

BANANARAMA
Pop-rock "girl group" from London, England: Sarah Dallin, Keren Woodward and Siobhan Fahey. Group name is a combination of the children's TV show *The Banana Splits* and the Roxy Music song "Pyjamarama." Fahey married Dave Stewart (Eurythmics) on 8/1/1987; left group in early 1988; replaced by Jacqui O'Sullivan (left in mid-1991). Fahey later formed the duo Shakespear's Sister.

BANANA SPLITS, The
Saturday morning TV series featuring four live-action animals: Fleegle (dog), Drooper (lion), Bingo (gorilla) and Snorky (elephant). Actual vocals on the records were performed by songwriters Ritchie Adams and Mark Barkan.

BAND, The
Rock group formed in Woodstock, New York: Robbie Robertson (vocals, guitar), Levon Helm (vocals, drums), Rick Danko (bass), Richard Manuel and Garth Hudson (keyboards). All from Canada (except Helm from Arkansas) and all were with Ronnie Hawkins' Hawks. Group's "farewell concert" on Thanksgiving Day in 1976 was documented in the Martin Scorcese movie *The Last Waltz*. Helm, Danko and Hudson reunited in 1993 with Jim Weider (guitar), Richard Bell (piano) and Randy Ciarlante (drums). Worked on albums and tours as Bob Dylan's backup band. Manuel committed suicide on 3/4/1986 (age 42). Danko died on 12/10/1999 (age 56).

BAND AID
A benefit recording to assist famine relief in Ethiopia. Organized by Bob Geldof of The Boomtown Rats, all-star group also included Bananarama, Phil Collins, Culture Club, Duran Duran, Frankie Goes To Hollywood, Heaven 17, Kool & The Gang, Paul McCartney, Spandau Ballet, Status Quo, Sting, The Style Council, Ultravox, U2, Wham! and Paul Young.

BANDIT
Rock band from England: Gerry Trew (vocals), Danny McIntosh (guitar), Tony Lester (bass) and Theodore Thunder (drums).

BAND OF GOLD
Dutch session vocalists and musicians assembled by producers Pete Wingfield and Paco Saval.

BAND OF THE BLACK WATCH, The
Military unit from Canada. Led by pipe major Bruce Bolton.

BANDY, Moe
Born Marion Bandy on 2/12/1944 in Meridian, Mississippi; raised in San Antonio, Texas. Country singer/guitarist. Played in his father's band, the Mission City Playboys; also worked as a rodeo rider. Regular on the local San Antonio TV show *Country Corner* in 1973. Started his own theater in Branson, Missouri.

BANG
Rock trio from Florida: Frank Ferrara (vocals, bass), Frank Gilcken (guitar) and Tony D'Lorio (drums).

BANG
Pop duo formed in London, England. Paul Calliris (vocals) and Billy Adams (keyboards) were born in Athens, Greece.

B ANGIE B
Born Angela Boyd in Morton, Mississippi. Black singer/dancer/songwriter with M.C. Hammer's posse.

BANGLES
Female pop-rock group from Los Angeles, California: sisters Vicki (lead guitar; born on 1/11/1958) and Debbi (drums; born on 8/22/1961) Peterson, Michael Steele (bass; born on 6/2/1955) and Susanna Hoffs (guitar; born on 1/17/1959). Originally named The Bangs. Steele was previously in The Runaways. Hoffs starred in the 1987 movie *The Allnighter*. Disbanded in September 1989. Vicki

Peterson married John Cowsill (of The Cowsills) on 10/25/2003.

BANKS, Darrell
Born Darrell Eubanks on 7/25/1937 in Mansfield, Ohio; raised in Buffalo, New York. Shot to death on 2/24/1970 (age 32) by an off-duty policeman in Detroit, Michigan. R&B singer/songwriter.

BANKS, Lloyd
Born Christopher Lloyd on 4/30/1982 in New Carrollton, Maryland; raised in Jamaica, Queens, New York. Male rapper. Member of G-Unit.

BANNER, David
Born Levell Crump in 1985 in Jackson, Mississippi. Male rapper.

BANZAII
Disco studio group from France.

BARBARA AND THE BROWNS
R&B family group from Memphis, Tennessee: sisters Barbara (lead), Roberta, Betty and Maurice Brown.

BARBARA And THE UNIQUES
R&B vocal trio from Chicago, Illinois: sisters Barbara and Gwen Livsey with Doris Lindsey.

BARBARIANS, The
Garage-rock band from Provincetown, Massachusetts: Victor "Moulty" Moulton (vocals, drums), Jeff Morris and Bruce Benson (guitars), and Jerry Causi (bass). Regulars on TV's *Shindig* and *The T.A.M.I. Show*. Moulton had a hook in place of his left hand which he lost in an explosion from a homemade lead-pipe-and-gasoline bomb.

BARBER('S), Chris, Jazz Band
Born on 4/17/1930 in Welwyn Garden City, Hertfordshire, England. Trombone player. His band featured Monty Sunshine on clarinet.

BARBER, Frank
Born in England. Composer/conductor/arranger.

BARBOUR, Keith
Born on 1/21/1941 in New York. Pop singer/songwriter. Formerly with The New Christy Minstrels. Married to TV actress Deidre Hall *(Our House* and *Days of Our Lives)* from 1972-77.

BARCLAY, Eddie
Born on 1/26/1921 in Paris, France. Died on 5/12/2005 (age 84). Head of the French recording company Compagnie Phonographique Française and own Barclay label.

BARDEUX
Female dance duo from Los Angeles, California: Stacy "Acacia" Smith and Jaz. Melanie Taylor replaced Jaz in 1989. Bardeux (pronounced: bar-DO) is plural for Bardot (as in actress Brigitte Bardot).

BARE, Bobby
Born on 4/7/1935 in Ironton, Ohio. Country singer/songwriter/guitarist. Drafted by the Army in 1958; left a demo tape of "The All American Boy" with Fraternity Records. The song was released erroneously as by Bill Parsons. Wrote songs for the

BARE, Bobby — cont'd
movie *Teenage Millionaire* (1961). Acted in the movie *A Distant Trumpet* in 1964. Own TV series in the mid-1980s.

BAREILLES, Sara
Born on 12/7/1979 in Eureka, California. Female singer/songwriter/pianist.

BARENAKED LADIES
Alternative-rock group from Toronto, Ontario, Canada: Steven Page (vocals), Ed Robertson (guitar), Kevin Hearn (keyboards), Jim Creeggan (bass) and Tyler Stewart (drums).

BAR-KAYS
Funk group from Memphis, Tennessee: Jimmy King (guitar), Ronnie Caldwell (organ), Phalon Jones (sax), Ben Cauley (trumpet), James Alexander (bass) and Carl Cunningham (drums). The plane crash that killed Otis Redding (on 12/10/1967 in Madison, Wisconsin) also claimed the lives of all the Bar-Kays except Alexander (not on the plane) and Cauley (survived the crash). Alexander re-formed the group with Larry Dodson (vocals), Barry Wilkins (guitar), Harvey Henderson (sax), Winston Stewart (organ) and Willie Hall (drums).

BARLOW, Gary
Born on 1/20/1971 in Frodsham, Cheshire, England. Former lead singer of Take That.

BARNES, Cheryl
Born in Cleveland, Ohio. Black singer/actress. Played "Hud's Fiancee" in the 1979 movie version of *Hair*.

BARNES, J.J.
Born James Jay Barnes on 11/30/1943 in Detroit, Michigan. First recorded for Kable in 1960. Member of The Holidays, 1966.

BARNES, Jimmy
Born in Newark, New Jersey. R&B singer.

BARNES, Jimmy
Born on 4/28/1956 in Glasgow, Scotland; raised in Australia. Lead singer of Cold Chisel.

BARNUM, H.B.
Born Hidle Brown Barnum on 7/15/1936 in Houston, Texas; raised in Los Angeles, California. Producer/arranger/songwriter. Member of The Dyna-Sores.

BARRETT, Richard
Born in 1936 in Philadelphia, Pennsylvania. Died of cancer on 8/3/2006 (age 70). Black singer/songwriter/pianist/producer. Key figure in the Philly soul sound. Discovered Frankie Lymon & The Teenagers, The Chantels, Little Anthony & The Imperials, and The Isley Brothers. Lead singer with the Valentines which included Dave "Baby" Cortez and Ronnie Bright (of "Mr. Bass Man" fame). Managed The Three Degrees.

BARRETTO, Ray
Born on 4/29/1929 in Brooklyn, New York. Died on 2/17/2006 (age 76). Latin percussionist. Member of The Blackout Allstars.

BARRON KNIGHTS, The
Novelty group from England: Anthony Osmond and Richard Palmer (vocals), Peter Langford (guitar), Butch Baker (bass) and Dave Ballinger (drums).

BARRY, Claudja
Born in Jamaica; raised in Toronto, Ontario, Canada. Black dance singer/actress. Appeared in the musicals *Hair* and *Catch My Soul*.

BARRY, Joe
Born Joseph Barrios on 7/13/1939 in Cut Off, Louisiana. Died of a heart attack on 8/31/2004 (age 65). White swamp-pop singer/guitarist.

BARRY, John
Born on 11/3/1933 in York, England. Prolific movie soundtrack composer/conductor. Married to Jane Birken from 1965-68.

BARRY, Len
Born Leonard Borisoff on 6/12/1942 in Philadelphia, Pennsylvania. Lead singer of The Dovells from 1957-63.

BARRY And The TAMERLANES
Pop vocal trio from Los Angeles, California: songwriters Barry DeVorzon, Terry Smith and Bodie Chandler. Arranged by Perry Botkin, Jr. DeVorzon founded the Valiant label and began his ongoing prolific songwriting career in the mid-1950s.

BARTLEY, Chris
Born on 4/17/1949 in Harlem, New York. Male R&B singer.

BASIA
Born Basia Trzetrzelewska on 9/30/1959 in Jaworzno, Poland. Female pop singer.

BASIE, Count
Born William Basie on 8/21/1904 in Red Bank, New Jersey. Died of cancer on 4/26/1984 (age 79). Legendary jazz, big band leader/pianist/organist. Appeared in many movies.

BASIL, Toni
Born Antonia Basilotta on 9/22/1943 in Philadelphia, Pennsylvania. Choreographer/actress/video director. Worked on the TV shows *Shindig* and *Hullabaloo*. Choreographed the movie *American Grafitti*. Appeared in the movie *Easy Rider*.

BASKERVILLE HOUNDS, The
Rock band from Cleveland, Ohio: Dante Rossi (vocals), Larry Meese (guitar), Jack Topper (organ), Bill Emery (bass) and Michael Macron (drums). Named after the famous Sherlock Holmes work by Sir Arthur Conan Doyle.

BASS, Fontella
Born on 7/3/1940 in St. Louis, Missouri. R&B vocalist/pianist/organist. Mother was a member of the Clara Ward Gospel Troupe. Sang in church choirs; with Oliver Sain's band, St. Louis; with Little Milton's blues show to 1964. Married to trumpet player Lester Bowie.

BASSEY, Shirley
Born on 1/8/1937 in Cardiff, Wales. R&B singer. Began professional career at age 16 as a member of the touring show *Memories Of Al Jolson*. Became a popular club attraction in America in 1961.

BATDORF & RODNEY
Pop duo: John Batdorf and Mark Rodney. Batdorf formed the group Silver in 1976.

BATES, Jeff
Born on 9/19/1963 in Bunker Hill, Mississippi. Country singer/songwriter/guitarist.

BAXTER, Duke
Born in Australia. White pop singer/songwriter.

BAXTER, Les
Born on 3/14/1922 in Mexia, Texas. Died of a heart attack on 1/15/1996 (age 73). Orchestra leader/arranger. Began as a conductor on radio shows in the 1930s. Member of Mel Torme's vocal group, the Mel-Tones. Musical arranger for Capitol Records (Nat King Cole, Margaret Whiting and others) in the 1950s. Composed over 250 scores for radio, television and movies.

BAY CITY ROLLERS
Pop-rock group from Edinburgh, Scotland: Les McKeown (vocals; born on 11/12/1955), brothers Alan (guitar; born on 6/20/1948) and Derek (drums; born on 3/19/1951) Longmuir, Eric Faulkner (guitar; born on 10/21/1955) and Stuart "Woody" Wood (bass; born on 2/25/1957). Alan Longmuir left in mid-1976; returned in 1978. Ian Mitchell (guitar) joined briefly in 1976.

BAZUKA
Instrumental studio group assembled by producer Tony Camillo.

BBMAK
Male pop trio from Liverpool, England: Mark Barry (born on 10/26/1978), Christian Burns (born on 1/18/1974) and Steve McNally (born on 7/4/1978).

B. BUMBLE & THE STINGERS
Los Angeles sessionmen that included Ernie Freeman (piano), Tommy Tedesco (guitar), Earl Palmer (drums) and Red Callender (bass) on their first two hits. "Nut Rocker" was first recorded by Freeman, Palmer and René Hall (guitar) as Jack B. Nimble And The Quicks ("Bubbled Under" in 1962 on Del-Rio); Rendezvous then released their newly recorded version featuring Palmer, Hall and Ali Hazan on piano. Pianist R.C. Gamble led a touring trio from Oklahoma as B. Bumble & The Stingers.

BEACH BOYS, The
The most popular American rock and roll group was formed in 1961 in Hawthorne, California. Consisted of brothers Brian Wilson (keyboards, bass; born on 6/20/1942), Carl Wilson (guitar; born on 12/21/1946) and Dennis Wilson (drums; born on 12/4/1944); their cousin Mike Love (lead vocals, saxophone; born on 3/15/1941), and Al Jardine (guitar; born on 9/3/1942). Known in high school as Kenny & The Cadets, Carl & The Passions, then The Pendletones. First recorded for X/Candix in 1961.

Ignited the surf-rock craze. Jardine replaced by David Marks from March 1962 to March 1963. Brian quit touring with group in December 1964; replaced briefly by Glen Campbell until Bruce Johnston (of Bruce And Terry) joined permanently in April 1965. Johnston and Campbell also recorded with the studio band Sagittarius in 1967. Love formed Celebration in 1977. Brian continued to write for and produce group; returned to stage in 1983. Daryl Dragon (of Captain & Tennille) was a keyboardist in their stage band. Dennis Wilson drowned on 12/28/1983 (age 39). Lineup of Carl, Brian, Mike, Alan and Bruce continued to perform. Carl Wilson died of cancer on 2/6/1998 (age 51). Carnie and Wendy Wilson, daughters of Brian Wilson, were members of Wilson Phillips.

BEASTIE BOYS
White rap-punk trio from Brooklyn, New York: Adam Horovitz, Adam Yauch and Mike Diamond. Horovitz starred in the movie *Lost Angels*; was married to actress Ione Skye (daughter of Donovan) from 1991-99. DJ Hurricane was their DJ. Group started own Grand Royal record label.

BEATLES, The
The world's #1 rock group was formed in Liverpool, England, in the late 1950s. Known in early forms as The Quarrymen, Johnny & the Moondogs, The Rainbows, and the Silver Beatles. Named The Beatles in 1960. Originally consisted of John Lennon (born on 10/9/1940), Paul McCartney (born on 6/18/1942) and George Harrison (guitars; born on 2/24/1943), Stu Sutcliffe (bass) and Pete Best (drums). Sutcliffe left in April 1961 (died of a brain hemorrhage on 4/10/1962); McCartney moved to bass. Best replaced by Ringo Starr (born on 7/7/1940) in August 1962. Group managed by Brian Epstein (died of a sleeping-pill overdose on 8/27/1967) and produced by George Martin (born on 1/3/1926). First U.S. tour in February 1964. Group starred in the movies *A Hard Day's Night* , *Help, Magical Mystery Tour and Let It Be*; contributed soundtrack to the animated movie *Yellow Submarine*. Started own Apple label in 1968. McCartney publicly announced group's dissolution on 4/10/1970. Lennon was shot to death on 12/8/1980 (age 40). Harrison died of cancer on 11/29/2001 (age 58).

BEATNUTS, The
Latin rap trio from Queens, New York: Les Fernandez, Jerry Tineo and Bert Smalls (left in 1996).

BEATS INTERNATIONAL
Dance group from England: Lester Noel and Lindy Layton (vocals), Andy Boucher (keyboards), Norman Cook (bass) and Luke Creswell (drums). Cook (who later recorded as Fatboy Slim) was bassist of The Housemartins and assembled The Mighty Dub Kats.

BEATTY, E.C.
Born Erson Calvin Beatty Jr. in 1930 in Charlotte, North Carolina. Pop singer/songwriter.

BEAU BRUMMELS, The
Rock band from San Francisco, California: Sal Valentino (vocals; born Sal Spanminato), Ron Elliott (guitar), Ron Meagher (bass) and John Petersen (drums). Petersen left in 1966 to join Harpers Bizarre.

BEAU COUP
Rock group from Cleveland, Ohio: brothers Frank and Tommy Amato, with Dennis Lewin and Bill March. Lewin is a distant cousin of Eric Carmen.

BEAU-MARKS, The
Rock and roll band from Montreal, Quebec, Canada: Ray Hutchinson (vocals, guitar), Mike Robitaille (guitar), Joey Frechette (leader, piano) and Gilles Tailleur (drums).

BEAUMONT, Jimmie
Born on 10/21/1940 in Pittsburgh, Pennsylvania. Lead singer of The Skyliners.

BEAUVOIR, Jean
Born in Chicago, Illinois (Haitian parents); raised in Brooklyn, New York. Male rock singer/bassist. Member of the Plasmatics and Little Steven and the Disciples Of Soul.

BECK
Born Beck David Campbell (later changed his last name to his mother's maiden name of Hansen) on 7/8/1970 in Los Angeles, California. Alternative-rock singer/songwriter/guitarist. Married actress Marissa Ribisi on 4/3/2004.

BECK, Jeff
Born on 6/24/1944 in Wallington, Surrey, England. Prolific rock guitarist. With The Yardbirds from 1964-66. Rod Stewart and Ron Wood (Faces, Rolling Stones) were members of the Jeff Beck Group from 1967-69. Member of supergroup The Honeydrippers.

BECK, Jimmy
Born on 12/30/1929 in Cleveland, Ohio. R&B saxophonist.

BECKHAM, Bob
Born on 7/8/1927 in Stratford, Oklahoma. Pop-country singer.

BECKMEIER BROTHERS
Duo from San Francisco, California: Freddie and Stevie Beckmeier. Freddie was a member of the Paul Butterfield Blues Band.

BEDINGFIELD, Daniel
Born on 12/3/1979 in New Zealand; raised in London, England. Pop singer/songwriter.

BEDINGFIELD, Natasha
Born on 11/26/1981 in Haywards Heath, Sussex, England; raised in Lewisham, London, England. Pop singer/songwriter. Sister of Daniel Bedingfield.

BEECHER, Johnny
Born John Johnson on 7/21/1931 in Donaldsonville, Louisiana. Also known as Plas Johnson. Alto saxophonist.

BEE GEES
Trio of brothers from Manchester, England: Barry Gibb (born on 9/1/1946) and twins Maurice and Robin Gibb (born on 12/22/1949). First performed in December 1955. To Australia in 1958; performed as the Gibbs, later as BG's, finally the Bee Gees. First recorded for Leedon/Festival in 1963. Returned to England in February 1967, with guitarist Vince Melouney and drummer Colin Peterson. Toured Europe and the U.S. in 1968. Melouney left in December 1968; Robin left for solo career in 1969. When Peterson left in August 1969, Barry and Maurice went solo. After eight months, the brothers reunited. Maurice was married to Lulu from 1969-73. Composed soundtracks for *Saturday Night Fever* and *Staying Alive*. Acted in the movie *Sgt. Pepper's Lonely Hearts Club Band*. Youngest brother, Andy Gibb, was a successful solo singer. Maurice died of heart failure on 1/12/2003 (age 53).

BEENIE MAN
Born Moses Davis on 8/22/1973 in Kingston, Jamaica. Reggae singer/rapper. Beenie is Jamaican slang for little.

BEFORE DARK
Female R&B vocal trio from Los Angeles, California: sisters Arike and Jeni Rice, with Mia LeFleur. Arike Rice was a member of Voices.

BEGA, Lou
Born David Lubega on 4/13/1975 in Munich, Germany (Sicilian mother/Ugandan father).

BEGINNING OF THE END, The
R&B group from the Bahamas: brothers Ray (organ), Roy (guitar) and Frank (drums) Munnings, with Fred Henfield (bass).

BELAFONTE, Harry
Born on 3/1/1927 in Harlem, New York (of Jamaican and West Indian parentage). Calypso singer/actor/activist. Rode the crest of the calypso craze to worldwide stardom. Starred in several movies. Became UNICEF goodwill ambassador in 1987. Father of actress Shari Belafonte.

BELEW, Adrian
Born Robert Steven Belew on 12/23/1949 in Covington, Kentucky. Prolific rock guitarist. Discovered by Frank Zappa. Sideman with Talking Heads, David Bowie, Tom Tom Club, Laurie Anderson, Paul Simon and others. Member of King Crimson from 1981-84.

BELL, Archie, & The Drells
Born on 9/1/1944 in Henderson, Texas. Lead singer of the Drells, an R&B vocal group from Leo Smith Junior High School in Houston. First recorded for Ovid in 1967. Recorded "Tighten Up" with group consisting of Bell, Huey "Billy" Butler, Joe Cross and James Wise. Later recordings consisted of Bell, Wise, Lee Bell and Willie Parnell.

BELL, Benny
Born Benjamin Samberg on 3/27/1906 in Brooklyn, New York. Died on 9/1/1999 (age 93). Risque singer/songwriter.

BELL, Drake
Born Jared Drake Bell on 6/27/1986 in Orange County, California. Pop singer/songwriter/actor. Appeared in several movies and TV shows. Best-known as "Drake Parker" on TV's *Drake & Josh*.

BELL, Madeline
Born on 7/23/1942 in Newark, New Jersey. Singer/actress. In cast of *Black Nativity;* toured England in the mid-1960s and remained there. Formed group Blue Mink, 1969-73. Commercial jingle singer since then. Also see Space.

BELL, Maggie
Born on 1/12/1945 in Glasgow, Scotland. Lead singer of the rock band Stone The Crows.

BELL, Randy
Pop-rock singer/songwriter.

BELL, Vincent
Born Vincent Gambella on 7/28/1935 in Brooklyn, New York. Veteran studio guitarist. Formerly with the East Coast vocal group The Gallahads. His "water sound" guitar was featured in Ferrante & Teicher's hit "Midnight Cowboy." Not to be confused with Vincent Lee Bell of The Ramrods.

BELL, William
Born William Yarborough on 7/16/1939 in Memphis, Tennessee. R&B singer/songwriter. Own Peachtree and Wilbe labels. With Rufus Thomas's band in 1953.

BELLAMY BROTHERS
Country duo from Darby, Florida: brothers Howard (born on 2/2/1946; guitar) and David Bellamy (born on 9/16/1950; guitar, keyboards). Made their professional debut in 1958. David wrote "Spiders And Snakes" hit for Jim Stafford.

BELL & JAMES
R&B duo of Leroy Bell and Casey James. Began as a songwriting team for Bell's uncle, producer Thom Bell.

BELL BIV DeVOE
R&B trio of New Edition members: Ricky Bell (born on 9/18/1967), Michael Bivins (born on 8/10/1968) and Ronnie DeVoe (born on 11/17/1967). Bivins produced Another Bad Creation, Boyz II Men and MC Brains, formed own record label, Biv 10, and assembled East Coast Family.

BELLE, Regina
Born on 7/17/1963 in Englewood, New Jersey. Featured female vocalist with The Manhattans, 1986-87.

BELLE EPOQUE
Female disco trio from Paris, France: Marcia Briscue, Evelyne Lenton and Judy Lisboa.

BELLE STARS, The
Female group from England: Jennie McKeown (vocals), Sarah-Jane Owen and Stella Barker (guitars), Miranda Joyce and Clare Hirst (saxophones), Lesley Shone (bass) and Judy Parsons (drums).

BELL NOTES, The
Rock and roll band from Long Island, New York: Carl Bonura (vocals, sax), Ray Ceroni (vocals, guitar), Lenny Giamblavo (bass), Peter Kane (piano) and John Casey (drums). Discovered by WADO DJ Alan Fredericks.

BELLS, The
Pop group from Montreal, Quebec, Canada: Jacki Ralph and Cliff Edwards (vocals), Charles Clarke (guitar), Dennis Will (keyboards), Michael Waye (bass) and Douglas Gravelle (drums).

BELLUS, Tony
Born Anthony Bellusci on 4/17/1936 in Chicago, Illinois. Pop singer/accordionist. First recorded for Shi-Fi in 1958.

BELLY
Alternative-rock group from Newport, Rhode Island: Tanya Donelly (vocals, guitar) with brothers Thomas (guitar) and Chris (drums) Gorman. Gail Greenwood (bass) joined by mid-1993. Donelly was a member of Throwing Muses (with stepsister Kristin Hersh) and The Breeders.

BELMONTS, The
Doo-wop trio from the Bronx, New York: Angelo D'Aleo, Fred Milano and Carlo Mastrangelo. Sang with Dion from 1957-60. Named after Belmont Avenue in the Bronx, New York. Frank Lyndon replaced Mastrangelo in May 1962.

BELVIN, Jesse
Born on 12/15/1933 in Texarkana, Texas; raised in Los Angeles, California. Died in a car crash on 2/6/1960 (age 26). Recorded with Marvin Phillips as "Jesse & Marvin." A pivotal figure in the development of the R&B sound on the West Coast. Co-wrote "Earth Angel" with Curtis Williams of The Penguins. Also see The Cliques, The Chargers, and The Shields.

BENATAR, Pat
Born Patricia Andrzejewski on 1/10/1953 in Brooklyn, New York; raised in Lindenhurst, Long Island, New York. Rock singer/songwriter. Married her producer/guitarist Neil Geraldo on 2/20/1982. Acted in the movie *Union City* and the 1989 ABC afterschool TV special *Torn Between Two Fathers*.

BENET, Eric
Born Eric Benet Jordan on 10/15/1970 in Milwaukee, Wisconsin. R&B singer/songwriter. Married to actress Halle Berry from 2001-05.

BENNETT, Boyd
Born on 12/7/1924 in Muscle Shoals, Alabama. Died on 6/2/2002 (age 77). Attended high school in Tennessee; formed first band there. Later became a DJ in Kentucky.

BENNETT, Joe, & The Sparkletones
Teen rock and roll band from Spartanburg, South Carolina: Joe Bennett (vocals, guitar; born in 1941), Howard Childress (guitar), Wayne Arthur (bass) and Irving Denton (drums).

BENNETT, Tony
Born Anthony Dominick Benedetto on 8/3/1926 in
Queens, New York. One of the top jazz vocalists of
the past 50 years. Worked local clubs while in high
school, sang in U.S. Army bands. Breakthrough with
Bob Hope in 1949 who suggested that he change
his then-stage name, Joe Bari, to Tony Bennett.
Audition record of "Boulevard Of Broken Dreams"
earned a Columbia contract in 1950. Appeared in
the movie *The Oscar*.

BENSON, George
Born on 3/22/1943 in Pittsburgh, Pennsylvania.
R&B-jazz guitarist. Played guitar from age eight.
Played in Brother Jack McDuff's trio in 1963. House
musician at CTI Records to early 1970s. Influenced
by Wes Montgomery. Member of Fuse One.

BENTLEY, Dierks
Born on 11/20/1975 in Phoenix, Arizona; raised in
Lawrenceville, New Jersey. Country singer/
songwriter/guitarist.

BENTON, Brook
Born Benjamin Franklin Peay on 9/19/1931 in
Lugoff, South Carolina; raised in Camden, South
Carolina. Died of spinal meningitis on 4/9/1988 (age
56). R&B singer/songwriter. In The Camden Jubilee
Singers. To New York in 1948, joined Bill Langford's
Langfordaires. With Jerusalem Stars in 1951. First
recorded under own name for Okeh in 1955.

BENZINO
Born Raymond Scott in Boston, Massachusetts.
Male rapper/producer.

BERGEN, Polly
Born Nellie Burgin on 7/14/1930 in Knoxville,
Tennessee. Singer/actress. Not related to actress
Candice Bergen.

BERLIN
Electro-pop group from Los Angeles, California:
Terri Nunn (vocals), Rick Olsen (guitar), Matt Reid
and David Diamond (keyboards), John Crawford
(bass) and Rod Learned (drums). Rob Brill replaced
Learned in early 1984. Pared down to a trio in 1985
with Nunn, Crawford and Brill. Nunn was a teen
actress, appearing on such TV shows as *Lou Grant*.

BERLIN PHILHARMONIC
Symphony orchestra conducted by Karl Böhm (born
on 8/28/1894 in Graz, Austria; died on 8/14/1981,
age 86).

BERMUDAS, The
White "girl group" from Los Angeles, California:
Rickie Page (wife of producer George Motola) and
her two daughters, Joanna and Becky Page. Rickie
was one of The Crypt-Kickers with Bobby "Boris"
Pickett.

BERNARD, Rod
Born on 8/12/1940 in Opelousas, Louisiana. Rock
and roll singer/guitarist.

BERNSTEIN, Elmer
Born on 4/4/1922 in Manhattan, New York. Died on
8/18/2004 (age 82). Composer/conductor for
numerous movies.

BERRY, Chuck
Born Charles Edward Anderson Berry on
10/18/1926 in St. Louis, Missouri. Acclaimed as one
of rock and roll's most influential artists. Muddy
Waters introduced Berry to Leonard Chess (Chess
Records) in Chicago. First recording, "Maybellene,"
was an instant success. Appeared in the movie
Rock, Rock, Rock in 1956 and several others.
Incarcerated for violating the Mann Act (1962-63)
and income tax evasion (1979). Movie
documentary/concert tribute to Berry, *Hail! Hail!
Rock 'N' Roll*, released in 1987.

BERTRAND, Plastic
Born Roger Jouret on 2/24/1958 in Brussels,
Belgium. Male punk rocker.

BETTERS, Harold
Born in Connellsville, Pennsylvania. Black jazz
trombonist.

BETTER THAN EZRA
Rock trio from New Orleans, Louisiana: Kevin Griffin
(vocals, guitar, songwriter), Tom Drummond (bass)
and Cary Bonnecaze (drums). Travis McNabb
replaced Bonnecaze by 1996.

BETTY BOO
Born Allison Clarkson on 3/6/1970 in London,
England. Female dance singer.

BEVERLEY SISTERS, The
Vocal trio from London, England: sisters Joy, Babs
and Teddie Beverley. Babs and Teddie are twins.

BEYONCE
Born Beyonce Knowles on 9/4/1981 in Houston,
Texas. R&B singer/songwriter/actress. Member of
Destiny's Child. Acted in the movies *Austin Powers
In Goldmember*, *The Fighting Temptations*, *The
Pink Panther* and *Dreamgirls*. Married Jay-Z on
4/4/2008.

B-52's, The
New-wave dance group from Athens, Georgia:
Cindy Wilson (guitar, vocals) and her brother Ricky
Wilson (guitar; died of AIDS on 10/12/1985, age
32), Kate Pierson (organ, vocals), Fred Schneider
(keyboards, vocals) and Keith Strickland (drums;
moved to guitar after Ricky's death). Cindy left in
1991; replaced on tour by Julee Cruise. Appeared
as the B.C. 52's in the movie *The Flintstones*. B-52
is slang for the bouffant hairstyle worn by Kate and
Cindy.

B.G.
Born Christopher Dorsey in 1980 in New Orleans,
Louisiana. Male rapper. B.G.: Baby Gangsta. Also
see Hot Boy$.

B.G. THE PRINCE OF RAP
Born Bernard Greene in Washington DC. Male
rapper.

BICE, Bo
Born Harold Bice on 11/1/1975 in Huntsville,
Alabama. Male singer. Finished in second place on
the 2005 season of TV's *American Idol*.

BIDDU ORCHESTRA
Born Biddu Appaiah in 1944 in Bangalore, India.
Male dance songwriter/producer/arranger. To
England, worked as a baker. In 1969, began
producing for Beacon Records.

BIG & RICH
Country duo formed in Nashville, Tennessee: "Big"
Kenny Alphin and John Rich (former member of
Lonestar).

BIG AUDIO DYNAMITE II
Rock group from England: Mick Jones (vocals,
guitar), Nick Hawkins (guitar), Gary Stonadge
(bass) and Chris Kavanagh (drums). Jones was
co-founder of The Clash; not to be confused with
Mick Jones of Foreigner.

BIG BOPPER
Born Jiles Perry Richardson on 10/24/1930 in
Sabine Pass, Texas. DJ at KTRM in Beaumont,
Texas. Wrote "Running Bear" for Johnny Preston.
Died with Buddy Holly and Ritchie Valens in the
2/3/1959 plane crash (age 28).

BIG BUB
Born Frederick Lee Drakeford in Englewood, New
Jersey. Black singer/rapper.

BIG COUNTRY
Pop-rock group from Dunfermline, Scotland: Stuart
Adamson (vocals, guitar), Bruce Watson (guitar),
Tony Butler (bass) and Mark Brzezicki (drums).
Adamson committed suicide on 12/16/2001 (age
43).

BIG MAYBELLE
Born Mabel Louise Smith on 5/1/1924 in Jackson,
Tennessee. Died of diabetes on 1/23/1972 (age 47).
R&B singer/pianist.

BIG MOUNTAIN
Multi-cultural reggae band from San Diego,
California: Quino (vocals, rhythm guitar), Jerome
Cruz (guitar), Manfred Reinke (keyboards), Gregory
Blakney (percussion), Lance Rhodes (drums) and
Lynn Copeland (bass).

BIG NOISE
Pop band group from Birmingham, England:
Anthony Fenelle (vocals), Huw Lucas (guitar), Paul
Johnson (keyboards), Linton Levy (sax), Tony
Jones (percussion), Gary Thompson (bass) and
Tony Lahiffe (drums).

BIG PIG
Rock group from Australia: male singers Nick
Disbray, Tony Antoniades, Tim Rosewarne and
Oleh Witer, with female singer Sherine, and
drummers Adrian Scaglione and Neil Baker.

BIG PUNISHER
Born Christopher Rios on 11/9/1971 in the Bronx,
New York. Died of a heart attack on 2/7/2000 (age
28). Male rapper.

BIG RIC
Rock group from Los Angeles, California: Joel
Porter (vocals), John Pondel (guitar), Kevin
DiSimone (keyboards) and Bud Harner (drums).

BIG SAMBO
Born James Young on 8/3/1937 in Beaumont,
Texas. Died on 6/10/1983 (age 45). Black
saxophonist/vocalist.

BIG SISTER
Born Vicki Walker in New Orleans, Louisiana; raised
in Chicago, Illinois. Dance singer.

BIG STAR
Pop-rock group from Memphis, Tennessee: Alex
Chilton (vocals; Box Tops), Chris Bell (guitar), Andy
Hummel (bass) and Jody Stephens (drums).

BIG TROUBLE
Female pop group formed in Los Angeles,
California: Bobbi Eakes (vocals), Rebecca Ryan
(keyboards), Julia Farey (bass) and Suzy Zarow
(drums). Formed by TV network executive Fred
Silverman. Eakes was Miss Georgia 1982 and later
played "Macy Alexander" on TV's The Bold & The
Beautiful.

BIG TYMERS
Rap duo from New Orleans, Louisiana: Mannie
Fresh and Bryan "Baby" Williams. Members of Cash
Money Millionaires.

BILAL
Born Bilal Oliver in 1979 in Philadelphia,
Pennsylvania. Male R&B singer.

BILK, Mr. Acker
Born Bernard Stanley Bilk on 1/28/1929 in
Pensford, Somerset, England. Clarinetist/composer.

BILLY & LILLIE
Black vocal duo of Billy Ford (born on 3/9/1925 in
Bloomfield, New Jersey) and Lillie Bryant (born on
2/14/1940 in Newburg, New York). Backing group:
Billy Ford's Thunderbirds.

BILLY JOE & THE CHECKMATES
Born Louis Bideu on 3/21/1919 in El Paso, Texas.
Worked as a comedian. Hosted own local Lew
Bedell Show in New York. Dubbed himself Billy Joe
Hunter in the early 1960s.

BILLY SATELLITE
Rock group from Oakland, California: Monty Byrom
(vocals), Danny Chauncey (guitar), Ira Walker
(bass) and Tom Falletti (drums).

BIMBO JET
Disco studio group from France. Assembled by
producer Laurent Rossi.

BINGOBOYS
Dance trio of DJs from Vienna, Austria: Klaus
Biedermann, Paul Pfab and Helmut Wolfgruber.
Princessa is a female rapper from New York.

BIRDLEGS & PAULINE
R&B group from Rockford, Illinois: husband-and-
wife Sidney Banks (born on 10/13/1929) and
Pauline Shivers Banks (born on 4/28/1933), with
brothers Mack Murphy and Floyd Murphy.

BIRKIN, Jane, & Serge Gainsbourg
Actress Birkin was born on 12/14/1946 in London, England. Married to John Barry from 1965-68. Singer/songwriter Lucien "Serge" Gainsbourg was born on 4/2/1928 in Paris, France. Died of heart failure on 3/2/1991 (age 62). Birkin and Gainsbourg were married from 1968-80.

BISCUIT
Born Steve Walker in Oakland, California. Male rapper. Began as a bodyguard for New Kids On The Block.

BISHOP, Elvin
Born on 10/21/1942 in Glendale, California; raised in Tulsa, Oklahoma. Lead guitarist with The Paul Butterfield Blues Band (1965-68).

BISHOP, Stephen
Born on 11/14/1951 in San Diego, California. Pop-rock singer/songwriter. Wrote several movie themes. Cameo role as the "Charming Guy With Guitar" in *National Lampoon's Animal House*.

BIZARRE INC featuring Angie Brown
Techno-dance trio of DJs from England: Andrew Meecham, Dean Meredith and Carl Turner. Featuring female session singer Angie Brown.

BIZ MARKIE
Born Marcel Hall on 4/8/1964 in Harlem, New York. Rapper/actor. Appeared in the movie *The Meteor Man*.

BJORK
Born Bjork Gudmundsdottir on 11/21/1965 in Reykjavik, Iceland. Female lead singer of the dance group The Sugarcubes.

BLACK('S), Bill, Combo
Born on 9/17/1926 in Memphis, Tennessee. Died of a brain tumor on 10/21/1965 (age 39). White bass guitarist/songwriter. Session work in Memphis; backed Elvis Presley (with Scotty Moore, guitar; D.J. Fontana, drums) on most of his early records. Formed own band in 1959. Labeled as "The Untouchable Sound." Larry Rogers and Bob Tucker led group after Black's death; recorded well into the 1970s.

BLACK, Cilla
Born Priscilla White on 5/27/1943 in Liverpool, England. Discovered by The Beatles' manager Brian Epstein while she was working as a coat checker/singer at Liverpool's Cavern Club.

BLACK, Clint
Born on 2/4/1962 in Long Branch, New Jersey; raised in Katy, Texas. Country singer/guitarist. Former construction worker. Married actress Lisa Hartman on 10/20/1991.

BLACK, Jay
Born David Blatt on 11/2/1938 in New York. Replaced John Traynor as lead singer of Jay & The Americans in mid-1962.

BLACK, Jeanne
Born Gloria Jeanne Black on 10/25/1937 in Pomona, California. Country-pop singer. Discovered by Cliffie Stone; sang with her sister Janie on Stone's TV show *Hometown Jamboree*.

BLACK, Oscar
Born in Newark, New Jersey. R&B singer.

BLACK, Terry
Born on 2/3/1949 in North Vancouver, British Columbia, Canada. Male singer. Married singer Laurel Ward in 1970.

BLACK BOX
Male Italian dance trio of producer Daniele Davoli and musicians Mirko Limoni and Valerio Semplici. Videos feature French model Katrin Quinol as lead singer; however, Martha Wash is the uncredited lead vocalist on all of the group's hits.

BLACKBYRDS, The
R&B group formed by Donald Byrd (born on 12/9/1932 in Detroit, Michigan) while teaching jazz at Howard University in Washington DC. Core members: Joe Hall (vocals, bass), Kevin Toney (vocals, keyboards) and Keith Killgo (vocals, drums).

BLACK CROWES, The
Rock and roll band from Atlanta, Georgia. Led by brothers Chris (vocals) and Rich (guitar) Robinson. Includes Jeff Cease (guitar), Johnny Colt (bass) and Steve Gorman (drums). Cease left in late 1991; replaced by Marc Ford (ex-Burning Tree). By 1994, Eddie Harsch (keyboards) joined. Chris Robinson was married to actress Kate Hudson (daughter of Goldie Hawn; 2000-07). The Robinson brothers are the sons of Stan Robinson.

BLACK EYED PEAS
Hip-hop group from Los Angeles, California: Will Adams (will.i.am), Allan Pineda (apl.de.ap), Jaime Gomez (taboo) and Stacy Ferguson (Fergie). Ferguson was a member of Wild Orchid.

BLACK FLAG
Hardcore punk group from Los Angeles, California: Henry Rollins (vocals; Rollins Band), Greg Ginn (guitar), Dez Cadena (guitar), Charles Dukowski (bass) and Roberto "Robo" Valverde (drums).

BLACKFOOT
Southern-rock band from Jacksonville, Florida: Rickey Medlocke (vocals, guitar), Charlie Hargrett (guitar), Greg Walker (bass) and Jakson Spires (drums). Medlocke and Walker were original members of Lynyrd Skynyrd. Spires died of a brain hemorrhage on 3/16/2005 (age 53).

BLACKFOOT, J.
Born John Colbert on 11/20/1946 in Greenville, Mississippi. R&B singer. Formerly with The Soul Children.

BLACKGIRL
Black female R&B vocal trio from Atlanta, Georgia: Nycolia "Tye-V" Turman, Pamela Copeland and Rochelle Stuart.

BLACKHAWK
Country vocal trio: Henry Paul (Outlaws), Van Stephenson and Dave Robbins. Stephenson died of cancer on 4/8/2001 (age 47).

BLACKJACK
Rock group formed in New York: Michael Bolotin (vocals), Bruce Kulick (guitar), Jimmy Haslip (bass) and Sandy Gennaro (drums). Bolotin began solo career in 1983 as Michael Bolton. Kulick joined Kiss in 1985.

BLACK LAB
Rock group from Berkeley, California: Paul Durham (vocals), Michael Belfer (guitar), Geoff Stanfield (bass) and Bryan Head (drums).

BLACK MOON
Rap trio from Brooklyn, New York: Kenyatta "Buckshot Shorty" Blake (lead vocals), 5 Ft. Excellerator and DJ Evil Dee of the Beat Minerz. Black Moon stands for Brothers Lyrically Acting, Combining Kicking Music Out On Nations. Buckshot Shorty is also a member of The Crooklyn Dodgers.

BLACK OAK ARKANSAS
Southern-rock band from Black Oak, Arkansas: Jim "Dandy" Mangrum (vocals), Ricky Reynolds, Jimmy Henderson and Stan Knight (guitars), Pat Daugherty (bass) and Wayne Evans (drums).

BLACKOUT ALLSTARS, The
All-star Latin group: Ray Barretto, Sheila E., Tito Puente, Tito Nieves, Paquito D'Rivera, Dave Valentin and Grover Washington Jr. Washington died of a heart attack on 12/17/1999 (age 56). Puente died of heart failure on 5/31/2000 (age 77).

BLACK ROB
Born Robert Ross in 1970 in Harlem, New York. Male rapper.

BLACK SABBATH
Heavy-metal rock band from Birmingham, England: Ozzy Osbourne (vocals; born on 12/3/1948), Tony Iommi (guitar; born on 2/19/1948), Terry "Geezer" Butler (bass; born on 7/17/1949) and William Ward (drums; born on 5/5/1948). Osbourne fired from band in January 1979; replaced by Ronnie James Dio. Numerous personnel changes over the years.

BLACK SHEEP
Rap duo from the Bronx, New York: Andres Titus and William McLean.

BLACKstreet
R&B/hip-hop group: Teddy Riley (vocals), Chauncey Hannibal, Levi Little and Dave Hollister. Riley, a prolific producer (Michael Jackson, Keith Sweat, Bobby Brown and more) and originator of the "new jack swing" style was a member of Guy and Kids At Work. Hollister is the cousin of K-Ci & JoJo of Jodeci. Hollister and Little left in late 1995; replaced by Eric Williams and Mark Middleton.

BLACKWELL
Pop-rock band from Houston, Texas: Glenn Gibson (vocals), Jimmy Smith (guitar), John Bundrick (keyboards), Terry Wilson (bass) and Randy Dehart (drums).

BLACKWELL, Charlie
Born on 5/11/1921 in Seattle, Washington. Percussionist, top sideman with many jazz greats (Stan Kenton, Dave Brubeck, Charlie Barnett and others).

BLADES OF GRASS, The
Pop group from New Jersey: Dave Gordon, Frank Dichiara, Bruce Ames and Marc Black.

BLAHZAY BLAHZAY
Rap duo from Brooklyn, New York: rapper Out Loud and producer DJ P.F. Cuttin.

BLAIR
Born Blair MacKichan in 1970 in London, England. White male dance-pop singer.

BLAKEY, Art, & The Jazz Messengers
Born on 10/11/1919 in Pittsburgh, Pennsylvania. Died of cancer on 10/16/1990 (age 71). Black jazz drummer. Played in Billy Eckstine's band from 1944-47.

BLANCHARD, Jack, & Misty Morgan
Husband-and-wife country duo. Both born in Buffalo, New York. Jack (born on 5/8/1942) plays saxophone and keyboards. Misty (born on 5/23/1945) plays keyboards. Met and married while working in Florida.

BLAND, Billy
Born on 4/5/1932 in Wilmington, North Carolina. R&B singer. Formed group the Four Bees in 1954. First recorded solo for Old Town in 1955.

BLAND, Bobby "Blue"
Born on 1/27/1930 in Rosemark, Tennessee. Blues singer/guitarist. Nicknamed "Blue." Sang in gospel group The Miniatures in Memphis, late 1940s. Member of the Beale Streeters which included Johnny Ace, B.B. King, Rosco Gordon, Earl Forest and Willie Nix in 1949. Driver and valet for B.B. King; appeared in the Johnny Ace Revue, early 1950s. First recorded in 1952 for the Modern label.

BLANE, Marcie
Born on 5/21/1944 in Brooklyn, New York. Pop singer.

BLAQ, Rufus
Born Rufus Moore in Youngstown, Ohio. Male rapper.

BLAQUE
Female R&B vocal trio from Atlanta, Georgia: Shamari Fears, Natina Reed and Brandi Williams.

BLAZE
Five-member pop-rock group from Cincinnati, Ohio.

BLEND, The
Rock group from Portland, Maine: Jim Drown (vocals, guitar), Steven Dore (guitar), Donnie Pomber (keyboards), Ken Holt (bass) and Skip Smith (drums). Drown died on 12/3/2002 (age 55).

BLENDELLS, The
Latin rock band from Los Angeles, California: Sal Murillo (vocals), Rudy Valona (guitar), Tommy Esparza (guitars), Don Cardenas (sax), Mike Rincon (bass) and Ron Chipres (drums). Valona died on 12/26/2003 (age 56).

BLENDERS, The
R&B vocal group from Chicago, Illinois: Hilliard "Johnny" Jones (formerly with the Five Chances), Albert Hunter, Goldie Coates, Delores Johnson and Gail Mapp (lead). Later recorded as The Candles on the Nike label.

BLESSID UNION OF SOULS
Interracial Adult Alternative group from Cincinnati, Ohio: Eliot Sloan (vocals, piano), Jeff Pence (guitar), Charly Roth (keyboards), Tony Clark (bass) and Eddie Hedges (drums). Group name taken from a line in the TV show *M*A*S*H*.

BLEU, Corbin
Born Corbin Bleu Reivers on 2/21/1989 in Brooklyn, New York (Jamaican father; American mother). Male singer/dancer/actor. Played "Chad Danforth" in the popular TV movie series *High School Musical*.

BLEYER, Archie
Born on 6/12/1909 in Corona, New York. Died of Parkinson's disease on 3/20/1989 (age 79). Arranger/music director for the radio and TV show *Arthur Godfrey and His Friends* from 1949-54. Founded Cadence Records. Married Chordettes member Janet Ertel in 1954.

BLIGE, Mary J.
Born Mary Jane Blige on 1/11/1971 in the Bronx, New York; spent first few years in Savannah, Georgia; mainly raised in Yonkers, New York. Recognized by most music critics as the R&B queen of the past 15 years. Iso see Case's "Touch Me Tease Me."

BLIND FAITH
Rock supergroup from England: Eric Clapton (The Yardbirds, Cream), Steve Winwood (Spencer Davis Group, Traffic), Ginger Baker (Cream) and Rick Grech (Family, Traffic). Formed and disbanded in 1969.

BLIND MELON
Male rock group formed in Los Angeles, California: Shannon Hoon (vocals), Rogers Stevens and Christopher Thorn (guitars), Brad Smith (bass) and Glen Graham (drums). Stevens, Smith and Graham are from West Point, Mississippi. Hoon died of a drug overdose on 10/21/1995 (age 28).

BLINK-182
Punk-rock trio from San Diego, California: Tom DeLonge (vocals, guitar), Mark Hoppus (vocals, bass) and Scott Raynor (drums). Travis Barker replaced Raynor in 1998. Also see (+44).

BLINKY
Born Sondra Williams in California. Female R&B singer. Recorded duets with Edwin Starr in 1969.

BLONDIE
New-wave rock group formed in New York: Debbie Harry (vocals; born on 7/1/1945), Chris Stein (born on 1/5/1950) and Frank Infante (guitars), Jimmy Destri (keyboards; born on 4/13/1954), Nigel Harrison (bass; born on 4/24/1951) and Clem Burke (drums; born on 11/24/1955). Harry had been in the folk-rock group Wind In The Willows. Disbanded in 1982; reunited in 1999.

BLOODHOUND GANG
Electro-rock group from Trappe, Pennsylvania: Jimmy Pop Ali (vocals), Lupus (guitar), Q-Ball (DJ), Evil Jared (bass) and Spanky G (drums).

BLOODROCK
Hard-rock band from Fort Worth, Texas: Jim Rutledge (vocals), Lee Pickens and Nick Taylor (guitars), Stevie Hill (keyboards), Eddie Grundy (bass) and Rick Cobb (drums). Rutledge headed own production company in the 1970s; produced Meri Wilson's "Telephone Man."

BLOODSTONE
R&B vocal group from Kansas City, Missouri: Charles Love, Willis Draffen, Charles McCormick and Harry Williams. Group starred in the 1975 movie *Train Ride To Hollywood*. Draffen died on 2/8/2002 (age 56).

BLOOD, SWEAT & TEARS
Rock-jazz group formed by Al Kooper (keyboards; born on 2/5/44; Royal Teens, Blues Project) in 1967. Nucleus consisted of Kooper, Steve Katz (guitar; born on 5/9/45; American Flyer; Blues Project), Bobby Colomby (drums; born on 12/20/44) and Jim Fielder (bass; born on 10/4/47). Kooper replaced by lead singer David Clayton-Thomas (born on 9/13/41) by 1969. Clayton-Thomas replaced by Jerry Fisher in 1972. Katz left in 1973. Clayton-Thomas rejoined in 1974. Colomby later worked as a television music reporter and an executive with Epic, Capitol, EMI and CBS.

BLOOM, Bobby
Born in 1945 in Brooklyn, New York. Died from an accidental shooting on 2/28/1974 (age 28). Pop singer/songwriter. Much session work in the 1960s.

BLOSSOMS, The
Female R&B backing vocal group for Elvis Presley, Paul Anka, Duane Eddy, Bobby Darin, Mamas & Papas, Beach Boys, Herb Alpert, Dionne Warwick and many others. Regulars on TV's *Shindig*. Members Darlene Love, Fanita James (nee Barrett) and Gloria Jones were members of Bob B. Soxx & The Blue Jeans. Also included twins Annette and Nanette Williams. Grazia Nitzsche (wife of Jack Nitzsche) sang on the sessions. Group actually performed two songs as by The Crystals.

BLOUNT, Tanya
Born on 9/25/1977 in Washington DC. Female R&B singer.

BLOW, Kurtis
Born Kurt Walker on 8/9/1959 in Harlem, New York. Pioneering rapper. Began as a disco DJ. Appeared in the movie *Krush Groove*.

BLOW MONKEYS, The
Pop-rock group from England: "Dr. Robert" Howard (vocals, guitar), Neville Henry (saxophone), Mick Anker (bass) and Tony Kiley (drums).

BLUE
Pop-rock group from Glasgow, Scotland: brothers Hugh (guitar) and David (keyboards) Nicholson, Ian McMillan (bass) and Charlie Smith (drums).

BLUE, David
Born Stuart David Cohen on 2/18/1941 in Providence, Rhode Island. Died while jogging on 12/2/1982 (age 41).

BLUE CHEER
Hard-rock trio formed in Boston, Massachusetts; later based in San Francisco, California: Dickie Peterson (vocals, bass), Leigh Stephens (guitar) and Paul Whaley (drums). One of the first "heavy metal" bands.

BLUE COUNTY
Country duo formed in Nashville, Tennessee: Aaron Benward (from Auburn, Indiana) and Scott Reeves (from Delight, Arkansas). Reeves played "Ryan McNeil" on TV's *The Young And The Restless.*

BLUE DIAMONDS, The
Vocal duo from Indonesia: brothers Rudy DeWolff (born on 12/5/1941; died on 12/18/2000, age 59) and Riem DeWolff (born on 4/15/1943). Immigrated to Holland in 1949.

BLUE HAZE
Reggae studio group assembled in England by producers Johnny Arthey and Phil Swern.

BLUE JAYS, The
R&B vocal group from Los Angeles, California: Leon Peels, Van Richardson, Alex Manigo and Leonard Davidson. Peels died of cancer on 4/12/1999 (age 62).

BLUE MAGIC
R&B vocal group from Philadelphia, Pennsylvania: Theodore Mills (lead), Vernon Sawyer, Wendell Sawyer, Keith Beaton and Richard Pratt.

BLUE MERCEDES
Pop duo from London, England: David Titlow (vocals) and Duncan Millar (keyboards).

BLUE MINK
Pop group from England: Madeline Bell and Roger Cook (vocals), Alan Parker (guitar), Roger Coulman (keyboards), Herbie Flowers (bass) and Barry Morgan (drums). Cook was one-half of David & Jonathan duo and co-founder of White Plains.

BLUENOTES, The
White male vocal group from Asheboro, North Carolina: Ralph Harrington, Pat Patterson, Tom Underwood and Joe Tanner (later an arranger/publisher; since deceased). Did backing vocals for George Hamilton IV.

BLUE OCTOBER
Rock band from Houston, Texas: brothers Justin (vocals, guitar) and Jeremy Furstenfeld (drums), with C.B. Hudson (guitar), Ryan Delahoussaye (keyboards) and Matt Noveskey (bass).

BLUE OYSTER CULT
Hard-rock group from Long Island, New York: Eric Bloom (vocals), Donald "Buck Dharma" Roeser (guitar), Allen Lanier (keyboards), and brothers Joe (bass) and Albert (drums) Bouchard. Rick Downey replaced Albert Bouchard in 1982. Downey left in 1984. Tommy Zvoncheck (keyboards) and Jimmy Wilcox (drums) joined in 1985. Bloom is a cousin of DJ Howard Stern.

BLUES BROTHERS
Duo of comedians John Belushi (as "Jake Blues") and Dan Aykroyd (as "Elwood Blues"). Originally created for TV's *Saturday Night Live.* Starred in their own movie. Belushi was born on 1/24/1949 in Wheaton, Illinois. Died of a drug overdose on 3/5/1982 (age 33). Aykroyd was born on 7/1/1952 in Ottawa, Ontario, Canada. Backing band included Paul Shaffer, and Steve Cropper and Donald "Duck" Dunn of Booker T. & The MG's. Actor John Goodman replaced Belushi for the *Blues Brothers 2000* movie.

BLUES IMAGE
Rock group from Tampa, Florida: Mike Pinera (vocals, guitar; Iron Butterfly), Frank "Skip" Konte (keyboards; Three Dog Night), Joe Lala (percussion), Malcolm Jones (bass) and Manuel Bertematti (drums).

BLUES MAGOOS
Psychedelic-rock group from the Bronx, New York: Emil "Peppy Castro" Thielhelm (vocals, guitar), Mike Esposito (guitar), Ralph Scala (keyboards), Ronnie Gilbert (bass) and Geoff Daking (drums). Originally known as the Bloos Magoos. Castro later became lead singer of Balance.

BLUES PROJECT, The
Blues-rock group from New York City, New York: Danny Kalb (guitar) and Roy Blumenfeld (drums). Vocalist Tommy Flanders left group in 1966. Guitarist Steve Katz and organist Al Kooper took over vocals. Katz and Kooper left to form Blood, Sweat & Tears in 1968.

BLUE STARS
Pop-jazz group formed in Paris, France. Lead vocals by Blossom Dearie (born on 4/28/1926 in East Durham, New York), a former big-band singer who sang with King Pleasure on his 1952 R&B hit "Moody Mood For Love."

BLUES TRAVELER
Blues-rock group from New York City, New York: John Popper (vocals, harmonica), Chan Kinchla (guitar), Bobby Sheehan (bass) and Brendan Hill (drums). Sheehan died of a drug overdose on 8/20/1999 (age 31); replaced by Chan's brother, Tad Kinchla.

BLUE SWEDE
Pop group from Sweden: Bjorn Skifs (vocals), Michael Areklew (guitar), Anders Berglund (keyboards), Hinke Ekestubbe (sax), Thomas Berglund (trumpet), Bosse Liljedahl (bass) and Jan Guldback (drums).

BLUE TRAIN
Rock group from Nottingham, Nottinghamshire, England: Tony Osborne (vocals), Alan Fearn (guitar), Simon Husbands (keyboards) and Paul Betts (drums).

BLUE ZONE U.K.
Dance trio formed in 1984 in Rochdale, England: Lisa Stansfield (vocals), Andy Morris (trumpet, keyboards) and Ian Devaney (trombone, keyboards). In 1989, Stansfield went solo, produced by Morris and Devaney.

BLUNT, James
Born James Blount on 2/22/1974 in Tidworth, Wiltshire, England. Adult Alternative singer/songwriter/guitarist/pianist.

BLUR
Pop-rock group from London, England: Damon Albarn (vocals), Graham Coxon (guitar), Alex James (bass) and Dave Rowntree (drums). Albarn later co-founder Gorillaz.

BMU (BLACK MEN UNITED)
All-star gathering of top R&B stars: R. Kelly, Tevin Campbell, Aaron Hall, Brian McKnight, Boyz II Men, Tony Toni Toné, Silk, Keith Sweat, Stokley (Mint Condition), H-Town, Christopher Williams, Portrait, Gerald Levert, Al B. Sure!, Damion Hall, Lil' Joe (Rude Boys), Intro, D.R.S., El DeBarge, After 7, Usher, Sovory, Joe, D'Angelo and Lenny Kravitz (guitar).

BO, Eddie
Born Edwin Bocage on 9/20/1930 in New Orleans, Louisiana. R&B singer/pianist/producer. Nicknamed "Spider."

BOB & EARL
R&B vocal duo: Bob Relf & Earl Nelson. Bobby Day sang with Earl Nelson (as Bob & Earl) in 1960; however, Day was not involved in either of Bob & Earl's charted hits. Earl Lee Nelson (wife's name was Jackie) recorded the hit "The Duck" as Jackie Lee. Earl was also lead singer on the Hollywood Flames' hit "Buzz-Buzz-Buzz."

BOBBETTES, The
Female R&B vocal group from Harlem, New York: sisters Emma and Jannie Pought, Laura Webb, Helen Gathers and Heather Dixon. Jannie Pought died in a car crash in September 1980 (age 36). Webb died of cancer on 1/8/2001 (age 59).

BOB B. SOXX & The Blue Jeans
Vocal trio formed by producer Phil Spector (The Teddy Bears). Bobby Sheen (The Alley Cats) with Darlene Love and Fanita James (both formerly with The Blossoms). Love and James later replaced by Gloria Jones (also with The Blossoms) and Carolyn Willis. Sheen died of pneumonia on 11/23/2000 (age 58).

BoDEANS
Rock and roll band from Waukesha, Wisconsin: Sam Llanas and Kurt Neumann (vocals, guitars), Michael Ramos (keyboards), Bob Griffin (bass) and Nick Kitsos (drums).

BODY HEAD BANGERZ
All-star rap group: Roy Jones Jr., Magic, Choppa, Giz, Swellz, Rated PG's and Big Perion.

BOFILL, Angela
Born on 5/2/1954 in the Bronx, New York (Cuban father; Puerto Rican mother); raised in Harlem, New York. Jazz-styled singer/songwriter. Trained in opera at the Manhattan School of Music. Father was lead singer for Cuban bandleader Machito.

BOHANNON, Hamilton
Born on 3/7/1942 in Newnan, Georgia. Drummer for Stevie Wonder from 1965-67. Bandleader/arranger for Motown tours until the mid-1970s.

BOLTON, Michael
Born Michael Bolotin on 2/26/1954 in New Haven, Connecticut. First recorded for Epic in 1968. Lead singer of Blackjack in the late 1970s. Began recording as Michael Bolton in 1983.

BOND, Johnny
Born Cyrus Bond on 6/1/1915 in Enville, Oklahoma. Died of a heart attack on 6/12/1978 (age 63). Country singer/songwriter/actor/author. Appeared in several movies.

BONDS, Gary (U.S.)
Born Gary Anderson on 6/6/1939 in Jacksonville, Florida; raised in Norfolk, Virginia. Black rock and roll singer/songwriter.

BONE CRUSHER
Born Wayne Hardnett on 8/23/1971 in Atlanta, Georgia. Male rapper.

BONE THUGS-N-HARMONY
Male rap group from Cleveland, Ohio: Anthony Henderson ("Krayzie Bone"; born on 6/17/1973), Charles Scruggs ("Wish Bone"; born on 2/17/1975), Bryon McCane ("Bizzy Bone"; born on 9/12/1976) and brothers Steven Howse ("Layzie Bone"; born on 9/23/1975) and Stanley Howse ("Flesh-N-Bone"; born on 6/10/1974; went solo in 1996). Steven and Stanley are brothers; Scruggs is their cousin. Discovered by Eazy-E. Previously known as Bone Enterprise.

BONEY M
Vocal group created in Germany by producer/composer Frank Farian. Farian sang solo on first recording in 1975; group formed later. Consisted of Marcia Barrett, Maizie Williams, Liz Mitchell and Bobby Farrell. All were from the West Indies. Farian created the Far Corporation in 1986 and Milli Vanilli in 1988.

BONHAM
British hard-rock group led by drummer Jason Bonham, the son of Led Zeppelin's drummer, the late John Bonham. Includes Daniel MacMaster (vocals), Ian Hatton (guitar) and John Smithson (keyboards, bass).

BONHAM, Tracy
Born on 3/16/1967 in Eugene, Oregon. Female rock singer/songwriter/guitarist.

BON JOVI
Rock group from Sayreville, New Jersey: Jon Bon Jovi (vocals; born on 3/2/1962), Richie Sambora (guitar; born on 7/11/1959), Dave Bryan (keyboards; born on 2/7/1962), Alec John Such (bass; born on 11/14/1956) and Tico Torres (drums; born on

BON JOVI — cont'd
10/7/1953). Such left in November 1994. Jon also pursued acting with roles in movies *Moonlight and Valentino* and *U571* and on TV's *Ally McBeal*. Sambora was married to actress Heather Locklear from 1994-2007.

BONNIE AND THE TREASURES
Born Charlotte Ann Matheny in 1945. Died of cancer in 1976 (age 31). Also recorded as Charlotte O'Hara and Bonnie Graham.

BONNIE LOU
Born Mary Kath on 10/27/1924 in Towanda, Illinois. Country singer/guitarist.

BONNIE SISTERS
Doo-wop "girl group" from Brooklyn, New York: Pat, Jean and Sylvia Bonnie. All were nurses at Bellevue Hospital. One of the first white female rock and roll vocal groups.

BONOFF, Karla
Born on 12/27/1951 in Los Angeles, California. Pop singer/songwriter/pianist.

BOOKER, Chuckii
Born on 12/19/1962 in Los Angeles, California. R&B multi-instrumentalist. Session keyboard work with Vanessa Williams, Gerald Albright and Troop. Godson of Barry White.

BOOKER, James
Born on 12/17/1939 in New Orleans, Louisiana. Died on 11/8/1983 (age 43). R&B-jazz pianist/organist. Nicknamed "Little Booker." First recorded for Imperial in 1954. With Dee Clark's band in 1960. Session work at Duke/Peacock in Houston.

BOOKER T. & THE MG'S
Interracial R&B band formed by sessionmen from Stax Records in Memphis, Tennessee. Consisted of Booker T. Jones (keyboards; born on 11/12/1944 in Memphis, Tennessee), Steve Cropper (guitar), Donald "Duck" Dunn (bass) and Al Jackson, Jr. (drums; murdered on 10/1/1975, age 39). MG stands for Memphis Group. Jones was in a band with classmate Maurice White of Earth, Wind & Fire. Cropper and Dunn had been in the Mar-Keys. Much session work. Recordings included horns by Andrew Love, Wayne Jackson and Joe Arnold, plus Isaac Hayes, piano. Group disbanded in 1971, and reorganized for a short time in 1973. Cropper and Dunn joined the Blues Brothers. Jones received music degree from Indiana University; married Priscilla Coolidge (sister of Rita); and did production work for Rita Coolidge, Earl Klugh, Bill Withers and Willie Nelson (his *Stardust* album).

BOOK OF LOVE
Electro-dance/pop group from New York: Susan Ottaviano (vocals), Ted Ottaviano and Lauren Roselli (keyboards), and Jade Lee (percussion). The Ottavianos are not related.

BOOM, Taka
Born Yvonne Stevens in 1954 in Chicago, Illinois. R&B singer. Sister of Chaka Khan.

BOOMKAT
Pop duo from Tuscon, Arizona: brother-and sister Kellin and Taryn Manning. Taryn acted in the movies *Crossroads* and *8 Mile*.

BOOMTOWN RATS, The
Rock group formed in Dublin, Ireland: Bob Geldof (vocals; born on 10/5/1951), Gerry Cott and Garry Roberts (guitars), Johnnie Fingers (keyboards), Pete Briquette (bass) and Simon Crowe (drums). Geldof organized Band Aid in 1984.

BOONE, Daniel
Born Peter Lee Stirling on 7/31/1942 in Birmingham, England. Pop singer/songwriter.

BOONE, Debby
Born on 9/22/1956 in Hackensack, New Jersey. Third daughter of Shirley and Pat Boone and granddaughter of Red Foley. Worked with the Boone Family from the mid-1960s, sang with sisters in the Boone Girls Gospel Quartet. Went solo in 1977. Popular Contemporary Christian artist. Married Gabriel Ferrer, the son of Rosemary Clooney and actor Jose Ferrer, on 9/1/1979.

BOONE, Pat
Born Charles Eugene Boone on 6/1/1934 in Jacksonville, Florida. To Tennessee in 1936. Direct descendant of Daniel Boone. Married country singer Red Foley's daughter, Shirley, on 11/7/1953. Won on *Arthur Godfrey's Talent Scouts* in 1954. First recorded for Republic Records in 1954. Graduated from New York's Columbia University in 1958. Hosted own TV show, *The Pat Boone-Chevy Showroom*, 1957-60. Appeared in 15 movies. Wrote several books. Toured with wife and daughters Cherry, Linda, Laura and Debby Boone in the mid-1960s. Hosted own syndicated show on Christian radio. Recording artist Nick Todd is his younger brother. Pat's trademark: white buck shoes. Comeback on charts in 1997 with an album covering heavy-metal tunes.

BORN JAMERICANS
Dancehall reggae duo: Horace "Edley Shine" Payne and Norman "Natch" Howell. Both were born in U.S. to Jamaican parents. Payne was raised in Washington DC; Howell was raised in Hartford, Connecticut.

BOSS
Female hardcore rap duo based in Los Angeles, California: Lichelle "Boss" Laws and Irene "Dee" Moore.

BOSTON
Hard-rock band from Boston, Massachusetts, spearheaded by Tom Scholz (guitars, keyboards, songwriter; born on 3/10/1947). His homemade demo tapes became the basis of Boston's first album in 1976 with Scholz recruiting members Brad Delp (vocals; born on 6/12/1951; died on 3/9/2007, age 55), Barry Goudreau (guitar; born on 11/29/1951), Fran Sheehan (bass; born on 3/26/1949) and Sib Hashian (drums; born on 8/17/1949). Goudreau formed Orion The Hunter in 1982. After a long absence from the charts, Boston returned in 1986 as a duo: Scholz and Delp. Delp and Goudreau spearheaded RTZ in 1991. Scholz's

BOSTON — cont'd

1994 Boston lineup: Fran Cosmo (Orion The Hunter) and Tommy Funderburk (vocals), Gary Pihl (guitar), David Sikes (bass) and Doug Huffman (drums). Scholz is an avid inventor with several patents.

BOSTON POPS ORCHESTRA

An American institution founded in 1885 by Henry Lee Higginson, conductor of the Boston Symphony Orchestra. Arthur Fiedler (born on 12/17/1894 in Boston, Massachusetts; trained in Germany; died on 7/10/1979, age 84) joined the orchestra in 1915 as a violist; began his reign as its conductor in 1930 and remained until his death. Local radio broadcasts of concerts began in 1952, then syndicated nationally from 1962-92. National public TV program *Evening at Pops* began in 1969. John Williams succeeded Fiedler in 1980. Keith Lockhart (former Cincinnati Pops conductor) succeeded Williams in 1995.

BOUNTY KILLER

Born Rodney Pryce on 6/26/1972 in Riverton City, Jamaica. Reggae singer.

BOURGEOIS TAGG

Rock group from Los Angeles, California: Brent Bourgeois (vocals, keyboards), Larry Tagg (vocals, bass), Lyle Workman (guitar), Scott Moon (synthesizer) and Michael Urbano (drums). Bourgeois was named vice president of A&R for Word Records in 1997.

BOWEN, Jimmy

Born on 11/30/1937 in Santa Rita, New Mexico. Formed The Rhythm Orchids at West Texas State University with Buddy Knox, Don Lanier and Dave "Dicky Doo" Alldred. Bowen became a producer and top record executive on the West Coast. Produced 20 of Dean Martin's hits, 1964-69. In 1984, became president of MCA Records in Nashville (renamed Universal Records in 1988).

BOWIE, David

Born David Jones on 1/8/1947 in Brixton, London, England. Left pupil paralyzed in a childhood fight resulting in appearance of different-colored eyes. From 1964-66, recorded with the bands King Bees, Manish Boys and Lower Third. First recorded solo in 1966. Joined Lindsay Kemp Mime Troupe in 1967. Formed short-lived trio Feathers in 1968. Adopted new personas (Ziggy Stardust, Alladin Sane, Thin White Duke) to accompany several of his musical phases. Married to Angie Barnett, the subject of The Rolling Stones' song "Angie," from 1970-80. Acted in several movies including *The Man Who Fell To Earth*, *Labyrinth* and *Absolute Beginners*; starred in *The Elephant Man* on Broadway. Formed the group Tin Machine in 1988. Married Somalian actress/supermodel Iman on 4/24/1992. Launched own Internet service provider, Bowienet, in 1998.

BOWLES, Rick

Born in Shelby, North Carolina. Pop singer/songwriter. Later co-wrote several country hits.

BOWLING FOR SOUP

Punk-rock band from Wichita Falls, Texas: Jaret Reddick (vocals, guitar), Chris Burney (guitar), Erik Chandler (bass) and Gary Wiseman (drums).

BOW WOW

Born Shad Moss on 3/9/1987 in Columbus, Ohio. Teen male rapper/actor. Starred in the movies *Like Mike* and *Roll Bounce;* also acted in the movies *All About The Benjamins* and *Johnson Family Vacation*. First recorded as Lil Bow Wow.

BOW WOW WOW

New-wave group assembled in London, England, by Malcolm McLaren (former Sex Pistols manager). Consisted of Annabella Lwin (vocals; born Myant Myant Aye in Burma), Matthew Ashman (guitar), Leroy Gorman (bass) and Dave Barbarossa (drums). The latter three were members of Adam And The Ants until 1980. Boy George had a brief stint with the group. Ashman died of diabetes on 11/21/1995 (age 35).

BOX TOPS, The

Pop-rock band from Memphis, Tennessee: Alex Chilton (vocals; born on 12/28/1950), Gary Talley (guitar; born on 8/17/1947), John Evans (organ), Bill Cunningham (bass; born on 1/23/1950) and Danny Smythe (drums). Evans and Smythe left in late 1967; replaced by Rick Allen and Tom Boggs. Disbanded in 1970. Chilton later formed the power-pop band Big Star. Cunningham is the brother of B.B. Cunningham of The Hombres. Boggs died of cancer on 5/5/2008 (age 63).

BOYCE, Tommy, & Bobby Hart

Top songwriting duo/production team. Boyce was born on 9/29/1939 in Charlottesville, Virginia. Died of a self-inflicted gunshot wound on 11/23/1994 (age 55). Hart was born on 2/18/1939 in Phoenix, Arizona. Writers of "Pretty Little Angel Eyes," "Come A Little Bit Closer," much of The Monkees material and others. Toured and recorded with The Monkees' Davy Jones and Mickey Dolenz in 1975.

BOYD, Eddie

Born on 11/25/1914 near Clarksdale, Mississippi. Died on 7/13/1994 (age 79). Blues singer/guitarist/pianist.

BOYER, Bonnie

Born on 7/28/1958 in San Francisco, California. Disco singer.

BOY KRAZY

Female pop vocal group from New York: Kimberly Blake, Johnna Lee Cummings, Josselyne Jones and Ruth Ann Roberts (a former Miss Junior America).

BOY MEETS GIRL

Songwriting/recording duo from Seattle, Washington: Shannon Rubicam and George Merrill. Married in 1988. Wrote Whitney Houston's hits "How Will I Know" and "I Wanna Dance With Somebody."

BOYS, The
R&B vocal group from Northridge, California: brothers Khiry, Hakeem, Tajh and Bilal Samad. All were members of performing gymnastic troupes. Ages 9-14 in 1988.

BOYS BAND, The
Country-rock trio from Hendersonville, Tennessee: Greg Gordon (vocals), B. James Lowry (guitar, vocals) and Rusty Golden (keyboards, vocals; son of William Golden of the Oak Ridge Boys).

BOYS CLUB
Duo formed in Minneapolis, Minnesota: vocalists Joe Pasquale and Gene Hunt (born Eugene Wolfgramm; formerly with his family group, The Jets).

BOYS DON'T CRY
Pop-rock group from England: Nick Richards (vocals), Nico Ramsden (guitar), Brian Chatton (keybaords), Mark Smith (bass) and Jeff Seopardi (drums).

BOYS IN THE BAND, The
Studio group led by Herman Lewis Griffin, the first husband of Mary Wells. Griffin (born on 11/25/1936 in Selma, Alabama; died of a heart attack on 11/11/1989, age 52) recorded in 1957, on H.O.B., the first song of Berry Gordy's Jobete Publishing.

BOYS LIKE GIRLS
Alternative-rock band from Andover, Massachusetts: Martin Johnson (vocals, guitar), Paul DiGiovanni (guitar), Bryan Donahue (bass) and John Keefe (drums).

BOYZ N DA HOOD
Male rap group formed in Atlanta, Georgia: Jay "Young Jeezy" Jenkins, Jacoby "Jody Breeze" White, Miguel "Big Gee" Scott and Lee "Big Duke" Dixon.

BOYZ II MEN
R&B vocal group from Philadelphia, Pennsylvania: Wanya Morris (born on 7/29/1973), Michael McCary (born on 12/16/1971), Shawn Stockman (born on 9/26/1972) and Nathan Morris (born on 6/18/1971). Discovered by Michael Bivins (New Edition, Bell Biv DeVoe). Appeared in the 1992 TV mini-series *The Jacksons: An American Dream*.

BRADLEY, Jan
Born Addie Bradley on 7/6/1943 in Byhalia, Mississippi; raised in Robbins, Illinois. R&B singer. First recorded for Formal in 1962. Became a social worker in 1976.

BRADLEY, Owen, Quintet
Born on 10/21/1915 in Westmoreland, Tennessee. Died on 1/7/1998 (age 82). Band leader/producer/organist/combo leader. Country A&R director for Decca from 1958-68. Vice president of MCA from 1968. His quintet included Hank Garland (guitar), E.R. "Dutch" McMillan (tenor horn), Bob Moore (bass) and Buddy Harmon (drums). Away From Me."

BRADSHAW, Terry
Born on 9/2/1948 in Shreveport, Louisiana. Pro football quarterback with the Pittsburgh Steelers from 1970-83. In the movies *Hooper*, *Smokey and the Bandit II* and *Cannonball Run*. Current TV football analyst (on Fox's *NFL Sunday*).

BRAIDS, The
Female R&B vocal duo from Oakland, California: Caitlin Cornwell and Zoe Ellis.

BRAINSTORM
Disco group from Detroit, Michigan: Belita Karen "B.B." Woods (vocals), Charles Overton, Jeryl Bright, Larry H. "Leap" Sims, Gerald "Jumpin' Jerry" Kent, Trenita Womack, E. Lamont "Stro" Johnson, Willie Wooten and Renell Gonsalves (son of famous Duke Ellington saxman Paul Gonsalves).

BRAITHWAITE, Daryl
Born on 1/11/1949 in Melbourne, Australia; raised in Randwick, Australia. Former lead singer of the Sherbs.

BRAM TCHAIKOVSKY
Rock trio from Lincolnshire, England: Peter Bramall (vocals, guitar; The Motors), Micky Broadbent (bass) and Keith Boyce (drums).

BRANCH, Michelle
Born on 7/2/1983 in Phoenix, Arizona; raised in Flagstaff and Sedona, Arizona. Adult Alternative pop-rock singer/songwriter/guitarist. Formed country duo, The Wreckers, with Jessica Harp.

BRAND NEW HEAVIES, The
Funk group from London, England: N'dea Davenport (vocals), Simon Bartholomew (guitar), Andrew Levy (bass) and Jan Kincaid (drums). Davenport left in 1996; replaced by Siedah Garrett.

BRAND NUBIAN
Rap trio from New Rochelle, New York: Maxwell Dixon ("Grand Puba"), Derek Murphy "Sadat X") and Lorenzo DeChalus ("Lord Jamar"). Dixon left in 1992; replaced by Terence Perry ("Sincere Allah"). Dixon returned in 1998.

BRANDON
Born in San Jose, California (of Latin and Danish parentage). Dance singer/multi-instrumentalist.

BRANDON, Bill
Born in 1944 in Huntsville, Alabama. Black vocalist/trumpeter/bassist/drummer.

BRANDY
Born Brandy Norwood on 2/11/1979 in McComb, Mississippi; raised in Los Angeles, California. Singer/actress. Star of the TV series *Moesha*. Played "Karla Wilson" in the 1998 movie *I Still Know What You Did Last Summer*. Sister of Ray J. One of the judges on the 2006 TV show *America's Got Talent*.

BRANIGAN, Laura
Born on 7/3/1957 in Brewster, New York. Died of a brain aneurysm on 8/26/2004 (age 47). Pop singer/actress. Played "Monica" in the 1984 movie *Delta Pi*.

BRASS CONSTRUCTION
Disco group from Brooklyn, New York: Randy Muller (vocals, keyboards), Joe Wong (guitar), Wayne Parris, Morris Price, Jesse Ward and Mickey Grudge (horn section), Sandy Billups (congas), Wade Williamston (bass) and Larry Payton (drums). Muller later formed Skyy.

BRASS RING, The
Studio group assembled by producer/arranger/saxophonist Phil Bodner (born on 6/13/1921).

BRAT PACK, The
Male dance vocal duo from New Jersey: Patrick Donovan and Ray Frazier.

BRAUN, Bob
Born Robert Brown on 4/20/1929 in Ludlow, Kentucky. Died of Parkinson's disease on 1/15/2001 (age 71). Hosted own TV show in Cincinnati.

BRAVERY, The
Alternative-rock band from New York: Sam Endicott (vocals, guitar), Michael Zakarin (guitar), John Conway (keyboards), Mike Hindirt (bass) and Anthony Burulcich (drums).

BRAVO ALL STARS
Collaboration of Backstreet Boys, The Boyz, Blümchen, Aaron Carter, Gil, The Moffatts, Mr. President, 'N Sync, R'N'G, Scooter, Sqeezer, and Touché. Benefitting the Nordoff-Robbins Music Therapy Foundation.

BRAXTON, Toni
Born on 10/7/1967 in Severn, Maryland. Female R&B singer. Recorded in 1990 with her younger sisters as The Braxtons. Married Keri Lewis (of Mint Condition) on 4/21/2001.

BRAXTONS, The
Vocal trio of sisters from Severn, Maryland: Tamar, Trina and Towanda Braxton. Began as a quintet, with Traci and Toni Braxton. Toni went solo in 1992; Traci went solo in 1995.

BREAD
Soft-rock group formed in Los Angeles, California. Consisted of leader David Gates (vocals, guitar, keyboards; born on 12/11/1940), James Griffin (guitar), Robb Royer (guitar) and Jim Gordon (drums). Originally called Pleasure Faire. Mike Botts replaced Gordon after first album. Royer replaced by Larry Knechtel (top sessionman, member of Duane Eddy's Rebels) in 1971. Disbanded in 1973; reunited briefly in 1976. All hits written and produced by Gates. Griffin died of cancer on 1/11/2005 (age 61). Botts died of cancer on 12/9/2005 (age 61).

BREAKFAST CLUB
Pop-dance group from Manhattan, New York: brothers Dan (vocals) and Eddie (guitar) Gilroy, Gary Burke (bass) and Stephen Bray (drums). Madonna was with the group for a short time in 1979 as the drummer. Bray co-produced Madonna's *True Blue* album.

BREAKING BENJAMIN
Hard-rock band from Wilkes-Barre, Pennsylvania: Ben Burnley (vocals, guitar), Aaron Fink (guitar),

Mark Klepaski (bass) and Jeremy Hummel (drums). Chad Szeliga replaced Hummel in late 2005.

BREATHE
Pop group from London, England: David Glasper (vocals), Marcus Lillington (guitar), Michael Delahunty (bass) and Ian Spice (drums). Delahunty left in 1988.

BREATHLESS
Rock group from Cleveland, Ohio: Jonah Koslen (vocals; Michael Stanley Band), Alan Greene (guitar), Mark Avsec (keyboards; Wild Cherry), Bob Benjamin (bass), and Rodney Psyka and Kevin Valentine (drums).

BRECKER BROTHERS, The
White jazz-funk duo of Philadelphia-born brothers Randy (trumpet; born on 11/27/1945) and Michael (reeds; born on 3/29/1949; died on 1/13/2007, age 57) Brecker. Both are prolific sessionmen. The brothers began recording together in their group, Dreams; also with Spyro Gyra.

BREEDERS, The
Rock group from Dayton, Ohio: twin sisters/guitarists/vocalists Kim and Kelley Deal, bassist Josephine Wiggs (native of Bedfordshire, England) and drummer Jim MacPherson. Kim was a member of the Pixies. Tanya Donelly (Throwing Muses, Belly) was an early member.

BREMERS, Beverly
Born on 3/10/1950 in Chicago, Illinois. Pop singer/actress.

BRENDA & THE TABULATIONS
R&B vocal group from Philadelphia, Pennsylvania: Brenda Payton, Jerry Jones, Eddie Jackson and Maurice Coates. Bernard Murphy was added in 1969. Reorganized in 1970 with vocalists Payton, Pat Mercer and Deborah Martin. Payton died on 6/14/1992 (age 46).

BRENNAN, Walter
Born on 7/25/1894 in Swampscott, Massachusetts. Died of emphysema on 9/21/1974 (age 80). Famous character actor. Appeared in several movies and TV shows.

BRENSTON, Jackie, & His Delta Cats
Born on 8/15/1930 in Clarksdale, Mississippi. Died of a heart attack on 12/15/1979 (age 49). Male singer/saxophonist with Ike Turner's Kings Of Rhythm.

BREWER, Teresa
Born Theresa Breuer on 5/7/1931 in Toledo, Ohio. Died on 10/17/2007 (age 76). Pop singer. Debuted on *Major Bowes Amateur Hour* at age five; toured with show until age 12. Appeared on *Pick & Pat* radio show. First recorded for London in 1949. In the movie *Those Redheads From Seattle*.

BREWER & SHIPLEY
Folk-rock duo formed in Los Angeles, California: Mike Brewer (born in 1944 in Oklahoma City, Oklahoma) and Tom Shipley (born in 1942 in Mineral Ridge, Ohio).

B RICH
Born Brian Rich in Baltimore, Maryland. Male rapper.

BRICK
Black disco-jazz group from Atlanta, Georgia: Jimmy Brown (sax), Reggie Hargis (guitar), Don Nevins (keyboards), Ray Ransom (bass) and Eddie Irons (drums). All share vocals. Session work in the early 1970s.

BRICKELL, Edie
Born on 3/10/1966 in Oak Cliff, Texas. Pop singer/songwriter. New Bohemians: Kenny Withrow (guitar), Brad Houser (bass) and John Bush (drums). Group disbanded in 1991. Brickell married Paul Simon on 5/30/1992.

BRICKMAN, Jim
Born on 11/20/1961 in Cleveland, Ohio. New Age pianist/songwriter.

BRIDGES, Alicia
Born on 7/15/1953 in Lawndale, North Carolina. Disco singer/songwriter.

BRIGGS, Lillian
Born Lillian Biggs in Allentown, Pennsylvania. Died of cancer on 4/11/1998 (age 64). White big band-styled singer. Discovered by Alan Freed while working in Joy Cayler's All-Girl Orchestra.

BRIGHT, Larry
Born Julian Ferebee Bright on 8/17/1934 in Norfolk, Virginia; raised in Corpus Christi, Texas. White soul singer/guitarist.

BRIGHTER SIDE OF DARKNESS
R&B vocal group from Chicago, Illinois: Darryl Lamont, Ralph Eskridge, Randolph Murphy and Larry Washington.

BRILEY, Martin
Born on 8/17/1949 in London, England. Rock singer/songwriter/guitarist.

BRISTOL, Johnny
Born on 2/3/1939 in Morganton, North Carolina. Died of a heart attack on 3/21/2004 (age 65). R&B singer/composer/producer. Teamed with Jackey Beavers, recorded as Johnny & Jackey for Tri-Phi, 1961. Teamed with Harvey Fuqua as Motown producers until 1973.

BRITISH LIONS
Rock group from Birmingham, England: John Fiddler (vocals), Ray Major (guitar), Morgan Fisher (keyboards), Pete "Overend" Watts (bass) and Dale "Buffin" Griffin (drums). Fisher, Watts and Griffin were members of Mott The Hoople.

BRITNY FOX
Hard-rock group from Philadelphia, Pennsylvania: "Dizzy" Dean Davidson (vocals), Michael Kelly Smith (guitar), Billy Childs (bass) and Johnny Dee (drums).

BROADWAY
R&B group led by vocalist Patti Williams.

BROCK, Chad
Born on 7/31/1963 in Ocala, Florida. Country singer/songwriter/guitarist.

B-ROCK & THE BIZZ
B-Rock is rap producer Baron Agee from Mobile, Alabama. The Bizz is a studio group assembled by Agee.

BRONSKI BEAT
Techno-pop trio from England: Jimmy Somerville (vocals), Steve Bronski and Larry Steinbachek (synthesizers). Somerville formed the Communards in 1986.

BROOD, Herman
Born on 11/5/1946 in Zwolle, Netherlands. Committed suicide on 7/11/2001 (age 54). Leader of Dutch rock band Wild Romance.

BROOKLYN BOUNCE
Dance group is actually German producers Matthias Menck and Dennis Böhn. Represented on stage by male singer Damon and female dancers Ulrica and Maeva.

BROOKLYN BRIDGE
Pop group from Long Island, New York, made up of a vocal quartet and seven-piece band. The Del-Satins are Johnny Maestro (lead vocals, The Crests), Fred Ferrara, Les Cauchi and Mike Gregorie (backing vocals). The Rhythm Method are Richie Macioce (guitar), Tom Sullivan and Joe Ruvio (saxophones), Shelly Davis (trumpet), Carolyn Wood (organ), Jimmy Rosica (bass) and Artie Catanzarita (drums).

BROOKLYN DREAMS
Disco trio from Brooklyn, New York: Joe "Bean" Esposito (vocals, guitar), Bruce Sudano (keyboards; Alive And Kicking) and Eddie Hokenson (drums). Sudano married Donna Summer on 7/16/1980.

BROOKS, Donnie
Born John Abohosh on 2/6/1936 in Dallas, Texas; raised in Ventura, California. Died of heart failure on 2/23/2007 (age 71). Pop singer.

BROOKS, Garth
Born Troyal Garth Brooks on 2/7/1962 in Luba, Oklahoma; raised in Yukon, Oklahoma. Country singer/guitarist. Attended Oklahoma State on a track scholarship (javelin). His immense popularity contributed to a resurgence of country music in the 1990s. Married Trisha Yearwood on 12/10/2005.

BROOKS, Meredith
Born on 6/12/1958 in Oregon City, Oregon. Rock singer/guitarist. Former member of The Graces.

BROOKS, Nancy
Pop-rock singer.

BROOKS & DUNN
Country duo of Kix Brooks (born on 5/12/1955 in Shreveport, Louisiana) and Ronnie Dunn (born on 6/1/1953 in Coleman, Texas).

BROS
Pop trio from Camberley, England: twin brothers Matt (vocals) and Luke (drums) Goss, with Craig Logan (bass). Group's name rhymes with "cross."

BROTHER BEYOND
Pop group from England: Nathan Moore (vocals), David White (guitar), Carl Fysh (keyboards) and Steve Alexander (drums).

BROTHERHOOD CREED
Rap duo from Los Angeles, California: Tyrone Ward and Sean McDuffie.

BROTHERHOOD OF MAN, The
Studio group from England featuring Tony Burrows, Johnny Goodison and Sunny Leslie (female singer). Burrows was lead singer of Edison Lighthouse, First Class, The Pipkins and White Plains. 1976 hit featured new members: Nicky Stevens, Sandra Stevens, Martin Lee and Lee Sheridan.

BROTHERS FOUR, The
Folk-pop group formed at the University of Washington: Dick Foley, Bob Flick, John Paine and Mike Kirkland.

BROTHERS IN RHYTHM
Duo of dance remixers: Steve Anderson and Dave Seaman.

BROTHERS JOHNSON, The
R&B-funk duo from Los Angeles, California: brothers George (guitar; born on 5/17/1953) and Louis Johnson (bass; born on 4/13/1955). Own band, the Johnson Three + 1, with brother Tommy and cousin Alex Weir. With Billy Preston's band to 1975. Duo split up in 1984.

BROTHER TO BROTHER
R&B group from St. Louis, Missouri: Michael Burton (vocals), Billy Jones (guitar), Frankie Prescott (bass) and Yogi Horton (drums).

BROWN, Al
Born on 5/22/1934 in Fairmont, West Virginia. Black singer/songwriter/producer. The Tunetoppers backing band formed in 1953.

BROWN, Alex
Female R&B singer.

BROWN, Arthur
Born Arthur Wilton on 6/24/1944 in Whitby, England. White theatrical rock singer. His band consisted of Sean Nicholas (guitar), Vince Crane (organ) and Carl Palmer (drums; Atomic Rooster, Emerson, Lake & Palmer, Asia). Since 1992, has been a partner in a music therapy practice known as Healing Songs Therapy. Crane committed suicide on 2/14/1989 (age 44).

BROWN, Bobby
Born on 2/5/1969 in Roxbury, Massachusetts. Member of New Edition. Appeared in the movies *Ghostbusters II*, *Panther* and *A Thin Line Between Love & Hate*. Established own Bosstown recording studio and label in Atlanta in 1991. Married to Whitney Houston, 1992-2007.

BROWN, Boots
Brown was actually black jazz trumpeter Shorty Rogers. Born Milton Rajonsky on 4/14/1924 in Lee, Massachusetts. Died of liver failure on 11/7/1994 (age 70). Worked with the big bands of Woody Herman and Stan Kenton.

BROWN, Buster
Born Wayman Glasco on 8/15/1911 in Cordele, Georgia. Died on 1/31/1976 (age 64). R&B singer/harmonica player.

BROWN, Charles
Born on 9/13/1922 in Texas City, Texas. Died of heart failure on 1/21/1999 (age 76). R&B singer/pianist. Joined Johnny Moore's Three Blazers in 1944, who first recorded the classic "Merry Christmas, Baby" in 1947.

BROWN, Chris
Born on 5/5/1989 in Tappahannock, Washington. Male teen R&B singer.

BROWN, Chuck, & The Soul Searchers
Funk group from Washington DC: Chuck Brown (vocals, guitar), John Buchanan and Curtis Johnson (keyboards), Don Tillery (trumpet), Leroy Fleming (sax), Gregory Gerran (congas), Jerry Wilder (bass) and Ricky Wellman (drums).

BROWN, Don
Born in 1949 in Minneapolis, Minnesota. Pop singer/songwriter/producer.

BROWN, Foxy
Born Inga Marchand on 9/6/1979 in Brooklyn, New York. Female rapper. Guest rapper on songs by Toni Braxton, Case, Jay-Z, L.L. Cool J and Total. "Foxy Brown" was an action movie character of the 1970s played by actress Pam Grier.

BROWN, Horace
Born in Charlotte, North Carolina. R&B singer.

BROWN, James
Born on 5/3/1933 in Barnwell, South Carolina; raised in Augusta, Georgia. Died of heart failure on 12/25/2006 (age 73). Formed own vocal group, the Famous Flames with Bobby Byrd. Cut a demo record of own composition "Please Please Please" in November 1955 at radio station WIBB in Macon. Signed to King/Federal Records in January 1956 and re-recorded the song. Cameo appearances in movies *The Blues Brothers* and *Rocky IV*. One of the originators of "Soul" music. His backing group, The JB's, featured various personnel, including Nat Kendrick, Bootsy Collins, Maceo Parker and Fred Wesley. On 12/15/1988, received a six-year prison sentence after leading police on an interstate car chase; released from prison on 2/27/1991.

BROWN, Jim Ed
Born on 4/1/1934 in Sparkman, Arkansas. Leader of The Browns. Hosted Nashville Network's TV talent show *You Can Be A Star!*.

BROWN, Jocelyn
Born on 11/25/1950 in Kinston, North Carolina. Female R&B singer. Backing vocalist for Luther Vandross, George Benson, John Lennon and many others. Singer with the dance groups Inner Life and Salsoul Orchestra.

BROWN, Louise
Born in Chicago, Illinois. Black lounge singer/pianist.

BROWN, Maxine
Born on 8/18/1939 in Kingstree, South Carolina. R&B singer. With gospel groups The Manhattans and The Royaltones in New York City in the late 1950s. Starred in the Broadway musical *Wild Women Don't Have The Blues*.

BROWN, Nappy
Born Napoleon Brown Culp on 10/12/1929 in Charlotte, North Carolina. Died on 9/20/2008 (age 78). R&B-gospel singer.

BROWN, Oscar Jr.
Born on 10/10/1926 in Chicago, Illinois. Died on 5/29/2005 (age 78). R&B-jazz singer. Radio actor while still a teenager. Hosted the TV series *Jazz Scene* in 1962.

BROWN, Peter
Born on 7/11/1953 in Blue Island, Illinois; later based in Miami, Florida. Disco singer/songwriter/keyboardist.

BROWN, Polly
Born on 4/18/1947 in Birmingham, England. White soul singer. Lead vocalist of Pickettywitch and Sweet Dreams.

BROWN, Randy
Born in Memphis, Tennessee. R&B singer/songwriter.

BROWN, Roy
Born on 9/10/1925 in New Orleans, Louisiana. Died of a heart attack on 5/25/1981 (age 55). R&B vocalist/pianist. One of the originators of the New Orleans R&B sound.

BROWN, Ruth
Born Ruth Weston on 1/12/1928 in Portsmouth, Virginia. Died on 11/17/2006 (age 78). R&B pioneer. Married singer/trumpeter Jimmy Brown in 1945. In late 1946, sang for one month with Lucky Millinder's band, then fired. Later heard by Duke Ellington, who alerted Herb Abramson of the then-new Atlantic Records. Abramson signed her to a contract. Became Atlantic Records' top-selling artist of the 1950s. Married for a time to Willis Jackson. In later years, had acting roles in the TV shows *Hello, Larry* and *Checking In*, plus several Broadway and Las Vegas musicals. Appeared in the movies *Under The Rainbow* and *Hairspray*. Starred in the 1988 musical *Black And Blue*.

BROWN, Sam
Born on 10/7/1964 in London, England. White female singer/songwriter. Backing vocalist for Small Faces, Mark Knopfler, Spandau Ballet and others since her teens. Daughter of U.K. singer/guitarist Joe Brown and singer Vicki Brown.

BROWN, Shirley
Born on 1/6/1947 in West Memphis, Arkansas; raised in St. Louis, Missouri. R&B singer.

BROWN, Sleepy
Born Patrick Brown in Atlanta, Georgia. R&B singer/songwriter.

BROWN, Zac, Band
Born in Dahlonega, Georgia. Male singer/songwriter/guitarist. His band: Jimmy DeMartini (fiddle), Coy Bowles (keyboards), John Hopkins (bass) and Chris Fryar (drums).

BROWN BOY
Born Dario Perez in Blythe, California. Latin male rapper.

BROWNE, Jackson
Born on 10/9/1948 in Heidelberg, Germany (U.S. Army base); raised in Los Angeles, California. Pop-rock singer/songwriter/guitarist/pianist. With Tim Buckley and Nico in 1967 in New York City. Returned to Los Angeles, concentrated on songwriting. His songs were recorded by Linda Ronstadt, Tom Rush, Joe Cocker, The Byrds, Johnny Rivers, Bonnie Raitt, and many others. Worked with the Eagles. Produced Warren Zevon's first album. Wife, Phyllis, committed suicide on 3/25/1976. A prominent activist against nuclear power.

BROWNS, The
Country vocal trio from Sparkman, Arkansas: Jim Ed Brown (born on 4/1/1934) and his sisters Maxine and Bonnie.

BROWNSTONE
Female R&B vocal trio from Los Angeles, California: Monica Doby, Nichole Gilbert and Charmayne Maxwell. Doby left group for health reasons in June 1995; replaced by Kina Cosper.

BROWN SUGAR
Born Clydie King on 8/21/1943 in Atlanta, Georgia. Female R&B singer. Formerly in The Raeletts.

BROWNSVILLE STATION
Rock trio from Ann Arbor, Michigan: Michael Lutz (vocals, bass), Michael "Cub" Koda (guitar) and Henry Weck (drums). Koda died of kidney failure on 7/1/2000 (age 51).

BRUBECK, Dave, Quartet
Born David Warren on 12/6/1920 in Concord, California. Leader of jazz quartet consisting of Brubeck (piano), Paul Desmond (alto sax), Joe Morello (drums) and Eugene Wright (bass). One of America's all-time most popular jazz groups on college campuses. Desmond died on 5/30/1977 (age 52).

BRUCE, Ed
Born William Edwin Bruce, Jr. on 12/29/1940 in Keiser, Arkansas; raised in Memphis, Tennessee. Country singer/songwriter/guitarist/actor. Did TV commercials as "The Tennessean." Played "Tom Guthrie" on TV's *Bret Maverick*. Hosted TV's *American Sports Cavalcade* and *Truckin' U.S.A.*

BRUCE AND TERRY
Bruce Johnston (later of The Beach Boys) and Terry Melcher (produced The Byrds, Paul Revere & The Raiders, Grapefruit). Both were later members of the studio group Sagittarius. Terry is the son of Doris Day and Marty Melcher, owner of Arwin Records. Melcher died of cancer on 11/19/2004 (age 62).

BRYAN, Luke
Born Thomas Luther Bryan in Leesburg, Georgia. Country singer/songwriter/guitarist.

BRYANT, Anita
Born on 3/25/1940 in Barnsdall, Oklahoma. Adult Contemporary singer. Second runner-up to Miss America in 1958.

BRYANT, Ray
Born Raphael Bryant on 12/24/1931 in Philadelphia, Pennsylvania. R&B-jazz pianist/bandleader. Uncle of *The Tonight Show* guitarist Kevin Eubanks.

BRYANT, Sharon
Born on 8/14/1956 in Westchester County, New York. Lead singer of Atlantic Starr from 1976-84. Married Rick Gallwey (former percussionist with the group Change) in 1984.

BRYSON, Peabo
Born Robert Peabo Bryson on 4/13/1951 in Greenville, South Carolina. R&B singer/producer. First recorded for Bang in 1970. Married Juanita Leonard, former wife of boxer Sugar Ray Leonard, in 1992.

BT
Born Brian Transeau on 10/4/1970 in Washington DC. Electronic keyboardist/producer.

B.T. EXPRESS
R&B-disco group from Brooklyn, New York. Earlier known as Brooklyn Trucking Express. Core members: Barbara Joyce Lomas (female vocals; left by 1977), brothers Louis (vocals, bass) and Bill (sax) Risbrook, Richard Thompson (guitar), Carlos Ward (flute) and Dennis Rowe (congas). Keyboardist Michael Jones, who was with the group from 1976-79, later recorded solo as techno-funk musician Kashif.

B2K
Male R&B vocal group from Los Angeles, California: Jarell "J-Boog" Houston, Mario "Raz-B" Thornton, Dreux "Lil Fizz" Frederic and Omari Grandberry. Group starred in the movie *You Got Served*.

BUBBLE PUPPY, The
Psychedelic-rock group from Houston, Texas: Rod Prince (vocals), Todd Potter (guitar), Roy Cox (bass) and David Fore (drums). Later recorded as Demian.

BUBLÉ, Michael
Born on 9/9/1975 in Burnaby, British Columbia, Canada. Adult Contemporary singer/songwriter.

BUCKCHERRY
Hard-rock group from Los Angeles, California: Josh Todd (vocals), Keith Nelson (guitar), Stevie D. (guitar), Jimmy Ashhurst (bass) and Xavier Muriel (drums).

BUCKETHEADS, The
Group is actually solo dance producer Kenny "Dope" Gonzalez (from Brooklyn, New York).

BUCKEYE
Rock group from Cleveland, Ohio: Ronn Price (vocals, bass), Thom Fowle (guitar), Gabriel Katona (keyboards) and Beaver Parker (drums).

BUCKINGHAM, Lindsey
Born on 10/3/1949 in Palo Alto, California. Rock guitarist/singer/songwriter. In group Fritz from 1967-71; with Stevie Nicks (Fritz lead singer) formed duo, Buckingham Nicks, in early 1970s. Both joined Fleetwood Mac in 1975. Buckingham left Fleetwood Mac in 1987. His grandfather founded Keystone Coffee; his father founded Alta Coffee. Buckingham's brother Gregg won a silver medal in swimming in the 1968 Olympics. Reunited with Fleetwood Mac in 1997.

BUCKINGHAMS, The
Rock band from Chicago, Illinois: Dennis Tufano (vocals; born on 9/11/1946), Carl Giammarese (guitar; born on 8/21/1947), Dennis Miccoli (keyboards), Nick Fortuna (bass; born on 5/1/1945) and Jon-Jon Poulos (drums; born on 3/31/1947; died of a drug overdose on 3/26/1980, age 32). Martin Grebb (born on 9/2/1946) replaced Miccoli in 1967. Tufano and Giammarese recorded as a duo in 1973. Grebb formed The Fabulous Rhinestones.

BUCKLEY, Jeff
Born on 11/17/1966 in Anaheim, California. Drowned on 5/29/1997 (age 30). Adult Alternative singer/songwriter/guitarist. Son of Tim Buckley.

BUCKNER & GARCIA
Novelty duo from Atlanta, Georgia: Jerry Buckner (keyboards) and Gary Garcia (vocals). Also recorded as Willis "The Guard" & Vigorish.

BUCKWHEAT
Pop group from Los Angeles, California: Debbie Campbell (vocals), Michael Smotherman (vocals, keyboards), Randy James (guitar), Mark Durham (bass) and Timmy Harrison (drums). Campbell died of cancer on 2/28/2004 (age 53).

BUD AND TRAVIS
Folk duo from San Francisco, California: Oliver "Bud" Dashiell (born on 9/28/1929; died of a brain tumor on 6/2/1989, age 59) and Travis Edmonson (born on 9/23/1932).

BUDDEN, Joe
Born on 8/31/1980 in Harlem, New York; raised in Jersey City, New Jersey. Male rapper.

BUENA VISTAS, The
Three-man, one-woman band that also recorded as Kathy Lynn & The Play Boys. Kathy Lynn is Kathy Lynn Keppen.

BUFFALO SPRINGFIELD, The
Superstar rock group formed in Los Angeles, California: Stephen Stills, Neil Young, Richie Furay, Dewey Martin and Bruce Palmer (replaced by Jim Messina after first two albums). Disbanded in 1968. Stills and Young with Crosby, Stills, Nash & Young. Furay and Messina formed Poco. Palmer died of a heart attack on 10/4/2004 (age 58).

BUFFETT, Jimmy
Born on 12/25/1946 in Pascagoula, Mississippi; raised in Mobile, Alabama. Singer/songwriter/guitarist. Has BS degree in journalism from the University of Southern Mississippi. After working in New Orleans, moved to Nashville in 1969. Nashville correspondent for *Billboard* magazine, 1969-70.

BUFFETT, Jimmy — cont'd
Settled in Key West in 1971. Author of several books. Appeared in the 1978 movie *FM*. Faithful fans known as "Parrotheads."

BUFFY
Female Latin pop-rock singer.

BUGGLES, The
New-wave duo from England: Geoff Downes and Trevor Horn. Both joined the group Yes in 1980. Downes joined Asia in 1981. Horn became a prolific producer.

BULL & THE MATADORS
R&B trio from Chicago, Illinois: JaMell "Bull" Parks (born on 6/7/1945), Milton Hardy and James Otis Love.

BULLDOG
Rock group from New York City, New York: Billy Hocher (vocals, bass), Eric Thorngren and Gene Cornish (guitars), John Turi (keyboards) and Dino Danelli (drums). Cornish and Danelli were members of The Rascals. Thorngren later became a prolific record mixer.

BULLENS, Cindy
Born on 11/30/1957 in West Newbury, Massachusetts. Pop-rock singer/guitarist.

BULLET
Studio group featuring lead singer Ernie Sorrentino from Brooklyn, New York. Sorrentino later formed duo The Bay Brothers with Lou Hokenson.

BULLETBOYS
Hard-rock group from Los Angeles, California: Marq Torien (vocals), Mick Sweda (guitar), Lonnie Vencent (bass) and Jimmy D'Anda (drums).

BUMBLE BEE UNLIMITED
Disco group from New York. Led by singer/songwriter Patrick Adams.

BUOYS, The
Rock band from Wilkes-Barre, Pennsylvania: Bill Kelly (vocals), Carl Siracuse (guitar), Fran Brozena (keyboards), Jerry Hludzik (bass) and Chris Hanlon (drums). Rupert Holmes (Street People) was their composer/arranger.

BURBANK, Gary
Born Billy Purser in July 1941 in Memphis, Tennessee. DJ at WHAS in Louisville, Kentucky, at the time of his hit.

BURCH, Vernon
Born on 7/28/1955 in Washington DC. R&B singer/songwriter/guitarist. Member of the Bar-Kays from 1970-74.

BURDON, Eric, & War
Born on 5/11/1941 in Walker, Newcastle, England. After leaving The Animals, Burdon teamed up with the Latin funk-rock band War for two albums. Starred in the movie *Comeback* and made a cameo appearance in *The Doors*.

BURKE, Solomon
Born on 3/21/1940 in Philadelphia, Pennsylvania. Soul singer. Preached and broadcast from own church, "Solomon's Temple," in Philadelphia from 1945-55 as the "Wonder Boy Preacher." Church was founded for him by his grandmother. The father of 21 children. First recorded for Apollo in 1954. Left music to attend mortuary school; returned in 1960. Also see The Soul Clan.

BURNETTE, Billy
Born on 5/8/1953 in Memphis, Tennessee. Son of Dorsey Burnette, nephew of Johnny Burnette, and cousin of Rocky Burnette. Member of Fleetwood Mac from 1987-1993. Writer of many country hits.

BURNETTE, Dorsey
Born on 12/28/1932 in Memphis, Tennessee. Died of a heart attack on 8/19/1979 (age 46). Older brother of Johnny Burnette and father of Billy Burnette. Recorded with brother Johnny in the Rock & Roll Trio from 1956-57 and as The Texans in 1961.

BURNETTE, Johnny
Born on 3/25/1934 in Memphis, Tennessee. Died in a boating accident on Clear Lake in California on 8/14/1964 (age 30). Johnny, older brother Dorsey Burnette, and Paul Burlison were rockabilly pioneers when they formed the Johnny Burnette Rock & Roll Trio. They released seven records on the Coral label, 1956-57. Recorded with brother Dorsey as The Texans in 1961. Father of Rocky Burnette.

BURNETTE, Rocky
Born Jonathan Burnette on 6/12/1953 in Memphis, Tennessee. Son of Johnny Burnette, nephew of Dorsey Burnette and cousin of Billy Burnette (of Fleetwood Mac).

BURNS, George
Born Nathan Birnbaum on 1/20/1896 in Brooklyn, New York. Died on 3/9/1996 (age 100). Popular radio, movie and TV comedian. Starred in several movies including *The Sunshine Boys* and *Oh God*.

BURRELL, Kenny
Born on 7/31/1931 in Detroit, Michigan. Jazz guitarist. Veteran sessionman with the Blue Note and Prestige labels. Featured guitarist on albums by Jimmy Smith and Kai Winding.

BURROWS, Tony
Born on 4/14/1942 in Exeter, England. Lead singer for the following groups: White Plains, First Class, Brotherhood Of Man, Edison Lighthouse and The Pipkins.

BURTNICK, Glen
Born on 4/8/1955 in New Brunswick, New Jersey. Pop-rock singer/guitarist. Member of Styx from 1990-2004.

BURTON, Jenny
Born on 11/18/1957 in Brooklyn, New York. Female R&B singer.

BURTON, Richard
Born Richard Jenkins on 11/10/1925 in Pontrydyfen, Wales. Died of a cerebral hemorrhage on 8/5/1984 (age 58). Leading actor from 1948-83. Twice married to and divorced from actress Elizabeth Taylor.

BUS BOYS, The
R&B group from Los Angeles, California: Gus Lounderman (vocals), brothers Brian (keyboards) and Kevin (bass) O'Neal, Victor Johnson (guitar), Michael Jones (keyboards) and Steve Felix (drums). Group appeared in the movie *48 HRS*.

BUSCH, Lou
Born on 7/18/1910 in Louisville, Kentucky. Died on 9/19/1979 (age 69). Pianist/orchestra leader. Also recorded as Joe "Fingers" Carr.

BUSH
Rock group from London, England: Gavin Rossdale (vocals, guitar; born on 10/30/1967), Nigel Pulsford (guitar; born on 4/11/1963), Dave Parsons (bass; born on 7/2/1965) and Robin Goodridge (drums; born on 9/10/1966). Rossdale married Gwen Stefani (lead singer of No Doubt) on 9/14/2002.

BUSH, Kate
Born on 7/30/1958 in Bexleyheath, Kent, England. Discovered by David Gilmour of Pink Floyd. Signed to EMI at age 16 while still at St. Joseph's Convent Grammar School. In 1993, directed movie *The Line, The Curve and The Cross* which was based on six songs from her album *The Red Shoes*.

BUSTA RHYMES
Born Trevor Smith on 5/20/1972 in Brooklyn, New York. Male rapper. Founder of rap group Leaders Of The New School and member of Flipmode Squad. Played "Freddie Harris" in the 2002 movie *Halloween: Resurrection*.

BUSTERS, The
Rock and roll band from Springfield, Massachusetts: Alan Orkins, John Chappel and Freddie Cole (guitars), Al Marczyk (sax), Jack Baker (bass) and Fran Parda (drums). Originally known as the Northern Lights, recorded "Typhoid" which was released as "Bust Out" by The Busters. Baker and Parda put together a new Busters touring group.

BUTANES, The
Black doo-wop group backed by Teddy McRae's Orchestra.

BUTCHER, Jon, Axis
Born in Boston, Massachusetts. Black rock singer/guitarist. The Axis included Thom Gimbel (keyboards), Jimmy Johnson (bass) and Derek Blevins (drums).

BUTLER, Billy
Born on 6/7/1945 in Chicago, Illinois. R&B singer/songwriter/guitarist. Younger brother of Jerry Butler.

BUTLER, Carl
Born on 6/2/1927 in Knoxville, Tennessee. Died on 9/4/1992 (age 65). Country singer. His wife, Pearl, who sang harmony, died on 3/1/1989 (age 61).

BUTLER, Champ
Born on 12/21/1926 in St. Louis, Missouri; raised in Los Angeles, California. Died on 3/8/1992 (age 65). Pop singer.

BUTLER, Jerry
Born on 12/8/1939 in Sunflower, Mississippi; raised in Chicago, Illinois. Older brother of Billy Butler. Sang in the Northern Jubilee Gospel Singers, with Curtis Mayfield. Later with the Quails. In 1957, Butler and Mayfield joined the Roosters with Sam Gooden and brothers Arthur and Richard Brooks. Changed name to The Impressions in 1957. Left for solo career in autumn of 1958. Also worked as the Cook County Commissioner in Illinois. Dubbed "The Ice Man." Hosted the popular PBS TV "Doo Wop" specials.

BUTLER, Jonathan
Born on 10/1/1961 in Capetown, South Africa; later based in London, England. R&B singer/songwriter/guitarist.

BUTTERFIELD, Paul
Born on 12/17/1942 in Chicago, Illinois. Died of heart failure on 5/4/1987 (age 44). White blues singer/harmonica player. Formed interracial blues band in Chicago in 1965.

BUTTHOLE SURFERS
Punk-rock group from San Antonio, Texas: Gibby Haynes (vocals), Paul Leary (guitar), Jeff Pinkus (bass) and King Coffey (drums).

BUZZCOCKS
Punk-rock group from Manchester, England: Pete Shelley (vocals, guitar), Steve Diggle (guitar), Steve Garvey (bass) and John Maher (drums).

B*WITCHED
Female vocal group from Dublin, Ireland: twin sisters Edele and Keavy Lynch, with Sinead O'Carroll and Lindsay Armaou.

BYRD, Bobby
Born on 8/15/1934 in Toccoa, Georgia. Died of cancer on 9/12/2007 (age 73). Founder/leader of James Brown's vocal group, The Famous Flames.

BYRD, Charlie
Born on 9/16/1925 in Chuckatuck, Virginia. Died of cancer on 11/30/1999 (age 74). Jazz and classical guitar virtuoso. Studied under classical master guitarist Segovia. With Woody Herman in 1959.

BYRD, Jerry
Born on 3/9/1920 in Lima, Ohio. Died on 4/11/2005 (age 85). Steel guitarist. Member of the guitar session band The Nashville Guitars.

BYRD, Russell
Born Bertrand Berns on 11/8/1929 in Brooklyn, New York. Died of a heart attack on 12/31/1967 (age 38). Producer/songwriter/co-owner of Bang Records. Wrote "Twist And Shout" and "Hang On Sloopy."

BYRD, Tracy
Born on 12/17/1966 in Beaumont, Texas; raised in Vidor, Texas. Male country singer/guitarist.

BYRDS, The
Folk-rock group formed in Los Angeles, California. Consisted of James McGuinn (12-string guitar; born on 7/13/1942), David Crosby (guitar; born on 8/14/1941), Gene Clark (percussion; born on 11/17/1944), Chris Hillman (bass; born on

BYRDS, The — cont'd
12/4/1944) and Mike Clarke (drums; born on 6/3/1946). McGuinn, who changed his first name to Roger in 1968, had been with Bobby Darin and the Chad Mitchell Trio. Clark had been with the New Christy Minstrels. All except Clarke had folk music background. First recorded as the Beefeaters for Elektra in 1964. Also recorded as the Jet Set. Professional debut in March 1965. Clark left after "Eight Miles High." Crosby left in 1968 to form Crosby, Stills & Nash. Re-formed in 1968 with McGuinn, Hillman, Kevin Kelly (drums) and Gram Parsons (guitar). Hillman and Parsons left that same year to form the Flying Burrito Brothers. McGuinn again re-formed with Clarence White (guitar), John York (bass) and Gene Parsons (drums). Reunions with original members in 1973 and 1979. Gram Parsons died of a heroin overdose on 9/19/1973 (age 26). Hillman with The Souther, Hillman, Furay Band in 1974. McGuinn, Clark & Hillman later recorded as a trio. In 1986, Hillman formed popular country group The Desert Rose Band. McGuinn, Crosby and Hillman reunited on stage on 2/24/1990 for a Roy Orbison tribute. Gene Clark died of natural causes on 5/24/1991 (age 46). Mike Clarke, also with the Flying Burrito Brothers and Firefall, died of liver failure on 12/19/1993 (age 47).

BYRNES, Edward
Born Edward Breitenberger on 7/30/1933 in Brooklyn, New York. Best known as "Kookie" on TV's *77 Sunset Strip*.

CABOOSE, The
Gospel-rock group: Gary Johns and Patricia Karr (vocals), Jackie Cook (guitar), Walt Ramsey (keyboards), Tom Cathey (bass) and Joel Williams (drums).

CABRERA, Ryan
Born on 7/18/1982 in Dallas, Texas. Pop singer/songwriter.

CADETS, The / JACKS, The
R&B vocal group from Los Angeles, California: Aaron Collins, Ted Taylor, William "Dub" Jones (bass man for The Coasters; died on 1/16/2000), Willie Davis and Lloyd McCraw. Recorded as both The Jacks on RPM with Davis as lead and The Cadets on Modern with Collins or Jones as lead. Collins and Davis joined The Flares in 1961. Collins' sisters, Betty and Rosie, recorded as The Teen Queens.

CADILLACS, The
Black doo-wop group formed in 1953 at P.S. 139 in Harlem, New York, as the Carnations. The first R&B vocal group to extensively use choreography in their stage routines. Consisted of Earl "Speedoo" Carroll (lead), LaVerne Drake, Earl Wade, Charles Brooks and Robert Phillips. Their first recording was the 1954 doo-wop classic "Gloria." By 1958, Drake and Brooks replaced by James Bailey and Bobby Spencer. Varying membership. Carroll joined The Coasters in 1961. Spencer was later the lead voice for Crazy Elephant. Bailey died in January 1980 (age 45).

CAESAR, Shirley
Born on 10/13/1938 in Durham, North Carolina. Billed as the "First Lady of Gospel Music."

CAESARS
Alternative-rock band from Borlänge, Sweden: Joakim Ahlund (vocals, guitar), Cesar Vidal (guitar), David Lindquist (bass) and Nino Keller (drums).

CAFFERTY, John, & The Beaver Brown Band
Rock group from Narragansett, Rhode Island: John Cafferty (vocals, guitar), Gary Gramolini (guitar), Robert Cotoia (keyboards), Michael Antunes (saxophone), Pat Lupo (bass) and Kenny Jo Silva (drums). Wrote and recorded the music for the soundtrack *Eddie And The Cruisers*. Cotoia died on 9/3/2004 (age 51).

CAGLE, Chris
Born Christian Cagle on 11/10/1968 in DeRidder, Louisiana; raised in Baytown, Texas. Male country singer/songwriter/guitarist.

CAILLAT, Colbie
Born on 5/28/1985 in Newbury Park, California; raised in Malibu, California. Female singer/songwriter/guitarist. Daughter of record producer Ken Caillat.

CAIN, Jonathan
Born on 2/26/1950 in Chicago, Illinois. Former keyboardist with The Babys. Joined Journey in 1981. Co-founded Bad English in 1989. Formerly married to Tané Cain.

CAIN, Tané
Born Tané McClure on 6/8/1959 in Pacific Palasades, California. Female singer/songwriter. Daughter of actor Doug McClure. Formerly married to Jonathan Cain. First name pronounced: tawnee.

CAIOLA, Al
Born Alexander Caiola on 9/7/1920 in Jersey City, New Jersey. White studio guitarist.

CAKE
Rock group from Sacramento, California: John McCrea (vocals, guitar), Greg Brown (guitar), Vince DiFiore (trumpet), Victor Damiani (bass) and Todd Roper (drums).

CALDWELL, Bobby
Born on 8/15/1951 in Manhattan, New York; raised in Miami, Florida. Multi-instrumentalist/songwriter. Wrote tracks for *New Mickey Mouse Club* TV show, commercials, and Peter Cetera and Amy Grant's "The Next Time I Fall."

CALE, J.J.
Born John W. Cale on 12/5/1938 in Oklahoma City, Oklahoma. Rock singer/songwriter/guitarist. Wrote Eric Clapton's "After Midnight" and "Cocaine." In high school bands with Leon Russell. Worked with Phil Spector and Delaney & Bonnie. Session work with Art Garfunkel, Bob Seger and Neil Young.

CALEN, Frankie
Born in Los Angeles, California. Teen pop singer.

CALIFORNIA RAISINS, The
Studio group produced by Ross Vannelli (producer of Earth, Wind & Fire and Howard Hewett; brother of Gino Vannelli). Features R&B vocalist/drummer Buddy Miles and vocalist Alfie Silas. Based on the Claymation characters of a California Raisin Growers' television commercial.

CALL, The
Rock group from California: Michael Been (vocals, guitar), Tom Ferrier (guitar), Greg Freeman (bass) and Scott Musick (drums). Jim Goodwin (keyboards) replaced Freeman in 1984.

CALLENDER, Bobby
Born in Orlando, Florida. Teen pop singer/songwriter.

CALLING, The
Rock group from Los Angeles, California: Alex Band (vocals), Aaron Kamin and Sean Woolstenhulme (guitars), Billy Mohler (bass) and Nate Wood (drums).

CALLOWAY
R&B duo from Cincinnati, Ohio: brothers Reggie and Vincent Calloway. Both founded Midnight Star and did production work for The Whispers, Natalie Cole, Gladys Knight and Teddy Pendergrass.

CALLOWAY, Cab
Born Cabell Calloway on 12/25/1907 in Rochester, New York; raised in Baltimore, Maryland. Died of a stroke on 11/18/1994 (age 86). Nicknamed "His Hi-De-Ho Highness Of Jive." Vocalist/bandleader/alto saxophonist/drummer. Gained fame at New York's Cotton Club in the 1930s. Appeared in many movies, including *The Blues Brothers*. Signature song is his 1931 hit "Minnie The Moocher."

CAMBRIDGE STRINGS AND SINGERS, The
British studio assemblage conducted and arranged by Dick Rowe and Malcolm Lockyer (died on 6/28/1976, age 53).

CAMEO
R&B-funk group founded by Larry Blackmon (vocals, drums, producer) as The New York City Players. In late 1982, Blackmon relocated the group to Atlanta, Georgia. Pared the group down to a trio of Blackmon, Tomi Jenkins and Nathan Leftenant.

CAMOUFLAGE
Dance trio from Germany: Marcus Meyn (vocals), Heiko Maile (keyboards) and Oliver Kreyssig (backing vocals; left band in 1990).

CAMP, Hamilton
Born on 10/30/1934 in London, England. Died of a heart attack on 10/2/2005 (age 70). Singer/actor. Cast member of the TV shows *He & She*, *Just Our Luck*, *Story Theater* and *Turn-On*.

CAMPBELL, Debbie
Born in 1951 in Fort Worth, Texas; later based in Los Angeles, California. Died of cancer on 2/28/2004 (age 53). Lead singer of Buckwheat.

CAMPBELL, Glen
Born on 4/22/1936 in Delight, Arkansas. Country-pop singer/songwriter/guitarist. With his uncle Dick Bills' band, 1954-58. To Los Angeles; recorded with The Champs in 1960. Became prolific studio musician; with The Hondells in 1964, The Beach Boys in 1965 and Sagittarius in 1967. Own TV show *The Glen Campbell Goodtime Hour*, 1968-72. In movies *True Grit*, *Norwood* and *Strange Homecoming*; voice in the animated movie *Rock-A-Doodle*.

CAMPBELL, Jim
Pop singer.

CAMPBELL, Jo Ann
Born on 7/20/1938 in Jacksonville, Florida. First recorded for El Dorado in 1957. In the movies *Johnny Melody*, *Go Johnny Go* and *Hey, Let's Twist*. Married country singer Troy Seals (cousin of Dan Seals) in the early 1960s; recorded together as Jo Ann & Troy in 1964.

CAMPBELL, Tevin
Born on 11/12/1976 in Waxahachie, Texas. R&B singer. Had first chart hit at the age of 13. Won role in 1988 for the TV show *Wally & The Valentines*. Discovered by Quincy Jones. Appeared in the movie *Graffiti Bridge*.

CAMP LO
Hip-hop duo from the Bronx, New York: Salahadeen Wallace and Saladine Wilds.

CAMP ROCK CAST
Recordings below feature various cast members of the highly popular Disney TV movie: Jonas Brothers, Demi Lovato, Aaryn Doyle, Meaghan Martin and Maria Barrera.

CAM'RON
Born Cameron Giles on 2/4/1976 in Harlem, New York. Male rapper/songwriter.

C & C MUSIC FACTORY
Dance group led by producers/songwriters Robert Clivilles (percussion; born on 8/30/1964) & David Cole (keyboards; born on 6/3/1962). Featured vocalists include Freedom Williams and Deborah Cooper (Fatback, Change). Martha Wash (Two Tons O' Fun, The Weather Girls) is the actual vocalist of "Gonna Make You Sweat," lip-synched in video by Liberian-born Zelma Davis. Cole died of spinal meningitis on 1/24/1995 (age 32).

CANDI
Dance group from Toronto, Ontario, Canada: Candy Pennella (vocals), Nino Milazzo (bass), Rich Imbrogno (keyboards) and Paul Russo (drums).

CANDLEBOX
Rock group from Seattle, Washington: Kevin Martin (vocals), Peter Klett (guitar), Bardi Martin (bass) and Scott Mercado (drums). The Martins are not related.

CANDY AND THE KISSES
Black vocal trio from Port Richmond, New York: sisters Candy (lead) and Suzanne Nelson, with schoolmate Jeanette Johnson.

CANDYMAN
Born John Shaffer on 6/25/1968 in Los Angeles, California. Male rapper.

CANDYMEN, The
Former backing band for Roy Orbison: Rodney Justo (vocals), John Adkins (guitar), Dean Daughtry (piano), Billy Gilmore (bass) and Bob Nix (drums). Daughtry joined the Classics IV. Justo, Daughtry and Nix later joined the Atlanta Rhythm Section. Adkins died in June 1989 (age 47).

CANE, Gary
Born in 1943 in Brooklyn, New York.

CANIBUS
Born Germaine Williams on 12/9/1974 in Jamaica; raised in New Jersey. Male rapper.

CANNED HEAT
Blues-rock group from Los Angeles, California: Bob "The Bear" Hite (vocals, harmonica), Al "Blind Owl" Wilson (guitar, harmonica, vocals), Henry Vestine (guitar), Larry Taylor (bass) and Frank Cook (drums). Cook replaced by Fito de la Parra in 1968. Vestine replaced by Harvey Mandel in 1969. Wilson died of a drug overdose on 9/3/1970 (age 27). Hite died of a drug-related heart attack on 4/6/1981 (age 36). Vestine died of heart failure on 10/20/1997 (age 52).

CANNIBAL AND THE HEADHUNTERS
Latino vocal group from Los Angeles, California: Frankie "Cannibal" Garcia, brothers Robert and Joe Jaramillo, and Richard Lopez. Garcia died on 1/21/1996 (age 49). Joe Jaramillo died on 5/24/2000 (age 51).

CANNON, Ace
Born on 5/5/1934 in Grenada, Mississippi. White saxophonist/songwriter. Worked with Bill Black's Combo.

CANNON, Freddy
Born Frederick Picariello on 12/4/1939 in Lynn, Massachusetts. Rock and roll teen idol. Local work with own band, Freddy Karmon & The Hurricanes. Nickname "Boom Boom" came from big bass drum-sound on his records. Band arrangements by Frank Slay on all Swan recordings.

CANNON, Nick
Born on 10/17/1980 in San Diego, California. R&B singer/actor. Regular on TV's *All That* (1998-2001). Starred in the 2002 movie *Drumline*. Married Mariah Carey on 4/30/2008.

CANTRELL, Blu
Born Tiffany Cobb on 10/1/1976 in Providence, Rhode Island. Female R&B singer.

CANTRELL, Lana
Born on 8/7/1943 in Sydney, Australia. Female singer/actress.

CANYON
Pop vocal group: Richard Carmichael, Randy Davidson, Bill Frazier and Mark Lance.

CAPALDI, Jim
Born on 8/24/1944 in Evesham, Worcestershire, England. Died of cancer on 1/28/2005 (age 60). Rock singer/drummer. Member of Traffic.

CAPITOLS, The
R&B vocal trio from Detroit, Michigan: Sam George (vocals, drums), Donald Storball (guitar) and Richard McDougall (keyboards). George was murdered on 3/17/1982 (age 39).

CAPLETON
Born Clifton Bailey on 4/13/1967 in Islington, St. Mary, Jamaica. Male dancehall-reggae DJ/singer/songwriter.

CAPRIS, The
Italian-American doo-wop group from Queens, New York: Nick Santamaria (lead), Mike Mincieli (1st tenor), Frank Reina (2nd tenor), Vinny Naccarato (baritone) and John Apostol (bass). Disbanded in 1959, re-formed when song "There's A Moon Out Tonight" was reissued on Lost-Nite in 1960 and became a hit in 1961.

CAPTAIN & TENNILLE
Pop duo: Daryl "The Captain" Dragon (born on 8/27/1942 in Los Angeles, California) and his wife, Toni Tennille (born on 5/8/1943 in Montgomery, Alabama). They married in 1974. Dragon is the son of noted conductor Carmen Dragon. Keyboardist with The Beach Boys; nicknamed "The Captain" by Mike Love. Duo had own TV show on ABC from 1976-77.

CAPTAIN HOLLYWOOD PROJECT
Captain Hollywood is dance producer Tony Harrison. Born on 8/9/1962 in Newark, New Jersey; raised in Detroit, Michigan. While in the Army, was stationed in Nuremburg, Germany, where he began entertainment career as a choreographer.

CARA, Irene
Born Irene Escalera on 3/18/1959 in the Bronx, New York. Dance singer/actress/pianist. Appeared in several movies and TV shows.

CARAVELLES, The
Female pop vocal duo from England: Andrea Simpson (born on 9/12/1946) and Lois Wilkinson (born on 4/3/1944).

CARDENAS, Luis
Born in Los Angeles, California. Rock singer/drummer.

CARDIGANS, The
Pop-rock group from Jönköping, Sweden: Nina Persson (vocals), Peter Svensson (guitar), Lars-Olof Johansson (keyboards), Magnus Sveningsson (bass) and Bengt Lagersburg (drums).

CARDINALS, The
R&B vocal group from Baltimore, Maryland: Ernie Warren, Meredith Brothers, Leon Hardy and Donald Johnson. Later joined by Jack Aydelotte as guitarist and fifth voice. Warren died on 7/30/2007 (age 78).

CAREFREES, The
Female vocal trio from England: Lyn Cornell, Betty Prescott and Barbara Kay.

CAREY, Mariah
Born on 3/27/1970 in Greenlawn, Long Island, New York. Her mother is Patricia Carey, former singer with the New York City Opera. Mariah sang backup for Brenda K. Starr. Married to Tommy Mottola, president of Sony Music Entertainment, from1993-98. Starred in the 2001 movie *Glitter*. Married Nick Cannon on 4/30/2008.

CAREY, Tony
Born on 10/16/1952 in Watsonville, California; later settled in West Germany. Ex-keyboardist with Rainbow and lead singer of Planet P.

CARGILL, Henson
Born on 2/5/1941 in Oklahoma City, Oklahoma. Died on 3/24/2007 (age 66). Country singer.

CARLILE, Brandi
Born on 6/1/1981 in Ravensdale, Washington. Female singer/songwriter/guitarist.

CARLISLE, Belinda
Born on 8/17/1958 in Hollywood, California. Lead singer of the Go-Go's, 1978-84. Married to Morgan Mason, son of the late actor James Mason.

CARLISLE, Bob
Born on 9/29/1956 in Santa Ana, California. Singer/songwriter/guitarist. Recorded Christian music on the Sparrow label.

CARLISLE, Steve
Pop background and radio jingle singer. Appeared in several movies.

CARLTON, Carl
Born on 10/22/1952 in Detroit, Michigan. R&B singer/songwriter.

CARLTON, Larry
Born on 3/2/1948 in Torrance, California. Top session guitarist. Frequent guest guitarist of The Crusaders, 1972-77. Fully recovered from a near-fatal gunshot wound suffered in a robbery attack in 1988. Married to Contemporary Christian artist Michelle Pillar.

CARLTON, Vanessa
Born on 8/16/1980 in Milford, Pennsylvania. Adult Contemporary singer/songwriter/pianist.

CARMEN, Eric
Born on 8/11/1949 in Cleveland, Ohio. Classical training at Cleveland Institute of Music from early years to mid-teens. Lead singer of the Raspberries from 1970-74. Wrote "That's Rock 'N' Roll" and "Hey Deanie" for Shaun Cassidy.

CARNES, Kim
Born on 7/20/1945 in Los Angeles, California. Female vocalist/pianist/composer. Member of The New Christy Minstrels with husband/co-writer Dave Ellingson and Kenny Rogers, late 1960s. Wrote and performed vocals for the Sugar Bears. Wrote for and performed in commercials. Co-wrote "Love Comes From Unexpected Places," which won the American Song Festival in 1977 and was later recorded by Barbra Streisand.

CAROSONE, Renato
Born on 1/2/1920 in Naples, Italy. Died on 5/20/2001 (age 81). Male singer.

CARPENTER, Mary Chapin
Born on 2/21/1958 in Princeton, New Jersey. Country singer/guitarist. Moved to Washington DC in 1974. Graduated from Brown University with an American Civilization degree.

CARPENTER, Thelma
Born on 1/15/1920 in Brooklyn, New York. Died on 5/15/1997 (age 77). Black singer with Teddy Wilson, Coleman Hawkins and Count Basie bands. On Eddie Cantor's radio show, 1945-46. Starred in Broadway's *Hello, Dolly!* In the movies *The Wiz* and *The Cotton Club.*

CARPENTERS
Brother-sister duo originally from New Haven, Connecticut: Richard (born on 10/15/1946) and Karen Carpenter (born on 3/2/1950; died of heart failure due to anorexia nervosa on 2/4/1983, age 32). Moved in 1963 to Downey, California. Richard played piano from age nine. Karen played drums in group with Richard and bass player Wes Jacobs in 1965. The trio recorded for RCA in 1966. After a period with the band Spectrum, the Carpenters recorded as a duo for A&M in 1969. Hosts of the TV variety show *Make Your Own Kind Of Music* in 1971. 1988 TV movie *The Karen Carpenter Story* was based on her life.

CARR, Cathy
Born Angela Catherine Cordovano on 6/28/1936 in the Bronx, New York. Died in November 1988 (age 52). Pop singer.

CARR, James
Born on 6/13/1942 in Coahoma, Mississippi; raised in Memphis, Tennessee. Died of cancer on 1/7/2001 (age 58). Soul-gospel singer.

CARR, Valerie
Born in 1936 in New York. Black singer.

CARR, Vikki
Born Florencia Martinez Cardona on 7/19/1941 in El Paso, Texas. Regular on TV's *Ray Anthony Show* in 1962.

CARRACK, Paul
Born on 4/22/1951 in Sheffield, Yorkshire, England. Lead singer of Ace (1973-76), Squeeze (1981, 1993) and Mike + The Mechanics (1985-1992). Keyboardist with Roxy Music (1978-80). With Nick Lowe & His Cowboy Outfit in 1985.

CARRADINE, Keith
Born on 8/8/1949 in San Mateo, California. Leading actor in many movies including *Pretty Baby*, *Nashville*, *The Long Riders* and others. Son of actor John Carradine; half-brother of actor David Carradine.

CARROLL, Andrea
Born Andrea DeCapite on 10/3/1946 in Cleveland, Ohio. Teen pop singer.

CARROLL, Bernadette
Born Bernadette Dalia on 6/21/1945 in Linden, New Jersey. Teen pop singer.

CARROLL, Bob
Born on 6/18/1918 in New York City, New York. White baritone singer. Sang with Charlie Barnet and Jimmy Dorsey in the 1940s.

CARROLL, Cathy
Born in Los Angeles, California. Teen pop singer.

CARROLL, David
Born Nook Schrier on 10/15/1913 in Chicago, Illinois. Arranger/conductor since 1951 for many top Mercury artists.

CARROLL, Dina
Born on 8/21/1968 in Newmarket, Suffolk, England (African-American father and Scottish mother). Dance-R&B singer.

CARROLL, Jason Michael
Born on 6/13/1978 in Houston, Texas; raised in Franklinton, North Carolina. Country singer/ songwriter.

CARROLL, Ronnie
Born Ronald Cleghorn on 8/18/1934 in Belfast, Ireland. Male singer.

CARROLL BROS.
Rock and roll band from Philadelphia, Pennsylvania: Pete Carroll (guitar), Dick Noble (organ/sax), Jimmy Chick (drums), Kenneth Dorn (sax) and Billy McGraw (bass).

CARS, The
Rock and roll band from Boston, Massachusetts: Ric Ocasek (vocals, guitar; born on 3/23/1949), Benjamin Orr (bass, vocals; born on 8/9/1947), Elliot Easton (guitar; born on 12/18/1953), Greg Hawkes (keyboards; born on 3/15/1950) and David Robinson (drums; born on 4/2/1953). Ocasek, Orr and Hawkes had been in trio in the early 1970s. Group named by Robinson; got start at the Rat Club in Boston. Disbanded in 1988. Ocasek appeared in the 1987 movie *Made In Heaven* and married supermodel/actress Paulina Porizkova on 8/23/1989. His son Christopher Otcasek is leader of Glamour Camp. Orr died of cancer on 10/3/2000 (age 53).

CARSON, Jeff
Born Jeff Herndon on 12/16/1964 in Tulsa, Oklahoma; raised in Gravette, Arkansas. Country singer/songwriter/guitarist.

CARSON, Kit
Born Lisa Morrow. Vocalist on Benny Goodman's 1946 hit "Symphony."

CARSON, Mindy
Born on 7/16/1927 in Queens, New York. Sang with Paul Whiteman in the 1940s.

CARTEL
Pop-punk band from Atlanta, Georgia: Will Pugh (vocals), Joe Pepper (guitar), Nic Hudson (guitar), Jeff Lett (bass) and Kevin Sanders (drums).

CARTER, Aaron
Born on 12/7/1987 in Tampa, Florida. Age 12 at the time of his first chart hit. Younger brother of Nick Carter of the Backstreet Boys and Leslie Carter.

CARTER, Clarence
Born on 1/14/1936 in Montgomery, Alabama. R&B singer/guitarist/songwriter. Blind since age one; self-taught on guitar at age 11. Teamed with vocalist/pianist Calvin Scott as Clarence & Calvin, recorded for Fairlane in the early 1960s. Carter went solo in 1966. Married for a time to Candi Staton.

CARTER, Deana
Born on 1/4/1966 in Nashville, Tennessee. Country singer/songwriter. Daughter of prominent session musician Fred Carter, Jr.

CARTER, Leslie
Born on 6/6/1986 in Tampa, Florida. Pop singer. Younger sister of Nick Carter of the Backstreet Boys. Older sister of Aaron Carter.

CARTER, Mel
Born on 4/22/1939 in Cincinnati, Ohio. Black Adult Contemporary singer/actor. Sang on local radio from age four; with Lionel Hampton on stage show at age nine. With Paul Gayten, Jimmy Scott bands. Joined Raspberry Singers gospel group in the early 1950s. With his mother's gospel group, The Carvetts, in the mid-1950s. Named Top Gospel Tenor in 1957. Recorded in late 1950s for Tri-State, Arwin, then Mercury. With Gospel Pearls in the early 1960s. Acted on TV's *Quincy*, *Sanford And Son*, *Marcus Welby, MD* and *Magnum P.I.*

CARTER, Ralph
Born on 5/30/1961 in Harlem, New York. Black dance singer/actor. Played "Michael Evans" on the TV series *Good Times*.

CARTER, Torrey
Born on 8/7/1976 in Detroit, Michigan. R&B singer/ rapper.

CARTOUCHE
Dance duo from Belgium: Myrelle Tholen and Jean-Paul Visser. Cartouche means "bullet" in French.

CARTRIDGE, Flip
Born William Meshel on 5/5/1946 in Brooklyn, New York. Pop singer. Later became an executive at Ariola America Records.

CASCADA
Dance trio formed in Germany: fronted by female vocalist Natalie Horler (born on 9/23/1981 in Bonn, Germany), with male musicians/producers Yann "Yanou" Peifer and Manuel "DJ Manian" Reuter. Group name is Spanish for "waterfall."

CASCADES, The
Pop group from San Diego, California: John Gummoe (vocals, guitar), Eddie Snyder (piano), David Wilson (sax), David Stevens (bass) and David Zabo (drums). Snyder hit the country charts in 1989 as "Eddie Preston." Wilson died of cancer on 11/14/2000 (age 63).

CASE
Born Casey Woodard on 1/10/1973 in Harlem, New York. Male R&B singer/songwriter.

CASEY, Al
Born on 10/26/1936 in Long Beach, California. Died on 9/17/2006 (age 69). Guitarist/pianist/bandleader/producer. Much session work with Lee Hazlewood productions, including Sanford Clark and Duane Eddy. Not to be confused with black guitarist of the same name.

CASH, Alvin
Born Alvin Welch on 2/15/1939 in St. Louis, Missouri. Died on 11/21/1999 (age 60). Soul-funk singer/dancer. Formed song/dance troupe The Crawlers in 1960, with brothers Robert, Arthur and George (ages 8 to 10). They never sang on any of Alvin's hits. Alvin moved to Chicago in 1963. First recorded for Mar-V-Lus in 1964. Cut "Twine Time" with backing band the Nightlighters from Louisville, who changed their name to the Registers.

CASH, Johnny
Born J.R. Cash on 2/26/1932 in Kingsland, Arkansas. Died of diabetes on 9/12/2003 (age 71). Legendary country singer/songwriter/guitarist. Brother Roy led the Dixie Rhythm Ramblers band in late 1940s. In U.S. Air Force, 1950-54. Formed trio with Luther Perkins (guitar) and Marshall Grant (bass) in 1955. First recorded for Sun in 1955. On *Louisiana Hayride* and *Grand Ole Opry* in 1957. Own TV show for ABC from 1969-71. Worked with June Carter from 1961; married her in March 1968. Carl Perkins and The Statler Brothers were members of his touring troupe from 1968-75. Daughter Rosanne Cash and stepdaughter Carlene Carter had successful singing careers. June Carter died of heart failure on 5/15/2003 (age 73).

CASH, Rosanne
Born on 5/24/1955 in Memphis, Tennessee. Daughter of Johnny Cash and Vivian Liberto. Raised by her mother in California, then moved to Nashville after high school graduation. Worked in the Johnny Cash Road Show. Married to Rodney Crowell from 1979-92. Moved to New York. Married producer John Leventhal in 1995. Released short-story collection *Bodies Of Water* in 1996.

CASH, Tommy
Born on 4/5/1940 in Dyess, Arkansas. Brother of Johnny Cash.

CASHMAN & WEST
Duo of pop record producers/songwriters/singers Dennis "Terry Cashman" Minogue (born on 7/5/1941) and Thomas "Tommy West" Picardo, Jr. (born on 8/17/1942). Produced all of Jim Croce's recordings. Recorded as Buchanan Brothers and Morning Mist.

CASH MONEY MILLIONAIRES
Rap collective of Cash Money label artists: Big Tymers, Juvenile and Lil' Wayne.

CASINOS, The
Pop vocal group from Cincinnati, Ohio: Gene Hughes (lead), Pete Bolton, Bob Armstrong, Tom Mathews, Ray White, Mickey Denton, Glen Hughes,

Joe Patterson and Bill Hawkins. Gene Hughes died in a car crash on 2/3/2004 (age 67).

CASLONS, The
White pop vocal group from Brooklyn, New York: Sal Mondeuri (lead), Richie Smith, Lou Smith, Joe Carvelli and Bernie Belkin.

CASSIDY
Born Barry Reese on 7/7/1982 in Philadelphia, Pennsylvania. Male rapper.

CASSIDY, David
Born on 4/12/1950 in Manhattan, New York. Son of actor Jack Cassidy and actress Evelyn Ward. Played "Keith Partridge," the lead singer of TV's *The Partridge Family*. Married to actress Kay Lenz from 1977-83. Co-starred with his half-brother Shaun Cassidy on Broadway's *Blood Brothers* in 1993.

CASSIDY, Shaun
Born on 9/27/1958 in Los Angeles, California. Son of actor Jack Cassidy and actress Shirley Jones of TV's *The Partridge Family*. Played "Joe Hardy" on TV's *The Hardy Boys*. Co-starred with his half-brother David Cassidy on Broadway's *Blood Brothers* in 1993. Cast member of the TV soap *General Hospital* in 1987. Married to model Ann Pennington, 1979-91.

CASSIE
Born Casandra Ventura on 8/26/1986 in New London, Connecticut. Female R&B singer/songwriter/former fashion model.

CASTAWAYS, The
Rock and roll band of teens from St. Paul, Minnesota: Richard Roby (vocals, bass), Robert Folschow and Roy Hensley (guitars), James Donna (keyboards) and Dennis Craswell (drums). Craswell later joined Crow.

CASTELLS, The
Adult Contemporary vocal group from Santa Rosa, California: Bob Ussery, Tom Hicks, Joe Kelly and Chuck Girard (later with The Hondells).

CASTLE, David
Born on 11/28/1952 in Overton, Texas. Pop singer/songwriter.

CASTLEMAN, Boomer
Owen "Boomer" Clarke of The Lewis & Clarke Expedition. Originally from Farmers Branch, Texas.

CASTLE SISTERS, The
Pop vocal trio.

CAST OF HAIRSPRAY
Features cast members of the 2007 movie musical: Nikki Blonsky, Zac Efron, Amanda Bynes, Elijah Kelly, John Travolta and Queen Latifah.

CAST OF RENT
Song below features Tracie Thoms as "Joanne Jefferson" and Jesse L. Martin as "Tom Collins" along with other cast members of the 2005 movie musical.

CASTOR, Jimmy
Born on 6/22/1943 in the Bronx, New York. R&B singer/saxophonist/composer/arranger. Formed the Jimmy Castor Bunch in 1972: Gerry Thomas (keyboards), Doug Gibson (bass), Harry Jensen (guitar), Lenny Fridie, Jr. (congas) and Bobby Manigault (drums).

CASTRO, Christian
Born on 12/8/1974 in Mexico City, Mexico. Latin singer/actor. Son of Mexican movie star Veronica Castro.

CASWELL, Johnny
Born in Philadelphia, Pennsylvania. Lead singer of Crystal Mansion.

CATE BROS.
White pop-rock duo of twins Ernie (vocals, piano) and Earl (guitar) Cate. Born on 12/26/42 in Fayetteville, Arkansas.

CATES, George
Born on 10/19/1911 in Brooklyn, New York. Died on 5/10/2002 (age 90). Arranger for Bing Crosby, Teresa Brewer, The Andrews Sisters and others. Musical director of TV's *Lawrence Welk Show* for 25 years.

CATHY & JOE
Pop vocal duo from New Orleans, Louisiana: Catherine Anne Bunn and Joseph J. Wegman.

CATHY JEAN & THE ROOMMATES
Born Cathy Jean Giordano on 9/8/1945 in Brooklyn, New York. The Roommates were a vocal quartet from Queens, New York: Steve Susskind (lead), Jack Sailson and Felix Alvarez (tenors) and Bob Minsky (bass).

CAT MOTHER & The All Night News Boys
Rock group from New York produced by Jimi Hendrix: Larry Packer (guitar), Bob Smith (piano), Charley Chin (banjo), Roy Michaels (bass) and Michael Equine (drums). All share vocals.

CAUSE & EFFECT
Pop duo based in Northern California: Sean Rowley (keyboards) and British-born Robert Rowe (vocals, guitar). Joined on tour by drummer Evan Parandes, then Richard Shepherd. Rowley died of asthma-related cardiac arrest on 11/12/1992 (age 23). Rowe, Shepherd and Keith David Milo continued as a trio.

CAVALIERE, Felix
Born on 11/29/1942 in Pelham, New York. Lead singer of The Rascals after a stint with Joey Dee & The Starliters.

CAZZ
Born Robert Lewis in Texas. R&B singer.

C COMPANY Featuring TERRY NELSON
Group of studio musicians led by DJ/singer Terry Nelson from Russellville, Alabama.

C.C.S.
Jazz-rock collective from England. Put together by a core trio of vocalists Alexis Korner (born on 4/19/1928; died of lung cancer on 1/1/1984, age 55) and Peter Thorup (born on 12/14/1948; died on

8/3/2007, age 58), with arranger John Cameron. Name stands for Collective Consciousness Society. Korner's Blues Inc., a pioneer blues-rock band of the early 1960s, featured Mick Jagger, Ginger Baker, Jack Bruce and other rock notables.

CEE-LO
Born Thomas Callaway on 5/30/1974 in Atlanta, Georgia. R&B singer/songwriter. Member of Goodie Mob and the lead singer of the duo Gnarls Barkley.

CELEBRATION featuring MIKE LOVE
Pop group formed in Los Angeles, California: Mike Love (vocals), Ron Altback (keyboards), Charles Lloyd (sax) and Dave "Doc" Robinson (bass). Love is lead singer of The Beach Boys. Altback and Robinson were members of King Harvest.

CELI BEE & THE BUZZY BUNCH
Disco group from Puerto Rico. Led by female singer Celinas Soto.

CELLARFUL OF NOISE
Rock group from Cleveland, Ohio. Led by singer/songwriter/keyboardist Mark Avsec (Wild Cherry).

CELLOS, The
Black doo-wop group from Manhattan, New York: Cliff "Monk" Williams (lead), Robert Thomas, Alton Campbell, William Montgomery and Alvin Williams.

CENTRAL LINE
R&B group from London, England: Linton Beckles (vocals, drums), Henry Defoe (guitar), Lipson Francis (keyboards) and Camelle Hinds (bass).

CERA, Michael
Born on 6/7/1988 in Brampton, Ontario, Canada. Male singer/actor. Played "Paulie Bleeker" in the 2007 movie *Juno*.

CERRONE
Born Jean-Marc Cerrone in 1952 in St. Michel, France. Dance composer/producer/drummer. A pioneer of the Euro-disco sound.

CETERA, Peter
Born on 9/13/1944 in Chicago, Illinois. Lead singer/bass guitarist of Chicago from 1967-85.

CHACKSFIELD, Frank
Born on 5/9/1914 in Battle, Sussex, England. Died on 6/9/1995 (age 81). Pianist/bandleader.

CHAD & JEREMY
Soft-rock duo from London, England: Chad Stuart (born on 12/10/1941) and Jeremy Clyde (born on 3/22/1941). Broke up in 1968. Re-formed briefly in 1982.

CHAIRMEN OF THE BOARD
R&B vocal group from Detroit, Michigan: General Norman Johnson, Danny Woods, Harrison Kennedy and Eddie Curtis. First recorded for Invictus in 1969. Johnson was leader of The Showmen from 1961-67; wrote "Patches," hit for Clarence Carter. Johnson went solo in 1976.

CHAKACHAS, The
Studio group from Belgium. Featuring saxophonist Victor Ingevald.

CHAM
Born Dameon Beckett in 1977 in Kingston, Jamaica. Male reggae singer/songwriter.

CHAMBERLAIN, Richard
Born George Richard Chamberlain on 3/31/1935 in Beverly Hills, California. Leading movie, theater and TV actor. Played lead role in TV's *Dr. Kildare*, 1961-66.

CHAMBERS BROTHERS, The
Black psychedlic-rock band from Lee County, Mississippi: brothers George Chambers (bass), Willie Chambers (guitar), Lester Chambers (harmonica) and Joe Chambers (guitar), with Brian Keenan (drums). All shared vocals. Keenan died of a heart attack on 10/5/1985 (age 42).

CHAMILLIONAIRE
Born Hakeem Seriki on 11/28/1979 in Houston, Texas. Male rapper/songwriter.

CHAMPAGNE
Pop group from Rotterdam, Holland: Paulette Bronkhorst, Trudie Huysdens, Jan Vredenburg and Bert van der Wiel.

CHAMPAIGN
R&B group from Champaign, Illinois: Pauli Carman and Rena Jones (vocals), Leon Reeder (guitar), Michael Day and Dana Walden (keyboards), Michael Reed (bass) and Rocky Maffit (drums).

CHAMPLIN, Bill
Born on 5/21/1947 in Oakland, California. Leader of San Francisco's Sons Of Champlin for 13 years. Member of Chicago since 1982.

CHAMPS, The
Rock and roll instrumental group from Los Angeles, California. Named after Gene Autry's horse, Champ. Originally consisted of studio musicians Dave Burgess (rhythm guitar), Buddy Bruce (lead guitar), Danny Flores (sax; later changed name to Chuck Rio; died on 9/19/2006, age 77), Cliff Hils (bass) and Gene Alden (drums). Shortly after "Tequila" became a hit, Bruce and Hils were replaced by Dale Norris and Joe Burnas. Eight months after recording "Tequila," Flores and Alden left; replaced by Jimmy Seals (sax) & Dash Crofts (drums), later a hit recording duo (Seals & Crofts). Other personnel changes followed; in 1960, guitarist Glen Campbell spent some time in the group.

CHAMPS' BOYS ORCHESTRA, The
Instrumental group from France. Assembled by producer Patrick Boceno.

CHANDLER, Gene
Born Eugene Dixon on 7/6/1940 in Chicago, Illinois. R&B singer/producer. Took last name from his favorite movie star, Jeff Chandler. Joined the Gaytones at Englewood High School in 1955. Joined his neighborhood vocal group The Dukays 1956. In the U.S. Army, Germany, 1957-60. Rejoined The Dukays in 1960; they first recorded for NAT in 1961. Group recorded "Duke Of Earl" while under contract to NAT; however, Vee-Jay purchased the recording and released the record as by Gene Chandler. Own label, Mr. Chand, 1969-73.

Gene, Jerry Butler, Lloyd Price and Ben E. King formed a corporation "The 4 Kings of Rhythm & Blues" in 1999.

CHANDLER, Karen
Born Eva Nadauld in Rexburg, Idaho. Formerly married to Jack Pleis. Sang with Benny Goodman under the name Eve Young in 1946.

CHANDLER, Kenny
Born Kenneth Bolognese on 11/21/1940 in Harrisburg, Pennsylvania. White pop singer. Also recorded as Kenny Beau.

CHANGE
European-American dance group formed in Italy by producers Jacques Fred Petrus and Mauro Malavasi. Led by Paolo Gianolio (guitar) and David Romani (bass). Luther Vandross sang lead on several songs of group's first charted album. Later group, based in New York, included lead vocals by James Robinson and Deborah "Crab" Cooper (later with C & C Music Factory). One-time band member Rick Gallwey married Sharon Bryant, former lead singer of Atlantic Starr.

CHANGING FACES
Female R&B vocal duo from Brooklyn, New York: Charisse Rose and Cassandra Lucas.

CHANGIN' TIMES, The
Songwriting/producing duo from New York: Artie Kornfeld and Steve Duboff. Kornfeld was a co-creator of the *Woodstock* music festival.

CHANNEL, Bruce
Born on 11/28/1940 in Jacksonville, Texas. Pop singer.

CHANNEL LIVE
Rap duo from New Jersey: Hokiem Green and Vincent Morgan.

CHANSON
Disco studio group. Lead vocals by James Jamerson, Jr. and David Williams. Jamerson's father was a prominent Motown bassist. Group name is French for song.

CHANTAY'S
Teen surf-rock group from Santa Ana, California: Bob Spickard (lead guitar), Brian Carman (rhythm guitar), Rob Marshall (piano), Warren Waters (bass) and Bob Welsh (drums).

CHANTELS, The
Female R&B vocal group from the Bronx, New York: Arlene Smith, Sonia Goring, Rene Minus, Jackie Landry and Lois Harris. Landry died of cancer on 12/23/1997 (age 56).

CHANTERS, The
Black teen doo-wop group from Queens, New York: Larry Pendergrass (lead), Fred Paige, Bud Johnson, Elliot Green and Bobby Thompson. Johnson's father is famous bandleader Buddy Johnson, who arranged their sessions. Group disbanded in the early 1960s. Not to be confused with Billy Butler's Chanters.

CHAPIN, Harry
Born on 12/7/1942 in Greenwich Village, New York. Died in a car crash on 7/16/1981 (age 38). Folk-rock singer/songwriter/guitarist.

CHAPLAIN, Paul
Born on 9/3/1934 in Webster, Massachusetts. Died on 5/13/1995 (age 61). Rock and roll singer/guitarist. His Emeralds: George Dibonaventura, Bob Prince and Bill Hickman.

CHAPMAN, Tracy
Born on 3/30/1964 in Cleveland, Ohio. Folk-R&B singer/songwriter/guitarist.

CHARGERS, The
R&B vocal group from Los Angeles, California: Benny Easley, brothers Dunbar and Johnny White, Jimmy Scott and Mitchell Alexander. Founded by Jesse Belvin.

CHARLENE
Born Charlene D'Angelo on 6/1/1950 in Hollywood, California. Pop-R&B singer.

CHARLES, Jimmy
Born in 1942 in Paterson, New Jersey. R&B singer. Won Apollo Amateur Contest in 1958.

CHARLES, Ray
Born Ray Charles Robinson on 9/23/1930 in Albany, Georgia; raised in Greenville, Florida. Died of liver disease on 6/10/2004 (age 73). Partially blind at age five; completely blind at seven (glaucoma). Studied classical piano and clarinet at State School for Deaf and Blind Children, St. Augustine, Florida, 1937-45. With local Florida bands; moved to Seattle in 1948. Formed the McSon Trio (also known as the Maxin Trio) with Gossady McGhee (guitar) and Milton Garred (bass). First recordings were very much in the King Cole Trio style. The Raeletts were Ray's credited and uncredited backing vocalists. Legendary performer, with many TV and movie appearances. Jamie Foxx won an Oscar for his portrayal of Ray Charles in the 2004 movie *Ray*.

CHARLES, Ray, Singers
Born Charles Raymond Offenberg on 9/13/1918 in Chicago, Illinois. Arranger/conductor for many TV shows including the *Perry Como Show*, *Glen Campbell Goodtime Hour* and *Sha-Na-Na*. Winner of two Emmys.

CHARLES, Sonny
Born in Fort Wayne, Indiana. R&B singer. Leader of The Checkmates, Ltd., which includes Bobby Stevens, Harvey Trees, Bill Van Buskirk and Marvin Smith. Smith died of a heart attack on 12/15/2007 (age 68).

CHARLES, Tommy
Born on 11/29/1929 in Chattanooga, Tennessee. Died on 8/8/1996 (age 66). Pop singer.

CHARLES & EDDIE
R&B vocal duo: Charles Pettigrew (from Philadelphia, Pennsylvania) and Eddie Chacon (from Oakland, California). Pettigrew died of cancer on 4/6/2001 (age 37).

CHARLIE
Rock group from England: Terry Thomas (guitar), Julian Colbeck (guitar), John Anderson (bass) and Steve Gadd (drums). Varying membership also included Bob Henrit (drums; Argent; joined by 1983) and Terry Slesser (vocals; joined in 1980). Henrit joined The Kinks by 1984.

CHARM
Born in Brooklyn, New York. Male rapper.

CHARMETTES, The
Female R&B vocal trio from Brooklyn, New York: Clara Byrd, Mittie Ponder and Betty Simmons.

CHARM FARM
Techno-pop group from Detroit, Michigan: Dennis White (vocals), Steve Zuccaro (guitar), Ken Roberts (keyboards), Dino Zoyes (bass) and Eric Meyer (drums).

CHARMS, The
R&B vocal group from Cincinnati, Ohio: Otis Williams, Richard Parker, Donald Peak, Joe Penn and Rolland Bradley. Group first recorded for Rockin' in 1953. Otis, not to be confused with the same-named member of The Temptations, later recorded country music.

CHARTBUSTERS, The
Rock and roll band from Washington DC: Vernon Sandusky (vocals, guitar), Vince Gideon (guitar), John Dubas (bass) and Mitch Corday (drums).

CHARTS, The
Black doo-wop group from Harlem, New York: Joe Grier (lead), Leroy Binns and Steven Brown (tenors), Glenmore Jackson (baritone) and Ross Buford (bass). Brown died on 1/20/1989 (age 48).

CHASE
Jazz-rock band organized by trumpeter Bill Chase (born in 1935 in Chicago, Illinois; formerly with Woody Herman and Stan Kenton). Varying lineup. Chase along with bandmates John Emma, Wallace Yohn and Walter Clark were killed in a plane crash on 8/9/1974 near Jackson, Minnesota.

CHASE, Ellison
Born in 1952 in Ohio. Male dance-rock singer. Backing vocalist for Patty Smyth.

CHASEZ, JC
Born Joshua Chasez on 8/8/1976 in Washington DC. Pop singer/songwriter. Member of *NSYNC.

CHATER, Kerry
Born on 8/7/1945 in Vancouver, British Columbia, Canada. Singer/songwriter. Original member of The Union Gap.

CHEAP TRICK
Rock group from Rockford, Illinois: Robin Zander (vocals; born on 1/23/1953), Rick Nielsen (guitar; born on 12/22/1946), Tom Petersson (bass; born on 5/9/1950) and Bun E. Carlos (drums; born Brad Carlson on 6/12/1951). Discovered by Aerosmith's producer Jack Douglas. Petersson replaced by Jon Brant in 1980; returned in 1988, replacing Brant.

CHECKER, Chubby
Born Ernest Evans on 10/3/1941 in Andrews, South Carolina; raised in Philadelphia, Pennsylvania. Did impersonations of famous singers. First recorded for Parkway in 1959. Dick Clark's then-wife Bobbie suggested that Evans change his name to Chubby Checker due to his resemblance to a teenage Fats Domino. Cover version of Hank Ballard's "The Twist" started worldwide dance craze. On 4/12/1964, married Miss World 1962, Dutch-born Catharina Lodders ("Loddy Lo" written for her). In the movies *Don't Knock The Twist* and *Twist Around The Clock*.

CHEECH & CHONG
Comedians Richard "Cheech" Marin (born on 7/13/1946 in Watts, California) and Thomas Chong (born on 5/24/1938 in Edmonton, Alberta, Canada). Their first four comedy albums were certifield gold sellers. Starred in movies since 1978. Chong, the father of actress Rae Dawn Chong, was the guitarist of Bobby Taylor & The Vancouvers. Duo split in the late 1980s. Cheech was a cast member of TV's *Golden Palace* and *Nash Bridges*.

CHEE-CHEE & PEPPY
Black teen duo of Keith "Chee-Chee" Bolling (born in 1957 in Frankfort, Pennsylvania) and Dorothy "Peppy" Moore (born in 1959 in Morristown, Pennsylvania). Duo formed by producer Jesse James.

CHEEKS, Judy
Born in Miami, Florida. Dance singer. Daughter of gospel singer/preacher Rev. Julius Cheeks. Cousin of Genobia Jeter.

CHEERS, The
Pop vocal trio from Los Angeles, California: Bert Convy, Gil Garfield and Sue Allen. Convy later became a popular TV personality; died of a brain tumor on 7/15/1991 (age 58).

CHEETAH GIRLS, The
Female pop vocal trio: Adrienne Bailon, Kiely Williams and Sabrina Bryan. The trio starred in the same-named Disney channel TV movies with Raven-Symoné. Bailon and Williams were members of 3LW.

CHEMAY, Joe, Band
Born on 3/22/1950 in Baltimore, Maryland. Pop-rock singer/bassist. Band included Billy Walker (guitar), John Hobbs (piano), Mike Meros (organ), Louis Conte (percussion) and Paul Leim (drums).

CHEMICAL BROTHERS, The
Techno-dance DJ duo from England: Tom Rowlands and Ed Simons.

CHER
Born Cherilyn Sarkasian on 5/20/1946 in El Centro, California. Adopted by stepfather at age 15 and last name changed to La Piere. Worked as backup singer for Phil Spector (The Teddy Bears). Recorded as "Bonnie Jo Mason" and "Cherilyn" in 1964. Recorded with Sonny Bono (born on 2/16/1935; died on 1/5/1998) as "Caesar & Cleo" in 1963, then as Sonny & Cher from 1965-73. Married to Bono from 1963-75. Married to Gregg Allman from 1975-78. Own TV series with Bono from 1971-74, 1976-77. Member of the group Black Rose in 1980. Acclaimed movie actress (won the 1987 Best Actress Oscar for *Moonstruck*).

CHERI
Female dance duo from Montreal, Quebec, Canada: Rosalind Hunt and Lyn Cullerier.

CHERIE
Born Cindy Almouzni in 1984 in Marseilles, France. Female pop singer.

CHERISH
Female R&B vocal group from Atlanta, Georgia: sisters Farrah, Neosha, Fallon and Felisha King (Fallon and Felisha are twins).

CHERRELLE
Born Cheryl Norton on 10/13/1958 in Los Angeles, California. R&B singer. Cousin of singer Pebbles.

CHERRY, Don
Born on 1/11/1924 in Wichita Falls, Texas. Studied voice after the service in mid-1940s. Vocalist with Jan Garber band in the late 1940s. Accomplished professional golfer.

CHERRY, Eagle-Eye
Born on 5/7/1969 in Stockholm, Sweden. Son of jazz trumpeter Don Cherry. Half-brother of Neneh Cherry.

CHERRY, Neneh
Born on 3/10/1964 in Stockholm, Sweden; raised in Brooklyn, New York. R&B-dance singer. Stepdaughter of jazz trumpeter Don Cherry. Half-sister of Eagle-Eye Cherry. Married composer/musician Cameron "Booga Bear" McVey in December 1990.

CHERRY PEOPLE, The
Pop-rock band from Washington DC: brothers Doug Grimes (vocals) and Chris Grimes (guitar), Edwin "Punky" Meadows (guitar), Jan Zukowski (bass) and Rocky Isaac (drums). Meadows later joined Angel.

CHERRY POPPIN' DADDIES
Retro-swing group from Eugene, Oregon: Steve Perry (vocals, guitar), Jason Moss (guitar), Dana Heitman, Sean Flannery and Ian Early (horns), Darren Cassidy (bass) and Tim Donahue (drums).

CHESNEY, Kenny
Born on 3/26/1968 in Knoxville, Tennessee; raised in Luttrell, Tennessee. Country singer/songwriter/guitarist. Married actress Renée Zellweger on 5/9/2005; marriage annulled on 9/16/2005.

CHESNUTT, Mark
Born on 9/6/1963 in Beaumont, Texas. Country singer/guitarist.

CHEVELLE
Rock trio from Chicago, Illinois: brothers Pete (vocals, guitar), Joe (bass) and Sam (drums) Loeffler.

CHIC

R&B-disco group formed in New York City, New York, by prolific producers Bernard Edwards (bass; born on 10/31/1952) and Nile Rodgers (guitar; born on 9/19/1952). Featured drummer Tony Thompson and vocalists Luci Martin and Norma Jean Wright. Wright began solo career in 1978 as Norma Jean; replaced by Alfa Anderson. Edwards recorded with the studio group Roundtree in 1978. Rodgers joined The Honeydrippers in 1984. Thompson joined the Power Station in 1985, and Edwards became their producer. Wright, along with supporting Chic member Raymond Jones, formed State Of Art in 1991. Rodgers and Edwards regrouped as Chic in 1992 with female lead vocalists/South Carolina natives Sylvester Logan Sharp and Jenn Thomas. Edwards died of pneumonia on 4/18/1996 (age 43). Thompson died of cancer on 11/12/2003 (age 48). Pronounced: sheek.

CHICAGO

Jazz-oriented rock group from Chicago, Illinois: Peter Cetera (vocals, bass; born on 9/13/1944), Terry Kath (vocals, guitar; born on 1/31/1946), Robert Lamm (vocals, keyboards; born on 10/13/1944), James Pankow (trombone; born on 8/20/1947), Lee Loughnane (trumpet; born on 10/21/1946), Walt Parazaider (sax; born on 3/14/1945) and Danny Seraphine (drums; born on 8/28/1948). Known as the Big Thing, then moved to Los Angeles in 1969 and changed name to Chicago Transit Authrity, then simply to Chicago later that year. Kath died of a self-inflicted gunshot on 1/23/1978 (age 31); replaced by Donnie Dacus (guitar, vocals; 1978-80). Bill Champlin (Sons Of Champlin; guitar, keyboards, vocals) joined in 1981. Cetera left in 1985; replaced by Jason Scheff (bass, vocals). Seraphine left in 1990. Original members Lamm, Loughnane, Pankow and Parazaider still performing as Chicago with Champlin, Scheff, Tris Imboden (drums) and Keith Howland (guitar).

CHICAGO BEARS SHUFFLIN' CREW, The

Actual members of the Chicago Bears football team (Super Bowl XX Champs) rapping about themselves. Featuring (in order): Walter Payton, Willie Gault, Mike Singletary, Jim McMahon, Otis Wilson, Steve Fuller, Mike Richardson, Richard Dent, Gary Fencik and William ("The Refrigerator") Perry.

CHICAGO LOOP, The

Rock group from Chicago, Illinois: Bob Slawson and Judy Navy (vocals), John Savanna (guitar), Barry Goldberg (piano), Carmen Riole (bass) and Jack Siomoms (drums).

CHICORY

Rock group from Maidstone, Kent, England: Peter Hewson (vocals), Rick Foster (guitar), Barry Mayger (bass) and Brian Shearer (drums). Known in England as Chicory Tip.

CHIFFONS, The

Female black "girl group" from the Bronx, New York. Formed while high school classmates; worked as backup singers in 1960. Consisted of Judy Craig, Barbara Lee Jones (born on 5/16/1947), Patricia Bennett (born on 4/7/1947) and Sylvia Peterson

(born on 9/30/1946). Jones died of a heart attack on 5/15/1992 (age 44). Also recorded as The Four Pennies on the Rust label.

CHILD, Desmond

Born John Charles Barrett Jr. on 10/28/1953 in Miami, Florida (Cuban mother/Hungarian father). Prolific producer/songwriter. Formed vocal group Rouge with Diane Grasselli, Myriam Valle and Maria Vidal in 1974.

CHILD, Jane

Born on 2/15/1969 in Scarborough, Ontario, Canada. Singer/songwriter/keyboardist.

CHILDS, Toni

Born on 7/20/1960 in Orange, California. Female rock singer.

CHI-LITES, The

R&B vocal group from Chicago, Illinois: Eugene Record (lead; born on 12/23/1940; died on 7/22/2005, age 64), Robert "Squirrel" Lester (tenor), Marshall Thompson (baritone) and Creadel "Red" Jones (bass). First recorded as the Hi-Lites on Daran in 1963. Eugene Record (husband of Barbara Acklin) went solo in 1976.

CHILLIWACK

Rock group from Vancouver, British Columbia, Canada: Bill Henderson (vocals, guitar, songwriter), Brian MacLeod (guitar), Ab Bryant (bass) and Rick Taylor (drums). Bryant and MacLeod later joined Headpins. Bryant was also with Prism. MacLeod died of brain cancer on 4/25/1992 (age 41).

CHIMES, The

White doo-wop group from Brooklyn, New York: Len Cocco, Pat DePrisco, Richard Mercado, Joe Croce and Pat McGuire.

CHIMES, The

Dance trio from Scotland: Pauline Henry (vocals), Mike Peden (bass) and James Locke (drums).

CHINGY

Born Howard Bailey on 3/9/1980 in St. Louis, Missouri. Male rapper.

CHIPMUNKS, The — see SEVILLE, David

CHOCOLATE MILK

R&B group formed in Memphis, Tennessee; later based in New Orleans, Louisiana: Frank Richard (vocals), Mario Tio (guitar), Robert Dabon (keyboards), Amadee Castanell (sax), Joe Foxx (trumpet) and Dwight Richards (drums).

CHOICE FOUR, The

R&B vocal group from Washington DC: Bobby Hamilton (lead), Ted Maduro, Pete Marshall and Charles Blagmore.

CHOIR, The

Rock band formed in Mentor, Ohio: Wally Bryson (vocals, guitar; Fotomaker), David Smalley (guitar), James Skeen (bass) and Jim Bonfanti (drums). Bryson, Smalley and Bonfanti went on to form the Raspberries with Eric Carmen.

CHOIRBOYS
Rock group from Sydney, Australia: Mark Gable (vocals), Brett Williams (guitar), Ian Hulme (bass) and Lindsay Tebbutt (drums).

CHOPPA
Born Darwin Turner in New Orleans, Louisiana. Male rapper.

CHORDETTES, The
Female vocal group from Sheboygan, Wisconsin: Janet Ertel, Carol Buschman, Lynn Evans and Margie Needham. With Arthur Godfrey from 1949-53. Ertel married Cadence record owner Archie Bleyer in 1954; her daughter Jackie was married to Phil Everly of The Everly Brothers. Ertel died of cancer on 11/22/1988 (age 75).

CHORDS, The
R&B vocal group from the Bronx, New York: brothers Carl Feaster and Claude Feaster, with Jimmy Keyes, Floyd McRae, William Edwards and Rupert Branker (piano). Claude Feaster died in November 1978 (age 45). Carl Feaster died on 1/23/1981 (age 50). Keyes died on 7/22/1995 (age 65).

CHRISTIAN, Chris
Born on 2/7/1951 in Abilene, Texas. Singer/ songwriter/producer. Member of Cotton, Lloyd and Christian. Began recording Christian music in 1977.

CHRISTIE
Pop-rock trio from England: Jeff Christie (vocals, bass), Vic Elmes (guitar) and Mike Blakely (drums). Blakely's brother, Alan, was a member of The Tremeloes.

CHRISTIE, Dean
Born in New York. Teen pop singer/songwriter.

CHRISTIE, Lou
Born Lugee Sacco on 2/19/1943 in Glenwillard, Pennsylvania. Joined vocal group the Classics; first recorded for Starr in 1960. Started long association with songwriter Twyla Herbert. Recorded as Lugee & The Lions for Robbee in 1961. Sang lead for Meco's The Cantina Band in 1981.

CHRISTIE, Susan
Born Beatrice Hill in Philadelphia, Pennsylvania. White teen pop singer.

CHRISTIÓN
R&B vocal duo from Oakland, California: Kenny Ski and Allen Anthony.

CHRISTOPHER, Gavin
Born in Chicago, Illinois. R&B singer/composer/producer. Brother of Shawn Christopher.

CHRISTOPHER, Shawn
Born in Chicago, Illinois. Sister of Gavin Christopher. Touring vocalist with Chaka Khan from 1982-85.

CHUBB ROCK
Born Richard Simpson on 5/28/1968 in Jamaica; raised in Brooklyn, New York. Male rapper.

CHUCKLEBUTT
Group of studio musicians from New Jersey led by producer Adam Marano.

CHUMBAWAMBA
Post-punk rock group from Leeds, England: Alice Nutter, Lou Watts, Danbert Nubacon, Paul Greco, Jude Abbott, Dunstan Bruce, Neil Ferguson and Harry Hamer.

CHUNKY A
Chunkston Arthur Hall is actually actor/comedian Arsenio Hall. Born on 2/12/57 in Cleveland, Ohio. Hosted own late night talk show (1989-1994) and starred in own sitcom (1997). Acted in the movies *Coming To America* and *Harlem Nights.* Hosted the 2002 revival of TV's *Star Search.*

CHURCH, The
Alternative pop-rock band from Canberra, Australia: Steve Kilbey (vocals, bass), Peter Koppes and Marty Willson-Piper (guitars), and Richard Ploog (drums).

CHURCH, Eric
Born on 5/3/1977 in Granite Falls, North Carolina. Country singer/songwriter.

CHURCH, Eugene
Born on 1/23/1938 in St. Louis, Missouri; raised in Los Angeles, California. Died of AIDS on 4/16/1993 (age 55). R&B singer/songwriter. Recorded with Jesse Belvin as The Cliques. Later worked in Texas as a hairdresser and sang gospel music.

CIARA
Born Ciara Harris on 10/25/1985 in Austin, Texas; raised in several different cities (father was with U.S. Army); eventually settled in Atlanta, Georgia. Female R&B singer/songwriter.

CINDERELLA
Hard-rock group from Philadelphia, Pennsylvania: Tom Keifer (vocals, guitar), Jeff LaBar (guitar), Eric Brittingham (bass) and Fred Coury (drums).

CIRCUS
Rock group from Cleveland, Ohio: Dan Hrdlicka (vocals, guitar), Mick Sabol (guitar), Phil Alexander (keyboards), Frank Salle (bass) and Tommy Dobeck (drums). Dobeck later joined the Michael Stanley Band.

CISYK, Kacey
Born Kvitka Cisyk on 4/4/1953 in Queens, New York. Died of cancer on 3/29/1998 (age 44). Female session singer.

CITIZEN KING
Rock group from Milwaukee, Wisconsin: Matt Sims (vocals, bass), Kristian Riley (guitar), Malcolm Michiles (DJ), Dave Cooley (keyboards) and DJ Brooks (drums).

CITY BOY
Pop-rock group from Birmingham, England: Lol Mason (vocals), Mike Slamer (guitar), Max Thomas (keyboards), Steve Broughton (percussion), Chris Dunn (bass) and Roy Ward (drums).

CITY HIGH
Black hip-hop trio from Willingboro, New Jersey: Claudette Ortiz, Robby Pardlo and Ryan Toby.

C.J. & CO.
Disco group from Detroit, Michigan: Cornelius Brown, Curtis Durden, Joni Tolbert, Connie Durden and Charles Clark.

CLANTON, Ike
Born in Baton Rouge, Louisiana. Brother of Jimmy Clanton. Touring bassist in 1959 with Duane Eddy's Rebels.

CLANTON, Jimmy
Born on 9/2/1940 in Baton Rouge, Louisiana. Rock and roll teen idol. Brother of Ike Clanton. Played in local bands, discovered by Ace Records while making a demo at Cosimo Matassa's studio in New Orleans. Recorded with famous New Orleans sessionmen, including Huey "Piano" Smith, Earl King (guitar) and Lee Allen (tenor sax). Toured with Dick Clark's Caravan Of Stars. Starred in the movie *Go, Johnny, Go!* in 1958. DJ in Lancaster, Pennsylvania, from 1972-76.

CLAPTON, Eric
Born Eric Patrick Clapp on 3/30/1945 in Ripley, England. Legendary rock-blues guitarist/vocalist. With The Roosters in 1963, The Yardbirds, 1963-65, and John Mayall's Bluesbreakers, 1965-66. Formed Cream with Jack Bruce and Ginger Baker in 1966. Formed Blind Faith in 1968; worked with John Lennon's Plastic Ono Band, and Delaney & Bonnie. Formed Derek and The Dominos in 1970. After two years of reclusion (1971-72), Clapton performed his comeback concert at London's Rainbow Theatre in January 1973. Began actively recording and touring again in 1974. Nicknamed "Slowhand" in 1964 while with The Yardbirds.

CLARK, Claudine
Born on 4/26/1941 in Macon, Georgia; raised in Philadelphia, Pennsylvania. Black singer/songwriter. First recorded for Herald in 1958. Also recorded for Swan as Joy Dawn.

CLARK, Dave, Five
Rock and roll band formed in Tottenham, England. By 1961 established lineup: Dave Clark (drums; born on 12/15/1939), Mike Smith (vocals, keyboards; born on 12/6/1943; died on 2/28/2008, age 64), Lenny Davidson (guitar; born on 5/30/1942), Denny Payton (sax; born on 8/11/1943; died on 12/17/2006, age 63) and Rick Huxley (bass; born on 8/5/1940). Clark had been a movie stuntman. First recorded for Ember and Piccadilly in 1962. In May 1964 made first of 18 appearances on *The Ed Sullivan Show*. In the movie *Having A Wild Weekend* (released abroad as *Catch Us If You Can*) in 1965. Announced breakup in August 1970; Clark and Smith recorded as Dave Clark & Friends until 1973. Clark co-wrote and produced the 1986 London stage musical *Time*.

CLARK, Dee
Born Delecta Clark on 11/7/1938 in Blytheville, Arkansas; raised in Chicago, Illinois. Died of a heart attack on 12/7/1990 (age 52). Male R&B singer. To Chicago in 1941. In Hambone Kids with Sammy McGrier and Ronny Strong; first recorded for Okeh in 1952. Joined R&B vocal group the Goldentones in 1953. Group became the Kool Gents; billed as The Delegates for Vee-Jay in 1956. First solo recording for Falcon in 1957.

CLARK, Petula
Born on 11/15/1932 in Epsom, Surrey, England. Adult Contemporary singer/actress. On radio at age nine; own show *Pet's Parlour* at age 11. TV series in England in 1950. First U.S. record release for Coral in 1953. Appeared in over 20 British movies from 1944-57; revived her movie career in the late 1960s, starring in *Finian's Rainbow* and *Goodbye Mr. Chips*.

CLARK, Roy
Born on 4/15/1933 in Meherrin, Virginia. Country singer/guitarist. Acted in the TV series *The Beverly Hillbillies*, appearing as both "Cousin Roy" and Roy's mother, "Big Mama Halsey." Clark and Buck Owens hosted TV's *Hee Haw* from 1969-86.

CLARK, Sanford
Born on 10/24/1935 in Tulsa, Oklahoma. Male singer/songwriter/guitarist.

CLARK, Terri
Born Terri Sauson (Clark is her stepfather's last name) on 8/5/1968 in Montreal, Quebec, Canada; raised in Medicine Hat, Alberta, Canada. Country singer/guitarist.

CLARKE, Allan
Born on 4/5/1942 in Salford, England. Lead singer of The Hollies.

CLARKE, Rozlyne
Born in Brooklyn, New York. Female dance singer.

CLARKE, Stanley
Born on 6/30/1951 in Philadelphia, Pennsylvania. R&B-jazz bassist/violinist/cellist. With Chick Corea in Return To Forever in 1973. Much session work, solo debut in 1974. Member of Fuse One in 1982 and Animal Logic in 1989.

CLARKE, Tony
Born on 4/13/1940 in Harlem, New York; raised in Detroit, Michigan. Murdered on 8/28/1971 (age 31). R&B singer/songwriter.

CLARK FAMILY EXPERIENCE, The
Bluegrass group from Rocky Mount, Virginia: brothers Alan (guitar), Ashley (fiddle), Austin (dobro), Adam (mandolin), Aaron (bass) and Andrew (drums) Clark.

CLARKSON, Kelly
Born on 4/24/1982 in Burleson, Texas. Female pop singer. Winner on the 2002 inaugural season of TV's *American Idol*.

CLASH, The
Punk-rock band from London, England: John "Joe Strummer" Mellor (vocals), Mick Jones (guitar), Paul Simonon (bass) and Nicky "Topper" Headon (drums). Political activists who wrote songs protesting racism and oppression. Headon left in May 1983; replaced by Peter Howard. Jones (not to

CLASH, The — cont'd
be confused with Mick Jones of Foreigner) left band in 1984 to form Big Audio Dynamite. Strummer disbanded The Clash in early 1986, and appeared in the 1987 movie *Straight To Hell*. Strummer died of heart failure on 12/22/2002 (age 50).

CLASSIC EXAMPLE
Male R&B vocal group from Boston, Massachusetts: Darin Campbell, Jami Thompson, Gerald Alston, Marvin Harris and Bunny Rose. Alston is no relation to the same-named lead singer of The Manhattans.

CLASSICS, The
Italian-American doo-wop group from Brooklyn, New York: Emil Stucchio (lead), Johnny Gambale, Tony Victor and Jamie Troy. First known as the Perennials. First recorded for Dart in 1959.

CLASSICS IV
Soft-rock group from Jacksonville, Florida: Dennis Yost (vocals), J.R. Cobb and Wally Eaton (guitars), Joe Wilson (bass) and Kim Venable (drums). Wilson was replaced by Dean Daughtry (of The Candymen). Cobb, Daughtry and producer Buddy Buie later joined the Atlanta Rhythm Section.

CLAY, Judy
Born Judy Guions on 9/12/1938 in St. Paul, North Carolina; raised in Fayetteville, North Carolina. Died of kidney failure on 7/19/2001 (age 62). Black singer. In backup group with Cissy Houston, Dionne Warwick and Dee Dee Warwick, for Don Covay, Wilson Pickett and many others.

CLAY, Otis
Born on 2/11/1942 in Waxhaw, Mississippi. R&B singer.

CLAY, Tom
Born Thomas Clague on 8/20/1929 in Binghamton, New York. Died of cancer on 11/22/1995 (age 66). Was a DJ at KGBS in Los Angeles when he created this recording.

CLAYTON, Adam, & Larry Mullen
Adam Clayton was born on 3/13/1960 (bass). Larry Mullen Jr. was born on 10/31/1961 in Dublin, Ireland (drums). Both are members of U2.

CLAYTON, Merry
Born Mary Clayton on 12/25/1948 in New Orleans, Louisiana. Session singer. In The Raeletts, Ray Charles' backing vocal group from 1967-69. Acted in the 1987 movie *Maid To Order*.

CLEAN LIVING
Country-rock group: Norman Schell (vocals, guitar), Al Anderson, Robert LaMountain and Robert LaPalm (guitars), Frank Shaw (bass) and Tim Griffin (drums). Anderson was also with The Wildweeds and NRBQ.

CLEFS OF LAVENDER HILL
Rock and roll band formed in Miami, Florida: Travis and Coventry Fairchild (born Joseph Ximenes and his sister Lorraine; singers/guitarists) and brothers Bill (bassist) and Fred (drums) Moss.

CLEFTONES, The
Black doo-wop group from Queens, New York: Herbie Cox (lead), Charlie James (first tenor), Berman Patterson (second tenor), William McClain (baritone) and Warren Corbin (bass). Originally called the Silvertones.

CLEMONS, Clarence
Born on 1/11/1942 in Norfolk, Virginia. Black saxophonist in Bruce Springsteen's E Street Band. Nicknamed "The Big Man."

CLEOPATRA
Black teen vocal trio from Manchester, England: sisters Cleopatra, Zainam and Yonah Higgins.

CLICK, The
Rap group from San Francisco, California: E-40, his brother D-Shot, sister Suga T, and cousin B-Legit.

CLICK FIVE, The
Punk-rock band from Boston, Massachusetts: Eric Dill (vocal, guitar), Joe Guese (guitar), Ben Romans (keyboards), Ethan Mentzer (bass) and Joey Zehr (drums).

CLIFF, Jimmy
Born James Chambers on 4/1/1948 in St. James, Jamaica. Reggae singer/songwriter. Starred in the movies *The Harder They Come* and *Club Paradise*.

CLIFFORD, Buzz
Born Reese Francis Clifford III on 10/8/1942 in Berwyn, Illinois. Teen pop-novelty singer.

CLIFFORD, Linda
Born in 1944 in Brooklyn, New York. R&B-dance singer.

CLIFFORD, Mike
Born on 11/6/1943 in Los Angeles, California. White pop singer/actor. In the 1970s Broadway production of *Grease*.

CLIMAX
White pop group from Los Angeles, California: Sonny Geraci (vocals, The Outsiders), Walter Nims (guitar), Virgil Weber (keyboards), Steve York (bass) and Robert Neilson (drums).

CLIMAX BLUES BAND
Blues-rock band from Stafford, England: Colin Cooper (vocals, sax), Peter Haycock (guitar, vocals), Derek Holt (bass) and John Cuffley (drums). Cooper died of cancer on 7/3/2008 (age 68).

CLIMIE FISHER
Pop-rock duo. Simon Climie (vocals) was born on 4/7/1960 in Fulham, London, England. Rob Fisher (keyboards) was born on 11/5/1959 in Cheltenham, Gloucestershire, England; died of complications following stomach surgery on 8/25/1999 (age 39). Fisher was a member of Naked Eyes.

CLINE, Patsy
Born Virginia Patterson Hensley on 9/8/1932 in Gore, Virginia. Killed in a plane crash (age 30) with Cowboy Copas and Hawkshaw Hawkins on 3/5/1963 near Camden, Tennessee. Jessica Lange portrayed Cline in the 1985 biographical movie *Sweet Dreams*.

CLINTON, George
Born on 7/22/1941 in Kannapolis, North Carolina. Highly prolific and influential funk music singer/ songwriter/producer. Formed the seminal Parliament/Funkadelic aggregation.

CLIPSE
Male rap duo from Virginia Beach, Virginia: brothers Gene "Malice" and Terrence "Pusha T" Thornton.

CLIQUE, The
Pop-rock group from Beaumont, Texas: Randy Shaw (vocals), David Dunham, Sid Templeton, Tommy Pena, John Kanesaw and Jerry Cope.

CLIQUES, The
R&B vocal duo: Jesse Belvin and Eugene Church.

CLOCKS
Rock group from Wichita, Kansas: Jerry Sumner (vocals, bass), Lance Threet (guitar), Gerald Graves (keyboards) and Steve Swaim (drums). Swaim died of liver failure on 3/18/2006 (age 51).

CLOONEY, Rosemary
Born on 5/23/1928 in Maysville, Kentucky. Died of cancer on 6/29/2002 (age 74). Sang with her sister Betty in Tony Pastor's orchestra in the late 1940s. Became one of the most popular singers of the early 1950s. Acted in several movies including *White Christmas*. Re-emerged in the late 1970s as a successful jazz and ballad singer and as a TV commercial actress. Married for a time to actor Jose Ferrer; their son Gabriel married Debby Boone, and their other son, actor Miguel, starred in the TV series *Lateline*. Her brother, Nick Clooney, is a popular TV broadcaster, and his son, George Clooney, is a popular TV and movie actor.

CLOUT
Rock group from Johannesburg, South Africa: Cindi Alter (vocals), Sandie Robbie and Inge Herbst (guitars), Jennie Garson (keyboards), Lee Tomlinson (bass) and Bones Brettell (drums).

CLOVERS, The
R&B vocal group from Washington DC: John "Buddy" Bailey (lead), Matthew McQuater, Harold Lucas, Harold Winely and Bill Harris. Bailey entered the U.S. Army in 1952; replaced by Billy Mitchell. Upon Bailey's return, Mitchell stayed in the group. Harris died of pancreatic cancer on 12/10/1988 (age 63). A Clovers unit with Lucas performed until 1992. Lucas died of cancer on 1/6/1994 (age 61). Mitchell died of a stroke on 11/5/2002 (age 71).

CLUB HOUSE
Italian dance-disco studio group.

CLUBLAND
Dance collaboration assembled by Swedish producer Jan Ekholm and British drummer Morgan King. Features female vocalist Zemya (pronounced: zem-i-ah) Hamilton (of Jamaican and Swedish parentage).

CLUB NOUVEAU
Dance group from Sacramento, California. Formed and fronted by Jay King producer/owner of King Jay Records; founded the Timex Social Club). Early lineup: vocalists Valerie Watson and Samuelle

Prater with Denzil Foster and Thomas McElroy. Prater, Foster and McElroy left in 1988; replaced by David Agent and Kevin Irving. Agent left in 1989. Foster and McElroy formed a prolific production duo and also recorded as FMob.

CLUB 69
Dance group assembled by Austrian producer Peter Rauhofer. Lead vocals by Suzanne Palmer and Kim Cooper.

COASTERS, The
R&B vocal group formed in Los Angeles, California, in late 1955 from elements of The Robins. Originally consisted of Carl Gardner (lead; ex-Robins; born on 4/29/1928), Billy Guy (baritone lead; born on 6/20/1936), Leon Hughes (tenor), Bobby Nunn (bass; ex-Robins; born on 9/20/1925) and Adolph Jacobs (guitar). Noted for serio-comic recordings, primarily of Leiber & Stoller songs. Cornelius Gunter (early member of The Flairs; brother of Shirley Gunter; born on 11/14/1938) joined in 1957; left in 1961. Will "Dub" Jones (ex-Cadets) replaced Nunn in late 1958 and is heard on "Charlie Brown" and "Along Came Jones." Earl "Speedoo" Carroll (ex-Cadillacs) joined group in 1961. Bobby Nunn died of a heart attack on 11/5/1986 (age 61). Gunter was shot to death on 2/26/1990 (age 51). Jones died on 1/16/2000 (age 71). Guy died of a heart attack on 11/5/2002 (age 66).

COATES, Odia
Born on 11/13/1941 in Vicksburg, Mississippi; raised in Los Angeles, California. Died of cancer on 5/19/1991 (age 49). Black female singer. Member of the Edwin Hawkins Singers. Sang with Paul Anka on four of his hits (1974-75).

COBB, Joyce
Born in Okmulgee, Oklahoma. R&B singer/ songwriter.

COCCIANTE, Richard
Born in 1946 in Saigon, Vietnam (Italian father/ French mother); raised in Rome, Italy. Adult Contemporary singer/songwriter.

COCHISE
Rock group from England: John Gilbert (vocals), Mick Grabham and B.J. Cole (guitars), Rick Wills (bass) and Willie Wilson (drums). Wills also a member of Foreigner, Roxy Music and Small Faces. Wilson also a member of Sutherland Brothers & Quiver.

COCHRAN, Anita
Born on 2/6/1967 in Pontiac, Michigan. Country singer/songwriter/guitarist.

COCHRAN, Eddie
Born Edward Ray Cochrane on 10/3/1938 in Albert Lea, Minnesota. Killed in a car crash on 4/17/1960 (age 21) in Chippenham, Wiltshire, England; accident also injured Gene Vincent. Influential rock and roll singer/guitarist. Moved to Bell Gardens, California, in 1953. Teamed with Hank Cochran (no relation) as the Cochran Brothers; first recorded as country act for Ekko Records in 1954. Appeared in movies *The Girl Can't Help It*, *Untamed Youth* and *Go, Johnny, Go!*

COCHRAN, Tammy
Born on 1/30/1972 in Austinburg, Ohio. Country singer/songwriter.

COCHRANE, Tom
Born on 5/13/1953 in Lynn Lake, Manitoba, Canada. Rock singer/songwriter. Formed Red Rider in 1976.

COCKBURN, Bruce
Born on 5/27/1945 in Ottawa, Ontario, Canada. Pop-rock singer/songwriter. Pronounced: CO-burn.

COCKER, Joe
Born John Robert Cocker on 5/20/1944 in Sheffield, Yorkshire, England. Own skiffle band, the Cavaliers, late 1950s, later reorganized as Vance Arnold & The Avengers. Assembled the Grease Band in the mid-1960s. Performed at Woodstock in 1969. Successful tour with 43-piece revue, Mad Dogs & Englishmen, in 1970. Notable spastic stage antics were based on Ray Charles's movements at the piano.

COCK ROBIN
Pop group from Los Angeles, California: Peter Kingsbery (vocals, bass), Anna LaCazio (vocals, keyboards), Clive Wright (guitars) and Louis Molino (drums).

C.O.D.'s, The
R&B vocal trio from Chicago, Illinois: Larry Brownlee, Robert Lewis and Carl Washington. Brownlee (died in 1978) wrote all of the group's songs; later became a member of The Lost Generation and Mystique. Ruby Andrews was a backing vocalist.

COE, David Allan
Born on 9/6/1939 in Akron, Ohio. Country singer/songwriter/guitarist/actor. Billed as "The Mysterious Rhinestone Cowboy" until 1978. Acted in such movies as *Take This Job And Shove It*, *The Last Days Of Frank And Jesse James* and *Stagecoach*.

COFFEY, Dennis
Born in 1940 in Detroit, Michigan. White session guitarist for Motown.

COFFEY, Kellie
Born on 4/22/1971 in Moore, Oklahoma. Country singer/songwriter.

COHN, Marc
Born on 7/5/1959 in Cleveland, Ohio. Pop-rock singer/songwriter/pianist. Married ABC-TV news anchor Elizabeth Vargas on 7/20/2002. Shot in the head during an attempted car jacking on 8/7/2005 (fully recovered).

COKO
Born Cheryl Gamble on 6/13/1974 in the Bronx, New York. R&B singer. Member of SWV.

COLD
Hard-rock group from Jacksonville, Florida: Ronald "Scooter" Ward (vocals, guitar), Stephen "Kelly" Hayes (guitar), Terry Balsamo (guitar), Jeremy Marshall (bass) and Sam McCandless (drums).

COLD BLOOD
Rock group from San Francisco, California. Core members: Lydia Pense (vocals), Michael Sasaki (guitar), Raul Matute (piano), Rod Ellicott (bass), Max Haskett (trumpet) and Danny Hull (sax). Haskett later joined Rubicon.

COLDPLAY
Alternative-rock band formed in London, England: Chris Martin (vocals), Jon Buckland (guitar), Guy Berryman (bass) and Will Champion (drums). Martin married actress Gwyneth Paltrow on 12/5/2003.

COLE, Ann
Born Cynthia Coleman on 1/24/1934 in Newark, New Jersey.

COLE, Bobby
Born in New York. Died from a fall on 12/19/1997. Singer/songwriter/pianist.

COLE, Cozy
Born William Cole on 10/17/1909 in East Orange, New Jersey. Died of cancer on 1/31/1981 (age 71). Lead drummer for many swing bands, including Benny Carter, Willie Bryant, Cab Calloway and Louis Armstrong.

COLE, Gardner
Born on 2/7/1962 in Flint, Michigan. White songwriter/singer/producer. Wrote Madonna's "Open Your Heart," Jody Watley's "Most Of All" and "Strange But True" for Times Two.

COLE, Jude
Born on 6/18/1960 in Carbon Cliff, Illinois; raised in East Moline, Illinois. Male singer/guitarist. Member of the rock band The Records from 1979-81.

COLE, Keyshia
Born on 10/15/1983 in Oakland, California. Female R&B singer/songwriter. Starred in own BET reality series *The Way It Is*.

COLE, Nat "King"
Born Nathaniel Adams Coles on 3/17/1919 in Montgomery, Alabama; raised in Chicago, Illinois. Died of lung cancer on 2/15/1965 (age 45). Own band, the Royal Dukes, at age 17. First recorded in 1936 in band led by brother Eddie. Toured with "Shuffle Along" musical revue; lived in Los Angeles. Formed The King Cole Trio in 1939: Nat (piano), Oscar Moore (guitar; later joined brother's group, Johnny Moore's Three Blazers) and Wesley Prince (bass; replaced several years later by Johnny Miller). Began solo career in 1950. In movies *St. Louis Blues*, *Cat Ballou*, and many other movie appearances. The first major African-American performer to star in a network (NBC) TV variety series (1956-57). His daughter Natalie Cole is a recording star.

COLE, Natalie
Born Stephanie Natalie Cole on 2/6/1950 in Los Angeles, California. Daughter of Nat "King" Cole. Professional debut at age 11. Married for a time to her producer, Marvin Yancy, Jr. Later married Andre Fischer, former drummer of Rufus and producer for Brenda Russell, Michael Franks and Andrae Crouch, until 1992. Hosted own syndicated variety TV show *Big Break* in 1990.

COLE, Paula
Born on 4/5/1968 in Rockport, Massachusetts. Adult Alternative singer/songwriter.

COLE, Samantha
Born on 10/31/1975 in Long Island, New York. Pop singer/songwriter. Former dancer on MTV's *The Grind.*

COLE, Tony
Adult Contemporary singer/guitarist/songwriter from England.

COLLAGE
Dance project assembled by Adam Marano, who spearheaded T.P.E. in 1991. Featured singer was Tony Monte. Both were students at Philadelphia's Temple University in 1993.

COLLAY & the Satellites
Collay is rock and roll singer/songwriter Anthony Callais (from New Orleans, Louisiana).

COLLECTIVE SOUL
Rock group from Stockbridge, Georgia: brothers Ed (vocals) and Dean (guitar) Roland with Ross Childress (guitar), Will Turpin (bass) and Shane Evans (drums).

COLLEGE BOYZ, The
Male rap group from Los Angeles, California: Rom, Squeak, The Q and DJ B-Selector.

COLLEY, Keith
Born in Connell, Washington. Pop singer. Later a record executive with the Challenge label.

COLLIER, Mitty
Born on 6/21/1941 in Birmingham, Alabama. R&B singer.

COLLINS, William "Bootsy"
Born on 10/26/1951 in Cincinnati, Ohio. R&B singer/bass player. Member of James Brown's group from 1969-71. Joined Parliament/Funkadelic aggregation in 1972. Later led Bootsy's Rubber Band.

COLLINS, Dave & Ansil
Reggae duo from Jamaica: Dave Barker (vocals) and Ansil Collins (keyboards).

COLLINS, Dorothy
Born Marjorie Chandler on 11/18/1926 in Windsor, Ontario, Canada. Died of a heart attack on 7/21/1994 (age 67). Star of TV's *Your Hit Parade.* Married to orchestra leader Raymond Scott from 1952-65.

COLLINS, Edwyn
Born on 8/23/1959 in Edinburgh, Scotland. Pop-rock singer/songwriter.

COLLINS, Judy
Born on 5/1/1939 in Seattle, Washington. Contemporary folk singer/songwriter. Began studying classical piano at age five. Moved to Los Angeles, then to Denver at age nine, where her father, Chuck Collins, was a radio personality. Classical debut at 13, playing with the Denver Businessmen's Symphony Orchestra. Discovered folk music at 15. Signed to Elektra in 1961.

Appeared in the New York Shakespeare Festival's production of *Peer Gynt.* Nominated for a 1974 Academy Award for co-directing *Antonia: A Portrait of the Woman,* a documentary about Judy's former classical mentor and a pioneer female orchestra conductor, Dr. Antonia Brico.

COLLINS, Lyn
Born on 6/12/1948 in Lexington, Texas. Died of a heart seizure on 3/13/2005 (age 56). With Charles Pikes & The Scholars in the mid-1960s. Joined the James Brown Revue in 1969. Billed as "The Female Preacher" and later as "The Sultry Siren of Funk."

COLLINS, Phil
Born on 1/30/1951 in Chiswick, London, England. Pop singer/multi-instrumentalist/composer. Stage actor as a young child; played the "Artful Dodger" in the London production of *Oliver.* With group Flaming Youth in 1969. Joined Genesis as its drummer in 1970; became lead singer in 1975. Also with jazz-rock group Brand X. First solo album in 1981. Starred in the 1988 movie *Buster* and appeared in *Hook* and *Frauds.* Left Genesis in April 1996.

COLLINS, Tyler
Born in Harlem, New York; raised in Detroit, Michigan. Female R&B singer.

COLOR ME BADD
Vocal group from Oklahoma City, Oklahoma: Bryan Abrams (born on 11/16/1969), Sam Watters (born on 7/23/1970), Mark Calderon (born on 9/27/1970) and Kevin Thornton (born on 6/17/1969). Formed while in high school in Oklahoma City.

COLOURHAUS
Pop duo of Australian vocalist Sherrié Krenn and British producer/guitarist Phil Radford (writer of "The Flame" by Cheap Trick). Krenn later became known as country singer Sherrié Austin.

COLTER, Jessi
Born Mirriam Johnson on 5/25/1943 in Phoenix, Arizona. Country singer/songwriter. Married to Duane Eddy from 1961-68. Married Waylon Jennings in October 1969.

COLTRANE, Chi
Born on 11/16/1948 in Racine, Wisconsin. Female rock singer/pianist. Pronounced: shy.

COLTRANE, John
Born on 9/23/1926 in Hamlet, North Carolina. Died of liver cancer on 7/17/1967 (age 40). Legendary jazz tenor saxophonist. With Dizzy Gillespie in the early 1950s, Miles Davis in 1955, Thelonious Monk in 1957, then solo. Married to Alice Coltrane from 1964-67 (his death).

COLUMBO, Chris, Quintet
Born on 6/17/1902 in Greenville, North Carolina; raised in Atlantic City, New Jersey. Died on 7/5/2002 (age 100). Jazz drummer; recorded with Duke Ellington and Louis Jordan.

COLVIN, Shawn
Born Shanna Colvin on 1/10/1956 in Vermillion, South Dakota. Female folk singer.

COMMANDER CODY & His Lost Planet Airmen
Born George Frayne on 7/19/1944 in Boise, Idaho; raised in Brooklyn, New York. Singer/keyboardist. His Lost Planet Airmen consisted of John Tichy, Don Bolton and Bill Kirchen (guitars), Andy Stein (fiddle, sax), Bruce Barlow (bass) and Lance Dickerson (drums). Dickerson died on 11/10/2003 (age 55).

COMMITMENTS, The
Group of Irish actors/musicians who starred in the movie of the same name: Robert Arkin, Michael Aherne, Angeline Ball, Maria Doyle, Dave Finnegan, Bronagh Gallagher, Felim Gormley, Glen Hansard, Dick Massey, Kenneth McCluskey, Johnny Murphy and Andrew Strong. All did their own performing.

COMMODORES
R&B group formed in Tuskegee, Alabama: Lionel Richie (lead singer; saxophone; born on 6/20/1949), William King (trumpet; born on 1/29/1949), Thomas McClary (guitar; born on 10/6/1950), Milan Williams (keyboards; born on 3/28/1948; died of cancer on 7/9/2006, age 58), Ronald LaPread (bass; born on 9/4/1950) and Walter "Clyde" Orange (drums; born on 12/9/1946). First recorded for Motown in 1972. In the movie *Thank God It's Friday*. Richie left the group in 1982.

COMMON
Born Lonnie Lynn on 3/13/1972 in Chicago, Illinois. Male rapper/songwriter. Originally performed as Common Sense.

COMMUNARDS
British rock duo consisting of Bronski Beat vocalist Jimmy Somerville and multi-instrumentalist Richard Coles.

COMO, Perry
Born Pierino Como on 5/18/1912 in Canonsburg, Pennsylvania. Died on 5/12/2001 (age 88). Owned barbershop in hometown. With Freddy Carlone band in 1933; with Ted Weems from 1936-42. In the movies *Something For The Boys*, *Doll Face*, *If I'm Lucky* and *Words And Music*, 1944-48. Own *Supper Club* radio series to late 1940s. Own TV shows (15 minutes) from 1948-55. Host of hourly TV shows from 1955-63. Winner of five Emmys. One of the most popular singers of the 20th century.

COMPANY B
Female dance trio from Miami, Florida: Lori Ledesma, Lezlee Livrano and Susan Johnson.

COMSTOCK, Bobby, & The Counts
Born on 12/29/1941 in Ithaca, New York. Rock and roll singer/songwriter/guitarist.

CONCRETE BLONDE
Rock trio from Los Angeles, California: Johnette Napolitano (vocals, bass), James Andrew Mankey (guitar) and Paul Thompson (drums).

CONDUCTOR
Rock group from Los Angeles, California. Led by singer Judy Comden.

CON FUNK SHUN
Funk group from Vallejo, California: Michael Cooper (vocals, guitar; born on 11/15/1952), Danny Thomas (keyboards), Karl Fuller, Paul Harrell and Felton Pilate (horns), Cedric Martin (bass) and Louis McCall (drums).

CONLEE, John
Born on 8/11/1946 in Versailles, Kentucky. Country singer/songwriter/guitarist. Worked as a mortician for six years, then a newsreader in Fort Knox. Moved to WLAC-Nashville in 1971; worked as a DJ and music director.

CONLEY, Arthur
Born on 1/4/1946 in Atlanta, Georgia. Died of cancer on 11/17/2003 (age 57). Soul singer/songwriter. Discovered by Otis Redding in 1965 (recorded for Redding's Jotis label). First recorded for NRC as Arthur & The Corvets. Also see The Soul Clan.

CONLEY, Earl Thomas
Born on 10/17/1941 in West Portsmouth, Ohio. Country singer/songwriter/guitarist. Served in the U.S. Army from 1960-62. Worked in a steel mill in Huntsville, Alabama, in the early 1970s. Also recorded as The ETC Band.

CONNICK, Harry Jr.
Born on 9/11/1967 in New Orleans, Louisiana. Jazz-pop pianist/singer/actor. Studied jazz under Ellis Marsalis, the father of Wynton and Branford Marsalis. Acted in the movies *Memphis Belle*, *Little Man Tate*, *Independence Day* and *Hope Floats*. Married model/actress Jill Goodacre in 1994. Has had 9 albums certified platinum since 1990.

CONNIFF, Ray
Born on 11/6/1916 in Attleboro, Massachusetts. Died of a stroke on 10/12/2002 (age 85). Trombonist/arranger with Bunny Berigan, Bob Crosby, Harry James, Vaughn Monroe and Artie Shaw bands. Arranger/conductor for many of Columbia Records' top vocalists during the 1950s and 1960s (Guy Mitchell, Johnny Mathis, Marty Robbins, etc.).

CONNOR, Chris
Born on 11/8/1927 in Kansas City, Missouri. Female jazz-styled singer; with Stan Kenton from 1952-53.

CONNOR, Sarah
Born on 6/13/1980 in Delmenhorst, Germany. White R&B singer.

CONNORS, Norman
Born on 3/1/1948 in Philadelphia, Pennsylvania. Jazz drummer with Archie Shepp, John Coltrane, Pharoah Sanders and others. Own group on Buddah in 1972.

CONSCIOUS DAUGHTERS, The
Female hardcore rap duo from Oakland, California: Carla Green and Karryl Smith.

CONSUMER RAPPORT
Dance group from New York, featuring Frank Floyd (pit singer in the musical *The Wiz*).

CONTI, Bill
Born on 4/13/1942 in Providence, Rhode Island. Composer/conductor for the first three *Rocky* movies; also for *The Karate Kid*, *Private Benjamin*, *For Your Eyes Only*, and an Oscar-winning score for *The Right Stuff*.

CONTINENTAL 4, The
R&B vocal group from Pittsburgh, Pennsylvania: Freddie Kelly (falsetto lead), Ronnie McGregor and Larry McGregor (tenors), and Anthony Burke (baritone).

CONTINENTAL MINIATURES
Pop group from Los Angeles, California: Kevin McCarthy (vocals), Rich Bytnar and Eric Ramon (guitars), Matt Walker (bass), David Kendrick (drums).

CONTINO, Dick
Born on 1/17/1930 in Fresno, California. Accordion virtuoso. Discovered by bandleader Horace Heidt and featured on his radio show in the late 1940s.

CONTOURS, The
R&B vocal group from Detroit, Michigan: Billy Gordon, Billy Hoggs, Joe Billingslea, Sylvester Potts, Huey Davis (guitar; died on 2/23/2002, age 63) and Hubert Johnson (died on 7/11/1981). Dennis Edwards, a member in 1967, joined The Temptations in 1968. Gordon was married to Georgeanna Tillman of The Marvelettes. Johnson was the cousin of Jackie Wilson.

CONTROLLERS, The
R&B vocal group from Fairfield, Alabama: brothers Reginald and Larry McArthur, with Lenard Brown and Ricky Lewis. Formed in 1965 as the Epics. Became the Soul Controllers in 1970.

CONWELL, Tommy, & The Young Rumblers
Born in Philadelphia, Pennsylvania. Rock singer/guitarist. The Young Rumblers: Chris Day (guitar), Rob Miller (keyboards; Hooters), Paul Slivka (bass) and Jim Hannum (drums).

COO COO CAL
Born Calvin Bellamy on 4/30/1970 in Milwaukee, Wisconsin. Male rapper.

COOK, David
Born on 12/20/1982 in Houston, Texas; raised in Blue Springs, Missouri. Male singer. Winner on the 2008 season of TV's *American Idol*.

COOKE, Sam
Born Samuel Cook (the "e" was added later) on 1/22/1931 in Clarksdale, Mississippi; raised in Chicago, Illinois. Died from a gunshot wound on 12/11/1964 (age 33); shot by a female motel manager under mysterious circumstances. Son of a Baptist minister. Sang in choir from age six. Joined gospel group the Highway Q.C.'s. Lead singer of the Soul Stirrers from 1950-56. First recorded secular songs in 1956 as "Dale Cook" on Specialty. String of hits on Keen label led to contract with RCA. Nephew is singer R.B. Greaves. Revered as the definitive soul singer.

COOKER
Born Norman DesRosiers in Chicago, Illinois. Pop singer/songwriter.

COOKIE & HIS CUPCAKES
Swamp-rock band from Louisiana: Huey "Cookie" Thierry (vocals, sax), Shelton Dunaway (sax), Sidney Reynaud (sax), Marshall LeDee (guitar), Ernest Jacobs (piano), Joe Landry (bass) and Ivory Jackson (drums). Cookie died on 9/23/1997 (age 61).

COOKIES, The
Female R&B vocal trio from Brooklyn, New York. Much backup work for Atlantic in mid-1950s, then for Neil Sedaka and Carole King in early 1960s. Sang background vocals on Little Eva's "The Loco-Motion." Formed in 1954 with Dorothy Jones, her cousin Beulah Roberston and Ethel "Darlene" McCrea. Margie Hendrix replaced Beulah in 1956. Margie and Darlene joined the The Raeletts in 1958. Darlene's sister Earl-Jean McCrea and Margaret Ross joined Dorothy in 1960. Margie died of a drug overdose on 7/14/1973 (age 38). Beulah died of cancer in 1987.

COOL BREEZE
Born Freddy Calhoun in Atlanta, Georgia. Male rapper.

COOLEY, Eddie
Born in Harlem, New York. R&B singer/songwriter. Wrote "Fever" (hit for Little Willie John, Peggy Lee, Rita Coolidge and The McCoys). His Dimples were a black female trio.

COOL HEAT
Group of New York studio musicians led by Bo Gentry and Kenny Laguna.

COOLIDGE, Rita
Born on 5/1/1944 in Nashville, Tennessee. Had own group, R.C. and the Moonpies, at Florida State University. Moved to Los Angeles in the late 1960s. Did backup work for Delaney & Bonnie, Leon Russell, Joe Cocker and Eric Clapton. With Kris Kristofferson from 1971, married to him from 1973-80. Known as "The Delta Lady," for whom Leon Russell wrote the song of the same name. In the 1983 movie *Club Med*.

COOLIO
Born Artis Ivey on 8/1/1963 in Los Angeles, California. Male rapper. Former member of WC And The MAAD Circle.

COOPER, Alice
Born Vincent Furnier on 2/4/1948 in Detroit, Michigan; raised in Phoenix, Arizona. Formed several groups (The Earwigs/The Spiders/The Nazz – not the Todd Rundgren band) before settling on Alice Cooper in 1968: Furnier (vocals), Glen Buxton (guitar), Michael Bruce (keyboards), Dennis Dunaway (bass) and Neal Smith (drums). Furnier went on to assume the Alice Cooper (a 17th-century witch) name for himself. Band split in 1974. Cooper went solo and became known for his bizarre stage antics. Appeared in the movies *Prince Of Darkness* and *Wayne's World*, among others. Buxton died on 10/19/1997 (age 49).

COOPER, Les
Born on 3/15/1931 in Norfolk, Virginia. Pianist/
arranger. Member of the doo-wop groups The
Empires and The Whirlers.

COOPER, Michael
Born on 11/15/1952 in Vallejo, California. R&B
singer/guitarist/songwriter/producer. Leader of Con
Funk Shun from 1972-87.

COOPER BROTHERS
Pop-rock group from Ottawa, Ontario, Canada:
brothers Richard (guitar) and Brian (bass) Cooper,
Terry King and Darryl Alguire (guitars), Charles
Robinson III (flute), Al Serwa (keyboards), and
Glenn Bell (drums). All but Serwa share vocals.

COPAS, Cowboy
Born Lloyd Estel Copas on 7/15/1913 in Blue Creek,
Ohio. Died in a plane crash on 3/5/1963 (age 49)
near Camden, Tennessee (with Patsy Cline and
Hawkshaw Hawkins). Country singer/fiddler/
guitarist.

COPE, Julian
Born on 10/21/1957 in Deri, South Wales; raised in
Tamworth, England. Former lead singer/songwriter/
bassist of the British group the Teardrop Explodes.

COPELAND, Ken
Born on 5/25/1937 in Gainesville, Texas. Later
became a televangelist with own Kenneth Copeland
Ministries.

COPPOLA, Imani
Born on 4/28/1976 in Long Island, New York.
Female singer/rapper.

COREA, Chick
Born Anthony Corea on 6/12/1941 in Chelsea,
Massachusetts. Jazz-rock pianist. Worked with Stan
Getz, Blue Mitchell, Sarah Vaughan and Gary
Burton before joining the Miles Davis band in 1968.

COREY
Born Corey Hodges on 11/13/1988 in Atlanta,
Georgia. Teen R&B singer.

COREY, Jill
Born Norma Jean Speranza on 9/30/1935 in
Avonmore, Pennsylvania. Married major league
baseball player Don Hoak. Regular on TV's *Your Hit
Parade* from 1957-58.

CORINA
Born Corina Ayala on 10/14/1963 in Manhattan,
New York. Female dance singer.

CORLEY, Al
Born on 5/22/1956 in Waynesville, Missouri.
Pop-rock singer/songwriter/actor. Played the
original "Steven Carrington" on TV's *Dynasty*.
Worked as a doorman at Studio 54 in the late
1970s.

CORLEY, Bob
Born on 5/29/1924 in Macon, Georgia. Died on
11/18/1971 (age 47). "Redneck" stand-up
comedian/songwriter/actor.

CORNBREAD & BISCUITS
Black comedy duo.

CORNELIUS BROTHERS & SISTER ROSE
R&B family trio from Dania, Florida: Edward, Carter
and Rose Cornelius. Carter died of a heart attack on
11/7/1991 (age 43).

CORNELL, Chris
Born on 7/20/1964 in Seattle, Washington.
Hard-rock singer/songwriter/guitarist. Lead singer of
Soundgarden and Audioslave.

CORNELL, Don
Born Luigi Varlaro on 4/21/1919 in Brooklyn, New
York. Died of emphysema on 2/23/2004 (age 84).
Popular singer/guitarist. From the late 1930s,
worked with Al Kavelin and Red Nichols. Achieved
great success with Sammy Kaye.

CORO
Born Jose Coro in New York; raised in Miami,
Florida. Black singer/actor. Appeared in Don
Johnson's "Heartbeat" video and TV's *Miami Vice*.

CORONA
Dance duo: Italian producer Francesco Bontempi
and Brazilian singer Olga DeSouza.

CORRS, The
Sibling pop group from Ireland: Andrea (lead
vocals), Jim (guitar), Sharon (violin) and Caroline
(drums) Corr.

CORSAIRS Featuring Jay "Bird" Uzzell
R&B vocal group from La Grange, North Carolina:
brothers Jay "Bird" (lead), James and "King" Moe
Uzzell, with cousin George Wooten.

CORTEZ, Dave "Baby"
Born David Cortez Clowney on 8/13/1938 in Detroit,
Michigan. R&B keyboardist/composer. Played organ
and sang with the vocal group The Pearls from
1955-57, and also with the Valentines, which
included Richard Barrett and Ronnie Bright (of "Mr.
Bass Man" fame), from 1956-57. Frequent session
work in New York. First recorded (as David
Clooney) for Ember in 1956.

CORY
Born Cory Braverman on 12/16/1949 in Brooklyn,
New York. Female singer/songwriter.

COSBY, Bill
Born on 7/12/1937 in Philadelphia, Pennsylvania.
Stand-up comedian/actor. Star of the highly-rated
TV series *The Cosby Show*. Four of his first five
albums won Grammys for "Best Comedy Album."

COSGROVE, Miranda
Born on 5/14/1993 in Los Angeles, California. Teen
actress/singer. Appeared in several TV shows; best
known as "Carly" on TV's *iCarly*.

COSTA, Don
Born on 6/10/1925 in Boston, Massachusetts. Died
on 1/19/1983 (age 57). Arranger for Vaughn
Monroe, Frank Sinatra, Vic Damone, The Ames
Brothers and many more. A&R director of
ABC-Paramount Records, then for United Artists
Records.

COSTELLO, Elvis
Born Declan McManus on 8/25/1954 in Paddington, London, England; raised in Liverpool, England. Leading eclectic rock singer. Adopted stage name Elvis Costello in 1976; Costello is his mother's maiden name. In 1977, formed backing band The Attractions: Steve "Nieve" Nason (keyboards), Bruce Thomas (bass; Sutherland Brothers & Quiver) and Peter Thomas (drums). Appeared in the 1987 movie *Straight To Hell*. Married to Cait O'Riordan, former bassist with The Pogues, from 1986-2002. Married singer Diana Krall on 12/6/2003.

COTTON, Gene
Born on 6/30/1944 in Columbus, Ohio. Pop-rock singer/songwriter/guitarist. Recording since 1967.

COTTON, Josie
Born Kathleen Josey on 5/15/1951 in Dallas, Texas. Pop-rock singer/actress. Appeared in the movie *Valley Girl*.

COTTON, LLOYD & CHRISTIAN
Soft-rock trio: Darryl Cotton, Michael Lloyd and Chris Christian.

COUNT FIVE
Psychedelic garage-rock band from San Jose, California: Kenn Ellner (vocals), John Michalski and Sean Byrne (guitars), Roy Chaney (bass) and Craig Atkinson (drums). Atkinson died on 10/13/1998 (age 50).

COUNTING CROWS
Rock group from San Francisco, California: Adam Duritz (vocals), David Bryson (guitar), Charlie Gillingham (piano), Matt Malley (bass) and Steve Bowman (drums). Ben Mize replaced Bowman in 1994. Guitarist Dan Vickrey joined in 1996.

COUNTRY COALITION
Country-rock group: Peggie Moje, Dick Bradley, Tom Riney and John Kurtz.

COUNTRY JOE & THE FISH
Born Joseph McDonald on 1/1/1942 in El Monte, California. Highly political rock singer/guitarist. The Fish: Barry Melton and David Cohen (guitars), Bruce Barthol (bass) and Chicken Hirsch (drums). Disbanded in 1970.

COURTNEY, Lou
Born in 1944 in Buffalo, New York. R&B singer/songwriter.

COURTSHIP, The
Pop-rock group from Texas.

COVAY, Don
Born on 3/24/1938 in Orangeburg, South Carolina. R&B singer/songwriter. Member of the Rainbows in 1955. Recorded as "Pretty Boy" with Little Richard's band for Atlantic in 1957. Formed The Goodtimers in 1960. Wrote "Chain Of Fools" (Aretha Franklin) and "Pony Time" (Chubby Checker). Also see The Soul Clan.

COVEN
Pop group from Chicago, Illinois: Jinx Dawson (female vocals), Oz (male vocals), Christopher

Nelson (guitar), John Hobbs (keyboards) and Steve Ross (drums).

COVER GIRLS, The
Female dance trio from New York City, New York: Louise Sabater, Caroline Jackson and Sunshine Wright (replaced by Margo Urban in 1989). New 1992 lineup: Jackson, Evelyn Escalera and Michelle Valentine.

COVINGTON, Bucky
Born William Covington on 11/8/1977 in Rockingham, North Carolina. Country singer. Finalist on the 2006 season of TV's *American Idol*.

COWBOY CHURCH SUNDAY SCHOOL, The
Producer Stuart Hamblen's family: his daughters Veeva Susanne (age 18) and Obee Jane "Lisa" (age 16) with his wife Suzy, plus two of the girls' friends. Recorded at 33-1/3 rpm so that the record sounds like children's voices at 45 rpm. Veeva married actor Harve Presnell.

COWBOY JUNKIES
Alternative-rock band from Toronto, Ontario, Canada: siblings Margo Timmins (vocals), Michael Timmins (guitar) and Peter Timmins (drums), with Alan Anton (bass).

COWSILLS, The
Family pop group from Newport, Rhode Island: brothers Bill, Bob, Paul, Barry and John, with their younger sister Susan and mother Barbara Cowsill. Bob, Paul, John and Susan reunited for touring in 1990. Susan married Peter Holsapple of The dB's on 4/18/1993. Group was the inspiration for TV's *The Partridge Family*. John married Vicki Peterson (of the Bangles) on 10/25/2003. Barbara died of emphysema on 1/31/1985 (age 56). Barry went missing during Hurricane Katrina on 9/1/2005; his body was found on 12/28/2005 (age 51). Bill died of emphysema on 2/18/2006 (age 58).

COX, Deborah
Born on 7/13/1974 in Toronto, Ontario, Canada. R&B singer/songwriter.

COYOTE SISTERS, The
White female vocal trio: Marty Gwinn, Leah Kunkel (sister of Mama Cass) and Renee Armand.

COZIER, Jimmy
Born on 10/15/1977 in Brooklyn, New York. R&B singer/songwriter.

CRABBY APPLETON
Pop-rock group from Los Angeles, California: Michael Fennelly (vocals, guitar), Casey Foutz (keyboards), Flaco Falcon (percussion), Hank Harvey (bass) and Phil Jones (drums). Named for the cartoon character on the original *Captain Kangaroo* TV show.

CRACKER
Rock trio from Redlands, California: David Lowery (vocals; Camper Van Beethoven), John Hickman (guitar) and Davey Faragher (bass). Faragher left by 1996; Bob Rupe (Faragher Bros.; bass) and Charlie Quintana (drums) joined.

CRADDOCK, Billy "Crash"
Born on 6/13/1939 in Greensboro, North Carolina. Country-rock singer. First recorded for Colonial in 1957. Nickname "Crash" came from his stock car racing hobby.

CRAMER, Floyd
Born on 10/27/1933 in Campti, Louisiana; raised in Huttig, Arkansas. Died of cancer on 12/31/1997 (age 64). Nashville's top session pianist. Played piano from age five. Moved to Nashville in 1955. Worked with Elvis Presley, Johnny Cash, Perry Como, Chet Atkins and many others.

CRAMPTON SISTERS, The
White doo-wop duo of sisters from Bloomfield, New Jersey. Peggy Crampton is one of the sisters.

CRANBERRIES, The
Pop-rock group from Limerick, Ireland: Dolores O'Riordan (vocals), brothers Noel (guitar) and Mike (bass) Hogan, and Fergal Lawler (drums). Group formed in 1990 as the Cranberry Saw Us. O'Riordan joined in 1991 and group shortened name to The Cranberries. O'Riordan married Don Burton, assistant tour manager for Duran Duran, on 7/18/1994.

CRANE, Les
Born Lesley Stein on 12/3/1933 in Long Beach, New York; later based in San Francisco, California. Died on 7/13/2008 (age 74). Hosted TV talk show *ABC's Nightlife* in 1964. Married to actress Tina Louise from 1966-70.

CRASH TEST DUMMIES
Pop-rock group from Winnipeg, Manitoba, Canada: brothers Brad (vocals) and Dan (bass) Roberts, with Ellen Reid (keyboards), Benjamin Darvill (harmonica) and Mitch Dorge (drums).

CRAWFORD, Johnny
Born on 3/26/1946 in Los Angeles, California. Teen pop singer/actor. One of the original Mouseketeers. Played Chuck Connors' son ("Mark McCain") on TV's *The Rifleman*, 1958-63.

CRAWFORD, Randy
Born Veronica Crawford on 2/18/1952 in Macon, Georgia; raised in Cincinnati, Ohio. R&B singer.

CRAWLER
Rock group from England formerly known as Back Street Crawler; shortened name after death of leader Paul Kossoff (Free; died of drug-induced heart failure on 3/19/1976). Consisted of Terry Wilson-Slesser (vocals), Geoff Whitehorn (guitar), John Bundrick (keyboards), Terry Wilson (bass) and Tony Braunagel (drums).

CRAY, Robert, Band
Born on 8/1/1953 in Columbus, Georgia. Blues-rock guitarist/vocalist. Played bass with fictional band, Otis Day & The Knights, in the movie *Animal House*. Band formed in 1974 as backing tour group for bluesman Albert Collins. Lineup from 1986-89: Peter Boe (keyboards), Richard Cousins (bass) and David Olson (drums).

CRAYTON, Pee Wee
Born Connie Crayton on 12/18/1915 in Rockdale, Texas; raised in Austin, Texas. Died of a heart attack on 6/25/1985 (age 69). Blues singer/guitarist.

CRAZY ELEPHANT
Bubblegum studio concoction by producers Jerry Kasenetz and Jeff Katz. Robert Spencer (The Cadillacs) on lead vocals. Joey Levine (Ohio Express, Reunion) on backing vocals. Touring group formed later.

CRAZY FROG
Novelty production based on a computer animation character created by Erik Wernquist. First made popular as a ringtone.

CRAZY OTTO
Born Fritz Schulz-Reichel on 7/4/1912 in Meiningen, Germany. Died on 2/14/1990 (age 77). Honky-tonk pianist. Wrote original German version of 1954 hit "The Man With The Banjo."

CRAZY TOWN
White rock-rap group from Los Angeles, California: Seth "Shifty Shellshock" Binzer and Bret "Epic" Mazur (vocals), DJ AM (DJ), Craig Tyler and Anthony Valli (guitars), Doug Miller (bass) and James Bradley (drums).

CREAM
All-star blues-rock trio from England: Eric Clapton (guitar), Jack Bruce (bass) and Ginger Baker (drums). Baker and Bruce had been in Alexis Korner's Blues Inc. (C.C.S.) and the Graham Bond Organization. Clapton and Bruce were in John Mayall's Bluesbreakers. After Cream disbanded, Clapton and Baker formed Blind Faith.

CREATIVE SOURCE
R&B-dance vocal group from Los Angeles, California: Don Wyatt, Celeste Rhodes, Steve Flanagan, Barbara Berryman and Barbara Lewis. Formed in 1972 by Ron Townson of The 5th Dimension.

CREED
Christian rock group formed in Tallahassee, Florida: Scott Stapp (vocals; born on 8/8/1973), Mark Tremonti (guitar; born on 4/18/1974), Brian Marshall (bass; born on 4/24/1974) and Scott Phillips (drums; born on 2/22/1973). Marshall left in late 2000. Group disbanded in June 2004. Tremonti, Marshall and Phillips formed Alter Bridge.

CREEDENCE CLEARWATER REVIVAL
Rock group formed in El Cerrito, California: John Fogerty (vocals, guitar; born on 5/28/1945), brother Tom Fogerty (guitar; born on 11/9/1941), Stu Cook (keyboards, bass; born on 4/25/1945) and Doug Clifford (drums; born on 4/24/1945). First recorded as the Blue Velvets for the Orchestra label in 1959. Recorded as the Golliwogs for Fantasy in 1964. Renamed Creedence Clearwater Revival in 1967. Tom Fogerty left for a solo career in 1971 and group disbanded in October 1972. Tom Fogerty died of respiratory failure on 9/6/1990 (age 48). Also see Don Harrison Band.

CRENSHAW, Marshall
Born on 11/11/1953 in Detroit, Michigan. Rockabilly singer/guitarist. Played John Lennon in the road show of *Beatlemania* in 1976. Appeared in the movie *Peggy Sue Got Married* and portrayed Buddy Holly in the 1987 movie *La Bamba*.

CRESCENDOS, The
White vocal group from Nashville, Tennessee: cousins George Lanius and James Lanius, Ken Brigham, Tom Fortner and Jim Hall.

CRESCENTS, The
Rock and roll instrumental band from Oxnard, California: female Chiyo Ishii (lead guitar), with Tom Bresh (guitar), Ray Reed (sax) and Tom Mitchell (bass). Bresh, the son of country singer Merle Travis, charted several country hits in the 1970s.

CRESPO, Elvis
Born on 7/30/1971 in Brooklyn, New York. Latin singer/songwriter.

CRESTS, The
Interracial doo-wop group formed in Manhattan, New York: Johnny Maestro (born Johnny Mastrangelo on 5/7/1939; shown as Mastro on all The Crests' hits; joined as lead singer in 1956), Harold Torres, Talmadge Gough, J.T. Carter and Patricia Van Dross. Discovered by Al Browne; first recorded for Joyce in 1957. Van Dross (older sister of Luther Vandross) left group in 1958. Maestro left for solo work in 1960; replaced by James Ancrum. Maestro later joined Brooklyn Bridge.

CRETONES, The
Rock group from Los Angeles, California: Mark Goldenberg (vocals, guitar), Steve Leonard (keyboards), Peter Bernstein (bass) and Steve Beers (drums).

CREW-CUTS, The
Pop vocal group from Toronto, Ontario, Canada: brothers John (lead; born on 8/28/1931) and Ray (bass; born on 11/28/1932) Perkins, Pat Barrett (tenor; born on 9/15/1931), and Rudi Maugeri (baritone; born on 1/27/1931; died of cancer on 5/7/2004, age 73). First called the Canadaires, changed name in 1954. Maugeri did vocal arrangements for the group. The group's huge #1 hit in the summer of 1954, "Sh-Boom," helped to usher in the rock & roll era. Disbanded in 1964. One of the first white vocal groups to "cover" R&B hits.

CREWE, Bob
Born on 11/12/1937 in Newark, New Jersey. Wrote many hit songs beginning with "Silhouettes" in 1957. One of the top producers of the 1960s. Wrote and produced most of the hits by The 4 Seasons. Head of several labels, publishing and production companies. Assembled The Bob Crewe Generation, an aggregation of studio musicians.

CRIME MOB
Rap group from Cedar Grove, Tennessee: Princess, Diamond, Lil Jay, Killa C, Jock and Cyco Black.

CRITTERS, The
Pop group from Plainfield, New Jersey: Don Ciccone (vocals, guitar), Jimmy Ryan (guitar), Chris Darway (organ), Kenny Gorka (bass) and Jack Decker (drums). Ciccone later joined The 4 Seasons.

CROCE, Jim
Born on 1/10/1943 in Philadelphia, Pennsylvania. Killed in a plane crash in Natchitoches, Louisiana, on 9/20/1973 (age 30). Singer/songwriter/guitarist. Recorded with wife Ingrid for Capitol in 1968. Lead guitarist on his hits, Maury Muehleisen, was killed in the same crash.

CROCHET, Cleveland
Born on 6/6/1921 in Hathaway, Louisiana. White fiddle player with his cajun band, the Hillbilly Ramblers.

CROCKETT, G.L.
Born George Crockett on 9/18/1928 in Carrollton, Mississippi. Died on 2/15/1967 (age 38). Blues singer.

CROOKLYN DODGERS, The
Rap group from Brooklyn, New York. Created by director Spike Lee for his movies *Crooklyn* and *Clockers*.

CROSBY, Bing
One of the most popular entertainers of the 20th century. Born Harry Lillis Crosby on 5/3/1903 in Tacoma, Washington. Died of a heart attack on 10/14/1977 (age 74) on a golf course near Madrid, Spain. Bing and singing partner Al Rinker were hired in 1926 by Paul Whiteman; with Harry Barris they became the Rhythm Boys and gained an increasing popularity. The trio split from Whiteman in 1930, and Bing sang briefly with Gus Arnheim's band. It was his early-1931 smash with Arnheim, "I Surrender, Dear," which earned Bing a CBS radio contract and launched an unsurpassed solo career. Over the next three decades the resonant Crosby baritone and breezy persona sold more than 300 million records and was featured in over 50 movies (won Academy Award for *Going My Way*, 1944). Married to actress Dixie Lee from 1930 until her death in 1952; their son Gary (died on 8/24/1995, age 62) began recording in 1950. Married to actress Kathryn Grant from 1957 until his death; their daughter Mary became an actress. Bing's youngest brother, Bob Crosby (died on 3/9/1993, age 80), was a popular swing-era bandleader.

CROSBY, Chris
Born in Los Angeles, California. Pop singer. Son of bandleader Bob Crosby. Nephew of Bing Crosby.

CROSBY, David
Born on 8/14/1941 in Los Angeles, California. Singer/guitarist with The Byrds from 1964-68 and later Crosby, Stills & Nash. Son of cinematographer Floyd Crosby (*High Noon*). Frequent troubles with the law due to drug charges. Movie cameos in *Backdraft*, *Hook* and *Thunderheart*; appeared on TV's *Roseanne*. Underwent a successful liver transplant on 11/19/1994. In early 2000, it was announced that he was the biological father (via artificial insemination) of two children for the couple of Melissa Etheridge and Julie Cypher.

CROSBY, STILLS & NASH
Folk-rock trio formed in Laurel Canyon, California. Consisted of David Crosby (guitar; born on 8/14/1941), Stephen Stills (guitar, keyboards, bass; born on 1/3/1945) and Graham Nash (guitar; born on 2/2/1942). Crosby had been in The Byrds, Stills had been in The Buffalo Springfield, and Nash was with The Hollies. Neil Young (guitar; born on 11/12/1945), formerly with Buffalo Springfield, joined group in 1970; left in 1974. Reunion in 1988. Crosby, Stills, Nash & Young reunited for a tour and album in 2000.

CROSS, Christopher
Born Christopher Geppert on 5/3/1951 in San Antonio, Texas. Pop-rock singer/songwriter/guitarist. Formed own group with Rob Meurer (keyboards), Andy Salmon (bass) and Tommy Taylor (drums) in 1973.

CROSS, Jimmy
Born on 11/17/1938 in Philadelphia, Pennsylvania. Died of a heart attack on 10/8/1978 (age 39). Produced the syndicated radio series *Country Concert*.

CROSS COUNTRY
Trio of Jay Siegel (lead vocals), with brothers Mitch (guitar) and Phil (percussion) Margo. All were members of The Tokens.

CROSSFADE
Rock band from Columbia, South Carolina: Tony Byroads (vocals), Ed Sloan (guitar), Mitch James (bass) and Brian Geiger (drums).

CROW
Rock-blues group from Minneapolis, Minnesota: Dave Waggoner (vocals), Dick Weigand (guitar), Kink Middlemist (organ), Larry Weigand (bass) and Denny Craswell (drums; The Castaways).

CROW, Sheryl
Born on 2/11/1962 in Kennett, Missouri. Adult Alternative rock singer/songwriter/guitarist. After attending the University of Missouri, worked as a grade school music teacher, until moving to Los Angeles in 1986. Worked as backing singer for Michael Jackson, Don Henley, George Harrison and others. Crow's compositions covered by Eric Clapton and Wynonna Judd.

CROWDED HOUSE
Pop trio formed in Melbourne, Australia: Neil Finn (vocals, guitar, piano), Nick Seymour (bass) and Paul Hester (drums). Finn and Hester were former members of Split Enz. Hester committed suicide on 3/26/2005 (age 46).

CROWELL, Rodney
Born on 8/7/1950 in Houston, Texas. Country singer/songwriter/guitarist. Married to Rosanne Cash from 1979-92.

CROWN HEIGHTS AFFAIR
R&B-disco group from New York: Phil Thomas (vocals), William Anderson (guitar), Howard Young (keyboards), Bert Reid, James Baynard and Raymond Reid (horn section), Muki Wilson (bass), and Raymond Rock (drums). Bert Reid died of cancer on 12/12/2004.

CROWS, The
R&B vocal group from Harlem, New York: Daniel "Sonny" Norton (lead), Harold Major (tenor), Bill Davis (baritone), Gerald Hamilton (bass) and Mark Jackson (guitar). Hamilton died in 1967 (age 33). Norton died in 1972 (age 39).

CRU
Rap trio from Brooklyn, New York: Chadio, Yogi and Mighty Ha.

CRUCIAL CONFLICT
Hip-hop group from Chicago, Illinois: Corey Johnson, Marrico King, Ralph Levertson and Wondosas Martin.

CRUDUP, Arthur "Big Boy"
Born on 8/24/1905 in Forest, Mississippi. Died of a stroke on 3/28/1974 (age 68). Blues singer/guitarist.

CRUISE, Erin
Born in Chicago, Illinois. Female dance singer.

CRUSADERS, The
Instrumental jazz-oriented group from Houston, Texas, as the Swingsters, in the early 1950s. To California in the early 1960s, name changed to The Jazz Crusaders. Became The Crusaders in 1971. Included Joe Sample (keyboards), Wilton Felder (reeds), Nesbert "Stix" Hooper (drums) and Wayne Henderson (trombone; left in 1975). Larry Carlton was a frequent guest guitarist from 1972-77.

CRUSH
Female pop-rock vocal duo from England: Donna Air and Jayni Hoy.

CRYAN' SHAMES, The
Rock and roll band from Hinsdale, Illinois: Tom Doody (vocals), Jim Fairs and Jerry Stone (guitars), Jim Pilster (tambourine), Dave Purple (bass) and Dennis Conroy (drums).

CRYSTAL, Billy
Born on 3/14/1947 in Long Beach, Long Island, New York. Actor/comedian. Cast member of TV's *Soap*, 1977-81, and a regular on *Saturday Night Live*, 1984-85. Star of the movies *Throw Momma From The Train*, *City Slickers I & II*, *When Harry Met Sally* and others.

CRYSTAL MANSION
Pop group from Philadelphia, Pennsylvania: Johnny Caswell (vocals), Ron Gentile (guitar), Sam Rota (keyboards), Jerry Marlow (bass) and Rick Morley (drums).

CRYSTALS, The
Rock and roll "girl group" from Brooklyn, New York: Barbara Alston, Dee Dee Kenniebrew, Mary Thomas, Patricia Wright and Myrna Gerrard. La La Brooks replaced Gerrard in 1962. Thomas left in 1962. Wright was replaced by Frances Collins in 1964. The Crystals and The Ronettes were producer Phil Spector's most successful 'wall of sound' girl groups.

C-SIDE
Male rap trio from Atlanta, Georgia: Kenny Kold, Gator and Bo-Q.

CSS
Dance-rock band from Sao Paulo, Brazil: Adriano Cintra, Luisa "Lovefoxxx" Matsushita, Luiza Sa, Ana Rezende and Carolina Parra. CSS: Cansei Ser Sexy.

CUBA, Joe, Sextet
Born Gilberto Calderon in 1931 in Manhattan, New York. Latin conga player. Other members of his sextet: Jose "Cheo" Feliciano (vocals, not to be confused with the solo star), Tommy Berrios (vibes), Nick Jimenez (piano), Jules Cordero (bass) and Jimmy Sabater (drums).

CUES, The
R&B vocal group from Brooklyn, New York: Jimmy Breedlove, Ollie Jones and Abel DeCosta (tenors), Robie Kirk ("Winfield Scott"; baritone) and Eddie Barnes (bass). Backing vocal group for many artists on Atlantic Records. DeCosta died on 11/2/1984 (age 60).

CUEVAS, Chris
Born on 2/8/1973 in Long Beach, Mississippi. White male pop singer. Junior Vocalist winner on TV's *Star Search*.

CUFF LINKS, The
Group is actually the overdubbed voice of pop singer Ron Dante (The Archies).

CUGINI
Born Donald Cugini on 5/7/1959 in Los Angeles, California. Pop singer/songwriter.

CULT, The
Rock group from England. Nucleus of evercharging lineup included Ian Astbury (vocals; born Ian Lindsay), Billy Duffy (guitar), Jamie Stewart (bass) and Les Warner (drums). Warner left in 1988; replaced by Matt Sorum (Guns N' Roses).

CULTURE BEAT
Dance group assembled by Germans Torsten Fenslau (DJ/producer; died in a car accident on 11/6/1993, age 29), Juergen "Nosie" Katzmann (composer/guitarist) and Peter Zweier (composer/engineer). Includes London vocalist Lana Evans and New Jersey rapper Jay Supreme.

CULTURE CLUB
Pop group formed in London, England: George "Boy George" O'Dowd (vocals; born on 6/14/1961), Roy Hay (guitar, keyboards; born on 8/12/1961), Michael Craig (bass; born on 2/15/1960) and Jon Moss (drums; born on 9/11/1957). Designer Sue Clowes originated distinctive costuming for the group. Boy George went solo in 1987.

CUMMINGS, Burton
Born on 12/31/1947 in Winnipeg, Manitoba, Canada. Lead singer of The Guess Who. Acted in the 1982 movie *Melanie*.

CUNHA, Rick
Born on 7/17/1944 in Washington DC. Session guitarist.

CUPID
Born Bryson Bernard on 10/10/1982 in Lafayette, Louisiana. Male rapper/songwriter.

CUPIDS, The
White doo-wop group from Brooklyn, New York. Group dissolved after the untimely death of lead singer Lenny Colton. The Camelots fulfilled the rest of The Cupids' recording obligations.

CURB, Mike, Congregation
Born on 12/24/1944 in Savannah, Georgia. Music mogul/politician. President of MGM Records, 1969-73. *Billboard's* producer (with Don Costa) of the year in 1972. Elected lieutenant governor of California in 1978; served as governor of California, 1980. Formed own company, Sidewalk Records, in 1964; became Curb Records in 1974 (*Billboard's* country label of the year in 2001).

CURE, The
Techno-rock group formed in England by Robert Smith (vocals, guitar; born on 4/21/1959) and Laurence "Lol" Tolhurst (drums; born on 2/3/1959). Since 1983, members have included Smith, Tolhurst (until 1990), Porl Thompson, Simon Gallup, Andy Anderson (1984), Boris Williams and Roger O'Donnell (1989). Perry Bamonte joined in 1992. Smith was also a touring member of Siouxsie And The Banshees in the early 1980s.

CURIOSITY KILLED THE CAT
Pop-rock group formed in London, England: Ben Volpeliere-Pierrot (vocals), Julian Brookhouse (guitar), Nick Thorpe (bass) and Miguel Drummond (drums).

CURRENT
Disco session group assembled by producer Joe Saraceno (The T-Bones).

CURRIE, Cherie & Marie
Identical twins born on 11/30/1959 in Encino, California. Cherie (formerly with the rock band The Runaways) appeared in the movies *Foxes* and *Wavelength*.

CURRINGTON, Billy
Born on 11/19/1973 in Savannah, Georgia; raised in Rincon, Georgia. Country singer/songwriter/guitarist.

CURRY, Clifford
Born on 11/4/1940 in Knoxville, Tennessee. R&B singer.

CURRY, Tim
Born on 4/19/1946 in Grappenhall, Cheshire, England. Actor/singer. Starred in many movies.

CURTIE & THE BOOMBOX
Female vocal group from Holland: Curtie Fortune (lead), Patricia Balrak, Judith Landry and Denise van der Hek.

CURTOLA, Bobby
Born on 4/17/1944 in Port Arthur, Ontario, Canada. Teen pop singer.

CUT 'N' MOVE
Dance group from Denmark: producer/musicians Per Holm and Jorn Kristensen with rapper Jens "M.C. Zipp" Larsen and female vocalist Thera Hoeymanss.

CUTTING CREW
Pop-rock group formed in England: Nick Van Eede (vocals), Kevin MacMichael (guitar), Colin Farley (bass) and Martin Beedle (drums). MacMichael died of cancer on 12/31/2002 (age 51).

CYCLONES
Instrumental rock and roll band led by Bill Taylor.

CYMANDE
Afro-rock band from the West Indies: Ray King (vocals), Pat Patterson (guitar), Peter Serreo and Derek Gibbs (saxophones), Mike Rose (flute), Joe Dee and Pablo Gonsales (percussion), and Sam Kelly (drums).

CYMARRON
Male pop vocal trio from Memphis, Tennessee: Richard Mainegra, Rick Yancey and Sherrill Parks.

CYMBAL, Johnny
Born on 2/3/1945 in Ochitree, Scotland. Died of a heart attack on 3/16/1993 (age 48). Pop singer/songwriter/producer. Also recorded as Derek.

CYNTHIA
Born Cynthia Torres on 5/6/1968 in the Bronx, New York. Dance singer. Recorded duet with Johnny Ortiz.

CYPRESS HILL
Rap trio from Los Angeles, California: Senen "Sen Dog" Reyes (Cuban-born; older brother of Mellow Man Ace), Louis "B-Real" Freese and Lawrence "Mixmaster Muggs" Muggerud (former member of The 7A3). Band named for Cypress Street in the Southgate section of Los Angeles. Appeared in the movie *The Meteor Man*.

CYRKLE, The
Pop group formed in Easton, Pennsylvania: Don Dannemann (vocals, guitar), Mike Losekamp (keyboards), Tom Dawes (bass) and Marty Fried (drums). Signed to Columbia and managed by The Beatles' manager Brian Epstein; named by John Lennon. Dawes died of a stroke on 10/13/2007 (age 64).

CYRUS, Billy Ray
Born on 8/25/1961 in Flatwoods, Kentucky. Country singer/actor. Played "Dr. Clint Cassidy" on the PAX-TV series *Doc* (2001-04). Father of TV's *Hannah Montana* star Miley Cyrus (plays her manager "Robbie Stewart" on the show).

CYRUS, Miley
Born Destiny Hope Cyrus on 11/23/1992 in Franklin, Tennessee. Teen idol singer/actress. Daughter of Billy Ray Cyrus. Star of the Disney TV series *Hannah Montana*. Legally changed her name to Miley Ray Cyrus in January 2008.

DA BRAT
Born Shawntae Harris on 4/14/1974 in Chicago, Illinois. Female rapper/songwriter. Discovered by her producer/songwriter Jermaine Dupri at a Kris Kross concert in Chicago.

DADDY DEWDROP
Born Richard Monda in 1952 in Cleveland, Ohio. Pop singer. Songwriter for the TV cartoon series *Sabrina & The Groovy Ghoulies*.

DADDY-O'S, The
Novelty session group produced by guitarist Billy Mure (of The Trumpeteers).

DADDY YANKEE
Born Raymond Ayala on 2/3/1977 in Rio Piedras, Puerto Rico. Leading artist of the reggaeton sound.

DAFT PUNK
Electronica-dance duo from Paris, France: Thomas Bangalter (Stardust) and Guy-Manuel de Homem-Christo.

D'AGOSTINO, Gigi
Born Luigino Di Agostino in Italy. Electronica-dance DJ/remixer/producer.

DAHL, Steve
Born on 11/20/1954 in La Canada, California. DJ in Chicago, Illinois. Organized the controversial "disco sucks demolition" at Chicago's Comiskey Park on 7/12/1979.

DAILY, E.G.
Born Elizabeth Daily on 9/11/1962 in Los Angeles, California. White dance singer/actress. Acted in the movies *Pee-Wee's Big Adventure* and *Valley Girl*. Performs voices for the animated TV series *Rugrats*.

DAKOTA MOON
Black pop group formed in Los Angeles, California: Ty Taylor (vocals), Joe Dean (guitar), Ray Artis (bass) and Mike Malloy (drums).

DALE, Alan
Born Aldo Sigismondi on 7/9/1925 in Brooklyn, New York. Died of heart failure on 4/20/2002 (age 76). Baritone singer formerly with Carmen Cavallaro. Hosted his own TV shows beginning in 1948. Starred in the 1956 movie *Don't Knock The Rock*.

DALE, Dick
Born Richard Monsour on 5/4/1937 in Boston, Massachusetts. Later based in Southern California. Influential surf-rock guitarist.

DALE & GRACE
Pop vocal duo: Dale Houston (born on 4/23/1940 in Seminary, Mississippi; died of heart failure on 9/27/2007, age 67) and Grace Broussard (born in 1939 in Prairieville, Louisiana).

DALLARA, Tony
Born on 6/30/1936 in Campobasso, Italy. Adult Contemporary singer.

DALTON, Kathy
Born in Memphis, Tennessee. Pop-country singer.

DALTREY, Roger
Born on 3/1/1944 in Hammersmith, London, England. Formed band The Detours, which later became The Who; Daltrey was The Who's lead singer. Starred in the movies *Tommy*, *Lisztomania*, *The Legacy* and *McVicar*.

DAMAGE
Male R&B vocal group from London, England: Andrez, Coree, Jade, Noel and Ras.

DAMIAN, Michael
Born Michael Damian Weir on 4/26/1962 in San Diego, California. While performing on *American Bandstand*, was discovered by the producers of TV soap opera *The Young & The Restless* and won the role of "Danny Romalotti" in 1981.

DAMIAN DAME
Black male-female duo. Damian was born Bruce Broadus in Battle Creek, Michigan. Died of cancer on 6/27/1996 (age 29). Dame was born Debra Hurd in Houston, Texas. Died in a car crash on 7/4/1994 (age 36).

DAMIANO, Joe
Born on 1/29/1939 in Philadelphia, Pennsylvania. White pop singer. Brother of Peter DeAngelis (produced for Frankie Avalon and Fabian).

DAMITA JO
Born Damita Jo DuBlanc on 8/5/1930 in Austin, Texas. Died on 12/25/1998 (age 68). R&B singer/songwriter. With Steve Gibson & The Red Caps (married to Gibson) from 1951-53 and 1959-60. Regular on Redd Foxx's TV variety series in 1977.

DAMNED, The
Punk-rock band from England: David Vanian (vocals), Roman Jugg (guitar), Bryn Merrick (bass) and Chris Miller (drums).

DAMN YANKEES
Superstar rock group: guitarist Ted Nugent (Amboy Dukes), bassist/vocalist Jack Blades (Night Ranger), guitarist/vocalist Tommy Shaw (Styx) and drummer Michael Cartellone. Shaw and Blades recorded as a duo in 1995.

DAMON('S), Liz, Orient Express
Damon is the leader of the three-woman, six-man Adult Contemporary vocal/instrumental group from Hawaii.

DAMONE, Vic
Born Vito Farinola on 6/12/1928 in Brooklyn, New York. Pop ballad singer. Appeared in the movies *Kismet*, *Meet Me In Las Vegas* and *Hell To Eternity*. Hosted own TV series (1956-57). Married to actress Diahann Carroll from 1987-96.

DANA
Born Dana Harris in Tampa, Florida. Female R&B singer.

DANA, Vic
Born on 8/26/1942 in Buffalo, New York. Adult Contemporary singer. Moved to California as a teen. Replaced Tony Butala (of The Lettermen) in the Los Angeles group Eddie Laurence & The Whatnotts in 1960.

DANCER, PRANCER & NERVOUS
Novelty production of "The Singing Reindeer" (similar to The Chipmunks).

DANDELION
Rock group from Philadelphia, Pennsylvania: brothers Kevin (vocals, guitar) and Mike (bass)

Morpurgo, Carl Hinds (guitar) and Dante Cimino (drums).

D'ANGELO
Born Michael D'Angelo Archer on 2/11/1974 in Richmond, Virginia. R&B singer/songwriter.

DANGER DANGER
Hard-rock group from Queens, New York: Ted Poley (vocals), Andy Timmons (guitar), Kasey Smith (keyboards), Bruno Ravel (bass) and Steve West (drums).

DANGERFIELD, Rodney
Born Jacob Cohen on 11/22/1921 in Babylon, Long Island, New York. Died of heart failure on 10/5/2004 (age 82). Popular stand-up comedian/actor who "gets no respect."

DANIELS, Charlie, Band
Born on 10/28/1936 in Wilmington, North Carolina. Country-rock singer/fiddle player. His band: Tom Crain (guitar), Joe "Taz" DiGregorio (keyboards), Charles Hayward (bass), and James W. Marshall & Fred Edwards (drums). Marshall and Edwards left in 1986; replaced by Jack Gavin. Daniels led the Jaguars from 1958-67. Went solo in 1968 and worked as a session musician in Nashville. Played on Bob Dylan's *Nashville Skyline* album. Group appeared in the movie *Urban Cowboy*. Began recording Christian music in 1994.

DANITY KANE
Female R&B vocal group assembled by Diddy for the reality TV series *Making The Band 3*: Shannon Bex, Aundrea Fimbres, Aubrey O'Day, Dawn Richard and Wanita "D. Woods" Woodgette.

DANKWORTH, Johnny
Born on 9/20/1927 in Woodford, Essex, England; raised in London, England. Alto saxophonist/jazz bandleader/composer. Married singer Cleo Laine in 1958.

DANLEERS, The
Black doo-wop group from Brooklyn, New York: Jimmy Weston (lead; died on 6/10/1993), Johnny Lee (first tenor), Willie Ephraim (second tenor), Nat McCune (baritone) and Roosevelt Mays (bass). Group was named after their manager, Danny Webb, who wrote "One Summer Night." Not to be confused with the R&B group, The Danderliers.

DANNY & THE JUNIORS
Rock and roll group from Philadelphia, Pennsylvania: Danny Rapp (lead; born on 5/10/1941; committed suicide on 4/5/1983, age 41), David White (first tenor), Frank Maffei (second tenor) and Joe Terranova (baritone). White later joined The Spokesmen. Group appeared in the 1958 movie *Let's Rock*.

DANNY WILSON
Pop trio from Dundee, Scotland: brothers Gary (vocals, guitar) and Kit (keyboards, percussion) Clark, with Ged Grimes (bass). Group named after the 1952 Frank Sinatra movie *Meet Danny Wilson*.

DANTE & the EVERGREENS
Born Donald Drowty on 9/8/1941 in Los Angeles, California. Pop singer. The Evergreens: Bill Young, future record producer Tony Moon and future Beverly Hills lawyer Frank D. Rosenthal.

DANZIG
Born Glenn Anzalone on 6/23/1955 in Lodi, New Jersey. Hard-rock singer/songwriter. His group: John Crist (guitar), Eerie Von (bass) and Chuck Biscuits (drums).

D'ARBY, Terence Trent
Born on 3/15/1962 in Manhattan, New York; later based in London, England. R&B-pop singer/songwriter/producer. Last name originally spelled Darby. Was a member of the U.S. Army boxing team.

DARENSBOURG, Joe
Born on 7/9/1906 in Baton Rouge, Louisiana. Died on 5/24/1985 (age 78). Black clarinetist with Jack Teagarden and Louis Armstrong.

DARIAN, Fred
Born on 6/16/1927 in Detroit, Michigan. Pop singer/songwriter/producer. Co-writer of Larry Verne's hit "Mr. Custer." Produced records for Dobie Gray.

DARIN, Bobby
Born Walden Robert Cassotto on 5/14/1936 in the Bronx, New York. Died of heart failure on 12/20/1973 (age 37). Pop-rock and roll vocalist/pianist/songwriter/entertainer. First recorded in 1956 with The Jaybirds (Decca). First appeared on TV in March 1956 on *The Tommy Dorsey Show*. Married to actress Sandra Dee from 1960-67. Nominated for an Oscar for his performance in the movie *Captain Newman, MD* (1963). Formed own record company, Direction. Kevin Spacey played Darin in his biopic *Beyond The Sea*.

DARLIN, Florraine
Born Florraine Panza on 1/20/1944 in Pittsburgh, Pennsylvania. Pop singer.

DARNELL, Larry
Born Leonard Donald on 12/21/1928 in Columbus, Ohio. Died of cancer on 7/3/1983 (age 54). R&B singer/dancer.

DARREN, James
Born James Ercolani on 6/8/1936 in Philadelphia, Pennsylvania. Pop singer/actor. Moved to Hollywood in 1955. In the movies *Rumble On The Docks*, *The Brothers Rico*, *Operation Mad Ball*, *Gunman's Walk*, *The Guns Of Navarone*, *Because They're Young* and *Let No Man Write My Epitaph*. Played "Moondoggie," Gidget's boyfriend, in *Gidget*, *Gidget Goes Hawaiian* and *Gidget Goes To Rome*. In the TV series *The Time Tunnel* from 1966-67 and *T.J. Hooker* from 1983-86.

DARTELLS, The
Rock and roll band from Oxnard, California: Doug Phillips (vocals, bass), Dick Burns, Corky Wilkie, Rich Peil, Randy Ray and Gary Peeler. Phillips died on 5/5/1995 (age 50). Burns died on 11/5/2007 (age 64).

DARUDE
Born Ville Virtanen on 1/28/1975 in Finland. Techno-dance DJ/producer.

DAS EFX
Hip-hop duo of Andre "Dray" Weston (born on 9/9/1970) and Willie "Skoob" Hines (born on 11/27/1970) formed at Virginia State. DAS is an acronym for Dray And Skoob (which is "books" spelled backward).

DASH, Sarah
Born on 8/18/1943 in Trenton, New Jersey. R&B singer. Original member of The Blue-Belles and LaBelle.

DASHBOARD CONFESSIONAL
Rock band from Boca Raton, Florida: Christopher Carrabba (vocals, guitar), John Lefler (guitar), Scott Shoenbeck (bass) and Mike Marsh (drums).

DAUGHTRY
Rock band: Chris Daughtry (born on 12/26/1979 in Roanoke Rapids, North Carolina; finalist on the 2006 season of TV's *American Idol*), Josh Steeley (guitar), Jeremy Brady (guitar), Josh Paul (bass) and Joey Barnes (drums).

DAVE DEE, DOZY, BEAKY, MICK & TICH
Pop band from Wiltshire, England: "Dave Dee" Harmon (vocals), Trevor "Dozy" Davies (guitar), John "Beaky" Dymond (guitar), Michael "Mick" Wilson (bass) and Ian "Tich" Amey (drums).

DAVID, Craig
Born on 5/5/1981 in Southampton, England. R&B singer/songwriter.

DAVID, F.R.
Born Robert Fitoussi on 1/1/1954 in Tunisia, Africa; raised in Paris, France. White pop singer/songwriter.

DAVID & DAVID
Pop-rock duo from Los Angeles, California: David Baerwald and David Ricketts.

DAVID & JONATHAN
Songwriting/producing/vocal duo from Bristol, England: Roger Greenaway (David) and Roger Cook (Jonathan). Both later were production team for White Plains. Cook founded Blue Mink. Greenaway also in The Pipkins.

DAVIDSON, Clay
Born on 4/4/1971 in Saltville, Virginia. Country singer/songwriter/guitarist.

DAVIE, Hutch
Born Robert Davie. Leading musical arranger during the 1950s and 1960s. Pianist on Jim Lowe's hit "The Green Door."

DAVINA
Born Davina Bussey in Detroit, Michigan. Female R&B singer/songwriter.

DAVIS, Alana
Born on 5/6/1974 in Manhattan, New York. Female pop-rock singer/songwriter.

DAVIS, Jimmy, & Junction
Born in Memphis, Tennessee. Rock singer/guitarist. His band Junction: Tommy Burroughs (guitar), John Scott (piano) and Chuck Reynolds (drums).

DAVIS, John
Born on 8/31/1952 in Philadelphia, Pennsylvania. Dance singer/songwriter/producer/arranger. In U.S. Naval Academy Band. Wrote score for the Broadway musical *Gotta Go Disco*.

DAVIS, Mac
Born on 1/21/1942 in Lubbock, Texas. Country-pop singer/songwriter/actor. Worked as a regional rep for Vee-Jay and Liberty Records. Wrote "In The Ghetto," "Memories" and "Don't Cry Daddy" for Elvis Presley. Also wrote "I Believe In Music" and "Watching Scotty Grow." Host of own musical variety TV series from 1974-76. Appearances in several movies, including *North Dallas Forty* in 1979.

DAVIS, Martha
Born on 1/15/1951 in Berkeley, California. Lead singer of The Motels.

DAVIS, Miles
Born on 5/26/1926 in Alton, Illinois. Died on 9/28/1991 (age 65). Innovative and legendary jazz trumpeter who influenced the jazz fusion movement. Married to funk singer Betty Davis (1968-69) and actress Cicely Tyson (1981-88).

DAVIS, Paul
Born on 4/21/1948 in Meridian, Mississippi. Died of a heart attack on 4/21/2008 (age 60). Pop-country singer/songwriter/producer. Survived a shooting in Nashville on 7/30/1986.

DAVIS, Sammy Jr.
Born on 12/8/1925 in Harlem, New York. Died of cancer on 5/16/1990 (age 64). One of America's all-time great entertainers. With father and uncle in dance act the Will Mastin Trio from the early 1940s. First recorded for Capitol in 1950. Lost his left eye and had his nose smashed in an auto accident near San Bernardino, California, on 11/19/54; returned to performing in January 1955. Frequent appearances on TV, Broadway and in movies.

DAVIS, Skeeter
Born Mary Frances Penick on 12/30/1931 in Dry Ridge, Kentucky. Died of cancer on 9/19/2004 (age 72). Country singer. Recorded with friend Betty Jack Davis as the Davis Sisters until Betty Jack was killed in a car accident on 8/2/1953. Married to TV's *Nashville Now* host, Ralph Emery (1960-64). Married to Joey Spampinato, the bassist of jazz-rock band NRBQ (1983-96).

DAVIS, Spencer, Group
Spencer was born on 7/14/1941 in Swansea, South Wales. Rock singer/rhythm guitarist. Formed his R&B-styled rock band in Birmingham, England in 1963. Featured Steve Winwood (lead vocals, lead guitar, keyboards), his brother Muff Winwood (bass) and Pete York (drums). Steve Winwood left in 1967 to form the group Traffic; later, a successful solo artist. Muff became senior director of A&R at CBS Records, U.K.

DAVIS, Tami
Born in Charleston, South Carolina. R&B singer.

DAVIS, Tim
Born on 11/29/1943 in Milwaukee, Wisconsin. Died on 9/20/1988 (age 44). Pop singer/drummer.

DAVIS, Tyrone
Born on 5/4/1938 in Greenville, Mississippi; raised in Saginaw, Michigan. Died of a stroke on 2/9/2005 (age 66). R&B singer. To Chicago in 1959. Worked as valet/chauffeur for Freddy King until 1962. Working local clubs when discovered by Harold Burrage. First recorded for Four Brothers in 1965 as Tyrone The Wonder Boy. His younger sister, Jean Davis, was a member of the group Facts Of Life.

DAY, Arlan
Born Alan Green in Manchester, England. White pop-jazz pianist/singer.

DAY, Bobby
Born Robert Byrd on 7/1/1930 in Ft. Worth, Texas. Died of cancer on 7/15/1990 (age 60). R&B singer/songwriter. To Watts, Los Angeles in 1948. Formed the Hollywood Flames in 1950. Group also recorded as The Flames in 1950. Day recorded with various Flames members as the Hollywood Four Flames, Jets, Tangiers, and The Satellites until 1957. Day then recorded solo; later in duo Bob & Earl in 1960.

DAY, Doris
Born Doris Kappelhoff on 4/3/1924 in Cincinnati, Ohio. Sang briefly with Bob Crosby in 1940 and shortly thereafter became a major star with the Les Brown band. Her great solo recording success was soon transcended by Hollywood as Day became the #1 box office star of the late 1950s and early 1960s. Star of own popular TV series from 1968-73. Her husband, Marty Melcher, owned Arwin Records; their son, Terry, was a member of The Rip Chords and Bruce And Terry, and a prolific producer (The Beach Boys).

DAY, Howie
Born on 1/15/1981 in Bangor, Maine. Adult Alternative singer/songwriter.

DAY, Morris
Born on 12/13/1957 in Springfield, Illinois; raised in Minneapolis, Minnesota. In local band Grand Central with schoolmate Prince. Leader of Minneapolis funk group The Time (Prince's former backing band). Acted in the movies *Purple Rain*, *The Adventures Of Ford Fairlane* and *Graffiti Bridge*.

DAYBREAK
Pop vocal group from Canada.

DAYE, Cory
Born on 4/25/1952 in the Bronx, New York. Female lead singer of Dr. Buzzard's Original Savannah Band.

DAYNE, Taylor
Born Leslie Wunderman on 3/7/1962 in Baldwin, Long Island, New York. White female dance-pop singer.

DA YOUNGSTA'S
Hip-hop trio from Philadelphia, Pennsylvania: brothers Taji and Qur'an Goodman, with Tarik Dawson.

DAYS OF THE NEW
Rock group from Louisville, Kentucky: Travis Meeks (vocals), Todd Whitener (guitar), Jesse Vest (bass) and Matt Taul (drums).

DAYTON
Funk group from Dayton, Ohio: Chris Jones (male vocals), Jennifer Matthews (female vocals), Shawn Sandridge (guitar), Craig Robinson (bass) and Kevin Hurt (drums).

DAY26
R&B vocal group assembled by P.Diddy for the reality TV series *Making The Band 4*: Brian Andrews, Robert Curry, Michael McCluney, Qwanell Mosley and Willie Taylor.

DAZE
Dance trio from Greve, Denmark: Trine Bix (female vocals), Jesper Tonnov and Lucas Sieber.

DAZZ BAND
Funk-dance band from Cleveland, Ohio: Bobby Harris (vocals, sax), Eric Fearman (guitar), Kevin Frederick (keyboards), Kenny Pettus (percussion), Pierre DeMudd and Sennie "Skip" Martin (horns), Michael Wiley (bass), and Isaac Wiley (drums). Martin joined Kool & The Gang in 1988.

DC TALK
Contemporary rock/hip-hop Christian trio from Washington DC: Toby McKeehan, Michael Tait and Kevin Smith.

DEADEYE DICK
Pop-rock trio from New Orleans, Louisiana: Caleb Guillotte (guitar), Mark Miller (bass) and Billy Landry (drums). All share vocals. Group name taken from a Kurt Vonnegut novel.

DEADLY NIGHTSHADE, The
Female disco band: Helen Hooke, Anne Bowen and Pamela Brandt.

DEAD OR ALIVE
Dance group from Liverpool, England: Pete Burns (vocals), Tim Lever (keyboards), Mike Percy (bass) and Steve Coy (drums).

DEAL, Bill, & The Rhondels
Brassy-rock band from Virginia Beach, Virginia: Bill Deal (vocals, organ), Bob Fisher (guitar), Mike Kerwin, Jeff Pollard, Ronny Rosenbaum and Ken Dawson (horns), Don Queinsenburry (bass) and Ammon Tharp (drums). Deal died of a heart attack on 12/10/2003 (age 59).

DEAN, Billy
Born on 4/2/1962 in Quincy, Florida. Country singer/songwriter/guitarist.

DEAN, Debbie
Born Reba Jeanette Smith on 2/1/1928 in Corbin, New York. Died on 2/17/2001 (age 73). Also recorded as Penny Smith, Debra Dixon and Debbie Stevens. Signed by Berry Gordy as the first white artist to chart on his Motown label.

DEAN, Jimmy
Born on 8/10/1928 in Plainview, Texas. Country singer/pianist/guitarist. With Tennessee Haymakers in Washington, DC in 1948. Own Texas Wildcats in 1952. Recorded for Four Star in 1952. Hosted own CBS-TV series, 1957-58; ABC-TV series, 1963-66. Business interests include a restaurant chain and a line of pork sausage. Married country singer Donna Meade on 10/27/1991.

DEAN, Kiley
Born Kiley Dean Bowlin in 1982 in Alma, Arkansas; raised in Orlando, Florida. Female singer.

DEAN & JEAN
Black vocal duo of Welton "Dean" Young and Brenda Lee "Jean" Jones from Dayton, Ohio. Jones died of cancer on 8/4/2001 (age 63).

DEAN & MARC
Brothers Dean and Marc Mathis who later joined with Larry Henley as The Newbeats. Backing vocalists for Dale Hawkins.

DeANDA, Paula
Born on 11/3/1989 in San Angelo, Texas. Teen pop singer/songwriter.

DEATH CAB FOR CUTIE
Pop-rock band from Bellingham, Washington: Benjamin Gibbard (vocals, guitar), Chris Walla (keyboards), Nick Harmer (bass) and Jason McGerr (drums). Gibbard is also one-half of the duo The Postal Service.

DeBARGE
R&B family group from Grand Rapids, Michigan: Eldra "El DeBarge" (vocals, keyboards; born on 6/4/1961), Mark (trumpet, saxophone; born on 6/19/1959), James (keyboards; born on 8/22/1963), Randy (bass; born on 8/6/1958) and Bunny (vocals; born on 3/15/1955). Brothers Bobby and Tommy were in Switch. James was briefly married to Janet Jackson in 1984.

DeBARGE, Chico
Born Jonathan DeBarge on 6/23/1966 in Grand Rapids, Michigan. DeBarge sibling, but not a member of the group DeBarge. Served six years in prison in the early 1990s for conspiracy to sell drugs.

DeBARGE, El
Born Eldra DeBarge on 6/4/1961 in Grand Rapids, Michigan. Male singer/songwriter. Member of DeBarge.

DeBURGH, Chris
Born Christopher Davison on 10/15/1948 in Buenos Aires, Argentina (of Irish parentage). Adult Contemporary singer/songwriter. DeBurgh was his mother's maiden name.

DeCARO, Nick
Born on 2/17/1924 in the Bronx, New York. Died on 11/5/1992 (age 68). Prolific record producer/arranger/conductor.

DeCASTRO SISTERS, The
Female vocal trio from Cuba: Peggy, Babette and Cherie DeCastro. Peggy died on 3/6/2004 (age 83).

DEE, Daisy
Born Desiree Rollocks in 1970 in Curacao, Brazil.
Female dance singer.

DEE, Jimmy, & The Offbeats
Rock and roll band from San Antonio, Texas. Led
by Jimmy D. Fore.

DEE, Joey, & the Starliters
Born Joseph DiNicola on 6/11/1940 in Passaic, New
Jersey. High school classmate of The Shirelles.
Joey first recorded for the Bonus and Scepter labels
in 1960. Joey & the Starliters became the house
band at the Peppermint Lounge, New York City in
September 1960. Actor Joe Pesci played guitar with
band briefly in 1961. Own club, The Starliter, in New
York City in 1964. Band then included, for a time,
three members who later formed The Young
Rascals, and Jimi Hendrix on guitar, 1965-66. In the
movies *Hey, Let's Twist* and *Two Tickets To Paris*.

DEE, Kiki
Born Pauline Matthews on 3/6/1947 in Bradford,
Yorkshire, England. Female pop-rock singer.

DEE, Lenny
Born Leonard DeStoppelaire on 1/5/1923 in
Chicago, Illinois. Male organist. Released over 60
organ instrumental albums from 1955-78.

DEE, Lola
Born in Chicago, Illinois. White pop vocalist.

DEE, Tommy
Born Thomas Donaldson on 7/15/1933 in Vicker,
Virginia. Died on 1/26/2007 (age 73). DJ at
KFXM-San Bernadino at the time of his only hit (first
recorded by Eddie Cochran). Later worked as a
producer/promoter/record company executive in
Nashville.

DEEE-LITE
Dance trio formed in New York: Super DJ Dmitry
Brill (from Kirovograd, Soviet Union), Jungle DJ
Towa "Towa" Tei (from Tokyo, Japan) and vocalist
Lady Miss Kier (Kier Kirby from Youngstown, Ohio).
Group's name inspired by the tune "It's De-lovely"
from the 1936 Cole Porter musical *Red, Hot & Blue*.
Brill and Kier are married.

DEE JAY & The Runaways
Rock and roll band from Spirit Lake, Iowa: "Dee"
Denny Storey (drums) and "Jay" John Senn (bass),
with Gary Lind (vocals), Chuck Colegrove (guitar),
Bob Godfredson (guitar) and Tom Vallie (organ).

DEELE, The
R&B group from Cincinnati, Ohio: Darnell Bristol
and Carlos Greene (vocals), Stanley Burke,
Kenneth "Babyface" Edmonds, Mark "L.A. Reid"
Rooney and Kevin Roberson. Babyface and L.A.
Reid later formed LaFace Records.

DEEP BLUE SOMETHING
Pop-rock group from Dallas, Texas: brothers Todd
(vocals, bass) and Toby (guitar) Pipes, Kirk Tatom
(guitar) and John Kirtland (drums).

DEEP FOREST
Experimental keyboard duo from France: Michel
Sanchez and Eric Mouquet.

DEEP PURPLE
Hard-rock group from England: Rod Evans (vocals),
Ritchie Blackmore (guitar), Jon Lord (keyboards),
Nicky Simper (bass) and Ian Paice (drums). Evans
and Simper left in 1969, replaced by Ian Gillan
(vocals) and Roger Glover (bass). Evans formed
Captain Beyond. Gillan and Glover left in late 1973;
replaced by David Coverdale (vocals) and Glenn
Hughes (bass). Blackmore left in early 1975 to form
Rainbow (which Glover later joined); replaced by
American Tommy Bolin (ex-James Gang guitarist;
died on 12/4/1976). Band split in July 1976.
Coverdale formed Whitesnake. Blackmore, Lord,
Paice, Gillan and Glover reunited in 1984. Hughes
joined Black Sabbath as vocalist in 1986. Gillan left
in 1989 to form Garth Rockett & The Moonshiners;
replaced by Joe Lynn Turner (ex-Rainbow), then
returned in 1992 to take Turner's place.

DEES, Rick
Born Rigdon Dees on 3/14/1950 in Jacksonville,
Florida. DJ working at WMPS-Memphis when he
conceived idea for "Disco Duck." Currently one of
America's top radio DJs (*Weekly Top 40*). Host of
TV's *Solid Gold* (1984) and his own late-night talk
show *Into The Night* (1990).

DEFAULT
Rock group from Vancouver, British Columbia,
Canada: Dallas Smith (vocals), Jeremy Hora
(guitar), David Benedict (bass) and Daniel Craig
(drums).

DEFINITION OF SOUND
Dance duo from London, England: Kevin Clark and
Don Weekes. Featured vocalist is Elaine Vassel.

DEF LEPPARD
Hard-rock group from Sheffield, Yorkshire, England:
Joe Elliott (vocals; born on 8/1/1959), Steve Clark
(born on 4/23/1960) and Pete Willis (guitars; born
on 2/16/1960), Rick Savage (bass; born on
12/2/1960) and Rick Allen (drums; born on
11/1/1963; lost his left arm in an auto accident on
12/31/1984). Phil Collen (born on 12/8/1957)
replaced Willis in late 1982. Clark died of
alcohol-related respiratory failure on 1/8/1991 (age
30). Guitarist Vivian Campbell (Whitesnake, Dio,
Riverdogs, Shadow King) joined in April 1992.

DeFRANCO FAMILY Featuring Tony DeFranco
Family teen pop vocal group from Port Colborne,
Ontario, Canada: Tony (born on 8/31/1959), Merlina
(born on 7/20/1957), Nino (born on 10/19/1956),
Marisa (born on 7/23/1955) and Benny (born on
7/11/1954) DeFranco.

DeGARMO, Diana
Born on 6/16/1987 in Snellville, Georgia. Female
singer. Finished in second place on the 2004
season of TV's *American Idol*.

DEGRAW, Gavin
Born on 2/4/1977 in South Fallsburg, New York.
Adult Alternative singer/songwriter.

DEGREES OF MOTION
Dance group from Brooklyn, New York: Biti, Kit
West, Balle Legend and Mariposa.

DEJA
R&B duo of writer/producer/musician Curt Jones and vocalist Starleana Young. First known as Symphonic Express. Both were members of Slave and Aurra. Mysti Day replaced Young in 1989.

DEJA VU
Dance group from England featuring female singer Tasmin.

DeJOHN SISTERS
Pop vocal duo from Chester, Pennsylvania: Julie (born on 3/18/1931) and Dux (born on 1/21/1933) DeGiovanni.

DEKKER, Desmond, & The Aces
Born Desmond Dacris on 7/16/1941 in Kingston, Jamaica. Died of a heart attack on 5/25/2006 (age 64). Leader of reggae trio with Barrington Howard and Winston Samuel.

DELACARDOS, The
R&B vocal group from Charlotte, North Carolina: Vernon Hill, Harold Ford, Robert Gates and Christopher Harris.

DEL AMITRI
Pop-rock group from Glasgow, Scotland: Justin Currie (vocals, bass), David Cummings and Iain Harvie (guitars), and Brian McDermott (drums).

DELANEY & BONNIE & FRIENDS
Vocal duo: Delaney Bramlett (born on 7/1/1939 in Pontotoc County, Mississippi) and wife Bonnie Lynn Bramlett (born on 11/8/1944 in Alton, Illinois). Married in 1967. Backing artists (Friends) included, at various times, Leon Russell, Rita Coolidge, Dave Mason, Eric Clapton, Duane Allman (Allman Brothers Band) and many others. Friends Bobby Whitlock, Carl Radle and Jim Gordon later became Eric Clapton's Dominos. Delaney & Bonnie dissolved their marriage and group in 1972. Their daughter Bekka was lead vocalist of The Zoo, then joined Fleetwood Mac in 1993. Also see The Shindogs.

DE LA SOUL
Alternative hip-hop trio from Amityville, Long Island, New York: Kelvin Mercer, David Jolicoeur and Vincent Mason.

DELEGATES, The
Novelty trio of Bob DeCarlo, Nick Cenci and Nick Kousaleous. DeCarlo was a DJ in Tampa, Florida. Cenci and Kousaleous owned the Co & Ce record label.

DELEGATION
R&B-disco trio based in England: Jamaicans Ricky Bailey and Ray Patterson, with Texan, Bruce Dunbar.

DELFONICS, The
R&B vocal group from Philadelphia, Pennsylvania: brothers William (born on 1/17/1945) and Wilbert (born on 10/19/1947) Hart, Ritchie Daniels and Randy Cain (born on 5/2/1945). First recorded for Moon Shot in 1967. Daniels left for the service in 1968, group continued as a trio. Cain was replaced by Major Harris in 1971. Harris went solo in 1974.

DEL FUEGOS, The
Rock group from Boston, Massachusetts: Dan Zanes (vocals, guitar), Warren Zanes (guitar), Tom Lloyd (bass) and Woody Giessman (drums).

DELINQUENT HABITS
Latino hip-hop trio from Los Angeles, California: Kemo (David Thomas) and Ives (Ivan Martin) with DJ/producer O.G. Style (Alejandro Martinez).

DELIVERANCE
Pop vocal trio from Three Hills, Alberta, Canada: brothers Paul, Danny and Ken Janz.

DELLS, The
R&B vocal group from Harvey, Illinois: Johnny Funches (lead), Marvin Junior (baritone lead; born on 1/31/1936), Verne Allison (tenor; born on 6/22/1936), Mickey McGill (baritone; born on 2/17/1937) and Chuck Barksdale (bass; born on 6/11/1935). First recorded as the El-Rays for Checker in 1953. Signed with Vee-Jay in 1955. Group remained intact into the 1980s, with the exception of Funches, who was replaced by Johnny Carter (ex-Flamingos; born on 6/2/1934) in 1960. Funches died on 1/23/1998 (age 62).

DELL-VIKINGS, The
Interracial doo-wop group formed at the Air Force Serviceman's Club in 1955 in Pittsburgh, Pennsylvania. "Come Go With Me" featured lead singer Norman Wright with Corinthian "Kripp" Johnson, Don Jackson, Clarence Quick and David Lerchey (the only white member). "Whispering Bells" featured Kripp Johnson as lead singer with Gus Backus (white tenor) replacing Don Jackson. Mercury signed the group (as Del Vikings) in May, 1957 with Gus Backus as lead singer and William Blakely replacing Kripp Johnson (died on 6/22/1990, age 57). Many personnel changes thereafter, including successful R&B singer Chuck Jackson. Quick died of a heart attack on 5/5/1983 (age 46). Lerchey died on 1/29/2005 (age 67).

DELMORE BROTHERS
Country duo from Elkmont, Alabama: brothers Alton (born on 12/25/1908; died on 6/8/1964, age 55) and Rabon Delmore (born on 12/3/1916; died on 12/4/1952, age 36). Both were singers/songwriters/guitarists/fiddle players.

DeLORY, Al
Born on 1/31/1930 in Los Angeles, California. Prolific producer/arranger/conductor. Sang in the pop trio The Balladeers.

DELPHS, Jimmy
Born in Toledo, Ohio. R&B singer.

DELTA RHYTHM BOYS
R&B vocal group formed at Langston University in Oklahoma; later transfered to Dillard University in New Orleans, Louisiana: Carl Jones, Traverse Crawford, Kelsey Pharr and Lee Gaines, with Rene DeKnight (guitar). Pharr died in 1960. Crawford died in 1975. Gaines died on 7/15/1987 (age 73).

DELUNA, Kat
Born Kathleen DeLuna on 11/17/1987 in the Bronx, New York. R&B-reggae singer/songwriter.

DeMARCO, Ralph
Born on 1/22/1943 in the Bronx, New York. Pop singer.

DeMATTEO, Nicky
Born in 1942 in Philadelphia, Pennsylvania. Male teen pop singer.

DEMENSIONS, The
White pop vocal group from the Bronx, New York: Lenny Del Giudice (Lenny Dell), Marisa Martelli, Howard Margolin and Charlie Peterson.

DEM FRANCHIZE BOYZ
Hip-hop group from Atlanta, Georgia: Maurice "Parlac" Gleaton, Bernard "Jizzal Man" Leverette, Jamal "Pimpin" Willingham and Gerald "Buddie" Tiller.

DEMUS, Chaka, & Pliers
Male dancehall reggae duo from Jamaica: John "Chaka Demus" Taylor and Everton "Pliers" Banner.

DENINE
Born Denine Latanzo in Philadelphia, Pennsylvania. White female dance singer.

DENNEY, Kevin
Born on 1/27/1976 in Monticello, Kentucky. Country singer/songwriter/guitarist.

DENNIS, Cathy
Born on 3/25/1969 in Norwich, Norfolk, England. White dance-pop singer/songwriter. Vocalist for D-Mob. Wrote Britney Spears' 2004 hit "Toxic."

DENNY, Martin (The Exotic Sounds of)
Born on 4/10/1911 in Manhattan, New York. Died on 3/2/2005 (age 93). Composer/arranger/pianist. Originated "The Exotic Sounds of Martin Denny" in Hawaii, featuring Arthur Lyman and Julius Wechter (Baja Marimba Band) on vibes and marimba.

DENVER, John
Born Henry John Deutschendorf on 12/31/1943 in Roswell, New Mexico. Died at the controls of a light plane that crashed off the California coast on 10/12/1997 (age 53). To Los Angeles in 1964. With the Chad Mitchell Trio from 1965-68. Wrote "Leaving On A Jet Plane." Starred in the 1977 movie *Oh, God*. Won an Emmy in 1975 for the TV special *An Evening with John Denver*.

DEODATO
Born Eumir Deodato on 6/21/1942 in Rio de Janeiro, Brazil. Dance keyboardist/composer/producer/arranger. Kool & The Gang's producer from 1979-82.

DEPECHE MODE
All-synthesized electro-pop group formed in Basildon, Essex, England: singer Dave Gahan (born on 5/9/1962) and synthesizer players Martin L. Gore (born on 7/23/1961), Vince Clarke (born on 7/3/1960) and Andy Fletcher (born on 7/8/1961). Clarke left in 1982 (formed Yaz, then Erasure), replaced by Alan Wilder (born on 6/1/1959; left in 1995). Group name is French for fast fashion. From 1997-on, group consists of Gahan, Gore and Fletcher.

DERRINGER, Rick
Born Richard Zehringer on 8/5/1947 in Celina, Ohio. Lead singer/guitarist of the rock band The McCoys. Performed on and produced sessions for both Edgar and Johnny Winter's bands; also a producer for "Weird Al" Yankovic.

DeSANTO, Sugar Pie
Born Umpeylia Balinton on 10/16/1935 in Brooklyn, New York; raised in San Francisco, California. Female R&B singer. Member of the James Brown Revue.

DeSARIO, Teri
Born in Miami, Florida. Female dance-pop singer/songwriter. Began recording Christian music in 1983.

DeSHANNON, Jackie
Born Sharon Myers on 8/21/1944 in Hazel, Kentucky. Soft-rock singer/songwriter. On radio at age six. First recorded (as Sherry Lee Myers) for Glenn in 1959. To Los Angeles in 1960. Attained prominence as a prolific songwriter (over 600 to date). Co-writer of mega-pop hit "Bette Davis Eyes." Toured with The Beatles for 26 concerts in 1964. In the movies *Surf Party*, *C'mon Let's Live A Little* and *Hide And Seek*. Married to Randy Edelman.

DESMOND, Johnny
Born Giovanni DeSimone on 11/14/1920 in Detroit, Michigan. Died on 9/6/1985 (age 64). Pop singer. Sang with Bob Crosby, Gene Krupa and Glenn Miller's military band. Featured on the *Breakfast Club* radio show and TV's *Your Hit Parade*.

DES'REE
Born Des'ree Weeks on 11/30/1968 in London, England (West Indian parentage). Black female singer/songwriter.

DESTINY'S CHILD
Female R&B vocal group from Houston, Texas: Beyoncé Knowles (born on 9/4/1981), Kelly Rowland (born on 2/11/1981), LaTavia Roberson (born on 11/1/1981) and LeToya Luckett (born on 3/11/1981). Roberson and Luckett left in early 2000; replaced by Farrah Franklin (born on 5/3/1981) and Michelle Williams (born on 7/23/1980). Franklin left shortly thereafter, leaving trio of Knowles, Rowland and Williams.

DETERGENTS, The
Novelty vocal trio from New York: Ron Dante (of The Archies and The Cuff Links), Tommy Wynn and Danny Jordan.

DETROIT EMERALDS
R&B vocal group from Little Rock, Arkansas: brothers Abrim, Ivory, Cleophus and Raymond Tilmon. In 1970, group reduced to trio of Abrim, Ivory and friend James Mitchell. 1977 group consisted of Abrim Tilmon, Paul Riser, Johnny Allen and Maurice King. "Sweet" James Epps, of the Fantastic Four, was a cousin of the Tilmon brothers. The group's backing band, from 1971-73, later recorded as Chapter 8. Abrim Tilmon died of a heart attack on 7/6/1982 (age 37).

DeVAUGHN, Raheem
Born in Newark, New Jersey; raised in Maryland.
Male R&B singer/songwriter.

DeVAUGHN, William
Born in 1948 in Washington DC. R&B singer/
songwriter/guitarist.

DEVICE
Pop-rock trio from Los Angeles, California: Paul
Engemann (vocals), Holly Knight (keyboards, bass,
vocals) and Gene Black (guitar). Engemann joined
Animotion in 1988. Prolific songwriter Knight was a
member of Spider.

DEVO
Robotic rock-dance group from Akron, Ohio:
brothers Mark (synthesizers) and Bob (vocals,
guitar) Mothersbaugh, brothers Jerry (bass) and
Bob (guitar) Casale, and Alan Myers (drums).

DeVOL, Frank
Born on 9/20/1911 in Moundsville, West Virginia;
raised in Canton, Ohio. Died of heart failure on
10/27/1999 (age 88). Prolific composer/conductor/
arranger. Composed the TV theme for *My Three
Sons*. Married to singer Helen O'Connell from
1991-93 (her death).

DEVONÉ
Born Devoné Shuford in Los Angeles, California.
Male dance singer.

DeVORZON, Barry, & Perry Botkin, Jr.
Songwriting/producing/arranging duo based in
California. DeVorzon was born on 7/31/1934 in
Brooklyn, New York. Founded Valiant Records.
Leader of Barry And The Tamerlanes. Began prolific
songwriting career in the mid-1950s. Botkin was
born on 4/16/1933 in Manhattan, New York. Son of
orchestra leader Perry Botkin, Sr.

DEVOTIONS, The
White doo-wop group from Queens, New York: Ray
Sanchez, Bob Weisbrod, Bob Hovorka, Frank Pardo
and Joe Pardo.

DEXTER, Terry
Born in 1978 in Detroit, Michigan. Black female
singer/songwriter.

DEXYS MIDNIGHT RUNNERS
Pop-rock group from Birmingham, England: Kevin
Rowland (vocals), Billy Adams (guitar), Brian
Maurice (sax), Paul Speare (flute), Jimmy Patterson
(trombone), Micky Billingham (piano), Giorgio
Kilkenny (bass) and Seb Shelton (drums).
Billingham was later with General Public.

DEY, Tracey
Born Nora Ferrari in Yonkers, New York. Pop
singer.

DeYOUNG, Cliff
Born on 2/12/1945 in Los Angeles, California. Adult
Contemporary singer/actor. Starred in the movie
Shock Treatment.

DeYOUNG, Dennis
Born on 2/18/1947 in Chicago, Illinois. Lead
singer/keyboardist of Styx.

D4L
Rap group from Atlanta, Georgia: Lefabian "Fabo"
Williams, Dennis "Mook B" Butler, Adrian "Stoney"
Parks and Carlos "Shawty Lo" Walker. D4L: Down
For Life.

D.H.T.
Electronic-dance duo from Belgium: female singer
Edmée Daenen and Flor "DJ Da Rick" Theeuwes.
D.H.T.: Danger House Trance.

DIABLOS, The
Vocal group from Detroit, Michigan: brothers Nolan
Strong and Jimmy Strong (cousins of Barrett
Strong), with Willie Hunter, Quentin Eubanks and
Bob Edwards. Nolan Strong died on 2/21/1977 (age
43). Edwards died on 3/17/2001 (age 63).

DIAMOND, Joel
Born on 2/20/1943 in Passaic, New Jersey.
Producer/songwriter/record industry executive.
Producer for Engelbert Humperdinck for 11 years.
Worked in music publishing for Mercury, CBS, and
his own company, Silver Blue Records/Productions.
Appeared in the movie *Crossover Dreams*.

DIAMOND, Leo
Born on 6/29/1915 in Brooklyn, New York. Died on
9/15/1966 (age 51). Arranger/lead harmonica player
for The Borrah Minevitch Harmonica Rascals,
1930-46.

DIAMOND, Neil
Born on 1/24/1941 in Brooklyn, New York. Pop-rock
singer/guitarist/prolific composer. Worked as
songplugger/staff writer in New York City; also
wrote under pseudonym Mark Lewis. His real name
is Neil Diamond, however he considered changing
his name to Noah Kaminsky early in his career. First
recorded for Duel in 1962 as the duo Neil & Jack
(Parker), then for Columbia in 1963 ("Clown Town").
Wrote for *The Monkees* TV show. Wrote score for
the movie *Jonathan Livingston Seagull*. Starred in
and composed the music for *The Jazz Singer* in
1980. America's top male vocalist from 1966-86.

DIAMOND REO
Rock group from Pittsburgh, Pennsylvania: Bob
McKeag (vocals, guitar), Frank Czuri (keyboards),
Norm Nardini (bass) and Robbie Johns (drums).

DIAMOND RIO
Country group formed in Nashville, Tennessee:
Marty Roe (vocals), Jimmy Olander (guitar), Gene
Johnson (mandolin), Dan Truman (piano), Dana
Williams (bass) and Brian Prout (drums).

DIAMONDS, The
White doo-wop group from Toronto, Ontario,
Canada: Dave Somerville (lead; born on 4/8/1934),
Ted Kowalski (tenor; born on 6/17/1935), Phil Levitt
(baritone; born on 9/6/1934) and Bill Reed (bass;
born on 1/11/1936; died on 10/22/2004, age 68).
Recorded for Coral in 1955. Debuted on Mercury in
January 1956. Michael Douglas replaced Levitt in
early 1958. Reed and Kowalski replaced in 1959 by
Evan Fisher and John Felten (killed in a plane crash
in 1982). Frequent personnel changes. Dave
teamed with Four Preps' co-founder, Bruce Belland,
as a duo from 1962-69. Bob Duncan (lead) joined in

DIAMONDS, The — cont'd

1978 and re-formed the group, after Felten's death, with new lineup. Group hit the country charts in 1987. The Diamonds and The Crew-Cuts (both from Toronto and both on Mercury) were two of the first white vocal groups to "cover" R&B hits.

DIBANGO, Manu

Born on 2/10/1934 in Cameroon, Africa. Jazz-R&B saxophonist/pianist.

DICK & DEEDEE

Pop vocal duo formed in Santa Monica, California: Dick Gosting and Deedee Sperling. Dick died from injuries suffered in a fall on 12/27/2003 (age 63).

DICKENS, "Little" Jimmy

Born on 12/19/1920 in Bolt, West Virginia. Country singer/guitarist.

DICKY DOO & THE DON'TS

Rock and roll band founded by Gerry Granahan in Brooklyn, New York. Group named after the nickname of Dick Clark's son, Dicky Doo. Group featured Harvey Davis (bass), Ray Gangi (guitar), Al Ways (sax) and Dave Alldred (ex-drummer of Buddy Knox and Jimmy Bowen's Rhythm Orchids).

DIDDLEY, Bo

Born Otha Ellas Bates McDaniels on 12/30/1928 in McComb, Mississippi; raised in Chicago, Illinois. Died of heart failure on 6/2/2008 (age 79). Highly influential rock and roll singer/guitarist. Adopted as an infant by his mother's cousin, Mrs. Gussie McDaniel. Moved to Chicago in 1934. Began recording in 1955 with the Chess/Checker label. Name "bo diddley" is a one-stringed African guitar.

DIDO

Born Florian Armstrong on 12/25/1971 in London, England. Female Adult Alternative singer/songwriter.

DIESEL

Rock group from the Netherlands: Rob Vunderink (vocals, guitar), Mark Boon (guitar), Frank Papendrecht (bass) and Pim Koopman (drums).

DIFFIE, Joe

Born on 12/28/1958 in Tulsa, Oklahoma; raised in Velma, Oklahoma. Country singer/songwriter/guitarist.

DIGABLE PLANETS

Hip-hop trio from New York: Ishmael "Butterfly" Butler, Mary Ann "Ladybug" Vierra and Craig "Doodle Bug" Irving.

DIGITAL UNDERGROUND

Hip-hop group from Oakland, California: Gregory Jacobs ("Humpty-Hump" and "Shock-G"), Ron Brooks ("Money B"), Earl Cook ("Schmoovy-Schmoov"), James Dight ("Chopmaster J") and DJ Fuze. Tupac (2Pac) Shakur was a member in 1991. Group appeared in the movie Nothing But Trouble.

DILATED PEOPLES

Hip-hop trio from Los Angeles, California: Michael "Evidence" Perretta, Rakaa "Iriscience" Taylor and Christopher "DJ Babu" Oroc.

DILLARDS, The

Country-rock group from Salem, Missouri: Rodney Dillard (vocals, guitar), Billy Ray Latham (banjo), Dean Webb (mandolin), Mitch Jayne (bass) and Paul York (drums).

DILLMAN BAND, The

Country-rock group: Steve Solmonson (vocals), Pat Frederick and Steve Seamans (guitars), Dik Shopteau (bass) and Dan Flaherty (drums).

DINNING, Mark

Born on 8/17/1933 in Drury, Oklahoma. Died of a heart attack on 3/22/1986 (age 52). Pop singer. Brother of the Dinning Sisters vocal trio. First recorded for MGM in 1957.

DINO

Born Dino Esposito on 7/20/1963 in Encino, California; raised in Hawaii and Connecticut. Pop-dance singer.

DINO, Kenny

Born on 7/12/1939 in Queens, New York; raised in Hicksville, Long Island, New York. Pop singer.

DINO, Paul

Born Paul Dino Bertuccini on 3/2/1935 in Philadelphia, Pennsylvania. Married for a time to Justine Correlli, a regular on TV's American Bandstand.

DINO, DESI & BILLY

Dino (Dean Martin's son, Dean Martin, Jr.), Desi (Lucille Ball and Desi Arnaz's son, Desiderio Arnaz IV) & Billy (a schoolmate from Beverly Hills, William Hinsche). Dino (formerly married to actress Olivia Hussey and to Olympic skater Dorothy Hamill) was killed on 3/21/1987 (age 35) when his Air National Guard jet crashed.

DINOSAUR JR.

Rock group formed in 1984 in Amherst, Massachusetts: Joseph Mascis (vocals, guitar), Mike Johnson (guitar) and Murph (drums). Murph left in late 1993; replaced by George Berz. Mascis acted in the movie Gas Food Lodging.

DIO

Hard-rock group formed by Ronnie James Dio (born Ronald Padavona on 7/10/1942 in Portsmouth, New Hampshire). Former lead singer of Black Sabbath and Rainbow. Dio consisted of Vivian Campbell (guitar), Jimmy Bain (bass) and Vinny Appice (drums; Black Sabbath).

DION (& The Belmonts)

Born Dion DiMucci on 7/18/1939 in the Bronx, New York. First recorded as Dion & The Timberlanes on Mohawk in 1957. Formed doo-wop group, Dion & The Belmonts, in the Bronx in 1958. Consisted of Dion (lead), Angelo D'Aleo (first tenor), Fred Milano (second tenor) and Carlo Mastrangelo (bass). Named for Belmont Avenue in the Bronx. D'Aleo was in the Navy in 1959 and missed some recording and picture sessions. Dion went solo in 1960 as did The Belmonts. Brief reunion with The Belmonts in 1967 and 1972, periodically since then. Began recording Christian music in 1981.

DION, Celine
Born on 3/30/1968 in Charlemagne, Quebec, Canada. Adult Contemporary singer. Youngest of 14 children. Began performing at age five. Wrote first song at age 12. Married her longtime manager, Rene Angelil, on 12/17/1994.

DIPLOMATS, The
R&B vocal group from Washington DC: Ervan Waters, William Collier, Samuel Culley and Tom Price.

DIRE STRAITS
Rock group formed in London, England: Mark Knopfler (vocals, guitar) and his brother David (guitar), with John Illsley (bass) and Pick Withers (drums). David left in mid-1980, replaced by Hal Lindes (left in 1985). Added keyboardist Alan Clark in 1982. Terry Williams replaced Withers in 1983. Guitarist Guy Fletcher added in 1984. Mark and Guy were also members of The Notting Hillbillies in 1990.

DIRKSEN, Senator Everett McKinley
Born on 1/4/1896 in Pekin, Illinois. Died on 9/7/1969 (age 73). U.S. senator from Illinois, 1950-69.

DIRTY VEGAS
Electronica trio from England: producers Ben Harris, Paul Harris and Steve Smith.

DISCO TEX & THE SEX-O-LETTES
Disco studio group assembled by producer Bob Crewe. Featuring lead voice Sir Monti Rock III (real name: Joseph Montanez).

DISHWALLA
Rock band from Santa Barbara, California: J.R. Richards (vocals), Rodney Cravens (guitar), Scott Alexander (bass) and George Pendergast (drums).

DIS 'N' DAT
R&B duo of sisters Tishea (Dis) and Tenesia (Dat) Bennett.

DISTURBED
Heavy-metal band from Chicago, Illinois: David Draiman (vocals), Dan Donegan (guitar), Steve "Fuzz" Kmak (bass) and Mike Wengren (drums).

DIVINE
Female R&B vocal trio from New Jersey: Nikki Bratcher, Kia Thornton and Tonia Tash.

DIVING FOR PEARLS
Pop-rock group from New York: Danny Malone (vocals), Yul Vazquez (guitar), Jack Moran (keyboards), David Weeks (bass) and Peter Clemente (drums).

DIVINYLS
Rock group from Australia: Christina Amphlett (vocals), Mark McEntee (guitar), Bjarne Olin (keyboards), Richard Grossman (bass) and J.J. Harris (drums). By 1991, group reduced to a duo of Amphlett and McEntee.

DIXIEBELLES, The
Black female trio from Memphis, Tennessee: Shirley Thomas, Mary Hunt and Mildred Pratcher. Backed by pianist Jerry Smith (as Cornbread & Jerry).

DIXIE CHICKS
Female country-pop trio from Lubbock, Texas: sisters Emily Robison (guitar, banjo; born on 8/16/1972) and Martie Maguire (fiddle, mandolin; born on 10/12/1969), with Natalie Maines (lead vocals; born on 10/14/1974). Several radio stations banned their songs after Maines made a controversial statement about President Bush in March 2003.

DIXIE CUPS, The
Black female "girl group" from New Orleans, Louisiana: Barbara Ann Hawkins, her sister Rosa Lee Hawkins and their cousin Joan Marie Johnson. Discovered and managed by singer/producer Joe Jones.

DIXIE DRIFTER, The
Born Enoch Gregory on 12/13/1936 in Harlem, New York. Died on 4/29/2000 (age 63). Black male DJ.

DIXON, Willie
Born on 7/1/1915 in Vicksburg, Mississippi. Died of heart failure on 1/29/1992 (age 76). Blues singer/songwriter/guitarist/producer. Member of the Big Three Trio. Wrote hundreds of blues songs and produced a majority of the Chicago blues records into the 1970s.

DJ COMPANY
Techno-dance group from Germany: producers Stefan Benz, Paul Strand and Louis Lasky, with January Ordu (female singer), and Michael Fielder and Brian Thomas (dancers).

DJ FELLI FEL
Born James Reigart in Rock Hill, South Carolina; raised in Atlanta, Georgia. Popular club and radio DJ.

D.J. JAZZY JEFF & THE FRESH PRINCE
Rap duo from Philadelphia, Pennsylvania: D.J. Jeff Townes (born on 1/22/1965) and rapper/actor Will Smith (born on 9/25/1968).

DJ KHALED
Born Khaled Khaled on 11/26/1967 in New Orleans, Louisiana. Male rapper/songwriter. DJ on Florida radio station WEDR-FM.

DJ KOOL
Born John Bowman in Washington DC. Male rapper.

DJ LAZ
Born Lazaro Mendez on 12/2/68 in Miami. Male rapper.

DJ MIKO
Born Monier Quartrarro in Milan, Italy. Male DJ.

DJ QUIK
Born David Blake on 1/18/1970 in Compton, California. Male rapper. Produced 2nd II None.

DJ SAMMY & YANOU Featuring Do
DJ Sammy was born Samuel Bouriah on 10/29/1969 in Mallorca, Spain. Electronica dance producer. Yanou is a member of Cascada. Do is female singer Dominque Van Hulst.

DJ TAZ
Born Tino Santron McInytosh in Atlanta, Georgia.
Male DJ/rapper.

DMX
Born Earl Simmons on 12/18/1970 in Baltimore,
Maryland; raised in Yonkers, New York. Male
rapper/actor. DMX is short for Dark Man X. Acted in
the movies *Belly*, *Romeo Must Die*, *Exit Wounds*
and *Cradle 2 The Grave*.

DOBKINS, Carl Jr.
Born Carl Edward Dobkins on 1/13/1941 in
Cincinnati, Ohio. Teen pop singer/songwriter.
"Junior" added to last name when Carl started
singing at age 16. First recorded for Fraternity in
1958. Left music, mid-1960s.

DOBSON, Fefe
Born on 2/27/1985 in Toronto, Ontario, Canada.
Black female rock singer/songwriter.

DOC BOX & B. FRESH
Male rap duo from Jacksonville, Florida. Discovered
by producer Joyce "Fenderella" Irby (of Klymaxx).

DR. ALBAN
Born Alban Nwapa on 8/26/1957 in Nigeria; later
based in Stockholm, Sweden. Dance DJ.

DOCTOR & THE MEDICS
Glam-rock group from London, England: Clive
"Doctor" Jackson (lead vocals), brothers Wendi
Anadin and Collette Anadin (backing vocals), Steve
Maguire (guitar), Richard Searle (bass) and Steve
"Vom" Ritchie (drums).

DR. BUZZARD'S ORIGINAL SAVANNAH BAND
Big-band swing-disco band formed in Brooklyn,
New York, by brothers Stony Browder (guitar) and
Thomas "August Darnell" Browder (bass). Featuring
Cory Daye (vocals), Andy Hernandez (vibraphone)
and Mickey Sevilla (drums). Darnell and Hernandez
left in 1980 to form Kid Creole & The Coconuts..

DR. DRE
Born Andre Young on 2/18/1965 in Compton,
California. Pioneer rapper/producer of gangsta rap
(G-funk sound). Co-founder of N.W.A. and World
Class Wreckin' Cru. Produced many hip-hop artists,
including Snoop Dogg, BlackStreet and Eminem.
Founded Death Row Records in 1992 and
Aftermath Records in 1996. Half-brother of Warren
G.

DOCTOR DRE & ED LOVER
Rap duo from Queens, New York: Andre "Doctor
Dre" Brown and James "Ed Lover" Roberts. Hosted
TV show *Yo! MTV Raps*. Starred in the movie
Who's The Man.

DR. FEELGOOD & THE INTERNS
Group is actually bluesman Willie "Piano Red"
Perryman. Born on 10/19/1911 in Hampton,
Georgia. Died of cancer on 7/25/1985 (age 73).

DR. HOOK
Pop group formed in Union City, New Jersey: Ray
Sawyer (vocals; born on 2/1/1937; dubbed "Dr.
Hook" because of eye patch), Dennis Locorriere
(vocals, guitar; born on 6/13/1949), George

Cummings (born on 7/28/1938) and Rik Elswit
(guitars; born on 7/6/1945), William Francis
(keyboards; born on 1/16/1942), Jance Garfat
(bass; born on 3/3/1944) and Jay David (drums;
born on 8/8/1942). John Wolters replaced David in
1973. Bob Henke replaced Cummings in 1975.
Group appeared in and performed the music for the
movie *Who Is Harry Kellerman And Why Is He
Saying Those Terrible Things About Me?* Wolters
died of cancer on 6/16/1997 (age 52).

DR. JOHN
Born Malcolm Rebennack on 11/20/1940 in New
Orleans, Louisiana. Known as "The Night Tripper."
White R&B-rock-blues singer/pianist. Leading artist
of the New Orleans sound while dressed in Mardi
Gras glitter.

DR. WEST'S MEDICINE SHOW & JUNK BAND
'Jug band' from California: Norman Greenbaum
(vocals, guitar), Bonnie Wallach (vocals), George
Ducay (harmonica), Jack Carrington (bass) and
Evan Engber (drums).

DODD, Deryl
Born on 4/12/1964 in Comanche, Texas; raised in
Dallas, Texas. Country singer/songwriter/guitarist.

DODDS, Nella
Born in Philadelphia, Pennsylvania. R&B singer.

DOGGETT, Bill
Born on 2/16/1916 in Philadelphia, Pennsylvania.
Died on 11/13/1996 (age 80). Leading jazz-R&B
organist/pianist. Formed own band in 1938,
recorded with the Jimmy Mundy Band in 1939. With
the Ink Spots, Illinois Jacquet, Lucky Millinder, Louis
Jordan, Ella Fitzgerald, Louis Armstrong, Coleman
Hawkins and many others. Formed own combo in
1952.

DOGG POUND, Tha
Rap duo from Los Angeles, California: Delmar "Dat
Nigga Daz" Arnaud and Ricardo "Kurupt The
Kingpin" Brown. Arnaud is a cousin of Nate Dogg
and Snoop Dogg.

DOG'S EYE VIEW
Rock group from Manhattan, New York: Peter
Stuart (vocals, guitar), Oren Bloedow (guitar), John
Abbey (bass) and Alan Bezozi (drums).

DOKKEN
Hard-rock group from Los Angeles, California: Don
Dokken (vocals; born on 6/29/1953), George Lynch
(guitar), Juan Croucier (bass) and Mick Brown
(drums). Jeff Pilson replaced Croucier in late 1983.
Disbanded in 1988. Lynch and Brown formed Lynch
Mob in 1990. Dokken, Lynch, Pilson and Brown
reunited as Dokken in late 1994.

DOLBY, Thomas
Born Thomas Morgan Dolby Robertson on
10/14/1958 in London, England. New-wave
singer/songwriter/keyboardist. Married actress
Kathleen Beller (played "Kirby Colby" on TV's
Dynasty) in 1988.

DOLCE, Joe
Born in 1947 in Painesville, Ohio. Novelty singer/
songwriter.

DOLENZ, Micky
Born on 3/8/1945 in Tarzana, California. Singer/drummer of The Monkees. Son of actor George Dolenz. Father of actress Amy Dolenz. Under the name Mickey Braddock, played "Corky" in the TV series *Circus Boy* from 1956-58.

DOLLA
Born Roderick Burton on 11/11/1987 in Chicago, Illinois; later based in Atlanta, Georgia. Male rapper.

DOLLAR
Pop duo from England: David Van Day and Theresa Bazzar.

DOLPHINS, The
Pop vocal trio: Carl Edmonson (lead), Paul Singleton and Marvin Lockhard. Edmonson was married to Linda Parrish of 2 Of Clubs.

DOMINGO, Plácido
Born on 1/21/1941 in Madrid, Spain. One of the world's leading operatic tenors. Emigrated to Mexico in 1950. Debuted at the New York Metropolitan Opera in 1968.

DOMINO
Born Shawn Ivy in 1972 in St. Louis, Missouri; raised in Long Beach, California. Male singer/rapper/songwriter.

DOMINO, Fats
Born Antoine Domino on 2/26/1928 in New Orleans, Louisiana. Legendary R&B singer/songwriter/pianist. Heavily influenced by Fats Waller and Albert Ammons. Joined the Dave Bartholomew band, mid-1940s. Signed to Imperial record label in 1949. His first recording "The Fat Man" reportedly was a million seller. Fats had a dozen Top 10 R&B hits (1950-55) prior to his first pop hit. Heard on many sessions cut by other R&B artists, including Lloyd Price and Joe Turner. In the movies *Shake, Rattle And Rock!*, *Jamboree!*, *The Big Beat* and *The Girl Can't Help It*. Teamed with co-writer Dave Bartholomew on majority of his hits.

DOMINOES, The
R&B vocal group formed in New York: Clyde McPhatter (lead tenor), Charlie White (tenor), Joe Lamont (baritone) and Bill Brown (bass), with Billy Ward (piano). James Van Loan replaced White in 1951. David McNeil replaced Brown in 1952. Jackie Wilson replaced McPhatter in 1953. Eugene Mumford replaced Wilson in 1957. Both McNeil and Mumford were members of The Larks. McPhatter died on 6/13/1972 (age 39). Mumford died on 5/10/1977 (age 51). Wilson died on 1/21/1984 (age 49). Ward died on 2/16/2002 (age 80).

DONALDS, Andru
Born in Kingston, Jamaica. Male reggae singer.

DONALDSON, Bo, & The Heywoods
Pop group from Cincinnati, Ohio: Bo Donaldson (keyboards), Mike Gibbons (vocals), Scott Baker (guitar), Gary Coveyou (reeds), Rick Joswick (percussion), David Krock (bass) and Nicky Brunetti (drums).

DONALDSON, Lou
Born on 11/1/1926 in Badin, North Carolina. Black jazz alto saxophonist. Leader of small combos in the East.

DON & JUAN
R&B vocal duo from Brooklyn, New York: Roland "Don" Trone and Claude "Juan" Johnson of The Genies. Don died in May 1982 (age 45). Juan died on 10/31/2002 (age 67).

DON & THE GOODTIMES
Rock and roll band from Portland, Oregon: Don Gallucci (vocals, piano; The Kingsmen), Joey Newman (guitar), Jeff Hawks (tambourine), Buzz Overman (bass) and Bobby Holden (drums).

DON, DICK N' JIMMY
"Cocktail music" trio: Don Sutton (piano; baritone), Dick Rock (bass; tenor) and Jimmy Cook (acoustic guitar; lead singer).

DONEGAN, Lonnie
Born Anthony Donegan on 4/29/1931 in Glasgow, Scotland. Died on 11/3/2002 (age 71). England's "King of Skiffle." Member of Chris Barber's Jazz Band in 1954.

DONNER, Ral
Born Ralph Donner on 2/10/1943 in Chicago, Illinois. Died of cancer on 4/6/1984 (age 41). Pop vocalist. Narrator for the movie *This Is Elvis*. His backing band known as The Starfires.

DONNIE & THE DREAMERS
Italian-American doo-wop group from the Bronx, New York: Louis "Donnie" Burgio, Andy Catalano, Frank Furstaci and Pete Vecchiarelli.

DONOVAN
Born Donovan Leitch on 5/10/1946 in Glasgow, Scotland; raised in Hatfield, England. Pop-rock-folk singer/songwriter/guitarist. Appeared in the movies *The Pied Piper Of Hamlin* and *Brother Sun, Sister Moon*. Father of actress Ione Skye and actor Donovan Leitch, Jr.

DOOBIE BROTHERS, The
Pop-rock group formed in San Jose, California: Patrick Simmons (vocals, guitar; born on 10/19/1948), Tom Johnston (lead vocals, guitar, keyboards; born on 8/15/1948), Tiran Porter (bass) and John Hartman (drums; born on 3/18/1950). Mike Hossack (percussion; born on 10/17/1946) added in 1972 (later replaced by Keith Knudsen). Jeff "Skunk" Baxter (slide guitar; born on 12/13/1948), formerly with Steely Dan, added in 1974. Michael McDonald (lead vocals, keyboards), added in 1975. Johnston left in 1978. Baxter and Hartman replaced by Cornelius Bumpus (keyboards, saxophone), John McFee (guitar) and Chet McCracken (drums) in 1979. Johnston wrote majority of hits from 1972-75; McDonald, from 1976-83. Disbanded in 1983. Re-formed in early 1988 with Johnston, Simmons, Hartman, Porter, Hossack, and Bobby LaKind (percussion; died of cancer on 12/24/1992). Bumpus died of a heart attack on 2/3/2004 (age 58). Knudsen died of pneumonia on 2/8/2005 (age 56).

DOOLITTLE BAND, The
Pop-country studio musicians from Nashville, Tennessee: Hilke Cornelious, Jeff Tweel and Jack 'Stackatrack' Groshmal.

DO OR DIE
Male rap trio from Chicago, Illinois: Dennis Rounk ("AK"), Anthony Round ("N.A.R.D." - which stands for Niggas Ain't Ready to Die) and Darnell Smith ("Belo Zero").

DOORS, The
Rock group formed in Los Angeles, California: Jim Morrison (vocals; born on 12/8/1943), Ray Manzarek (keyboards; born on 2/12/1939), Robby Krieger (guitar; born on 1/8/1946) and John Densmore (drums; born on 12/1/1944). Controversial onstage performances by Morrison caused several arrests and cancellations. Group appeared in the 1969 movie *A Feast Of Friends*. Morrison left group on 12/12/1970; died of heart failure in Paris on 7/3/1971 (age 27). Group disbanded in 1973. 1991 movie based on group's career, *The Doors*, starred Val Kilmer as Morrison.

DORE, Charlie
Born in 1956 in Pinner, Middlesex, England. Female singer/songwriter.

DORMAN, Harold
Born on 12/23/1931 in Drew, Mississippi; raised in Sledge, Mississippi. Died on 10/8/1988 (age 56). Rock and roll singer.

DORSEY, Jimmy
Born on 2/29/1904 in Shenandoah, Pennsylvania. Died of cancer on 6/12/1957 (age 53). Esteemed alto sax and clarinet soloist/bandleader. Recorded with his brother Tommy Dorsey in the Dorsey Brothers Orchestra, 1928-35 and 1953-56.

DORSEY, Lee
Born Irving Lee Dorsey on 12/24/1924 in New Orleans, Louisiana. Died of emphysema on 12/1/1986 (age 61). R&B singer. Prizefighter in the early 1950s as "Kid Chocolate." Major hits produced by Allen Toussaint and Marshall Sehorn.

DORSEY, Tommy
Born on 11/19/1905 in Mahanoy Plane, Pennsylvania. Choked to death on 11/26/1956 (age 51). Esteemed trombonist/band leader. Tommy and brother Jimmy Dorsey recorded together as the Dorsey Brothers Orchestra from 1928-35 and 1953-56. They hosted a musical variety TV show, *Stage Show*, 1954-56. Warren Covington fronted band after Tommy's death.

DOUBLE
Pop duo from Switzerland: Felix Haug (vocals, guitar) and Kurt Maloo (keyboards).

DOUBLE DEE featuring Dany
Dance duo from Italy: Davide Domenella and Donato "Dany" Losito.

DOUBLE EXPOSURE
Disco group from Philadelphia, Pennsylvania: James Williams, Leonard "Butch" Davis, Charles Whittington and Joseph Harris.

DOUBLE IMAGE
Techno-rock band.

DOUCETTE
Rock group from Montreal, Quebec, Canada: Jerry Doucette (vocals, guitar), Mark Olson (keyboards), Donnie Cummings (bass) and Duris Maxwell (drums).

DOUG E. FRESH & THE GET FRESH CREW
Born Douglas Davis on 9/17/1966 in St. Thomas, Virgin Islands; raised in Brooklyn, New York. Male rapper. The Get Fresh Crew: Barry Bee and Chill Will. Early records also featured Slick Rick as M.C. Ricky D. Member of The Stop The Violence Movement.

DOUGLAS, Carl
Born in 1942 in Jamaica; raised in California. Disco singer.

DOUGLAS, Carol
Born Carol Strickland on 4/7/1948 in Brooklyn, New York. Disco singer. Member of The Chantels in the early 1970s. Cousin of Sam Cooke.

DOUGLAS, Mike
Born Michael Dowd on 8/11/1925 in Chicago, Illinois. Died on 8/11/2006 (age 81). Singer with Kay Kyser's band from 1945-50. Hosted own TV talk show from 1961-80.

DOUGLAS, Ronny
Born Ralph Bruce Douglas in New York. R&B singer/songwriter.

DOVALE, Debbie
Born in 1951 in Pittsburgh, Pennsylvania. Teen pop singer.

DOVE, Ronnie
Born on 9/7/1935 in Herndon, Virginia; raised in Baltimore, Maryland. White Adult Contemporary singer. Nearly all of Dove's hits were produced by Phil Kahl (vice president of Diamond Records). First recording on own Dove label in 1958 as Ronnie Dove and the Bell-Tones.

DOVELLS, The
Rock and roll vocal group from Philadelphia, Pennsylvania. Originally called the Brooktones. Consisted of Leonard Borisoff ("Len Barry"; born on 6/12/1942), Arnie Silver, Jerry Gross ("Jerry Summers"), Mike Freda ("Mike Dennis") and Jim Meeley ("Danny Brooks"). Brooks left in 1962. Barry left in late 1963 and recorded solo. Group continued as a trio. Recorded as The Magistrates for MGM in 1968.

DOVE SHACK
Hip-hop vocal trio from Long Beach, California: Mark Makonie, Anthony Blount and Gary Brown.

DOWELL, Joe
Born on 1/23/1940 in Bloomington, Indiana. Pop singer. Signed to Mercury's Smash label by Shelby Singleton, Jr.

DOWN A.K.A. KILO
Born Juan Martinez in Oxnard, California. Mexican-American rapper.

DOWNING, Al
Born on 1/9/1940 in Centralia, Oklahoma; raised in Lenapah, Oklahoma. Died of leukemia on 7/4/2005 (age 65). Black singer/songwriter/pianist. Session work with Wanda Jackson. First recorded for White Rock in 1958. Later pursued a country career.

DOWNING, Will
Born in 1964 in Brooklyn, New York. R&B singer/songwriter/producer.

DOZIER, Lamont
Born on 6/16/1941 in Detroit, Michigan. R&B singer/songwriter/producer. Recorded as Lamont Anthony for Anna in 1961. With the brothers Brian and Eddie Holland in highly successful songwriting/production team for Motown. Trio left Motown in 1968 and formed own Invictus/Hot Wax labels.

DRAFI
Born Drafi Deutscher on 5/9/1946 in Berlin, Germany. Died on 6/9/2006 (age 60). Male pop singer/producer.

DRAGON
Pop-rock group from Auckland, New Zealand: Marc Hunter (vocals), Robert Taylor (guitar), Ivan Thompson and Paul Hewson (keyboards), Todd Hunter (bass), and Neil Story (drums). Hewson died of a drug overdose in 1985. Hunter died of cancer on 7/17/1998 (age 44).

DRAGONFORCE
Hard-rock band formed in London, England: ZP "Zippy" Theart (vocals), Herman Li (guitar), Sam Totman (guitar), Vadim Pruzhanov (keyboards), Frederic Leclercq (bass) and Dave Mackintosh (drums).

DRAKE, Charlie
Born Charles Springall on 6/19/1925 in London, England. Died on 12/23/2006 (age 81). Actor/comedian.

DRAKE, Guy
Born on 7/24/1904 in Weir, Kentucky. Died on 6/17/1984 (age 79). Country singer/comedian.

DRAKE, Pete
Born Roddis Drake on 10/8/1932 in Atlanta, Georgia. Died on 7/29/1988 (age 55). Session steel guitarist.

DRAMA
Born Terrence Cook in 1980 in Atlanta, Georgia. Male rapper. Drama stands for Drastic Retaliation Against My Adversaries.

DRAMATICS, The
R&B vocal group from Detroit, Michigan: Ron Banks, William Howard, Larry Demps, Willie Ford and Elbert Wilkins. Howard and Wilkins replaced by L.J. Reynolds and Lenny Mayes in 1973. Mayes died on 11/7/2004 (age 53).

DRAPER, Rusty
Born Farrell Draper on 1/25/1923 in Kirksville, Missouri. Died of pneumonia on 3/28/2003 (age 80). Male singer/songwriter/guitarist. Known as "Ol' Redhead."

DREAM
Female pop vocal group from Los Angeles, California: Holly Arnstein, Melissa Schuman, Ashley Poole and Diana Ortiz.

DREAM, The
Born Terius Nash in North Carolina; raised in Atlanta, Georgia. Male rapper. Married to Nivea from 2004-07.

DREAM ACADEMY, The
Pop-rock trio from England: Nick Laird-Clowes (guitar, vocals), Gilbert Gabriel (keyboards) and Kate St. John (vocals).

DREAMLOVERS, The
R&B vocal group from Philadelphia, Pennsylvania: Tommy Ricks, Cleveland Hammock, Morris Gardner, and brothers Cliff and Ray Dunn. Backup vocal group for most of Chubby Checker's hits. Named after Bobby Darin's hit record.

DREAM WEAVERS, The
Adult Contemporary vocal group from Miami, Florida: Wade Buff, Gene Adkinson, Lee Turner, Eddie Newson, Sally Sanborn, Mary Carr and Mary Rude.

DRESSLAR, Len
Born Elmer Dresslar on 3/25/1925 in Evanston, Illinois. Died of cancer on 10/16/2005 (age 80). Singer/actor. The memorable voice ("Ho Ho Ho") of the Jolly Green Giant commercials.

DREW, Patti
Born on 12/29/1944 in Charleston, South Carolina. Lead singer of black vocal group The Drew-Vels; included her sisters Lorraine and Erma Drew, and bass singer Carlton Black (married to Erma). Patti first recorded under her own name for Quill in 1966. Left music in 1971.

DREWS, J.D.
Born Jurgen Drews on 4/2/1948 in Berlin, Germany. Progressive rock singer.

DREXLER, Jorge
Born on 9/21/1964 in Montevideo, Uruguay. Latin singer/songwriter.

DRIFTERS, The
R&B vocal group formed to showcase lead singer Clyde McPhatter on Atlantic in 1953. Included Gerhart and Andrew Thrasher, Bill Pinkney and McPhatter (who went solo in 1955). The Drifters had 11 Top 10 R&B hits (1953-55) prior to their first pop hit. Group continued with various lead singers through 1958. In 1959, manager George Treadwell disbanded the group and brought in The Five Crowns and renamed them The Drifters. New lineup included Ben E. King (lead; born on 9/23/1938), Doc Green (baritone; born on 10/8/1934), Charlie Thomas (tenor; born on 4/7/1937) and Elsbeary Hobbs (bass; born on 8/4/1936). Green died on 3/10/1989 (age 54). Hobbs died on 5/31/1996 (age 59). Pinkney died on 7/4/2007 (age 81). The majority of The Drifters' pop hits were sung with three different lead singers: Ben E. King (1959-60), Rudy Lewis (1961-63) and Johnny Moore (1957, 1964-66). Lewis died of a heart attack on 5/20/1964 (age 27). Moore died of respiratory failure on

DRIFTERS, The — cont'd
12/30/1998 (age 64). Leiber & Stoller produced their hits from 1959-63. Many personnel changes throughout career and several groups have used the name in later years.

D.R.S.
Male R&B vocal group from Sacramento, California: Endo, Pic, Jail Bait, Deuce Deuce and Blunt. D.R.S.: Dirty Rotten Scoundrels.

DRU DOWN
Born Danyle Robinson in Oakland, California. Male rapper.

DRU HILL
Male R&B vocal group from Baltimore, Maryland: Mark "Sisqo" Andrews (born on 11/9/1978), James "Woody" Green, Tamir "Nokio" Ruffin (born on 1/21/1979) and Larry "Jazz" Anthony. Green left in March 1999. Group named after Druid Hill Park in Baltimore.

DRUPI
Born Giampiero Anelli on 8/10/1947 in Pavia, Italy. Male singer.

DRUSKY, Roy
Born on 6/22/1930 in Atlanta, Georgia. Died of emphysema on 9/23/2004 (age 74). Country singer/guitarist.

"D" TRAIN
R&B-dance duo from Brooklyn, New York: James "D Train" Williams (vocals) and Hubert Eaves III (keyboards).

D12
Rap group from Detroit, Michigan: Marshall Mathers ("Eminem"), DeShaun Holton ("Proof"), Denaun Porter ("Kon Artis"), Rufus Johnson ("Bizzare"), Ondre Moore ("Swift") and Von Carlisle ("Kuniva"). D-12 is short for Dirty Dozen. Holton was shot to death on 4/11/2006 (age 30).

DUALS
Rock and roll instrumental duo from Los Angeles, California: Henry Bellinger and Johnny Lageman.

DUARTE, Ryan
R&B singer/songwriter.

DUBS, The
R&B vocal group from Harlem, New York: Richard Blandon (lead singer), Cleveland Still, Bill Carlyle, Tommy Grate and Jake Miller. Blandon died on 12/20/1991 (age 57).

DUDLEY, Dave
Born David Pedruska on 5/3/1928 in Spencer, Wisconsin. Died of a heart attack on 12/22/2003 (age 75). Country singer/guitarist.

DUFF, Hilary
Born on 9/28/1987 in Houston, Texas. Actress/singer. Played the title character in both the TV series and movie *Lizzie McGuire*.

DUFFY
Born Aimee Duffy on 6/23/1984 in Bangor, Gwynedd, Wales. Female singer/songwriter.

DUICE
Male rap duo: Ira "LA Sno" Brown (from California) and Anthony "Creo-D" Darlington (from Barbados).

DUKE, Doris
Born Doris Curry in Sandersville, Georgia. R&B singer. Recorded as Doris Willingham for Hy-Monty in 1967.

DUKE, George
Born on 1/12/1946 in San Rafael, California. Jazz-rock keyboardist. Own group in San Francisco during the mid-1950s. With the Don Ellis Big Band and Jean-Luc Ponty. With Frank Zappa's Mothers Of Invention from 1971-75. Also with Cannonball Adderley from 1972-75. Own group from 1977. With Stanley Clarke in the Clarke/Duke Project. The California Raisins' lead vocalist.

DUKE, Patty
Born Anna Marie Duke on 12/14/1946 in Elmhurst, New York. Movie and TV actress. Married to actor John Astin from 1972-85.

DUKE & THE DRIVERS
Rock group from Boston, Massachusetts: Tom Swift (vocals), Sam Deluxe and Cadillac Jack (guitars), Rhinestone Mudflaps (sax), Koko Dee (bass) and Bobby Blue Sky (drums).

DUKE JUPITER
Rock group from Rochester, New York: Marshall James Styler (vocals, keyboards), Greg Walker (guitar), George Barajas (bass) and David Corcoran (drums). Barajas died on 8/17/1982 (age 33). Rickey Ellis (bass) joined in 1983.

DUNCAN, Johnny
Born on 10/5/1938 in Dublin, Texas. Died of a heart attack on 8/14/2006 (age 67). Country singer/songwriter/guitarist.

DUNDAS, David
Born on 4/2/1945 in Oxford, Oxfordshire, England. Pop singer/actor/commercial jingle writer.

DUNN & McCASHEN
Rock duo of singers/guitarists/songwriters Don Dunn and Tony McCashen.

DUPREE, Robbie
Born Robert Dupuis on 12/23/1946 in Brooklyn, New York. Soft-rock singer/songwriter.

DUPREES, The
Italian-American doo-wop group from Jersey City, New Jersey: Joey Vann, Mike Arnone, Tom Bialablow, Joe Santollo and John Salvato. Santollo died of a heart attack on 6/4/1981 (age 37). Vann died on 2/28/1984 (age 40). Arnone died on 10/27/2005 (age 63). Group also recorded as I.A.P. CO.

DUPRI, Jermaine
Born Jermaine Dupri Mauldin on 9/23/1973 in Asheville, North Carolina; raised in Atlanta, Georgia. Rapper/prolific producer. Started performing as an on-stage dancer at the age of 10. Started own So So Def Record label. Discovered Kris Kross and Da Brat. Acted in the movies *In Too Deep* and *The New Guy*.

DURAN DURAN
Synth-pop-dance band from Birmingham, England: Simon LeBon (vocals; born on 10/27/1958), Andy Taylor (guitar; born on 2/16/1961), Nick Rhodes (keyboards; born Nicholas James Bates on 6/8/1962), John Taylor (bass; born on 6/20/1960) and Roger Taylor (drums; born on 4/26/1960). None of the Taylors are related. Group named after a villain in the Jane Fonda movie *Barbarella*. In 1984, Andy and Roger left the group. In 1985, Andy and John recorded with supergroup The Power Station; Simon, Nick and Roger recorded as Arcadia. Duran Duran reduced to a trio in 1986 of Simon, Nick and John. Expanded to a quintet in 1990 with the addition of guitarist Warren Cuccurullo (Missing Persons) and drummer Sterling Campbell (left by 1993; joined Soul Asylum in 1995). The original lineup reunited in 2004. Huge popularity helped by their distinctive MTV music videos.

DURANTE, Jimmy
Born on 2/10/1893 in Brooklyn, New York. Died of pneumonia on 1/29/1980 (age 86). Legendary comedian. Appeared in numerous movies and TV shows.

DUSK
Studio group created by Dawn's producers, Hank Medress and Dave Appell. Lead vocals by Peggy Santiglia of The Angels.

DUVALL, Huelyn
Born on 8/18/1939 in Garner, Texas; raised in Huckabay, Texas. Male rockabilly singer.

DWELE
Born Andwele Gardner in Detroit, Michigan. Male R&B singer/songwriter/producer.

DYKE & THE BLAZERS
R&B-funk group from Buffalo, New York: Arlester "Dyke" Christian (vocals; songwriter), Alvester "Pig" Jacobs (guitar), Bernard Williams and Clarence Towns (saxophones), Alvin Battle (bass) and Willie Earl (drums). Dyke was shot to death in Phoenix on 3/13/1971 (age 28).

DYLAN, Bob
Born Robert Zimmerman on 5/24/1941 in Duluth, Minnesota; raised in Hibbing, Minnesota. Highly influential, legendary singer/songwriter/guitarist/ harmonica player. Innovator of folk-rock style. Took stage name from poet Dylan Thomas. To New York City in December 1960. Worked Greenwich Village folk clubs. Signed to Columbia Records in October 1961. Motorcycle crash on 7/29/1966 led to short retirement. Subject of documentaries *Don't Look Back* and *Eat The Document*. Acted in movies *Pat Garrett And Billy The Kid*, *Renaldo And Clara* (also directed) and *Hearts Of Fire*. Newly-found Christian faith reflected in his recordings of 1979-81. Member of the supergroup Traveling Wilburys. His son Jakob is lead singer of The Wallflowers.

DYNAMICS, The
R&B group from Detroit, Michigan: Samuel Stevenson, Isaac "Zeke" Harris, George White and Fred "Sonny" Baker.

DYNAMIC SUPERIORS
R&B-dance group from Washington DC: Tony Washington, George Spann, George Peterbark, Michael McCalphin and Maurice Washington.

DYNA-SORES, The
R&B group featuring H.B. Barnum, Jimmy Norman and guitarist/vocalist/arranger Réne Hall.

DYNASTY
R&B-dance trio from Los Angeles, California: Kevin Spencer, Nidra Beard and Linda Carriere.

DYNATONES, The
White instrumental pop group from Clarksburgh, West Virginia: Ray Figlar (fife, sax), Gary Van Scyoc (bass), Eddie Evans (piano; replaced by Pat Wallace) and Jack Wolfe (drums).

DYSON, Ronnie
Born on 6/5/1950 in Washington DC; raised in Brooklyn, New York. Died of heart failure on 11/10/1990 (age 40). R&B singer. Acted in the Broadway musical *Hair* and the movie *Putney Swope*.

D'ZYRE
Dance duo from Glendale, Illinois: Troy Guy and Andrea Salazar.

EAGLES
Soft-rock group formed in Los Angeles, California: Glenn Frey (vocals, guitar; born on 11/6/1948), Don Henley (vocals, drums; born on 7/22/1947), Randy Meisner (bass; born on 3/8/1946) and Bernie Leadon (guitar; born on 7/19/1947). Meisner founded Poco; Leadon had been in the Flying Burrito Brothers; and Frey and Henley were with Linda Ronstadt. Debut album recorded in England in 1972. Don Felder (guitar; born on 9/21/1947) added in 1975. Leadon replaced by Joe Walsh (born on 11/20/1947) in 1975. Meisner replaced by Timothy B. Schmit (born on 10/30/1947) in 1977. Frey and Henley were the only members to play on all recordings. Disbanded in 1982. Henley, Frey, Felder, Walsh and Schmit reunited in 1994. Felder left by 2003. Henley, Frey, Walsh and Schmit began their "Farewell 1 Tour" in 2004. Their album *Eagles/Their Greatest Hits 1971-1975* is the all-time biggest selling album in U.S. history with over 29 million copies sold to date.

EAMON
Born Eamon Doyle on 9/19/1984 in Staten Island, New York. Male R&B singer/songwriter.

EARL, Stacy
Born on 12/28/1962 in Boston, Massachusetts. Female dance singer.

EARL-JEAN
Born Earl-Jean McCrea in Brooklyn, New York. Female R&B singer. Member of The Cookies from 1960-65. Younger sister of Ethel "Darlene" McCrea, also of The Cookies and The Raeletts.

EARLS, The
White doo-wop group from the Bronx, New York: Larry Chance, Bob Del Din, Eddie Harder, and Jack Wray.

EARTH OPERA
Pop-rock group from Boston, Massachusetts: Peter Rowan (vocals, guitar; The Rowans), David Grisman (mandolin), John Nagy (bass) and Paul Dillon (drums).

EARTH, WIND & FIRE
R&B-funk group formed in Chicago, Illinois, by producer/songwriter/singer/percussionist/kalimba player Maurice White (born on 12/19/1944). In 1969, White, former session drummer for Chess Records and member of The Ramsey Lewis Trio, formed the Salty Peppers; recorded for Capitol. Maurice's brother Verdine White (born on 7/25/1951) was the group's bassist. Eighteen months later, the brothers hired a new band and recorded as Earth, Wind & Fire — named for the three elements of Maurice's astrological sign. Co-lead singer Philip Bailey (born on 5/8/1951) joined in 1971. Group generally contained 8 to 10 members, with frequent personnel shuffling. In the movies *That's the Way of the World* and *Sgt. Pepper's Lonely Hearts Club Band*. Elaborate stage shows featured an array of magic acts and pyrotechnics. Also see Wade Flemons and Ronnie Laws.

EAST COAST FAMILY
Grouping of artists assembled by Michael Bivins (New Edition, Bell Biv DeVoe). Features Bivins, Another Bad Creation, Boyz II Men, and M.C. Brains, plus newcomers Whytgize, Yvette Brown, Hayden Hajdu, Cali Brock, Tam Rock, Lady V, Tom Boyy, 1010, Fruit Punch, Anthony Velasquez, and Mark Finesse.

EASTERHOUSE
Rock duo from Manchester, England: brothers Andy (vocals) and Ivor (guitar) Perry.

EAST L.A. CAR POOL
Disco group led by conga player Jack J. Gold.

EASTON, Sheena
Born Sheena Orr on 4/27/1959 in Bellshill, Scotland. Pop singer/actress. Acted on TV's *Miami Vice*.

EASTSIDAZ, Tha
Rap duo from Long Beach, California: Tray Deee and Goldie Loc.

EASYBEATS, The
Rock group formed in Sydney, Australia: Steven Wright (vocals), George Young and Harry Vanda (guitars), Dick Diamonde (bass) and Gordon Fleet (drums). Young is the older brother of AC/DC's Angus and Malcolm Young. Young and Vanda went on to form Flash & The Pan.

EASY STREET
Rock group from England: Peter Marsh (vocals), Ken Nicol (guitar), Jim Hall (bass) and Richard Burgess (drums).

EAZY-E
Born Eric Wright on 9/7/1963 in Compton, California. Died of AIDS on 3/26/1995 (age 31). Rapper/producer. Formerly with N.W.A.

EBONYS, The
R&B vocal group from Camden, New Jersey: Jenny Holmes, David Beasley, James Tuten and Clarence Vaughan.

ECHOES, The
White vocal trio from Brooklyn, New York: Tommy Duffy, Harry Doyle and Tom Morrissey.

ECKSTINE, Billy
Born on 7/8/1914 in Pittsburgh, Pennsylvania. Died of heart failure on 3/8/1993 (age 78). R&B singer/guitarist/trumpeter. One of the most distictive baritones in popular music. Nicknamed "Mr. B." His son Ed was the president of Mercury Records.

ECSTASY, PASSION & PAIN
R&B-dance group from New York: Barbara Roy (vocals, guitar), Billy Gardner (organ), Alan Tizer (percussion), Joseph Williams (bass) and Althea "Cookie" Smith (drums).

EDDIE, John
Born in 1959 in Richmond, Virginia; raised in New Jersey. Pop-rock singer/songwriter.

EDDIE & BETTY
Black husband-and-wife pop-jazz piano and vocal duo: Eddie and Betty Cole. Eddie is an older brother of Nat King Cole, who made his recording debut with Eddie Cole's Solid Swingers in 1936 on Decca. Eddie played "The Baron" on TV's *Bourbon Street Beat*.

EDDIE & THE TIDE
Rock group from Berkeley, California: Eddie Rice (vocals), Johnny Perri (guitar), Cazz McCaslin (keyboards), George Diebold (bass) and Scott Mason (drums).

EDDY, Duane
Born on 4/26/1938 in Corning, New York. Began playing guitar at age five. To Phoenix in 1955; began long association with producer/ songwriter Lee Hazlewood. First recorded as Jimmy & Duane (Jimmy Delbridge) in 1955 on Hazlewood's label, Eb X. Preston. Backing band, The Rebels, included top sessionmen: pianist Larry Knechtel (later with Bread); saxmen Plas Johnson, Jim Horn and Steve Douglas (died on 4/19/93, age 55); guitarists Al Casey, his wife Corki Casey and Donnie Owens; and drummers Jimmy Troxel and Mike Bermani. Appeared in movies *Because They're Young*, *A Thunder Of Drums*, *The Wild Westerners*, *The Savage Seven* and *Kona Coast*. Married to Jessi Colter from 1961-68. Originated the "twangy" guitar sound with his '56 red Gretsch 6120 guitar.

EDELMAN, Randy
Born on 6/10/1947 in Paterson, New Jersey. Pop singer/songwriter/pianist. Married to Jackie DeShannon.

EDEN'S CRUSH
Female pop-dance vocal group: Ana Maria Lombo (from Columbia), Ivette Sosa (from New Jersey), Maile Misajon (from California), Nicole Scherzinger (from Hawaii) and Rosanna Tavarez (from New York). Group assembled for TV series *PopStars*.

EDISON LIGHTHOUSE
Studio group from England. Featuring lead singer Tony Burrows (also of The Brotherhood Of Man, First Class, The Pipkins and White Plains).

EDMONDS, Kevon
Born in Indianapolis, Indiana. Male R&B singer. Former member of After 7. Brother of Babyface. Also see Milestone.

EDMUNDS, Dave
Born on 4/15/1944 in Cardiff, Wales. Rock and roll singer/songwriter/guitarist/producer. Formed Love Sculpture in 1967. Formed rockabilly band Rockpile in 1976. Produced for Shakin' Stevens, Brinsley Schwarz and Stray Cats.

EDSELS, The
Black doo-wop group from Campbell, Ohio: George Jones, Marshall Sewell, James Reynolds, and brothers Larry and Harry Green. Jones died on 9/27/2008 (age 71).

EDWARD BEAR
Pop trio from Toronto, Ontario, Canada: Larry Evoy (vocals, drums), Roger Ellis (guitar) and Paul Weldon (keyboards). Took name from a character in *Winnie The Pooh*.

EDWARDS, Bobby
Born Robert Moncrief on 1/18/1926 in Anniston, Alabama. Country singer.

EDWARDS, Dennis
Born on 2/3/1943 in Birmingham, Alabama. Lead singer of The Contours in 1967. Lead singer of The Temptations from 1968-77, 1980-84 and 1987-present.

EDWARDS, Jimmy
Born James Bullington on 2/9/1933 in Senath, Missouri. Rock and roll singer/songwriter.

EDWARDS, Jonathan
Born on 7/28/1946 in Aitkin, Minnesota; raised in Virginia. Pop-country singer/songwriter. Formed bluegrass band Sugar Creek in 1965.

EDWARDS, Tom
DJ at WERE Radio in Cleveland, Ohio, 1951-59. Owner of Record Heaven record store in Cleveland. Died on 7/24/1981 (age 58).

EDWARDS, Tommy
Born on 2/17/1922 in Richmond, Virginia. Died on 10/23/1969 (age 47). Black Adult Contemporary singer/pianist/songwriter. Began performing at age nine. First recorded for Top in 1949.

EDWARDS, Vincent
Born Vincent Edward Zoine on 7/7/1928 in Brooklyn, New York. Died of cancer on 3/11/1996 (age 67). Actor/singer. Star of TV's *Ben Casey*.

EELS
Rock trio formed in Los Angeles, California: Mark Everett (vocals, guitar), Tommy Walter (bass) and Butch Norton (drums).

E-40
Born Earl Stevens on 11/15/1967 in Vallejo, California. Male rapper. Leader of The Click.

EGAN, Walter
Born on 7/12/1948 in Jamaica, New York. Pop-rock singer/guitarist/songwriter.

EIFFEL 65
Male dance trio from Italy: Jeffrey Jey, Maurizio Lobina and Gabry Ponte.

8TH DAY, The
Eight-piece R&B band from Detroit, Michigan: Melvin Davis (vocals, drums), Lynn Harter (vocals), Michael Anthony and Bruce Nazarian (guitars), Carole Stallings (electric violin), Anita Sherman (vibes), Jerry Paul (percussion) and Tony Newton (bass).

EIGHTH WONDER
Pop-dance group from England: Patsy Kensit (vocals), Jamie Kensit (guitar), Geoff Beauchamp (bass) and Steve Grantley (drums). Patsy acted in the movies *Absolute Beginners* and *Lethal Weapon II*; married to Dan Donovan (Big Audio Dynamite) from 1988-91, Jim Kerr (Simple Minds) from 1992-96 and Liam Gallagher (Oasis) from 1997-2000.

EIGHT SECONDS
Pop-rock group from Canada: Andres del Castillo (vocals), Marc Parent (guitar), Frank Levin (keyboards), March Cesare (bass) and Scott Milks (drums).

ELASTICA
Rock group from London, England: Justine Frischmann (vocals), Donna Matthews (guitar), Annie Holland (bass) and Justin Welch (drums). Holland left in the fall of 1995.

ELBERT, Donnie
Born on 5/25/1936 in New Orleans, Louisiana; raised in Buffalo, New York. Died on 1/26/1989 (age 52). R&B singer/songwriter.

EL CHICANO
Latin group formed in Los Angeles, California. Core members: Mickey Lesperon (guitar), Andre Baeza (congas), Bobby Espinosa (organ), Freddie Sanchez (bass) and Johnny De Luna (drums). Singers included Ersi Arvizu, and brothers Rudy, Steve and Jerry Salas. Rudy and Steve Salas later formed Tierra.

EL COCO
Disco studio group led by producers Laurin Rinder and W. Michael Lewis.

EL DORADOS, The
R&B vocal group from Chicago, Illinois: Pirkle Lee Moses (lead), Arthur Bassett, Louis Bradley, Jewel Jones and James Maddox. Moses died of a brain tumor on 12/16/2000 (age 63). Their 1956 recording "Bim Bam Boom" influenced the title of an early 1970s Oldies magazine.

ELECTRIC BOYS
Male rock group from Sweden: Conny Bloom (vocals), Franco Santunione (guitar), Andy Christell (bass) and Niclas Sigevall (drums).

ELECTRIC EXPRESS, The
R&B-funk band produced by Slack Johnson.

ELECTRIC INDIAN, The
Instrumental group assembled from top Philadelphia studio musicians. Some members later joined MFSB.

ELECTRIC LIGHT ORCHESTRA
Orchestral rock band formed in Birmingham, England, by Roy Wood (born on 11/8/1946), Bev Bevan (born on 11/25/1945) and Jeff Lynne (The Move; born on 12/30/1947). Wood left after first album, leaving Lynne as group's leader. Much personnel shuffling from then on. From a group size of eight in 1971, the 1986 ELO consisted of three members: Lynne (vocals, guitar, keyboards), Bevan (drums) and Richard Tandy (keyboards, guitar). Bevan also recorded with Black Sabbath in 1987. Lynne was a member of the supergroup Traveling Wilburys.

ELECTRIC PRUNES, The
Psychedelic-rock group from Los Angeles, California: James Lowe (vocals), Ken Williams and James Spagnola (guitars), Mark Tulin (bass) and Preston Ritter (drums).

ELECTRONIC
Dance duo from Manchester, England: Bernard Sumner (of New Order) and Johnny Marr (of The Smiths).

ELEGANTS, The
White doo-wop group from Staten Island, New York: Vito Picone (lead), Arthur Venosa, Frank Tardogna, Carmen Romano and James Moschella. All were veterans of other groups.

ELEPHANT MAN
Born O'Neil Bryan in 1974 in Kingston, Jamaica. Dancehall reggae singer.

ELEPHANT'S MEMORY
Jazz-rock group from New York: Michal Shapiro (female vocals), Stan Bronstein (male vocals, sax), Richard Ayers (guitar), Richard Sussman (piano), Myron Yules (trombone), John Ward (bass) and Rick Frank (drums). Backing band for John Lennon.

ELEVENTH HOUR, The
Disco group featuring lead singers Michael Gray and Kenneth Kerr.

ELGART, Larry
Born on 3/20/1922 in New London, Connecticut. Alto saxophonist. Brother of Les Elgart.

ELGART, Les
Born on 8/3/1917 in New Haven, Connecticut. Died on 7/29/1995 (age 77). Trumpeter/bandleader. Brother of Larry Elgart. Les's recording of "Bandstand Boogie" was used as the opening theme for Dick Clark's 1950s daily TV show.

ELGINS, The
R&B vocal group from Detroit, Michigan: Saundra Mallett Edwards, Johnny Dawson, Cleotha Miller, Robert Fleming and Norbert McClean. Originally called The Downbeats.

ELLEDGE, Jimmy
Born on 1/8/1943 in Nashville, Tennessee. Discovered by Chet Atkins. Regular at The Pillars nightclub in Biloxi, Mississippi.

ELLIMAN, Yvonne
Born on 12/29/1951 in Honolulu, Hawaii. Played "Mary Magdalene" for the concept album and in the rock opera and movie *Jesus Christ Superstar*. Backing singer for Eric Clapton.

ELLINGTON, Duke
Born Edward Kennedy Ellington on 4/29/1899 in Washington DC. Died of cancer on 5/24/1974 (age 75). Legendary jazz bandleader/composer/arranger.

ELLIOTT, Missy "Misdemeanor"
Born on 7/1/1971 in Portsmouth, Virginia. Female rapper/singer/songwriter/producer. Former member of the group Sista.

ELLIS, Joey B., & Tynetta Hare
Rapper/producer Ellis was born in Philadelphia, Pennsylvania. Female singer Hare was born in Charlotte, North Carolina (member of Soft Touch).

ELLIS, Ray
Born on 7/28/1923 in Philadelphia, Pennsylvania. Saxophonist/arranger/conductor.

ELLIS, Shirley
Born Shirley Elliston in 1941 in the Bronx, New York. R&B singer/songwriter.

ELLIS, Terry
Born on 9/5/1963 in Houston, Texas. Female R&B singer. Member of En Vogue.

ELLISON, Lorraine
Born in 1935 in Philadelphia, Pennsylvania. Died on 8/17/1985 (age 50). R&B singer/songwriter.

ELMO & ALMO
Duo of songwriters Gary "Elmo" Bonner and Alan "Almo" Gordon. Wrote "Happy Together" for The Turtles.

ELMO & PATSY
Husband-and-wife team of Elmo Shropshire and Patsy Trigg; originally known as The Homestead Act. In the movie *The Right Stuff*. Divorced in 1985.

ELUSION
Black female vocal group consisting of two sets of identical twins: Tamica Johnson and Tonya Johnson (from Los Angeles, California) and Michelle Harris and Marie Harris (from San Diego, California).

EMERICK, Scotty
Born on 6/11/1973 in Hollywood, Florida; raised in Vero Beach, Florida. Country singer/songwriter/guitarist.

EMERSON DRIVE
Country band from Grande Prairie, Alberta, Canada: Brad Mates (vocals), Danick Dupelle (guitar), Chris Hartman (keyboards), Pat Allingham (fiddle), Jeff Loberg (bass) and Mike Melancon (drums). Hartman and Loberg left in 2002; replaced by Dale Wallace and Patrick Bourque. Allington left in 2003;

EMERSON DRIVE — cont'd
replaced by David Pichette. Bourque died on 9/25/2007 (age 29).

EMERSON, LAKE & PALMER
Progressive rock trio from England: Keith Emerson (with The Nice; keyboards), Greg Lake (King Crimson; vocals, bass, guitars; born on 11/10/1948) and Carl Palmer (Atomic Rooster, Crazy World of Arthur Brown; drums). Group split up in 1979, with Palmer joining supergroup Asia. Emerson and Lake re-grouped in 1986 with new drummer Cozy Powell (Whitesnake). Palmer returned in 1987, replacing Powell, who joined Black Sabbath in 1990. Powell died in a car crash on 4/5/1998 (age 50).

EMF
Dance-rock-techno-funk group from Forest of Dean, Gloucestershire, England: James Atkin (vocals), Ian Dench (guitar), Derry Brownson (keyboards, percussion), Zac Foley (bass) and Mark Decloedt (drums). Foley died of a drug overdose on 1/3/2002 (age 31).

EMILIA
Born Emilia Rydberg on 1/5/1978 in Sweden. Female dance singer.

EMINEM
Born Marshall Mathers III on 10/17/1972 in Kansas City, Missouri; raised in Detroit, Michigan. White male rapper/actor. Protege of Dr. Dre. First recorded with the rap group Soul Intent in 1995. Created his alter ego, Slim Shady, for his 1999 album *The Slim Shady LP*. Starred in the 2002 movie *8 Mile*.

EMMERSON, Les
Born on 9/17/1944 in Toronto, Ontario, Canada. Lead singer/guitarist of Five Man Electrical Band.

EMOTIONS, The
White doo-wop group from Brooklyn, New York: Joe Favale (lead), Tony Maltese, Larry Cusamanno, Joe Nigro and Dom Colluri.

EMOTIONS, The
Female R&B vocal trio from Chicago, Illinois: sisters Wanda (lead), Sheila and Jeanette Hutchinson. First worked as a child gospel group called the Heavenly Sunbeams. Left gospel, became The Emotions in 1968. Jeanette replaced by cousin Theresa Davis in 1970, and later by sister Pamela. Jeanette returned to the group in 1978.

EMPEROR'S, The
R&B group from Harrisburg, Pennsylvania: Edgar Moore (vocals), Donald Brantley, Calvin Tyrone "Ty" Moss, Ronnie Bowers, Milton Brown Jr. and Steve Stephens.

ENCHANTERS, The
White doo-wop group from New York.

ENCHANTERS, The
R&B trio from Philadelphia, Pennsylvania: Zola Pearnell, Samuel Bell and Charles Boyer. Also backed Garnet Mimms.

ENCHANTMENT
R&B vocal group from Detroit, Michigan: Ed Clanton, Bobby Green, Davis Banks, Emanuel Johnson and Joe Thomas.

ENEA, Laura
Born on 11/16/1966 in White Plains, New York (of Italian parentage). Began singing in Italy; won the Miss Italia Pagent Talent Competition.

ENGLAND DAN & JOHN FORD COLEY
Pop duo from Austin, Texas: Dan Seals (born on 2/8/1948) and John Ford Coley (born on 10/13/1948). In the late 1960s, both were members of Southwest F.O.B. Dan, later a top country artist, is the brother of Jim Seals of Seals & Crofts and cousin of country singers Johnny Duncan, Troy Seals (Jo Ann & Troy) and Brady Seals (Little Texas). Coley appeared in the 1987 movie *Scenes From The Goldmine*.

ENGLISH, Jackie
Born in Los Angeles, California. Female dance singer.

ENGLISH, Scott
Born on 1/10/1943 in Brooklyn, New York. Pop singer/songwriter.

ENGLISH CONGREGATION, The
Pop vocal group from England. Led by singer Brian Keith.

ENGVALL, Bill
Born on 7/27/1957 in Galveston, Texas. Country comedian/actor. Played "Bill Pelton" on TV's *The Jeff Foxworthy Show*.

ENIGMA
Born Michael Cretu on 5/18/1957 in Bucharest, Romania; later based in Germany. Dance producer. Worked with Vangelis and The Art Of Noise. Featured vocalist is Cretu's wife, Sandra.

ENRIQUEZ, Jocelyn
Born on 12/28/1974 in San Francisco, California. Female R&B-dance singer.

ENTOUCH
Male R&B vocal duo of Eric McCaine (from Mt. Vernon, New York) and Free (from the Bronx, New York).

ENUFF Z'NUFF
Rock group from Chicago, Illinois: Chip Z'Nuff (bass), Donnie Vie (vocals), Derek Frigo (guitar) and Vikki Foxx (drums). Frigo died on 5/28/2004 (age 36).

ENUR
Born Rune Kolsch in 1979 in Copenhagen, Denmark. Male DJ/producer.

EN VOGUE
Female R&B vocal group from Oakland, California: Terry Ellis (born on 9/5/1966), Dawn Robinson (born on 11/28/1968; Lucy Pearl), Cindy Herron (born on 9/26/1965) and Maxine Jones (born on 1/16/1966). Herron married pro baseball player Glenn Braggs in June of 1993 and acted in the movie *Juice*. Reduced to a trio when Robinson went

EN VOGUE — cont'd
solo in 1997. Robinson married Andre Allen (of IV Xample) in May 2003.

ENYA
Born Eithne Ni Bhraonain (Gaelic spelling of Brennan) on 5/17/1961 in County Donegal, Ireland. From 1980-82, she was a member of her siblings' folk-rock group, Clannad.

E.O.L.
R&B vocal group from Washington DC: Ike, John, Priest and Scooter.

EPIC SPLENDOR, The
Pop-rock band from Long Island, New York: Paul Masarti (vocals), Vic Canone (guitar), Charlie (organ), Larry Jack (bass) and Eddie Garguilo (drums).

EPMD
Long Island rap duo: Erick Sermon and Parrish Smith (born on 5/13/1968). EPMD: Erick and Parrish Making Dollars. By 1993, duo broke up and Sermon recorded solo and Smith recorded as PMD.

EPPS, Preston
Born in 1931 in Oakland, California. Black bongo player.

EQUALS, The
Interracial British-Jamaican rock group: twin brothers Derv (vocals) and Lincoln (guitar) Gordon, with Eddy Grant and Patrick Lloyd (guitars), and John Hall (drums).

ERASURE
Techno-rock-dance duo from England: Andy Bell (vocals) and Vince Clarke (instruments). Clarke was a member of Depeche Mode and one-half of the duo Yaz.

ERIC B. & RAKIM
Rap duo: DJ Eric Barrier (from Elmhurst, New York) and rapper William Griffin, Jr. (from Long Island, New York).

ERUPTION
Techno-funk-dance group of Jamaican natives based in London: Precious Wilson and Lintel (vocals), brothers Gregory and Morgan Petrineau (guitars), Horatio McKay (keyboards), and Eric Kingsley (drums).

ESCAPE CLUB, The
Pop-rock group formed in London, England: Trevor Steel (vocals), John Holliday (guitar), Johnnie Christo (bass) and Milan Zekavica (drums).

ESPN Presents
ESPN is America's leading cable sports network. The medley below is based on their best-selling series of albums.

ESQUIRES, The
R&B vocal group from Milwaukee, Wisconsin: brothers Gilbert and Alvis Moorer, Millard Edwards, Sam Pace and Shawn Taylor.

ESSEX, The
R&B vocal group formed by members of the U.S. Marine Corps at Camp LeJeune, North Carolina: Anita Humes, Walter Vickers, Rodney Taylor, Billy Hill and Rudolph Johnson.

ESSEX, David
Born David Cook on 7/23/1947 in Plaistow, London, England. Portrayed "Christ" in the London production of *Godspell*. Star of British movies since 1970.

ESTEFAN, Gloria / Miami Sound Machine
Latin pop-dance group from Miami, Florida: Gloria Estefan (born Gloria Fajardo on 9/1/1957 in Havana, Cuba; raised in Miami), her husband Emilio Estefan (keyboards), Juan Avila (bass) and Enrique Garcia (drums). Group later grew to nine members. Gloria and Emilio married on 9/2/1978; both were in a serious bus crash on 3/20/1990. Gloria played "Isabel Vasquez" in the movie *Music Of The Heart*.

ESTELLE
Born Estelle Swaray on 1/18/1980 in Hammersmith, West London, England (African mother/Latin father). Female singer/rapper/songwriter.

ESTUS, Deon
Born in Detroit, Michigan. R&B singer/bassist.

ETERNAL
Female R&B vocal group from London, England: sisters Easther and Vernie Bennett, with Louise Nurding and Kelle Bryan.

ETERNALS, The
White doo-wop group from the Bronx, New York: Charles Girona (lead), Ernest Sierra and Fred Hodge (tenors), Arnie Torres (baritone) and Alex Miranda (bass).

ETERNITY'S CHILDREN
Pop group from Biloxi, Mississippi: Linda Lawley (vocals), Jerry Bounds and Johnny Walker (guitars), Bruce Blackman (keyboards), Charlie Ross (bass) and Roy Whitaker (drums). Blackman later formed Starbuck and Korona.

ETHERIDGE, Melissa
Born on 5/29/1961 in Leavenworth, Kansas. Adult Alternative pop-rock singer/songwriter/guitarist.

E.U.
Funk group from Washington DC. Led by singer/bassist Gregory Elliott. E.U.: Experience Unlimited.

EUBANKS, Jack
Born in Nashville, Tennessee. Country session guitarist/producer.

EUCLID BEACH BAND
Pop duo from Cleveland, Ohio: Richard Reising and Peter Hewlett.

EUROGLIDERS
Pop-rock group from Perth, Australia: Grace Knight (vocals), Crispin Akerman (guitar), Amanda Vincent and Bernie Lynch (keyboards), Ron Francois (bass) and John Bennetts (drums).

EUROPE
Hard-rock group from Stockholm, Sweden: Joey Tempest (vocals), Kee Marcello (guitar), Mic Michaeli (keyboards), John Leven (bass) and Ian

EUROPE — cont'd
Haugland (drums). Founding guitarist John Norum went solo in 1987.

EURYTHMICS
Synth-pop duo: Annie Lennox (born on 12/25/1954 in Aberdeen, Scotland; vocals, keyboards, flute, composer) and David A. Stewart (born on 9/9/1952 in England; keyboards, guitar, synthesizer, composer). Both had been in The Tourists from 1977-80. Formed duo in December 1980. Stewart was married to Siobhan Fahey of Bananarama from 1987-96. Duo split in 1990.

EVAN & JARON
Pop-rock duo of identical twin brothers: Evan and Jaron Lowenstein. Born on 3/18/1974 in Atlanta, Georgia.

EVANESCENCE
Rock group from Little Rock, Arkansas: Amy Lee (vocals), Ben Moody (guitar), Josh LeCompt (bass) and Rocky Gray (drums).

EVANS, Faith
Born on 6/10/1973 in Lakeland, Florida; raised in Newark, New Jersey. Female R&B singer/songwriter. Married to rapper The Notorious B.I.G. from 1994-97.

EVANS, Paul
Born on 3/5/1938 in Brooklyn, New York. Pop singer/songwriter. First recorded for RCA in 1957. Wrote hits "When" for the Kalin Twins, "Roses Are Red" for Bobby Vinton, "I Gotta Know" and "The Next Step Is Love" for Elvis Presley. Wrote the score for the Broadway show *Loot* and the movie *Live Young*.

EVANS, Sara
Born on 2/5/1971 in New Franklin, Missouri. Country singer/songwriter.

EVE
Born Eve Jeffers on 11/10/1978 in Philadelphia, Pennsylvania. Female rapper/songwriter. Star of the Fox TV series *The Opposite Sex*.

EVERCLEAR
Rock trio formed in Portland, Oregon: Art Alexakis (vocals, guitar), Craig Montoya (bass) and Greg Eklund (drums).

EVERETT, Betty
Born on 11/23/1939 in Greenwood, Mississippi. Died on 8/19/2001 (age 61). R&B singer/pianist. Performed in gospel choirs. To Chicago in the late 1950s. First recorded for Cobra in 1958. Toured England in the mid-1960s.

EVERLAST
Born Erik Schrody on 8/18/1969 in Valley Stream, New York. White rock-hip-hop singer/songwriter. Former member of House Of Pain. Played "Rhodes" in the movie *Judgment Night*.

EVERLY BROTHERS, The
Rock and roll-pop-country vocal duo/guitarists/songwriters: brothers Don (born Isaac Donald on 2/1/1937 in Brownie, Kentucky) and Phil (born on 1/19/1939 in Chicago, Illinois). Parents were folk

and country singers. Don (beginning at age eight) and Phil (age six) sang with parents through high school. Invited to Nashville by Chet Atkins and first recorded there for Columbia in 1956. Signed to Archie Bleyer's Cadence Records in 1957. Phil married for a time to the daughter of Janet Bleyer (Chordettes). Duo split up in July 1973 and reunited in September 1983. Don's daughter Erin was married for a short time to Axl Rose of Guns N' Roses in 1990.

EVERY FATHER'S TEENAGE SON
Bill Dean recites a teenager's response to Victor Lundberg's Top 10 hit.

EVERY MOTHERS' SON
Pop-rock group from New York: brothers Dennis (vocals) and Larry (guitar) Larden, Bruce Milner (organ), Schuyler Larsen (bass) and Christopher Augustine (drums).

EVERYTHING
Ska-rock group from Sperryville, Virginia: Craig Honeycutt (vocals, guitar), Rich Bradley, Wolfe Quinn and Steve Van Dam (horns), David Slankard (bass) and Nate Brown (drums).

EVERYTHING BUT THE GIRL
Pop-dance duo formed in London, England: Tracey Thorn (vocals) and Ben Watt (guitar, keyboards, vocals). Group name taken from a furniture store sign on England's Hull University campus.

EVERYTHING is EVERYTHING
Pop-rock duo: Danny Weiss and Chris Hills.

EVE 6
Rock trio from Los Angeles, California: Max Collins (vocals, bass), Jon Siebels (guitar) and Tony Fagenson (drums).

EXCELLENTS, The
White doo-wop group from Brooklyn, New York: John Kuse (lead), George Kuse, Denis Kestenbaum, Joel Feldman, Phil Sanchez and Chuck Epstein.

EXCELS, The
White doo-wop group from the Bronx, New York: Fred Orange (lead), Benito Travieso, Raphael Diaz, Harry Hilliard and Joe Robles.

EXCITERS, The
R&B vocal group from Jamaica, New York: Herb Rooney, his wife Brenda Reid, Carol Johnson and Lillian Walker. Rooney and Reid are the parents of prolific producer Antonio "L.A." Reid (of The Deele). Johnson died on 5/7/2007 (age 62).

EX-GIRLFRIEND
Female R&B vocal group from Brooklyn, New York: Julia Roberson, Monica Boyd, Tisha Hunter and Stacy Francis.

EXILE
Pop-country group formed in Richmond, Kentucky: Jimmy Stokley (vocals), J.P. Pennington (vocals, guitar), Buzz Cornelison (keyboards), Sonny Lemaire (bass) and Steve Goetzman (drums).

EXPOSE
Female dance trio based in Miami, Florida: Ann Curless (born on 10/7/1965), Jeanette Jurado (born on 11/14/1966) and Gioia Bruno (born on 6/11/1965). Assembled by producer/songwriter Lewis Martineé. Kelly Moneymaker replaced Bruno in 1992.

EXTREME
Pop-rock group from Boston, Massachusetts: Gary Cherone (vocals), Nuno Bettencourt (guitar; born in Portugal), Pat Badger (bass) and Paul Geary (drums). Cherone became lead singer of Van Halen in September 1996.

EYE TO EYE
Pop duo: vocalist Deborah Berg from Seattle, Washington, and pianist Julian Marshall (of Marshall Hain) from England.

FABARES, Shelley
Born Michele Fabares on 1/19/1944 in Santa Monica, California. Pop singer/actress. Niece of actress Nanette Fabray. Starred with Elvis Presley in three of his movies. Played teenager "Mary Stone" on *The Donna Reed Show*. Married to record producer Lou Adler from 1964-67. Cast member of several TV series since 1972, among them *One Day At A Time* and *Coach*. Married actor Mike Farrell on 1/31/1984.

FAB 5, The
Gathering of rap acts Heltah Skeltah and Originoo Gunn Clappaz.

FABIAN
Born Fabian Forte on 2/6/1943 in Philadelphia, Pennsylvania. Rock and roll teen idol. Discovered at age 14 (because of his good looks and intriguing name) by a chance meeting with Bob Marcucci, owner of Chancellor Records. Began acting career in 1959 with the movie *Hound Dog Man*. His son, Christian Forte, wrote the screenplay for the 1997 movie *Albino Alligator*.

FABIAN, Lara
Born Lara Crokaert on 1/9/1970 in Etterbeek, Belgium. Female Adult Contemporary singer/songwriter.

FABOLOUS
Born John Jackson on 11/18/1979 in Brooklyn, New York. Male rapper.

FABRIC, Bent
Born Bent Fabricius-Bjerre on 12/7/1924 in Copenhagen, Denmark. Male pianist.

FABU
Female R&B duo: Janine Williams and Christina Hayes.

FABULOUS COUNTS
Funk band from Detroit, Michigan: Mose Davis (vocals, organ), Leroy Emmanuel (guitar), Demetrus Cates (sax), Jim White (sax), Raoul Keith Mangrum (percussion) and Andrew Gibson (drums). Recorded as The Counts for Westbound Records. Also recorded as Lunar Funk.

FABULOUS POODLES
Rock group from England: Tony DeMeur (vocals, guitar), Bobby Valentino (violin), Richie Robertson (bass) and Bryn Burrows (drums).

FABULOUS RHINESTONES, The
Rock trio from Chicago, Illinois: Kal David (vocals, guitar), Harvey Brooks (bass) and Martin Grebb (vocals, keyboards; The Buckinghams).

FABULOUS THUNDERBIRDS, The
Male blues-rock group from Austin, Texas: Kim Wilson (vocals, harmonica), Jimmie Vaughan (guitar; older brother of Stevie Ray Vaughan), Keith Ferguson (bass) and Fran Christina (drums). Preston Hubbard replaced Ferguson in late 1981. Vaughan appeared in the 1989 movie *Great Balls Of Fire* and recorded with Stevie Ray as The Vaughan Brothers in 1990. Ferguson died of liver failure on 4/29/1997 (age 49).

FACENDA, Tommy
Born on 11/10/1939 in Portsmouth, Virginia. Backup vocals with Gene Vincent from 1957-58. Nicknamed "Bubba." Discovered by Frank Guida, who wrote Facenda's hit and discovered Gary (U.S.) Bonds. First recorded for Nasco in 1958. Later became a firefighter in Virginia.

FACE TO FACE
Rock group from Boston, Massachusetts: Laurie Sargent (vocals), brothers Angelo and Stuart Kimball (guitars), John Ryder (bass) and William Beard (drums).

FACHIN, Eria
Born in 1960 in Hamilton, Ontario, Canada. Died of cancer on 5/9/1996 (age 36). Female dance singer.

FACTS OF LIFE
R&B vocal trio formed by Millie Jackson, originally known as The Gospel Truth: Jean Davis (younger sister of Tyrone Davis), Keith William (Imperials, Flamingos) and Chuck Carter.

FAGEN, Donald
Born on 1/10/1948 in Passaic, New Jersey. Backup keyboardist/vocalist with Jay & The Americans. At New York's Bard College, formed band with Walter Becker and drummer-turned-comic actor Chevy Chase. Fagen and Becker formed Steely Dan in 1972.

FAGIN, Joe
Born in Liverpool, England. Pop singer/songwriter/bassist.

FAIR, Yvonne
Born in 1942 in Virginia. Died on 3/6/1994 (age 51). R&B-dance singer. Toured with James Brown Revue. Appeared in the movie *Lady Sings The Blues*. Married to Sammy Strain of The O'Jays.

FAIRCHILD, Barbara
Born on 11/12/1950 in Knobel, Arkansas. Country singer/songwriter.

FAIRGROUND ATTRACTION
Pop group from England: Eddi Reader (female vocals), Mark Nevin (guitar), Simon Edwards (bass) and Roy Dodds (drums).

FAITH, Adam
Born Terence Nelhams on 6/23/1940 in Acton, London, England. Died of a heart attack on 3/7/2003 (age 62). Pop singer/actor.

FAITH, Percy
Born on 4/7/1908 in Toronto, Ontario, Canada. Died of cancer on 2/9/1976 (age 67). Orchestra leader. Moved to the U.S. in 1940. Joined Columbia Records in 1950 as conductor/arranger for company's leading singers (Tony Bennett, Doris Day, Rosemary Clooney, Johnny Mathis and others).

FAITH BAND
Pop-rock group from Indianapolis, Indiana: Carl Storie (vocals), David Bennett (guitar), John Cascella (keyboards), Mark Cawley (bass) and David Barnes (drums).

FAITHFULL, Marianne
Born on 12/29/1946 in Hampstead, London, England. Discovered by The Rolling Stones' manager, Andrew Loog Oldham. Involved in a long, tumultuous relationship with Mick Jagger. Appeared in several stage and screen productions. Married British art gallery owner John Dunbar, Vibrators bassist Ben Brierly and American playwright Giorgio Dellaterza.

FAITH, HOPE & CHARITY
R&B-dance vocal trio from Tampa, Florida: Brenda Hilliard, Albert Bailey and Zulema Cusseaux. Cusseaux went solo in 1971. Hilliard and Bailey continued as a duo until 1974 when joined by Diane Destry.

FAITHLESS
Electronica-dance group from London, England: Rollo Armstrong, Sister Bliss, Jamie Catto and Maxi Jazz.

FAITH NO MORE
Rock group from San Francisco, California: Michael "Vlad Dracula" Patton (vocals), Jim Martin (guitar), Roddy Bottum (keyboards), Billy Gould (bass) and Mike Bordin (drums).

FALCO
Born Johann Holzel on 2/19/1957 in Vienna, Austria. Died in a car crash on 2/6/1998 (age 40). Male dance singer/songwriter. Took his name from professional skier Falco Weisspflog.

FALCON, Billy
Born on 7/13/1956 in Valley Stream, New York. Rock singer/songwriter/guitarist.

FALCONS, The
R&B vocal group from Detroit, Michigan: Eddie Floyd (lead vocals; replaced in 1961 by Wilson Pickett), Bonny "Mack" Rice, Joe Stubbs (brother of the Four Tops' Levi Stubbs), Willie Schofield and Lance Finney. Stubbs died on 1/19/1998 (age 57). Backing band, Ohio Untouchables, later became Ohio Players.

FALL OUT BOY
Punk-pop band from Wilmette, Illinois: Patrick Stump (vocals, guitar), Joe Trohman (guitar), Pete Wentz (bass) and Andy Hurley (drums). Wentz married Ashlee Simpson on 5/17/2008.

FALTERMEYER, Harold
Born on 10/5/1952 in Munich, Germany. Keyboardist/songwriter/arranger/producer. Arranged and played keyboards on the movie scores of *Midnight Express, American Gigolo* and *Top Gun.*

FALTSKOG, Agnetha
Born on 4/5/1950 in Jonkoping, Sweden. Member of Abba.

FAME, Georgie
Born Clive Powell on 6/26/1943 in Leigh, Lancashire, England. Began as a pianist with Billy Fury's backup group, The Blue Flames (became their lead singer in 1962 after Fury dropped them).

FAMILY, The
R&B group from Minneapolis featuring The Time members St. Paul (Paul Peterson), Jerome Benton and Jellybean Johnson. Female vocalist Susannah is the twin sister of Wendy Melvoin (Prince's Revolution, Wendy & Lisa), sister of the late Jonathan Melvoin (The Smashing Pumpkins) and the daughter of jazz pianist Mike Melvoin (The Plastic Cow).

FANCY
Pop-rock group from England: Helen Caunt (vocals), Ray Fenwick (guitar), Alan Hawkshaw (keyboards), Mo Foster (bass) and Henry Spinetti (drums). Caunt and Spinetti left after "Wild Thing"; replaced by Annie Kavanagh (vocals) and Les Binks (drums).

FANNY
Female rock group from Los Angeles, California: sisters June (vocals, guitar) and Jean (vocals, bass) Millington, Nicole Barclay (keyboards) and Alice DeBuhr (drums). Jean and Alice left in 1974; replaced by Patti Quatro (bass; sister of Suzi Quatro) and Brie Howard (drums).

FANTASIA
Born Fantasia Barrino on 6/30/1984 in High Point, North Carolina. Female R&B singer. Winner on the 2004 season of TV's *American Idol.*

FANTASTIC FOUR
R&B vocal group from Detroit, Michigan: "Sweet" James Epps, Robert and Joseph Pruitt, and Toby Childs. Robert Pruitt and Childs later replaced by Cleveland Horne and Ernest Newsome. Epps was cousin of the Tilmon brothers of the Detroit Emeralds. Epps died of a heart attack on 9/7/2000.

FANTASTIC JOHNNY C, The
Born Johnny Corley on 4/28/1943 in Greenwood, South Carolina. R&B singer. Produced and managed by Jesse James.

FANTASTICS, The
R&B group from Brooklyn, New York: Don Haywood, Jerome Ramos, John Cheetom and Alfred Pitts. Don, Jerome and John were members of The Velours.

FANTASY
Rock group from Miami, Florida: Vincent DeMeo (guitar), Lydia Miller (female vocals), Mario Russo (organ), David Robbins (bass) and Greg Kimple (drums).

FARAGHER BROS., The
Soft-rock group from Redlands, California: brothers Danny, Jimmy, Tommy, Davey, Marty and Pammy Faragher. Davey joined Cracker in 1992.

FAR CORPORATION
Far: name of producer Frank Farian's studio in Rosbach, Germany. This assemblage of European and American musicians contains three members of Toto: Bobby Kimball (lead vocals), Steve Lukather (guitars) and David Paich (keyboards). Robin McAuley (McAuley Schenker Group) was also a member. Farian created Boney M and Milli Vanilli.

FARDON, Don
Born Donald Maughn on 8/19/1943 in Coventry, West Midlands, England. Lead singer of British rock group The Sorrows ("Bubbled Under" in 1965).

FARGO, Donna
Born Yvonne Vaughan on 11/10/1945 in Mount Airy, North Carolina. Recorded for Ramco in 1969. Worked as a high school teacher until June 1972. Fargo was stricken with multiple sclerosis in 1979.

FARM, The
Pop-rock-dance group from Liverpool, England: Peter Hooton (vocals), Steve Grimes and Keith Mullin (guitars), Ben Leach (keyboards), Carl Hunter (bass) and Roy Boulter (drums).

FARNHAM, John
Born on 7/1/1949 in Dagenham, Essex, England; raised in Australia. Lead singer of Little River Band from 1983-87.

FARRIS, Dionne
Born in 1969 in Bordentown, New Jersey. Female R&B singer. Former member of Arrested Development.

FARROW, Cee
Born in Germany. Male synth-pop-dance singer.

FASCINATIONS, The
Female R&B vocal group from Detroit, Michigan: Shirley Walker, Joanne Levell, Bernadine Boswell and Fern Bledsoe.

FASTBALL
Rock trio from Austin, Texas: Miles Zuniga (vocals, guitar), Tony Scalzo (vocals, bass) and Joey Shuffield (drums).

FASTER PUSSYCAT
Hard-rock group from Los Angeles, California: Taime Downe (vocals), Greg Steele and Brent Muscat (guitars), Eric Stacy (bass), and Mark Michals (drums). Group name taken from the 1965 action movie *Faster Pussycat! Kill! Kill!*

FATBACK
Funk group from New Jersey: Bill Curtis (vocals, drums), Johnny King (guitar), Saunders McCrae (keyboards), Earl Shelton, George Williams, George

Adam and Richard Cromwell (horns) and Johnny Flippin (bass).

FAT BOYS
Rap trio from Brooklyn, New York: Mark "Prince Markie Dee" Morales (born on 2/19/1960), Darren "The Human Beat Box" Robinson and Damon "Kool Rock-ski" Wimbley. Combined weight of over 750 pounds. Appeared in the 1987 movie *Disorderlies*. Robinson died of cardiac arrest on 12/10/1995 (age 28).

FATBOY SLIM
Born Norman Cook on 7/31/1963 in Bromley, London, England. Techno-house instrumentalist. Former member of The Housemartins, Beats International and The Mighty Dub Kats.

FATHER MC
Born Timothy Brown in Harlem, New York. Dancehall reggae singer. Dropped the MC from his name in mid-1993.

FAT JOE
Born Joseph Cartagena on 8/19/1970 in the Bronx, New York. Male rapper. Member of Terror Squad.

FAVORITE ANGEL
Pop duo from Boston, Massachusetts: songwriter/guitarist Joe McGee and singer Gigi.

FEATHER
Pop group from Los Angeles, California: Steve Woodard, Barry Collings, Roger White, Larry Sims and Peter Bregante. Woodard died of respiratory failure on 10/8/2000 (age 53).

FEATHERS, Charlie
Born on 6/12/1932 in Holly Springs, Mississippi. Died of a stroke on 8/29/1998 (age 66). Rockabilly pioneer on King Records.

FEIST
Born Leslie Feist on 2/13/1976 in Amherst, Nova Scotia, Canada. Female singer/songwriter.

FELDER, Don
Born on 9/21/1947 in Gainesville, Florida. Singer/songwriter/guitarist. Member of the Eagles.

FELDMAN, Victor, Quartet
Born on 4/7/1934 in London, England. Died on 5/12/1987 (age 53). Jazz pianist/vibist. Worked with Cannonball Adderley and Miles Davis. Quartet consisted of Feldman (piano), Buddy Collette (sax), Leroy Vinnegar (bass) and Ron Jefferson (drums).

FELICIANO, José
Born on 9/8/1945 in Lares, Puerto Rico; raised in Spanish Harlem, New York. Blind since birth. Virtuoso acoustic guitarist. First performed at age nine. First recorded for Spanish language TV series in the mid-1960s. Appeared in several TV shows and own specials. Composed score for TV's *Chico & The Man*.

FELLER, Dick
Born on 1/2/1943 in Bronaugh, Missouri. Country singer/songwriter/guitarist.

FELLINI, Suzanne
Born on 8/6/1955 in Manhattan, New York. Rock singer/actress.

FELONY
Rock group from Los Angeles, California: brothers Jeffrey Scott (vocals) and Curly Joe (guitar) Spry, Danny Sands (keyboards), Louis Ruiz (bass) and Arty Blea (drums).

FELTS, Narvel
Born Albert Narvel Felts on 11/11/1938 near Keiser, Arkansas; raised near Bernie, Missouri. Rockabilly-country singer/songwriter/guitarist.

FENDER, Freddy
Born Baldemar Huerta on 6/4/1937 in San Benito, Texas. Died of cancer on 10/14/2006 (age 69). Mexican-American singer/guitarist. First recorded in Spanish under his real name for Falcon in 1956. In the movie *The Milagro Beanfield War*. Joined the Texas Tornados in 1990.

FENDERMEN, The
Rock and roll duo of Phil Humphrey (from Stoughton, Wisconsin) and Jim Sundquist (from Niagara, Wisconsin); both were born on 11/26/1937. Formed at the University of Wisconsin-Madison. Named after the Fender guitar.

FERGIE
Born Stacy Ferguson on 3/27/1975 in Whittier, California; raised in Hacienda Heights, California. Female singer/songwriter/actress. Regular on TV's *Kids Incorporated* from 1984-89; also acted in other TV shows and movies. Member of the groups Wild Orchid and Black Eyed Peas.

FERGUSON, Helena
Born in Detroit, Michigan. Female R&B singer.

FERGUSON, Jay
Born on 5/10/1947 in Burbank, California. Before going solo, formed and led the rock groups Spirit and Jo Jo Gunne.

FERGUSON, Johnny
Born on 3/22/1937 in Nashville, Tennessee. Pop singer. Worked as a DJ in the late 1950s.

FERGUSON, Maynard
Born on 5/4/1928 in Verdun, Quebec, Canada. Died of liver failure on 8/23/2006 (age 78). White jazz trumpeter. Moved to the U.S. in 1949. Played for Charlie Barnet and then Stan Kenton's Band (1950-56). Chuck Mangione played in Ferguson's band.

FERKO STRING BAND
String band from Philadelphia, Pennsylvania; directed by William Connors. String bands parade annually in Philadelphia's famed New Year's Day Mummers Parade. The Nu Tornados and the Quaker City Boys were also Philadelphia string bands.

FERRANTE & TEICHER
Piano duo: Arthur Ferrante (born on 9/7/1921 in Manhattan, New York) and Louis Teicher (born on 8/24/1924 in Wilkes-Barre, Pennsylvania; died of a heart attack on 8/3/2008, age 83). Met as children

while attending Manhattan's Juilliard School. First recorded for Columbia in 1953.

FERRAS
Born Ferras Alqaisi in 1982 in Gillespie, Illinois; later based in Los Angeles, California. Male singer/ songwriter/keyboardist.

FERRY, Bryan
Born on 9/26/1945 in County Durham, England. Pop-rock singer/songwriter. Lead singer of Roxy Music. Married to socialite Lucy Helmore from 1982-2003.

FESTIVAL
Disco studio group assembled by producer Boris Midney.

FEVER TREE
Psychedelic-rock group from Houston, Texas: Dennis Keller (vocals), Michael Knust (guitar), Rob Landes (piano), E.E. Wolfe (bass) and John Tuttle (drums). Knust died of heart failure on 9/15/2003 (age 54).

FEW GOOD MEN, A
R&B vocal group from Atlanta, Georgia: Aaron Hilliard, David Morris, Tony Amey and Demail Burks.

FIASCO, Lupe
Born Wasalu Jaco on 2/17/1982 in Chicago, Illinois. Male rapper/songwriter.

FIDELITY'S, The
Black male doo-wop group from Albany, New York: Emmett Smith (lead), Maurice Newton and Robert McCann (tenors), Earl Thorpe (bass) and Arthur Manning (baritone).

FIELD, Sally
Born on 11/6/1946 in Pasadena, California. Prolific TV/movie actress.

FIELD MOB
Male rap duo from Albany, Georgia: Darion "Smoke" Crawford and "Shawn Jay" Johnson.

FIELDS, Ernie
Born on 8/26/1905 in Nacogdoches, Texas. Died on 5/11/1997 (age 91). Black trombonist/pianist/ bandleader/arranger.

FIELDS, Richard "Dimples"
Born in 1942 in New Orleans, Louisiana; raised in San Francisco, California. Died of a stroke on 1/12/2000 (age 57). R&B singer/songwriter/ producer.

FIESTAS, The
R&B vocal group from Newark, New Jersey: Tommy Bullock (lead), Eddie Morris (tenor), Sam Ingalls (baritone) and Preston Lane (bass).

5TH DIMENSION, The
Adult Contemporary-R&B vocal group formed in Los Angeles, California: Marilyn McCoo (born on 9/30/1943), Billy Davis, Jr. (born on 6/26/1940), Florence LaRue (born on 2/4/1944), LaMonte McLemore (born on 9/17/1939) and Ron Townson (born on 1/20/1933). McLemore and McCoo had been in the Hi-Fi's; Townson and Davis had been

5TH DIMENSION, The — cont'd
with groups in St. Louis. First called the Versatiles (recorded on the Bronco label in 1966). McCoo and Davis were married on 7/26/1969 and recorded as a duo since 1976. Townson died of kidney failure on 8/2/2001 (age 68).

FIFTH ESTATE, The
Pop band from Stamford, Connecticut: Wayne Wadhams (vocals, keyboards), Rick Engler (guitar), Bill Shute (guitar), Doug Ferrara (bass), and Ken Evans (drums). Wadhams died on 8/19/2008 (age 61).

50 CENT
Born Curtis Jackson on 7/6/1975 in Jamaica, Queens, New York. Male rapper/songwriter. Member of G-Unit. Starred in the 2005 movie *Get Rich Or Die Tryin'*.

FIGURES ON A BEACH
Techno-rock group from Boston, Massachusetts: Anthony Kaczynski (vocals), John Rolski (guitar), Christopher Ewen (keyboards), Percy Tell (bass) and Michael Smith (drums).

FILTER
Industrial-rock duo from Cleveland, Ohio: Richard Patrick (vocals, guitar, bass) and Brian Liesegang (keyboards, drums). Both worked with Trent Reznor in Nine Inch Nails.

FINE YOUNG CANNIBALS
Rock trio from Birmingham, England: Roland Gift (vocals) and English Beat members David Steele (bass) and Andy Cox (guitar). Band name taken from the 1960 movie *All The Fine Young Cannibals*. Group appeared in the movie *Tin Men*. Gift acted in the movies *Sammy And Rosie Get Laid* and *Scandal*.

FINGER ELEVEN
Rock band from Burlington, Ontario, Canada: brothers Scott Anderson (vocals) and Sean Anderson (bass), Rick Jackett (guitar), James Black (guitar) and Rob Gommerman (drums).

FINNEGAN, Larry
Born John Lawrence Finneran on 8/10/1938 in Brooklyn, New York. Died of a brain tumor on 7/22/1973 (age 34). Pop singer/songwriter.

FIONA
Born Fiona Flanagan on 9/13/1961 in Manhattan, New York. Female rock singer/actress. Co-starred in the 1987 movie *Hearts Of Fire*.

FIORILLO, Elisa
Born on 2/28/1969 in Philadelphia, Pennsylvania. Female dance singer.

FIRE & RAIN
Pop duo from Tucson, Arizona: Patti McCarron and Manny Freiser. Named after James Taylor's 1970 hit.

FIREBALLS, The
Rock and roll band from Raton, New Mexico: Chuck Tharp (vocals; born on 2/3/1941; died of cancer on 3/17/2006, age 65), George Tomsco (lead guitar; born on 4/24/1940), Dan Trammell (rhythm guitar;

born on 7/14/1940), Stan Lark (bass; born on 7/27/1940) and Eric Budd (drums; born on 10/23/1938). First recorded for Kapp in 1958. Trammell left group in 1959. Doug Roberts (died on 11/18/1981) replaced Budd in 1962. Tharp quit group in 1960 and was replaced by Jimmy Gilmer (vocals, piano). Gilmer was introduced to The Fireballs by their record producer Norman Petty at his famed studio in Clovis, New Mexico.

FIREFALL
Soft-rock group from Boulder, Colorado: Rick Roberts (vocals; born on 8/31/1949), Larry Burnett (born on 11/8/1951) and Jock Bartley (guitars; born on 5/16/1950), Mark Andes (Spirit, Jo Jo Gunne; bass; born on 2/19/1948), and Mike Clarke (Byrds; drums; born on 6/3/1946). David Muse (keyboards; born on 7/27/1949) joined in 1977. Andes joined Heart in 1980. Roberts and Clarke were members of the Flying Burrito Brothers. Clarke died of liver failure on 12/19/1993 (age 49).

FIREFLIES
White doo-wop group formed by Gerry Granahan (Dicky Doo And The Don'ts) and Lee Reynolds (died of cancer). Varying membership included Ritchie Adams (lead), Vinnie Reynolds (died of a heart attack, age 22), Paul Giacalone and Johnny Visceli. Adams (born Richard Adam Ziegler) wrote "Tossin' And Turnin'" for Bobby Lewis.

FIREFLY
Disco studio group assembled by Kenny Nolan.

FIREHOUSE
Pop-metal band from Charlotte, North Carolina: C.J. Snare (vocals), Bill Leverty (guitar), Perry Richardson (bass) and Michael Foster (drums).

FIRE INC.
Rock group assembled for the movie *Streets Of Fire*.

FIRM, The
All-star rock group from England: Paul Rodgers (Free, Bad Company), Jimmy Page (Yardbirds, Led Zeppelin, Honeydrippers; guitar), Tony Franklin (bass) and Chris Slade (Manfred Mann; drums). Disbanded in 1986. Franklin joined Blue Murder in 1989. Slade joined AC/DC in 1990. Rodgers joined The Law in 1991.

FIRST CHOICE
Female R&B-dance vocal trio from Philadelphia, Pennsylvania: Rochelle Fleming, Annette Guest and Joyce Jones. By 1977, Jones left and Ursula Herring joined.

FIRST CLASS
Pop studio group formed in England: Tony Burrows (lead vocals), John Carter, Del John and Chas Mills (backing vocals), Spencer James (guitar), Robin Shaw (bass) and Eddie Richards (drums). Burrows was also the vocalist on hits by The Brotherhood Of Man, Edison Lighthouse, The Pipkins and White Plains.

FISCHER, Lisa
Born in Brooklyn, New York. R&B-dance singer.

FISCHOFF, George
Born on 8/3/1938 in South Bend, Indiana.
Pianist/songwriter. Wrote "98.6" for Keith and "Lazy
Day" for Spanky & Our Gang.

FISHER, Eddie
Born Edwin Jack Fisher on 8/10/1928 in Philadelphia, Pennsylvania. At Copacabana night club in
New York at age 17. With Buddy Morrow and
Charlie Ventura in 1946. On Eddie Cantor's radio
show in 1949. In the Armed Forces Special
Services, 1952-53. Married to Debbie Reynolds
from 1955-59. Other marriages to Elizabeth Taylor
(1959-64) and Connie Stevens (1967-69). Daughter
with Debbie is actress/author Carrie Fisher.
Daughters with Connie are singer Tricia Leigh
Fisher and actress Joely Fisher. Own *Coke Time*
15-minute TV series, 1953-56. In movies *All About
Eve* (1950), *Bundle Of Joy* (1956) and *Butterfield 8*
(1960).

FISHER, Mary Ann
Born on 2/23/1923 in Henderson, Kentucky. Died on
3/14/2004 (age 81). Female R&B singer. Backing
vocalist on several Ray Charles recordings.

FISHER, Miss Toni
Born in 1931 in Los Angeles, California. Died of a
heart attack on 2/12/1999 (age 67). Pop singer.

FISHER, Tricia Leigh
Born on 12/26/1968 in Burbank, California. Pop
singer/actress. Daughter of Connie Stevens and
Eddie Fisher. Acted in the movies *Stick* and *Book of
Love*. Half sister of actress Carrie Fisher.

FITZGERALD, Ella
Born on 4/25/1917 in Newport News, Virginia. Died
of diabetes on 6/15/1996 (age 79). The
most-honored jazz singer of all time. Discovered
after winning on the *Harlem Amateur Hour* in 1934,
she was hired by Chick Webb and in 1938 created a
popular sensation with "A-Tisket, A-Tasket."
Following Webb's death in 1939, Ella took over the
band for three years. Winner of the *Down Beat* poll
as top female vocalist more than 20 times and
winner of 12 Grammys, she remains among the
undisputed royalty of 20th-century popular music.

FIVE
Pop vocal group from England: Rich Neville, Scott
Robinson, Richard Breen, Jason Brown and Sean
Conlon.

FIVE AMERICANS, The
Rock and roll band from Dallas, Texas: Michael
Rabon (vocals; Gladstone), Norman Ezell (guitar),
John Durrill (keyboards), James Grant (bass) and
James Wright (drums). Wright married Robin of Jon
& Robin and The In Crowd in 1970. Grant died of a
heart attack on 11/29/2004 (age 61).

FIVE BLOBS, The
Group is actually the overdubbed vocals of Bernie
Nee (born on 12/4/1922; died in February 1974, age
51).

FIVE BY FIVE
Rock group from Magnolia, Arkansas: Ron Plants
(vocals, guitar), Larry Andrew (guitar), Tim Milam
(organ), Bill Merritt (bass) and Doug Green (drums).

5 CHANELS, The
Black female doo-wop group from New York.
Changed name from The Chanels to The 5 Chanels
to avoid confusion with the Harlem doo-wop group
The Channels.

FIVE DU-TONES, The
R&B vocal group from St. Louis, Missouri: Andrew
Butler (lead), Willie Guest, LeRoy Joyce, Frank
McCurrey and James West. Also see South Shore
Commission.

FIVE EMPREES, The
Pop-rock band from Benton Harbor, Michigan: Don
Cook (vocals), Ron Pelkey (guitar), Tony Cantania
(guitar), Bill Schueneman (bass), and Mike DeRose
(drums).

FIVE FLIGHTS UP
Black male pop group. Featuring lead singer J.B.
Bingham.

FIVE FOR FIGHTING
Born John Ondrasik in 1968 in Los Angeles,
California. Adult Contemporary
singer/songwriter/guitarist. Name refers to a penalty
in hockey.

FIVE KEYS, The
R&B vocal group from Newport News, Virginia:
brothers Rudy and Bernie West, Ripley Ingram,
Maryland Pierce and Ramon Loper. Ingram died on
3/23/1995 (age 65). Rudy West died of a heart
attack on 5/14/1998 (age 65).

FIVE MAN ELECTRICAL BAND
Rock group from Ottawa, Ontario, Canada: Les
Emmerson (vocals, guitar), Ted Gerow (piano),
Brian Rading (bass) and brothers Rick (percussion)
and Mike (drums) Belanger.

504 BOYZ
All-star rap trio from New Orleans, Louisiana:
Master P ("Nino Brown"), Silkk The Shocker ("Vito")
and Mystikal ("G Money"). 504 is the area code for
New Orleans.

"5" ROYALES, The
R&B vocal group from Winston-Salem, North
Carolina: cousins Lowman Pauling, Clarence
Pauling and Windsor King, with brothers Eugene
and John Tanner. Lowman Pauling died in
December 1973 (age 47). Eugene Tanner died on
12/29/1994 (age 58). Clarence Pauling died on
5/6/1995 (age 67).

FIVE SATINS, The
R&B vocal group from New Haven, Connecticut:
Fred Parris (lead), Al Denby, Jim Freeman, Eddie
Martin and Jessie Murphy (piano). Parris was
stationed in the Army in Japan when "In The Still Of
The Nite" charted, and the group re-formed with Bill
Baker (died of lung cancer on 8/10/1994, age 58) as
lead singer. Parris returned in January 1958,
replacing Baker.

FIVE SPECIAL
R&B vocal group from Detroit, Michigan: Bryan
Banks (lead), Steve Harris, Greg Finley, Mike Pettilo
and Steve Boyd. Banks is the brother of Ron Banks
of The Dramatics.

FIVE STAIRSTEPS, The
R&B group from Chicago, Illinois: brothers Clarence, Jr., James, Kenneth and Dennis Burke with their sister Alohe. Later joined by their five-year-old brother Cubie. Managed by their father and produced by Curtis Mayfield; later became The Invisible Man's Band.

FIVE STAR
Family R&B-dance vocal group from Romford, Essex, England: Deniece (lead singer), Stedman, Doris, Lorraine and Delroy Pearson. Their father, Buster Pearson, was a guitarist with Otis Redding.

5000 VOLTS
Disco trio from England: Tina Charles, Martin Jay and Tony Eyers.

FIXX, The
Techno-pop group from London, England: Cy Curnin (vocals), Jamie West-Oram (guitar), Rupert Greenall (keyboards), Charlie Barrett (bass) and Adam Woods (drums). Barrett left in early 1983; replaced by Alfred Agies. Agies left in 1985; replaced by Dan Brown.

FLACK, Roberta
Born on 2/10/1939 in Black Mountain, North Carolina; raised in Arlington, Virginia. Singer/pianist. Played piano from an early age. Music scholarship to Howard University at age 15; classmate of Donny Hathaway. Worked as a high school music teacher in North Carolina. Discovered by jazz musician Les McCann. Signed to Atlantic in 1969.

FLAME, The
Pop-rock group from Durban, South Africa: brothers Rikki, Steve and Brother Fataar, with Terry "Blondie" Chaplin. Rikki (drums) and Blondie (guitar) also played with The Beach Boys, 1971-75.

FLAMING EMBER, The
White R&B-rock group from Detroit, Michigan: Joe Sladich (guitar), Bill Ellis (piano), Jim Bugnel (bass) and Jerry Plunk (drums).

FLAMING LIPS, The
Rock group from Oklahoma City, Oklahoma: Wayne Coyne (vocals), Ron Jones (guitar), Michael Ivins (bass) and Steven Drozd (drums).

FLAMINGOS, The
R&B vocal group from Chicago, Illinois: cousins Zeke and Jake Carey, Tommy Hunt, Nate Nelson, Johnny Carter and Paul Wilson. Carter replaced Johnny Funches in The Dells in 1960. Hunt went solo in 1961. Nelson joined The Platters in 1966; died of heart disease on 6/1/1984 (age 52). Wilson died in May 1988 (age 53). Jake Carey died of a heart attack on 12/10/1997 (age 74). Zeke Carey died of cancer on 12/24/1999 (age 66).

FLARES, The
R&B vocal group from Los Angeles, California: Aaron Collins (lead), Willie Davis, Tommy Miller and George Hollis. Collins and Davis had been in The Cadets/The Jacks; Miller and Hollis had been in The Ermines and The Flairs. Produced by The Platters manager/songwriter, Buck Ram.

FLASH
Rock group from England: Colin Carter (vocals), Peter Banks (guitar; Yes, After The Fire), Ray Bennett (bass) and Michael Hough (drums).

FLASH & THE PAN
Pop duo formed in Australia: George Young and Harry Vanda (both formerly with The Easybeats). George's younger brothers, Angus and Malcolm Young, are members of AC/DC.

FLASH CADILLAC & THE CONTINENTAL KIDS
Fifties-styled rock and roll act from Colorado: Sam "Flash Cadillac" McFadin (vocals, guitar), Linn "Spike" Phillips (guitar), Kris "Angelo" Moe (keyboards), Dwight "Spider" Bement (sax), Warren "Butch" Knight (bass) and Jeff "Wally" Stewart (drums; replaced in 1975 by Paul "Wheaty" Wheatbread). Bement and Wheatbread were with Gary Puckett & The Union Gap. Group appeared as the prom band in the movie *American Graffiti*. Phillips died in 1993 (age 47). McFadin died of a heart attack on 8/31/2001 (age 49). Moe died on 7/8/2005 (age 55).

FLATT & SCRUGGS
Influential bluegrass duo. Lester Flatt (guitar) was born on 6/19/1914 in Overton County, Tennessee; died on 5/11/1979 (age 64). Earl Scruggs (banjo) was born on 1/6/1924 in Cleveland County, North Carolina. Duo formed in 1948 while both were members of Bill Monroe's band. Regulars on TV's *Beverly Hillbillies*. Separated in early 1969.

FLAVOR
Rock trio from Frederick, Maryland: Gary St. Clair (vocals, bass), Demetri Callas (guitar) and Danny Conway (drums).

FLAVOR UNIT MCs, The
Rap ensemble assembled by Queen Latifah, CEO of Flavor Unit Records. Features Heavy D, Treach (Naughty By Nature), Dres (Black Sheep), D-Nice, Chip-Fu (Fu-Schnickens), Freddie Foxx, and The Almighty RSO.

FLEETWOOD MAC
Pop-rock group formed in England by Peter Green (guitar; born on 10/29/1946), Mick Fleetwood (drums; born on 6/24/1947) and John McVie (bass; born on 11/26/1945), along with guitarist Jeremy Spencer (born on 7/4/1948). Many lineup changes followed as group headed toward rock superstardom. Green and Spencer left in 1970. Christine McVie (keyboards; born on 7/12/1943) joined in August 1970. Bob Welch (guitar; born on 7/31/1946) joined in April 1971, stayed through 1974. Group relocated to California in 1974, whereupon Americans Lindsey Buckingham (guitar; born on 10/3/1949) and Stevie Nicks (vocals; born on 5/26/1948) joined in January 1975. Buckingham left in summer of 1987. Guitarists/vocalists Billy Burnette (son of Dorsey Burnette) and Rick Vito joined in July 1987. Christine McVie and Nicks quit touring with the band at the end of 1990. Vito left in 1991. In early 1993, Nicks and Burnette left. In late 1993, Bekka Bramlett (leader of The Zoo and daughter of Delaney & Bonnie Bramlett) and Dave Mason joined Mick, John and Christine in band.

FLEETWOOD MAC — cont'd
The classic lineup of Fleetwood, John & Christine McVie, Buckingham and Nicks reunited in May 1997. Christine McVie retired from the group prior to their 2003 album and tour.

FLEETWOODS, The
Pop vocal trio from Olympia, Washington: Gary Troxel (born on 11/28/1939), Gretchen Christopher (born on 2/29/1940) and Barbara Ellis (born on 2/20/1940).

FLEMONS, Wade
Born on 9/25/1940 in Coffeyville, Kansas; raised in Battle Creek, Michigan. Died of cancer on 10/13/1993 (age 53). Black electric pianist of Maurice White's pre-Earth, Wind & Fire group, the Salty Peppers, 1969.

FLETCHER, Darrow
Born on 1/23/1951 in Inkster, Michigan. Male R&B singer/songwriter.

FLETCHER, Lois
Pop-folk singer. Former member of The Back Porch Majority.

FLEX
Born Felix Gomez on 8/26/1979 in Panama. Latin male rapper.

FLINT, Shelby
Born on 9/17/1939 in North Hollywood, California. Female pop singer/songwriter.

FLIRTATIONS, The
Female R&B vocal trio formed in England: sisters Shirley and Earnestine Pearce (from South Carolina), with Viola Billups (from Alabama).

FLOATERS, The
R&B vocal group from Detroit, Michigan: brothers Paul and Ralph Mitchell, Charles Clarke and Larry Cunningham.

FLOBOTS
Alternative-rock/hip-hop band from Denver, Colorado: James "Jonny 5" Laurie and Brer Rabbit (vocals), Andy Guerro (guitar), Joe Ferrone (trumpet), Mackenzie Roberts (viola), Jesse Walker (bass) and Kenny Ortiz (drums).

FLOCK OF SEAGULLS, A
New wave group from Liverpool, England: brothers Mike (vocals, keyboards) and Ali (drums) Score, Paul Reynolds (guitar) and Frank Maudsley (bass).

FLOETRY
Female R&B vocal duo: Marsha Ambrosius (born in London, England) and Natalie Stewart (born in Atlanta, Georgia).

FLOOD, Dick
Born on 11/13/1932 in Philadelphia, Pennsylvania. Pop-country singer/songwriter. Performed with Billy Graves on Jimmy Dean's CBS-TV show as The Country Lads.

FLO RIDA
Born Tramar Dillard on 12/16/1979 in Opa-locka, Florida; raised in Carol City, Florida. Male rapper/songwriter.

FLOYD, Eddie
Born on 6/25/1937 in Montgomery, Alabama; raised in Detroit, Michigan. R&B singer/songwriter. Original member of The Falcons, 1955-61. Eddie's uncle, Robert West, founded the Lu Pine record label.

FLOYD, King
Born on 2/13/1945 in New Orleans, Louisiana. Died of diabetes on 3/6/2006 (age 61). R&B singer/songwriter. First recorded for Original Sound in 1965.

FLYING BURRITO BROTHERS
Country-rock group from Los Angeles, California. Various members included Gram Parsons, Chris Hillman and Mike Clarke (all from The Byrds), Bernie Leadon (later with the Eagles) and Rick Roberts (later with Firefall). Parsons died of a drug overdose on 9/19/1973 (age 26). Clarke died of liver failure on 12/19/1993 (age 49).

FLYING LIZARDS, The
New wave group from England: Patti Palladin (vocals), David Cunningham (guitar, keyboards), Steve Beresford (bass) and J.J. Johnson (drums).

FLYING MACHINE, The
Studio project of British pop songwriters/producers Tony MacAuley and Geoff Stephens. Touring group featured Tony Newman as lead vocalist. Not to be confused with James Taylor's group.

FLYLEAF
Christian rock band formed in Belton, Texas: Lacey Mosley (vocals), Sameer Bhattacharya (guitar), Jared Hartmann (guitar), Pat Seals (bass) and James Culpepper (drums).

FOCUS
Progressive-rock group formed in Amsterdam, Holland: Jan Akkerman (guitar), Thijs van Leer (keyboards, flute), Martin Dresdan (bass) and Hans Cleuver (drums).

FOGELBERG, Dan
Born on 8/13/1951 in Peoria, Illinois. Died of prostate cancer on 12/16/2007 (age 56). Soft-rock singer/songwriter/guitarist. Worked as a folk singer in Los Angeles, California. With Van Morrison in the early 1970s. Session work in Nashville, Tennessee. Fogelberg's backing group is Fools Gold.

FOGERTY, John
Born on 5/28/1945 in Berkeley, California. Rock singer/songwriter/multi-instrumentalist. With his brother Tom in the Blue Velvets in 1959. Group became the Golliwogs and recorded for Fantasy in 1964. Group renamed Creedence Clearwater Revival in 1967. Went solo in 1972 and recorded as The Blue Ridge Rangers.

FOGHAT
Rock group formed in England: "Lonesome" Dave Peverett (vocals, guitar), Rod Price (guitar), Tony Stevens (bass) and Roger Earl (drums). Peverett, Stevens and Earl were with Savoy Brown. Peverett died of pneumonia on 2/7/2000 (age 57). Price died of head trauma on 3/22/2005 (age 57).

FOLDS, Ben
Born on 9/12/1966 in Winston-Salem, North Carolina. Adult Alternative singer/songwriter/pianist. His trio included Robert Sledge (bass) and Darren Jessee (drums).

FOLEY, Ellen
Born in 1951 in St. Louis, Missouri. Rock singer/actress. Vocalist on Meat Loaf's *Bat Out Of Hell* album. Acted in several movies and TV shows.

FOLEY, Red
Born Clyde Foley on 6/17/1910 in Blue Lick, Kentucky. Died of a heart attack on 9/19/1968 (age 58). Country singer/songwriter. Father of Betty Foley. On the *WLS National Barn Dance* from 1930-37 and the *Renfro Valley Show* from 1937-39. Hosted the *Ozark Jubilee* series on ABC-TV from 1954-60. Regular on TV's *Mr. Smith Goes To Washington*. Pat Boone married his daughter Shirley on 11/7/1953.

FOLK IMPLOSION
Rock duo from San Francisco, California: Lou Barlow (vocals, bass) and John Davis (guitar, drums).

FONSI, Luis
Born on 4/15/1978 in Puerto Rico; raised in Orlando, Florida. Latin singer.

FONTAINE, Eddie
Born on 3/6/1934 in Jersey City, New Jersey. Rock and roll singer/actor. Played "Pete D'Angelo" on TV's *The Gallant Men*.

FONTANE SISTERS, The
Pop vocal trio from New Milford, New Jersey: sisters Marge, Bea and Geri, whose family name is Rosse. Backed Perry Como on many of his hits from 1949-52.

FOO FIGHTERS
Rock group formed in Seattle: Dave Grohl (vocals, guitar; born on 1/14/1969), Pat Smear (guitar; born on 8/5/1959), Nate Mendel (bass; born on 12/2/1968) and William Goldsmith (drums; born on 7/4/1972). Taylor Hawkins (born on 2/10/1968) replaced Goldsmith in 1997. Franz Stahl (born on 10/30/1961) replaced Smear in 1998. Chris Shiflett replaced Stahl in 2000. Grohl was drummer for Nirvana. Group name taken from the fiery UFO-like apparitions seen by U.S. pilots during World War II.

FOOLS, The
Rock group from Boston, Massachusetts: Mike Girard (vocals), brothers Stacey (guitar) and Chris (drums) Pedrick, Rich Bartlett (guitar) and Doug Forman (bass).

FOOLS GOLD
Backing group for Dan Fogelberg: Denny Henson (vocals, guitar), Doug Livingston (piano), Tom Kelly (bass) and Ron Grinel (drums).

FORBERT, Steve
Born on 12/15/1954 in Meridian, Mississippi. Folk-rock singer/songwriter. Moved to New York City in 1976.

FORCE M.D.'S
R&B vocal group from Staten Island, New York: brothers Stevie and Antoine Lundy, Jesse Daniels, Trisco Pearson and Charles Nelson. Nelson died of a heart attack on 3/10/1995 (age 30). Antoine Lundy died of ALS on 1/18/1998 (age 33). M.D.: Musical Diversity.

FORD, Frankie
Born Francis Guzzo on 8/4/1939 in Gretna, Louisiana. Rock and roll singer. Appeared with Sophie Tucker, Ted Lewis and Carmen Miranda at local shows at an early age. Appeared in the movie *American Hot Wax*.

FORD, Lita
Born Carmelita Ford on 9/19/1958 in London, England; raised in Los Angeles, California. Rock singer/guitarist. Member of The Runaways from 1975-79.

FORD, "Tennessee" Ernie
Born Ernest Jennings Ford on 2/13/1919 in Bristol, Tennessee. Died of liver disease on 10/17/1991 (age 72). Country singer. Revered as America's favorite hymn singer. Began career as a DJ. Host of musical variety TV shows, 1955-65. Favorite expression: "Bless your little pea-pickin' hearts."

FORD, Willa
Born Amanda Lee Williford on 1/22/1981 in Ruskin, Florida. Female pop singer.

FOREIGNER
British-American rock group formed in New York: Mick Jones (guitar; born on 12/27/1944), Lou Gramm (vocals; born on 5/2/1950), Ian McDonald (guitar, keyboards; born on 6/25/1946), Ed Gagliardi (bass; born on 2/13/1952), Al Greenwood (keyboards; born on 10/20/1951) and Dennis Elliott (drums; born on 8/18/1950). Gagliardi, Gramm and Greenwood are from New York. Most of material written by Jones (Spooky Tooth) and Gramm. Rick Wills (Cochise, Roxy Music, Small Faces) replaced Gagliardi in 1979. Greenwood and McDonald (King Crimson) left in 1980. Gramm left in 1991 to form Shadow King; replaced by Johnny Edwards. Gramm returned in mid-1992. Wills left in 1992 to join Bad Company; Elliott left to open woodworking business. Jones not to be confused with Mick Jones of The Clash and Big Audio Dynamite.

FOREST FOR THE TREES
Group is actually solo alternative pop-rock singer/songwriter/producer Carl Stephenson (co-writer of Beck's "Loser").

FORMATIONS, The
R&B vocal group from Philadelphia, Pennsylvania: Victor Drayton, Jerry Akines, Ernie Brooks, Reggie Turner and John Bellman.

FOR REAL
Female R&B vocal group from Los Angeles, California: Josina Elder, Wendi Williams, LaTanyia Baldwin and Necia Bray.

FORREST, Jimmy
Born on 1/24/1920 in St. Louis, Missouri. Died on 8/26/1980 (age 60). Tenor saxophonist.

FOR SQUIRRELS
Rock group from Gainesville, Florida: John Francis Vigliatura (vocals), Travis Michael Tooke (guitar), William Richard White (bass) and Thomas Jacob Griego (drums). Vigliatura (age 20) and White (age 22) were killed in a car crash on 9/8/95. Tooke and Griego went on to form Subrosa.

FORTE, John
Born in Brooklyn, New York. Male rapper.

FORT MINOR
Solo side project for Linkin Park member Mike Shinoda. Combines electronic beats with hip-hop music.

FORTUNE
Male pop-rock group: Larry Greene (vocals), Bobby Birch, Richard Fortune, Nick Fortune and Roger Scott Craig.

FORTUNES, The
Pop group formed in England: Glen Dale Garforth and Barry Pritchard (vocals, guitars), David Carr (keyboards), Rod Allen Bainbridge (bass) and Andy Brown (drums). Pritchard died of heart failure on 1/11/1999 (age 54). Bainbridge died of liver cancer on 1/10/2008 (age 63).

49ERS
Dance group from Italy featuring producer/DJ Gianfranco Bortolotti and vocalist Dawn Mitchell.

FORUM, The
Pop-folk trio from Pasadena, California: Phil Campos, Rene Nole and Riselle Bain.

FOSTER, Bruce
Born in Trenton, New Jersey. Pop-rock singer/songwriter/keyboardist. Claims to be a descendant of composer Stephen Foster.

FOSTER, David
Born on 11/1/1949 in Victoria, British Columbia, Canada. Prolific producer/composer/keyboardist. Member of the groups Skylark and Attitudes. Wrote and produced hits for Chicago, Barbra Streisand, Celine Dion, Whitney Houston and many others. Married songwriter/actress Linda Thompson in 1991.

FOTOMAKER
Pop-rock group from New York: Wally Bryson and Lex Marchesi (guitars), Frankie Vinci (keyboards), Gene Cornish (bass) and Dino Danelli (drums). All share vocals. Bryson was a member of The Raspberries. Cornish and Danelli were members of The Rascals and Bulldog.

FOUNDATIONS, The
Interracial R&B-pop group formed in England: Clem Curtis (vocals), Allan Warner (guitar), Eric Allendale, Pat Burke and Michael Elliott (horns), Anthony Gomez (keyboards), Peter McBeth (bass) and Tim Harris (drums). Colin Young replaced Curtis in 1968. Group disbanded in 1970.

FOUNTAIN, Pete
Born on 7/3/1930 in New Orleans, Louisiana. Top jazz clarinetist. With Al Hirt, 1956-57. Performed on Lawrence Welk's weekly TV show, 1957-59. Own club in New Orleans, The French Quarter Inn.

FOUNTAIN, Roosevelt
Born in Detroit, Michigan. Black funk-jazz band leader.

FOUNTAINS OF WAYNE
Pop-rock duo from New York: Chris Collingwood (vocals, guitar) and Adam Schlesinger (keyboards, bass). By 2003, added Jody Porter (guitar) and Brian Young (drums).

FOUR ACES
Vocal group from Chester, Pennsylvania: Al Alberts (lead; born on 3/28/1928), Dave Mahoney (tenor; born on 7/7/1928), Sod Vaccaro (baritone; born on 10/1/1931) and Lou Silvestri (bass; born on 6/10/1930). Worked Ye Olde Mill near Philadelphia, late 1940s. First recorded for Victoria in 1951. Group has undergone several personnel changes over the years.

FOUR BLAZES
R&B group from Chicago, Illinois: Tommy Braden (bass), William "Shorty" Hill (guitar), Floyd McDaniel (guitar) and Paul "Jelly" Holt (drums). All shared vocals. Braden died in 1957. McDaniel died of a heart attack on 7/23/1995 (age 80).

4 BY FOUR
R&B vocal group from Queens, New York: brothers Damen and Lance Heyward, Steve Gray, and Jeraude Jackson.

FOUR COINS, The
Vocal group from Canonsburg, Pennsylvania: brothers Michael and George Mahramas, George Mantalis, and Jim Gregorakis. In the 1957 movie *Jamboree!*

FOUR DATES, The
Pop vocal backing group for Frankie Avalon and Fabian. Johnny October, lead singer.

FOUR ESQUIRES, The
Vocal group from Boston, Massachusetts: Bill Courtney, Frank Mahoney, Bob Golden and Wally Gold (died of heart failure on 6/7/1998, age 70).

FOUR-EVERS, The
White vocal group from Brooklyn, New York: Joe Di Benedetto (lead), John Capriani, Steve Tudanger and Nick Zagami.

FOUR FRESHMEN, The
Jazz-styled vocal/instrumental group from Indianapolis, Indiana: brothers Ross and Don Barbour, their cousin Bob Flanigan and Ken Albers. Don Barbour died in a car crash on 10/5/1961 (age 32).

FOUR JACKS & A JILL
Pop group from South Africa: Glenys "Jill" Lynne (vocals), Bruce Bark (guitar), Till Hannamann (keyboards), Clive Harding (bass) and Anthony Hughes (drums).

FOUR KNIGHTS, The
Black vocal group from Charlotte, North Carolina: Gene Alford (lead; died in 1960), Clarence Dixon (baritone), Oscar Broadway (bass) and John Wallace (tenor; died in 1978).

FOUR LADS, The
Vocal group from Toronto, Ontario, Canada: Bernie Toorish (lead tenor), Jimmie Arnold (second tenor), Frankie Busseri (baritone) and Connie Codarini (bass). Sang in choir at St. Michael's Cathedral in Toronto. Worked local hotels and clubs. Worked Le Ruban Bleu in New York City. Signed as backup singers by Columbia in 1950. Backed Johnnie Ray on several of his hits.

4 NON BLONDES
Pop-rock group from San Francisco, California: Linda Perry (vocals), Roger Rocha (guitar), Christa Hillhouse (bass) and Dawn Richardson (drums).

4 OF US, The
Rock group from Newry, Ireland: brothers Brendan (vocals), Paul (keyboards) and Declan (drums) Murphy, with John McCandless (bass).

4 P.M. (For Positive Music)
R&B vocal group from Baltimore, Maryland: brothers Rene and Roberto Pena, with Larry McFarland and Marty Ware.

4.0
R&B vocal group from Atlanta, Georgia: Tony "T-Bone" Hightower, Sammy "Cat Daddy" Crumbley, Jason "JJ" Sylvain and Ron "Hollywood" Jackson. Pronounced: Four Point Oh.

FOUR PREPS, The
Pop vocal group from Hollywood, California: Bruce Belland, Glen Larson, Ed Cobb and Marvin Inabnett (born on 7/29/1938). Belland, who was later in duo with Dave Somerville of The Diamonds, is the father of Tracey and Melissa Belland of Voice Of The Beehive. Larson's production company was a creative force behind numerous TV series during the 1970s. Inabnett died of a heart attack on 3/7/1999 (age 60). Cobb died of leukemia on 9/19/1999 (age 61).

4 SEASONS, The
Vocal group formed in Newark, New Jersey. In 1955, lead singer Frankie Valli (Francis Castelluccio; born on 5/3/1937) formed the Variatones with twin brothers Nick and Tommy (born on 6/19/1928) DeVito, and Hank Majewski. Changed name to The Four Lovers in 1956. Bob Gaudio (of The Royal Teens; born on 11/17/1942) joined as keyboardist/songwriter in 1959, replacing Nick DeVito. Nick Massi (born on 9/19/1927) replaced Majewski, and their 1961 lineup was set: Valli, Gaudio, Massi and Tommy DeVito. Group had been doing session work for their producer Bob Crewe and took their new name from a New Jersey bowling alley, The Four Seasons. In 1965, Nick Massi was replaced by the group's arranger Charlie Calello and then by Joe Long. In 1971, Tommy DeVito retired, and Gaudio left (as a performer) the following year. Numerous personnel changes from then on. The songwriting/producing/arranging team of Bob Crewe, Bob Gaudio and Charlie Calello and the "sound" of Frankie Valli helped rank The 4 Seasons as one of the top American groups of the 1960s. Massi died of cancer on 12/24/2000 (age 73). Also recorded as The Wonder Who? The group's musical biography is the basis for the hit Broadway show *Jersey Boys* which opened on 11/6/2005.

FOUR SONICS, The
R&B vocal group from Detroit, Michigan: Willie Frazier, Steve Gaston, Eddy Daniels and James "Jay" Johnson.

FOUR SPORTSMEN, The
R&B vocal group: Norman Brown, John Mobley, William Simpson and Jim Taylor.

4 THE CAUSE
R&B vocal group from Chicago, Illinois: brother-and-sister J-Man and Ms. Lady, with cousins Shorty and Bennie.

FOUR TOPS
Legendary R&B vocal group from Detroit, Michigan: Levi Stubbs (lead singer; born on 6/6/1936), Renaldo "Obie" Benson (born on 6/14/1937), Lawrence Payton (born on 3/2/1938) and Abdul "Duke" Fakir (born on 12/26/1935). First recorded for Chess in 1956, then Red Top and Columbia, before signing with Motown in 1963. Stubbs was the voice of Audrey II (the voracious vegetation) in the 1986 movie *Little Shop of Horrors*. Payton died of cancer on 6/20/1997 (age 59). Benson died of cancer on 7/1/2005 (age 68). The Supremes, The Temptations, The Miracles and the Four Tops were the "big 4" of the Motown "group sound."

FOUR TUNES, The
R&B vocal group formed in Harlem, New York: Danny Owens, Pat Best, Jimmy Gordon and Jimmie Nabbie. Group first recorded as The Sentimentalists. Nabbie died on 9/12/1992 (age 72). Gordon died on 10/27/1993 (age 80). Best died on 10/14/2004 (age 81).

FOUR VOICES, The
Male vocal group: Allan Chase (tenor), Frank Fosta (bass), Sal Mayo (tenor) and Bill McBride (baritone). Mitch Miller signed the group to Columbia after seeing them on *Arthur Godfrey's Talent Scouts* TV show. Recorded original version of "Sealed With A Kiss" in 1960 (Columbia 41699).

IV XAMPLE
R&B vocal group from Los Angeles, California: brothers Robert (B.C.) and Raymond Chevis, with Andre Allen and Lucious. Allen married Dawn Robinson (of En Vogue and Lucy Pearl) in May 2003.

FOX
Pop group from England: Noosha Fox (vocals), Herbie Armstrong and Kenny Young (guitars), Pete Solley (keyboards), Gary Taylor (bass) and Jim Frank (drums).

FOX, Charles
Born on 10/30/1940 in Manhattan, New York. Composer/conductor/pianist.

FOX, Samantha
Born on 4/15/1966 in London, England. Dance singer. Rose to stardom as a topless model for the U.K. *Daily Sun* newspaper.

FOXWORTHY, Jeff
Born on 9/6/1958 in Atlanta, Georgia; raised in Hapeville, Georgia. Comedian/actor/author. Starred in own TV sitcom, 1995-97. Began hosting own radio countdown show in April 1999. Host of TV game show *Are You Smarter Than A 5th Grader?*

FOXX, Inez
Born on 9/9/1942 in Greensboro, North Carolina. Female singer. Accompnaied vocally on most of her hits by brother Charlie Foxx. Charlie died on 9/18/1998 (age 68).

FOXX, Jamie
Born Eric Bishop on 12/13/1967 in Terrell, Texas. R&B singer/actor/comedian. Star of own TV series *The Jamie Foxx Show* from 1996-2001. Won Best Actor Oscar for portraying Ray Charles in the 2004 movie *Ray*.

FOXY
Latino dance band from Miami, Florida: Ish "Angel" Ledesma (vocals, guitar), Charlie Murciano (keyboards), Richie Puente (percussion), Arnold Paseiro (bass) and Joe Galdo (drums). Four of group's five members came to Florida with the Cuban emigres of 1959. Ledesma later founded and produced Oxo and Company B. Puente is son of luminary Latin bandleader Tito Puente; died on 7/18/2004 (age 48).

FRAGMA
Trio of electronic dance producers from Europe: brothers Dirk and Marco Duderstadt with Ramon Zenker.

FRAMPTON, Peter
Born on 4/22/1950 in Beckenham, Kent, England. Rock singer/songwriter/guitarist. Joined British band The Herd at age 16 before forming Humble Pie in 1969, which he left in 1971 to form Frampton's Camel. Went solo in 1974. Played "Billy Shears" in the 1978 movie *Sgt. Pepper's Lonely Hearts Club Band*. Near-fatal car crash on 6/29/1978 temporarily sidelined his career.

FRANCIS, Connie
Born Concetta Rosa Maria Franconero on 12/12/1938 in Newark, New Jersey. First recorded for MGM in 1955. From 1961-65, appeared in the movies *Where The Boys Are*, *Follow The Boys*, *Looking For Love* and *When The Boys Meet The Girls*. Connie stopped performing after she was raped on 11/8/1974. Began comeback with a performance on *Dick Clark's Live Wednesday* TV show in 1978.

FRANKE & THE KNOCKOUTS
Soft-rock group from New Brunswick, New Jersey: Franke Previte (vocals), Billy Elworthy (guitar), Blake Levinsohn (keyboards), Leigh Foxx (bass) and Claude LeHenaff (drums).

FRANKEE
Born Jennifer Graziano in 1983 in Staten Island, New York. Female singer/songwriter.

FRANKIE GOES TO HOLLYWOOD
Dance-rock group from Liverpool, England: Holly Johnson and Paul Rutherford (vocals), Brian Nash (guitar), Mark O'Toole (bass) and Peter Gill (drums).

Group's name inspired by publicity recounting Frank Sinatra's move into the movie industry.

FRANKIE J
Born Francisco Javier Bautista on 12/14/1978 in Tijuana, Mexico; raised in San Diego, California. Latino singer/songwriter/producer.

FRANKLIN, Aretha
Born on 3/25/1942 in Memphis, Tennessee; raised in Detroit, Michigan. Revered as the all-time Queen of Soul Music. Daughter of famous gospel preacher Rev. Cecil L. Franklin, pastor of Detroit's New Bethel Baptist Church. Greatly influenced as a child by family friends/gospel stars Rev. James Cleveland and Clara Ward. First recorded for JVB/Battle in 1956. Signed to Columbia Records in 1960 by legendary talent scout John Hammond. Dramatic turn in style and success after signing with Atlantic in 1966 and working with producer Jerry Wexler. Her sisters Carolyn and Erma Franklin also recorded. Married to her manager/co-writer Ted White, 1961-1969, and actor Glynn Turman, 1978-84. Appeared in the 1980 movie *The Blues Brothers*.

FRANKLIN, Doug, with the Bluenotes
Teen pop singer with a white male vocal quartet from North Carolina.

FRANKLIN, Erma
Born on 3/13/1938 in Memphis, Tennessee; raised in Detroit, Michigan. Died of cancer on 9/7/2002 (age 64). Sister of Aretha Franklin.

FRANKLIN, Kirk
Born on 1/26/1970 in Fort Worth, Texas. Gospel singer/choir leader. Also see God's Property.

FRANKS, Michael
Born on 9/18/1944 in La Jolla, California. Jazz-pop singer/songwriter.

FRANTICS, The
Instrumental rock and roll band from Seattle, Washington: Ron Petersen (guitar), Chuck Schoning (piano), Bob Hosko (sax), Jim Manolides (bass) and Don Fulton (drums).

FRANZ FERDINAND
Punk-rock band from Glasgow, Scotland: Alex Kapranos (vocals, guitar), Nick McCarthy (guitar), Bob Hardy (bass) and Paul Thomson (drums). Group named after the Austrian archduke whose murder helped spark World War I.

FRASER, Andy
Born on 8/7/1952 in London, England. Rock singer/bassist. Formerly with John Mayall's Bluesbreakers and Free.

FRATELLIS, The
Alternative-rock trio from Glasgow, Scotland: John Lawler (vocals, guitar), Barry Wallace (bass) and Gordon McRory (drums).

FRAY, The
Alternative pop-rock band from Denver, Colorado: Isaac Slade (vocals, piano), Joe King (guitar), Dave Welsh (bass) and Ben Wysocki (drums).

FRAZIER, Dallas
Born on 10/27/1939 in Spiro, Oklahoma; raised in Bakersfield, California. Country singer/songwriter/multi-instrumentalist. Wrote "Alley-Oop."

FREAK NASTY
Born Eric Timmons in Puerto Rico; raised in New Orleans, Louisiana. Male rapper.

FREBERG, Stan
Born on 8/7/1926 in Pasadena, California. Began career doing impersonations on Cliffie Stone's radio show in 1943. Did cartoon voices for the major movie studios. His first in a long string of brilliant satirical recordings was "John And Marsha" in 1951. Launched highly successful advertising career in early 1960s; winner of numerous Clio Awards (outstanding achievement award of the radio and TV ad industry).

FRED, John
Born John Fred Gourrier on 5/8/1941 in Baton Rouge, Louisiana. Died on 4/15/2005 (age 63). Formed The Playboys in 1956 as a white band playing R&B music. John played basketball and baseball at LSU and Southeastern Louisiana University.

FREDDIE & THE DREAMERS
Lead singer Freddie Garrity was born on 11/14/1936 in Manchester, England; died of emphysema on 5/19/2006 (age 69). Formed The Dreamers in 1961 with Derek Quinn (lead guitar), Roy Crewsdon (guitar), Peter Birrell (bass) and Bernie Dwyer (drums). Dwyer died of cancer on 12/4/2002 (age 62).

FREE
Rock group formed in England: Paul Rodgers (vocals), Paul Kossoff (guitar), Andy Fraser (bass) and Simon Kirke (drums). Kossoff and Fraser left in 1972, replaced by Tetsu Yamauchi (bass, later with Faces) and John "Rabbit" Bundrick (keyboards). Kossoff (died of drug-induced heart failure on 3/19/1976) formed Back Street Crawler. Rodgers and Kirke formed Bad Company in 1974. Rodgers was lead singer of The Firm (1984-85) and The Law (1991).

FREEMAN, Bobby
Born on 6/13/1940 in San Francisco, California. Black rock and roll singer. Formed vocal group the Romancers, at age 14, and later formed R&B group the Vocaleers.

FREEMAN, Ernie
Born on 8/16/1922 in Cleveland, Ohio. Died of a heart attack on 5/16/1981 (age 58). Black pianist/arranger/producer. Prominent sessionman; on recordings by Frank Sinatra, Dean Martin, Sammy Davis, Jr. and Connie Francis. Piano player on The Platters' hit recording "The Great Pretender." Recorded as "B. Bumble" on all records under that name except "Nut Rocker." Musical director at Reprise Records for 10 years. Retired in the late 1970s.

FREE MOVEMENT, The
R&B vocal group from Los Angeles, California: brothers Adrian and Claude Jefferson, Godoy

Colbert, Cheryl Conley, Josephine Brown and Jennifer Gates.

FREEWAY
Born Leslie Pridgen on 7/8/1979 in Philadelphia, Pennsylvania. Male rapper.

FREHLEY, Ace
Born Paul Frehley on 4/27/1951 in the Bronx, New York. Lead guitarist of Kiss until 1983. Formed own band, Frehley's Comet. Returned to Kiss in 1996.

FRENCH, Don
Born on 3/31/1940 in Wayne, Pennsylvania. Pop singer/guitarist. Later became a stockbroker.

FRENCH, Nicki
Born on 9/26/1964 in Carlisle, Cumbria, England; raised in Tenterden, Kent, England. Female dance singer.

FRENTE!
Pop-rock group from Melbourne, Australia: Angie Hart (vocals), Simon Austin (guitar), Tim O'Connor (bass) and Mark Picton (drums). Band name is Spanish for "Front."

FRESH, Mannie
Born Byron Thomas on 3/20/1974 in New Orleans, Louisiana. Male rapper. Member of Big Tymers and Cash Money Millionaires.

FREY, Glenn
Born on 11/6/1948 in Detroit, Michigan. Soft-rock singer/songwriter/guitarist. Founding member of the Eagles. Appeared in episodes of TV's *Miami Vice* and *Wiseguy*; starred in the short-lived CBS-TV series *South of Sunset* in 1993. Formed Longbranch Pennywhistle with J.D. Souther.

FRICKE, Janie
Born on 12/19/1947 in South Whitley, Indiana. Country singer. Former backing singer for RCA record label. Sang numerous commercial jingles. Later a regular on TNN's *The Statler Brothers Show*.

FRIDA
Born Anni-Frid Lyngstad on 11/15/1945 in Narvik, Norway. Member of Abba.

FRIEDMAN, Dean
Born on 4/21/1955 in Paramus, New Jersey. Pop singer/songwriter/pianist.

FRIEND & LOVER
Husband-and-wife pop vocal duo: Jim Post (born on 10/28/1939 in Houston, Texas) and Cathy Post (born Cathy Conn on 5/30/1945 in Chicago, Illinois).

FRIENDS OF DISTINCTION, The
R&B vocal group from Los Angeles, California: Floyd Butler, Harry Elston, Jessica Cleaves and Barbara Jean Love. Butler died of a heart attack on 4/29/1990 (age 49).

FRIJID PINK
Male rock group from Detroit, Michigan: Kelly Green (vocals), Gary Thompson (guitar), Tom Beaudry (bass) and Rich Stevens (drums).

FRIZZELL, Lefty
Born William Orville Frizzell on 3/31/1928 in Corsicana, Texas. Died of a stroke on 7/19/1975 (age 47). Country singer/songwriter/guitarist His brother David was also a top country star.

FROGMEN, The
Instrumental rock and roll band from Los Angeles, California: Dennis Fowley, Larry Bartone, Ray Sullivan, Michael Anderson, Larry Wnuk and Jim Young.

FROST
Born Arturo Molina on 5/31/1964 in Los Angeles, California. Raised on military bases in Guam and Germany. Hispanic rapper. Formerly known as Kid Frost. Member of Latin Alliance.

FROST, Max, & The Troopers
Studio group featuring lead singer Paul Wybier. Produced by Mike Curb.

FROST, Thomas & Richard
Born Thomas and Richard Martin in San Mateo, California. Pop singing/songwriting duo of brothers.

FROZEN GHOST
Pop-rock duo from Canada: Arnold Lanni (vocals, guitar, keyboards) and Wolf Hassel (bass). Both were members of the group Sheriff.

FRUIT DE LA PASSION
Dance group featuring lead singer Joe Pugas.

FUEL
Rock group from Harrisburg, Pennsylvania: Brett Scallions (vocals), Carl Bell (guitar), Jeff Abercrombie (bass) and Kevin Miller (drums).

FUGEES
Two-man, one-woman hip-hop group: rappers/ producers/cousins Wyclef Jean and Pras Michel (both are of Haitian descent), and rapper/singer Lauryn Hill (from East Orange, New Jersey). Fugees is short for refugees.

FULLER, Bobby, Four
Born on 10/22/1942 in Baytown, Texas. Died mysteriously of asphyxiation on 7/18/1966 (age 23). Band, formed in El Paso, consisted of Bobby (vocals, guitar) and his brother Randy (bass), with Jim Reese (guitar) and DeWayne Quirico (drums).

FULLER, Jerry
Born Jerrell Lee Fuller on 11/19/1938 in Fort Worth, Texas. Pop-country singer/songwriter.

FULL FORCE
Rap group from Brooklyn, New York: brothers Brian George, Paul Anthony George and "Bow Legged" Lou George, with their cousins Gerry Charles, Hugh "Junior" Clarke and Curt Bedeau. Assembled and produced Lisa Lisa & Cult Jam. Production work for numerous others.

FULSOM, Lowell
Born on 3/31/1921 in Tulsa, Oklahoma. Died of heart failure on 3/7/1999 (age 77). Blues vocalist/guitarist. Also known as Tulsa Red. First recorded for Big Town in 1946. Teamed up with pianist Lloyd Glenn. His band, at one time, included Ray Charles, Stanley Turrentine and Billy Brooks.

FUN & GAMES, The
Rock band from Houston, Texas: brothers Rock Romano (trumpet) and Joe Romano (bass), Paul Guille (guitar), Joe Dugan (keyboards), Sam Irwin (tambourine) and Carson Graham (drums). All share vocals.

FUN FACTORY
Dance group: French vocalist Marie-Annette with rapper Rod D., Italian dancer Toni Cottura and German dancer Steve Browarczyk.

FUNKDOOBIEST
Rap trio from Los Angeles, California: Ralph "DJ Ralph M" Medrano, Jason "Sondoobie" Vasquez and Tyrone "Tomahawk Funk" Pachenco.

FUNKMASTER FLEX
Born Aston Taylor in Brooklyn, New York. Black rap DJ/producer.

FUNKY COMMUNICATION COMMITTEE
Country-pop group: Dennis Clifton (vocals, guitar), J.B. Christman (vocals, keyboards), Steve Gooch (guitar), Lonnie Ledford (bass) and Jim "Be-Bop" Evans (drums). Clifton died of cancer on 1/1/2008 (age 54).

FUNKY GREEN DOGS
Techno-dance trio from New York: producers Oscar Gaetan and Ralph Falcon, with singer Pamela Williams.

FUNKY KINGS
Rock group formed in Los Angeles, California: Jules Shear, Jack Tempchin and Richard Stekol (vocals, guitars), Mike Finnigan (keyboards), Bill Bodine (bass) and Frank Cotinola (drums).

FUN LOVIN' CRIMINALS
Eclectic hip-hop trio formed in Manhattan, New York: Huey Morgan (vocals, guitar), Brian Leiser (bass, keyboards) and Steve Borgovini (drums).

FURAY, Richie
Born on 5/9/1944 in Yellow Springs, Ohio. Member of Buffalo Springfield, Poco, and The Souther, Hillman, Furay Band. Began recording Christian music in 1976.

FURTADO, Nelly
Born on 12/2/1978 in Victoria, British Columbia, Canada (of Portugese parentage). Female alternative pop-rock singer/songwriter.

FURYS, The
Black vocal group from Los Angeles, California: Jerome Evans (lead singer), Jimmy Green, Melvin White, George Taylor and Robert Washington. Evans died of a heart attack on 11/30/2003 (age 65).

FU-SCHNICKENS
Hip-hop trio from Brooklyn, New York: Larry "Poc-Fu" Maturine, Roderick "Chip-Fu" Roachford (The Flavor Unit MCs) and James "Moc-Fu" Jones. FU stands for "For Unity" and Schnicken is a term invented by the group to signify coalition.

FUZZ, The
Female R&B vocal trio from Washington DC: Sheila Young, Barbara Gilliam and Val Williams.

GABRIEL
Rock group from Seattle, Washington: Terry Lauber (vocals), Frank Butorac (guitar), Gary Ruhl (bass) and Michael Kinder (drums).

GABRIEL, Peter
Born on 2/13/1950 in Woking, Surrey, England. Lead singer of Genesis from 1966-75. Scored movies *Birdy* and *The Last Temptation Of Christ*. In 1982, financed the World of Music Arts and Dance (WOMAD) festival.

GABRIEL & The Angels
Rock and roll band from Camden, New Jersey: Rick "Gabriel" Kellis (vocals), George Jones (guitar), Pete Colangelo (trumpet), Richie Bruno (bass) and Al Hobbs (drums). Backing vocals by a black female trio named The Swans.

GABRIELLE
Born Louise Gabrielle Bobb on 4/16/1970 in London, England. Black female dance singer.

GADABOUTS, The
R&B vocal group from Chicago, Illinois: Johnnie Barr, Eddie Hayes, Larry Craig and Bill Putnam.

GADSON, Mel
Born on 7/21/1937 in Sarasota, Florida. Pop singer.

GAGNON, Andre
Born in 1942 in Pacome-de-Kamouraska, Quebec, Canada. Dance pianist/composer.

GALE, Sunny
Born Selma Segal on 2/20/1927 in Clayton, New Jersey; raised in Philadelphia, Pennsylvania. At age 16, placed in the finals of the Miss Philadelphia Beauty Contest. Began career with Hal McIntyre's band.

GALENS, The
Pop vocal group from Los Angeles, California: Galen, Bob Hubener, Charlene Knight (lead singer) and George Ross.

GALLAGHER & LYLE
Pop-rock duo from Largs, Ayrshire, Scotland: Benny Gallagher & Graham Lyle. Both formerly with McGuiness Flint.

GALLAHADS, The
White vocal group from New Jersey: Frank Kreisel, Jackie Vincent, Bob Alexander and Vincent Gambella (later recorded as Vincent Bell).

GALLERY
Pop group from Detroit, Michigan: Jim Gold (vocals), Brent Anderson (lead guitar), Cal Freeman (steel guitar), Bill Nova (percussion), Dennis Korvarik (bass) and Danny Brucato (drums).

GALLOP, Frank
Born on 6/30/1900 in Brooklyn, New York. Died in May 1988 (age 87). Best known as the announcer on Perry Como's TV shows during the 1950s.

GAME, The
Born Jayceon Taylor on 11/29/1979 in Compton, California. Male rapper.

GAMMA
Rock group formed by guitarist Ronnie Montrose after breakup of Montrose. Also included Davey Pattison (vocals), Mitchell Froom (keyboards), Glenn Letsch (bass) and Denny Carmassi (drums). Carmassi left in late 1982 to join Heart. Froom, also a record producer, was married to Suzanne Vega from 1995-98.

GANG STARR
Rap duo from Brooklyn, New York: Christopher "DJ Premier" Martin and Keith "Guru" Elam.

GANT, Pvt. Cecil
Born on 4/4/1913 in Nashville, Tennessee. Died of pneumonia on 2/4/1951 (age 37). Singer/pianist. Billed as "The G.I. Sing-Sation."

GANTS, The
Garage-rock band from Greenwood, Mississippi: Sid Herring (vocals), Johnny Sanders (guitar), Vince Montgomery (bass) and Don Wood (drums).

GAP BAND, The
R&B-funk trio from Tulsa, Oklahoma: brothers Ronnie, Robert and Charlie Wilson (lead singer). Group named for three streets in Tulsa: Greenwood, Archer and Pine. Cousins of Bootsy Collins. Charlie was a member of the Eurythmics' backing band.

GARBAGE
Rock group formed in Madison, Wisconsin: Shirley Manson (vocals, guitar; native of Edinburgh, Scotland), Doug Erikson (guitar, bass, keyboards), Steve Marker (guitar) and Butch Vig (drums). Vig produced albums for Nirvana, Soul Asylum, Sonic Youth and Smashing Pumpkins.

GARCIA, Jerry
Born on 8/1/1942 in San Francisco, California. Died of a heart attack on 8/9/1995 (age 53). Founder/ lead guitarist of the Grateful Dead. Produced and acted in the movie *Hells Angels Forever*. Ben & Jerry's Cherry Garcia ice cream named after him.

GARDNER, Dave
Born on 6/11/1926 in Jackson, Tennessee. Died of a heart attack on 9/22/1983 (age 57). Comedian known as "Brother Dave."

GARDNER, Don, & Dee Dee Ford
R&B vocal duo from Philadelphia, Pennsylvania. Gardner formed his own group, the Sonotones with Jimmy Smith, in 1953 and recorded for Gotham and Bruce. Ford also plays organ and piano.

GARFUNKEL, Art
Born on 11/5/1941 in Forest Hills, New York. One-half of Simon & Garfunkel duo. Appeared in movies *Catch 22*, *Carnal Knowledge* and *Bad Timing*. Has Master's degree in mathematics from Columbia University.

GARI, Frank
Born on 4/1/1942 in Brooklyn, New York. Teen pop singer.

GARLAND, Judy
Born Frances Gumm on 6/10/1922 in Grand Rapids, Minnesota. Died of an accidental sleeping pill overdose on 6/22/1969 (age 47). Star of MGM movie musicals from 1935-54. Most famous movie role was "Dorothy" in 1939's *The Wizard Of Oz*. Hosted own TV variety series, 1963-64. Married to David Rose from 1941-45. Married to director Vincente Minnelli from 1945-51; their daughter is Liza Minnelli.

GARNETT, Gale
Born on 7/17/1942 in Auckland, New Zealand. Came to the U.S. in 1951. Made singing debut in 1960. Acted in several movies and TV shows.

GARRETT, Lee
Born in Mississippi. R&B singer/songwriter. Blind since birth. Teamed with Stevie Wonder to write "It's A Shame" hit for the Spinners.

GARRETT, Leif
Born on 11/8/1961 in Hollywood, California. Teen pop singer/actor. Appeared in several movies, including all three *Walking Tall* movies.

GARRETT, Scott
Born on 11/5/1932 in Pittsburgh, Pennsylvania. Pop singer.

GARRETT, Siedah
Born on 6/24/1960 in Los Angeles, California. Black female singer/songwriter. Joined the Brand New Heavies in 1996.

GARY, John
Born John Gary Strader on 11/29/1932 in Watertown, New York. Died of cancer on 1/4/1998 (age 65). Adult Contemporary singer on Don McNeill's radio program, *Breakfast Club*.

GARY & DAVE
Pop duo from Canada: Gary Weeks (born on 5/22/1950) and Dave Beckett (born on 7/5/1949).

GARY & THE HORNETS
Pop-rock band of young brothers from Franklin, Ohio: Gary Calvert (vocals, guitar; born in 1955), Gregg Calvert (bass; born in 1952) and Steve Calvert (born in 1959).

GARY O'
Born Gary O'Connor in Toronto, Ontario, Canada. Rock singer/songwriter.

GARY'S GANG
Dance group from Queens, New York: Gary Turnier (drums), Eric Matthew (vocals, guitar), Al Lauricella and Rino Minetti (keyboards), Bill Catalano (percussion), Bob Forman (sax) and Jay Leon (trombone).

GATES, David
Born on 12/11/1940 in Tulsa, Oklahoma. Began career as a session musician, then a songwriter/producer before becoming the lead singer of Bread. Wrote The Murmaids' hit "Popsicles & Icicles."

GATLIN, Larry, & The Gatlin Brothers
Born on 5/2/1948 in Seminole, Texas. Country singer/songwriter/guitarist. Leader of The Gatlin Brothers.

GAYE, Marvin
Born on 4/2/1939 in Washington DC. R&B singer/songwriter/producer. Fatally shot by his father after a quarrel on 4/1/1984 (one day before his 45th birthday). Sang in his father's Apostolic church. In vocal groups the Rainbows and Marquees. Joined Harvey Fuqua in the re-formed Moonglows. Moved to Detroit in 1960. Session work as a drummer at Motown; married to Berry Gordy's sister Anna, 1961-75. First recorded under own name for Tamla in 1961. In seclusion for several months following the death of Tammi Terrell in 1970. Problems with drugs and the IRS led to his moving to Europe for three years. His daughter Nona Gaye also recorded.

GAYE, Nona
Born on 9/4/1974 in Washington DC. Female R&B singer. Daughter of Marvin Gaye.

GAYLE, Crystal
Born Brenda Gail Webb on 1/9/1951 in Paintsville, Kentucky; raised in Wabash, Indiana. Sister of country singers Loretta Lynn, Jay Lee Webb and Peggy Sue.

GAYLORDS, The
Italian-American vocal trio: Ronnie Gaylord (Fredianelli), Burt Holiday (Bonaldi) and Don Rea. Formed trio while students at the University of Detroit. Ronnie died of cancer on 1/25/2004 (age 74).

GAYNOR, Gloria
Born Gloria Fowles on 9/7/1949 in Newark, New Jersey. Dance-disco singer.

GAYTEN, Paul
Born on 1/29/1920 in Kentwood, Louisiana. Died of bleeding ulcers on 3/26/1991 (age 71). R&B vocalist/pianist/bandleader. Backup singer on many R&B hits for such artists as Clarence Henry, Annie Laurie and Bobby Charles.

G-CLEFS, The
R&B vocal group from Roxbury, Massachusetts: brothers Teddy, Chris, Timmy and Arnold Scott, with Ray Gibson.

G. DEP
Born Trevell Coleman in Harlem, New York. Male rapper.

GEDDES, David
Born David Idema on 7/1/1950 in Ann Arbor, Michigan. Pop singer.

GEGGY TAH
Rock trio from Los Angeles, California: singers/multi-instrumentalists Tommy Jordan and Greg Kurstin, with drummer Daren Hahn.

GEIGER, Teddy
Born John Theodore Geiger II on 9/16/1988 in Buffalo, New York; raised in Pittsford, New York. Male singer/songwriter/guitarist.

GEILS, J., Band
Rock band from Boston, Massachusetts: Jerome Geils (guitar; born on 2/20/1946), Peter Wolf (vocals; born on 3/7/1946), Magic Dick Salwitz (harmonica; born on 5/13/1945), Seth Justman (keyboards; born on 1/27/1951), Danny Klein (bass; born on 5/13/1946) and Stephen Jo Bladd (drums; born on 7/13/1942). Wolf left for a solo career in January 1983.

GELDOF, Bob
Born on 10/5/1951 in Dublin, Ireland. Leader of The Boomtown Rats. Played "Pink" in the Pink Floyd movie *The Wall*. Organized British superstar benefit group Band Aid and earned a Nobel Peace Prize nomination.

GENE & DEBBE
Pop vocal duo: Gene Thomas (born on 12/28/1938 in Palestine, Texas) and Debbe Neville.

GENE & EUNICE
Black duo of Forest Gene Wilson (from San Antonio, Texas) and Eunice Levy (from Texarkana, Texas). Gene also recorded as "Gene Forrest." Eunice died on 5/26/2002 (age 71). Gene died on 7/24/2003 (age 71).

GENE LOVES JEZEBEL
Techno-rock group formed in England: twin brothers Jay and Michael Aston (vocals), James Stevenson (guitar), Peter Rizzo (bass) and Chris Bell (drums). Michael Aston left in early 1989.

GENERAL PUBLIC
Pop group from Birmingham, England: Dave Wakeling (vocals, guitar), Ranking Roger (vocals, keyboards), Kevin White (guitar), Micky Billingham (keyboards; Dexys Midnight Runners), Horace Panter (bass) and Stoker (drums). Wakeling and Roger had been in English Beat. General Public disbanded in March 1987. Wakeling and Roger reunited in 1994.

GENESIS
Formed as a progressive-rock group in England: Peter Gabriel (vocals; born on 2/13/1950), Anthony Phillips (guitar), Tony Banks (keyboards; born on 3/27/1950), Mike Rutherford (guitar, bass; born on 10/2/1950) and Chris Stewart (drums; replaced by John Silver in 1968, then John Mayhew in 1969). Phillips and Mayhew left in 1970; replaced by Steve Hackett (guitar) and Phil Collins (drums; born on 1/30/1951). Gabriel left in June 1975, with Collins replacing him as new lead singer. Hackett went solo in 1977, leaving group as a trio: Collins, Rutherford and Banks. Added regular members for touring: Americans Chester Thompson (drums), in 1977, and Daryl Stuermer (guitar), in 1978. Collins also recorded in jazz-fusion group Brand X. Rutherford also in own group, Mike + The Mechanics, formed in 1985. Hackett later formed group GTR. Collins announced his departure from the group in April 1996; Ray Wilson joined as lead singer in June 1997.

GENIES, The
R&B vocal group from Brooklyn, New York: Roy Hammond (lead), Claude Johnson, Bill Gains, Alexander Faison and Fred Jones. Claude ("Juan")

Johnson later teamed with Roland ("Don") Trone as Don & Juan.

GENIUS / GZA
Born Gary Grice on 8/22/1966 in Brooklyn, New York. Male rapper. Member of Wu-Tang Clan. Pronounced: jizz-ah.

GENTLE PERSUASION
Female R&B vocal group.

GENTRY, Bobbie
Born Roberta Streeter on 7/27/1944 in Chickasaw County, Mississippi; raised in Greenwood, Mississippi. Country singer/songwriter/guitarist. Formerly married to Jim Stafford.

GENTRYS, The
Garage-rock band from Memphis, Tennessee: Larry Raspberry, Jimmy Hart and Bruce Bowles (vocals), Bobby Fisher (guitar), Jimmy Johnson (trumpet), Pat Neal (bass) and Larry Wall (drums). Hart later became a professional wrestling manager, known as "The Mouth of The South."

GEORGE, Barbara
Born on 8/16/1942 in New Orleans, Louisiana. R&B singer/songwriter.

GEORGE, Robin
Born in Wolverhampton, West Midlands, England. Rock singer/guitarist.

GEORGIA SATELLITES
Rock group from Atlanta, Georgia: Dan Baird (born on 12/12/1953) and Rick Richards (vocals, guitars), Rich Price (bass), and Mauro Magellan (drums). Group disbanded in 1991. Richards joined Izzy Stradlin & The Ju Ju Hounds.

GEORGIO
Born Georgio Allentini in San Francisco, California. Black dance-funk singer/songwriter/keyboardist/guitarist.

GERARD, Danyel
Born Gerard Daniel Kherlakian on 3/7/1939 in Paris, France. Pop singer/songwriter.

GERARDO
Born Gerardo Mejia on 4/16/1965 in Guayaquil, Ecuador; raised in Glendale, California. Latino rapper/actor. Raps in Spanglish (half Spanish, half English). Appeared in the movies *Can't Buy Me Love* and *Colors*. A&R director for Interscope Records.

GERONIMO, Mic
Born in Queens, New York. Male rapper.

GERRARD, Donny
Born in Canada. Black lead singer of the pop group Skylark.

GERRY & THE PACEMAKERS
Merseybeat pop-rock group from Liverpool, England: Gerry Marsden (vocals, guitar; born on 9/24/1942), Leslie Maguire (piano; born on 12/27/1941), John Chadwick (bass; born on 5/11/1943) and Freddie Marsden (drums; born on 10/23/1940; died on 12/9/2006, age 66). The Marsden brothers had been in skiffle bands;

GERRY & THE PACEMAKERS — cont'd
Gerry had own rock band, Mars-Bars. Signed in 1962 by The Beatles' manager, Brian Epstein.

GESTURES, The
Garage-rock band from Mankato, Minnesota: Dale Menten (vocals, guitar), Gus Dewey (guitar), Tom Klugherz (bass) and Bruce Waterson (drums).

GETO BOYS, The
Rap group from Houston, Texas: Richard "Bushwick Bill" Shaw, William "Willie D" Dennis, Brad "Scarface" Jordan, and Collins "DJ Ready Red" Lyaseth (left group in early 1991; replaced by "Big Mike" Barnett). Shaw, a Jamaican-born dwarf, lost his right eye in a shooting on 5/10/1991.

GET WET
Pop group featuring lead singer Sherri Beachfront.

GETZ, Stan
Born Stan Gayetzsky on 2/2/1927 in Philadelphia, Pennsylvania. Died of cancer on 6/6/1991 (age 64). Legendary jazz tenor saxophonist. Played with Stan Kenton (1944-45), Jimmy Dorsey (1945-46), Benny Goodman (1946) and Woody Herman (1947-49). Leader of the Brazilian-born "Bossa Nova" rage of the 1960s.

GHOSTFACE KILLAH
Born Dennis Coles on 5/9/1970 in Staten Island, New York. Male rapper/songwriter. Member of Wu-Tang Clan.

GHOST TOWN DJ'S
DJ rap-dance duo from Atlanta, Georgia: Rodney Terry and Carlton Mahoney.

GIANT
Rock group formed in Nashville, Tennessee: brothers Dan (vocals, guitar) and David (drums) Huff, Mike Brignardello (bass) and Alan Pasqua (keyboards).

GIANT STEPS
British pop duo: vocalist Colin Campsie and multi-instrumentalist George McFarlane. Both initially worked together as members of the British band Grand Hotel, then as Quick.

GIBB, Andy
Born on 3/5/1958 in Manchester, England. Died of heart failure on 3/10/1988 (age 30). Moved to Australia when six months old, then back to England at age nine. Youngest brother of Barry Gibb, Robin Gibb and Maurice Gibb (the Bee Gees). Hosted TV's Solid Gold from 1981-82.

GIBB, Barry
Born on 9/1/1946 in Manchester, England. Member of the Bee Gees.

GIBB, Robin
Born on 12/22/1949 in Manchester, England. Twin brother of the Bee Gees' Maurice Gibb.

GIBBONS, Steve, Band
Rock group from England: Steve Gibbons (vocals, guitar), Bob Wilson (guitar), Trevor Burton (bass) and Bob Lamb (drums).

GIBBS, Georgia
Born Frieda Lipschitz on 8/17/1919 in Worcester, Massachusetts. Died of leukemia on 12/9/2006 (age 87). Sang on the Lucky Strike radio show from 1937-38. With Hudson-DeLange band, then with Frankie Trumbauer (1940) and Artie Shaw (1942). On the Garry Moore-Jimmy Durante radio show in the late 1940s, where Moore dubbed her "Her Nibs, Miss Gibbs."

GIBBS, Terri
Born on 6/15/1954 in Miami, Florida; raised in Grovetown, Georgia. Country singer/pianist. Blind since birth.

GIBSON, Debbie
Born on 8/31/1970 in Brooklyn, New York; raised in Merrick, Long Island, New York. Pop singer/songwriter/pianist/actress. Playing piano since age five and songwriting since age six. Acted in the Broadway shows Les Miserables and Grease.

GIBSON, Don
Born on 4/3/1928 in Shelby, North Carolina. Died on 11/17/2003 (age 75). Country singer/songwriter/guitarist.

GIBSON, Ginny
Born Virginia Gorski on 4/9/1928 in St. Louis, Missouri. Pop singer on TV's Your Hit Parade, 1957-58.

GIBSON, Johnny
Born in Detroit, Michigan. R&B instrumentalist. Also recorded as the Johnny Gibson Trio.

GIBSON, Steve
Born on 10/17/1914 in Lynchburg, Virginia. Began recording with the Five Red Caps in 1943. His Red Caps: Romaine Brown, Emmett Matthews, Dave Patillo and Jimmy Springs. Gibson's wife Damita Jo was featured singer, 1951-53 and 1959-60.

GIBSON BROTHERS
Dance trio of brothers from the West Indies: Chris (guitar, percussion), Patrick (vocals, drums) and Alex (vocals, keyboards) Gibson.

GIDEA PARK featuring Adrian Baker
Group is actually British singer/producer Adrian Baker.

GIGGLES
Born Maria Respeto on 11/6/1970 in the Bronx, New York. Female dance singer.

GILBERTO, Astrud
Born on 3/30/1940 in Salvador, Brazil. Female singer. Married to Joao Gilberto from 1960-64.

GILBERTO, Joao
Born on 6/10/1931 in Juazeiro, Brazil. Male singer. Father of Bebel Gilberto. Married to Astrud Gilberto from 1960-64.

GILDER, Nick
Born on 12/21/1951 in London, England; raised in Vancouver, British Columbia, Canada, at age 10. Founding member of the rock band Sweeney Todd.

GILKYSON, Terry, & The Easy Riders
Folk trio: Terry Gilkyson, Rich Dehr and Frank Miller. Gilkyson died of an aneurysm on 10/15/1999 (age 83).

GILL, Johnny
Born on 5/22/1966 in Washington DC. Sang in family gospel group, Wings Of Faith, from age five. Joined New Edition in 1988. His brother Randy and cousin Jermaine Mickey are members of II D Extreme. Also see LSG.

GILL, Vince
Born on 4/12/1957 in Norman, Oklahoma. Country singer/guitarist. Member of Pure Prairie League from 1979-83. Married to Janis Oliver of the Sweethearts Of The Rodeo from 1980-97. Married Amy Grant on 3/10/2000.

GILLETTE
Born Sandra Gillette on 9/16/1973 in Chicago, Illinois. Female rapper.

GILLEY, Mickey
Born on 3/9/1936 in Natchez, Mississippi; raised in Ferriday, Louisiana. Country singer/pianist. First cousin to both Jerry Lee Lewis and TV evangelist Jimmy Swaggart. Co-owner of Gilley's nightclub in Pasadena, Texas, from 1971-89. Gilley and the club were featured in the movie *Urban Cowboy*.

GILMAN, Billy
Born on 5/24/1988 in Westerly, Rhode Island; raised in Hope Valley, Rhode Island. Country singer (age 12 in 2000).

GILMOUR, David
Born on 3/6/1946 in Cambridge, England. Rock singer/guitarist. Member of Pink Floyd.

GILREATH, James
Born on 11/14/1936 in Prairie, Mississippi. Died in a tractor accident on 9/7/2003 (age 66). Pop singer/songwriter/guitarist.

GILSTRAP, Jim
Born in Texas. R&B singer. Backing vocalist for Quincy Jones and Stevie Wonder.

GINA G
Born Gina Gardiner on 8/3/1970 in Brisbane, Queensland, Australia. Female dance singer.

GINA GO-GO
Born Gina Gomez in London, England. Female dance singer.

GIN BLOSSOMS
Alternative-rock group from Tempe, Arizona: Robin Wilson (vocals), Jesse Valenzuela and Scott Johnson (guitars), Bill Leen (bass) and Phillip Rhodes (drums). Early guitarist Doug Hopkins died of a self-inflicted gunshot wound on 12/5/1993 (age 32).

GINO & GINA
Brother-sister pop vocal duo from Brooklyn, New York: Aristedes and Irene Giosasi. Aristedes co-wrote "Sorry (I Ran All The Way Home)."

GINUWINE
Born Elgin Lumpkin on 10/15/1970 in Washington DC. Male R&B singer/songwriter.

GIRLFRIENDS, The
Female R&B vocal trio from Los Angeles, California: Gloria Goodson, Nannette Jackson and Carolyn Willis (Bob B. Soxx & The Blue Jeans, The Honey Cone).

GIUFFRIA
Rock group from California: Gregg Giuffria (keyboards; Angel), David Glen Eisley (vocals), Craig Goldy (guitar), Chuck Wright (Quiet Riot; bass) and Alan Krigger (drums). Lanny Cordola (Ozzy Osbourne's band) and David Sikes replaced Goldy and Wright in late 1985. Giuffria, Wright and Cordola joined House Of Lords in 1988.

GLADIOLAS, The
R&B group formed as the Royal Charms in 1955: Maurice Williams (lead singer), Earl Gainey, William Massey, Willie Jones and Norman Wade. Name changed to Maurice Williams & The Zodiacs in 1959.

GLADSTONE
Pop group from Tyler, Texas: H.L. Voelker (vocals), Michael Rabon and Doug Rhone (guitars), Jerry Scheff (bass) and Ron Tutt (drums). Rabon was leader of The Five Americans.

GLAHÉ, Will
Born on 2/12/1902 in Elberfeld, Germany. Died on 11/21/1989 (age 87). Accordionist/composer/ conductor.

GLASER BROTHERS, Tompall & The
Country vocal trio from Spalding, Nebraska: brothers Tompall (born on 9/3/1933), Chuck and Jim Glaser.

GLASS BOTTLE, The
Pop group from New Jersey: Gary Criss (male vocals), Carol Denmark (female vocals), Dennis Dees (guitar), Charles Moore (keyboards) and Jon Melia (drums).

GLASS HOUSE, The
R&B vocal group from Detroit, Michigan: Larry Mitchell, Pearl Jones, Scherrie Payne, Ty Hunter and Eric Dunham. Hunter (born in 1943; died on 2/24/1981) was in The Originals. Payne was in The Supremes and is the sister of Freda Payne.

GLASS MOON
Pop-rock group from Raleigh, North Carolina: Dave Adams (vocals, keyboards), Jaime Glaser (guitar), Nestor Nunez (bass) and Chris Jones (drums).

GLASS TIGER
Pop-rock group from Canada: Alan Frew (vocals), Al Connelly (guitar), Sam Reid (keyboards), Wayne Parker (bass) and Michael Hanson (drums).

GLAZER, Tom
Born on 9/3/1914 in Philadelphia, Pennsylvania. Died on 2/21/2003 (age 88). Novelty folk singer. Hosted own ABC radio program, 1945-47. Composed score for the 1957 movie *A Face In The Crowd*.

GLEASON, Jackie
Born Herbert John Gleason on 2/26/1916 in Brooklyn, New York. Died of cancer on 6/24/1987 (age 71). Legendary movie and TV comedian. Father of actress Linda Miller. Grandfather of actor Jason Patric. From 1953-56, had 11 consecutive Top 10 hit albums of lushly-recorded orchestral "mood music."

GLENCOVES, The
Folk trio from Long Island, New York: singers/guitarists Don Connors and Bill Byrne, with singer Brian Bolger.

GLITTER, Gary
Born Paul Gadd on 5/8/1944 in Banbury, Oxfordshire, England. Glam-rock singer. Backing band is The Glitter Band. In 2006 sentenced to three years in prison in Vietnam after his child molestation trial.

GLITTER BAND, The
Glam-rock group formed in England as a backing band for Gary Glitter: John Springate (vocals, guitar), Harvey Ellison (sax), Gerry Shephard (bass) and Peter Phipps (drums). Shephard died on 5/6/2003 (age 51).

GLORIES, The
Female R&B vocal trio from Harlem, New York: Francis Yvonne Gearing, Betty Stokes and Mildred Vaney.

GNARLS BARKLEY
Collaboration between R&B producer Brian "Danger Mouse" Burton and singer Thomas "Cee-Lo" Callaway (of Goodie Mob).

GOANNA
Rock group from Australia: Shane Howard (vocals), Warrick Harwood and Graham Davidge (guitars), Peter Coughlan (bass) and Robert Ross (drums).

GODDESS
Female dance singer from Amsterdam, Netherlands. Former backing singer for Joe Cocker and Falco.

GODLEY & CREME
Duo from Manchester, England: Kevin Godley (born on 10/7/1945) and Lol Creme (born on 9/19/1947). Both were members of Hotlegs and 10cc.

GODSMACK
Hard-rock group formed in Boston, Massachusetts: Salvatore "Sully" Erna (vocals; born on 2/7/1968), Tony Rombola (guitar; born on 11/24/1964), Robbie Merrill (bass; born on 6/13/1963) and Tommy Stewart (drums; born on 5/26/1966). Shannon Larkin (born on 4/24/1967) replaced Stewart in late 2002.

GODSPELL
The original cast from the Broadway rock musical *Godspell*.

GOD'S PROPERTY
Funk-rap-gospel collective of 50 young singers (ages 16-26) founded by Linda Searight in Dallas, Texas. Members of mentor Kirk Franklin's Nu Nation.

GOFFIN, Louise
Born in Brooklyn, New York. Pop singer/songwriter. Daughter of one of pop music's most prolific songwriting teams, Gerry Goffin and Carole King.

GO-GO'S
Female rock group formed in Los Angeles, California: Belinda Carlisle (vocals), Jane Wiedlin (guitar), Charlotte Caffey (guitar), Kathy Valentine (bass) and Gina Schock (drums). Disbanded in 1984. Reunited briefly in 1990 and again in 1994. Caffey formed The Graces in 1989.

GOLD, Andrew
Born on 8/2/1951 in Burbank, California. Pop-rock singer/songwriter. Son of soundtrack composer Ernest Gold (*Exodus*) and singer Marni Nixon. Session and arranging work for Linda Ronstadt since the early 1970s. In pop duo Wax in 1986.

GOLDE, Frannie
Born in Chicago, Illinois. Pop singer/songwriter.

GOLDEN EARRING
Rock group from The Hague, Netherlands: Barry Hay (vocals), George Kooymans (guitar), Rinus Gerritsen (bass) and Cesar Zuiderwijk (drums).

GOLDFINGER
Rock group from Santa Monica, California: John Feldman (vocals, guitar), Charlie Paulson (guitar), Simon Williams (bass) and Darrin Pfeiffer (drums).

GOLDSBORO, Bobby
Born on 1/18/1941 in Marianna, Florida. Pop singer/songwriter/guitarist. To Dothan, Alabama, in 1956. Toured with Roy Orbison, 1962-64. Own syndicated TV show from 1972-75, *The Bobby Goldsboro Show*.

GOMM, Ian
Born on 3/17/1947 in Ealing, London, England. Pop-rock singer/songwriter/guitarist.

GONE ALL STARS
Instrumental rock and roll-R&B studio band arranged by record company mogul George Goldner.

GONZALEZ
Disco group formed in London, England: Linda Taylor and Alan Marshall (vocals), Jim Cansfield (guitar), Roy Davies (keyboards), Bobby Stignac (percussion), Mick Eve, Chris Mercer, Bud Beadle, Colin Jacas, Ron Carthy and Martin Drover (horn section), Hugh Bullen (bass) and Sergio Castillo (drums).

GOOD CHARLOTTE
Rock band from Waldorf, Maryland: twin brothers Joel (vocals) and Benji (guitar) Madden, with Billy Martin (guitar), Paul Thomas (bass) and Aaron Escolopio (drums). Chris Wilson replaced Escolopio in 2000. Dean Butterworth replaced Wilson in 2006.

GOODEES, The
Female pop vocal trio from Memphis, Tennessee: Judy Williams, Kay Evans and Sandra Johnson.

GOODFELLAZ
R&B vocal trio from Brooklyn, New York: Angel Vasquez, DeLouie Avant and Ray Vencier.

GOODIE MOB
Male hip-hop group from Atlanta, Georgia: Cee-Lo (Gnarls Barkley), Khujo, T-Mo and Big Gipp.

GOODIES, The
Comedy trio from England: Graeme Garden, Tim Brooke-Taylor and Bill Oddie. Had own show on BBC-TV from 1970-81.

GOODMAN, Dickie
Born Richard Goodman on 4/19/1934 in Brooklyn, New York. Died of a self-inflicted gunshot wound on 11/6/1989 (age 55). Goodman and partner Bill Buchanan originated the novelty "break-in" recordings featuring bits of the original versions of Top 40 hits interwoven throughout the recording (all of the hits listed below are "break-in" records). Goodman was also a comedy writer for Jackie Mason and head of music department at 20th Century Fox. Buchanan died of cancer on 8/1/1996 (age 66).

GOODMEN, The
Electronic production duo from Amsterdam, Netherlands: Gaston Steenkist and René Horst.

GOOD QUESTION
R&B-dance duo from Philadelphia, Pennsylvania: brothers Sean and Marc Douglas.

GOOD 2 GO
Female pop-rap vocal group from Los Angeles, California: Melissa Miller, Natalie Fernie, Kathy Webb, Cindy Shows and Missy Newman.

GOODWIN, Don
Born in Canada. Pop singer/songwriter.

GOODWIN, Ron
Born on 2/17/1925 in Plymouth, England. Died on 1/8/2003 (age 77). Arranger/composer/conductor.

GOODY GOODY
Disco production by Vincent Montana (Montana Orchestra/Salsoul Orchestra) featuring Denise Montana, lead singer.

GOO GOO DOLLS
Rock trio from Buffalo, New York: Johnny Rzeznik (vocals, guitar), Robby Takac (bass) and Mike Malinin (drums). Although their recording of "Iris" was not released as a single, its 18 weeks at #1 on the *Billboard Hot 100 Airplay* chart is the most weeks at #1 ever on any *Billboard Hot 100* chart.

GOOSE CREEK SYMPHONY
Country-rock group: Ritchie Hart (vocals, guitar), Paul Howard (guitar), Bob Henke (keyboards), Ellis Schweid (fiddle), Chris Mostert (sax), Dave Birkett (bass) and Dennis Kenmore (drums).

GORDON, Barry
Born on 12/21/1948 in Brookline, Massachusetts. Acted in several TV shows.

GORDON, Lonnie
Born in the Bronx, New York. Female dance singer.

GORDON, Robert
Born in 1947 in Washington DC. Rockabilly singer. Lead singer of the New York punk band Tuff Darts.

GORDON, Roscoe
Born on 4/10/1928 in Memphis, Tennessee. Died of a heart attack on 7/11/2002 (age 74). R&B singer/guitarist/pianist.

GORE, Lesley
Born on 5/2/1946 in Manhattan, New York; raised in Tenafly, New Jersey. The leading solo singer of the "girl group" sound. Discovered by Quincy Jones while singing at a hotel in Manhattan. In the movies *Girls On The Beach*, *Ski Party* and *The T.A.M.I. Show*. Sister of Michael Gore.

GORE, Michael
Born on 3/5/1951 in Manhattan, New York; raised in Tenafly, New Jersey. Prolific songwriter. Brother of Lesley Gore.

GORILLAZ
Animated hip-hop/rock group created by Jamie Hewlett and Damon Albarn (of Blur): 2-D (vocals, keyboards), Noodle (guitar), Murdoc (bass) and Russel (drums).

GORILLA ZOE
Born Alonzo Mathis in Atlanta, Georgia. Male rapper/songwriter.

GORKY PARK
Rock group from Russia: Nikolai Noskov (vocals), Alexei Belov and Jan Ianenkov (guitars), "Big" Sasha Minkov (bass) and "Little" Sasha Lvov (drums). Group named after a famous park in Moscow.

GORME, Eydie
Born Edith Gormezano on 8/16/1931 in the Bronx, New York. Vocalist with the big bands of Tommy Tucker and Tex Beneke in the late 1940s. Featured on Steve Allen's *The Tonight Show* from 1953. Married Steve Lawrence on 12/29/1957. They recorded as the duo Parker & Penny in 1979.

GOSDIN, Vern
Born on 8/5/1934 in Woodland, Alabama. Country singer/songwriter/guitarist. Joined the Gosdin Family radio show from Birmingham in the early 1950s. Moved to California in 1960 and formed The Golden State Boys with his brother Rex Gosdin; they later recorded together as The Gosdin Bros.

GOULET, Robert
Born on 11/26/1933 in Lawrence, Massachusetts (French Canadian parents). Died of lung failure on 10/20/2007 (age 73). Began concert career in Edmonton, Alberta, Canada. Broadway/movie/TV actor. Launched career as "Sir Lancelot" in the hit Broadway musical *Camelot*.

GO WEST
Pop-rock duo from England: Peter Cox (vocals) and Richard Drummie (guitar, vocals).

GQ
R&B-dance group from the Bronx, New York: Emmanuel Rahiem LeBlanc (vocals, guitar), Herb Lane (keyboards), Keith Crier (bass) and Paul Service (drums). Group became a trio with the departure of Service in 1980.

GRACES, The
Female rock vocal trio formed in Los Angeles, California: Charlotte Caffey (guitarist of the Go-Go's), Meredith Brooks and Gia Ciambotti.

GRACIE, Charlie
Born Charles Graci on 5/14/1936 in Philadelphia, Pennsylvania. Rock and roll singer/guitarist. Began playing the guitar in 1946. Appeared on the *Paul Whiteman Teen Show* in 1950. First recorded for Cadillac in 1951. Regular on *Bandstand* (later: *American Bandstand*) from 1952-58. Toured England in 1957 and 1979.

GRACIN, Josh
Born on 10/18/1980 in Westland, Michigan. Country singer/songwriter. Finalist on the 2003 season of TV's *American Idol*. Served as a lance corporal in the United States Marines.

GRADUATES
White doo-wop group from Buffalo, New York: John Cappello, Bruce Hammond, Fred Mancuso and Jack Scorsone.

GRAHAM, Larry
Born on 8/14/1946 in Beaumont, Texas; raised in Oakland, California. Bass player with Sly & The Family Stone from 1966-72. Formed Graham Central Station in 1973: Graham (vocals, bass), David Vega (guitar), Hershall Kennedy and Robert Sam (keyboards), Willie Sparks and Patrice Banks (percussion). Graham went solo in 1980.

GRAMM, Lou
Born Lou Grammatico on 5/2/1950 in Rochester, New York. Lead singer of Foreigner.

GRAMMER, Billy
Born on 8/28/1925 in Benton, Illinois. Country singer/guitarist. Performed regularly on *The Jimmy Dean Show*, CBS-TV, 1957-58. Prominent session musician in Nashville.

GRANAHAN, Gerry
Born on 6/17/1939 in Pittston, Pennsylvania. To New York City at age 17. First recorded for Atco as Jerry Grant. Formed Dicky Doo And The Don'ts and The Fireflies. Formed Caprice Records in 1958 and produced many top hits.

GRANATA, Rocco
Born on 8/16/1938 in Figline Vigliaturo, Italy; moved to Belgium at age 10. Singer/songwriter/accordionist.

GRAND CANYON
Novelty duo from Atlanta, Georgia: Ed Brown and Jeff McKee.

GRAND FUNK RAILROAD
Hard-rock group formed in Flint, Michigan: Mark Farner (guitar; born on 9/29/1948), Mel Schacher (bass; born on 4/3/1951) and Don Brewer (drums; born on 9/3/1948). Band name inspired by Michigan landmark the Grand Trunk Railroad. Brewer and Farner had been in Terry Knight and The Pack; Schacher was bassist with ? & The Mysterians. Knight became producer/manager for Grand Funk, until his firing in March 1972. Craig Frost (keyboards) added in 1973. Disbanded in 1976.

Re-formed in 1981, with Farner, Brewer and Dennis Bellinger (bass). Disbanded again shortly thereafter. Farner began recording Christian music in 1988.

GRANDMASTER FLASH
Grandmaster Flash is pioneer rap DJ/producer Joseph Saddler (born on 1/1/1958 in Barbados; raised in the Bronx, New York). Rapper Melle Mel (Melvin Glover) was part of the original Furious Five rap/dance posse with Kidd Creole (Nathaniel Glover — no relation to the August Darnell character), Rahiem (Guy Todd Williams), Cowboy (Keith Wiggins; died on 9/8/1989; age 28) and Scorpio.

GRANDMASTER SLICE
Born in South Boston, Virginia. Male rapper.

GRAND PUBA
Born Maxwell Dixon on 3/4/1966 in the Bronx, New York; raised in New Rochelle, New York. Male rapper. Former member of Brand Nubian.

GRANT, Amy
Born on 11/25/1960 in Augusta, Georgia. Pop singer/songwriter. Began career as a top Contemporary Christian singer. Married to singer/songwriter Gary Chapman from 1982-99. Married Vince Gill on 3/10/2000.

GRANT, Earl
Born on 1/20/1933 in Idabelle, Oklahoma. Died in a car crash on 6/11/1970 (age 37). Black singer/songwriter/pianist.

GRANT, Eddy
Born Edmond Grant on 3/5/1948 in Plaisance, Guyana; raised in London, England. Rock-reggae singer. Member of The Equals.

GRANT, Gogi
Born Myrtle Arinsberg on 9/20/1924 in Philadelphia, Pennsylvania; raised in Los Angeles, California. Female pop singer.

GRANT, Janie
Born Rose Marie Casilli on 9/27/1944 in Jersey City, New Jersey. Teen pop singer/songwriter.

GRAPEFRUIT
Psychedelic-rock group from England: John Perry (vocals), brothers Pete (guitar) and Geoff (drums) Swettenham, and George Alexander (bass).

GRASS ROOTS, The
Pop-rock group formed in Los Angeles, California: Rob Grill (vocals, bass; born on 11/30/1944), Warren Entner (born on 7/7/1944) and Creed Bratton (guitars; born on 2/8/1943), and Rick Coonce (drums; born on 8/1/1947). New lineup in 1971 included Entner, Grill, Reed Kailing and Virgil Webber (guitars), and Joel Larson (drums). Bratton plays "Creed" on TV's *The Office*.

GRATEFUL DEAD
Legendary improvisatory-style rock group formed in San Francisco, California: Jerry Garcia (vocals, guitar; born on 8/1/1942), Bob Weir (vocals, guitar; born on 10/16/1947), Ron "Pigpen" McKernan (organ, harmonica), Phil Lesh (bass) and Bill Kreutzmann (drums). Mickey Hart (2nd drummer) and Tom Constanten (keyboards) added in 1968.

GRATEFUL DEAD — cont'd

Constanten left in 1970; Hart in 1971. Keith Godchaux (piano) and his wife Donna (vocals) joined in 1972. Pigpen died of a liver ailment on 3/8/1973 (age 27). Hart returned in 1975. Brent Mydland (keyboards) added in 1979, replacing Keith and Donna Godchaux. Mydland was a member of Silver. Keith Godchaux died on 7/23/1980 (age 32) from injuries suffered in a motorcycle accident. Weir and Mydland also recorded as Bobby & The Midnites. Mydland died on 7/26/1990 (age 37) of a drug overdose; Bruce Hornsby then took over keyboards on tour until Tubes keyboardist Vince Welnick joined band. Garcia died of a heart attack on 8/9/1995 (age 53). Welnick died on 6/2/2006 (age 55). Incessant touring band with faithful followers known as "Deadheads."

GRAVEDIGGAZ

Male rap group: Robert Diggs (a.k.a. RZA; also of Wu-Tang Clan), Anthony Berkeley, Paul Huston and Arnold Hamilton. Huston also produced De La Soul. Berkeley died of cancer on 7/15/2001 (age 35).

GRAVES, Billy

Born in Delaware. Rock and roll singer. Performed with Dick Flood on Jimmy Dean's CBS-TV show as The Country Lads.

GRAVES, Carl

Born in Calgary, Alberta, Canada. R&B singer. With the group Skylark in 1973.

GRAVITY KILLS

Techno-rock group from Jefferson City, Missouri: Jeff Scheel (vocals), Matt Dudenhoeffer (guitar), Douglas Firley (keyboards) and Kurt Kerns (bass, drums).

GRAY, Claude

Born on 1/25/1932 in Henderson, Texas. Country singer/guitarist. Standing 6'5", known as "The Tall Texan."

GRAY, David

Born on 6/13/1968 in Sale, England; raised in Solva, Wales. Folk-rock singer/songwriter/guitarist.

GRAY, Dobie

Born Lawrence Darrow Brown on 7/26/1940 in Brookshire, Texas. Black singer/songwriter. Acted in the Los Angeles production of *Hair*.

GRAY, Macy

Born Natalie McIntyre on 9/9/1970 in Canton, Ohio. Female R&B singer/songwriter.

GRAY, Maureen

Born in 1949 in Philadelphia, Pennsylvania. Teen R&B singer.

GREAN, Charles Randolph

Born on 10/1/1913 in Manhattan, New York. Died of heart failure on 12/20/2003 (age 90). Conductor/arranger. Married singer Betty Johnson.

GREAT WHITE

Hard-rock group formed in Los Angeles, California: Jack Russell (vocals), Mark Kendall (guitar), Lorne Black (bass) and Gary Holland (drums). Audie Desbrow replaced Holland in 1986. Michael Lardie (keyboards) joined in 1987. Tony Montana replaced Black in 1987. Many personnel changes since 1991. The band's pyrotechnic show at a Rhode Island club set off a fire that killed nearly 100 people on 2/21/2003, including the band's guitarist, Ty Longley.

GREAVES, R.B.

Born Ronald Bertram Greaves on 11/28/1944 at the USAF Base in Georgetown, British Guyana. Half Native American raised on a Seminole reservation in California. Nephew of Sam Cooke.

GRECCO, Cyndi

Born on 5/19/1952 in Manhattan, New York. Pop singer.

GRECO, Buddy

Born Armando Greco on 8/14/1926 in Philadelphia, Pennsylvania. Former pianist/vocalist with Benny Goodman ("It Isn't Fair" in 1950).

GREEN, Al

Born on 4/13/1946 in Forrest City, Arkansas. Soul singer/songwriter. With gospel group the Greene Brothers. To Grand Rapids, Michigan in 1959. First recorded for Fargo in 1960. In group The Creations from 1964-67. Sang with his brother Robert Green and Lee Virgins in the group Soul Mates from 1967-68. Went solo in 1969. Wrote most of his songs. Returned to gospel music in 1980.

GREEN, Garland

Born Garfield Green on 6/24/1942 in Leland, Mississippi. R&B singer/pianist.

GREEN, Pat

Born on 4/5/1972 in San Antonio, Texas; raised in Waco, Texas. Country singer/songwriter/guitarist.

GREEN, Vivian

Born in 1979 in Philadelphia, Pennsylvania. R&B singer/songwriter.

GREENBAUM, Norman

Born on 11/20/1942 in Malden, Massachusetts. Pop-rock singer/songwriter. Member of Dr. West's Medicine Show & Junk Band.

GREENBERG, Steve

Pop-novelty singer. Not to be confused with Steven Greenberg of Lipps, Inc.

GREEN DAY

Punk-rock trio formed in Rodeo, California: Billie Joe Armstrong (vocals, guitar), Mike Dirnt (bass; born Mike Pritchard) and Frank "Tre Cool" Wright (drums).

GREENE, Barbara

Born in Chicago, Illinois. R&B singer.

GREENE, Jack

Born on 1/7/1930 in Maryville, Tennessee. Country singer/songwriter/guitarist. Known as the "Jolly Green Giant."

GREENE, Lorne

Born on 2/12/1915 in Ottawa, Ontario, Canada. Died of heart failure on 9/11/1987 (age 72). Star of TV's *Bonanza* and *Battlestar Galactica*.

GREEN JELLY
Novelty hard-rock group formed in Kenmore, New York: Moronic Dictator (lead vocals), Joey Blowey, Rootin', Jesus Quisp, Coy Roy, Sadistica, Hotsy Menshot, Tin Titty, Sven Seven, Reason Clean, Mother Eucker, Roof D.H. and Daddy Longlegs.

GREENWICH, Ellie
Born on 10/23/1940 in Brooklyn, New York; raised in Long Island, New York. With former husband Jeff Barry, wrote and produced many of the top hits of the 1960s. Recorded as The Butterflys and sang backup on Cyndi Lauper's *She's So Unusual* album. Also see Tony Orlando & Dawn and The Raindrops.

GREENWOOD, Lee
Born on 10/27/1942 in Los Angeles, California. Country singer/songwriter/multi-instrumentalist.

GREENWOOD COUNTY SINGERS, The
Folk group formed in Los Angeles, California: brothers Van Dyke Parks and C. Carson Parks, with Dave Backhaus, Reg Bannister, Al Johnston, Pat Peyton, Tom Robbins, Sandy Mosely and Gaile Foote. Johnston and Robbins left in 1965.

GREER, John
Born on 11/23/1923 in Hot Springs, Arkansas. Died on 5/12/1972 (age 48). R&B singer/tenor saxophonist.

GREGG, Bobby
Born Robert Grego in Philadelphia, Pennsylvania. White jazz-R&B drummer. Performed with Steve Gibson & The Red Caps from 1955-60. Also performed on several Bob Dylan albums.

GREY & HANKS
R&B-dance vocal duo from Chicago, Illinois: Zane Grey and Len Ron Hanks.

GRIFFIN, Clive
Born in London, England; raised in Reigate, Surrey, England. Former session singer.

GRIFFIN, Merv
Born on 7/6/1925 in San Mateo, California. Died of prostate cancer on 8/12/2007 (age 82). Popular TV talkshow host/TV producer. Owner of TV's all-time most popular game shows *Jeopardy!* and *Wheel Of Fortune*, and an Atlantic City casino. Featured singer with Freddy Martin, 1948-52 ("I've Got A Lovely Bunch of Coconuts").

GRIFFITH, Andy
Born on 6/1/1926 in Mount Airy, North Carolina. Actor/comedian. Starred in several movies and Broadway shows. Star of TV's *The Andy Griffith Show* and *Matlock*.

GRIFFITHS, Marcia
Born in 1954 in Kingston, Jamaica. Reggae singer. Member of Bob Marley's backing vocal group, the I Threes, from 1974-81.

GRIGGS, Andy
Born on 8/13/1973 in Monroe, Louisiana. Country singer/songwriter/guitarist.

GRIN
Rock trio formed in Maryland: Nils Lofgren (vocals, guitar), Bob Gordon (bass) and Bob Berberich

(drums). Lofgren was a member of Bruce Springsteen's E Street Band, 1984-85.

GROBAN, Josh
Born on 2/27/1981 in Los Angeles, California. Classical-styled Adult Contemporary singer.

GROCE, Larry
Born on 4/22/1948 in Dallas, Texas. Pop-folk singer/songwriter. Wrote children's songs for Walt Disney Records.

GROOVE THEORY
Male-female R&B duo: Bryce Wilson and Amel Larrieux. Wilson, then known as Bryce Luvah, was a member of Mantronix.

GROSS, Henry
Born on 4/1/1951 in Brooklyn, New York. Pop-rock singer/songwriter/guitarist.

GROUP HOME
Rap duo from Brooklyn, New York: James "Melachi The Nutcracker" Felder and James "Lil' Dap" Heath.

GTR
Rock group formed in England: Max Bacon (vocals), Steve Hackett and Steve Howe (guitars), Phgil Spalding (bass) and Jonathan Mover (drums). Hackett was with Genesis. Howe was with Yes and Asia. Group name is short for guitar.

GUARALDI, Vince, Trio
Born on 7/17/1932 in San Francisco, California. Died of a heart attack on 2/6/1976 (age 43). Pianist/leader of own jazz trio. Formerly with Woody Herman and Cal Tjader. Wrote the music for the *Peanuts* TV specials.

GUCCI MANE
Born Radric Davis on 2/2/1980 in Birmingham, Alabama; later based in Decatur, Georgia. Male rapper.

GUERILLA BLACK
Born Charles Williamson in Chicago, Illinois; raised in Mississippi and Los Angeles, California. Male rapper.

GUESS WHO, The
Rock group formed in Winnipeg, Manitoba, Canada: Allan "Chad Allan" Kobel (vocals, guitar), Randy Bachman (guitar; born on 9/27/1943), Bob Ashley (piano), Jim Kale (bass; born on 8/11/1943) and Garry Peterson (drums; born on 5/26/1945). Recorded as The Reflections and Chad Allan & The Expressions. Ashley replaced by new lead singer Burton Cummings (born on 12/31/1947) in 1966. Allan left shortly thereafter. Bachman left in 1970 to form Bachman-Turner Overdrive; replaced by Kurt Winter and Greg Leskiw (guitars). Leskiw and Kale left in 1972; replaced by Don McDougall (guitar) and Bill Wallace (bass). Domenic Troiano (guitar; The James Gang) replaced both Winter and McDougall in 1973. Group disbanded in 1975; several reunions since then. Winter died of a bleeding ulcer on 12/14/1997 (age 51). Troiano died of cancer on 5/25/2005 (age 59).

GUETTA, David
Born in France. White DJ/producer.

GUIDRY, Greg
Born on 1/23/1950 in St. Louis, Missouri. Died in a car fire on 7/28/2003 (age 53). Pop singer/ songwriter/pianist.

GUITAR, Bonnie
Born Bonnie Buckingham on 3/25/1923 in Auburn, Washington. Own group in the early 1950s. Worked as session guitarist in Los Angeles in the mid-1950s. Owner of Dolphin/Dolton Records in Seattle in 1958. Played on several Fleetwoods' recordings.

GUITAR SLIM
Born Edward Jones on 12/10/1926 in Greenwood, Mississippi; raised in New Orleans, Louisiana. Died of pneumonia on 2/7/1959 (age 32). Blues singer/ guitarist.

GUNHILL ROAD
Pop-rock trio: Glenn Leopold, Gil Roman and Steven Goldrich.

G UNIT
Male superstar rap trio from Jamaica, Queens, New York: 50 Cent, Lloyd Banks and Young Buck.

GUNS N' ROSES
Hard-rock group formed in Los Angeles, California: William "Axl Rose" Bailey (vocals; born on 2/6/1962), Saul "Slash" Hudson (born on 7/23/1965) and Jeffrey "Izzy Stradlin" Isbell (born on 4/8/1962; guitars), Michael "Duff" McKagan (bass; born on 2/5/1964) and Steven Adler (drums; born on 1/22/1965). Axl Rose married Erin Everly (daughter of Don Everly of The Everly Brothers) on 4/27/1990; she filed for divorce three weeks later. Adler left in 1990; replaced by Matt Sorum (who had toured with The Cult). Keyboardist Dizzy Reed joined in 1990. Stradlin' left in late 1991; replaced by Gilby Clarke (of Kill For Thrills). Slash was married to model Renee Surran from 1992-97. Clarke left band in January 1995. Slash, Sorum and Clarke recorded in 1995 in Slash's Snakepit.

GUTHRIE, Arlo
Born on 7/10/1947 in Brooklyn, New York. Folk singer/songwriter. Son of legendary folk music artist Woody Guthrie. Starred as himself in the 1969 movie *Alice's Restaurant*, which was based on his 1967 song "Alice's Restaurant Massacree." Often performed in concert with Pete Seeger.

GUTHRIE, Gwen
Born on 7/9/1950 in Newark, New Jersey. Died of cancer on 2/4/1999 (age 48). R&B-dance singer/ songwriter. Background singer for many top artists.

GUY
R&B trio from Harlem, New York: Teddy Riley, with brothers Damion and Aaron Hall. By age 20, in 1988, Riley (ex-member of R&B group Kids At Work) was already a renowned producer. Trio disbanded in 1991; reunited in 1999. Riley formed BLACKstreet in 1993.

GUY, Buddy
Born George Guy on 7/30/1936 in Lettsworth, Louisiana. Blues singer/guitarist. Popular concert attraction. Father of Shawnna.

GUY, Jasmine
Born on 3/10/1964 in Boston, Massachusetts; raised in Atlanta, Georgia. Black female actress/ singer. Played "Whitley Gilbert" on TV's *A Different World*. Began career with the Alvin Ailey Dance Troupe. Dancer in TV show *Fame*. Starred in several off-Broadway shows. In movies *School Daze* and *Harlem Nights*.

GUYS NEXT DOOR
Pop group formed for their own Saturday morning NBC-TV show: Patrick J. Dancy, Eddie Garcia, Bobby Leslie, Damon Sharpe and Chris Wolfe.

G-WIZ
Rap group from Los Angeles, California: Jamahl Harris, Ron Martin, Craig Cummins and Kevin Williams.

GYM CLASS HEROES
Alternative hip-hop band from Geneva, New York: Travis McCoy (vocals), Disashi Lumumba-Kasongo (guitar), Eric Roberts (bass) and Matt McGinley (drums).

GYPSY
Rock group formed in Minneapolis, Minnesota: James "Owl" Walsh (vocals, keyboards), James Johnson and Enrico Rosenbaum (guitars), Doni Larson (bass), and Jay Epstein (drums). Walsh re-formed the group in 1978 as the James Walsh Gypsy Band.

GYRL
Female R&B vocal group: sisters Miyoko and Jamila, with Tai and Jeanae.

HACKETT, Buddy
Born on 8/31/1924 in Brooklyn, New York. Died of diabetes on 6/30/2003 (age 78). Long-time popular comedian.

HADDAWAY
Born Nester Haddaway on 1/9/1965 in Tobago, West Indies; raised in Chicago, Illinois. Black dance singer/choreographer.

HAGAR, Sammy
Born on 10/13/1947 in Monterey, California. Rock singer/songwriter/guitarist. Lead singer of Montrose (1973-75) and Van Halen (1985-96). Also recorded in a quartet with Neal Schon (Journey), Kenny Aaronson (Stories) and Michael Shrieve (Santana).

HAGGARD, Merle
Born on 4/6/1937 in Bakersfield, California. Country singer/songwriter/guitarist. Served nearly three years in San Quentin prison on a burglary charge, 1957-60. Signed to Capitol Records in 1965 and then formed backing band, The Strangers.

HAHN, Joyce
Born on 1/31/1929 in Eatonia, Saskatchewan, Canada. Ballad singer.

HAIRCUT ONE HUNDRED
Pop-rock group from Beckenham, Kent, England: Nick Heyward (vocals), Graham Jones (guitar), Phil Smith (saxophone), Mark Fox (percussion), Les Nemes (bass) and Blair Cunningham (drums).

HALEY, Bill, & His Comets
Born on 7/6/1925 in Highland Park, Michigan. Died
of a heart attack on 2/9/1981 (age 55). Began
career as a singer with a New England country
band, the Down Homers. Formed the Four Aces of
Western Swing in 1948. In 1949 formed the
Saddlemen, who recorded on various labels before
signing with the Essex label (as Bill Haley and the
Saddlemen) in 1952; signed with Decca in 1954.
The original Comets band backing Haley on "Rock
Around The Clock," recorded on 4/12/1954, were
Danny Cedrone (lead guitar; died of a heart attack
on 7/10/1954), Joey D'Ambrosio (sax), Billy
Williamson (steel guitar), Johnny Grande (piano;
died on 6/2/2006, age 76), Marshall Lytle (bass) and
Billy Gussack (session drums; Dick Richards was
their live drummer). D'Ambrosio, Richards and Lytle
left in September 1955 to form the Jodimars.
Comets lineup on subsequent recordings included
Williamson, Grande, Rudy Pompilli (sax; died on
2/5/1976, age 47), Al Rex (bass; born Al Piccarelli),
Ralph Jones (drums) and Franny Beecher (lead
guitar). They also recorded as The Kingsmen in
1958. Haley's 1953 hit "Crazy Man, Crazy" was the
first rock and roll hit on the pop charts and his 1955
hit "Rock Around The Clock" was the first #1 rock
and roll hit on the pop charts..

HALL, Aaron
Born on 8/10/1964 in Brooklyn, New York. R&B
singer. Member of the New York City trio Guy which
included his younger brother Damion Hall.

HALL, Daryl
Born Daryl Franklin Hohl on 10/11/1946 in
Philadelphia, Pennsylvania. One-half of Hall &
Oates duo.

HALL, Daryl, & John Oates
Daryl Hall (born on 10/11/1946) and John Oates
(born on 4/7/1948 in New York City, New York) met
while students at Temple University in 1967. Hall
sang backup for many top soul groups before
teaming up with Oates in 1972.

HALL, Jimmy
Born on 4/26/1949 in Mobile, Alabama. Leader of
the Southern rock band Wet Willie.

HALL, John, Band
Born on 10/25/1948 in Baltimore, Maryland. Rock
singer/guitarist. Leader of Orleans. Band includes
Bob Leinbach (keyboards), John Troy (bass) and
Eric Parker (drums). Hall was elected to the U.S.
House of Representatives (in New York) in 2006.

HALL, Lani
Born on 11/1/1945 in Chicago, Illinois. Lead vocalist
with Sergio Mendes & Brasil '66. Married to Herb
Alpert.

HALL, Larry
Born on 6/30/1940 in Hamlett, Ohio. Died of cancer
on 9/24/1997 (age 57). Teen rock and roll singer.

HALL, Tom T.
Born on 5/25/1936 in Olive Hill, Kentucky. Country
music storyteller. Wrote "Harper Valley P.T.A." hit
for Jeannie C. Riley and "Little Bitty" hit for Alan
Jackson. Hosted *Pop Goes The Country* TV series.

HALLORAN, Jack, Singers
Born on 1/10/1916 in Rock Rapids, Iowa. Died of a
stroke on 1/24/1997 (age 81). Conductor/arranger.
Member of The Ray Conniff Singers.

HALLYDAY, David
Born David Smet on 8/14/1966 in Boulogne-
Billancourt, France; raised in Los Angeles,
California. Actor/singer. Son of French superstars,
Sylvie Vartan & Johnny Hallyday. Starred in the
movie *He's My Girl*. Married to actress/model
Estelle LeFebure from 1989-2000.

HALOS, The
R&B vocal group from Harlem, New York: Harold
Johnson, Al Cleveland, Phil Johnson and Arthur
Crier. Backing group on Curtis Lee's "Pretty Little
Angel Eyes" and Barry Mann's "Who Put The
Bomp." Crier died of heart failure on 7/22/2004 (age
59).

HAMBLEN, Stuart
Born Carl Stuart Hamblen on 10/20/1908 in
Kellyville, Texas. Died on 3/8/1989 (age 80).
Singer/songwriter/actor. On radio from age 17.
Moved to Hollywood in the early 1930s and
appeared in many western movies and on radio with
own band. Ran for president on Prohibition Party
ticket in 1952.

HAMILTON, Anthony
Born on 6/29/1971 in Charlotte, North Carolina.
R&B singer/songwriter.

HAMILTON, Bobby
Born Robert Caristo on 10/5/1939 in Locust Valley,
Long Island, New York. Rock and roll singer/
songwriter.

HAMILTON, George IV
Born on 7/19/1937 in Winston-Salem, North
Carolina. Country-folk-pop singer/songwriter/
guitarist. Toured with Buddy Holly, Gene Vincent
and The Everly Brothers. Own TV series on ABC in
1959, and in Canada in the late 1970s. The
Bluenotes were Hamilton's backing vocalists.

HAMILTON, Roy
Born on 4/16/1929 in Leesburg, Georgia; raised in
Jersey City, New Jersey. Died of a stroke on
7/20/1969 (age 40). R&B ballad singer. Moved to
Jersey City at age 14. Sang with the Searchlight
Gospel Singers in 1948.

HAMILTON, Russ
Born Ronald Hulme in 1934 in Liverpool, England.
Pop singer/songwriter.

HAMILTON, JOE FRANK & REYNOLDS
Pop vocal trio: Dan Hamilton, Joe Frank Carollo and
Tommy Reynolds. Trio were members of The
T-Bones. Reynolds left group in 1972 and was
replaced by Alan Dennison. Although Reynolds had
left, group still recorded as Hamilton, Joe Frank &
Reynolds until July 1976. Hamilton died on
12/23/1994 (age 48).

HAMLISCH, Marvin
Born on 6/2/1944 in Brooklyn, New York.
Pianist/composer/conductor. Wrote "The Way We
Were" and "Nobody Does It Better."

110

HAMMEL, Karl Jr.
Pop-rockabilly singer. First recorded for Gone in 1958.

HAMMER, Jan
Born on 4/17/1948 in Prague, Czechoslovakia. Jazz-rock keyboard virtuoso. Toured with Sarah Vaughan as conductor/keyboardist. Member of Mahavishnu Orchestra until 1973.

HAMMOND, Albert
Born on 5/18/1944 in London, England; raised in Gibraltar, Spain. Pop singer/songwriter. Member of the Magic Lanterns in 1971. Wrote nine Top 10 pop hits, including "Nothing's Gonna Stop Us Now" and "The Air That I Breathe."

HAMPSHIRE, Keith
Born on 11/23/1945 in East Dulwich, London, England; raised in Calgary, Alberta, Canada. Pop singer/songwriter.

HAMPTON, Lionel
Born on 4/20/08 in Louisville, Kentucky; raised in Birmingham and Chicago. Died of heart failure on 8/31/2002 (age 94). Legendary black jazz vibraphonist. First recorded with the Reb Spikes band for Hollywood in 1924. Worked with Les Hite, then Benny Goodman from 1936-40; own band thereafter. The first jazz musician to feature vibes. Appeared in several movies. Theme song: "Flying High."

HANCOCK, Herbie
Born on 4/12/1940 in Chicago, Illinois. Jazz electronic keyboardist. Pianist with the Miles Davis band, 1963-68. Won an Oscar in 1987 for his *Round Midnight* movie score. Also scored the 1988 movie *Colors*. Wrote Mongo Santamaria's "Watermelon Man."

HANDY, John
Born on 2/3/1933 in Dallas, Texas. Jazz saxophonist.

HANSARD, Glen, & Marketa Irglova
Male singer Hansard was born on 4/21/1970 in Dublin, Ireland. Female singer Irglova was born on 2/28/1988 in Valasske Mezirici, Czechoslovakia.

HANSON
Teen pop-rock trio of brothers from Tulsa, Oklahoma: Isaac (age 16 in 1997; guitar), Taylor (age 14; keyboards) and Zac (age 11; drums) Hanson. All share vocals.

HANSON, Jennifer
Born on 8/10/1973 in La Habra, California. Country singer/songwriter.

HAPPENINGS, The
Pop vocal group from Paterson, New Jersey: Bob Miranda (lead), Tom Giuliano (tenor), Ralph DiVito (baritone) and Dave Libert (bass). Originally the Four Graduates, recorded for Rust in 1963. Bernie LaPorta replaced DiVito in mid-1967.

HAPPY MONDAYS
Dance-rock group formed in Manchester, England: brothers Shaun (vocals) and Paul (bass) Ryder, Mark Day (guitar), Paul Davis (keyboards), Mark Berry (percussion) and Gary Whelan (drums).

HARDCASTLE, Paul
Born on 12/10/1957 in London, England. Contemporary jazz keyboardist/producer.

HARDEN TRIO, The
Country vocal trio from England, Arkansas: siblings Bobby, Robbie and Arlene Harden.

HARDIN, Tim
Born on 12/23/1941 in Eugene, Oregon. Died of a drug overdose on 12/29/1980 (age 39). Folk-blues singer/songwriter. Relative of notorious outlaw John Wesley Hardin.

HARDTIMES, The
Pop-rock band from San Diego, California: Rudy Romero, Bill Richardson, Bob Morris, Lee Kiefer and Paul Wheatbread. Regulars on Dick Clark's daily ABC-TV show *Where The Action Is*. Wheatbread later joined Gary Puckett & The Union Gap and Flash Cadillac & The Continental Kids.

HARDY, Hagood
Born on 2/26/1937 in Angola, Indiana; raised in Toronto, Ontario, Canada. Died of cancer on 1/1/1997 (age 59). Male vibraphonist. Sideman for Herbie Mann and George Shearing.

HARLEY, Steve
Born Steven Nice on 2/27/1951 in London, England. Ex-journalist turned rock singer. Cockney Rebel: Jim Cregan (guitar), Duncan MacKay (keyboards), George Ford (bass) and Stuart Elliott (drums).

HARMONICATS
Harmonica trio formed in Chicago, Illinois: Jerry Murad (died on 5/11/1996, age 80), Al Fiore (died on 10/25/1996, age 73) and Don Les (died on 8/25/1994, age 79).

HARNELL, Joe
Born Joseph Hittelman on 8/2/1924 in the Bronx, New York. Died of heart failure on 7/14/2005 (age 80). "Bossa Nova" conductor/arranger.

HARPER, Janice
Born in Flushing, New York. Adult Contemporary singer.

HARPERS BIZARRE
Adult Contemporary vocal group from Santa Cruz, California: Ted Templeman, Eddie James, Dick Yount, John Petersen and Dick Scoppettone. Petersen was a member of The Beau Brummels. Templeman later produced many albums for The Doobie Brothers and Van Halen.

HARPO, Slim
Born James Moore on 1/11/1924 in Lobdell, Louisiana. Died of a heart attack on 1/31/1970 (age 46). Blues singer/harmonica player. Also known as Harmonica Slim.

HARPTONES, The
Black doo-wop group from Harlem, New York: Willie Winfield, William James, Jimmie Beckum, Bill Brown and Nicky Clark.

HARRIET
Born Harriet Roberts in 1966 in Sheffield, Yorkshire, England. Female dance singer.

HARRIS, Betty
Born in 1939 in Orlando, Florida; raised in Alabama. R&B singer.

HARRIS, Eddie
Born on 10/20/1936 in Chicago, Illinois. Died of cancer on 11/5/1996 (age 60). Jazz tenor saxophonist. Wrote much of the music for TV's *The Bill Cosby Show* and several books of music theory.

HARRIS, Emmylou
Born on 4/2/1947 in Birmingham, Alabama. Country-rock singer/guitarist. Sang backup with Gram Parsons until his death in 1973.

HARRIS, Major
Born on 2/9/1947 in Richmond, Virginia. R&B singer. With The Jarmels in the early 1960s. With The Delfonics from 1971-74.

HARRIS, Richard
Born on 10/1/1930 in Limerick, Ireland. Died of cancer on 10/25/2002 (age 72). Began prolific acting career in 1958. Portrayed "King Arthur" in the long-running stage production and movie version of *Camelot*. Played "Headmaster Albus Dumbledore" in *Harry Potter and the Sorcerer's Stone*.

HARRIS, Rolf
Born on 3/30/1930 in Perth, Australia. White novelty singer. Played piano from age nine. Moved to England in the mid-1950s. Developed his unique "wobble board sound" out of a sheet of masonite. Own BBC-TV series from 1970.

HARRIS, Sam
Born on 6/4/1961 in Cushing, Oklahoma. Pop singer/actor. Winner of TV's *Star Search* male vocalist category in 1984.

HARRIS, Thurston
Born on 7/11/1931 in Indianapolis, Indiana. Died of a heart attack on 4/14/1990 (age 58). Black singer/songwriter. First recorded with the R&B group The Lamplighters in 1953.

HARRIS, Tony
Male R&B-rock and roll singer.

HARRIS, Wynonie
Born on 8/24/1915 in Omaha, Nebraska. Died of throat cancer on 6/14/1969 (age 53). Highly influential male blues singer. Nicknamed "Mr. Blues." Vocalist for Lucky Millinder's band from 1944-45.

HARRISON, Don, Band
Rock group formed in California: Don Harrison (vocals), Russell DaShiell (guitar), Stu Cook (bass) and Doug Clifford (drums). Cook and Clifford were members of Creedence Clearwater Revival.

HARRISON, George
Born on 2/24/1943 in Wavertree, Liverpool, England. Died of cancer on 11/29/2001 (age 58). Formed his first group, the Rebels, at age 13. Joined John Lennon and Paul McCartney in The Quarrymen in 1958; group later evolved into The

Beatles, with Harrison as lead guitarist. Organized the Bangladesh benefit concerts at Madison Square Garden in 1971. Member of the supergroup Traveling Wilburys. Harrison's most popular recordings as The Beatles' lead singer included "Something," "While My Guitar Gently Weeps" and "Here Comes The Sun."

HARRISON, Noel
Born on 1/29/1934 in London, England. Singer/actor. Son of actor Rex Harrison.

HARRISON, Wilbert
Born on 1/5/1929 in Charlotte, North Carolina. Died of a stroke on 10/26/1994 (age 65). R&B singer/songwriter.

HARRY, Debbie
Born on 7/1/1945 in Miami, Florida; raised in Hawthorne, New Jersey. Lead singer of Blondie. In several movies and in several episodes of TV's *Wiseguy*.

HART, Beth
Born on 1/24/1972 in Santa Monica, California. Blues-rock singer/songwriter.

HART, Corey
Born on 5/31/1962 in Montreal, Quebec, Canada; raised in Malaga, Spain and Mexico City, Mexico. Male pop singer/songwriter/keyboardist.

HART, Freddie
Born Fred Segrest on 12/21/1926 in Loachapoka, Alabama. Country singer/songwriter/guitarist.

HART, Rod
Born in Beulah, Michigan. Male singer/songwriter.

HARTMAN, Dan
Born on 12/8/1950 in Harrisburg, Pennsylvania. Died of a brain tumor on 3/22/1994 (age 43). Singer/songwriter/multi-instrumentalist/producer. Member of the Edgar Winter Group from 1972-76. Writer/producer of several disco club anthems in the late '70s. Own studio, the Schoolhouse, in Westport, Connecticut.

HARVEY, PJ
Born Polly Jean Harvey on 10/9/1969 in Yeovil, England. Female singer/guitarist. Had own trio, also named PJ Harvey, which included bassist Stephen Vaughan and drummer Rob Ellis.

HARVEY BOYS, The
Pop vocal group.

HARVEY DANGER
Rock group from Seattle, Washington: Sean Nelson (vocals), Jeff Lin (guitar), Aaron Huffman (bass) and Evan Sult (drums).

HATFIELD, Bobby
Born on 8/10/1940 in Beaver Dam, Wisconsin. Died on 11/5/2003 (age 63). Teamed with Bill Medley as The Righteous Brothers.

HATFIELD, Juliana
Born on 7/2/1967 in Wiscasset, Maine. Female rock singer/guitarist. Originally recorded as The Juliana Hatfield 3. Attended Berklee College of Music where

HATFIELD, Juliana — cont'd
she was a member of the Blake Babies. Also played
bass with The Lemonheads.

HATHAWAY, Donny
Born on 10/1/1945 in Chicago, Illinois; raised in St.
Louis, Missouri. Committed suicide by jumping from
the 15th floor of New York City's Essex House hotel
on 1/13/1979 (age 33). R&B singer/songwriter/
keyboardist/producer/arranger. Gospel singer since
age three. Attended Washington DC's Howard
University on a fine arts scholarship; classmate of
Roberta Flack. Sang the theme of TV show *Maude*.
His wife Eulalah was a classical singer. Their
daughter Lalah Hathaway began her solo recording
career in 1990.

HAVENS, Richie
Born on 1/21/1941 in Brooklyn, New York. Black
folk singer/guitarist. Opening act of the 1969
Woodstock concert. Since the 1980s, sang
commercial jingles for Amtrak, McDonald's and
others.

HAWKES, Chesney
Born on 9/22/1971 in Windsor, Berkshire, England.
Pop-rock singer. Son of Len "Chip" Hawkes of The
Tremeloes.

HAWKINS, Dale
Born Delmar Hawkins on 8/22/1936 in Goldmine,
Louisiana. Rockabilly singer/guitarist. His lead
guitarists included James Burton, Roy Buchanan
and Scotty Moore. Record production work since
1965. First cousin to Ronnie Hawkins. The first
white rocker to play at the Apollo Theater.

HAWKINS, Edwin, Singers
Born on 8/18/1943 in Oakland, California. Formed
gospel group with Betty Watson in 1967 as the
Northern California State Youth Choir. Consisted of
46 black men and women. Dorothy Morrison was
lead singer and Odia Coates was a member.

HAWKINS, Erskine
Born on 7/26/1914 in Birmingham, Alabama. Died
on 11/11/1993 (age 79). Black trumpeter/composer/
band leader. Nicknamed the "Twentieth Century
Gabriel." Member of the 'Bama State Collegians, at
State Teacher's College, in Montgomery, which
became the Erskine Hawkins band in 1934. Very
popular at the Savoy Ballroom in New York City.
Featured brothers Dud and Paul Bascomb on
trumpet and tenor sax.

HAWKINS, Hawkshaw
Born Harold Hawkins on 12/22/1921 in Huntington,
West Virginia. Died in the plane crash with Patsy
Cline and Cowboy Copas on 3/5/1963 (age 41).
Country singer. Married Jean Shepard.

HAWKINS, Jennell
Born Jennell Grimes on 4/8/1938 in Los Angeles,
California. R&B singer/keyboardist.

HAWKINS, Ronnie
Born on 1/10/1935 in Huntsville, Arkansas. White
rockabilly singer/songwriter. Formed The Hawks in
1952. Moved to Canada in 1958. Assembled group
later known as The Band. First cousin to Dale
Hawkins.

HAWKINS, Roy
Born in Oakland, California. Singer/pianist.

HAWKINS, Screamin' Jay
Born Jalacy J. Hawkins on 7/18/1929 in Cleveland,
Ohio. Died of an aneurysm on 2/12/2000 (age 70).
R&B singer/songwriter/pianist. Former amatuer
boxing champion. Known for his bizarre antics and
props used in his stage shows.

HAWKINS, Sophie B.
Born Sophie Ballantine Hawkins on 11/1/1967 in
Manhattan, New York. Adult Contemporary
singer/songwriter.

HAWKS
Rock group from Otho, Iowa: Dave Hearn (vocals),
Kirk Kaufman and Dave Steen (guitars), Frank
Wiewel (bass), and Larry Adams (drums).

HAWLEY, Deane
Born William Dean Hawley on 12/18/1937 in Los
Angeles, California. Died on 12/25/2002 (age 65).
Pop singer.

HAY, Colin James
Born on 6/29/1953 in Scotland; raised in Melbourne,
Australia. Lead singer/guitarist of Men At Work.

HAYES, Bill
Born on 6/5/1926 in Harvey, Illinois. Hayes was a
regular on Sid Caesar's TV series *Your Show of
Shows*. Played "Doug Williams" on the TV soap
opera *Days Of Our Lives*.

HAYES, Darren
Born on 5/8/1972 in Brisbane, Queensland,
Australia. One-half of Savage Garden duo.

HAYES, Isaac
Born on 8/20/1942 in Covington, Tennessee. Died
on 8/10/2008 (age 65). R&B singer/songwriter/
keyboardist/actor. Session musician for Otis
Redding and other artists on the Stax label. Teamed
with songwriter David Porter to compose "Soul
Man," "Hold On! I'm A Comin'" and many others.
Composed movie scores for *Shaft*, *Tough Guys*,
Truck Turner and *Robin Hood: Men In Tights*. Acted
in the movie *Flipper*. Supplies the voice for "Chef"
on the animated TV series *South Park*.

HAYES, Peter Lind, & Mary Healy
Husband-and-wife vocal duo. Hayes was born on
6/25/1915 in San Francisco, California; died on
4/21/1998 (age 82). Healy was born on 4/14/1918 in
New Orleans, Louisiana. Married in 1940. Starred in
their own NBC-TV series, 1950-51.

HAYES, Wade
Born on 4/20/1969 in Bethel Acres, Oklahoma.
Country singer/songwriter/guitarist.

HAYMAN, Richard
Born on 3/27/1920 in Cambridge, Massachusetts.
Conductor/arranger/harmonica soloist. Long-time
associate conductor of the Boston Pops Orchestra.

HAYMES, Dick
Born on 9/13/1916 in Buenos Aires, Argentina (of
British parents); raised in Paris, France, and in New
Jersey. Died on 3/28/1980 (age 63). Ballad singer
with Harry James ("I'll Get By"), Benny Goodman

HAYMES, Dick — cont'd
and Tommy Dorsey in the early 1940s. Appeared in various movies from 1944-51. Married briefly to actress Rita Hayworth. His daughter Stephanie Haymes (with his fifth wife, singer Fran Jeffries) married rock songwriter Bernie Taupin in 1993.

HAYSI FANTAYZEE
Pop vocal duo from England: Kate Garner and Jeremiah Healy.

HAYWARD, Justin
Born on 10/14/1946 in Swindon, Wiltshire, England. Lead singer/guitarist of The Moody Blues.

HAYWOOD, Leon
Born on 2/11/1942 in Houston, Texas. R&B singer/songwriter/keyboardist.

HAZARD, Robert
Born in 1948 in Philadelphia, Pennsylvania. Died of cancer on 8/5/2008 (age 60). Rock singer/songwriter. Wrote Cyndi Lauper's "Girls Just Want To Have Fun."

HAZLEWOOD, Lee
Born Barton Lee Hazlewood on 7/9/1929 in Mannford, Oklahoma; raised in Texas. Died of kidney cancer on 8/4/2007 (age 78). Male singer/songwriter/producer.

HEAD, Murray
Born on 3/5/1946 in London, England. Pop singer/actor. Appeared on the 1970 rock concept album *Jesus Christ Superstar.* Played juvenile lead in the 1971 movie *Sunday, Bloody Sunday.*

HEAD, Roy
Born on 9/1/1941 in Three Rivers, Texas. Rock-country singer/guitarist. Head's backing band, The Traits, included Johnny Winter.

HEADBOYS, The
Rock group from Edinburgh, Scotland: Lou Lewis (guitar), Calum Malcolm (keyboards), George Boyter (bass) and Davy Ross (drums). All share vocals.

HEAD EAST
Rock group from St. Louis, Missouri: John Schlitt (vocals), Michael Somerville (guitar), Roger Boyd (keyboards), Dan Birney (bass) and Steve Huston (drums).

HEADLEY, Heather
Born on 10/5/1974 in Barataria, Trinidad; raised in Fort Wayne, Indiana. R&B singer/actress. Starred in the Broadway musical *Aida.*

HEADPINS
Rock group from Canada: Darby Mills (female vocals), Brian MacLeod (guitar), Ab Bryant (bass) and Bernie Aubin (drums). MacLeod and Bryant were with Chilliwack. Bryant was also with Prism. MacLeod died of cancer on 4/25/92.

HEALEY, Jeff, Band
Born Norman Jeffrey Healey on 3/25/1966 in Toronto, Ontario, Canada. Died of cancer on 3/2/2008 (age 41). Blues-rock singer/guitarist. Blind since age one. Formed own group with Joe

Rockman (bass) and Tom Stephen (drums). Band appeared in the 1989 movie *Road House.*

HEAP, Jimmy
Born on 3/3/1922 in Taylor, Texas. Died on 12/4/1977 (age 55). Perk Williams was lead singer of Heap's country band, The Melody Masters.

HEART
Rock group formed in Seattle, Washington: sisters Ann Wilson (vocals; born on 6/19/1950) and Nancy Wilson (guitar, keyboards; born on 3/16/1954), brothers Roger (born on 2/14/1950) and Mike Fisher (guitars), Steve Fossen (bass; born on 11/15/1949) and Mike DeRosier (drums; born on 8/24/1951). The Fishers left in 1979. Howard Leese (guitar) joined in 1980. Fossen and DeRosier left by 1982; replaced by Mark Andes (of Spirit, Jo Jo Gunne and Firefall) and Denny Carmassi (of Gamma). In 1990, former members Fossen, DeRosier and Roger Fisher joined Alias. Andes left by 1993. Carmassi left in 1994 to join Whitesnake. Nancy married movie director Cameron Crowe on 7/27/1986. Ann and Nancy's brother, Karl Wilson, played guitar for Merrilee Rush.

HEART & SOUL ORCHESTRA, The
Disco studio group assembled by DJ/VJ Frankie Crocker.

HEARTBEATS, The
R&B vocal group from Queens, New York: James "Shep" Sheppard, Wally Roker, Walter Crump, Robbie Adams and Vernon Walker. Group disbanded in 1960. Sheppard formed Shep & The Limelites in 1961; was murdered on 1/24/1970 (age 34).

HEARTLAND
Country group from Huntsville, Alabama: Jason Albert (vocals), brothers Craig Anderson (guitar) and Todd Anderson (drums), Mike Myerson (guitar), Chuck Crawford (fiddle) and Keith West (bass).

HEARTS, The
Female R&B vocal group from Harlem, New York: Joyce James, Joyce Peterson, Jeanette "Baby" Washington and Zell Sanders. Sanders, the mother of Johnnylouise Richardson of Johnnie & Joe, produced group's records. Not to be confused with Lee Andrews's male group of the same name.

HEARTSFIELD
Rock band from Chicago, Illinois: J.C. Heartsfield (vocals), Fred Dobbs, Perry Cordell and Phil Lucafo (guitars), Greg Biela (bass), and Artie Baldacci (drums).

HEATH, Ted
Born Edward Heath on 3/30/1900 in London, England. Died on 11/18/1969 (age 69). Trombonist/bandleader.

HEATHER B.
Born Heather Gardener on 11/13/1970 in Jersey City, New Jersey. Female rapper. One of the first-season cast members of MTV's *The Real World* in 1992.

HEATHERLY, Eric
Born on 2/21/1970 in Chattanooga, Tennessee.
Country-rockabilly singer/songwriter/guitarist.

HEATHERTON, Joey
Born Johanna Heatherton on 9/14/1944 in Rockville
Centre, Long Island, New York. Movie/TV actress.

HEATWAVE
Multi-national, interracial R&B-dance group formed
in Germany. Core members: brothers Johnnie and
Keith Wilder (vocals), Eric Johns and William Jones
(guitars), Rod Temperton and Calvin Duke
(keyboards), Derek Bramblz (bass), and Ernest
Berger (drums). Temperton left in late 1978 and
went on to become a prolific songwriter ("Rock With
You," "Baby Come To Me," among others). Johnnie
Wilder died on 5/13/2006 (age 56).

HEAVEN BOUND with Tony Scotti
Pop producer/backing vocalist Scotti with Joan
Medora (lead vocals), Eddie Medora, Tommy Oliver
and Michael Lloyd (Leif Garrett's producer). Tony
appeared in the movie *Valley Of The Dolls.*

HEAVEN 17
Electro-pop-dance trio from England: Glenn
Gregory (vocals) and former Human League
co-founders/synthesists Martyn Ware and Ian Craig
Marsh.

HEAVY D & THE BOYZ
Born Dwight Meyers on 5/24/1967 in Jamaica;
raised in Mt. Vernon, New York. Male rapper.
Former president of Uptown Records. Played
"Peaches" in the movie *The Cider House Rules.*
The Boyz consisted of Glen Parrish, Troy Dixon and
Edward Ferrell. Dixon died from an accidental fall
on 7/15/1990 (age 22).

HEBB, Bobby
Born on 7/26/1938 in Nashville, Tennessee. Black
singer/songwriter/multi-instrumentalist. Featured on
the *Grand Ole Opry* at age 12. His brother Hal was
a member of The Marigolds.

HEDGEHOPPERS ANONYMOUS
Rock band from England: Mick Tinsley (vocals),
John Stewart (guitar), Alan Laud (guitar), Ray
Honeybull (bass) and Leslie Dash (drums).

HEFTI, Neal
Born on 10/29/1922 in Hastings, Nebraska. Died of
a heart attack on 10/11/2008 (age 85). Conductor/
trumpeter. Gained fame as arranger for Woody
Herman (1944-46), Harry James and Count Basie,
then as composer of TV themes.

HEIGHT, Ronnie
Born on 3/2/1937 in Seattle, Washington. Pop
singer. Started career as lead first tenor of vocal
group the Five Checks.

HEIGHTS, The
Band made up of cast members from the Fox-TV
network prime time TV show of the same name:
Jamie Walters and Shawn Thompson (vocals), Alex
Desert, Ken Garito, Cheryl Pollack, Charlotte Ross,
Zachary Throne and Tarisa Valenza. Show was
based on fictional adventures featuring the band.

HELL, Richard, & The Voidoids
Born Lester Meyers on 10/2/1949 in Lexington,
Kentucky. Punk-rock singer/bassist. Formerly
married to Patty Smyth. The Voidoids consisted of
guitarists Robert Quine and Ivan Julian with
drummer Marc Bell.

HELLOGOODBYE
Pop-rock band from Huntington Beach, California:
Forrest Kline (vocals, guitar), Jesse Kurvink
(keyboards), Marcus Cole (bass) and Chris Profeta
(drums).

HELLO PEOPLE
White-faced, mime-rock group: Greg Geddes,
Robert Sedita, N.D. Smart and Laurence Tasse.

HELMS, Bobby
Born on 8/15/1935 in Bloomington, Indiana. Died of
emphysema on 6/19/1997 (age 61). Country
singer/guitarist. Appeared on father's local TV show.

HELTAH SKELTAH
Male rap duo from Brooklyn, New York: Tawl Sean
(a.k.a. Ruck or Sparsky) and Da Rockness Monsta
(a.k.a. Rock or Dutch).

HENDERSON, Joe
Born in 1937 in Como, Mississippi; raised in Gary,
Indiana. Died of a heart attack on 11/7/1964 (age
27). R&B singer.

HENDERSON, Michael
Born on 7/7/1951 in Yazoo City, Mississippi; raised
in Detroit, Michigan. R&B singer/bass player. To
Detroit in the early 1960s. Worked as a session
musician. Toured with Stevie Wonder and Aretha
Franklin. Featured vocalist on Norman Connors's
records.

HENDERSON, Willie
Born on 8/9/1941 in Pensacola, Florida. Black
producer/music director for Brunswick/Dakar in
Chicago, Illinois.

HENDRICKS, Bobby
Born on 2/22/1938 in Columbus, Ohio. R&B singer.
Lead singer with The Swallows in 1956. With The
Drifters in 1958 (sang lead on "Drip Drop").

HENDRIX, Jimi
Born on 11/27/1942 in Seattle, Washington. Died of
a drug overdose on 9/18/1970 (age 27). Legendary
psychedelic-blues-rock guitarist. Began career as a
studio guitarist. Played with Joey Dee & The
Starliters. In 1965, formed own band, Jimmy James
& The Blue Flames. In 1966, discovered by The
Animals' bassist Chas Chandler at New York City's
Cafe Wha?, who invited Hendrix to London, where
he created The Jimi Hendrix Experience with Noel
Redding (bass; died on 5/12/2003, age 57) and
Mitch Mitchell (drums). Formed new group in 1969,
Band of Gypsys, with Buddy Miles (drums) and Billy
Cox (bass).

HENDRYX, Nona
Born on 10/9/1944 in Trenton, New Jersey. Member
of Patti LaBelle & The Blue-Belles from 1961-77.

HENLEY, Don
Born on 7/22/1947 in Gilmer, Texas. Soft-rock singer/songwriter/drummer. Own band, Shiloh, in the early 1970s. Worked with Glenn Frey in Linda Ronstadt's backup band, then the two formed the Eagles with Randy Meisner and Bernie Leadon. Went solo in 1982. Married model Sharon Summerall on 5/20/1995.

HENRY, Clarence
Born on 3/19/1937 in Algiers, Louisiana. R&B singer/pianist/songwriter. With Bobby Mitchell's R&B band from 1953-55. Nicknamed "Frog Man" because of his frog sounds in his hit "Ain't Got No Home."

HENSON, Jim
Born on 9/24/1936 in Greenville, Mississippi. Died of a sudden virus on 5/16/1990 (age 53). Creator of The Muppets, that famous crew of puppets starring in TV's *Sesame Street* and *The Muppet Show*, also in the movies *The Muppet Movie* and *The Great Muppet Caper*. Henson was the voice for both Ernie and Kermit.

HERMAN, Keith
Pop-rock singer/songwriter/guitarist.

HERMAN, Woody
Born on 5/16/1913 in Milwaukee, Wisconsin. Died of heart failure on 10/29/1987 (age 74). Saxophonist/clarinetist of dance bands beginning in 1929. Formed own band in 1936. One of the most innovative and contemporary of all big band leaders.

HERMAN'S HERMITS
Teen pop-rock group from Manchester, England: Peter "Herman" Noone (vocals; born on 11/5/1947), Derek Leckenby (born on 5/14/1943) and Keith Hopwood (guitars; born on 10/26/1946), Karl Green (bass; born on 7/31/1947), and Barry Whitwam (drums; born on 7/21/1946). Group name derived from cartoon character Sherman of TV's *The Bullwinkle Show*. Noone left in 1972 for a solo career; formed Los Angeles-based group The Tremblers in late 1970s. Noone hosted own show on music video TV channel VH-1. Leckenby died of cancer on 6/4/1994 (age 51).

HERNANDEZ, Marcos
Born in 1982 in Phoenix, Arizona; raised in Dallas, Texas. Latin singer.

HERNANDEZ, Patrick
Born on 4/6/1949 in Paris, France. Disco singer/songwriter.

HERNDON, Ty
Born Boyd Tyrone Herndon on 5/2/1962 in Meridian, Mississippi; raised in Butler, Alabama. Country singer/songwriter/guitarist.

HESITATIONS, The
R&B vocal group from Cleveland, Ohio: brothers George "King" and Charles Scott, Fred Deal, Robert Sheppard, Arthur Blakely, Phillip Dorroh and Leonard Veal. George Scott was accidentally shot to death in February 1968 (age 38).

HEWETT, Howard
Born on 10/1/1957 in Akron, Ohio. Lead vocalist of Shalamar, 1979-85. Married to Nia Peeples from 1989-93.

HEWITT, Jennifer Love
Born on 2/21/1979 in Waco, Texas. Pop singer/actress. Starred on TV's *Party Of Five* and *Ghost Whisperer* and in such movies as *I Know What You Did Last Summer*, *Can't Hardly Wait*, *Heartbreakers* and *The Tuxedo*.

HEYETTES, The
Female novelty-pop vocal trio: Julia Tillman, Maxine Willard and Jessica Smith.

HEYWOOD, Eddie
Born on 12/4/1915 in Atlanta, Georgia. Died on 1/2/1989 (age 73). Black jazz pianist/composer/arranger. Played professionally by age 14. Own band in New York City in 1941. Worked with Billie Holiday. To the West Coast in 1947, with own trio.

HIBBLER, Al
Born on 8/16/1915 in Tyro, Mississippi. Died on 4/24/2001 (age 85). Black vocalist. Blind since birth, studied voice at Little Rock's Conservatory for the Blind. First recorded with Jay McShann for Decca in 1942. With Duke Ellington, 1943-51. Also recorded with Harry Carney, Tab Smith, Mercer Ellington and Billy Strayhorn.

HI-C
Born in 1972 in Louisiana; raised in California. Male rapper.

HICKEY, Ersel
Born on 6/27/1934 in Brighton, New York. Died of cancer on 7/12/2004 (age 70). Rockabilly singer/guitarist.

HICKS, Erik
R&B singer/songwriter.

HICKS, Taylor
Born on 10/7/1976 in Birmingham, Alabama. Winner on the 2006 season of TV's *American Idol*.

HI-FI FOUR, The
White pop vocal group from Toronto, Ontario, Canada: Jack McNicol, Don Wainman, Doug Harman and John Van Evera.

HI-FIVE
R&B vocal group from Waco, Texas: Tony Thompson, Roderick Clark, Russell Neal, Marcus Sanders and Toriano Easley. Treston Irby replaced Easley in late 1991. Thompson died of a drug overdose on 6/1/2007 (age 31).

HIGGINS, Bertie
Born Elbert Higgins on 12/8/1944 in Tarpon Springs, Florida. Soft-rock singer/songwriter. First recorded for ABC in 1964. Worked as a drummer with Tommy Roe, 1964-66.

HIGH INERGY
Female R&B vocal group from Pasadena, California: sisters Vernessa and Barbara Mitchell, Linda Howard and Michelle Rumph. Vernessa left in 1978; group continued as a trio.

HIGH KEYES, The
R&B vocal group from Brooklyn, New York: Troy Keyes (lead singer), Jimmy Williams, Bobby Haggard and Cliff Rice.

HIGHLIGHTS, The
White vocal group from Chicago, Illinois: Frank Pizani (lead; born on 1/24/1935), brothers Frank and Tony Calzaretta, Bill Melshimer, and Jerry Oleski.

HIGH SCHOOL MUSICAL CAST
Various cast members of the highly popular Disney TV movie: Zac Efron, Vanessa Hudgens, Ashley Tisdale, Lucas Grabeel, Corbin Bleu and Monique Coleman.

HIGHWAYMEN, The
Folk group formed in Middletown, Connecticut: Dave Fisher, Bob Burnett, Chan Daniels, Steve Trott and Steve Butts. Daniels died of pneumonia on 8/2/1975 (age 35).

HILL, Bunker
Born David Walker on 5/5/1941 in Washington DC. R&B singer. Member of Mighty Clouds Of Joy.

HILL, Dan
Born on 6/3/1954 in Toronto, Ontario, Canada. Adult Contemporary singer/songwriter.

HILL, David
Born David Hess on 9/19/1936 in Brooklyn, New York. Pop singer/songwriter. Starred in the movie *Last House On The Left*.

HILL, Faith
Born on 9/21/1967 in Jackson, Mississippi. Country singer. Adopted at less than a week old and raised as Audrey Faith Perry in Star, Mississippi. Married Tim McGraw on 10/6/1996.

HILL, Jessie
Born on 12/9/1932 in New Orleans, Louisiana. Died of heart failure on 9/17/1996 (age 63). R&B singer/drummer/pianist. With Huey (Piano) Smith to 1958.

HILL, Jordan
Born on 4/17/1978 in Knoxville, Tennessee. White female teen pop singer.

HILL, Lauryn
Born on 5/25/1975 in South Orange, New Jersey. Black singer/actress. Member of The Fugees. Acted on TV's *As The World Turns* and in the movie *Sister Act 2*.

HILL, Z.Z.
Born Arzel Hill on 9/30/1935 in Naples, Texas. Died of a heart attack on 4/27/1984 (age 48). Blues singer/guitarist. Formed Hill Records in 1970.

HILLSIDE SINGERS, The
Adult Contemporary vocal group: Lori Ham, Mary Mayo, Joelle Marino, Bill Marino, Frank Marino, Laura Marino, Rick Shaw, Ron Shaw and Susan Wiedinman. The Marinos are siblings. Mary Mayo was the wife of producer Al Ham; Lori Ham is their daughter. Rick and Ron Shaw are brothers; Ron went on to a country music career.

HILLTOPPERS, The
White vocal group formed in Bowling Green, Kentucky: Jimmy Sacca, Don McGuire, Seymour Spiegelman and Billy Vaughn. Vaughn left for own conducting career in 1955; replaced by Chuck Schrouder. Spiegelman died on 2/13/1987 (age 56). Vaughn died of cancer on 9/26/1991 (age 72).

HILSON, Keri
Born on 10/27/1982 in Atlanta, Georgia. Female R&B singer/songwriter.

HILTON, Paris
Born on 2/17/1981 in Manhattan, New York. Female singer/actress/socialite. One of the heirs to the Hilton Hotel dynasty. Starred in the 2003 reality series *The Simple Life* with friend Nicole Richie (adopted daughter of Lionel Richie); also acted in several movies. In June 2007, served time in jail on a probation violation.

HIM
Goth-rock band from Finland: Ville Valo (vocals), Mikko "Linde" Lindström (guitar), Emerson Burton (keyboards), Migé Amour (bass) and Gas Lipstick (drums). HIM: His Infernal Majesty.

HINDER
Alternative-rock band from Oklahoma City, Oklahoma: Austin Winkler (vocals), Joe Garvey (guitar), Mark King (guitar), Mike Rodden (bass) and Cody Hanson (drums).

HINE, Eric
Born in England. Pop-rock singer/songwriter/keyboardist.

HINTON, Joe
Born on 11/15/1929 in Evansville, Indiana. Died of cancer on 8/13/1968 (age 38). R&B singer. With the Chosen Gospel Singers. Lead singer of the Spirit Of Memphis (gospel group).

HIPPIES, The (Formerly The Tams)
White doo-wop group from Philadelphia, Pennsylvania. Not to be confused with the Atlanta R&B group, The Tams.

HIPSWAY
Pop group from Scotland: Graham Skinner (vocals), Pim Jones (guitar), John McElhone (bass) and Harry Travers (drums). McElhone later joined Texas.

HIRT, Al
Born Alois Maxwell Hirt on 11/7/1922 in New Orleans, Louisiana. Died of liver failure on 4/27/1999 (age 76). Trumpet virtuoso. Toured with Jimmy and Tommy Dorsey, Ray McKinley and Horace Heidt. Formed own Dixieland combo (with Pete Fountain) in the late 1950s.

HI TEK 3 Featuring Ya Kid K
Dance trio from Belgium: Kovali, El Sati and Yosev. Ya Kid K is the female rapper of Technotronic.

HITMAN SAMMY SAM
Born Sammy King in Atlanta, Georgia. Male rapper.

HIT MASTERS
Band of anonymous studio musicians.

HI-TOWN DJ'S
Rap group from Florida: Kalo, Derrick Rahming, Matt Young, Teeze, JP and Chyna Doll.

HIVES, The
Rock group from Fagersta, Sweden: brothers Pelle (vocals) and Niklas (guitar) Almqvist, Vigilante Carlstroem (guitar), Dr. Matt Destruction (bass) and Chris Dangerous (drums).

HO, Don
Born on 8/13/1930 in Kakaako, Oahu, Hawaii. Died of heart failure on 4/14/2007 (age 76). Adult Contemporary singer/actor. Father of Hoku.

HODGE, Chris
Born in England. Pop-rock singer/songwriter.

HODGES, Eddie
Born on 3/5/1947 in Hattiesburg, Mississippi. Pop singer/actor. Appeared in many movies and TV shows.

HODGES, JAMES & SMITH
Female R&B vocal trio from Detroit, Michigan: Pat Hodges, Denita James and Jessica Smith.

HODGSON, Roger
Born on 5/21/1950 in Portsmouth, England. Lead singer of Supertramp.

HOFFS, Susanna
Born on 1/17/1959 in Newport Beach, California. Former lead singer of The Bangles. Starred in the 1987 movie *The Allnighter*. Her mother is movie director Tamara Hoffs. Married M. Jay Roach, a TV producer/ movie director (*Austin Powers*), on 4/17/1993.

HOGAN, Brooke
Born Brooke Bollea on 5/2/1988 in Tampa, Florida. Teen female singer. Daughter of legendary professional wrestler Terry "Hulk Hogan" Bollea. Appeared with the rest of her family on the VH-1 reality series *Hogan Knows Best*.

HOG HEAVEN
Rock group formerly known as Tommy James's Shondells: Eddie Gray (guitar), Ronnie Rosman (keyboards), Mike Vale (bass) and Pete Lucia (drums). All share vocals.

HOKU
Born Hoku Ho on 6/10/1981 in Oahu, Hawaii. Teen pop-rock singer. Daughter of singer/actor Don Ho.

HOLDEN, Ron
Born on 8/7/1939 in Seattle, Washington. Died of a heart attack on 1/22/1997 (age 57). R&B singer.

HOLE
Rock group formed in Los Angeles, California: Courtney Love (vocals, guitar), Eric Erlandson (guitar), Kristen Pfaff (bass) and Patty Schemel (drums). Love acted in the movies *Sid & Nancy*, *Straight To Hell*, *Feeling Minnesota* and *The People Vs. Larry Flynt*. Love was married to Kurt Cobain (Nirvana) from 2/24/1992 until his death on 4/8/1994. Pfaff was found dead in her bathtub on 6/16/1994 (age 27). Melissa Auf Der Maur replaced Pfaff.

HOLIDAY, Billie
Born Eleanor Gough on 4/7/1915 in Philadelphia, Pennsylvania. Died on 7/17/1959 (age 44). Legendary jazz singer. Nicknamed "Lady Day." Subject of the 1972 movie *Lady Sings The Blues* starring Diana Ross.

HOLIDAY, Chico
Born Ralph Vergolino on 8/24/1934 in Waukesha, Wisconsin. Rock and roll singer.

HOLIDAY, J.
Born in 1985 in Washington DC. Male R&B singer/songwriter.

HOLIDAY, Jimmy
Born on 7/24/1934 in Durant, Mississippi; raised in Waterloo, Iowa. Died of heart failure on 2/15/1987 (age 52). R&B singer/songwriter.

HOLIDAY, Tasha
Born in Atlantic City, New Jersey. Female R&B singer.

HOLIDAYS, The
R&B vocal trio from Detroit, Michigan: Edwin Starr, J.J. Barnes and Steve Mancha. Each recorded solo.

HOLIEN, Danny
Born on 1/29/1949 in Red Wing, Minnesota. Folk-rock singer/songwriter/guitarist.

HOLLAND, Amy
Born on 5/15/1955 in Los Angeles, California. Pop singer. Married to Michael McDonald.

HOLLAND, Brian
Born on 2/15/1941 in Detroit, Michigan. Singer/ songwriter/producer. Teamed with brother Eddie Holland and Lamont Dozier in successful songwriting/production team for Motown; wrote many of Motown's greatest hits. Trio left Motown in 1968 and formed own Invictus/Hot Wax labels.

HOLLAND, Eddie
Born on 10/30/1939 in Detroit, Michigan. Singer/ songwriter/producer. Member of Motown's hit production trio with brother Brian Holland and Lamont Dozier; wrote many of Motown's greatest hits. Co-founder of the Invictus/Hot Wax label.

HOLLIDAY, Jennifer
Born on 10/19/1960 in Riverside, Texas. R&B singer/actress. Appeared in several Broadway musicals.

HOLLIES, The
Pop-rock group from Manchester, England: Allan Clarke (vocals; born on 4/5/1942), Graham Nash (born on 2/2/1942) and Tony Hicks (guitars; born on 12/16/1945), Eric Haydock (bass; born on 2/3/1943), and Bobby Elliott (drums; born on 12/8/1941). Haydock left in 1966; replaced by Bernie Calvert (first heard on "Bus Stop"). Nash left in December 1968 to join David Crosby and Stephen Stills in new trio; replaced by Terry Sylvester, formerly in The Swinging Blue Jeans. Shuffling personnel since then. Clarke, Nash, Hicks and Elliott regrouped briefly in 1983.

HOLLISTER, Dave
Born in Chicago, Illinois. R&B/hip-hop singer/
songwriter. Former member of BLACKstreet.

HOLLOWAY, Brenda
Born on 6/21/1946 in Atascadero, California. R&B
singer/songwriter. Later a backup singer for Joe
Cocker.

HOLLOWAY, Loleatta
Born on 11/5/1946 in Chicago, Illinois. Female disco
singer.

HOLLY, Buddy / The Crickets
Born Charles Hardin Holley on 9/7/1936 in Lubbock,
Texas. One of rock and roll's most popular,
legendary and innovative performers. Began
recording western and pop demos with Bob
Montgomery in 1954. Signed to Decca label in
January 1956 and recorded in Nashville as Buddy
Holly & The Three Tunes (Sonny Curtis, lead guitar;
Don Guess, bass; and Jerry Ivan Allison, drums). In
February 1957, Holly assembled his backing group,
The Crickets (Allison; Niki Sullivan, rhythm guitar;
and Joe B. Mauldin, bass), for recordings at
Norman Petty's studio in Clovis, New Mexico.
Signed to Brunswick and Coral labels (subsidiaries
of Decca Records). Because of contract
arrangements, all Brunswick records were released
as The Crickets, and all Coral records were
released as Buddy Holly. Holly split from The
Crickets in the fall of 1958. Holly (age 22), Ritchie
Valens and the Big Bopper were killed in a plane
crash near Mason City, Iowa, on 2/3/1959. Gary
Busey starred in the 1978 biographical movie *The
Buddy Holly Story*.

HOLLYRIDGE STRINGS, The
Arranged and conducted by Stu Phillips, later of the
Golden Gate Strings.

HOLLYWOOD ARGYLES
Gary Paxton recorded "Alley-Oop" as a solo artist;
since he was still under contract to Brent Records,
where he recorded as Flip of "Skip & Flip," he made
up the name Hollywood Argyles after street signs at
Hollywood & Argyle. After the song was a hit,
Paxton assembled a Hollywood Argyles group.
Formed Garpax Records. Paxton is now a gospel
artist.

HOLLYWOOD FLAMES
R&B vocal group from Los Angeles, California: Earl
Nelson and Bobby Day (both of Bob & Earl), David
Ford, Clyde Tillis and Curtis Williams (former
member of The Penguins). Day died on 7/15/1990
(age 60).

HOLLYWOOD STARS, The
Rock group from Los Angeles, California: Mark
Anthony (vocals), Rueben De Fuentes and Steve
DeLacy (guitars), Michael Rummans (bass), and
Bobby Drier (drums).

HOLM, Michael
Born Lothar Walter on 7/29/1943 in Stettin,
Germany. Adult Contemporary singer/songwriter/
producer.

HOLMAN, Eddie
Born on 6/3/1946 in Norfolk, Virginia; raised in New
York and Philadelphia, Pennsylvania. R&B singer/
songwriter. Recorded for Leopard in the early
1960s.

HOLMES, Clint
Born on 5/9/1946 in Bournemouth, England; raised
in Farnham, New York. Adult Contemporary singer.

HOLMES, Jake
Born on 12/28/1939 in San Francisco, California.
Folk-rock singer/songwriter.

HOLMES, Leroy
Born Alvin Holmes on 9/22/1913 in Pittsburgh,
Pennsylvania. Died on 7/27/1986 (age 72).
Orchestra conductor/arranger.

HOLMES, Richard "Groove"
Born on 5/2/1931 in Camden, New Jersey. Died of
prostate cancer on 6/29/1991 (age 60). Black jazz
organist. Discovered by Les McCann. Recorded
with Joe Pass, Gene Ammons and Clifford Scott.

HOLMES, Rupert
Born on 2/24/1947 in Northwich, Cheshire, England;
raised in Manhattan, New York. Pop singer/
songwriter. Member of Street People. Wrote the
Broadway musical *Drood*. Created the TV show
Remember WENN for American Movie Classics
cable channel.

HOLY, Steve
Born on 2/23/1972 in Dallas, Texas. Country
singer/songwriter.

HOMBRES, The
Rock group from Memphis, Tennessee: B.B.
Cunningham (vocals, organ), Gary McEwen (guitar),
Jerry Masters (bass) and Johnny Hunter (drums).
Hunter committed suicide in February 1976 (age
34). Cunningham's brother, Bill, was a member of
The Box Tops.

HOMER & JETHRO
Country comedy duo from Knoxville, Tennessee.
Henry "Homer" Haynes (guitar; born on 7/27/1920;
died on 8/7/1971, age 51) and Kenneth "Jethro"
Burns (mandolin; born on 3/10/1920; died on
2/4/1989, age 68). Jethro went on to work with
popular folk singer Steve Goodman after Homer's
death.

HOME TEAM
Rap duo from Brooklyn, New York; later relocated to
Miami, Florida: brothers Debonaire and Drugzie.

HONDELLS, The
Producer Nick Venet and arranger Gary Usher
recorded various studio musicians in Southern
California under different group names. "Little
Honda" featured Usher, Chuck Girard (The Castells;
vocals), Glen Campbell and Richie Podolor (Richie
Allen; guitars), Hal Blaine (drums) and Ritchie Burns
(backing vocals). Usher (Sagittarius; died of cancer
on 5/25/1990, age 51) later formed touring group
with Burns (lead vocals), Wayne Edwards (drums)
and varying members. Randy Thomas sang lead on
"Younger Girl."

HONEYCOMBS, The
Rock and roll band from London, England: Dennis D'ell (vocals), Allan Ward and Martin Murray (guitars), John Lantree (bass) and his sister Ann "Honey" Lantree (drums).

HONEY CONE, The
Female R&B vocal trio from Los Angeles, California: Carolyn Willis (member of The Girlfriends and Bob B. Soxx & The Blue Jeans), Edna Wright (sister of Darlene Love) and Shellie Clark (former Ikette and regular on the TV series *The Jim Nabors Hour* from 1969-70). Willis left in 1973; replaced by Denise Mills.

HONEYCONES, The
Five-man rock and roll band.

HONEYDRIPPERS, The
A rock superstar gathering: vocalist Robert Plant (Led Zeppelin), with guitarists Jimmy Page (The Yardbirds, Led Zeppelin, The Firm), Jeff Beck (The Yardbirds) and Nile Rodgers (Chic).

HONEYMOON SUITE
Rock group from Toronto, Ontario, Canada: Johnnie Dee (vocals), Dermot Grehan (guitar), Ray Coburn (keyboards), Garry Lalonde (bass) and Dave Betts (drums). Rob Preuss replaced Coburn in 1987.

HOOBASTANK
Hard-rock group from Agoura Hills, California: Doug Robb (vocals), Dan Estrin (guitar), Markku Lappalainen (bass) and Chris Hesse (drums).

HOOKER, John Lee
Born on 8/22/1917 in Coahoma County, Mississippi. Died on 6/21/2001 (age 83). Legendary blues singer/guitarist. Featured in the movie *The Blues Brothers*.

HOOTERS
Pop-rock group from Philadelphia, Pennsylvania: Eric Bazilian (vocals, guitar), Rob Hyman (vocals, keyboards), John Lilley (guitar), Andy King (bass) and David Uosikkinen (drums). Fran Smith Jr. replaced King in early 1989. Bazilian and Hyman were arrangers/musicians/backing vocalists on Cyndi Lauper's album *She's So Unusual*. Hooter: nickname of Hyman's keyboard-harmonica.

HOOTIE & THE BLOWFISH
Pop-rock group formed in South Carolina: Darius Rucker (vocals; born on 5/13/1966), Mark Bryan (guitar; born on 5/6/1967), Dean Felber (bass; born on 6/9/1967) and Jim Sonefeld (drums; born on 10/20/1964).

HOPKIN, Mary
Born on 5/3/1950 in Pontardawe, Glamorganshire, Wales. Discovered by the model Twiggy. Recorded with the group Hobby Horse in 1972 for Bell Records. Married to producer Tony Visconti (worked with David Bowie) from 1971-81.

HORNE, Jimmy "Bo"
Born on 9/28/1949 in West Palm Beach, Florida. R&B-disco singer.

HORNE, Lena
Born on 6/30/1917 in Brooklyn, New York. Singer/actress. Star of many MGM musicals from 1942-56. Received a Tony award for her one-woman Broadway show *Lena Horne: The Lady And Her Music*. Her 1943 recording of "Stormy Weather" (as performed by her in the movie of the same title) was selected for a Grammy Hall of Fame award.

HORNER, James
Born on 8/14/1953 in London, England. Scored several movies including the 1997 blockbuster *Titanic*.

HORNSBY, Bruce, & The Range
Born on 11/23/1954 in Williamsburg, Virginia. Pop-rock singer/songwriter/pianist. The Range: George Marinelli and David Mansfield (guitars), Joe Puerta (bass) and John Molo (drums). Puerta was a member of Ambrosia. Hornsby later toured as a member of the Grateful Dead and The Other Ones. Wrote the hits "Jacob's Ladder" (Huey Lewis) and "The End Of The Innocence" (Don Henley).

HORTON, Jamie
Born Gayla Peevey on 3/8/1943 in Oklahoma City, Oklahoma. Teen female pop singer. Recorded the novelty song "I Want A Hippopotamus For Christmas" under her real name in 1953.

HORTON, Johnny
Born on 4/30/1925 in Los Angeles, California; raised in Tyler, Texas. Died in a car crash on 11/5/1960 (age 35). Singer/songwriter/guitarist. Known as "The Singing Fisherman." Married to Billie Jean Horton, widow of Hank Williams, from 1953 until his death.

HOT
Interracial female vocal trio from Los Angeles, California: Gwen Owens, Cathy Carson and Juanita Curiel.

HOT BOY$
All-star rap group from New Orleans, Louisiana: B.G., Juvenile, Lil Wayne and Young Turk.

HOT BUTTER
Group is actually Stan Free (Moog synthesizer player).

HOT CHOCOLATE
Interracial rock-soul group formed in London, England: Errol Brown (vocals), Harvey Hinsley (guitar), Larry Ferguson (keyboards), Patrick Olive (bass) and Tony Connor (drums).

HOTEL
Pop-rock group from Birmingham, Alabama: Marc Phillips (vocals, keyboards), Tommy Colton and Mike Reid (guitars), Lee Bargeron (keyboards), George Creasman (bass) and Michael Cadenhead (drums).

HOTLEGS
Pop-rock trio from Manchester, England: Eric Stewart (of The Mindbenders), Kevin Godley and Lol Creme. Group evolved into 10cc. Godley & Creme later recorded as a duo.

HOT SAUCE
R&B vocal trio from Detroit, Michigan: Ronda Washington, Glynton Ashley and William Callaway. Washington also recorded solo as Hot Sauce.

HOT STYLZ
Male rap trio from Chicago, Illinois: Raydio G, Krazee and Meatball.

HOUGH, Julianne
Born on 7/20/1988 in Salt Lake City, Utah. Female singer/dancer. Winner (along with partner Apolo Ohno) on the fourth season and (along with partner Hélio Castroneves) on the fifth season of TV's *Dancing With The Stars*.

HOUSE OF LORDS
Hard-rock group: James Christian (vocals), Lanny Cordola (guitar), Gregg Giuffria (keyboards), Chuck Wright (bass) and Ken Mary (drums). Cordola was with Ozzy Osbourne. Giuffria and Wright were both with Giuffria; Wright was also with Quiet Riot. Mary was with Alice Cooper. Michael Guy replaced Cordola in 1990.

HOUSE OF PAIN
White hip-hop group from Los Angeles, California: Erik "Everlast" Schrody (born on 8/18/1969), "Danny Boy" O'Connor and Leor "DJ Lethal" DiMant. Both Schrody and O'Connor were born in the U.S. of Irish parentage. DiMant was born in Latvia.

HOUSTON
Born Houston Summers in Belize; raised in Los Angeles, California. Male R&B singer/songwriter.

HOUSTON, Cissy
Born Emily Drinkard on 9/30/1933 in Newark, New Jersey. R&B singer. Lead singer of The Sweet Inspirations from 1967-70. Mother of Whitney Houston.

HOUSTON, David
Born on 12/9/1938 in Bossier City, Louisiana. Died of a brain aneurysm on 11/30/1993 (age 54). Country singer/songwriter/guitarist.

HOUSTON, Marques
Born on 8/4/1981 in Los Angeles, California. R&B singer. Member of Immature.

HOUSTON, Thelma
Born on 5/7/1946 in Leland, Mississippi. R&B-dance singer/actress.

HOUSTON, Whitney
Born on 8/9/1963 in Newark, New Jersey. R&B singer/actress. Daughter of Cissy Houston and cousin of Dionne Warwick and Dee Dee Warwick. Began singing career at age 11 with the gospel group New Hope Baptist Junior Choir. As a teen, worked as a backing vocalist for Chaka Khan and Lou Rawls. Pursued modeling career in 1981, appearing in *Glamour* magazine and on the cover of *Seventeen*. Married to Bobby Brown, 1992-2007. Starred in the movies *The Bodyguard*, *Waiting To Exhale* and *The Preacher's Wife*.

HOWARD, Adina
Born on 11/14/1974 in Grand Rapids, Michigan. Female R&B singer.

HOWARD, Eddy
Born on 9/12/1914 in Woodland, California. Died on 5/23/1963 (age 48). Singer with the Dick Jurgens band from 1934-40. Composer of "My Last Goodbye" and "Careless."

HOWARD, Jan
Born Lula Grace Johnson on 3/13/1930 in West Plains, Missouri. Country singer/songwriter. Married to Harlan Howard from 1957-67. Toured with Bill Anderson, Johnny Cash and Tammy Wynette.

HOWARD, Miki
Born in 1962 in Chicago, Illinois. Black female session singer/songwriter. Former lead singer of Side Effect. Portrayed Billie Holiday in the movie *Malcolm X*.

HOWARD, Rebecca Lynn
Born on 4/24/1979 in Salyersville, Kentucky. Country singer/songwriter.

HOWARD, Terrence (Djay) & Taraji P. Henson (Shug)
Male-female R&B duo. Howard was born on 3/11/1969 in Chicago, Illinois. Henson was born on 9/11/1970 in Washington DC. Both acted in several movies.

HOWELL, Reuben
Pop singer/songwriter.

HOWLIN' WOLF
Born Chester Arthur Burnett on 6/10/1910 in West Point, Mississippi. Died of cancer on 1/10/1976 (age 65). Legendary blues singer/guitarist.

H-TOWN
R&B vocal trio from Houston, Texas: brothers Shazam and Keven "Dino" Conner, with Darryl Jackson. Keven Conner died in a car crash on 1/28/2003 (age 28).

HUDGENS, Vanessa
Born on 12/14/1988 in Salinas, California. Teen actress/singer. Played "Gabriella Montez" in the TV movie *High School Musical*.

HUDSON, David
Born in Miami, Florida. R&B singer.

HUDSON, Jennifer
Born on 9/12/1981 in Chicago, Illinois. R&B singer/actress. Won the Best Supporting Actress Oscar for playing "Effie White" in the 2006 movie *Dreamgirls*.

HUDSON, "Pookie"
Born James Hudson on 6/11/1934 in Des Moines, Iowa; raised in Gary, Indiana. Died of cancer on 1/16/2007 (age 72). R&B singer. Lead singer of The Spaniels.

HUDSON & LANDRY
Comedy duo of DJs Bob Hudson and Ron Landry from Los Angeles, California. Split up in 1976. Hudson died on 9/20/1997 (age 66). Landry died on 9/16/2002 (age 64).

HUDSON BROTHERS
Pop vocal trio from Portland, Oregon: Bill, Brett and Mark Hudson. Hosted own TV variety show during the summer of 1974; also hosted kiddie TV show *The Hudson Brothers Razzle Dazzle Comedy Show*. Bill was married to actress Goldie Hawn from 1976-79 (their daughter is actress Kate Hudson).

HUES CORPORATION, The
R&B-disco vocal trio formed in Los Angeles, California: St. Clair Lee, Fleming Williams (died in 1992) and Ann Kelley. Williams replaced by Tommy Brown after "Rock The Boat." Brown replaced by Karl Russell in 1976. Group named after Howard Hughes.

HUEY
Born Lawrence Franks on 1/1/1989 in Kinloch, Missouri. Male rapper.

HUGH, Grayson
Born in Connecticut. Blue-eyed soul singer/ songwriter/pianist.

HUGHES, Fred
Born in Arkansas. R&B singer/songwriter.

HUGHES, Freddie
Born on 8/20/1943 in Berkeley, California; raised in Oakland, California. R&B singer.

HUGHES, Jimmy
Born in Florence, Alabama. R&B singer. Cousin of Percy Sledge.

HUGHES/THRALL
Rock duo of singer/bassist Glenn Hughes (Trapeze, Deep Purple) and guitarist Pat Thrall (Automatic Man, Asia, Pat Travers Band).

HUGO & LUIGI
Producers/songwriters/label executives Hugo Peretti (born on 12/6/1916; died on 5/1/1986, age 69) and Luigi Creatore (born on 12/21/1920). Owned record labels Roulette and Avco/Embassy.

HULIN, T.K.
Born Alton James Hulin on 8/16/1943 in St. Martinville, Louisiana. Pop singer.

HULLABALLOOS, The
Rock and roll band from England: Ricky Knight (vocals, guitar), Andy Woonton (guitar), Geoff Mortimer (bass) and Harry Dunn (drums).

HUM
Rock group from Champaign, Illinois: Matt Talbott (vocals), Tim Lash (guitar), Jeff Dimpsey (bass) and Bryan St. Pere (drums).

HUMAN BEINZ, The
Rock group from Youngstown, Ohio: Dick Belly (vocals, guitar), Joe Markulin (guitar), Mel Pachuta (bass) and Mike Tateman (drums).

HUMAN LEAGUE, The
Electro-pop trio from Sheffield, Yorkshire, England: lead singer/synthesist Philip Oakey (born on 10/2/1955), with female vocalists Joanne Catherall (born on 9/18/1962) and Susanne Sulley (born on 3/22/1963). Early members Martyn Ware and Ian Craig Marsh left to form Heaven 17.

HUMBLE PIE
Hard-rock group formed in Essex, England: Peter Frampton (guitar, vocals; The Herd), Steve Marriott (vocals, guitar; Small Faces; died on 4/20/1991, age 44), Greg Ridley (bass; Spooky Tooth) and Jerry Shirley (drums). Frampton left in October 1971; replaced by Clem Clempson (Rough Diamond). Disbanded in 1975. Reunited from 1980-81 with Marriott, Shirley, Bobby Tench (guitar) and Anthony Jones (bass).

HUMPERDINCK, Engelbert
Born Arnold Dorsey on 5/2/1936 in Madras, India; raised in Leicester, England. First recorded for Decca in 1958. Met Tom Jones's manager, Gordon Mills, in 1965, who suggested his name change to Engelbert Humperdinck (a famous German opera composer). Starred in his own musical variety TV series in 1970.

HUMPHREY, Della
Born in 1956 in Miami, Florida. Female R&B singer.

HUMPHREY, Paul, & His Cool Aid Chemists
Born on 10/12/1935 in Detroit, Michigan. Black jazz session drummer. Member of Afrique. The Cool Aid Chemists were Clarence MacDonald, David T. Walker (also in Afrique) and Bill Upchurch.

HUNT, Tommy
Born Charles Hunt on 6/18/1933 in Pittsburgh, Pennsylvania. R&B singer. With The Five Echoes, 1952-53. First recorded for Sabre in 1953. In The Flamingos, 1956-61. Moved to Wales in 1970.

HUNTER, Alfonzo
Born in Chicago, Illinois. R&B singer/saxophonist.

HUNTER, Ian
Born on 6/3/1939 in Oswestry, England. Singer/guitarist. Leader of Mott The Hoople from 1969-74.

HUNTER, Ivory Joe
Born on 10/10/1914 in Kirbyville, Texas. Died of cancer on 11/8/1974 (age 60). R&B singer/ songwriter/pianist. First recorded in 1933 (a cylinder record for the Library Of Congress). Own radio shows, KFDM-Beaumont, Texas, early 1940s. Own record labels, Ivory and Pacific, 1944. Signed by King Records, 1947; MGM, 1950.

HUNTER, John
Born in Chicago, Illinois. Rock singer/keyboardist/ songwriter.

HUNTER, Tab
Born Arthur Kelm on 7/11/1931 in Brooklyn, New York. Singer/actor. Star of many movies from 1950-92.

HURRICANE CHRIS
Born Chris Dooley in 1989 in Shreveport, Louisiana. Male rapper.

HURT, Jim
Pop-dance singer.

HUSKER DU
Punk-rock trio from Minneapolis, Minnesota: Bob Mould (vocals, guitar), Greg Norton (bass) and Grant Hart (drums). Mould later formed Sugar.

HUSKY, Ferlin
Born on 12/3/1925 in Flat River, Missouri. Country singer/songwriter/guitarist. Recorded as Terry Preston in the early 1950s; also did humorous recordings as Simon Crum.

HUTCH, Willie
Born Willie Hutchinson on 12/6/1944 in Los Angeles, California; raised in Dallas, Texas. Died on 9/19/2005 (age 60). R&B singer/producer/songwriter.

HUTSON, Leroy
Born on 6/4/1945 in Newark, New Jersey. Male singer/songwriter/producer. Member of The Impressions from 1971-73.

HUTTON, Danny
Born on 9/10/1942 in Buncrana, Ireland; raised in Los Angeles, California. Member of Three Dog Night.

HYDE, Paul, & The Payola$
Pop-rock group from Canada: Paul Hyde (vocals), Bob Rock (guitar), Alex Boynton (bass) and Chris Taylor (drums; Roachford). Hyde and Rock later recorded as the duo Rock and Hyde.

HYLAND, Brian
Born on 11/12/1943 in Queens, New York. Teen idol pop singer. Own group, the Delphis, at age 12. In production company with Del Shannon in 1970.

HYMAN, Dick
Born on 3/8/1927 in Manhattan, New York. Pianist/composer/conductor/arranger. Toured Europe with Benny Goodman in 1950. Staff pianist at WMCA and WNBC-New York from 1951-57. Music director of *Arthur Godfrey And His Friends* from 1958-62.

HYMAN, Phyllis
Born on 7/6/1950 in Philadelphia, Pennsylvania; raised in Pittsburgh, Pennsylvania. Committed suicide on 6/30/1995 (age 44). R&B-dance singer/actress/model. Starred in the Broadway musical *Sophisticated Ladies*.

IAN, Janis
Born Janis Eddy Fink on 4/7/1951 in Brooklyn, New York. Contemporary-folk singer/songwriter/pianist/guitarist.

IAN VAN DAHL Featuring Marsha
Female electronica-dance trio from Belgium: Marsha Theeuwen, Diana Dander and Jeanine Tiemissen. Annemie Coenen replaced Theeuwen in early 2002.

ICE CUBE
Born O'Shea Jackson on 6/15/1969 in Los Angeles, California. Male rapper/actor. Former member of N.W.A. Acted in the movies *Boyz N The Hood*, *Trespass*, *Higher Learning*, *Friday*, *Anaconda* and *Barbershop*.

ICEHOUSE
Rock group formed in Sydney, Australia: Iva Davies (vocals, guitar), Anthony Smith (keyboards), Keith Welsh (bass) and John Lloyd (drums). Numerous personnel changes through the 1980s, with Davies the only constant. Group name is Australian slang for an insane asylum.

ICE-T
Born Tracy Morrow on 2/16/1958 in Newark, New Jersey; raised in Los Angeles, California. Male rapper/actor. Acted in several movies; cast member of TV's *Law & Order: Special Victims Unit*. Formed own Rhyme Syndicate label in 1988. Formed controversial speed-metal band, Body Count, in 1992. Star of the TV series *Players*.

ICICLE WORKS
Rock trio from Liverpool, England: Robert Ian McNabb (vocals, guitar), Chris Layhe (bass) and Chris Sharrock (drums).

ICONZ
Rap group from Miami, Florida: Luc Duc, Stage McCloud, Bull Dog, Chapter, Tony Manshino, Screwface and Supastar.

ICY BLU
Born Laurel Urchick on 6/1/1974 in Austin, Texas. White female rapper.

IDEAL
R&B vocal group from Houston, Texas: J-Dante, Maverick, PZ and Swab.

IDES OF MARCH, The
Rock group from Chicago, Illinois: Jim Peterik (vocals, guitar), Ray Herr (guitar), Larry Millas (keyboards), John Larson and Chuck Soumar (horns), Bob Bergland (bass), and Mike Borch (drums). Group named after a line in Shakespeare's *Julius Caesar*. Peterik later played keyboards for Survivor.

IDOL, Billy
Born William Broad on 11/30/1955 in Stanmore, Middlesex, England. Leader of the London punk band Generation X from 1977-81. Suffered serious leg injuries in a motorcycle crash on 2/6/1990. Appeared in the movies *The Doors* and *The Wedding Singer*.

IFIELD, Frank
Born on 11/30/1937 in Coventry, Warwickshire, England; raised in New South Wales, Australia. Pop singer.

IGLESIAS, Enrique
Born on 5/8/1975 in Madrid, Spain; raised in Miami, Florida. Latin singer. Son of Julio Iglesias. Younger brother of Julio Iglesias Jr.

IGLESIAS, Julio
Born on 9/23/1943 in Madrid, Spain. Latin singer. Soccer goalie for the pro Real Madrid team until temporary paralysis from a car crash. Father of Julio Iglesias Jr. and Enrique Iglesias.

IIO
Electronic-dance duo from New York: female singer Nadia Ali and male producer Markus Moser.

IKETTES, The
Female R&B trio formed for the Ike & Tina Turner Revue. Atco group consisted of Delores Johnson (lead), Eloise Hester and "Joshie" Jo Armstead. Modern group consisted of Vanetta Fields,

IKETTES, The — cont'd
Robbie Montgomery and Jessie Smith; later known as The Mirettes.

ILL AL SKRATCH
Male rap duo from Brooklyn, New York: ILL (I Lyrical Lord) and Al Skratch.

ILLEGAL
Male rap duo from Atlanta, Georgia: Malik Edwards and Jamal Phillips. Discovered by Lisa Lopes of TLC.

ILLUSION, The
Rock group from Long Island, New York: John Vinci (vocals), Richie Cerniglia (guitar), Mike Maniscalco (keyboards), Chuck Adler (bass) and Mike Ricciardella (drums).

IMAJIN
Male R&B vocal group: Jamal Hampton, Talib Kareem, Olamide Faison and John Fitch.

IMBRUGLIA, Natalie
Born on 2/4/1975 in Sydney, Australia. Alternative pop-rock singer/songwriter. Married Daniel Johns (lead singer of Silverchair) on 12/31/2003.

IMMATURE
Teen male R&B vocal trio from Los Angeles, California: Marques Houston, Jerome Jones and Kelton Kessee. Houston acted on TV's *Sister, Sister*. Group later shortened name to IMx.

IMPACT
R&B group from Baltimore, Maryland: Damon Otis Harris (vocals), John Simms, Charles Timmons and Donald Tilghman. Harris was a member of The Temptations from 1971-75.

IMPALAS, The
Doo-wop group from Brooklyn, New York: Joe "Speedo" Frazier, Richard Wagner, Lenny Renda and Tony Carlucci. All members, except black lead singer Frazier, are white.

IMPRESSIONS, The
R&B group formed in Chicago, Illinois: Jerry Butler (born on 12/8/1939), Curtis Mayfield (born on 6/3/1942), Sam Gooden (born on 9/2/1939) and brothers Arthur and Richard Brooks. Originally known as The Roosters. Butler left for a solo career in 1958; replaced by Fred Cash (born on 10/8/1940). The Brooks brothers left in 1962, leaving Mayfield as the trio's leader. Mayfield left in 1970 for a solo career; replaced by Leroy Hutson. In 1973, Hutson was replaced by Reggie Torian and Ralph Johnson. Johnson joined Mystique in 1976. Group did movie soundtrack for *Three The Hard Way* (1974). Butler, Mayfield, Gooden and Cash reunited for a tour in 1983. Mayfield died on 12/26/1999 (age 57).

INC., The
All-star rap group assembled by Murder Inc. label head and producer Irv Gotti.

INCREDIBLE BONGO BAND, The
Instrumental studio band assembled by producer Michael Viner in Los Angeles, California.

IN CROWD, The
White vocal trio: Ron Hicklin, Stan Farber and Al Capps. Hicklin and Farber were members of The Eligibles (Bubbled Under in 1959).

INCUBUS
Hard-rock group from Calabasas, California: Brandon Boyd (vocals), Mike Einziger (guitar), Chris Kilmore (DJ), Alex Katunich (bass) and Jose Pasillas (drums). Ben Kenney replaced Katunich in 2003.

INDECENT OBSESSION
Pop group from Brisbane, Australia: David Dixon (vocals), Andrew Coyne (guitar), Michael Szumowski (keyboards) and Darryl Simms (drums). Band's name taken from a Colleen McCullough novel.

INDEPENDENTS, The
R&B vocal group from Chicago, Illinois: Chuck Jackson, Maurice Jackson, Helen Curry and Eric Thomas. Chuck (no relation to Maurice) and Marvin Yancey, Jr. were producers/writers for the group; later teamed in production work, especially for Natalie Cole, to whom Yancey was once married. Chuck Jackson, not to be confused with the same-named solo singer, is the brother of civil rights leader the Rev. Jesse Jackson.

INDIA.ARIE
Born India Arie Simpson on 10/3/1975 in Denver, Colorado; raised in Atlanta, Georgia. Female contemporary R&B singer/songwriter/guitarist.

INDIGO GIRLS
Folk-rock duo from Decatur, Georgia: singers/songwriters/guitarists Amy Ray (born on 4/12/1964) and Emily Saliers (born on 7/22/1963).

INDUSTRY
Rock group from Long Island, New York: Jon Carin (vocals), Brian Unger (guitar), Rudy Perrone (bass) and Mercury Caronia (drums).

INFORMATION SOCIETY
Techno-dance band formed in Minneapolis, Minnesota: Kurt Harland (vocals), Paul Robb (guitar), Amanda Kramer (keyboards) and James Cassidy (bass). Reduced to a trio in 1990 with departure of Kramer.

INGMANN, Jorgen, & His Guitar
Born Jorgen Ingmann-Pedersen on 4/26/1925 in Copenhagen, Denmark. Male guitarist.

INGRAM, Jack
Born on 11/15/1970 in Houston, Texas. Country singer/guitarist.

INGRAM, James
Born on 2/16/1952 in Akron, Ohio. R&B singer/songwriter/pianist.

INGRAM, Luther
Born on 11/30/1937 in Jackson, Tennessee. Died of diabetes on 3/19/2007 (age 69). R&B singer/songwriter.

INK SPOTS
R&B vocal group from Indianapolis: Ivory "Deek" Watson, Charlie Fuqua, Orville "Hoppy" Jones and Bill Kenny. Jones died on 10/18/1944 (age 39); replaced by Bill Kenny's brother, Herb Kenny. Watson left in 1945 to form The Four Tunes. The Kenny brothers left in 1952. Watson died on 11/4/1969 (age 60). Fuqua died on 12/21/1971 (age 61). Bill Kenny died on 3/23/1978 (age 67). Herb Kenny died on 7/11/1992 (age 78).

INMAN, Autry
Born Robert Autry Inman on 1/6/1929 in Florence, Alabama. Died on 9/6/1988 (age 59). Country singer/songwriter.

INMATES, The
Rock group from England: Bill Hurley (vocals), Peter "Gunn" Staines and Tony Oliver (guitars), Ben Donnelly (bass) and Jim Russell (drums).

INNER CIRCLE
Reggae group formed in Kingston, Jamaica: Calton Coffie (vocals), Touter Harvey, Lancelot Hall, brothers Ian and Roger Lewis, and Lester Adderly (left by mid-1994).

INNER CITY
Techno-funk-dance group led by producer/ songwriter/mixer Kevin Saunderson (from Detroit, Michigan) and female vocalist Paris Grey (from Glencove, Illinois).

INNERLUDE
Male R&B vocal trio from San Jose, California: brothers James and Eric Visperas, with Cyrus Mallare.

INNOCENTS, The
Pop trio from Sun Valley, California: James West (lead singer), Al Candelaria (bass) and Darron Stankey (guitar, tenor). Backup vocal group for Kathy Young. First recorded as The Echoes for Andex in 1959.

INOJ
Born Ayanna Porter on 11/27/1976 in Madison, Wisconsin. Female R&B singer. Given pet name of Joni, spelled backwards is Inoj. Pronounced: i-no-jay.

INSANE CLOWN POSSE
White rap duo from Detroit, Michigan Joe "Violent J" Bruce and Joe "Shaggy 2 Dope" Utsler. Both wear clown makeup.

INSTANT FUNK
Dance-funk band from Philadelphia, Pennsylvania: James Carmichael (vocals), brothers Kim (guitar) and Scotty (drums) Miller, George Bell (guitar), Dennis Richardson (keyboards), Charles Williams (percussion), Larry Davis (trumpet), Johnny Onderline (sax) and Raymond Earl (bass). Former backup band for Bunny Sigler.

INTONATION featuring JOEE
Pop group fronted by Toronto, Ontario, Canada, native Joee. In 1988, Joee appeared on TV's *Star Search*.

INTRIGUES, The
R&B vocal group from Philadelphia, Pennsylvania: Alfred Brown, Ronald Hamilton, James Harris and James Lee.

INTRO
R&B vocal trio from New York: Kenny Greene, Clinton Wike and Jeff Sanders. Intro stands for Innovative New Talent Reaching Out.

INTRUDERS
Instrumental rock and roll trio from Hammonton, New Jersey: guitarists/brothers George and Augie Mitchell, with drummer Joe Rebardo.

INTRUDERS, The
R&B vocal group from Philadelphia, Pennsylvania: Sam "Little Sonny" Brown, Eugene "Bird" Daughtry (born on 10/29/1939; died on 12/25/1994, age 55), Phil Terry (born on 11/1/1943) and Robert "Big Sonny" Edwards (born on 2/22/1942). First recorded for Gowen in 1961.

INXS
Rock group from Sydney, Australia: Michael Hutchence (vocals; born on 1/22/1960), Kirk Pengilly (guitar, saxophone; born on 7/4/1958), Garry Beers (bass, born on 6/22/1957) and brothers Tim (guitar; born on 8/16/1957), Andy (keyboards, guitar; born on 3/27/1959) and Jon (drums; born on 8/10/1961) Farriss. Hutchence starred in the movies *Dogs In Space* and *Frankenstein Unbound*; formed the group Max Q. Jon Farriss was married to actress Leslie Bega (TV's *Head Of The Class*) from 1992-97. Hutchence committed suicide on 11/22/1997 (age 37). Canadian Jason Dean "J.D. Fortune" Bennison became new lead singer in 2005 after winning the reality TV series *Rock Star: INXS*.

IRBY, Joyce "Fenderella"
Born in Florida. Former member of Klymaxx.

IRIS, Donnie
Born Dominic Ierace on 2/28/1943 in Beaver Falls, Pennsylvania. Rock singer/songwriter/guitarist. Former member of The Jaggerz. Toured briefly with Wild Cherry.

IRISH ROVERS, The
Irish-born folk group formed in Calgary, Alberta, Canada: brothers Will (vocals, drums) and George (guitar) Millar, their cousin Joe Millar (bass), Jimmy Ferguson (vocals) and Wilcil McDowell (accordian). Ferguson died in October 1997 (age 57).

IRON BUTTERFLY
Hard-rock group from San Diego, California: Doug Ingle (vocals, keyboards), Erik Braunn (guitar), Lee Dorman (bass) and Ron Bushy (drums). Braunn left in late 1969; replaced by Mike Pinera (leader of Blues Image) and Larry Reinhardt. Split in mid-1971. Braunn and Bushy regrouped in early 1975 with Phil Kramer (bass) and Howard Reitzes (keyboards). Kramer, who later earned a physics degree and became a multimedia executive, mysteriously disappeared on 2/12/95; his remains were found at the bottom of a Malibu canyon on 5/29/1999. Braunn died of heart failure on 7/25/2003 (age 52).

IRONHORSE
Rock group from Canada: Randy Bachman (vocals, guitar; The Guess Who, Bachman-Turner Overdrive), Tom Sparks (guitar), John Pierce (bass) and Mike Baird (drums).

IRON MAIDEN
Hard-rock group formed in London, England: Paul Di'anno (vocals), Dave Murray and Adrian Smith (guitars), Steve Harris (bass) and Clive Burr (drums). Bruce Dickinson replaced Di'anno in early 1982. Nicko McBrain replaced Burr in early 1983.

IRWIN, Big Dee
Born Difosco Ervin on 7/8/1932 in Harlem, New York. Died of heart failure on 8/27/1995 (age 63). R&B singer. Former lead singer of The Pastels.

IRWIN, Russ
Born in 1968 in Huntington Hills, Long Island, New York. Pop-rock singer/songwriter.

ISAAK, Chris
Born on 6/26/1956 in Stockton, California. Rockabilly singer/songwriter/guitarist. Attended college in Japan. Acted in several movies; starred in own cable network TV situation comedy series.

ISLANDERS, The
Pop instrumental duo of Randy Starr (guitar) and Frank Metis (accordion).

ISLE OF MAN
Multi-ethnic pop group (members are from France, Nicaragua, Italy and U.S.): Robere Parlez (vocals), Raun (guitar), Jamie Roberto (bass) and Ronnie Lee Sage (drums).

ISLEY BROTHERS, The
Highly influential R&B-rock-funk trio of brothers from Cincinnati, Ohio: O'Kelly, Rudolph and Ronald Isley. Moved to New York in 1957 and first recorded for Teenage Records. Trio added their younger brothers Ernie (guitar, drums) and Marvin (bass, percussion) Isley and brother-in-law Chris Jasper (keyboards) in September 1969. Formed own T-Neck label the same year. Ernie, Marvin and Chris began recording as the trio Isley, Jasper, Isley in 1984. O'Kelly died of a heart attack on 3/31/1986 (age 48); Ronald and Rudolph continued on as The Isley Brothers through 1990. Ronald, Ernie and Marvin reunited as The Isley Brothers in 1991. Ronald became the featured member beginning in 1989 with brother Ernie on lead guitar. Ronald married Angela Winbush on 6/26/1993.

ISLEY, JASPER, ISLEY
Trio from Cincinnati, Ohio: brothers Ernie Isley (guitar, drums) and Marvin Isley (bass, percussion), with brother-in-law Chris Jasper (keyboards). All shared vocals. All were members of The Isley Brothers from 1973-84.

ISYSS
Female R&B vocal group from Los Angeles, California: Lamyia Good, Letecia Harrison, Ardena Clark and Quierra Davis-Martin.

I TO I
Dance trio from Amsterdam, Netherlands: producers Edward Smidt and Ewart van Horst with vocalist Susan (toured as vocalist with Candy Dulfer).

IT'S A BEAUTIFUL DAY
Folk-rock group from San Francisco, California. Core members: David LaFlamme (male vocals, violin), Pattie Santos (female vocals), Fred Webb (keyboards) and Val Fuentes (drums). LaFlamme left in 1973. Santos died in a car crash on 12/14/1989 (age 40).

IVES, Burl
Born on 6/14/1909 in Huntington Township, Illinois. Died on 4/14/1995 (age 85). Actor/author/folk singer. Played semi-pro football. Began Broadway career in the late 1930s. Own CBS radio show *The Wayfaring Stranger* in 1944. Appeared in many movies, including *Our Man In Havana*, *East Of Eden*, *Cat On A Hot Tin Roof* and *The Big Country*. Narrated the 1964 animated TV classic *Rudolph The Red-Nosed Reindeer* from which his recording of "A Holly Jolly Christmas" became an instant Christmas classic.

IVORY
Born in Brooklyn, New York. Male R&B-funk singer.

IVY LEAGUE, The
British songwriting team of John Carter and Ken Lewis. Wrote "Little Bit O' Soul" and "Can't You Hear My Heartbeat."

IVY THREE, The
Pop vocal trio formed in Long Island, New York: Charles Koppelman, Art Berkowitz and Don Rubin.

JACKS, Susan
Born Susan Pesklevits in Vancouver, British Columbia, Canada. Married Terry Jacks and recorded with him as The Poppy Family; divorced in 1973.

JACKS, Terry
Born on 3/29/1944 in Winnipeg, Manitoba, Canada. Recorded with his wife Susan Jacks as The Poppy Family.

JACKSON, Alan
Born on 10/17/1958 in Newnan, Georgia. Country singer/songwriter/guitarist. Former car salesman and construction worker. Formed own band, Dixie Steel. Signed to Glen Campbell's publishing company in 1985.

JACKSON, Bull Moose
Born Benjamin Jackson on 4/22/1919 in Cleveland, Ohio. Died of cancer on 7/31/1989 (age 70). R&B singer/saxophonist. Joined Lucky Millinder in 1943 as a replacement for Wynonie Harris. Own band with Millinder sidemen in 1947. One of the first major stars of R&B.

JACKSON, Chuck
Born on 7/22/1937 in Latta, South Carolina; raised in Pittsburgh, Pennsylvania. R&B singer. Cousin of singer Ann Sexton. Left college in 1957 to work with the Raspberry Singers gospel group. With The Dell-Vikings from 1957-59. First recorded solo as Charles Jackson for Clock in 1959.

JACKSON, Deon
Born on 1/26/1946 in Ann Arbor, Michigan. R&B singer/clarinetist/drummer.

JACKSON, Earnest
R&B singer/guitarist.

JACKSON, Freddie
Born on 10/2/1956 in Harlem, New York. R&B singer/songwriter. Backup singer for Melba Moore, Evelyn King and others. Member of R&B group Mystic Merlin.

JACKSON, J.J.
Born Jerome Louis Jackson on 4/8/1941 in Brooklyn, New York. R&B singer/songwriter. Became permanent resident of England in 1969. Not to be confused with the former MTV DJ.

JACKSON, Janet
Born Janet Damita Jo Jackson on 5/16/1966 in Gary, Indiana. R&B singer/actress. Sister of The Jacksons (youngest of nine children). Regular on TV's *Good Times*, *Diff'rent Strokes* and *Fame*. Co-starred in the movies *Poetic Justice* and *Nutty Professor 2: The Klumps*. Married to James DeBarge (of DeBarge) from 1984-85. Secretly married to producer Rene Elizondo from 1991-2000.

JACKSON, Jermaine
Born on 12/11/1954 in Gary, Indiana. Fourth eldest of The Jacksons. Vocalist/bassist of The Jackson 5 until group left Motown in 1976. Married to Hazel Gordy (daughter of Berry Gordy) from 1973-87. Rejoined The Jacksons in 1984 for the group's *Victory* album and tour.

JACKSON, Joe
Born on 8/11/1954 in Burton-on-Trent, England. Singer/songwriter/pianist, featuring an ever-changing music style. Moved to New York City in 1982.

JACKSON, LaToya
Born on 5/29/1956 in Gary, Indiana. Sister of The Jacksons. The fifth of nine children.

JACKSON, Mahalia
Born on 10/26/1911 in New Orleans, Louisiana. Died of heart failure on 1/27/1972 (age 60). Legendary gospel singer. Began recording for Apollo Records in the mid-1940s.

JACKSON, Michael
Born on 8/29/1958 in Gary, Indiana. The seventh of nine children. Became lead singer of his brothers' group, The Jackson 5 (later known as The Jacksons), at age five. Played "The Scarecrow" in the 1978 movie musical *The Wiz*. His 1988 autobiography, *Moonwalker*, became a movie the same year. Signed a $1 billion multimedia contract with Sony Software on 3/20/1991. Married to Elvis Presley's daughter, Lisa Marie Presley, from 1994-96. Eccentric and bizarre mannerisms and a media frenzy over his child molestation charges led the career of "The King of Pop" into a tailspin since 1996.

JACKSON, Mick
Born on 11/2/1947 in Yorkshire, England. White R&B singer. Later based in Germany.

JACKSON, Millie
Born on 7/15/1944 in Thomson, Georgia; raised in Newark, New Jersey. R&B singer/songwriter. To Newark, New Jersey, in 1958. Worked as a model in New York City. Professional singing debut at Club Zanzibar in Hoboken, New Jersey, in 1964. First recorded for MGM in 1970. Founded and produced the trio Facts Of Life.

JACKSON, Rebbie
Born Maureen Jackson on 5/29/1950 in Gary, Indiana. Eldest of the nine-sibling Jackson family. Worked with The Jacksons from 1974-77, then went solo.

JACKSON, Stonewall
His real name. Born on 11/6/1932 in Emerson, North Carolina. Country singer/guitarist/pianist. Descended from General Thomas Jonathan "Stonewall" Jackson.

JACKSON, Walter
Born on 3/19/1938 in Pensacola, Florida; raised in Detroit, Michigan. Died of a cerebral hemorrhage on 6/20/1983 (age 45). R&B singer. Contracted polio at an early age; performed on crutches.

JACKSON, Wanda
Born on 10/20/1937 in Maud, Oklahoma. Country-rockabilly singer/songwriter/guitarist. First recorded for Decca in 1954. Toured with Elvis Presley from 1955-56.

JACKSON 5, The
R&B group of brothers from Gary, Indiana: Michael Jackson (born on 8/29/1958), Jermaine Jackson (born on 12/11/1954), Marlon Jackson (born on 3/12/1957), Tito Jackson (born on 10/15/1953) and Jackie Jackson (born on 5/4/1951). First recorded for Steeltown in 1967. Known as The Jackson 5 from 1968-75, then changed name to The Jacksons. Jermaine replaced by Randy (born on 10/29/1961) in 1976. Jermaine rejoined the group for 1984's highly publicized *Victory* album and tour. Marlon left for a solo career in 1987. Their sisters Rebbie Jackson, LaToya Jackson and Janet Jackson backed the group; each had solo hits. Michael and Janet emerged with superstar solo careers in the 1980s. Group lineup in 1989: Jackie, Tito, Jermaine and Randy Jackson. Boyz II Men appeared in the 1992 TV mini-series *The Jacksons: An American Dream*.

JACKYL
Hard-rock band from Atlanta, Georgia: Jesse James Dupree (vocals), Jimmy Stiff (guitar), Jeff Worley (guitar), Tom Bettini (bass) and Chris Worley (drums). Stiff left in 2001. Roman Glick replaced Bettini in 2001.

JACOBS, Debbie
Born in Baltimore, Maryland. Black disco singer.

JACOBS, Dick
Born on 3/29/1918 in Brooklyn, New York. Died of cancer on 5/20/1988 (age 70). Music director of TV's *Your Hit Parade* from 1957-58. A&R director for Coral and Brunswick Records. Author of *Who Wrote That Song*.

JACOBS, Hank
Born in 1946 in Los Angeles, California. R&B organist.

JADAKISS
Born Jayson Phillips on 3/27/1975 in Yonkers, New York. Male rapper/actor. Member of The Lox and Ruff Ryders. Played "Killer Ben" in the 2003 movie *Ride Or Die*.

JADE
Female R&B vocal trio: Joi Marshall and Tonya Kelly (both born in Chicago, Illinois), with Di Reed (born in Houston, Texas).

JAGGED EDGE
R&B vocal group from Atlanta, Georgia: identical twin brothers Brian and Brandon Casey, with Richard Wingo and Kyle Norman.

JAGGER, Mick
Born Michael Phillip Jagger on 7/26/1943 in Dartford, Kent, England. Lead singer of The Rolling Stones. Appeared in the movies *Ned Kelly* and *Freejack*. Married to model Bianca Jagger from 1971-80. Married actress/model Jerry Hall from 1990-99.

JAGGERZ, The
Pop-rock group from Pittsburgh, Pennsylvania: Donnie Iris (vocals, trumpet), Jimmy Ross (vocals, trombone), Billy Maybray (vocals, bass), Benny Faiella (guitar), Thom Davis (organ) and Jim Pugliano (drums). Maybray died of cancer on 12/5/2004 (age 60).

JAGS, The
Rock group from Scarborough, England: Nick Watkinson (vocals, guitar), John Alder (guitar), Steve Prudence (bass) and Alex Baird (drums).

JAHEIM
Born Jaheim Hoagland on 5/26/1978 in New Brunswick, New Jersey. Male R&B vocalist.

JA-KKI
Interracial R&B-disco group from Flint, Michigan. Named after lead singer Jacqueline (sole female member).

JAM, The
Punk-rock trio from Woking, England: Paul Weller (vocals, bass; born on 5/25/1958), Bruce Foxton (guitar; born on 9/1/1955) and Rick Buckler (drums; born on 12/6/1955). Disbanded in 1982. Weller formed The Style Council.

JAMES
Rock group from Manchester, England: Tim Booth (vocals), James Gott (guitar), Mark Hunter (keyboards), Saul Davies (violin), Andy Diagram (trumpet), Jim Glennie (bass) and David Baynton-Power (drums).

JAMES, Bob
Born on 12/25/1939 in Marshall, Missouri. Jazz-fusion keyboardist.

JAMES, Elmore
Born Elmore Brooks on 1/27/1918 in Richland, Mississippi. Died of a heart attack on 5/24/1963 (age 45). Influential blues singer/guitarist.

JAMES, Etta
Born Jamesetta Hawkins on 1/25/1938 in Los Angeles, California. R&B pioneer. Nicknamed "Miss Peaches." First recorded for Modern in 1954. Recorded duets with Harvey Fuqua of The Moonglows as Etta & Harvey. Frequent bouts with heroin addiction; finally cured in the late 1970s.

JAMES, Jesse
Born James McClelland on 3/1/1943 in Eldorado, Arkansas. R&B singer/record producer. Also see The Fantastic Johnny C.

JAMES, Jimmy, & The Vagabonds
Born on 9/15/1940 in Jamaica. R&B singer. The Vagabonds: Count Prince Miller (vocals), Wallace Wilson (guitar), Carl Noel (keyboards), Matt Fredericks and Milton James (horns), Phil Chen (bass) and Rupert Balgobin (drums).

JAMES, Joni
Born Giovanna Carmello Babbo on 9/22/1930 in Chicago, Illinois. Worked as a dancer from age 12; model during high school. Toured Canada as a dancer in the late 1940s. First recorded for Sharp in 1952. Married her orchestral arranger/conductor (1958-61) Tony Acquaviva (died on 9/27/1986, age 61).

JAMES, Rick
Born James Johnson on 2/1/1948 in Buffalo, New York. Died of a heart attack on 8/6/2004 (age 56). Funk-rock singer/songwriter/guitarist. In Mynah Birds band with Neil Young in the late 1960s. To London; formed the band Main Line. Returned to the U.S. and formed Stone City Band; produced Teena Marie, Mary Jane Girls, Eddie Murphy and others. In mid-1994, sentenced to five years in prison for assaults on two women; released from prison in August 1996.

JAMES, Sonny
Born James Loden on 5/1/1929 in Hackleburg, Alabama. Country singer/songwriter/guitarist. Nicknamed "The Southern Gentleman." Brought to Capitol Records in Nashville by Chet Atkins. In the movies *Second Fiddle To A Steel Guitar*, *Nashville Rebel*, *Las Vegas Hillbillies* and *Hillbillys In A Haunted House*.

JAMES, Tommy, & The Shondells
Born Thomas Jackson on 4/29/1947 in Dayton, Ohio; raised in Niles, Michigan. Formed pop group The Shondells at age 12. Recorded "Hanky Panky" on the Snap label in 1963. James relocated to Pittsburgh in 1965 after a DJ there popularized "Hanky Panky." Original master was sold to Roulette, whereupon James recruited Pittsburgh group The Raconteurs to become the official Shondells. Consisted of Eddie Gray (guitar), Ronnie Rosman (organ), Mike Vale (bass) and Pete Lucia (drums). Group split from James in 1970; recorded as Hog Heaven.

JAMES BOYS, The
R&B studio band produced by Jesse James of Philadelphia, Pennsylvania. Arranged by pianist Bobby Martin, also included Norman Harris, Roland and Karl Chambers, Ronnie Baker and Earl Young. Later recorded as The Family and MFSB.

JAMES GANG, The
Rock group from Cleveland, Ohio: Joe Walsh (vocals, guitar, keyboards), Dale Peters (bass) and Jim Fox (drums). Walsh (later in the Eagles) left in late 1971; replaced by Dominic Troiano and Roy Kenner. Troiano joined the Guess Who in 1973; replaced by Tommy Bolin (died on 12/4/1976, age 25). Many personnel changes from 1974 until group disbanded in 1976. Troiano died of cancer on 5/25/2005 (age 59).

JAMESON, Nick
Born in Missouri. Pop-rock singer/bassist. Former member of Foghat.

JAMESTOWN MASSACRE
Rock group from Chicago, Illinois: Dave Bickler (vocals), Len Fogerty (guitar), Mark Ayers (keyboards), Gary Manata (bass) and Jim Smith (drums). Bickler later joined Survivor.

JAMIES, The
Pop vocal group from Dorchester, Massachusetts: Tom Jameson, his sister Serena Jameson, Jeannie Roy and Arthur Blair.

JAMIROQUAI
Interracial alternative dance group led by singer/songwriter Jason Kay (born on 12/30/1969 in Stretford, Manchester, England).

JAMUL
Rock group from San Diego, California: Steve Williams (vocals), Bob Desnoyers (guitar), John Fergus (bass) and Ron Armstrong (drums).

JAN & DEAN
Surf-pop-rock male vocal duo from Los Angeles, California. Jan Berry (born on 4/3/1941) and Dean Torrence (born on 3/10/1940) formed group called the Barons while attending high school in Los Angeles. Jan & Dean and Barons' member Arnie Ginsburg recorded "Jennie Lee" in Jan's garage. Dean left for a six-month Army Reserve stint, whereupon Jan signed with Arwin (label owned by Doris Day's husband, Marty Melcher) and released the record as by Jan & Arnie. Upon Dean's return from the service, Arnie (not to be confused with the famed DJ of the same name) joined the Navy, and Jan & Dean signed with the Dore label. Dean sang lead on The Beach Boys's 1966 hit "Barbara Ann." Jan was critically injured in an auto accident on 4/12/1966. Duo made a comeback in 1978 after their biographical movie *Dead Man's Curve* aired on TV. Jan died of a seizure on 3/26/2004 (age 62).

JAN & KJELD
Duo of brothers from Copenhagen, Denmark: Jan Wennick (born on 7/27/1946) and Kjeld Wennick (born on 2/3/1944).

JANE'S ADDICTION
Rock group from Los Angeles, California: Perry Farrell (vocals), Dave Navarro (guitar), Chris Chaney (bass) and Stephen Perkins (drums). Farrell and Perkins were also members of Porno For Pyros. Navarro was a member of Red Hot Chili Peppers; married actress Carmen Electra on 11/22/2003.

JANIS, Johnny
Born on 3/20/1920 in Chicago, Illinois. Pop singer.

JANKOWSKI, Horst
Born on 1/30/1936 in Berlin, Germany. Died of cancer on 6/29/1998 (age 62). Jazz pianist.

JARMELS, The
R&B vocal group from Richmond, Virginia: Nathaniel Ruff, Ray Smith, Paul Burnett, Earl Christian and Tom Eldridge. Named for a street in Harlem. Major Harris was later a member. Eldridge died on 6/19/2000 (age 59). Burnett died on 3/21/2001 (age 55).

JARREAU, Al
Born on 3/12/1940 in Milwaukee, Wisconsin. R&B/jazz-styled singer. Has master's degree in psychology from the University of Iowa. Worked clubs in San Francisco with George Duke.

JARS OF CLAY
Christian alternative pop group formed in Illinois: Dan Haseltine (vocals), Steve Mason and Matt Odmark (guitars), and Charlie Lowell (keyboards).

JA RULE
Born Jeffrey Atkins on 2/29/1976 in Queens, New York. Male rapper/actor. Appeared in the movies *The Fast And The Furious* and *Half Past Dead*.

JARVIS, Carol
Teen pop singer. Daughter of Los Angeles DJ Al Jarvis (died in 1970).

JAVIER
Born Javier Colon in 1978 in Hartford, Connecticut. R&B singer/songwriter/guitarist.

JAY, Morty, & The Surferin' Cats
Studio duo of Morty Jay (arranger from New York) and Mack Wolfson (songwriter). Wolfson was later the head of Golden Crest Records.

JAYA
Born Maria Buffington in 1970 in Manila, Philippines. To California in 1985. Discovered by Stevie B.

JAY & THE AMERICANS
Pop-rock vocal group formed in New York: John "Jay" Traynor (an early member of The Mystics), Sandy Yaguda (born on 1/30/1943), Kenny Vance (born on 12/9/1943; later a Hollywood musical director) and Howie Kane (born on 6/6/1942). Guitarist Marty Sanders (born on 2/28/1941) joined during production of their first album in 1961. Traynor left after their first hit; replaced by lead singer Jay Black (born David Blatt on 11/2/1938) in 1962.

JAY & THE TECHNIQUES
Interracial R&B-rock group from Allentown, Pennsylvania: Jay Proctor (lead singer; born on 10/28/1940), Karl Landis, Ronnie Goosly, John Walsh, George Lloyd, Chuck Crowl and Dante Dancho.

JAYE, Jerry
Born Gerald Jaye Hatley on 10/19/1937 in Manila, Arkansas. Rockabilly singer.

JAYMES, Jesse
Born in Roslyn, New York. White male rapper.

JAYNETTS, The
Female R&B group from the Bronx, New York.
Formed by producer/composer/owner of J&S
Records Zelma "Zell" Sanders. Consisted of Ethel
Davis, Mary Sue Wells, Yvonne Bushnell and Ada
Ray. Johnnie Louise Richardson (ex-Johnnie & Joe)
was Sanders's daughter and a touring member of
the group; died from a stroke on 10/25/1988.

JAY-Z
Born Shawn Carter on 12/4/1969 in Brooklyn, New
York. Male rapper/songwriter/record
executive/producer. Founded the Roc-A-Fella
record label. President of Def Jam Records and part
owner of the New Jersey Nets NBA team. Appeared
in the movie *State Property*. Married Beyoncé on
4/4/2008. The highest ranked rap artist in this book.

JB's, The
James Brown's super-funk backup band led by Fred
Wesley, also of Parliament/Funkadelic. Also
recorded as Nat Kendrick And The Swans and
Maceo And The Macks.

JEAN, Wyclef
Born on 10/17/1972 in Croix Des Bouquets, Haiti;
raised in Brooklyn, New York. Hip-hop singer/
songwriter/guitarist/producer. Member of The
Fugees.

JEAN & THE DARLINGS
Female R&B vocal trio of from Arkansas: sisters
Jean Dolphus and Delores "Dee" Dolphus, with
Phefe Harris.

JEFFERSON
Born Geoff Turton on 3/11/1944 in Birmingham,
England. Male singer. Lead singer for the U.K. band
Rockin' Berries.

JEFFERSON AIRPLANE / STARSHIP
Rock group formed as Jefferson Airplane in San
Francisco, California: Marty Balin (born on
1/30/1942) and Grace Slick (vocals; born on
10/30/1939), Paul Kantner (vocals, guitar; born on
3/17/1941), Jorma Kaukonen (guitar; born on
12/23/1940), Jack Casady (bass; born on
4/13/1944) and Spencer Dryden (drums; born on
4/7/1938; died of cancer on 1/11/2005, age 66).
Original drummer Skip Spence formed Moby Grape.
Dryden left in 1970 to join New Riders Of The
Purple Sage; replaced by Joey Covington. Casady
and Kaukonen left by 1974 to go full time with Hot
Tuna. Balin left in 1971; rejoined in 1975, by which
time group was renamed Jefferson Starship and
consisted of Slick, Kantner, Papa John Creach
(violin; died on 2/22/1994, age 76), David Freiberg
(bass), Craig Chaquico (guitar), Pete Sears (bass)
and John Barbata (drums). Slick left group from
June 1978 to January 1981. In 1979, singer Mickey
Thomas joined (replaced Balin), along with Aynsley
Dunbar (John Mayall's Bluesbreakers, Mothers Of
Invention, Journey) who replaced Barbata. Don
Baldwin (formerly with Snail) replaced Dunbar (later
with Whitesnake) in 1982. Kantner left in 1984, and,
due to legal difficulties, band's name was shortened
to Starship, whose lineup included Slick, Thomas,

Sears, Chaquico and Baldwin. Slick left in early
1988. Kantner, Balin and Casady formed the KBC
Band in 1986. In 1989, the original 1966 lineup of
Balin, Slick, Kantner, Kaukonen and Casady
reunited as Jefferson Airplane with Kenny Aronoff
(from John Cougar Mellencamp's band) replacing
Dryden. Continuing as Starship were Thomas,
Chaquico, Baldwin, Brett Bloomfield (bass) and
Mark Morgan (keyboards). Starship disbanded in
1990.

JEFFREY, Joe, Group
Born in Buffalo, New York. R&B singer/guitarist.

JEFFREYS, Garland
Born on 6/29/1943 in Brooklyn, New York. Black
rock singer.

JELLYBEAN
Born John Benitez on 11/7/1957 in the Bronx, New
York. Renowned dance club DJ/remixer/producer of
Puerto Rican descent. Remixing career took off with
his "Flashdance" and "Maniac" remixes, later to
include many of Madonna's hits.

JELLY BEANS, The
Black "girl group" from Jersey City, New Jersey:
sisters Elyse and Maxine Herbert, Alma Brewer,
Diane Taylor and Charles Thomas.

JELLYFISH
Rock group from San Francisco, California: Andy
Sturmer (vocals, drums), Jason Falkner (guitar),
and brothers Chris (bass) and Roger (keyboards)
Manning.

JENKINS, Donald, & The Delighters
Born in Chicago, Illinois. R&B singer. The
Delighters: Walter Granger and Ronnie Strong.

JENNINGS, Lyfe
Born Chester Jennings in 1978 in Toledo, Ohio.
Male R&B singer/songwriter/guitarist. Served a
prison sentence for arson from 1993-2002.

JENNINGS, Waylon
Born on 6/15/1937 in Littlefield, Texas. Died of
diabetes on 2/13/2002 (age 64). While working as a
DJ in Lubbock, Texas, Jennings befriended Buddy
Holly. Holly produced Jennings's first record "Jole
Blon" in 1958. Jennings then joined with Holly's
backing band as bass guitarist on the fateful "Winter
Dance Party" tour in 1959. Established himself in
the mid-1970s as a leader of the "outlaw"
movement in country music. Married Jessi Colter on
10/26/1969. In the movies *Nashville Rebel* and
MacKintosh And T.J. Narrator for TV's *The Dukes
Of Hazzard*.

JENSEN, Kris
Born Peter Jensen on 4/4/1942 in New Haven,
Connecticut. Pop singer/guitarist.

JERRYO
Born Jerry Murray in Chicago, Illinois.
Singer/dancer. Tom (of Tom and Jerrio) is Robert
"Tommy Dark" Tharp.

JERU THE DAMAJA
Born Kendrick Jeru Davis in Brooklyn, New York.
Male rapper.

JESTERS, The
R&B vocal group from Harlem, New York: Adam Jackson, Lenny McKay, Noel Grant, Leo Vincent and Jimmy Smith.

JESUS & MARY CHAIN, The
Alternative pop-rock band from East Kilbride, Scotland. Led by brothers William and Jim Reid.

JESUS JONES
Alternative pop-rock group formed in London, England: Mike Edwards (vocals, guitar), Jerry DeBorg (guitar), Iain Baker (keyboards), Al Jaworski (bass) and Simon Matthews (drums).

JET
Hard-rock group from Melbourne, Australia: brothers Nick Cester (guitar) and Chris Cester (drums), with Cameron Muncey (vocals, guitar) and Mark Wilson (bass).

JETHRO TULL
Progressive-rock band formed in Luton, England. Led by Ian Anderson (vocals, flute) and Martin Barre (guitar). Band named after 18th-century agriculturist/inventor of the seed drill. Lineups from 1971 through 1977 included Anderson, Barre, John Evan (piano), Clive Bunker (drums; replaced by Barriemore Barlow by 1972) and Jeffrey Hammond-Hammond (bass; replaced in 1976 by John Glascock who died in 1979).

JETS, The
Family group from Minneapolis, Minnesota (eight brothers and sisters): Leroy (born on 7/19/1965), Eddie (born on 8/14/1966), Eugene (born on 9/24/1967), Haini (born on 1/25/1968), Rudy (born on 3/1/1969), Kathi (born on 9/6/1970), Elizabeth (born on 8/19/1972) and Moana Wolfgramm (born on 10/13/1973). Their parents are from the South Pacific country of Tonga. All members play at least two instruments. Eugene left group and formed duo Boys Club in 1988.

JETT, Joan, & The Blackhearts
Born Joan Larkin on 9/22/1958 in Philadelphia, Pennsylvania. Rock singer/guitarist. Member of The Runaways from 1975-78. The Blackhearts: Ricky Byrd (guitar), Gary Ryan (bass) and Lee Crystal (drums). Ryan and Crystal left in 1987; replaced by Kasim Sulton (bass; Utopia) and Thommy Price (drums). Jett starred in the 1987 movie *Light Of Day* as the leader of a rock band called The Barbusters.

JEWEL
Born Jewel Kilcher on 5/23/1974 in Payson, Utah; raised in Homer, Alaska. Adult Alternative singer/songwriter/guitarist. Wrote own book of poetry. Played "Sue Lee Shelley" in the movie *Ride With The Devil*. Married rodeo champion Ty Murray on 8/7/2008.

JEWELL
Born in Los Angeles, California. Female rapper. Discovered and produced by Dr. Dre.

JEWELL, Buddy
Born on 4/2/1961 in Lepanto, Arkansas. Country singer/songwriter. Winner of TV's first *Nashville Star* talent series in 2003.

JEWELS, The
Female R&B vocal group from Washington DC: Sandra Bears, Grace Ruffin, Margie Clark and Martha Harvin. Ruffin is the first cousin of Billy Stewart.

JIBBS
Born Jovan Campbell on 11/1/1990 in St. Louis, Missouri. Teen rapper.

JIGSAW
Pop group from England: Des Dyer (vocals, drums), Tony Campbell (guitar), Clive Scott (keyboards) and Barrie Bernard (bass).

JIM & JEAN
Husband-and-wife pop duo: Jim Glover and Jean Glover.

JIM & MONICA
Pop vocal duo from Chicago, Illinois.

JIMENEZ, Jose
Born William Szathmary on 10/5/1924 in Quincy, Massachusetts. Became known as Bill Dana. Head comedy writer for Steve Allen's TV show (created the Latin American comic character Jose Jimenez). Star of own TV series from 1963-65.

JIMMY EAT WORLD
Rock group from Mesa, Arizona: Jim Adkins (vocals), Tom Linton (guitar), Rick Burch (bass) and Zach Lind (drums).

JINKINS, Gus
Born Gus Jenkins on 3/24/1931 in Birmingham, Alabama. Black singer/pianist.

JINNY
Born in Italy. Female dance singer.

JIVE BOMBERS, The
R&B vocal group from Harlem, New York: Clarence Palmer, Earl Johnson, Al Tinney and William "Pee Wee" Tinney. Al Tinney died of cancer on 12/11/2002 (age 81).

JIVE BUNNY & THE MASTERMIXERS
Dance group from England: DJ Les Hemstock and mixers John Pickles, his son Andy Pickles and Ian Morgan.

JIVE FIVE, The
R&B vocal group from Brooklyn, New York: Eugene Pitt (lead singer; born on 11/6/1937), Jerome Hanna and Billy Prophet (tenors), Richard Harris (baritone) and Norman Johnson (bass). After Johnson's death in 1970, group name changed to Jyve Fyve.

JIVIN' GENE
Born Gene Bourgeois in Port Arthur, Texas. Rock and roll singer/songwriter/guitarist.

J.J. FAD
Female rap trio from Los Angeles, California: Juana Burns, Dania Birks and Michelle Franklin. J.J. FAD stands for Just Jammin' Fresh And Def.

J-KWON
Born Jerrell Jones on 12/3/1982 in St. Louis, Missouri. Male rapper.

JoBOXERS
Pop group formed in London, England: Dig Wayne (vocals), Rob Marche (guitar), Dave Collard (keyboards), Chris Bostock (bass) and Sean McLusky (drums).

JODECI
Two pairs of brothers/R&B singers from Charlotte, North Carolina: Cedric "K-Ci" (born on 9/2/1969) and Joel "JoJo" (born on 6/10/1971) Hailey, with Dalvin (born on 7/23/1971) and Donald "DeVante Swing" (born on 9/29/1969) DeGrate. The Haileys are cousins of Dave Hollister (BLACKstreet). K-Ci & JoJo began as a successful duo in 1996. Group name pronounced: joe-deh-see.

JOE
Born Joseph L. Thomas on 7/5/1973 in Columbus, Georgia; raised in Opelika, Alabama. R&B singer/ songwriter/guitarist.

JOEL, Billy
Born William Martin Joel on 5/9/1949 in the Bronx, New York; raised in Hicksville, Long Island, New York. Pop-rock singer/songwriter/pianist. Member of The Hassles in the late 1960s. Involved in a serious motorcycle accident in Long Island in 1982. Married to supermodel Christie Brinkley from 1985-94. Joel's songs were the basis for the Broadway musical *Movin' Out* for which he won a Tony award for Best Orchestrations.

JOE PUBLIC
R&B vocal group from Buffalo, New York: Kevin Scott, Joe Carter, Joe Sayles and Dwight Wyatt.

JOHN, Elton
Born Reginald Kenneth Dwight on 3/25/1947 in Pinner, Middlesex, England. Pop-rock singer/ songwriter/pianist. Formed his first group Bluesology. Took the name of Elton John from the first names of Bluesology members Elton Dean and Long John Baldry. Teamed up with lyricist Bernie Taupin beginning in 1967. Formed Rocket Records in 1973. Played the "Pinball Wizard" in the movie version of *Tommy*.

JOHN, Little Willie
Born William Edgar John on 11/15/1937 in Cullendale, Arkansas; raised in Detroit, Michigan. Died of a heart attack in Washington State Prison on 5/26/1968 (age 30). R&B singer. Brother of Mable John (of The Raeletts). Convicted of manslaughter in 1966.

JOHN, Mable
Born on 11/3/1930 in Bastrop, Louisiana; raised in Detroit, Michigan. R&B singer. Member of The Raeletts. Sister of Little Willie John.

JOHN, Robert
Born Robert John Pedrick on 1/3/1946 in Brooklyn, New York. Pop singer. First recorded at age 12 for Big Top Records. In 1963 recorded as lead singer with Bobby & The Consoles.

JOHN & ERNEST
R&B novelty duo: John Free and Ernest Smith.

JOHNNIE & JOE
R&B duo from the Bronx, New York: Johnnie Louise Richardson (died of a stroke on 10/25/1988) and Joe Rivers. Johnnie was the daughter of the late J&S Records owner Zelma "Zell" Sanders and a touring member of The Jaynetts.

JOHNNY & THE EXPRESSIONS
R&B group led by Johnny Matthews.

JOHNNY & THE HURRICANES
Rock and roll instrumental group from Toledo, Ohio: leader Johnny "Paris" Pocisk (saxophone), Paul Tesluk (organ), Dave Yorko (guitar), Lionel "Butch" Mattice (bass) and Tony Kaye (drums; replaced in late 1959 by Bo Savich). First recorded for Twirl in 1958. Paris had own Attila label from 1965-70. Savich died of cancer on 1/4/2002 (age 62). Pocisk died of leukemia on 5/1/2006 (age 65).

JOHNNY HATES JAZZ
Pop trio formed in England: Clark Datchler (vocals), Calvin Hayes (keyboards, drums) and Mike Nocito (guitar, bass). Hayes is the son of producer Mickie Most.

JOHNNY O.
Born Johnny Ortiz in the Bronx, New York. Dance singer.

JOHNNY T. ANGEL
Born in Canada. Pop singer.

JOHNS, Sammy
Born on 2/7/1946 in Charlotte, North Carolina. Pop singer/songwriter/guitarist.

JOHNSON, Betty
Born on 3/16/1929 in Burlington, North Carolina. Pop singer. Married to musical conductor Charles Randolph Grean. Regular on Don McNeill's daily *Breakfast Club* radio show, and on NBC-TV's *The Tonight Show* starring Jack Parr.

JOHNSON, Bubber
R&B singer/pianist/songwriter Robert Johnson.

JOHNSON, Buddy
Born Woodrow Wilson Johnson on 1/10/1915 in Darlington, South Carolina. Died of a brain tumor on 2/9/1977 (age 62). Black orchestra leader/pianist.

JOHNSON, Carolyn Dawn
Born on 4/30/1971 in Grand Prairie, Alberta, Canada. Country singer/songwriter/guitarist.

JOHNSON, Don
Born on 12/15/1949 in Flatt Creek, Missouri. Actor/singer. Played "Sonny Crockett" on TV's *Miami Vice* and title role on TV's *Nash Bridges*. Starred in several movies. Twice married to and divorced from actress Melanie Griffith.

JOHNSON, Holly
Born William Johnson on 2/9/1960 in Liverpool, England. Male singer. At age 16, joined Big In Japan as bassist. Lead singer of Frankie Goes To Hollywood, 1980-87.

JOHNSON, Jack
Born on 5/18/1975 in Oahu, Hawaii. Adult Alternative pop-rock singer/songwriter/guitarist. Former professional surfer.

JOHNSON, Jamey
Born in Enterprise, Alabama; raised in Montgomery, Alabama. Male country singer/songwriter.

JOHNSON, Jesse
Born on 5/29/1960 in Rock Island, Illinois. Lead guitarist of The Time.

JOHNSON, Kevin
Born in Rockhampton, Queensland, Australia. Pop singer/songwriter/guitarist.

JOHNSON, Lonnie
Born Alonzo Johnson on 2/8/1889 in New Orleans, Louisiana. Died of a stroke on 6/16/1970 (age 81). Blues singer/guitarist. Staff musician at Okeh label from 1925-32. Recorded with Louis Armstrong and Duke Ellington. Guitar style highly influential to later jazz and blues guitarists.

JOHNSON, Lou
Born in 1941 in Harlem, New York. R&B singer.

JOHNSON, Marv
Born on 10/15/1938 in Detroit, Michigan. Died on 5/16/1993 (age 54). R&B singer/songwriter/pianist. With the Serenaders vocal group, mid-1950s. First recorded for Kudo in 1958. Worked in sales and promotion for Motown in the early 1970s. Recognized as a co-creator of the Motown sound with Berry Gordy.

JOHNSON, Michael
Born on 8/8/1944 in Alamosa, Colorado; raised in Denver, Colorado. Adult Contemporary singer. Studied classical guitar in 1966 in Spain. In the Chad Mitchell Trio with John Denver in 1968.

JOHNSON, Puff
Born on 12/10/1972 in Detroit, Michigan; raised in Los Angeles, California. Female R&B singer.

JOHNSON, Rozetta
Born in Tuscaloosa, Alabama. Female R&B singer.

JOHNSON, Syl
Born Sylvester Thompson on 7/1/1936 in Holly Springs, Mississippi; raised in Chicago, Illinois. R&B singer/songwriter/guitarist. Recorded for Federal Records, 1959-62. Father of Syleena Johnson.

JOHNSTON, Freedy
Born on 3/7/1961 in Kinsley, Kansas; later based in New York. Male Adult Alternative pop-rock singer/songwriter.

JOHNSTON, Sabrina
Born in New Jersey. Female dance singer.

JOHNSTON, Tom
Born on 8/15/1948 in Visalia, California. Lead singer/guitarist of The Doobie Brothers.

JOINER, ARKANSAS JUNIOR HIGH SCHOOL BAND
There never was a junior high school in Joiner, Arkansas. Group is actually a band of studio musicians led by Ernie Freeman. Joiner is the hometown of Liberty Records president Al Bennett. Also see Sir Chauncey.

JOJO
Born Joanna Levesque on 12/20/1990 in Foxboro, Massachusetts. Female teen pop singer.

JO JO GUNNE
Rock group from Los Angeles, California: Jay Ferguson (vocals, keyboards), brothers Matthew (guitar) and Mark (bass) Andes, and Curly Smith (drums). Both Ferguson and Mark Andes had been in Spirit. Group named after the 1958 Chuck Berry hit. Mark Andes was later with Firefall and Heart.

JOLI, France
Born in 1963 in Montreal, Quebec, Canada. White female dance singer.

JOMANDA
Female R&B-dance vocal trio from New Jersey: Joanne Thomas, Cheri Williams and Renee Washington.

JON & ROBIN
Duo of Jon Abnor and Javonne "Robin" Braga (who married James Wright of The Five Americans in 1970).

JON & VANGELIS
Duo of Jon Anderson (lead singer of Yes; born on 10/25/1944 in Lancashire, England) and Vangelis (born on 3/29/1943 in Valos, Greece).

JONAS BROTHERS
Teen pop-rock trio from Wyckoff, New Jersey: brothers Kevin (age 17), Joseph (age 16) and Nicholas (age 13) Jonas.

JON B
Born Jonathan Buck on 11/11/1974 in Rhode Island. R&B singer/songwriter.

JONELL
Born Shannon Jonell Showes in Cincinnati, Ohio. Female R&B singer/rapper.

JONES, Davy
Born on 12/30/1945 in Manchester, England. Member of The Monkees. Played "The Artful Dodger" in Broadway's *Oliver*.

JONES, Donell
Born on 5/22/1973 in Chicago, Illinois. R&B singer/songwriter.

JONES, Etta
Born on 11/25/1928 in Aiken, South Carolina. Died of cancer on 10/16/2001 (age 72). Jazz singer with Earl Hines's orchestra from 1949-52.

JONES, George
Born on 9/12/1931 in Saratoga, Texas. Legendary country singer/songwriter/guitarist. Married to Tammy Wynette from 1969-75. Recorded rockabilly music under pseudonyms Hank Smith and Thumper Jones.

JONES, Glenn
Born in 1961 in Jacksonville, Florida. R&B singer/songwriter.

JONES, Grace
Born Grace Mendoza on 5/19/1948 in Spanishtown, Jamaica; raised in Syracuse, New York. Dance singer/actress/model. Acted in several movies.

JONES, Hannah
Born in England. Black female dance singer.

JONES, Howard
Born John Howard Jones on 2/23/1955 in Southampton, Hampshire, England. Pop singer/songwriter/keyboardist.

JONES, Jack
Born on 1/14/1938 in Los Angeles, California. One of the top Adult Contemporary singers of the 1960s. Son of actress Irene Hervey and actor/singer Allan Jones. First recorded for Capitol in 1959. Performed the theme for the *Love Boat* TV series. Married to actress Jill St. John from 1967-69.

JONES, Jim
Born Joseph Jimmy Jones on 7/15/1976 in the Bronx, New York. Male rapper/songwriter. Member of The Diplomats.

JONES, Jimmy
Born on 6/2/1937 in Birmingham, Alabama. R&B singer.

JONES, Joe
Born on 8/12/1926 in New Orleans, Louisiana. R&B singer/songwriter. Pianist/valet for B.B. King in the early 1950s. First recorded for Capitol in 1954. Produced and managed The Dixie Cups and Alvin Robinson.

JONES, Kay Cee
Born Ruthie Reece on 12/20/1929 in Childress, Texas. White female singer. Appeared in the movie *Gentlemen From Arizona*. Once married to songwriter/movie historian Eddie Brandt.

JONES, Linda
Born on 1/14/1944 in Newark, New Jersey. Died of diabetes on 3/14/1972 (age 28). Soul singer. First recorded for MGM/Cub as Linda Lane in 1963.

JONES, Mike
Born on 1/6/1981 in Houston, Texas. Rapper/songwriter.

JONES, Norah
Born on 3/30/1979 in Manhattan, New York; raised in Dallas, Texas. Jazz-styled singer/pianist. Daughter of legendary sitar player Ravi Shankar.

JONES, Oran "Juice"
Born on 3/28/1957 in Houston, Texas; raised in Harlem, New York. R&B singer/rapper.

JONES, Quincy
Born on 3/14/1933 in Chicago, Illinois; raised in Bremerton, Washington. Songwriter/conductor/producer/arranger. Began as a jazz trumpeter with Lionel Hampton, 1950-53. Music director for Mercury Records in 1961, then vice president in 1964. Wrote scores for many movies, 1965-73. Scored TV series *Roots* in 1977. Arranger/producer for hundreds of successful singers and orchestras. Produced Michael Jackson's mega-albums *Off The Wall*, *Thriller* and *Bad*. Established own Qwest label in 1981. Line producer for the movie *The Color Purple*. Married to actress Peggy Lipton (TV's *Mod Squad*) from 1974-89. His biographical movie *Listen Up: The Lives Of Quincy Jones* was released in 1990.

JONES, Rickie Lee
Born on 11/8/1954 in Chicago, Illinois. Female jazz-styled singer/songwriter. Moved to Los Angeles in 1977.

JONES, Shae
Born on 7/27/1978 in Kansas City, Missouri. Female R&B singer.

JONES, Tamiko
Born Barbara Tamiko Ferguson in 1945 in Kyle, West Virginia; raised in Detroit, Michigan. First recorded for Atlantic in 1966. Moved to London; married to John Abbey (publisher of *Blues & Soul* magazine). Smokey Robinson's manager in 1991.

JONES, Tom
Born Thomas Jones Woodward on 6/7/1940 in Pontypridd, South Wales. Worked local clubs as Tommy Scott; formed own trio The Senators in 1963. Began solo career in London in 1964. Host of own TV musical variety series from 1969-71.

JONESES, The
R&B-disco group from Pittsburgh, Pennsylvania: Glenn Dorsey, Harold Taylor, Cy Brooks and Ernest Holt.

JONES GIRLS, The
Female R&B vocal trio from Detroit, Michigan: sisters Shirley, Brenda and Valorie Jones. Backup singers for Lou Rawls, Teddy Pendergrass and Aretha Franklin. With Diana Ross from 1975-78. Valorie died on 12/2/2001 (age 45).

JOOSE
Male R&B vocal group from Oklahoma: Leonardo Pettis, Rocky McKaufman, Trell Lewis and Jay Farmer.

JOPLIN, Janis
Born on 1/19/1943 in Port Arthur, Texas. Died of a heroin overdose on 10/4/1970 (age 27). White blues-rock singer. Nicknamed "Pearl." Moved to San Francisco in 1966; joined Big Brother & The Holding Company. Left band to go solo in 1968. The Bette Midler movie *The Rose* was inspired by Joplin's life.

JORDAN, Jeremy
Born Don Henson on 9/19/1973 in Hammond, Indiana; raised in Calumet City, Illinois. Teen pop singer. Relative of Tobin Mathews.

JORDAN, Louis
Born on 7/8/1908 in Brinkley, Arkansas. Died of a heart attack on 2/4/1975 (age 66). R&B/big band vocalist/saxophonist. Innovative, humorous, extremely popular vocal style paved the way for later R&B styles. Appeared in the movies *Follow The Boys*, *Beware*, *Meet Miss Bobby Sox* and *Swing Parade of 1946*.

JORDAN, Montell
Born on 12/3/1968 in Los Angeles, California. Male R&B singer/songwriter.

JORDAN, Sass
Born on 12/23/1962 in Birmingham, England; raised in Montreal, Quebec, Canada. Female rock singer. One of the judges on the TV talent show *Canadian Idol*.

JORDY
Born Jordy Lemoine on 1/14/1988 in Paris, France. Age 5 in 1993. His father, Claude, is a record producer.

JOSEPH, Margie
Born in 1950 in Gautier, Mississippi. R&B singer.

JOURNEY
Rock group formed in San Francisco, California: Neal Schon (born on 2/27/1954) and George Tickner (guitars), Gregg Rolie (keyboards, vocals; born on 6/17/1947), Ross Valory (bass; born on 2/2/1949) and Aynsley Dunbar (drums; born on 1/10/1946; John Mayall, Mothers Of Invention). Schon and Rolie had been in Santana. Tickner left in 1975. Steve Perry (lead vocals; born on 1/22/1949) added by 1978. In 1979, Steve Smith replaced Dunbar, who later joined Jefferson Starship, then Whitesnake. Jonathan Cain (ex-keyboardist of The Babys) added in 1981, replacing Rolie. In 1986 group pared down to a three-man core: Perry, Schon and Cain. The latter two hooked up with Bad English in 1989. Smith, Valory and Rolie joined The Storm in 1991. Schon with Hardline in 1992. Reunion in 1996 of Perry, Schon, Cain, Valory and Smith. Steve Augeri replaced Perry in 2001.

JOY, Roddie
Born Rita Coleman in Detroit, Michigan. Female R&B singer.

JOY DIVISION
Post-punk group formed in Manchester, England: Ian Curtis (vocals), Bernard Albrecht (guitar), Peter Hook (bass) and Stephen Morris (drums). Curtis committed suicide on 5/18/1980 (age 23). Group became New Order, recruiting keyboardist/guitarist Gillian Gilbert in December 1980.

JOY OF COOKING
Country-rock group from Berkeley, California: Terry Garthwaite (vocals), Toni Brown (vocals, keyboards), Ron Wilson (percussion), Jeff Neighbor (bass) and Fritz Kasten (drums).

J-SHIN
Born Jonathan Shinhoster in Miami, Florida. R&B singer.

J'SON
Born J'son Tyrel Thomas on 5/14/80 in Los Angeles, California. R&B singer.

JUANES
Born Juan Aristizabal on 8/9/1972 in Medellin, Colombia. Latin singer.

JUDAS PRIEST
Heavy metal band formed in Birmingham, England: Rob Halford (vocals), K.K. Downing and Glenn Tipton (guitars), Ian Hill (bass), and Dave Holland (drums). Halford left band in mid-1992 to form the rock group Fight.

JUDDS, The
Country duo from Ashland, Kentucky: Naomi Judd (born Diana Ellen Judd on 1/11/1946) and her daughter Wynonna Judd (born Christina Ciminella on 5/30/1964). Moved to Hollywood in 1968. Moved to Nashville in 1979. Naomi's chronic hepatitis forced duo to split at the end of 1991. Naomi's daughter and Wynonna's half-sister is actress Ashley Judd.

JULIE
Born Julie Budd in Manhattan, New York. Singer/actress. Played "Stella Summers" in the movie *The Devil And Max Devlin*.

JUMP 'N THE SADDLE
Country-pop group from Chicago, Illinois: Peter Quinn (vocals, harmonica), T.C. Furlong and Barney Schwartz (guitars), Tom Trinka (sax), Rick Gorley (bass) and Vincent Dee (drums).

JUNGKLAS, Rob
Born in Boston, Massachusetts. Rock singer/songwriter/guitarist.

JUNIOR
Born Norman Giscombe on 11/10/1961 in London, England. Funk singer/songwriter.

JUNIOR M.A.F.I.A.
Gathering of four rap acts: Lil' Kim, Klepto, Snakes (Trife & Larceny) and The Sixes (Little Caesar, Chico & Nino Brown). Proteges of The Notorious B.I.G. M.A.F.I.A.: Masters At Finding Intelligent Attitudes.

JUSTIS, Bill
Born on 10/14/1926 in Birmingham, Alabama. Died on 7/15/1982 (age 55). Session saxophonist/arranger/producer. Led house band for Sun Records.

JUST US
Pop duo of New York City producers Chip Taylor and Al Gorgoni.

JUVENILE
Born Terius Gray on 3/25/1975 in New Orleans, Louisiana. Male rapper.

KADISON, Joshua
Born on 2/8/1963 in Los Angeles, California. Adult Contemporary singer/songwriter/pianist.

KAEMPFERT, Bert
Born on 10/16/1923 in Hamburg, Germany. Died on 6/21/1980 (age 56). Multi-instrumentalist/bandleader/producer/arranger for Polydor Records in Germany. Composed "Strangers In The Night" and "Spanish Eyes" among others. Produced first Beatles recording session in Hamburg ("Cry For A Shadow"/"Ain't She Sweet").

KAI
Male R&B vocal group from San Francisco, California: Andrey Silva, Errol Viray, Andrew Gapuz, A.C. Lorenzo and Leo Chan.

KAJAGOOGOO
Pop-synth group formed in Leighton Buzzard, Hertfordshire, England: Christopher "Limahl" Hamill (vocals; left in late 1983), Steve Askew (guitar), Stuart Neale (keyboards), Nick Beggs (bass) and Jez Strode (drums).

KALIN TWINS
White pop vocal duo of twins Herbert Kalin and Harold Kalin. Born on 2/16/1934 in Port Jervis, New York. Harold died in a car crash on 8/23/2005 (age 71). Herbert died of a heart attack on 7/21/2006 (age 72).

KALLEN, Kitty
Born on 5/25/1922 in Philadelphia, Pennsylvania. Big band singer with Jack Teagarden, Jimmy Dorsey, Harry James and Artie Shaw.

KALLMANN, Gunter
Born on 11/19/1927 in Berlin, Germany. Choral director.

KAMON, Karen
Female pop singer. Married to producer Phil Ramone, who worked with Billy Joel and many others.

KAMOZE, Ini
Born on 10/9/1957 in Jamaica. Male dancehall reggae singer/author. Name means "mountain of the true God."

KANDI
Born Kandi Burruss on 5/17/1976 in Atlanta, Georgia. Female R&B singer/songwriter. Former member of Xscape.

KANE, Big Daddy
Born Antonio Hardy on 9/10/1968 in Brooklyn, New York. Rap singer/lyricist for Cold Chillin' Records. Wrote songs for Roxanne Shante and Biz Markie. Toured as Shante's DJ in 1985. Kane is an acronym for King Asiatic Nobody's Equal. Appeared in the movies *The Meteor Man* and *Posse*.

KANE, Madleen
Born in Sweden. Female disco singer produced by Giorgio Moroder.

KANE GANG, The
Soul-styled pop trio formed in England: vocalists Martin Brammer and Paul Woods with guitarist David Brewis. Band's name derived from the movie *Citizen Kane*.

KANO
Disco group from Italy: Rosanna Casale, Lella Esposito, Piero Cairo, Bruno Gergonzi, Luciano Nenzatti and Stefano Pulga.

KANSAS
Pop-rock group from Topeka, Kansas: Steve Walsh (vocals, keyboards; born on 6/15/1951), Kerry Livgren (guitar, keyboards; born on 9/18/1949), Rich Williams (guitar), Robby Steinhardt (violin), Dave Hope (bass; born on 10/7/1949) and Phil Ehart

(drums). Walsh left in 1981 and formed Streets; replaced by John Elefante (later a prolific Christian rock producer/artist). Livgren became a popular Contemporary Christian artist in the 1980s. Revised lineup in 1986: Walsh, Ehart, Williams, Steve Morse (guitarist from The Dregs) and Billy Greer (bass).

KAOMA
Multi-national group of singers, musicians and dancers based in Paris, France. Fronted by keyboardist/arranger Jean-Claude Bonaventure.

KAPLAN, Gabriel
Born on 3/31/1945 in Brooklyn, New York. Comedian/actor. Star of TV's *Welcome Back Kotter*.

KARDINAL OFFISHALL
Born Jason Harrow in Toronto, Ontario, Canada. Male rapper/producer.

KAREN, Kenny
Born in Montreal, Quebec, Canada. Pop singer/songwriter/actor. Played "David Miller" in the 1978 movie *If Ever I See You Again*.

KARL, Frankie, & The Dreams
R&B vocal group from Detroit, Michigan. Led by Frankie Karl Springs.

KaSANDRA
Born John Anderson on 7/30/1936 in Panama City, Florida. R&B singer/songwriter.

KASENETZ-KATZ SINGING ORCHESTRAL CIRCUS
Bubblegum rock aggregation assembled by producers Jerry Kasenetz and Jeff Katz. Featured members from The 1910 Fruitgum Co./The Ohio Express/The Music Explosion.

KASHIF
Born Michael Jones in 1959 in Brooklyn, New York. Techno-funk singer/musician. Member of B.T. Express from 1976-79.

KATALINA
Born in Chicago, Illinois; raised in California. Female dance singer.

KATFISH
Rock band from Lewiston, Maine. Led by singer/ guitarist Nick Knowlton.

KATRINA & THE WAVES
Pop-rock band formed in Cambridge, England: Katrina Leskanich (vocals; born in Topeka, Kansas), Kimberley Rew (guitar), Vince Dela Cruz (bass) and Alex Cooper (drums).

KAY, John
Born Joachim Krauledat on 4/12/1944 in Tilsit, Germany. Leader of Steppenwolf.

KAYAK
Rock group from Holland: Max Werner (vocals), Johan Slager (guitar), Ton Scherpenzeel (keyboards), Theo DeJong (bass) and Charles Schouten (drums).

KAYE, Mary, Trio
Adult Contemporary vocal trio: Mary (died on 2/17/2007, age 83), her brother Norman, and Frankie Ross (died on 5/9/1995, age 70).

KAYE, Sammy
Born on 3/13/1910 in Lakewood, Ohio. Died of cancer on 6/2/1987 (age 77). Leader of popular "sweet" dance band with the slogan "Swing and Sway with Sammy Kaye." Also played clarinet and alto sax.

KAYLI, Bob
Born Robert Gordy on 7/15/1931 in Detroit, Michigan. Brother of Motown founder Berry Gordy, Jr. Executive with Motown's music publishing firm, Jobete, from 1961-85. Appeared in the 1972 movie *Lady Sings The Blues*.

KBC BAND
Rock trio of former Jefferson Airplane bandmates: Paul Kantner (guitar), Marty Balin (vocals) and Jack Casady (bass).

KC & THE SUNSHINE BAND
Disco group from Hialeah, Florida. Formed by Harry Wayne "KC" Casey (vocals, keyboards; born on 1/31/1951) and Richard Finch (bass; born on 1/25/1954). Other members included Jerome Smith (guitar), Fermin Coytisolo (congas), Robert Johnson (drums), and Ronnie Smith, Denvil Liptrot, James Weaver and Charles Williams (horn section). Jerome Smith died in a construction accident on 7/28/2000 (age 47).

K-CI & JOJO
Brothers Cedric "K-Ci" and Joel "JoJo" Hailey from Charlotte, North Carolina. K-Ci was born on 9/2/1969; JoJo was born on 6/10/1971. Both were founding members of the R&B vocal group Jodeci.

K-DOE, Ernie
Born Ernest Kador on 2/22/1936 in New Orleans, Louisiana. Died on 7/5/2001 (age 65). R&B singer/ songwriter. Recorded with the Blue Diamonds on Savoy in 1954. First solo recording for Specialty in 1955.

KEANE
Alternative-rock trio from Battle, East Sussex, England: Tom Chaplin (vocals), Tim Rice-Oxley (piano) and Richard Hughes (drums).

KEANE BROTHERS, The
Pop duo: brothers Tom (piano; born on 3/13/1964) and John (drums; born on 4/26/1965) Keane. Sons of label owner Bob Keane. Duo hosted own summer replacement variety show on CBS-TV in 1977.

KEARNEY, Mat
Born on 2/1/1978 in Eugene, Oregon. Contemporary Christian singer/songwriter/guitarist.

KEEDY
Born Kelly Keedy on 7/26/1965 in Abilene, Texas. Female dance singer.

KEITH
Born James Keefer on 5/7/1949 in Philadelphia, Pennsylvania. Pop singer/songwriter.

KEITH, Lisa
Born in Minneapolis, Minnesota. Adult Contemporary singer/songwriter. Vocalist on Herb Alpert's "Keep Your Eye On Me," "Diamonds" and "Making Love In The Rain."

KEITH, Toby
Born Toby Keith Covel on 7/8/1961 in Clinton, Oklahoma; raised in Moore, Oklahoma. Country singer/songwriter/guitarist. Former rodeo hand, oil field worker and semi-pro football player.

KELIS
Born Kelis Rogers on 8/21/1979 in Harlem, New York. Female R&B singer/rapper/songwriter. Married Nas on 1/8/2005.

KELLEM, Manny
Born on 11/1/1916 in Philadelphia, Pennsylvania. Died on 11/5/2002 (age 86). Prolific record producer.

KELLER, Jerry
Born on 6/20/1937 in Fort Smith, Arkansas; raised in Tulsa, Oklahoma. Pop singer/songwriter.

KELLEY, Josh
Born in Augusta, Georgia. Pop singer/songwriter/ guitarist.

KELLUM, Murry
Born on 12/31/1942 in Jackson, Tennessee and raised in Plain, Texas. Died in a plane crash on 9/30/1990 (age 47). Country singer/songwriter.

KELLY, Casey
Born Daniel Cohen in Baton Rouge, Louisiana. Pop singer/songwriter/pianist/guitarist.

KELLY, Monty
Born on 6/8/1910 in Modesto, California. Died on 3/15/1971 (age 60). Conductor/arranger.

KELLY, Paul
Born on 6/19/1940 in Miami, Florida. R&B singer/ songwriter.

KELLY, R.
Born Robert Kelly on 1/8/1967 in Chicago, Illinois. R&B singer/songwriter/producer/multi-instrumentalist. Married Aaliyah on 7/31/1994 (marriage later annulled). Public Announcement was his assembly of backing singers and dancers.

KEM
Born Kem Owens in Nashville, Tennessee; raised in Detroit, Michigan. Male R&B singer/songwriter.

KEMP, Johnny
Born in Nassau, Bahamas; raised in Harlem, New York. R&B singer/songwriter/actor/dancer.

KEMP, Tara
Born on 5/11/1964 in San Francisco, California. R&B singer/songwriter/pianist.

KENDALLS, The
Father-and-daughter country duo from St. Louis, Missouri: Royce (born on 9/25/1934) and Jeannie (born on 11/30/1954) Kendall (real last name: Kuykendall). Royce died of a heart attack on 5/22/1998 (age 63).

KENDALL SISTERS, The
Rock and roll duo from Ohio: sisters Polly and Dolly Kendall.

KENDRICK, Nat, & The Swans
James Brown's backup band, also known as The JB's. Consisted of J.C. Adams, Bobby Roach, Fats Gonder, Bernard Odum and Nat Kendrick (drums).

KENDRICKS, Eddie
Born on 12/17/1939 in Union Springs, Alabama; raised in Birmingham, Alabama. Died of cancer on 10/5/1992 (age 52). Joined the R&B group the Primes in Detroit in the late 1950s. Group later evolved into The Temptations; Kendricks sang lead from 1960-71. Kendricks later dropped the letter "s" from his last name.

KENNEDY, Mike
Born Michael Kogel on 4/25/1945 in Berlin, Germany. Lead singer of Los Bravos.

KENNEDY, Ray
Born in Philadelphia, Pennsylvania. Pop-rock singer/songwriter.

KENNER, Chris
Born on 12/25/1929 in Kenner, Louisiana. Died of a heart attack on 1/28/1976 (age 46). Male R&B singer/songwriter. First recorded for Baton in 1956.

KENNY G
Born Kenny Gorelick on 6/5/1956 in Seattle, Washington. Soprano/tenor saxophonist. Joined Barry White's Love Unlimited Orchestra at age 17. Graduated Phi Beta Kappa and Magna Cum Laude from the University of Washington with an accounting degree.

KENT, Al
Born Al Hamilton in 1937 in Detroit, Michigan. R&B singer/guitarist/producer. In the mid-1950s, member of group The Nitecaps with his brother Ronnie Savoy.

KENTON, Stan
Born on 12/15/1911 in Wichita, Kansas. Died of a stroke on 8/25/1979 (age 67). Progressive-jazz bandleader/pianist/composer. Organized his first jazz band in 1941. Third person named to the Jazz Hall of Fame. His theme song "Artistry In Rhythm" was chosen for a Grammy Hall of Fame award.

KERR, Anita, Singers
Born Anita Grilli on 10/31/1927 in Memphis, Tennessee. Soprano session singer. The rest of her Quartet: Gil Wright (tenor), Dottie Dillard (alto) and Louis Nunley (baritone).

KERSH, David
Born on 12/9/1970 in Humble, Texas. Country singer/songwriter.

KERSHAW, Nik
Born on 3/1/1958 in Bristol, Somerset, England. Pop-rock singer/songwriter/multi-instrumentalist.

KERSHAW, Sammy
Born on 2/24/1958 in Abbeville, Louisiana; raised in Kaplan, Louisiana. Country singer. Married Lorrie Morgan on 9/29/2001 (since separated).

KEYES, Troy
Born on 3/13/1940 in Pantego, North Carolina; raised in Brooklyn, New York. R&B singer. Lead singer with The High Keyes.

KEYS, Alicia
Born Alicia Cook on 1/25/1980 in Hell's Kitchen, Manhattan, New York (Irish-Italian mother/Jamaican father). R&B singer/songwriter/keyboardist.

K5
Dance group assembled by producer Kevin "KJ" Shiver: vocalists Tammy Wright and Tessa Nollenberger with instrumentalists Mark Hibbard and Christian Orshal.

KHAN, Chaka / RUFUS
Born Yvette Marie Stevens on 3/23/1953 in Great Lakes, Illinois. Became lead singer of Rufus in 1972. Rufus members Andre Fischer and Kevin Murphy were with The American Breed. Recorded solo and with Rufus since 1978. Sister of vocalists Taka Boom and Mark Stevens (Jamaica Boys). Khan's daughter Milini is a member of Pretty In Pink.

KHIA
Born Khia Chambers in Philadelphia, Pennsylvania; raised in Tampa, Florida. Female rapper.

KIARA
R&B duo from Detroit, Michigan: Gregory Charley (vocals, bass) and John Winston (guitar, backing vocals). Kiara (pronounced: kee-air-a) is Swahili for change.

KID, Joey
Born in the Bronx, New York. Dance singer. Cousin of George LaMond.

KID 'N PLAY
Rap duo: Christopher "Kid" Reid (born in Bronx, New York) and Christopher "Play" Martin (born in Queens, New York). Starred in the *House Party* movies and *Class Act*. Starred in own Saturday morning cartoon show.

KID ROCK
Born Robert Ritchie on 1/17/1971 in Romeo, Michigan. White hip-hop/rock singer.

KIDS NEXT DOOR, The
Pop vocal group featuring Mary Sinclair.

KIHN, Greg, Band
Born on 7/10/1949 in Baltimore, Maryland. White pop-rock singer/songwriter/guitarist. His band consisted of Dave Carpender (guitar), Gary Phillips (keyboards), Steve Wright (bass) and Larry Lynch (drums). Greg Douglass replaced Carpender in late 1982. Kihn went solo in late 1984.

KILGORE, Theola
Born on 12/6/1925 in Shreveport, Louisiana; raised in Oakland, California. Died on 5/15/2005 (age 79). Female gospel-blues singer.

KILLER MIKE
Born Michael Render in Adamsville, Georgia. Male rapper.

KILLERS, The
Alternative-rock band from Las Vegas, Nevada: Brandon Flowers (vocals, keyboards), David Keuning (guitar), Mark Stoermer (bass) and Ronnie Vannucci (drums).

KIM, Andy
Born Androwis Jovakim on 12/5/1952 in Montreal, Quebec, Canada. His parents were from Lebanon. Pop singer/songwriter. Recorded briefly in the early 1980s as Baron Longfellow on Ice Records. Teamed with Jeff Barry to write "Sugar, Sugar."

KIMBALL, Cheyenne
Born on 7/27/1990 in Frisco, Texas. Female singer/songwriter/guitarist. Won *America's Most Talented Kid* TV talent competition in 2003. Starred in the 2006 MTV reality series *Cheyenne*.

KIMBERLY, Adrian
Artist is actually a Don Everly (Everly Brothers) production, recorded on Don's own label.

KIMBERLYS, The
Country vocal group from Oklahoma: brothers Harold and Carl Kimberly, with their spouses, sisters Verna and Vera Kimberly.

KIMMEL, Tom
Born Thomas Hobbs in 1953 in Memphis, Tennessee. Rock singer/songwriter.

KING
Pop-rock group from Coventry, England: Paul King (vocals), Jim Lantsbery (guitar), Mick Roberts (keyboards), Tony Wall (bass) and Adrian Lillywhite (drums).

KING, Albert
Born Albert Nelson on 4/25/1923 in Indianola, Mississippi; raised in Forrest City, Arkansas. Died of a heart attack on 12/21/1992 (age 69). Blues singer/guitarist. Known for playing his Gibson Flying V guitar.

KING, Anna
Born Anna Williams on 12/9/1937 in Philadelphia, Pennsylvania. Died on 10/21/2002 (age 64). Former female vocalist with the James Brown Revue.

KING, B.B.
Born Riley King on 9/16/1925 in Itta Bena, Mississippi. Legendary blues singer/guitarist. Moved to Memphis in 1946. Own radio show on WDIA-Memphis, 1949-50, where he was dubbed "The Beale Street Blues Boy," later shortened to "Blues Boy," then simply "B.B." First recorded for Bullet in 1949.

KING, Ben E.
Born Benjamin Earl Nelson on 9/28/1938 in Henderson, North Carolina; raised in Harlem, New York. Worked with The Moonglows for six months while still in high school. Joined the Five Crowns in 1957, which became the new Drifters in 1959. Wrote lyrics to "There Goes My Baby," his first lead performance with The Drifters. Went solo in May 1960. Also see The Soul Clan.

KING, Carole
Born Carole Klein on 2/9/1942 in Brooklyn, New York. Singer/songwriter/pianist. Neil Sedaka wrote his 1959 hit "Oh! Carol" about her. Married to lyricist Gerry Goffin, 1958-68. In 1971, won four Grammys. King and Goffin's daughter, Louise Goffin, began a solo career in 1979. One of the most successful female songwriters of the rock era.

KING, Claude
Born on 2/5/1923 in Keithville, Louisiana. Country singer/songwriter/guitarist. Acted in the movies *Swamp Girl* and *Year of The Yahoo*.

KING, Diana
Born on 11/8/1970 in St. Catherine, Jamaica. Reggae-dancehall singer/songwriter.

KING, Evelyn "Champagne"
Born on 6/29/1960 in the Bronx, New York; raised in Philadelphia, Pennsylvania. Disco singer. Employed as a cleaning woman at Sigma Sound Studios when discovered. Originally nicknamed "Bubbles;" then "Champagne."

KING, Freddy
Born Frederick Christian on 9/3/1934 in Gilmer, Texas. Died of a heart attack on 12/28/1976 (age 42). Influential blues singer/guitarist. Moved to Chicago in 1950. Released albums as Freddie King.

KING, Jonathan
Born Kenneth King on 12/6/1944 in London, England. Pop singer/songwriter/producer. Formed U.K. Records in 1972. Produced Hedgehoppers Anonymous.

KING, Peggy
Born on 2/16/1930 in Greensburg, Pennsylvania. Adult Contemporary singer. Regular on TV's *The George Gobel Show*, 1954-56. In the 1957 movie *Zero Hour*.

KING, Rev. Martin Luther
Born on 1/15/1929 in Atlanta, Georgia. Assassinated on 4/4/1968 (age 39) in Memphis, Tennessee. America's civil rights leader. Nobel prize winner in 1964. The third Monday in January is a principal U.S. holiday: Martin Luther King Day.

KING, Sleepy
Male R&B singer/organist.

KING, Teddi
Born Theodora King on 9/18/1929 in Boston, Massachusetts. Died on 11/18/1977 (age 48). Female jazz-styled singer.

KINGBEES, The
Rock trio from Los Angeles, California: Jamie James (vocals, guitar), Michael Rummons (bass) and Rex Roberts (drums).

KING CRIMSON
Progressive-rock group formed in England by eccentric guitarist Robert Fripp. Group featured an ever-changing lineup of top British artists. 1970 lineup: Fripp (guitar, keyboards), Greg Lake (vocals, bass; Emerson, Lake & Palmer), Ian McDonald (flute; Foreigner) and Mike Giles (drums).

KING CURTIS
Born Curtis Ousley on 2/7/1934 in Fort Worth, Texas. Stabbed to death on 8/13/1971 (age 37). R&B saxophonist. With Lionel Hampton in 1950. Moved to New York City; did session work. First own recording on Gem in 1953. Also recorded solo as the Rinky Dinks in 1962 on Enjoy and as The Ramrods in 1963 on R&H. Played on sessions for Bobby Darin, Aretha Franklin, Brook Benton, Nat

KING CURTIS — cont'd
King Cole, McGuire Sisters, Andy Williams, The Coasters, The Shirelles and hundreds of others. Also see Pat and the Satellites.

KINGDOM COME
Hard-rock group: Lenny Wolf (vocals; from Hamburg, Germany), Danny Stag and Rick Steier (guitars), Johnny Frank (bass) and James Kottak (drums).

KING HARVEST
Pop-rock group from Olcott, New York: Ron Altback (vocals, piano), Eddie Tuleja (guitar), Rod Novack (sax), Dave Robinson (trombone), Tony Cahill (bass) and David Montgomery (drums). Altback and Robinson later joined Celebration featuring Mike Love.

KING JUST
Born Adrian Angevin in Staten Island, New York. Male rapper.

KINGOFTHEHILL
Rock-funk group from St. Louis, Missouri: Frankie Muriel (vocals), Jimmy Griffin (guitar), George Potsos (bass) and Vito Bono (drums).

KING PINS, The
R&B vocal group from Clarksdale, Mississippi: brothers Andrew, Curtis and Robert Kelly with Charles Lee and Offe Reece.

KINGS, The
Rock group from Toronto, Ontario, Canada: David Diamond (vocals, bass), Aryan Zero (guitar), Sonny Keyes (keyboards) and Max Styles (drums).

KINGSMEN, The
Rock and roll band from Portland, Oregon: Jack Ely (vocals, guitar), Mike Mitchell (guitar), Don Gallucci (piano), Bob Nordby (bass) and Lynn Easton (drums). After release of "Louie Louie" (featuring lead vocal by Ely), Easton took over leadership of band and replaced Ely as lead singer. One of America's premier 1960s garage bands. Gallucci later formed Don And The Goodtimes.

KINGS OF LEON
Rock band from Nashville, Tennessee: brothers Caleb Followill (vocals, guitar), Jared Followill (bass) and Nathan Followill (drums), with their cousin Matthew Followill (guitar).

KINGS OF THE SUN
Hard-rock group from Sydney, Australia: brothers Jeffrey (vocals) and Clifford (drums) Hoad, Glen Morris (guitar), and Anthony Ragg (bass).

KINGSTON, Sean
Born Kisean Anderson on 2/3/1990 in Miami, Florida; raised in Kingston, Jamaica. R&B singer/songwriter/rapper.

KINGSTON TRIO, The
Folk trio formed in San Francisco, California: Dave Guard (born on 11/19/1934; died of cancer on 3/22/1991, age 56), Bob Shane (born on 2/1/1934) and Nick Reynolds (born on 7/27/1933; died of acute respiratory disease on 10/1/2008, age 75). Big break came at San Francisco's Purple Onion,

where the group stayed for eight months. Guard left in 1961 to form the Whiskeyhill Singers; John Stewart (died of a stroke on 1/19/2008, age 68) replaced him. Disbanded in 1968, Shane formed New Kingston Trio. Originators of the folk music craze of the 1960s.

KINKS, The
Rock group formed in London, England: Ray Davies (lead vocals, guitar; born on 6/21/1944) and his brother Dave Davies (lead guitar, vocals; born on 2/3/1947). Original lineup also included Peter Quaife (bass; born on 12/27/1943) and Mick Avory (drums; born on 2/15/1944). Numerous personnel changes during the 1970s. Ray appeared in the 1986 movie *Absolute Beginners*. Longtime members included the Davies brothers, Ian Gibbons (keyboards; 1979-88, 1996), Jim Rodford (bass; from 1978) and Bob Henrit (drums; from 1984; Charlie). Henrit and Rodford were members of Argent.

KINLEYS, The
Country vocal duo of identical twin sisters Heather and Jennifer Kinley (born on 11/5/1970 in Philadelphia, Pennsylvania).

KINNEY, Fern
Born in Jackson, Mississippi. Female R&B-dance singer.

KINSU
Born in Brooklyn, New York. Male hardcore rapper.

KIRBY, Kathy
Born on 10/20/1940 in Ilford, Essex, England. Pop singer.

KIRK, Jim
Born in Los Angeles, California. Vice president of TM Communications, a radio syndication organization. Wrote the original moog synthesizer theme music for radio's *American Top 40*.

KISS
Hard-rock theatrical group formed in New York: Gene Simmons (bass; born on 8/25/1949), Paul Stanley (guitar; born on 1/20/1952), Ace Frehley (lead guitar; born on 4/27/1951) and Peter Criss (drums; born on 12/20/1947). All shared vocals. Noted for elaborate makeup and highly theatrical stage shows; Simmons was made up as "The Bat Lizard," Stanley as "Star Child," Frehley as "Space Man" and Criss as "The Cat." Criss replaced by Eric Carr in 1981. Frehley replaced by Vinnie Vincent in 1982. Group appeared without makeup for the first time in 1983 on album cover *Lick It Up*. Mark St. John replaced Vincent in 1984. Bruce Kulick, brother of Bob Kulick of Balance, replaced St. John in 1985. Carr died of cancer on 11/24/1991 (age 41). St. John died on 4/5/2007 (age 51). Drummer Eric Singer joined in 1991. Original members reunited in 1996.

KISSING THE PINK
Synth-pop-dance group from England. Featuring singer/guitarist Nick Whitecross. Shortened name to KTP in 1985.

KISSOON, Mac & Katie
Brother-and-sister pop duo from Port-of-Spain, Trinidad. Mac was born Gerald Farthing on 11/11/1943. Katie was born Kathleen Farthing on 3/11/1951. Moved to England in the late 1950s.

KIX
Hard-rock group from Hagerstown, Maryland: Steve Whiteman (vocals), Ronnie Younkins and Brian Forsythe (guitars), Donnie Purnell (bass) and Jimmy Chalfant (drums).

KLAATU
Pop trio from Toronto, Ontario, Canada: Dee Long (vocals, guitar), Terry Draper (keyboards) and John Woloschuck (drums). Anonymous first release led to speculation that they were The Beatles. Name taken from alien character in the classic 1951 sci-fi movie *The Day The Earth Stood Still*.

KLEEER
R&B-disco group from New York: Isabelle Coles (vocals), Paul Crutchfield (vocals, percussion), Richard Lee (guitar), Norman Durham (bass) and Woody Cunningham (drums).

KLF, The
Pop-electronica-dance duo formed in England. Previously known as The Timelords: Bill Drummond (founding member of Big In Japan; former manager of Echo & The Bunnymen and Teardrop Explodes) and Jimmy Cauty (formerly with Zodiac Mindwarp). KLF stands for Kopyright Liberation Front.

KLINT, Pete, Quintet
Garage-rock band from Mason City, Iowa: Pete Klint (vocals, guitar), Mike Hesselink (guitar), John Peterson (keyboards), Jamie Wornson (bass) and Bill Morisky (drums).

KLIQUE
R&B vocal trio: Howard Huntsberry, Isaac Suthers and his sister Deborah Hunter. Huntsberry portrayed Jackie Wilson in the movie *La Bamba*.

KLOWNS, The
Four-man, two-woman group produced by Jeff Barry. Actor Barry Bostwick was a member. Group hosted own ABC-TV special on 11/15/1970.

KLYMAXX
Female R&B group from Los Angeles, California: Lorena Porter (vocals), Cheryl Cooley (guitar), Lynn Malsby and Robbin Grider (keyboards), Joyce "Fenderella" Irby (bass, vocals), and Bernadette Cooper (drums, vocals).

K.M.C. KRU
Rap duo from Lansing, Michigan: Tracy "T The Sarge" Edmond and Ken "The Butcher" White.

KNACK, The
Rock group formed in Los Angeles, California: Doug Fieger, Berton Averre (guitar), Prescott Niles (bass) and Bruce Gary (drums). Disbanded in 1982. All members but Gary reunited in 1986, replaced by drummer Billy Ward. Fieger was a member of the Detroit rock trio Sky. Gary died of cancer on 8/22/2006 (age 55).

KNICKERBOCKERS, The
Rock group from Bergenfield, New Jersey: Bill "Buddy Randell" Crandall (vocals, sax; The Royal Teens), brothers Bob "Beau Charles" Cecchino (guitar; vocals) and "Johnny Charles" Cecchino (bass, vocals), and Jimmy Walker (drums). Walker replaced Bill Medley, for a time, in The Righteous Brothers. Band named after Knickerbocker Avenue in their hometown. Crandall died in 1998.

KNIGHT, Frederick
Born on 8/15/1944 in Birmingham, Alabama. R&B singer/songwriter/producer.

KNIGHT, Gladys, & The Pips
R&B family group from Atlanta, Georgia: Gladys Knight (born on 5/28/1944), her brother Merald "Bubba" Knight and sister Brenda, and cousins William and Eleanor Guest. Named "Pips" for their manager, cousin James "Pip" Woods. First recorded for Brunswick in 1958. Brenda and Eleanor replaced by cousins Edward Patten and Langston George in 1959. Langston left group in 1962 and group has remained a quartet with the same members ever since. Due to legal problems, Gladys could not record with the Pips from 1977-80. Gladys played "Diana Richmond" on the 1985 TV series *Charlie & Co.* Patten died of a stroke on 2/25/2005 (age 65).

KNIGHT, Holly
Female singer/songwriter. Former member of the rock groups Spider and Device. Wrote Tina Turner's "Better Be Good To Me," Heart's "Never," Aerosmith's "Rag Doll," Animotion's "Obsession," Pat Benatar's "Love Is A Battlefield" and others.

KNIGHT, Jean
Born on 1/26/1943 in New Orleans, Louisiana. Female R&B singer.

KNIGHT, Jordan
Born on 5/15/1970 in Worcester, Massachusetts. Pop singer. Former member of New Kids On The Block.

KNIGHT, Robert
Born on 4/21/1945 in Franklin, Tennessee. R&B singer. Recorded for Dot in 1960.

KNIGHT, Sonny
Born Joseph Smith on 5/17/1934 in Maywood, Illinois. Died on 9/5/1998 (age 64). R&B singer/songwriter/pianist. Wrote the book *The Day The Music Died* in 1981 under his real name.

KNIGHT, Terry, & The Pack
Rock group from Flint, Michigan: Terry Knight (vocals), Curt Johnson (guitar), Bob Caldwell (organ), Mark Farner (bass) and Don Brewer (drums). Knight (real name: Richard Terrance Knapp) formed, managed and produced Grand Funk Railroad, which included Farner and Brewer. Knight was stabbed to death on 11/1/2004 (age 61).

KNIGHT BROS, The
R&B duo from Washington DC: Richard Dunbar and Jerry Diggs.

KNIGHTSBRIDGE STRINGS, The
Ensemble of 34 strings conducted by British conductor-arrangers Reg Owen and Malcolm Lockyer (died on 6/28/1976, age 53).

KNOBLOCK, Fred
Born J. Fred Knobloch on 4/28/1953 in Jackson, Mississippi. Member of the country trios Schuyler, Knobloch & Overstreet (SKO) and Schuyler, Knobloch & Bickhardt (SKB).

KNOCKOUTS, The
Rock and roll band from Lyndhust, New Jersey: Bob D'Andrea (vocals), Eddie Parenti (guitar), Bob Collada (piano) and Harry Venuta (drums).

KNOC-TURN'AL
Born Royal Harbor in Los Angeles, California. Male rapper. Protege of Dr. Dre.

KNOX, Buddy
Born on 7/20/1933 in Happy, Texas. Died of cancer on 2/14/1999 (age 65). White rock and roll singer/guitarist. Formed the rock and roll band The Rhythm Orchids at West Texas State University: Knox (guitar), Jimmy Bowen (bass), Donny Lanier (guitar) and Dave "Dicky Doo" Alldred (drums). Formed own record label, Triple-D, named after KDDD radio in Dumas, Texas.

KNUCKLES, Frankie
Born on 1/18/1955 in the Bronx, New York. Record mixer. Moved to Chicago, Illinois, in 1977. Worked at Chicago's Warehouse club and remixed hits by Chaka Khan and Pet Shop Boys. Dubbed the "Godfather of House" music.

KOFFEE BROWN
Male-female R&B duo from Minneapolis, Minnesota: Fonz and Vee.

KOFFMAN, Moe, Quartette
Born Morris Koffman on 12/28/1928 in Toronto, Ontario, Canada. Died of cancer on 3/28/2001 (age 72). Saxophonist with several U.S. big bands from 1950-55. Other members of his quartette: Ed Bickert (guitar), Hugh Currie (bass) and Ron Rully (drums).

KOKOMO
Born James J. Wisner on 12/8/1931 in Philadelphia, Pennsylvania. Pianist/arranger/producer/songwriter.

KOLBY, Diane
Born in Texas. White singer/songwriter/guitarist.

KONGAS
Disco studio group assembled by Cerrone.

KONGOS, John
Born on 9/6/1945 in Johannesburg, South Africa. Pop-rock singer/songwriter.

KON KAN
Dance duo from Toronto, Ontario, Canada: Barry Harris (piano, guitar) and Kevin Wynne (vocals). Became a one-man band when Wynne left in 1989. Name derived from the opposite of Can Con, as in Canadian Content.

KOOL & THE GANG
R&B-funk group formed in Jersey City, New Jersey: Robert "Kool" Bell (bass; born on 10/8/1950), his brother Ronald Bell (sax; born on 11/1/1951), Claydes Smith (guitar; born on 9/6/1948; died on 6/20/2006, age 57), Rick Westfield (keyboards), Dennis Thomas (sax; born on 2/9/1951), Robert Mickens (trumpet) and George Brown (drums; born on 1/5/1949). All shared vocals. Added lead singer James "J.T." Taylor in 1978. Earl Toon replaced Westfield in 1978. Taylor left in 1988.

KOOL G RAP
Born Nathaniel Wilson on 7/20/1968 in Elmhurst, Queens, New York. Name is short for Kool Genius of Rap.

KOOL MOE DEE
Born Mohandas DeWese on 8/8/1962 in Harlem, New York. Male rapper. Formerly with the Treacherous Three.

KORGIS, The
Pop trio formed in England: James Warren and Andy Davis (both formerly with Stackridge), with Stuart Gordon.

KORN
Alternative-metal band from Huntington Beach, California: Jonathan Davis (vocals), Brian Welch and James "Munkey" Shaffer (guitars), Reggie "Fieldy" Arvizu (bass) and David Silveria (drums). Welch left band in 2005. Joey Jordison replaced Silveria in 2006.

KORONA
Born Bruce Blackman in Greenville, Mississippi. Leader of Eternity's Children and Starbuck.

K.P. & ENVYI
Female rap duo: Kia "K.P." Philips and Susan "Envyi" Hedgepeth.

KRAFTWERK
Progressive-rock group formed in Dusseldorf, Germany: Ralf Hutter (keyboards), Florian Schneider (woodwinds), Klaus Roeder (guitar) and Wolfgang Flur (drums).

KRAMER, Billy J., With The Dakotas
Born William Ashton on 8/19/1943 in Bootle, Merseyside, England. Pop singer. The Dakotas consisted of Michael Maxfield and Robin MacDonald (guitars), Ray Jones (bass) and Tony Mansfield (drums).

KRAUSS, Alison, & Union Station
Born on 7/23/1971 in Decatur, Illinois; raised in Champaign, Illinois. Country singer/bluegrass fiddler. Union Station is her backing band: Dan Tyminski (guitar), Ron Block (banjo), Adam Steffey (mandolin) and Barry Bales (bass).

KRAVITZ, Lenny
Born on 5/26/1964 in Brooklyn, New York. R&B-rock singer/songwriter/guitarist. Married to actress Lisa Bonet (played "Denise Huxtable" on TV's *The Cosby Show*) from 1987-93. Son of actress Roxie Roker (played "Helen Willis" on TV's *The Jeffersons*).

KRAYZIE BONE
Born Anthony Henderson in Cleveland, Ohio. Male rapper. Member of Bone Thugs-N-Harmony.

KREVIAZUK, Chantal
Born on 5/18/1973 in Winnipeg, Manitoba, Canada. Female Adult Alternative singer/pianist.

KRIS KROSS
Male teen rap duo from Atlanta, Georgia: Chris "Mack Daddy" Kelly (born on 5/1/1978) and Chris "Daddy Mack" Smith (born on 1/10/1979). Appeared in the movie *Who's The Man?*

KRISTINE W
Born Kristine Weitz on 6/8/1962 in Pasco, Washington. Dance singer/songwriter.

KRISTOFFERSON, Kris
Born on 6/22/1936 in Brownsville, Texas. Singer/songwriter/actor. Attended England's Oxford University on a Rhodes scholarship. Married to Rita Coolidge from 1973-80. Wrote "Me And Bobby McGee," "For The Good Times" and "Help Me Make It Through The Night." Has starred in many movies since 1972.

KROEGER, Chad
Born on 11/15/1974 in Hanna, Alberta, Canada. Lead singer of Nickelback.

KROKUS
Hard-rock band from Solothurn, Switzerland: Marc Storace (vocals), Fernando Von Arb and Mark Kohler (guitars), Chris Von Rohr (bass) and Steve Pace (drums). Pace was replaced by Jeff Klaven in 1984. Von Rohr left in 1984.

KRS-ONE
Born Laurence Krisna Parker on 8/20/1965 in Harlem, New York. Co-founder of Boogie Down Productions. Brother-in-law of female rapper Harmony.

K'S CHOICE
Rock group from Belgium: Sarah Bettens (vocals), her brother Gert Bettens (vocals, keyboards), Jan Van Sichem (guitar) and Bart Van Der Zeeuw (drums).

K7
Born Louis Sharpe on 8/25/1969 in Harlem, New York. Male rapper/dancer. Former member of TKA.

KUBAN, Bob, & The In-Men
Pop-rock group from St. Louis, Missouri: Bob Kuban (drums), Walter Scott (vocals), Ray Schulte (guitar), Greg Hoeltzel (keyboards), Pat Hixton (trumpet), Harry Simon (sax), Skip Weisser (trombone) and Mike Krenski (bass). Scott disappeared on 12/27/1983; his ex-wife and her husband were charged with Scott's murder after his body was found three years later with a gunshot wound to the back.

KUF-LINX
Black vocal quintet: John Jennings, George McFadden, Leo Manley, Gaines Steele and Zena Aya. Jennings and McFadden were with the gospel group The Jubilaires.

KULA SHAKER
Rock group from London, England: Crispian Mills (vocals, guitar), Jay Darlington (keyboards), Alonza Bevan (bass) and Paul Winter-Hart (drums). Mills is the son of actress/singer Hayley Mills.

KULIS, Charlie
Born in New York. Pop singer/guitarist.

KUMBIA KINGS
Latin group: Jason Cano, Roy Ramirez and Andrew Maes (vocals), Jorge Pena (percussion), Alex Ramirez and Cruz Martinez (keyboards), A.B. Quintanilla (bass) and Robert Del Moral (drums). Quintanilla is the brother of Selena.

KUT KLOSE
Female R&B vocal trio from Atlanta, Georgia: Athena Cage, Tabitha Duncan and LaVonn Battle.

KWELI, Talib
Born Talib Kweli Greene in Brooklyn, New York. Male rapper. Member of Black Star.

K.W.S.
Dance trio from Nottingham, England: Chris King, Winnie Williams and "Mystic Meg" St. Joseph.

KYPER
Born Randall Kyper in Baton Rouge, Louisiana. Male rapper.

LABAN
Pop-dance duo from Denmark: vocalists Lecia Jonsson and Ivan Pedersen.

LaBELLE, Patti / LaBELLE / BLUE-BELLES
Born Patricia Holt on 5/24/1944 in Philadelphia, Pennsylvania. R&B singer. Began singing career as leader of the Ordettes which evolved into The Blue Belles. The quartet, formed in Philadelphia in 1962, included Nona Hendryx, Sarah Dash and Cindy Birdsong. Birdsong left in 1967 to join The Supremes. Group continued as a trio. In 1971, group shortened its name to LaBelle. In 1977, group disbanded and Patti recorded solo.

LA BOUCHE
Black male-female dance duo: Lane McCray and Melanie Thornton. Thornton died in a plane crash on 11/24/2001 (age 34); replaced by Kayo Shekoni. La Bouche is French for "mouth."

LaBOUNTY, Bill
Born on 5/3/1950 in Los Angeles, California. Pop singer/songwriter/pianist.

LACHEY, Nick
Born on 11/9/1973 in Harlan, Kentucky. Pop singer/songwriter. Member of 98°. Married to Jessica Simpson from 2002-06 (they appeared as themselves in the 2003 MTV reality series *Newlyweds*).

L.A.D. Featuring Darvy Traylor
Creation of Los Angeles-based producer Richard "Rikko" Preuss. Group features singers/rappers Darvy Traylor, Derrick Wilson, Larry Goldsmith and Reggie Smith.

LADD, Cheryl
Born Cheryl Stoppelmoor on 7/12/1951 in Huron, South Dakota. Singer/actress. Starred in several movies and TV shows. Married to David Ladd (son of actor Alan Ladd) from 1974-80. Married producer/songwriter Brian Russell (Brian & Brenda) in 1981.

LADY ANTEBELLUM
Country trio formed in Augusta, Georgia: Charles Kelley (male vocals), Hillary Scott (female vocals) and Dave Haywood (guitar). Scott is the daughter of country singer Linda Davis.

LADY FLASH
Female R&B vocal trio: Lorraine Mazzola (lead), Monica Burruss and Debra Byrd. Backing vocal group for Barry Manilow. Mazzola was in Reparata And The Delrons from 1966-73.

LADY GAGA
Born Stefania Germanotta in March 1986 in Yonkers, New York. Dance singer/songwriter.

LADY OF RAGE, The
Born Robin Allen in Farmville, Virginia. Female rapper.

LADY SOVEREIGN
Born Louise Harman on 12/19/1985 in Wembley, London, England. White female rapper/songwriter.

LAFAYETTES, The
Pop-rock band from Baltimore, Maryland: Frank Bonarrigo (vocals), Lee Bonner (guitar), Jamie Hess (keyboards), Dick Svehla (alto sax), Bob Kirschner (tenor sax), Steve Taylor (bass) and Ben Proctor (drums).

LAFLAMME, David
Born on 4/5/1941 in Salt Lake City, Utah. Rock singer/electric violinist. Leader of the San Francisco "flower-rock" group It's A Beautiful Day.

LA FLAVOUR
Pop-disco group featuring lead singer Craig DeBock.

LaFORGE, Jack
Born on 8/8/1924 in Manhattan, New York. Pianist/composer/conductor.

L.A. GUNS
Hard-rock group from Los Angeles, California: Philip Lewis (vocals), Tracii Guns and Mick Cripps (guitars), Kelly Nickels (bass), and Steve Riley (drums).

LAI, Francis
Born on 4/26/1932 in Nice, France. Male composer/conductor.

LAID BACK
Synth-pop duo from Denmark: Tim Stahl (keyboards) and John Guldberg (guitar).

LAINE, Frankie
Born Francesco LoVecchio on 3/30/1913 in Chicago, Illinois. Died on 2/6/2007 (age 93). First recorded for Exclusive in 1945. Signed to the Mercury label in 1947. Dynamic singer whose popularity lasted well into the rock era.

LAISSEZ FAIRE
Female dance trio from New York: Marlo Falcone, Gina Cardinale and Jennifer Castiello.

L.A. JETS
Rock group from Los Angeles, California: Karen Lawrence (vocals), Harlin McNees (guitar), Ron Cindrich (bass) and John DeSautels (drums).

LAKE
Progressive-rock group from Hamburg, Germany: James Hopkins-Harrison (vocals), Alex Conti (guitar), Geoffrey Peacey (keyboards), Martin Tiefensee (bass) and Dieter Ahrendt (drums). Hopkins-Harrison died of a drug overdose on 5/16/1991 (age 41).

LAKE, Greg
Born on 11/10/1948 in Bournemouth, Dorset, England. Guitarist/bassist with King Crimson and Emerson, Lake & Palmer.

LAKESIDE
R&B-funk group from Dayton, Ohio: Tiemeyer McCain, Thomas Shelby, Otis Stokes and Mark Wood (vocals), Steve Shockley (guitar), Norman Beavers (keyboards), Fred Lewis (percussion), Marvin Craig (bass) and Fred Alexander (drums).

LAMAS, Lorenzo
Born on 1/20/1958 in San Francisco, California. Son of actress Arlene Dahl and actor Fernando Lamas (died on 10/9/1982, age 67). Played "Lance" on TV's *Falcon Crest* and starred in *Renegade*.

LAMB, Kevin
Rock singer/guitarist/keyboardist. Session work for the British group Rare Bird, 1970-76.

LAMBERT, Miranda
Born on 11/10/1983 in Longview, Texas; raised in Lindale, Texas. Country singer/songwriter/guitarist. Placed third on the first season of TV's *Nashville Star* talent series in 2003.

LaMOND, George
Born George Garcia on 2/25/1967 in Washington DC; raised in the Bronx, New York. Dance singer. Cousin of Joey Kid.

LANCE, Herb, & The Classics
Herb was born on 6/14/1925 in Pittsburgh, Pennsylvania; died in December 1987 (age 52). The Classics are an Italian-American doo-wop quartet.

LANCE, Major
Born on 4/4/1939 in Winterville, Mississippi; raised in Chicago, Illinois. Died of heart disease on 9/3/1994 (age 55). R&B singer. First recorded for Mercury in 1959. Lived in Britain, 1972-74. Had own Osiris label with Al Jackson of Booker T. & The MG's in 1975. In prison for selling cocaine, 1978-81.

LANE, Mickey Lee
Born Mickey Lee Schreiber on 2/2/1941 in Rochester, New York. Rock and roll singer/songwriter.

LANE, Robin, & The Chartbusters
Born in 1947 in Los Angeles, California; later based in in Boston, Massachusetts. Female rock singer. Daughter of Dean Martin's pianist, Ken Lane.

LANE, Robin, & The Chartbusters — cont'd
The Chartbusters: Asa Brebner (guitar), Leroy
Radcliffe (keyboards), Scott Baerenwald (bass) and
Tim Jackson (drums).

LANE BROTHERS, The
Pop vocal trio from Brooklyn, New York: brothers
Pete, Frank and Art Loconto.

lang, k.d.
Born Kathryn Dawn Lang on 11/2/1961 in Consort,
Alberta, Canada. Eclectic singer/songwriter.

LANIER & CO.
R&B singer Farris Lanier, Jr.

LANSON, Snooky
Born Roy Landman on 3/27/1914 in Memphis,
Tennessee. Died of cancer on 7/2/1990 (age 76).
Star of TV's *Your Hit Parade* (1950-57).

LANZA, Mario
Born Alfredo Cocozza on 1/31/1921 in Philadelphia,
Pennsylvania. Died of a heart attack on 10/7/1959
(age 38). Became the most popular operatic tenor
since Caruso, with his voice featured in seven
movies, though no theatrical operas.

LARKS, The
R&B vocal group from Philadelphia, Pennsylvania:
Jackie Marsh (lead), Calvin Nichols (tenor), Earl
Oxeindine (baritone) and Weldon McDougal III
(bass). Named for the Lark cigarette. Backed
Barbara Mason on several of her recordings.

LARKS, The
R&B vocal group from Los Angeles, California.
Originally named Don Julian & The Meadowlarks:
Don Julian, Ted Walters and Charles Morrison.
Julian died of pneumonia on 11/6/1998 (age 61).

LaROSA, Julius
Born on 1/2/1930 in Brooklyn, New York. Regular
singer on *Arthur Godfrey And His Friends* TV show
until he was fired on the air on 10/19/1953. Popular
DJ in New York (WNEW) for many years. Had two
Top 5 hits in 1953: "Anywhere I Wander" and "Eh,
Cumpari."

LARRIEUX, Amel
Born in Manhattan, New York. Female R&B
singer/songwriter. Former member of Groove
Theory.

LARSEN, Blaine
Born on 2/2/1986 in Tacoma, Washington. Country
singer/songwriter/guitarist.

LARSEN-FEITEN BAND
Top session musicians Neil Larsen (keyboards) and
Buzz Feiten (guitar). Feiten, a former member of the
Paul Butterfield Blues Band, The Rascals and
Stevie Wonder's band, joined Mr. Mister in 1989.

LARSON, Nicolette
Born on 7/17/1952 in Helena, Montana; raised in
Kansas City, Missouri. Died of a cerebral edema on
12/16/1997 (age 45). Session vocalist with Neil
Young, Emmylou Harris, Linda Ronstadt, Van Halen
and many others. Married session drummer Russ
Kunkel.

LaRUE, D.C.
Born David Charles L'Heureux on 4/26/1948 in
Meriden, Connecticut. Disco singer/songwriter.

LA'S, The
Rock group from Liverpool, England: brothers Lee
(vocals) and Neil (drums) Mavers, with Peter Camell
(guitar), and John Power (bass). Group name is
slang for lads.

LaSALLE, Denise
Born Denise Craig on 7/16/1939 in LeFlore County,
Mississippi. R&B singer/songwriter. Moved to
Chicago in the early 1950s. First recorded for
Tarpen (Chess) in 1967. Had own Crajon
Productions with husband Bill Jones from 1969.

LASGO
Dance trio from Belgium: Evi Griffin, Peter Luts and
David Vervoort.

LAS KETCHUP
Female pop vocal trio from Cordoba, Spain: sisters
Lola, Lucía and Pilar Muñoz.

LASLEY, David
Born on 8/20/1947 in Branch, Michigan. Singer/
songwriter.

LASSIES, The
Female pop vocal trio.

LAST, James
Born on 4/17/1929 in Bremen, Germany.
Producer/arranger/conductor.

LAST GOODNIGHT, The
Rock band from Enfield, Connecticut: Kurtis
Henneberry (vocals), Mike Nadeau (guitar), Anton
Yarack (guitar), Ely Rise (keyboards), Leif
Christensen (bass) and Larone McMillan (drums).

LAST WORD, The
Rock band from Miami, Florida: Johnny Lombardo
(vocals), Mike Byrnes (guitar), Steve Sechak
(keyboards) and Ricky Cook (drums).

L.A. STYLE
Techno-rave creation of Dutch producer/musician
Denzil Slemming.

LaTANYA
Born in Chicago, Illinois. Female R&B singer.

LATIMORE
Born Benjamin Latimore on 9/7/1939 in Charleston,
Tennessee. R&B singer/songwriter.

LATIN ALLIANCE Featuring War
All-star rap trio: Kid Frost, Mellow Man Ace and
A.L.T.

LaTOUR
Born William LaTour in Chicago, Illinois. Techno-
dance artist.

LATTIMORE, Kenny
Born on 4/10/1970 in Washington DC. R&B singer.
Married Chanté Moore on 1/1/2002.

LATTISAW, Stacy
Born on 11/25/1966 in Washington DC. Female R&B singer. Recorded her first album at age 12. Childhood friend of Johnny Gill. Her younger brother Jerry is a member of Me-2-U.

LAUPER, Cyndi
Born on 6/22/1953 in Brooklyn, New York; raised in Queens, New York. Recorded an album for Polydor Records in 1980 with the group Blue Angel. Supported by the Hooters, 1983-84. In the movies *Vibes* and *Life With Mikey*. Married actor David Thornton on 11/24/1991.

LAUREN, Rod
Born Roger Lawrence Strunk on 3/26/1940 in Tracy, California. Died in a fall (possible suicide) on 7/11/2007 (age 67). Lauren was groomed by RCA in 1960 to be a hot new teen idol. Acted in several low-budget movies.

LAURIE, Annie
Born in Atlanta, Georgia. R&B singer. Joined Paul Gayten's band in 1947; had three Top 10 R&B hits with him: "Since I Fell For You" (1947), "Cuttin' Out" (1949) and "I'll Never Be Free" (1950).

LAURIE, Linda
Born Linda Gertz in Brooklyn, New York. Novelty-pop singer/songwriter. Wrote Helen Reddy's "Leave Me Alone (Ruby Red Dress)." Sang the theme to the Saturday morning TV series *Land of the Lost*. Linda is the voice of "Ambrose."

LAURIE SISTERS, The
Female vocal trio.

LAURNEÁ
Born Laurneá Wilkinson in Omaha, Nebraska; raised in Los Angeles, California. Female R&B singer.

LaVERNE & SHIRLEY
Duo of Penny Marshall and Cindy Williams; stars of the TV series *LaVerne & Shirley*. Marshall was born on 10/15/1942 in the Bronx, New York. Directed many movies including *Big*, *Awakenings* and *A League Of Their Own*. Married to actor/director Rob Reiner from 1971-79. Williams was born on 8/22/1947 in Van Nuys, California. Played Ron Howard's girlfriend in the movie *American Graffiti*.

LAVIGNE, Avril
Born on 9/27/1984 in Belleville, Ontario, Canada; raised in Napanee, Ontario, Canada. Teen pop-rock female singer/songwriter. Married Deryck Whibley (lead singer of rock group Sum 41) on 7/15/2006. Co-wrote Kelly Clarkson's hit "Breakaway."

LAWRENCE, Billy
Born in St. Louis, Missouri. Female R&B singer/songwriter/producer.

LAWRENCE, Eddie
Born Lawrence Eisler on 3/2/1919 in Brooklyn, New York. Comedian/actor/author/playwright.

LAWRENCE, Joey
Born on 4/20/1976 in Montgomery, Pennsylvania. Teen actor/singer. Acted on TV's *Gimme A Break*, *Blossom* and *Brotherly Love*.

LAWRENCE, Steve
Born Sidney Leibowitz on 7/8/1935 in Brooklyn, New York. Regular performer on Steve Allen's *The Tonight Show* for five years. First recorded for King in 1952. Married singer Eydie Gorme on 12/29/1957; they recorded as Parker & Penny in 1979. Steve and Eydie remain a popular nightclub act.

LAWRENCE, Tracy
Born on 1/27/1968 in Atlanta, Texas; raised in Foreman, Arkansas. Country singer. In May 1991, he was shot four times in an attempted holdup in Nashville; fully recovered.

LAWRENCE, Vicki
Born on 3/26/1949 in Inglewood, California. Regular on Carol Burnett's CBS-TV series from 1967-78. Also starred in TV's *Mama's Family* from 1982-87. Married to songwriter/singer Bobby Russell from 1972-74.

LAWS, Debra
Born on 9/10/1956 in Houston, Texas. R&B singer. Sister of Eloise Laws and Ronnie Laws.

LAWS, Eloise
Born Lavern Eloise Laws on 11/6/1943 in Houston, Texas. R&B singer. Sister of Debra Laws and Ronnie Laws.

LAWS, Ronnie
Born on 10/3/1950 in Houston, Texas. R&B-jazz saxophonist. Brother of Debra Laws and Eloise Laws. With Earth, Wind & Fire from 1972-73.

LAWSON, Melissa
Born in 1976 in Arlington, Texas. Country singer. Winner on the sixth season of TV's *Nashville Star* talent series in 2008.

LAYNE, Joy
Born in 1941 in Chicago, Illinois. Teen female pop singer.

LAZY RACER
Pop-rock group: Tim Renwick and Kelly Harland (vocals), Bill Lamb (guitar), Tim Gorman (keyboards), Dave Markee (bass) and Henry Spinetti (drums).

L.B.C. CREW
Rap group from Long Beach, California: Tray Dee, South Sentrell, Lil' Style, LT, Soopafly and Technique. Assembled by Snoop Dogg. Tray Dee later joined Tha Eastsidaz.

LEACH, Billy
Born William Leech on 1/9/1911 in Pittsburgh, Pennsylvania. Died on 11/11/1997 (age 86). Began singing career at age 14 on Pittsburgh's KDKA radio. Worked with Art Kassel, Raymond Scott and Guy Lombardo. On Chicago's WBBM radio for 21 years.

LEAPY LEE
Born Lee Graham on 7/2/1942 in Eastbourne, England. Acted on stage and TV in England.

LEAVES, The
Garage-rock band from Northridge, California: Robert Arlin (vocals), John Beck (guitar), Robert Lee Reiner (guitar), Jim Pons (bass) and Tom Ray (drums). Pons was later a brief member of The Turtles.

LEAVILL, Otis
Born Otis Leavill Cobb on 2/8/1937 in Dewy Rose, Georgia. Died of a heart attack on 7/17/2002 (age 65). R&B singer/songwriter.

LeBLANC & CARR
Soft-rock duo: Lenny LeBlanc (bass; born on 6/17/1951 in Leominster, Massachusetts) and Pete Carr (lead guitar; born on 4/22/1950 in Daytona Beach, Florida). Both were session musicians at Muscle Shoals, Alabama. Lenny later recorded Contemporary Christian music.

LE CLICK
Male-female techno-dance duo: Robert Haynes and Kayo Shekoni.

LED ZEPPELIN
Hard-rock band formed in England: Robert Plant (vocals; born on 8/20/1948), Jimmy Page (guitar; born on 1/9/1944), John Paul Jones (bass, keyboards; born on 1/3/1946) and John Bonham (drums; born on 5/31/1948). First known as the New Yardbirds. Page had been in The Yardbirds, 1966-68. Plant and Bonham had been in a group called Band Of Joy. Led Zeppelin's U.S. tour in 1973 broke many box office records. Formed own Swan Song label in 1974. In concert movie *The Song Remains The Same* in 1976. Bonham died of asphyxiation on 9/25/1980 (age 33). Group disbanded in December 1980. Plant and Page formed The Honeydrippers in 1984. Page also with The Firm (1984-86). Bonham's son Jason formed group Bonham in 1989. Their first 9 albums sold over 90 million copies in the U.S.

LEE, Brenda
Born Brenda Mae Tarpley on 12/11/1944 in Lithonia, Georgia. Signed to Decca Records in 1956 and sang a mix of country and rockabilly music until her pop ballad break-through on the *Hot 100* in 1960. Her main producer from 1958-on was Owen Bradley. Became known as "Little Miss Dynamite." Successful country singer from 1971-85.

LEE, Curtis
Born on 10/28/1941 in Yuma, Arizona. Pop singer/ songwriter.

LEE, Dick
Born Richard Lee Beurer on 2/20/1933 in Philadelphia, Pennsylvania. Pop ballad singer. Nicknamed "The Golden Boy."

LEE, Dickey
Born Dickey Lipscomb on 9/21/1936 in Memphis, Tennessee. Pop-country singer/songwriter. First recorded for Tampa Bay Records and then Sun Records in 1957.

LEE, Jackie
Born in May 1932 in Philadelphia, Pennsylvania. Nicknamed "Mr. Hot Piano."

LEE, Jackie
Born Earl Nelson on 9/8/1928 in Lake Charles, Louisiana. R&B singer. One-half of Bob & Earl duo. Took name from his wife's middle name, Jackie, and his middle name, Lee. Sang lead on the Hollywood Flames' "Buzz-Buzz-Buzz."

LEE, Johnny
Born John Lee Ham on 7/3/1946 in Texas City, Texas; raised in Alta Loma, Texas. Country singer/songwriter. Married to actress Charlene Tilton from 1982-84.

LEE, Julia
Born on 10/31/1902 in Boonville, Missouri. Died of a heart attack on 12/8/1958 (age 56). R&B-jazz vocalist/pianist. With father's band from age four. Joined brother George E. Lee's band from 1920-33. First recorded for Merritt in 1927. Worked up until the time of her death. Noted for her risque style of recordings.

LEE, Larry
Born in 1947 in Springfield, Missouri. Member of the Ozark Mountain Daredevils.

LEE, Laura
Born Laura Lee Newton on 3/9/1945 in Chicago, Illinois. R&B singer/songwriter.

LEE, Michele
Born Michele Dusick on 6/24/1942 in Los Angeles, California. Actress/singer. Played "Karen MacKenzie" on TV's *Knots Landing*.

LEE, Murphy
Born Tohri Harper on 12/19/1982 in St. Louis, Missouri. Male rapper. Member of St. Lunatics.

LEE, Peggy
Born Norma Egstrom on 5/26/1920 in Jamestown, North Dakota. Died of a heart attack on 1/21/2002 (age 81). Jazz singer with Jack Wardlow band (1936-40), Will Osborne (1940-41) and Benny Goodman (1941-43). Went solo in March 1943. In movies *Mister Music* (1950), *The Jazz Singer* (1953) and *Pete Kelly's Blues* (1955). Co-wrote many songs with husband Dave Barbour (married, 1943-52). Awarded nearly $4 million in court for her singing in the animated movie *Lady And The Tramp*.

LEE, Tommy
Born Thomas Lee Bass on 10/3/1962 in Athens, Greece; raised in West Covina, California. Rock singer/songwriter/drummer. Former member of Mötley Crüe. Married to actress Heather Locklear from 1986-93. Married to actress Pamela Anderson from 1995-98. Starred in his own TV reality series *Tommy Lee Goes to College* in 2005.

LEE, Tracey
Born in Philadelphia, Pennsylvania. Male rapper.

LEE & PAUL
Songwriters Lee Pockriss (born on 1/20/1927 in Brooklyn, New York) and Paul Vance (born on 11/4/1929 in Brooklyn, New York). Wrote "Calcutta," "Itsy Bitsy Teenie Weenie Yellow Polkadot Bikini" and many other hits.

LEFEVRE, Raymond
Born on 11/20/1929 in Calais, France. Died on 6/27/2008 (age 78). Conductor/pianist/flutist.

LEFT BANKE, The
Rock group from Manhattan, New York: Steve Martin (vocals), Rick Brand (guitar), Michael Brown (piano; Stories), Tom Finn (bass) and George Cameron (drums).

LEGACY OF SOUND featuring Meja
Dance group from Sweden. Featuring producers Bag and Snowman, with female singer Meja.

LEGEND, John
Born John Stephens on 12/28/1978 in Springfield, Ohio; later based in Philadelphia, Pennsylvania. Adult R&B-smooth jazz singer/songwriter/pianist.

LeGRAND, Michel
Born on 2/24/1932 in Paris, France. Conductor/ arranger/pianist.

LEIBER & STOLLER
One of the all-time most successful songwriting teams in rock and roll history. Jerry Leiber was born on 4/25/1933 in Baltimore, Maryland. Mike Stoller was born on 3/13/1933 in Belle Harbor, Queens, New York. Met and started prolific songwriting partnership in 1950 in Los Angeles, California.

LEILA K with Rob 'n' Raz
Born Leila Khalifi in Stockholm, Sweden, of Moroccan descent. Female rapper/dancer.

LEKAKIS, Paul
Born on 10/22/1965 in Yonkers, New York. Disco singer/model/dancer.

LEMMONS, Billy
Born on 2/16/1943 in Atlanta, Georgia. Died of heart failure on 7/14/2006 (age 63). Country singer/ songwriter. Record promotion man with several different companies.

LEMONHEADS, The
Rock group formed in Boston, Massachusetts, by Evan Dando (vocals, guitar; born on 3/4/1967). Numerous personnel changes with Dando the only constant.

LEMON PIPERS, The
Psychedelic/bubblegum rock group from Oxford, Ohio: Ivan Browne (vocals, guitar), Bill Bartlett (guitar; Ram Jam), R.G. Nave (organ), Steve Walmsley (bass) and Bill Albaugh (drums). Albaugh died on 1/20/1999 (age 53).

LEN
Alternative-rock group from Toronto, Ontario, Canada: Marc Costanzo (vocals), his sister Sharon Costanzo, D. Rock, DJ Moves, Planet Pea and Drunkness Monster.

LENNON, John
Born on 10/9/1940 in Woolton, Liverpool, England. Shot to death on 12/8/1980 in Manhattan, New York (age 40). Founding member of The Beatles. Married to Cynthia Powell (1962-68); their son is Julian Lennon. Met Yoko Ono in 1966; married her on 3/20/1969. Formed Plastic Ono Band in 1969. To New York City in 1971. Fought deportation from the U.S., 1972-76, until he was granted a permanent visa.

LENNON, Julian
Born John Charles Julian Lennon on 4/8/1963 in Liverpool, England. Pop-rock singer/songwriter/ keyboardist. Son of Cynthia and John Lennon. First child to be born to any of The Beatles.

LENNON SISTERS, The
Pop vocal group from Venice, California: sisters Dianne (born on 12/1/1939), Peggy (born on 4/8/1941), Kathy (born on 8/2/1943) and Janet (born on 6/15/1946) Lennon. With Lawrence Welk from 1955-68.

LENNOX, Annie
Born on 12/25/1954 in Aberdeen, Scotland. Member of The Tourists. Lead singer of the Eurythmics. Appeared in the movie *Edward II* and TV movie *The Room*. Married to movie director Uri Fruchtman from 1988-2000.

LEONETTI, Tommy
Born on 9/10/1929 in Bergen, New Jersey. Died of cancer on 9/15/1979 (age 50). Vocalist with Charlie Spivak and other big bands. Featured singer on TV's *Your Hit Parade*, 1957-58.

LE PAMPLEMOUSSE
Disco studio group led by producers Laurin Rinder and W. Michael Lewis. Group name is French for "The Grapefruit."

LE ROUX
Rock group from Louisiana: Jeff Pollard (vocals), Tony Haseldon (guitar), Rod Roddy (piano), Bobby Campo (horns), Leon Medica (bass) and David Peters (drums).

LESCHEA
Born in Brooklyn, New York. Female singer. Pronounced: la-SHAY.

LES COMPAGNONS DE LA CHANSON
"The Companions Of Song." Vocal group from France: Fred Mella, Jean-Pierre Calvert, Jacob Jaubert, Guy Bourguignon, Jo Frachon and Marc Herrand. Sometimes accompanied Edith Piaf.

LESLIE, Ryan
Born Anthony Ryan Leslie on 9/25/1978 in Washington DC; raised in Stockton, California. R&B singer/songwriter.

LESTER, Ketty
Born Revoyda Frierson on 8/16/1938 in Hope, Arkansas. R&B singer/actress. Acted in several movies and TV shows.

LeTOYA
Born LeToya Luckett on 3/11/1981 in Houston, Texas. Female R&B singer/songwriter. Former member of Destiny's Child.

LETTERMEN, The
Vocal group formed in 1958 in Los Angeles, California: Tony Butala (born on 11/20/1938), Jim Pike (born on 11/6/1936) and Bob Engemann (born on 2/19/1936). Played the part of Paul Whiteman's Rhythm Boys in the Las Vegas review *Newcomers Of 1928*. First recorded for Warner Bros. in 1960.

LETTERMEN, The — cont'd

Engemann replaced by Gary Pike (Jim's brother) in 1968. Tony sang with the Mitchell Boys Choir in the 1951 movie *On Moonlight Bay* and the 1954 movie *White Christmas*. Tony also sang with Connie Stevens in the group The Fourmost in 1954. Tony still performs with a touring Lettermen group today. Bob's nephew and niece recorded as Christopher Paul And Shawn.

LETTERS TO CLEO

Pop-rock group from Boston, Massachusetts: Kay Hanley (vocals), Michael Eisenstein and Greg McKenna (guitars), Scott Riebling (bass), and Stacy Jones (drums; American Hi-Fi).

LEVEL 42

Pop-rock-dance group formed in London, England: Mark King (vocals, bass), brothers Boon (guitar) and Phil (drums) Gould, and Mike Lindup (keyboards). The Goulds left in October 1987; replaced by Alan Murphy (guitar) and Gary Husband (drums). Murphy died of AIDS on 10/19/1989 (age 35).

LEVERT

R&B vocal/instrumental trio from Cleveland, Ohio: brothers Gerald Levert (vocals) and Sean Levert (vocals, percussion), with Marc Gordon (vocals, keyboards). The Leverts are the sons of Eddie Levert (of The O'Jays). Gerald died of a heart attack on 11/10/2006 (age 40). Sean died on 3/30/2008 (age 39).

LEVERT, Gerald

Born on 7/13/1966 in Cleveland, Ohio. Died of a heart attack on 11/10/2006 (age 40). Lead singer of R&B trio Levert (with his brother Sean Levert and Marc Gordon). Son of The O'Jays' Eddie Levert, Sr. Discovered the R&B group Troop. Also see LSG.

LEVINE, Hank

Born on 6/9/1932 in Pittsburgh, Pennsylvania. Conductor/producer/arranger. Assembled the studio band The Miniature Men.

LEWIS, Aaron

Born on 4/13/1972 in Boston, Massachusetts. Rock singer. Lead singer of Staind.

LEWIS, Barbara

Born on 2/9/1943 in Salem, Michigan; raised in South Lyon, Michigan. R&B singer/songwriter/multi-instrumentalist.

LEWIS, Blake

Born on 7/21/1981 in Redmond, Washington. Finished in second place on the 2007 season of TV's *American Idol*.

LEWIS, Bobby

Born on 2/17/1933 in Indianapolis, Indiana; raised in Detroit, Michigan. R&B singer/songwriter.

LEWIS, Donna

Born on 8/6/1973 in Cardiff, Wales. Adult Contemporary singer/songwriter.

LEWIS, Ephraim

Born in 1968 in Birmingham, England (Jamaican parents). Committed suicide on 3/18/1994 (age 26). Male R&B singer.

LEWIS, Gary, & The Playboys

Born Gary Levitch on 7/31/1945 in Brooklyn, New York. Pop singer/drummer. Son of comedian Jerry Lewis. The Playboys consisted of Al Ramsey and John West (guitars), David Walker (keyboards) and David Costell (bass).

LEWIS, Glenn

Born in Toronto, Ontario, Canada. R&B singer/songwriter.

LEWIS, Huey, & The News

Born Hugh Cregg III on 7/5/1950 in New York; raised in Danville, California. Joined the country-rock group Clover in the late 1970s. Formed the News in San Francisco: Lewis (vocals, harmonica), Chris Hayes (guitar), Johnny Colla (sax, guitar), Sean Hopper (keyboards), Mario Cipollina (bass; brother of Quicksilver Messenger Service guitarist John Cipollina) and Bill Gibson (drums). Lewis acted in the movie *Short Cuts* and had a cameo appearance in *Back To The Future*.

LEWIS, Jerry

Born Joseph Levitch on 3/16/1926 in Newark, New Jersey. Comedian/actor. Father of Gary Lewis. Formed comedy duo with Dean Martin in 1946. Starred in many movies from 1949-95.

LEWIS, Jerry Lee

Born on 9/29/1935 in Ferriday, Louisiana. Played piano since age nine, professionally since age 15. First recorded for Sun in 1956. Appeared in the movie *Jamboree!* in 1957. Career waned in 1958 after marriage to 13-year-old cousin, Myra Gale Brown, daughter of his bass player. Made comeback in country music beginning in 1968. Nicknamed "The Killer," Lewis has been surrounded by personal tragedies in the past two decades, survived several serious illnesses. Cousin to country singer Mickey Gilley and TV evangelist Jimmy Swaggart. Jerry's early career is documented in the 1989 movie *Great Balls Of Fire* starring Dennis Quaid.

LEWIS, Leona

Born on 4/3/1985 in Islington, London, England. Female R&B singer. Winner on the British TV talent show *The X Factor*.

LEWIS, Ramsey

Born on 5/27/1935 in Chicago, Illinois. R&B-jazz pianist. First recorded for Argo in 1958. His trio included Eldee Young (bass) and Isaac "Red" Holt (drums). Disbanded in 1965. Young and Holt then formed The Young-Holt Trio. Lewis re-formed his trio with Cleveland Eaton (bass) and Maurice White (drums). White later formed Earth, Wind & Fire. Young died on 2/12/2007 (age 71).

LEWIS, Shirley

Born in London, England. Black dance singer. Worked with Elton John, mid-1980s. Sister of singer Linda Lewis.

LEWIS, Smiley
Born Overton Amos Lemons on 7/5/1913 in DeQuincy, Louisiana. Died of cancer on 10/7/1966 (age 53). R&B singer/guitarist.

LEWIS & CLARKE EXPEDITION, The
Folk duo: Travis Lewis (Michael Martin Murphey) and Owen "Boomer" Clarke (Boomer Castleman).

LFO
White pop vocal trio from Orlando, Florida: Rich Cronin, David Brian and Brad Young. Brian and Young left in 1999; replaced by Brad Fischetti and Devin Lima. LFO: Lyte Funky Ones.

LIA, Orsa
Born in Virginia. Female pop singer. Sang several TV jingles in the mid-1970s.

LIFEHOUSE
Rock trio from Malibu, California: Jason Wade (vocals, guitar), Sergio Andrade (bass) and Rick Woolstenhulme (drums). Bryce Soderberg replaced Andrade in 2004.

LIGGINS, Joe, And His "Honeydrippers"
Born on 7/9/1916 in Guthrie, Oklahoma. Died of a stroke on 7/31/1987 (age 71). R&B singer/pianist/ bandleader. Older brother of Jimmy Liggins.

LIGHT, Enoch
Born on 8/18/1907 in Canton, Ohio. Died on 7/31/1978 (age 70). Conductor of own orchestra, The Light Brigade, since 1935. Pioneer in stereo recording. President of Grand Award label and managing director for Command Records.

LIGHTER SHADE OF BROWN, A
Hispanic rap duo from Riverside, California: Robert Gutierrez and Bobby Ramirez.

LIGHTFOOT, Gordon
Born on 11/17/1938 in Orillia, Ontario, Canada. Adult Contemporary-folk singer/songwriter/guitarist. Worked on *Country Hoedown*, CBC-TV series. Teamed with Jim Whalen as the Two Tones in the mid-1960s. Wrote hit "Early Morning Rain" for Peter, Paul and Mary. First recorded for Chateau in 1962.

LIGHTHOUSE
Rock group from Toronto, Ontario, Canada. Featured a fluctuating lineup of at least 10 members. Core members: Bob McBride (vocals), Skip Prokop (vocals, drums; The Paupers), Ralph Cole (guitar), Paul Hoffert (keyboards), Howard Shore (sax), Louie Yacknin (bass), Don Dinovo (viola) and Dick Armin (cello). Shore went on to become the original musical director of TV's *Saturday Night Live*. McBride died on 2/20/1998 (age 51).

LIGHTNING SEEDS, The
Group is actually singer/producer Ian Broudie (born on 8/4/1958 in Liverpool, England).

LIL' BOOSIE
Born Torence Hatch on 11/14/1983 in Baton Rouge, Louisiana. Male rapper/songwriter.

LIL' FLIP
Born Wesley Weston on 3/3/1981 in Houston, Texas. Male rapper.

LIL JON & THE EAST SIDE BOYZ
Born Jonathan Smith on 1/27/1971 in Clarksdale, Mississippi; raised in Atlanta, Georgia. Male rapper/ songwriter/producer. Creator of "crunk" style of rap music. The East Side Boyz: "Big Sam" Norris and Wendell "Lil Bo" Neal. Lil Jon became a popular guest rapper in 2003.

LIL' KEKE
Born Marcus Edwards in Houston, Texas. Male rapper.

LIL' KIM
Born Kimberly Jones on 7/11/1974 in Brooklyn, New York. Female rapper/songwriter. Nicknamed "Queen Bee." Member of Junior M.A.F.I.A. Acted in the movies *She's All That*, *Gang Of Roses* and *Juwanna Man*. Known for her provocative outfits and attitude. Convicted of perjury and sentanced to one year in prison in 2005.

LIL LOUIS
Born Louis Burns in Chicago, Illinois. Noted DJ of Chicago dance club scene. Son of blues guitarist Bobby Sims.

LIL MAMA
Born Niatia Kirkland on 10/4/1989 in Harlem, New York. Female rapper.

LIL' MO
Born Cynthia Loving on 3/10/1976 in Long Island, New York. Female R&B singer.

LIL ROB
Born Roberto Flores in 1975 in San Diego, California. Hispanic rapper/songwriter.

LIL' ROMEO
Born Percy Romeo Miller on 8/19/1989 in New Orleans, Louisiana. Pre-teen male rapper. Son of Master P.

LIL SCRAPPY
Born Darryl Richardson on 1/19/1984 in North Trenton, New Jersey; raised in Atlanta, Georgia. Male rapper/songwriter.

LIL' SUZY
Born Suzanne Casale in 1980 in the Bronx, New York. Dance singer. Appeared on TV's *Star Search*.

LIL' TROY
Born Troy Birklett on 2/24/1966 in Houston, Texas. Male rapper.

LIL WAYNE
Born Dwayne Carter on 9/27/1982 in New Orleans, Louisiana. Male rapper/songwriter.

LIL' ZANE
Born Zane Copeland Jr. on 7/11/1982 in Yonkers, New York; raised in Atlanta, Georgia. Male rapper. Shortened name to Zane in 2003.

LIMAHL
Born Christopher Hamill on 12/19/1958 in England. Former lead singer of Kajagoogoo.

LIMELITERS, The
Folk trio formed in Hollywood, California: Glenn Yarbrough, Lou Gottlieb and Alex Hassilev. Yarbrough went solo in 1963; replaced by Ernie Sheldon. Gottlieb died of cancer on 7/11/1996 (age 72).

LIMITED WARRANTY
Pop-rock group from Minneapolis, Minnesota: Dale Goulett (vocals, guitar), Greg Sotebeer (vocals, bass), Erik Newman (guitar), Paul Hartwig (keyboards) and Jerry Brunskill (drums).

LIMMIE & FAMILY COOKIN'
White pop family trio from Canton, Ohio: sisters Martha Stewart and Jimmy Thomas, and brother Limmie Snell.

LIMP BIZKIT
Alternative-metal band from Jacksonville, Florida: Fred Durst (vocals), Wes Borland (guitar), Sam Rivers (bass) and John Otto (drums).

LIND, Bob
Born on 11/25/1942 in Baltimore, Maryland. Folk-rock singer/songwriter.

LINDEN, Kathy
Born in Moorestown, New Jersey. Pop singer.

LINDISFARNE
Folk-rock group from England: Alan Hull (vocals), Ray Jackson (guitar), Simon Crowe (mandolin), Rod Clements (bass) and Ray Laidlaw (drums). Group's name is an island off of Northumberland, U.K. Hull died of a heart attack on 11/18/1995 (age 50).

LINDSAY, Mark
Born on 3/9/1942 in Eugene, Oregon. Lead singer/ saxophonist of Paul Revere & The Raiders. Also recorded with Raider, Keith Allison, and Steve Alaimo as The Unknowns.

LINEAR
Pop trio from Miami, Florida: Charlie Pennachio (vocals), Wyatt Pauley (guitar) and Joey Restivo (percussion).

LINER
Pop trio: brothers Tom (vocals, bass) and Dave (drums) Farmer, with Eddie Golga (guitar).

LINES, Aaron
Born on 11/17/1977 in Fort McMurray, Alberta, Canada. Country singer/songwriter/guitarist.

LINK
Born Lincoln Browder on 10/12/1964 in Dallas, Texas. Male rapper.

LINKIN PARK
Alternative-metal band from Los Angeles, California: Chester Bennington (vocals), Mike Shinoda (rap vocals), Joseph "Mr. Hahn" (DJ), Brad Delson (guitar), David "Phoenix" Farrell (bass) and Rob Bourdon (drums).

LINKLETTER, Art
Born Arthur Kelly on 7/17/1912 in Moose Jaw, Saskatchewan, Canada. Popular radio and TV personality. Hosted own shows *Art Linkletter's*

House Party (later known as *The Linkletter Show*) and several others.

LIPPS, INC.
Funk-dance project from Minneapolis, Minnesota. Formed by white producer/songwriter/multi-instrumentalist Steven Greenberg. Vocals by black singer Cynthia Johnson. Pronounced: lip-synch.

LIQUID GOLD
Disco group from England: Ellie Hope (vocals), Syd Twynham (guitar), Ray Knott (bass) and Wally Rothe (drums).

LIQUID SMOKE
White R&B-rock group from North Carolina: Sandy Pantaleo (vocals), Vince Fersak (guitar), Benny Ninmann (keyboards), Mike Archeleta (bass) and Chas Kimbrell (drums).

LISA LISA & CULT JAM
R&B-dance trio from Harlem, New York: Lisa Velez (vocals; born on 1/15/1967), Alex "Spanador" Moseley (guitar) and Mike Hughes (drums). Assembled and produced by Full Force.

LIT
Rock group from Los Angeles, California: brothers A.J. (vocals) and Jeremy (bass) Popoff, Kevin Blades (bass) and Allen Shellenberger (drums).

LITTLE ANTHONY & THE IMPERIALS
R&B vocal group from Brooklyn, New York: Anthony Gourdine (born on 1/8/1940), Ernest Wright, Tracy Lord, Glouster Rogers and Clarence Collins. Gourdine first recorded on Winley in 1955 with The DuPonts. Formed The Chesters in 1957, then changed name to The Imperials in 1958. Sammy Strain, who joined group in 1964, left in 1975 to join The O'Jays. Gourdine became an Inspirational artist in 1980.

LITTLE BIG TOWN
Country vocal group from Georgia: Karen Fairchild, Kimberly Roads, Phillip Sweet and Jimi Westbrook.

LITTLE BILL & The Bluenotes
Pop group from Tacoma, Washington: "Little Bill" Engelhart (vocals), Lassie Aanes, Frank Dutra, Tom Geving, Buck Mann and Buck Ormsby.

LITTLE CAESAR
Hard-rock band formed in Los Angeles, California: Ron Young (vocals), Apache and Louren Molinare (guitars), Fidel Paniagua (bass), and Tom Morris (drums). Group named after a 1930 gangster movie. Young had cameo in movie *Terminator 2: Judgment Day*.

LITTLE CAESAR & The Consuls
Garage-rock band from Toronto, Ontario, Canada: Bruce Morshead (vocals, keyboards), Ken Pernokis (guitar), Norm Sherrat (sax), Tommy Wilson (bass) and Gary Wright (drums).

LITTLE CAESAR & The Romans
R&B vocal group from Los Angeles, California: Carl "Little Caesar" Burnett, David Johnson, Early Harris, Leroy Sanders and Johnny Simmons.

LITTLE DIPPERS, The
One-time studio session recording produced by Buddy Killen; featuring Floyd Cramer (piano), Bob Moore (bass), Hank Garland (lead guitar), Kelso Herston (rhythm guitar), Buddy Harmon (drums) and the Anita Kerr Singers (vocals). Killen later formed a quartet to lip-synch the song on the Dick Clark show.

LITTLE EVA
Born Eva Narcissus Boyd on 6/29/1943 in Belhaven, North Carolina. Died of cancer on 4/10/2003 (age 59). Discovered by songwriters Carole King and Gerry Goffin while Eva was babysitting their daughter Louise Goffin.

LITTLE FEAT
Eclectic rock band formed in Los Angeles, California: Lowell George (vocals), Paul Barrere (guitar), Bill Payne (keyboards), Kenny Gradney (bass), Sam Clayton (percussion) and Richard Hayward (drums). Disbanded in April 1979. George died of drug-related heart failure on 6/29/1979 (age 34). Regrouped in 1988, adding Craig Fuller (vocals, guitar) and Fred Tackett (guitar).

LITTLE JO ANN
Born Jo Ann Morse in 1955 (age seven in 1962). Female singer.

LITTLE JOE & THE THRILLERS
R&B vocal group from Philadelphia, Pennsylvania: Joe Cook, Farris Hill, Richard Frazier, Donald Burnett and Harry Pascle.

LITTLE JOEY & The Flips
Born Joseph Hall on 5/13/1939 in Philadelphia, Pennsylvania. Died in September 1972 (age 33). R&B singer. The Flips: James Meagher, John Smith, Jeff Leonard and Fred Gerace.

LITTLE MILTON
Born James Milton Campbell on 9/7/1934 in Inverness, Mississippi. Died of a stroke on 8/4/2005 (age 70). Blues singer/guitarist. Recorded with Ike Turner at Sun Records, 1953-54. In concert movie *Wattstax*.

LITTLE RICHARD
Born Richard Penniman on 12/5/1932 in Macon, Georgia. R&B-rock and roll singer/pianist. Talent contest win led to first recordings for RCA Victor in 1951. Worked with the Tempo Toppers, 1953-55. Appeared in three early rock and roll movies: *Don't Knock The Rock*, *The Girl Can't Help It* and *Mister Rock 'n' Roll* and the 1986 comedy *Down And Out In Beverly Hills*. Earned theology degree in 1961 and was ordained a minister. Left R&B for gospel music, 1959-62, and again in the mid-1970s. One of the key figures in the transition from R&B to rock and roll.

LITTLE RIVER BAND
Pop-rock group formed in Australia: Glenn Shorrock (vocals; born on 6/30/1944), Rick Formosa (born on 9/1/1954), Beeb Birtles (guitar; born on 11/28/1948) and Graham Goble (guitar; born on 5/15/1947), Roger McLachlan (bass), and Derek Pellicci (drums; born on 2/18/1953). McLachlan replaced by George McArdle in 1977 and Formosa replaced by David

Briggs in 1978. In 1983, Shorrock replaced by John Farnham (born on 7/1/1949) and Briggs replaced by Steve Housden. By 1985, Pellicci replaced by Steven Prestwich, and Birtles had left and keyboardist David Hirschfelder joined. Pellicci and Shorrock returned in 1987. By 1992, Goble had left and Peter Beckett, ex-leader of Player, had joined. Band named after a resort town near Melbourne.

LITTLE SISTER
Female R&B vocal trio formed by Sly Stone: Vanetta Stewart (Sly's sister), Mary Rand and Elva Melton.

LITTLE STEVEN & THE DISCIPLES OF SOUL
Born Steven Lento (later adopted his stepfather's last name) on 11/22/1950 in Boston, Massachusetts; raised in New Jersey. Formed Southside Johnny & The Jukes with co-lead singer Johnny Lyon in 1974. Joined Bruce Springsteen's E Street Band in 1975. Organized Artists United Against Apartheid. Plays "Silvio Dante" on TV's *The Sopranos*. Wrote "Little Steven's Underground Garage" column for *Billboard*. Also see Jean Beauvoir.

LITTLE TEXAS
Country group from Arlington, Texas: Tim Rushlow (vocals), Porter Howell and Dwayne O'Brien (guitars), Brady Seals (keyboards), Duane Propes (bass) and Del Gray (drums). Seals is the cousin of Jim (Seals & Crofts) and "England" Dan Seals and nephew of Troy Seals (Jo Ann & Troy). Seals was replaced by Jeff Huskins in 1995.

LITTLE WALTER
Born Marion Walter Jacobs on 5/1/1930 in Marksville, Louisiana. Died of injuries from a street fight on 2/15/1968 (age 37). Blues singer/harmonica player.

LIVE
Rock group from York, Pennsylvania: Edward Kowalczyk (vocals), Chad Taylor (guitar), Patrick Dahlheimer (bass) and Chad Gracey (drums).

LIVERPOOL FIVE
Rock band formed in Liverpool, England; later based in Spokane, Washington: Steve Laine (vocals), Ken Cox (guitar), Ron Henley (keyboards), Dave "Burgess" McKuminskey (bass) and Jimmy May (drums).

LIVING COLOUR
Black rock group from Brooklyn, New York: Corey Glover (vocals), Vernon Reid (guitar), Muzz Skillings (bass) and William Calhoun (drums). Glover played "Francis" in the movie *Platoon*.

LIVING IN A BOX
Soul-styled pop-dance trio from Sheffield, Yorkshire, England: Richard Darbyshire (vocals), Marcus Vere (keyboards) and Anthony Critchlow (drums).

LIVIN' JOY
Italian techno-dance group featuring American lead singer Janice Robinson (left group in April 1995). New lead singer Tameka Star joined in 1996.

LL COOL J
Born James Todd Smith on 1/14/1968 in Bay Shore, Long Island, New York; raised in Queens, New York. Male rapper/actor. Highly influential hip-hop artist. Stage name is abbreviation for Ladies Love Cool James. Has appeared in several movies and TV shows.

LLOYD
Born Lloyd Polite on 1/3/1986 in New Orleans, Louisiana; raised in Atlanta, Georgia. R&B singer.

LOBO
Born Roland Kent LaVoie on 7/31/1943 in Tallahassee, Florida. Pop singer/songwriter/ guitarist. Played with the Legends in Tampa in 1961. The Legends included Jim Stafford, Gerald Chambers, Gram Parsons and Jon Corneal. Lobo is Spanish for wolf. Lavoie formed own publishing company, Boo Publishing, in 1974.

LOCAL H
Rock duo from Zion, Illinois: Scott Lucas (vocals, guitar, bass) and Joe Daniels (drums).

LOCKE, Kimberley
Born on 1/3/1978 in Hartsville, Tennessee. Black female singer. Finalist on the 2003 season of TV's *American Idol*.

LOCKLIN, Hank
Born Lawrence Hankins Locklin on 2/15/1918 in McLellan, Florida. Country singer/songwriter/ guitarist. Elected mayor of McLellan in the early 1960s. Own TV series in Houston and Dallas in the 1970s.

LOEB, Lisa
Born on 3/11/1968 in Bethesda, Maryland; raised in Dallas, Texas. Adult Alternative pop-rock singer/songwriter/guitarist. Nine Stories consisted of Tim Bright (guitar), Joe Quigley (bass) and Jonathan Feinberg (drums).

LOGGINS, Dave
Born on 11/10/1947 in Mountain City, Tennessee. Pop-country singer/songwriter. Cousin of Kenny Loggins.

LOGGINS, Kenny
Born on 1/7/1948 in Everett, Washington. Pop-rock singer/songwriter/guitarist. Cousin of Dave Loggins. In band Gator Creek with producer Michael Omartian (later with Rhythm Heritage), later in Second Helping. Worked as a songwriter for Wingate Music; wrote Nitty Gritty Dirt Band's "House At Pooh Corner." Signed as a solo artist with Columbia in 1971 where he met and recorded with Jim Messina from 1972-76 (as Loggins & Messina).

LOGGINS & MESSINA
Duo of Kenny Loggins e bio) and Jim Messina (born on 12/5/1947 in Maywood, California; raised in Harlingen, Texas). Messina was a member of Buffalo Springfield and Poco.

LOHAN, Lindsay
Born on 7/2/1986 in Cold Spring Harbor, New York. Actress/teen pop star. Starred in the movies *The*

Parent Trap, Freaky Friday and *Confessions of a Teenage Drama Queen*.

LO-KEY?
Funk group from Minneapolis, Minnesota: Prof T. and Dre (vocals), Lance Alexander (keyboards), T-Bone (bass) and "D" (drums).

LOLITA
Born Ditta Einzinger on 1/17/1931 in St. Poelten, Austria. Female singer.

LONDON, Julie
Born Julie Peck on 9/26/1926 in Santa Rosa, California. Died of a stroke on 10/18/2000 (age 74). Singer/actress. Played "Dixie McCall" on TV's *Emergency*. Married to Jack Webb from 1945-53.

LONDON, Laurie
Born on 1/19/1944 in London, England. Teen male singer.

LONDONBEAT
R&B-dance vocal trio of Americans Jimmy Helms and George Chandler, with Trinidad native Jimmy Chambers. Backed by British producer/multi-instrumentalist Willy M.

LONDON QUIREBOYS, The
Hard-rock band formed in London, England: Jonathan "Spike" Gray (vocals), Guy Bailey (guitar), Guy Griffin (guitar), Chris Johnstone (keyboards), Nigel Mogg (bass) and Ian Wallace (drums).

LONE JUSTICE
Country-rock group from Los Angeles, California: Maria McKee (vocals), Ryan Hedgecock (guitar), Marvin Etzioni (bass) and Dan Heffington (drums). Etzioni and Heffington left in early 1986; Shane Fontayne (guitar), Bruce Brody (keyboards), Gregg Sutton (bass) and Rudy Richman (drums) joined.

LONESTAR
Country group from Nashville, Tennessee: Richie McDonald (vocals, guitar), John Rich (vocals, bass), Michael Britt (guitar), Dean Sams (keyboards) and Keech Rainwater (drums). Rich left in January 1998; later formed Big & Rich.

LONG, Shorty
Born Frederick Earl Long on 5/20/1940 in Birmingham, Alabama. Drowned in a boating accident on the Detroit River on 6/29/1969 (age 29). R&B singer/songwriter. Moved to Detroit in 1959. First recorded for Tri-Phi in 1962.

LONGET, Claudine
Born on 1/29/1942 in Paris, France. Female singer/actress. Married to Andy Williams from 1961-69. Charged with criminal negligence (served 30 days in jail) in the shooting of boyfriend, Olympic skier Vladimir "Spider" Sabich on 3/21/1976.

LOOKING GLASS
Pop-rock group formed in New Jersey: Elliot Lurie (vocals, guitar), Larry Gonsky (keyboards), Piet Sweval (bass; Starz) and Jeff Grob (drums). Sweval died on 1/23/1990 (age 41).

LOON
Born Chauncey Hawkins on 6/20/1975 in Harlem, New York. Male rapper.

LOOSE ENDS
R&B-dance trio formed in London, England: Carl McIntosh (vocals, guitar), Steve Nichol and Jane Eugene.

LOPEZ, Denise
Born in Queens, New York. Female dance singer.

LOPEZ, Jennifer
Born on 7/24/1969 in the Bronx, New York (of Puerto Rican parents). Singer/actress/dancer. In 1990 was a "Fly Girl" dancer on TV's *In Living Color*. Movie break came as the star of *Selena* in 1997; other movies include *Out Of Sight*, *The Cell*, *The Wedding Planner*, *Enough* and *Maid In Manhattan*. Married to professional dancer Cris Judd briefly in 2001. Engaged to actor Ben Affleck from 2002-04. Married Marc Anthony on 6/5/2004.

LOPEZ, Trini
Born Trinidad Lopez on 5/15/1937 in Dallas, Texas. Pop-folk singer/guitarist. Discovered by Don Costa while performing at PJs nightclub in Los Angeles. Played "Pedro Jiminez" in the movie *The Dirty Dozen*.

LORAIN, A'Me
Born in Simi Valley, California. White female pop-dance singer.

LORBER, Jeff
Born on 11/4/1952 in Philadelphia, Pennsylvania. Jazz fusion keyboardist.

LORD ROCKINGHAM'S XI
Studio rock and roll band led by Harry Robinson (born in Scotland). Included Cherry Wainer (organ), Benny Green and Red Price (saxophones), and Rory Blackwell (drums). Green died on 6/22/1998 (age 71).

LORDS OF THE UNDERGROUND
Black rap trio from Newark, New Jersey: Al "Mr. Funkyman" Wardrick, Dupre "Do It All" Kelly and Bruce "Lord Jazz" Colston.

LORD TARIQ & PETER GUNZ
Black rap duo from Brooklyn, New York: Sean Hamilton ("Lord Tariq") and Peter Panky ("Peter Gunz").

LORELEIS, The
Female pop vocal duo from Wyandotte, Michigan: Peggy Reinagle and Gail Menafee.

LORENZ, Trey
Born on 1/19/1969 in Florence, South Carolina. Male R&B singer.

LORING, Gloria
Born on 12/10/1946 in Manhattan, New York. Played "Liz Curtis" on the TV soap *Days Of Our Lives*. Married to actor Alan Thicke from 1970-83. Mother of singer Robin Thicke. Recorded in 1977 as Cody Jameson.

LOS BRAVOS
Rock group formed in Spain: Mike Kogel (vocals; born in Germany), Tony Martinez (guitar), Manuel Fernandez (organ), Miguel Danus (bass) and Pablo Gomez (drums). Kogel also recorded as Mike Kennedy.

LOS DEL MAR
Studio group from Canada featuring lead singer Wil Veloz. Formed to 'cover' the Los Del Rio version below.

LOS DEL RIO
Flamenco guitar duo from Seville, Spain: Antonio Romero Monge and Rafael Ruiz Perdigones. Formed duo in the 1960s. In 1993, they wrote and recorded "Macarena," which became a worldwide dance craze after it was remixed by the Miami production team of the Bayside Boys.

LOS INDIOS TABAJARAS
Indian guitar instrumental duo from Ceara, Brazil: brothers Natalicio (born Musiperi) and Antenor (born Herundy) Lima.

LOS LOBOS
Hispanic-American rock group from Los Angeles, California: David Hildago (vocals), Cesar Rosas (guitar), Steve Berlin (saxophone), Conrad Lozano (bass) and Louie Perez (drums).

LOS LONELY BOYS
Rock trio of brothers from San Angelo, Texas: Henry Garza (guitar), Joey "JoJo" Garza (bass) and Ringo Garza (drums). All share vocals.

LOS POP TOPS
Pop group formed in Madrid, Spain: Phil Trim (lead vocals; born in Trinidad), Jose Lipiani, Alberto Vega, Ray Gomez, Ignacio Perez, Juan Luis Angulo and Enrique Gomez.

LOST BOYZ
Rap group from Queens, New York: Terrance Kelly ("Mr. Cheeks"), Ronald Blackwell ("Spigg Nice"), Raymond Rogers ("Freekie Tah") and Eric Ruth ("Pretty Lou"). Rogers was shot to death on 3/29/1999 (age 28).

LOST GENERATION, The
R&B vocal group from Chicago, Illinois: brothers Lowrell (lead) and Fred Simon, Larry Brownlee (of The C.O.D.'s; died in 1978) and Jesse Dean. Disbanded in 1974. Lowrell began recording solo (as Lowrell) in 1978.

LOSTPROPHETS
Rock group formed in Wales: Ian Watkins (vocals), Mike Lewis (guitar), Lee Gaze (guitar), Stuart Richardson (bass) and Mike Chiplin (drums).

LOST TRAILERS, The
Country band formed in Atlanta, Georgia: Ryder Lee (vocals, keyboards), Stokes Nielson (vocals, guitar), Manny Medina (guitar), Andrew Nielson (bass) and Jeff Potter (drums).

LOS UMBRELLOS
Dance trio from Denmark. Male singer Al Agami is originally from the African nation of Lado. The female singers are Grith Hojfeldt and Mai-Britt.

LOUDERMILK, John D.
Born on 3/31/1934 in Durham, North Carolina. Pop-country singer/songwriter/multi-instrumentalist. Wrote "Waterloo," "Tobacco Road," "Indian Reservation" and many others. Recorded as Johnny Dee and Ebe Sneezer in 1957.

LOUIE LOUIE
Born Louis Cordero in Los Angeles, California. Dance singer/songwriter. Played Madonna's boyfriend in her "Borderline" video.

LOUVIN, Charlie
Born Charlie Loudermilk on 7/7/1927 in Rainsville, Alabama. Country singer/songwriter/guitarist. One-half of The Louvin Brothers. First cousin of John D. Loudermilk.

LOVATO, Demi
Born Demetria Lovato on 8/20/1992 in Dallas, Texas. Teen singer/actress. Also see Camp Rock Cast.

LOVE
Psychedelic folk-rock group from Los Angeles, California. One of the first integrated rock acts. Core members from 1966-68: Arthur Lee (vocals), John Echols and Bryan MacLean (guitars), and Ken Forssi (bass). Forssi died of cancer on 1/5/1998 (age 63). MacLean died of a heart attack on 12/25/1998 (age 52). Lee died of leukemia on 8/3/2006 (age 61).

LOVE, Darlene
Born Darlene Wright on 7/26/1938 in Los Angeles, California. Lead singer of backing group The Blossoms. Sang lead on two songs by The Crystals and with Bob B. Soxx & The Blue Jeans. Phil Spector suggested that she change her name to Darlene Love. Her sister, Edna Wright, was a member of The Honey Cone. Starred in the off-Broadway show *Leader of The Pack*. Played Danny Glover's wife in all four *Lethal Weapon* movies.

LOVE, Monie
Born Simone Johnson on 7/2/1970 in London, England; raised in Brooklyn, New York. Black dance club singer/songwriter.

LOVE, Ronnie
Born Ronald Dunbar in Detroit, Michigan. R&B singer/songwriter/producer. Later became a staff writer for the Invictus record label. Worked with Holland-Dozier-Holland and George Clinton's P-Funk Empire.

LOVE, Toby
Born Octavio Rivera in 1984 in the Bronx, New York. Latin singer/rapper.

LOVE & KISSES
Disco studio group assembled by European producer Alec Costandinos. Consisted of singers Don Daniels, Elaine Hill, Dianne Brooks and Jean Graham.

LOVE & MONEY
Pop trio from Scotland: James Grant (vocals, guitar), Bobby Paterson (bass) and Paul McGeechan (keyboards). Paterson died on 7/23/2006 (age 49).

LOVE & ROCKETS
Pop-rock trio formed in England: Daniel Ash (vocals, guitar), David J (bass) and Kevin Haskins (drums).

LOVE CHILDS AFRO CUBAN BLUES BAND
Disco studio group assembled by Michael Zager.

LOVE GENERATION, The
Pop group formed in Los Angeles, California: brothers Tom and John Bahler, Mitch Gordon, Jim Wasson, Marilyn Miller and Ann White.

LOVELESS, Patty
Born Patricia Ramey on 1/4/1957 in Pikeville, Kentucky. Country singer/songwriter/guitarist.

LOVELITES, The
Female R&B vocal trio from Chicago, Illinois: sisters Patti Hamilton and Rozena Petty, with Ardell McDaniel.

LOVERBOY
Rock group formed in Canada: Mike Reno (vocals; born on 1/8/1955), Paul Dean (guitar; born on 2/19/1946), Scott Smith (bass; born on 2/13/1955), Matt Frenette (drums; born on 3/7/1954) and Doug Johnson (keyboards; left by 1989). Smith drowned on 11/30/2000 (age 45).

LOVERS, The
Husband-and-wife R&B duo: Alden "Tarheel Slim" Bunn (born on 9/24/1924 in Bailey, North Carolina; died of pneumonia on 8/21/1977, age 52) and Anna "Little Ann" Sandford.

LOVERS, The
Disco studio group from Philadelphia, Pennsylvania.

LOVE SPIT LOVE
Rock group featuring brothers/former Psychedelic Furs Richard (vocals) and Tim (bass) Butler, with Richard Fortus (guitar) and Frank Ferrer (drums).

LOVE TRIBE
Dance studio group assembled by producers Dewey Bullock, Latanza Waters and Victor Mitchell.

LOVETT, Lyle
Born on 11/1/1957 in Houston, Texas; rasied in Klein, Texas. Country singer/songwriter/guitarist. Acted in several movies. Married to actress Julia Roberts from 1993-95.

LOVETTE, Eddie
Born in Jamaica. Reggae singer/songwriter.

LOVE UNLIMITED
Female R&B vocal trio from San Pedro, California: sisters Glodean and Linda James, with Diane Taylor. Barry White, who was married to Glodean from 1974-88, was their manager and producer.

LOVE UNLIMITED ORCHESTRA
Disco studio orchestra conducted and arranged by Barry White. Formed to back Love Unlimited; also heard on some of White's solo hits. Kenny G was a member at age 17.

LOVIN' SPOONFUL, The
Jug-band rock group formed in New York: John Sebastian (lead vocals, songwriter, guitarist, harmonica; born on 3/17/1944), Zal Yanovsky (lead guitar; born on 12/19/1944; died of a heart attack on 12/13/2002, age 57), Steve Boone (bass; born on 9/23/1943) and Joe Butler (drums; born on 9/16/1941). Sebastian had been with the Even

LOVIN' SPOONFUL, The — cont'd
Dozen Jug Band; did session work at Elektra.
Yanovsky and Sebastian were members of the
Mugwumps with Mama Cass Elliot and Denny
Doherty (later with The Mamas & The Papas).
Yanovsky replaced by Jerry Yester (keyboards) in
1967. Disbanded in 1970.

LOW, Andy Fairweather
Born on 8/8/1948 in Ystrad Mynach, Wales. Rock
singer/guitarist.

LOWE, Bernie
Born on 11/22/1917 in Philadelphia, Pennsylvania.
Died on 9/1/1993 (age 75). Founder/chief producer
of Cameo-Parkway Records. Wrote the #1 hits
"Teddy Bear" and "Butterfly."

LOWE, Jim
Born on 5/7/1927 in Springfield, Missouri.
DJ/vocalist/composer. DJ in New York City when he
recorded "The Green Door" in 1956.

LOWE, Nick
Born on 3/24/1949 in Walton, Surrey, England.
Pop-rock singer/songwriter/guitarist. With Brinsley
Schwarz (1970-75) and Rockpile. Married to
Carlene Carter from 1979-90. Produced albums for
Elvis Costello, Graham Parker and others.

LOX, The
Rap trio from Yonkers, New York: David Styles,
Shawn "Sheek" Jacobs and Jayson "Jadakiss"
Phillips. Group name is short for Living Off
Xperience.

LSG
All-star R&B trio: Gerald Levert, Keith Sweat and
Johnny Gill.

L.T.D.
R&B-funk group from Greensboro, North Carolina:
Jeffrey Osborne (vocals, drums), John McGhee
(guitar), Abraham Miller, Lorenzo Carnegie, Carle
Vickers and Jake Riley (horns), Billy Osborne and
Jimmy Davis (keyboards), Henry Davis (bass), and
Alvino Bennett (drums). The Osborne brothers left
after "Shine On." L.T.D. stands for Love,
Togetherness and Devotion.

L'TRIMM
Female rap duo: Tigra (from New York) and Bunny
D. (from Chicago, Illinois).

LUCAS
Born Lucas Secon in 1970 in Copenhagen,
Denmark. Male rapper/producer.

LUCAS, Carrie
Born in Los Angeles, California. R&B-disco singer.

LUCAS, Frank
Born in Louisiana; later based in San Bernardino,
California. R&B singer.

LUCAS, Matt
Born on 7/19/1935 in Memphis, Tennessee.
"Blue-eyed soul" singer/drummer.

LUCY PEARL
All-star R&B trio: Raphael Saadiq (Tony Toni Toné),
Dawn Robinson (En Vogue) and Ali Shaheed

Muhammad (A Tribe Called Quest). Joi replaced
Robinson in 2001. Robinson married Andre Allen (of
IV Xample) in May 2003.

LUDACRIS
Born Christopher Bridges on 9/11/1977 in
Champaign, Illinois; raised in Atlanta, Georgia.
Rapper/songwriter/actor. Appeared in the movies
The Wash, *2 Fast 2 Furious*, *Crash* and *Hustle &
Flow*.

LUHRMANN, Baz
Born Bazmark Luhrmann on 9/17/1962 in New
South Wales, Australia. Produced and directed the
movies *Romeo & Juliet* (1996) and *Moulin Rouge*
(2001).

LUKE, Robin
Born on 3/19/1942 in Los Angeles, California. Male
teen rock and roll singer/songwriter.

LULU
Born Marie Lawrie on 11/3/1948 in Glasgow,
Scotland. Pop singer/actress. Married to Maurice
Gibb (of the Bee Gees) from 1969-73. Appeared in
the 1967 movie *To Sir With Love*. Hosted own U.K.
TV show in 1968.

LUMAN, Bob
Born on 4/15/1937 in Blackjack, Texas; raised in
Nacogdoches, Texas. Died on 12/27/1978 (age 41).
Country-rockabilly singer/songwriter/guitarist. First
recorded for Imperial in 1957.

LUMIDEE
Born Lumidee Cedeno in Harlem, New York (Puerto
Rican parents). Female singer/rapper/songwriter.

LUND, Art
Born on 4/1/1915 in Salt Lake City, Utah. Died on
5/31/1990 (age 75). Baritone with Benny Goodman
during the 1940s as both Art Lund and Art London.
Starred in the classic 1956 Broadway musical *The
Most Happy Fella*.

LUNDBERG, Victor
Born on 9/2/1923 in Grand Rapids, Michigan. Died
on 2/14/1990 (age 66). News reader at WMAX in
Grand Rapids.

LUNDI, Pat
Dance singer/actress. Appeared in the Broadway
musical *Don't Bother Me, I Can't Cope*.

LUNIZ
Rap duo from Oakland, California: Jerold
"Yukmouth" Ellis and Garrick "Knumskull" Husband.

LUSCIOUS JACKSON
Female pop-rock group from Manhattan, New York:
Jill Cunniff (vocals, bass), Gabrielle Glaser (vocals,
guitar), Vivian Trimble (keyboards) and Kate
Schellenbach (drums). Named after the former pro
basketball player.

LUSTRA
Punk-rock group formed in Boston, Massachusetts:
Chris Baird (vocals, bass), Nick Cloutman (vocals,
guitar), Travis Lee (guitar) and Phil Matthews
(drums).

LUTCHER, Nellie
Born on 10/15/1912 in Lake Charles, Louisiana; later based in Los Angeles, California. Died on 6/8/2007 (age 94). Singer/songwriter/pianist/ bandleader. Sister of Joe Lutcher.

LV
Born Larry Sanders in Los Angeles, California. R&B singer/songwriter. Former member of South Central Cartel. L.V. stands for Large Variety.

LY - DELLS, The
White male doo-wop trio from Philadelphia, Pennsylvania: Gary Young, Chuck Hatfield and Paul O'Lone.

LYMAN, Arthur, Group
Born on 2/2/1932 in Kauai, Hawaii. Died of cancer on 2/24/2002 (age 70). Played vibraphone, guitar, piano and drums. Formerly with Martin Denny.

LYME & CYBELLE
Male/female pop-rock duo: Warren Zevon and Victoria Santangelo (later acted on Broadway as Laura Kenyon).

LYMON, Frankie, & The Teenagers
R&B vocal group from the Bronx, New York. Lead singer Lymon was born on 9/30/1942; died of a drug overdose on 2/27/1968 (age 25). Other members included Herman Santiago and Jimmy Merchant (tenors), Joe Negroni (baritone; died on 9/5/1978, age 37) and Sherman Garnes (bass; died on 2/26/1977, age 36). Group appeared in the movies *Rock, Rock, Rock* and *Mister Rock 'n' Roll*.

LYNN, Barbara
Born Barbara Lynn Ozen on 1/16/1942 in Beaumont, Texas. R&B singer/songwriter/guitarist.

LYNN, Cheryl
Born on 3/11/1957 in Los Angeles, California. R&B-disco singer. Discovered on TV's *The Gong Show*.

LYNN, Donna
Teen pop singer.

LYNN, Loretta
Born Loretta Webb on 4/14/1935 in Butcher Holler, Kentucky. Country singer/songwriter/guitarist. Sister of Crystal Gayle and Country singers Jay Lee Webb and Peggy Sue; distant cousin of country singer Patty Loveless. The 1980 movie *Coal Miner's Daughter* was based on Loretta's autobiography.

LYNN, Vera
Born Vera Welch on 3/20/1917 in East Ham, London, England. The most popular female singer in England during World War II.

LYNNE, Gloria
Born Gloria Wilson on 11/23/1931 in Harlem, New York. Black jazz-styled vocalist.

LYNNE, Jeff
Born on 12/30/1947 in Birmingham, England. Leader of Electric Light Orchestra and The Move. Otis Wilbury of the supergroup Traveling Wilburys. Production work for George Harrison, Roy Orbison, Tom Petty and Del Shannon.

LYNYRD SKYNYRD
Southern-rock group formed by Ronnie Van Zant (lead singer; born on 1/15/1949), Gary Rossington (guitar) and Allen Collins (guitar) while they were in junior high in Jacksonville, Florida. Named after their gym teacher Leonard Skinner. Changing lineup featured drummers Bob Burns, Rickey Medlocke (later of Blackfoot) and Artimus Pyle; bassists Larry Junstrom (later of 38 Special), Greg Walker (later of Blackfoot), Leon Wilkeson and Ed King (Strawberry Alarm Clock); pianist Billy Powell; and guitarist Steve Gaines. Plane crash on 10/20/1977 in Gillsburg, Mississippi, killed Van Zant and members Steve and his sister Cassie Gaines (vocals). Gary and Allen formed the Rossington Collins Band in 1980 with Wilkeson and Powell; split in 1982. Rossington and vocalist Johnny Van Zant (the younger brother of Ronnie and Donnie [lead singer of 38 Special] Van Zant) regrouped with old and new band members for the 1987 Lynyrd Skynyrd Tribute Tour. Collins (paralyzed in a car accident in 1986) died of pneumonia on 1/23/1990 (age 37). Rossington, Van Zant, Pyle, Wilkeson, King and Powell regrouped in 1991 with Randall Hall (guitar) and Custer (drums). Pyle left by 1993; replaced by Mike Estes. Custer left by 1994 and Owen Hale joined. Wilkeson died on 7/27/2001 (age 49).

LYSETTE
Born Lysette Titi in Washington DC. Female R&B singer.

LYTLE, Johnny
Born on 10/13/1932 in Springfield, Ohio. Died of kidney failure on 12/15/1995 (age 63). Jazz vibraphonist. Worked with jazz greats Louis Armstrong, Miles Davis and Lionel Hampton, among others.

LYTTLE, Kevin
Born on 9/14/1976 in St. Vincent, West Indies. Reggae-styled singer.

M
Born Robin Scott on 4/1/1947 in England. Male new-wave singer.

MA, Remy
Born Remy Smith on 5/30/1981 in the Bronx, New York. Female rapper/songwriter. Member of Terror Squad.

MABLEY, Moms
Born Loretta Mary Aiken on 3/19/1894 in Brevard, North Carolina. Died on 5/23/1975 (age 81). Bawdy comedienne/actress. Adopted the name Jackie Mabley from her first boyfriend. In the movies *Boarding House Blues*, *Emperor Jones* and *Amazing Grace*.

MacARTHUR, James
Born on 12/8/1937 in Los Angeles, California; raised in Nyack, New York. Actor/singer. Adopted son of actress Helen Hayes and playwright Charles MacArthur. Played "Danny Williams" on TV's *Hawaii Five-O*. Acted in several movies and Broadway shows.

MacDONALD, Ralph
Born on 3/15/1944 in Harlem, New York. Black
session percussionist/bandleader.

MACEO & THE MACKS
The JB's spin-off funk group led by Maceo Parker
(tenor sax; member of Parliament/Funkadelic).

MacGREGOR, Byron
Born Gary Mack on 3/3/1948 in Calgary, Alberta,
Canada. Died on 1/3/1995 (age 46). News director
at CKLW-Detroit when he did the narration for
"Americans." Narration was originally written and
delivered as an editorial by Gordon Sinclair for
CFRB-Toronto on 6/5/73.

MacGREGOR, Mary
Born on 5/6/1948 in St. Paul, Minnesota. Adult
Contemporary singer/songwriter.

MACHINE
Disco group from the Bronx, New York: Clare Bathe
(vocals), Jay Stovall (vocals, guitar), Kevin Nance
(keyboards), Melvin Lee (bass) and Lonnie
Ferguson (drums).

MACK, Craig
Born on 9/3/1971 in North Trenton, New Jersey.
Male rapper.

MACK, Lonnie
Born Lonnie McIntosh on 7/18/1941 in Harrison,
Indiana. Rockabilly guitarist/R&B-styled singer. Own
country band in 1954. Lead guitarist of band for
country singer Troy Seals (Jo Ann & Troy) in the
early 1960s. Rediscovered in 1968. Session work
with James Brown, The Doors and Freddy King.
Retired from music, 1971-85.

MACK, Warner
Born Warner McPherson on 4/2/1935 in Nashville,
Tennesee; raised in Mississippi. Country singer/
guitarist.

MACK 10
Born Dedrick Rolison on 8/9/1971 in Inglewood,
California. Male rapper. Discovered by Ice Cube.
Married T-Boz on 8/19/2000.

MacKENZIE, Gisele
Born Gisele LaFleche on 1/10/1927 in Winnipeg,
Manitoba, Canada. Died of cancer on 9/5/2003 (age
76). Star of TV's *Your Hit Parade* from 1953-57.

MacRAE, Gordon
Born on 3/12/1921 in East Orange, New Jersey.
Died of cancer on 1/24/1986 (age 64). Sang with
Horace Heidt (1942-43) and recorded numerous
duets with Jo Stafford. Starred in the movie
musicals *Oklahoma!* and *Carousel*. Actresses
Sheila and Meredith were his wife and daughter,
respectively.

MAD COBRA
Born Ewart Everton Brown on 3/31/1968 in
Kingston, Jamaica; raised in St. Mary's, Jamaica.
Reggae rapper.

MADDOX, Johnny
Born on 8/4/1929 in Gallatin, Tennessee.
Honky-tonk pianist.

MADIGAN, Betty
Born in Washington DC. Adult Contemporary
singer.

MADISON AVENUE
Male/female dance duo from Melbourne, Australia:
producer Andy Van Dorsselaer and singer Cheyne
Coates.

MAD LADS, The
R&B vocal group from Detroit, Michigan: John Gary
Williams, Julius Green, William Brown and Robert
Phillips. Williams and Brown replaced by Sam
Nelson and Quincy Clifton Billops, Jr. (later with
Ollie & The Nightingales and The Ovations) from
1966-69. Brown's brother Bertrand was a member
of The Newcomers (later known as Kwick).

MAD LION
Born Oswald Preist in London, England; raised in
Jamaica. Male dancehall rapper. Based in Brooklyn.

MADNESS
Ska-rock group formed in London, England:
Graham McPherson (vocals), Chris Foreman
(guitar), Mike Barson (keyboards), Carl Smyth
(trumpet), Lee Thompson (sax), Mark Bedford
(bass) and Dan Woodgate (drums).

MADONNA
Born Madonna Louise Ciccone on 8/16/1958 in Bay
City, Michigan. Moved to New York in 1977;
performed with the Alvin Ailey dance troupe.
Member of the Breakfast Club in 1979. Formed her
own band, Emmy, in 1980. Married to actor Sean
Penn from 1985-89. Acted in the movies
Desperately Seeking Susan, *Dick Tracy*, *A League
Of Their Own*, *Body Of Evidence*, *Evita* and *Swept
Away*, among others. Appeared in Broadway's
Speed-The-Plow. Released concert tour
documentary movie *Truth Or Dare* in 1991.
Released her graphic and erotic book *Sex* in 1992.
Married British movie director Guy Ritchie on
12/22/2000.

MAGAZINE 60
Electro-pop group from France.

MAGGARD, Cledus
Born Jay Huguely in Quick Sand, Kentucky. Former
actor. Worked at Leslie Advertising in Greenville,
South Carolina, when he recorded "The White
Knight." Later worked as a story editor for TV's
Magnum P.I.

MAGIC LANTERNS
Rock band from Warrington, England: Jimmy
Bilsbury (vocals), Peter Shoesmith (guitar), Ian
Moncur (bass) and Allan Wilson (drums). The latter
three left in 1969; replaced by Alistair Beveridge
and Paul Garner (guitars), Mike Osbourne (bass)
and Paul Ward (drums).

MAGIC MUSHROOMS, The
Garage-rock band from Philadelphia, Pennsylvania:
Stu Freeman (vocals, guitar), Ted Cahill (guitar),
Dick Richardson (keyboards), Charles Ingersol
(bass) and Joe Lacavera (drums).

MAGISTRATES, The
Group consisted of three members of The Dovells: Arnie Silver, Jerry Gross ("Jerry Summers") and Mike Freda ("Mike Dennis"). Features the voice of Jean Hillary.

MAGNIFICENT BASTARDS, The
Side project of Scott Weiland, leader of Stone Temple Pilots. Group consists of Weiland (vocals), Zander Schloss (Thelonious Monster, Red Hot Chili Peppers) and Jeff Nolan (guitars), and Bob Thomson (bass).

MAGNIFICENT MEN, The
White R&B-styled group from Harrisburg, Pennsylvania: David Bupp (vocals), Terry Crousore (guitar), Tommy Hoover (organ), Tom Pane (saxophone), Buddy King (trumpet), Jimmy Seville (bass) and Bob "Puff" Angelucci (drums). Hoover died on 1/20/2008 (age 61).

MAG 7
R&B pre-teen vocal group. Features lead singers Antuan and Ray Ray.

MAHARIS, George
Born on 9/1/1928 in Astoria, New York. Actor/singer. Played "Buz Murdock" on TV's *Route 66.*

MAIN INGREDIENT, The
R&B vocal trio formed in Harlem, New York: Donald McPherson, Luther Simmons and Tony Sylvester. McPherson died of leukemia on 7/4/1971; replaced by Cuba Gooding. Gooding's son, Cuba Jr., is a prominent movie actor. Sylvester died on 11/26/2006 (age 65).

MAI TAI
Female black dance trio from Amsterdam, Netherlands: Jettie Wells, Carolien De Windt and Mildred Douglas.

MAJORS, The
R&B vocal group from Philadelphia, Pennsylvania: Ricky Cordo (lead), Eugene Glass, Frank Troutt, Ronald Gathers and Idella Morris.

MAKEBA, Miriam
Born Zensi Miriam Makeba on 3/4/1932 in Johannesburg, South Africa. Black folk singer. Married to Hugh Masekela (1964-66) and black-power activist Stokeley Carmichael (1968-78).

MALAIKA
Born in Seattle, Washington. Black female dance singer.

MALLOY, Mitch
Born in Dickinson, North Dakota. Rock singer/ songwriter.

MALMKVIST, Siw - Umberto Marcato
Female singer Malmkvist was born on 12/31/1936 in Landskrona, Sweden. Male singer Umberto was born in Italy.

MALO
Latin-rock group from San Francisco, California. Core members: Arcelio Garcia (vocals), Jorge Santana (guitar; brother of Carlos Santana),

Richard Kermode (keyboards) and Pablo Tellez (bass). Malo is Spanish for "Bad."

MALTBY, Richard
Born on 6/26/1914 in Chicago, Illinois. Died on 8/19/1991 (age 77). Trumpeter/composer/ bandleader.

MAMA CASS
Born Ellen Naomi Cohen on 9/19/1941 in Baltimore, Maryland. Died of a heart attack (despite rumors, she did not choke to death) on 7/29/1974 (age 32). Member of The Mamas & The Papas. Her sister Leah Kunkel is a member of The Coyote Sisters.

MAMAS & THE PAPAS, The
Folk-pop group formed in Los Angeles, California: John Phillips (born on 8/30/1935 in Paris Island, South Carolina); Michelle Phillips (born on 6/4/1944 in Long Beach, California); Denny Doherty (born on 11/29/1940 in Halifax, Nova Scotia, Canada) and Cass Elliot (see Mama Cass bio above). Disbanded in 1968, reunited briefly in 1971. John and Michelle were married from 1962-70; their daughter is Chynna Phillips of the Wilson Phillips trio. John is also the father of actress MacKenzie Phillips. Michelle Phillips later became a successful actress; briefly married to Dennis Hopper in 1970. Mama Cass died of a heart attack on 7/29/1974 (age 32). John Phillips died of heart failure on 3/18/2001 (age 65). Doherty died on 1/19/2007 (age 66).

MAMMA MIA! CAST
Recordings below feature actresses from the cast of the 2008 movie *Mamma Mia!*: Meryl Streep, Amanda Seyfried, Ashely Lilley and Rachael McDowall.

MANÁ
Latin rock group from Mexico: Fher Olvera (vocals), Sergio Vallin (guitar), Juan Calleros (bass) and Alex Gonzalez (drums).

MANCHESTER, Melissa
Born on 2/15/1951 in the Bronx, New York. Adult Contemporary singer/pianist/composer. Father was a bassoon player with the New York Metropolitan Opera Orchestra. She studied songwriting under Paul Simon at the University School of the Arts in the early 1970s. Former backup singer for Bette Midler.

MANCINI, Henry
Born on 4/16/1924 in Cleveland, Ohio; raised in Aliquippa, Pennsylvania. Died of cancer on 6/14/1994 (age 70). Leading movie and TV composer/arranger/conductor. Staff composer for Universal Pictures, 1952-58. Winner of four Oscars and 20 Grammys. Married Ginny O'Connor, an original member of Mel Torme's Mel-Tones.

MANDRELL, Barbara
Born on 12/25/1948 in Houston, Texas; raised in Oceanside, California. Country singer. Moved to Nashville in 1971. Host of own TV variety series *Barbara Mandrell & The Mandrell Sisters*, 1980-82. Suffered severe injuries in an auto accident in 1984, from which she fully recovered. Acted on TV's *Sunset Beach* in 1997.

MANDRILL
Latin jazz-rock group from Brooklyn, New York: brothers Louis "Sweet Lou" (trumpet), Richard "Dr. Ric" (sax) and Carlos "Mad Dog" (flute) Wilson, Omar Mesa (guitar), Claude "Coffee" Cave (keyboards), Fudgie Kae (bass) and Charlie Pardo (drums).

MANFRED MANN
Born Manfred Lubowitz on 10/21/1940 in Johannesburg, South Africa. Formed pop-rock group in England: Mann (keyboards), Paul Jones (vocals; born on 2/24/1942), Michael Vickers (guitar; born on 4/18/1941), Tom McGuinness (bass; born on 12/2/1941) and Mike Hugg (drums; born on 8/11/1942). Mike D'Abo replaced Jones in 1967. McGuinness left to form McGuinness Flint in 1970. Manfred Mann formed his new Earth Band in 1971: Mann, Mick Rogers (vocals), Colin Pattenden (bass) and Chris Slade (drums). Rogers replaced by Chris Thompson (vocals, guitar) in 1976. Pattenden replaced by Pat King in June 1977. Thompson also recorded with own group Night in 1979. Lineup in 1979: Mann, Thompson, King, Steve Waller (guitar, vocals) and Geoff Britton (drums). King replaced by Matt Irving in 1981. Earth Band dissolved in 1986.

MANGIONE, Chuck
Born on 11/29/1940 in Rochester, New York. Flugelhorn player/bandleader/composer. Recorded with older brother Gaspare ("Gap") as The Jazz Brothers for Riverside in 1960. To New York City in 1965; played with Maynard Ferguson, Kai Winding, and Art Blakey's Jazz Messengers.

MANHATTAN BROTHERS
Vocal group from Johannesburg, South Africa: Nathan Mdledle, Joseph Mogotsi, Rufus Khoza and Ronnie Sehume. Miriam Makeba was a member from 1954 to late 1956.

MANHATTANS, The
R&B vocal group from Jersey City, New Jersey: George "Smitty" Smith (lead vocals), Winfred "Blue" Lovett (bass; born on 11/16/1943), Edward "Sonny" Bivins (born on 1/15/1942) and Kenneth "Wally" Kelly (tenors; born on 1/9/1943) and Richard Taylor (baritone). Smith replaced by Gerald Alston in 1971. First recorded for Piney in 1962. Taylor (aka Abdul Rashid Talhah) left in 1976. Smith died of spinal meningitis on 12/16/1970. Taylor died following a lengthy illness on 12/7/1987 (age 47). Featured female vocalist Regina Belle began solo career in 1987. Alston went solo in 1988.

MANHATTAN TRANSFER, The
Versatile vocal harmony group formed in Manhattan, New York: Tim Hauser, Alan Paul, Janis Siegel and Laurel Masse. Cheryl Bentyne replaced Masse in 1979. Group hosted own TV variety show on CBS in 1975.

MANILOW, Barry
Born Barry Alan Pincus on 6/17/1943 in Brooklyn, New York. Pop singer/pianist/composer. Studied at New York's Juilliard School. Music director for the WCBS-TV series Callback. Worked at New York's Continental Baths bathhouse/nightclub in New York as Bette Midler's accompanist in 1972; later

produced her first two albums. First recorded solo as Featherbed. Wrote jingles for Dr. Pepper, Pepsi, State Farm Insurance, Band-Aids and McDonald's ("You Deserve A Break Today," which he also sang).

MANN, Aimee
Born on 9/8/1960 in Richmond, Virginia. Former lead singer of 'Til Tuesday. Married Michael Penn on 12/29/1997.

MANN, Barry
Born Barry Iberman on 2/9/1939 in Brooklyn, New York. One of pop music's most prolific songwriters in a partnership with wife Cynthia Weil, including "You've Lost That Lovin' Feelin'," "(You're My) Soul & Inspiration," "Kicks," "Hungry," "We Gotta Get Out Of This Place," and many others. Established own publishing company, Dyad Music.

MANN, Carl
Born on 8/24/1942 in Huntingdon, Tennessee. Rockabilly singer/pianist.

MANN, Gloria
Born in Philadelphia, Pennsylvania. Pop-rock and roll singer. Her son, Bob Rosenberg, is the leader of Will To Power.

MANN, Herbie
Born Herbert Jay Solomon on 4/16/1930 in Brooklyn, New York. Died of cancer on 7/1/2003 (age 73). Renowned jazz flutist. First recorded with Mat Mathews Quintet for Brunswick in 1953. First recorded as a solo for Bethlehem in 1954.

MANN, Johnny, Singers
Born on 8/30/1928 in Baltimore, Maryland. Musical director for Joey Bishop's TV talk show.

MANONE, Wingy
Born Joseph Mannone on 2/13/1904 in New Orleans, Louisiana. Died on 7/9/1982 (age 78). Trumpeter/bandleader. Lost right arm at age eight in streetcar accident. Composed "Tar Paper Stomp" which Glenn Miller later made famous in revised form as "In The Mood."

MANSON, Marilyn
Born Brian Warner on 1/5/1969 in Canton, Ohio. Hard-rock singer/songwriter. Noted for his controversial stage performances. His band includes: Scott "Daisy Berkowitz" Putesky (guitar), Steve "Madonna Wayne Gacy" Bier (keyboards), Jeordi "Twiggy Ramirez" White (bass) and Ken "Ginger Fish" Wilson (drums).

MANTOVANI
Born Annunzio Paolo Mantovani on 11/15/1905 in Venice, Italy. Died on 3/29/1980 (age 74). Played classical violin in England before forming his own orchestra in the early 1930s. Had first U.S. chart hit in 1935, "Red Sails In The Sunset" (#2). Achieved international fame 20 years later with his 40-piece orchestra and distinctive "cascading strings" sound.

MANTRONIX (Featuring Wondress)
Hip-hop/dance duo from Brooklyn, New York: Curtis "Mantronik" Kahleel and M.C. Tee. Bryce Wilson replaced Tee in 1989. Wilson later formed Groove Theory.

MARA, Tommy
Born in Waterbury, Connecticut. Adult Contemporary singer.

MARATHONS, The
The Olympics' Arvee label needed a new single, but since The Olympics were on tour, the label brought in The Vibrations, who were under contract with the Chess/Checker label. The Vibrations recorded "Peanut Butter," and Arvee released it as by The Marathons. Chess discovered the fraud and stopped the Arvee release and then released a re-recorded version on their subsidiary label, Argo. Arvee followed up with a new song by The Marathons, recorded by an unknown non-Vibrations group.

MARCELS, The
R&B doo-wop group from Pittsburgh, Pennsylvania: Cornelius "Nini" Harp (lead singer), Ronald "Bingo" Mundy and Gene Bricker (tenors), Richard Knauss (baritone) and Fred Johnson (bass). Knauss replaced by Fred's brother, Allen Johnson (died on 9/28/1995), and Bricker replaced by Walt Maddox, mid-1961. Mundy left in late 1961.

MARCH, Little Peggy
Born Margaret Battivio on 3/8/1948 in Lansdale, Pennsylvania. Lived in Germany from 1969-81. Youngest female singer to have a #1 single on the pop charts.

MARCHAN, Bobby
Born Oscar James Gibson on 4/30/1930 in Youngstown, Ohio. Died on 12/5/1999 (age 69). Lead singer with Huey "Piano" Smith & The Clowns.

MARCY JOE
Born Marcy Rae Sockel on 1/4/1944 in Pittsburgh, Pennsylvania. Teen pop singer.

MARCY PLAYGROUND
Rock trio from Manhattan, New York: John Wozniak (vocals, guitar), Dylan Keefe (bass) and Dan Reiser (drums).

MARDONES, Benny
Born on 11/9/1948 in Cleveland, Ohio. Pop singer/songwriter.

MARESCA, Ernie
Born on 4/21/1939 in the Bronx, New York. Rock and roll singer/songwriter. Wrote "Runaround Sue," "The Wanderer," "Lovers Who Wander" and "Donna The Prima Donna" for Dion.

MARÍ, Teairra
Born Teairra Maria Thomas on 12/2/1987 in Detroit, Michigan. Female R&B singer.

MARIE, Teena
Born Mary Christine Brockert on 3/5/1956 in Santa Monica, California; raised in Venice, California. White funk singer/songwriter.

MARIE & REX
R&B duo: Marie Knight and Rex Garvin. Marie teamed with Sister Rosetta Tharpe from 1947-54.

MARILLION
Rock group from Aylesbury, England: Derek "Fish" Dick (vocals), Steve Rothery (guitar), Mark Kelly (keyboards), Pete Trewavas (bass) and Ian Mosley (drums).

MARIMBA CHIAPAS
Marimba band from Mexico. Led by brothers Francisco and Ricardo Sanchez.

MARIO
Born Mario Barrett on 8/27/1986 in Baltimore, Maryland; raised in Teaneck, New Jersey. Teen R&B singer/rapper.

MARK-ALMOND
Pop-rock duo from England: Jon Mark and Johnny Almond.

MARKETTS, The
Surf-rock instrumental band from Hollywood, California: Ben Benay (guitar), Mike Henderson (sax), Richard Hobriaco (keyboards), Ray Pohlman (bass) and Gene Pello (drums).

MAR-KEYS
White R&B instrumental band from Memphis, Tennessee: Charles Axton (tenor sax), Wayne Jackson (trumpet), Don Nix (baritone sax), Jerry Lee "Smoochie" Smith (keyboards), Steve Cropper (guitar), Donald "Duck" Dunn (bass) and Terry Johnson (drums). Staff musicians at Stax/Volt. Cropper and Dunn later joined Booker T. & The MG's; also backing work for the Blues Brothers. Axton died in January 1974 (age 32).

MARKHAM, Pigmeat
Born Dewey Markham on 4/18/1904 in Durham, North Carolina. Died of a stroke on 12/13/1981 (age 77). Black comedian. Regular on TV's *Laugh-In* (1968-69).

MARK II, The
Pop-rock and roll instrumental duo: Wayne Cogswell and Ray Peterson.

MARK IV, The
Comedy duo from Chicago, Illinois: Eddie Mascari and Erwin "Dutch" Wenzlaff. First recorded as The Mark IV. Mascari died on 7/26/1991 (age 65).

MARKS, Guy
Born Mario Scarpa on 10/31/1923 in Philadelphia, Pennsylvania. Died on 11/28/1987 (age 64). Comedic impressionist.

MARKY MARK & The Funky Bunch
Born Mark Wahlberg on 6/5/1971 in Dorchester, Massachusetts. Singer/rapper/actor. Starred in movies since 1994. Younger brother of Donnie Wahlberg of New Kids On The Block. The Funky Bunch is DJ Terry Yancey and three male and two female dancers.

MARLEY, Bob, & The Wailers
Born on 2/6/1945 in Rhoden Hall, Jamaica. Died of cancer on 5/11/1981 (age 36). Legendary reggae singer/songwriter/guitarist. The Wailers included Peter Tosh and Bunny Wailer; both left in 1974. His 1984 album *Legend* has been on *Billboard's* Album charts for over 900 weeks! Father of Ziggy Marley. In 1990, Marley's birthday proclaimed a national holiday in Jamaica.

MARLEY, Damian "Jr. Gong"
Born on 7/21/1978 in Kingston, Jamaica. Reggae singer. Son of Bob Marley.

MARLEY, Ziggy, & The Melody Makers
Family reggae group from Kingston, Jamaica. Children of the late reggae master Bob Marley: David "Ziggy" (vocals, guitar), Stephen, Sharon and Cedella Marley.

MARLO, Micki
Female pop singer. Former magazine pin-up model. First recorded for Capitol in 1954. Appeared in the 1957 Broadway musical *Follies*.

MARLOWE, Marion
Born on 3/7/1929 in St. Louis, Missouri. Featured singer on *Arthur Godfrey And His Friends* from 1950-55.

MARMALADE, The
Pop group from Scotland: Thomas "Dean Ford" McAleese (vocals), Junior Campbell (guitar), Patrick Fairley (piano), Graham Knight (bass) and Alan Whitehead (drums).

MAROON 5
Alternative pop-rock band from Los Angeles, California: Adam Levine (vocals, guitar), James Valentine (guitar), Jesse Carmichael (keyboards), Mickey Madden (bass) and Ryan Dusick (drums).

M/A/R/R/S
Electro-funk group from England featuring two pairs of brothers: Martyn and Steve Young, with Alex and Rudi Kane. Includes mixers: Chris "CJ" Mackintosh and DJ Dave Dorrell.

MARSHALL, Amanda
Born on 8/29/1972 in Toronto, Ontario, Canada. Adult Alternative singer/songwriter.

MARSHALL HAIN
Pop-rock duo from England: Julian Marshall and Kit Hain. Marshall later formed the duo Eye To Eye.

MARSHALL TUCKER BAND, The
Southern-rock group from Spartanburg, South Carolina: Doug Gray (vocals; born on 5/22/1948), brothers Toy (guitar; born on 11/13/1947) and Tommy Caldwell (bass; born on 11/9/1949), George McCorkle (guitar; born on 10/11/1946), Jerry Eubanks (sax, flute; born on 3/19/1950) and Paul Riddle (drums; born in 1953). Tommy Caldwell died in a car crash on 4/28/1980 (age 30); replaced by Franklin Wilkie. Toy Caldwell left in 1985; died of respiratory failure on 2/25/1993 (age 45). McCorkle died on 6/29/2007 (age 60). Marshall Tucker was the owner of the band's rehearsal hall.

MARS VOLTA, The
Progressive-rock band from El Paso, Texas: Cedric Bixler-Zavala (vocals), Omar Rodriguez-Lopez (guitar), Isaiah "Ikey" Owens (keyboards), Marcel Rodriguez (percussion), Juan Alderete (bass) and Jon Theodore (drums).

MARTERIE, Ralph
Born on 12/24/1914 in Naples, Italy; raised in Chicago, Illinois. Died on 10/8/1978 (age 63). Very popular early 1950s band leader; played trumpet in the 1940s for Enric Madriguera and other bands. Had three Top 10 hits from 1953-54: "Pretend," "Caravan" and "Skokiaan."

MARTHA & THE MUFFINS
Rock group from Toronto, Ontario, Canada: led by Martha Johnson (vocal) and Mark Gane (guitars). Numerous personnel changes. Member Jocelyn Lanois is the sister of Daniel Lanois, noted producer of U2 and Peter Gabriel.

MARTHA & THE VANDELLAS
Female R&B vocal trio from Detroit, Michigan: Martha Reeves (born on 7/18/1941), Annette Beard and Rosalind Ashford (born on 9/2/1943). Reeves had been in The Del-Phis, recorded for Checkmate. Worked at Motown as an A&R secretary and sang backup. Vandellas sang backup on several of Marvin Gaye's hits. Beard left group in 1963; replaced by Betty Kelly (born on 9/16/1944; formerly with The Velvelettes). Group disbanded from 1969-71; re-formed with Martha and sister Lois Reeves, and Sandra Tilley in 1971. Martha Reeves went solo in late 1972.

MARTIKA
Born Marta Marrero on 5/18/1969 in Whittier, California. Latin singer/actress. Starred on TV's *Kids, Incorporated*. Appeared in the 1982 movie musical *Annie*.

MARTIN, Andrea
Born in 1975 in Brooklyn, New York. R&B singer/songwriter.

MARTIN, Billie Ray
Born in Hamburg, Germany. Female dance singer.

MARTIN, Bobbi
Born Barbara Martin on 11/29/1938 in Brooklyn, New York; raised in Baltimore, Maryland. Died of cancer on 5/2/2000 (age 61). Adult Contemporary singer/songwriter.

MARTIN, Dean
Born Dino Crocetti on 6/7/1917 in Steubenville, Ohio. Died of respiratory failure on 12/25/1995 (age 78). All-time great Adult Contemporary singer/actor. To California in 1937; worked local clubs. Teamed with comedian Jerry Lewis in Atlantic City in 1946. First movie, *My Friend Irma*, in 1949. Team broke up after 16th movie, *Hollywood Or Bust*, in 1956. Appeared in many movies since then. Own TV series from 1965-74. His son Dino (killed in a military jet crash in 1987) was in Dino, Desi & Billy.

MARTIN, Derek
Born in 1938 in Detroit, Michigan. R&B singer.

MARTIN, Eric
Born on 10/10/1960 in San Francisco, California. Pop-rock singer. Lead singer of rock group Mr. Big since 1988.

MARTIN, George
Born on 1/3/1926 in London, England. The Beatles' producer from 1962-70. Also produced Billy J. Kramer, Gerry And The Pacemakers, America, Jeff Beck and others. Knighted by Queen Elizabeth II in 1996.

MARTIN, Keith
Born in Washington DC. R&B singer. Toured as a background vocalist with Johnny Gill and M.C. Hammer.

MARTIN, Marilyn
Born on 5/4/1954 in Jellico, Tennessee; raised in Louisville, Kentucky. Adult Contemporary singer/ songwriter. Former session singer.

MARTIN, Moon
Born John Martin in 1950 in Oklahoma. Rock and roll singer/songwriter/guitarist. Wrote Robert Palmer's hit "Bad Case Of Loving You." Moved to Los Angeles in 1968. Lead guitarist of group Southwind. Jude Cole was a member of Martin's band.

MARTIN, Ricky
Born Enrique Martin Morales on 12/24/1971 in San Juan, Puerto Rico. Latin singer/actor. Member of Menudo from 1984-89. Acted on the TV soap *General Hospital* and on Broadway in *Les Miserables*.

MARTIN, Steve
Born on 6/8/1945 in Waco, Texas; raised in Garden Grove, California. Popular TV and movie comedian/ actor. Comedy writer for the *Smothers Brothers Comedy Hour* TV show and others; frequent appearances on *Saturday Night Live*. Starred in numerous movies. Married to actress Victoria Tennant from 1986-94.

MARTIN, Tony
Born Alvin Morris on 12/25/1912 in San Francisco, California. Singer/actor. Starred in over 30 movies from 1936-56. Hosted own TV show from 1954-56. Married actress/dancer Cyd Charisse in 1948.

MARTIN, Trade
Born on 11/19/1943 in Union City, New Jersey. Teen pop singer.

MARTIN, Vince
Born on 3/17/1937 in Brooklyn, New York. Teen folk singer.

MARTINDALE, Wink
Born Winston Martindale on 12/4/1933 in Jackson, Tennessee. DJ since 1950. Own TV shows starting with *Teenage Dance Party*. Host of *Tic Tac Dough*, *Gambit*, *Debt* and other TV game shows.

MARTINE, Layng
Born on 3/24/1942 in Greenwich, Connecticut. Male pop singer/songwriter.

MARTINEZ, Angie
Born on 1/9/1972 in the Bronx, New York (Puerto Rican parents). Female rapper. Radio personality at Hot 97 in New York.

MARTINEZ, Nancy
Born on 8/26/1960 in Quebec City, Quebec, Canada. Dance singer/actress.

MARTINEZ, Rosco
Born in Oriente Holguin, Cuba; raised in Plantation, Florida. Latin pop singer/songwriter.

MARTINO, Al
Born Alfred Cini on 10/7/1927 in Philadelphia, Pennsylvania. Adult Contemporary singer. Encouraged by success of boyhood friend Mario Lanza. Winner on *Arthur Godfrey's Talent Scouts* in 1952. Played singer "Johnny Fontane" in the 1972 movie *The Godfather*.

MARVELETTES, The
Female R&B vocal group from Inkster, Michigan: Gladys Horton, Georgeanna Marie Tillman Gordon (married Billy Gordon of The Contours), Wanda Young (married Bobby Rogers of The Miracles), Katherine Anderson and Juanita Cowart. Young and Horton both sang lead. Cowart left in 1962. Gordon left in 1965; died of lupus on 1/6/1980 (age 35). Horton left in 1967; replaced by Anne Bogan (later a member of Love, Peace & Happiness and New Birth). Disbanded in 1969. Also recorded as The Darnells.

MARVELOWS, The
R&B vocal group from Chicago, Illinois: Melvin Mason, Willie Stevenson, Frank Paden, Johnny Paden and Jesse Smith. Smith died of cancer on 9/4/2007 (age 65).

MARX, Richard
Born on 9/16/1963 in Chicago, Illinois. Pop-rock singer/songwriter. Professional jingle singer since age five. Backing singer for Lionel Richie. Married Cynthia Rhodes (of Animotion) on 1/8/1989.

MARY JANE GIRLS
Black female funk-dance group: Joanne McDuffie, Candice Ghant, Kim Wuletich and Yvette Marina. Formed and produced by Rick James. Marina is the daughter of disco singer Pattie Brooks.

MARY MARY
Black female gospel vocal duo from Inglewood, California: sisters Erica and Tina Atkins.

MAS, Carolyne
Born on 10/20/1955 in Bronxville, New York; raised in Long Island, New York. Rock singer/guitarist.

MA$E
Born Mason Betha on 8/27/1974 in Jacksonville, Florida; raised in Harlem, New York. Male rapper. In 2000 became a pastor and leader of Sane Ministries in Atlanta, Georgia.

MASEKELA, Hugh
Born on 4/4/1939 in Witbank, South Africa. Trumpeter/bandleader/arranger. Married to Miriam Makeba from 1964-66.

MASHMAKHAN
Rock group from Montreal, Quebec, Canada: Pierre Senecal (vocals, keyboards), Rayburn Blake (guitar), Brian Edwards (bass) and Jerry Mercer (drums). Mercer later joined April Wine.

MASKMAN & THE AGENTS, The
R&B novelty vocal group: Harmon "Maskman" Bethea, Tyrone Gray, Paul Williams and Johnny Hood.

MASON, Barbara
Born on 8/9/1947 in Philadelphia, Pennsylvania.
R&B singer/songwriter.

MASON, Dave
Born on 5/10/1946 in Worcester, West Midlands,
England. Soft-rock singer/songwriter/guitarist.
Original member of Traffic. Joined Delaney &
Bonnie for a short time in 1970. Joined Fleetwood
Mac for a short time in 1993. Wrote Joe Cocker's hit
"Feelin' Alright."

MASON, Vaughan, & Crew
Disco-funk group from Brooklyn, New York. Led by
multi-instrumentalist Mason, former manager of The
21st Century and engineer for B.T. Express. Mason
formed Raze in 1988. Lead singer of the Crew was
Jerome Bell.

MASQUERADERS, The
R&B group from Texas: Lee Hatim, Robert
Wrightsil, David Sanders, Harold Thomas and
Sammy Hutchinson.

MASSEY, Wayne
Born in Glendale, California. Singer/actor. Played
"Johnny Drummond" on TV's *One Life To Live*
(1980-84). Married country singer Charly McClain in
July 1984.

MASS PRODUCTION
Disco-funk group from Richmond, Virginia: Agnes
"Tiny" Kelly (female vocals), Larry Marshall (male
vocals), LeCoy Bryant (guitar), James "Otiste"
Drumgole (trumpet), Gregory McCoy (sax), Tyrone
Williams (keyboards), Emanual Redding
(percussion), Kevin Douglas (bass) and Ricardo
Williams (drums).

MASTA ACE INCORPORATED
Masta Ace is rapper Duval Clear from Brownsville,
New York. Member of The Crooklyn Dodgers. His
posse includes Lord Digga and rap trio Eyceurokk
(Master Eyce, Uneek and Diesalrokk).

MASTER P
Born Percy Miller on 4/29/1969 in New Orleans,
Louisiana. Gangsta rapper/producer. Member of
504 Boyz and Tru. Founder of the No Limit record
label. Played professional basketball for the CBA's
Fort Wayne Fury in 1998. Brother of Silkk The
Shocker. Father of Lil' Romeo.

MASTERS, Sammy
Born Samuel Lawmaster on 7/18/1930 in
Sasakawa, Oklahoma. Rock and roll singer. Moved
to Los Angeles, California, in 1947. Appeared on
Cal's Corral TV show from 1959-72.

MATCHBOX TWENTY
Rock band from Orlando, Florida: Rob Thomas
(vocals; born on 2/14/1972), Kyle Cook (guitar; born
on 8/29/1975), Adam Gaynor (guitar; born on
11/26/1963), Brian Yale (bass; born on 10/24/1968)
and Paul Doucette (drums; born on 8/22/1972).

MATHEWS, Tobin
Born Willy Henson in Calumet City, Illinois. Rock
and roll singer/guitarist. Relative of Jeremy Jordan.

MATHIESON, Muir
Born on 1/24/1911 in Stirling, Scotland. Died on
8/2/1975 (age 64). Conductor/arranger.

MATHIS, Johnny
Born on 9/30/1935 in Gilmer, Texas; raised in San
Francisco, California. Studied opera from age 13.
Track scholarship at the San Francisco State
College. Invited to Olympic tryouts; chose singing
career instead. Discovered by George Avakian of
Columbia Records. To New York City in 1956.
Initially recorded as a jazz-styled singer. Columbia
A&R executive Mitch Miller switched him to singing
pop ballads.

MATISYAHU
Born Matthew Miller on 6/30/1979 in West Chester,
Pennsylvania; raised in White Plains, New York.
Hasidic reggae rapper/singer. Name is Hebrew for
"Gift of God." Wears traditional Hasidic clothing and
raps in English, Hebrew and Yiddish.

MATTEA, Kathy
Born on 6/21/1959 in South Charleston, West
Virginia; raised in Cross Lanes, West Virginia.
Country singer/songwriter/guitarist. Discovered in
1983 while working as a waitress in Nashville.

MATTHEWS, Dave, Band
Dave was born on 1/9/1967 in Johannesburg, South
Africa; raised in New York. Adult Alternative rock
singer/guitarist/songwriter. Acted in the movies
Where The Red Fern Grows, *Because Of
Winn-Dixie* and *Lake City*. His band: LeRoi Moore
(sax), Boyd Tinsley (violin), Stefan Lessard (bass)
and Carter Beauford (drums). Since 1995, they
have been one of the most popular touring bands
on college campuses. Moore died on 8/19/2008
(age 46).

MATTHEWS, Ian
Born Ian Matthews MacDonald on 6/16/1946 in
Scunthorpe, Lincolnshire, England. Founder of
Fairport Convention and Matthews' Southern
Comfort. From 1984-87, in A&R for Island and
Windham Hill record labels.

MATYS BROS., The
Polka band from Chester, Pennsylvania: brothers
Emil Matys (sax; born on 7/22/1924; died on
5/5/2008, age 83), Walter Matys (accordian; born on
4/5/1917; died on 2/8/1988, age 70), John Matys
(bass) and Eugene Matys (born on 7/1/1922; died
on 10/12/1993, age 71).

MAUDS, The
Pop group from Chicago, Illinois: Jimmy Rogers
(vocals), Fuzzy Fuscaldo (guitar), Timmy Coniglio
(trumpet), Billy Winter (bass) and Phil Weinberg
(drums).

MAURIAT, Paul
Born on 3/4/1925 in Marseilles, France; raised in
Paris, France. Died on 11/3/2006 (age 81).
Orchestra leader.

MAX, Christopher
Born in Seattle, Washington. R&B singer.

MAX-A-MILLION
Techno-funk trio from Chicago, Illinois: A'Lisa B (female vocals), Duran Estevez and Tommye.

MAXWELL
Born Maxwell Musze on 5/23/1973 in Brooklyn, New York. R&B singer/songwriter/producer.

MAXWELL, Diane
Born on 5/24/1942 in Los Angeles, California. Teen pop singer.

MAXWELL, Robert
Born on 4/19/1921 in Brooklyn, New York. Jazz harpist/composer. With NBC Symphony under Toscanini at age 17. Also recorded as Mickey Mozart and Harmony Jones.

MAY, Billy
Born on 11/10/1916 in Pittsburgh, Pennsylvania. Died of a heart attack on 1/22/2004 (age 87). Arranger/conductor/sideman for many of the big bands. After leading his own band in the early 1950s, Billy went on to arrange/conduct for Frank Sinatra and compose movie scores.

MAYALL, John
Born on 11/29/1933 in Macclesfield, Cheshire, England. Blues-rock singer. His band, the Blues Breakers, spawned many of Britain's leading rock musicians, including Eric Clapton, John McVie and Mick Taylor.

MAYER, John
Born on 10/16/1977 in Fairfield, Connecticut; later based in Atlanta, Georgia. Adult Alternative pop-rock singer/songwriter/guitarist.

MAYER, Nathaniel
Born on 2/10/1944 in Detroit, Michigan. R&B singer/songwriter.

MAYFIELD, Curtis
Born on 6/3/1942 in Chicago, Illinois. Died on 12/26/1999 (age 57). R&B singer/songwriter/producer. Leader of The Impressions from 1957-70. Started own Curtom record label in 1968. Played "Pappy" in the movie *Short Eyes*. Paralyzed from the chest down when a stage lighting tower fell on him before a concert on 8/13/1990.

MAYFIELD, Percy
Born on 8/12/1920 in Minden, Louisiana. Died of a heart attack on 8/11/1984 (age 64). R&B singer/songwriter/pianist. Wrote the classic "Hit The Road Jack."

MAZE Featuring Frankie Beverly
R&B group formed in Philadelphia, Pennsylvania: Frankie Beverly (vocals), Wayne Thomas (guitar), Sam Porter (keyboards), Ronald Lowry (percussion), Robin Duhe (bass) and McKinley Williams (drums).

MAZZY STAR
Alternative-rock duo from California: songwriter/guitarist David Roback and vocalist Hope Sandoval. Roback was a member of Rain Parade and Opal.

MC BRAINS
Born James Davis in 1975 in Cleveland, Ohio. Male rapper.

MC BREED
Born Eric Breed in Flint, Michigan. Male rapper.

MC EIHT
Born Aaron Tyler on 5/22/1971 in Los Angeles, California. Male rapper. Leader of Compton's Most Wanted. Played "A-Wax" in the movie *Menace II Society*. EIHT stands for "Experienced In Hardcore-Thumpin'."

MC5
Hard-rock band from Detroit, Michigan: Rob Tyner (vocals), Wayne Kramer and Fred "Sonic" Smith (guitars), Michael Davis (bass) and Dennis Thompson (drums). Tyner died of a heart attack on 9/17/1991 (age 46). Smith married Patti Smith in 1980; died of a heart attack on 11/4/1994 (age 45). MC5 is short for Motor City Five.

M.C. HAMMER
Born Stanley Kirk Burrell on 3/30/1963 in Oakland, California. Rapper/producer/founder/leader of The Posse, an eight-member group of dancers, DJs and singers. Burrell was an Oakland A's batboy in the 1970s; his nickname "The Little Hammer" stemmed from his resemblance to baseball great "Hammerin'" Hank Aaron. Oaktown's 3-5-7 and Ace Juice are members of The Posse. Dropped the M.C. from his name in mid-1991; re-added it in 1995.

M.C. LUCIOUS
Born in Fort Lauderdale, Florida. Female rapper/dance singer.

MC LYTE
Born Lana Moorer on 10/11/1971 in Queens, New York; raised in Brooklyn, New York. Female rapper.

MC NAS-D & DJ FRED
Rap-bass music duo from Tampa, Florida: Darnell Williams (born on 8/15/1971) and Frederick Gray (born on 7/28/1967).

MC REN
Born Lorenzo Patterson in Los Angeles, California. Male rapper. Former member of N.W.A.

MC SERCH
Born Michael Berrin in Queens, New York. White rapper. Former member of 3rd Bass.

MC SKAT KAT & The Stray Mob
MC Skat Kat is an animated character featured in Paula Abdul's "Opposites Attract" video. Created by Michael Patterson and Candace Reckinger. The Stray Mob are Fatz, Taboo, Leo, Micetro, Katleen and Silk.

McANALLY, Mac
Born Lyman McAnally on 7/15/1957 in Red Bay, Alabama. Pop singer/songwriter/guitarist.

McAULEY SCHENKER GROUP
Hard-rock group led by Irish vocalist Robin McAuley (former leader of Far Corporation) and West German-born guitarist Michael Schenker (brother Rudolf is a member of Scorpions). Schenker was also a member of Contraband in 1991.

McBRIDE, Martina
Born Martina Schiff on 7/29/1966 in Medicine Lodge, Kansas; raised in Sharon, Kansas. Country singer.

McCAIN, Edwin
Born on 1/20/1970 in Greenville, South Carolina. Adult Alternative pop-rock singer/songwriter/guitarist.

McCALL, C.W.
Born William Fries on 11/15/1928 in Audubon, Iowa. The character "C.W. McCall" was created for the Mertz Bread Company. Fries was its advertising man. Elected mayor of Ouray, Colorado in the early 1980s.

McCALL, Toussaint
Born in 1934 in Monroe, Louisiana. R&B singer/songwriter/organist.

McCANN, Les
Born on 9/23/1935 in Lexington, Kentucky. Jazz keyboardist/singer.

McCANN, Lila
Born on 12/4/1981 in Steilacoom, Washington. Teen Country singer.

McCANN, Peter
Born on 1/29/1950 in Bridgeport, Connecticut. Pop singer/songwriter/pianist. Wrote Jennifer Warnes' hit "Right Time Of The Night."

McCARTNEY, Jesse
Born on 4/9/1987 in Manhattan, New York. Teen idol singer/songwriter. Member of Dream Street.

McCARTNEY, Paul / Wings
Born James Paul McCartney on 6/18/1942 in Allerton, Liverpool, England. Founding member/bass guitarist of The Beatles. Writer of over 50 Top 10 singles. Married Linda Eastman on 3/12/1969. First solo album in 1970. Formed group Wings in 1971 with Linda (keyboards, backing vocals), Denny Laine (guitar; Moody Blues) and Denny Seiwell (drums). Henry McCullough (guitar) joined in 1972. Seiwell and McCullough left in 1973. In 1975, Joe English (drums) and Thunderclap Newman guitarist Jimmy McCulloch (died of heart failure on 9/27/1979, age 26) joined; both left in 1977. Wings officially disbanded in April 1981. McCartney starred in own movie *Give My Regards To Broad Street* (1984). Knighted by Queen Elizabeth II in 1997. Linda died of cancer on 4/17/1998 (age 56). Married to ex-model Heather Mills, 2002-08.

McCLAIN, Alton, & Destiny
Female disco vocal trio: Alton McClain, Delores Warren and Robyrda Stiger. Warren died in a car crash on 2/22/1985 (age 32).

McClain, Charly
Born Charlotte McClain on 3/26/1956 in Jackson, Tennessee; raised in Memphis, Tennessee. Country singer/songwriter. Married singer Wayne Massey in July 1984.

McCLINTON, Delbert
Born on 11/4/1940 in Lubbock, Texas. Played harmonica on Bruce Channel's hit "Hey Baby."

Leader of The Ron-Dels. Recorded as a duo with Glen Clark.

McCLURE, Bobby
Born on 4/21/1942 in Chicago, Illinois; raised in St. Louis, Missouri. Died on 11/13/1992 (age 50). R&B singer.

McCOMAS, Brian
Born on 5/23/1972 in Bethesda, Maryland; raised in Harrison, Arkansas. Country singer/songwriter.

McCOO, Marilyn, & Billy Davis, Jr.
Husband-and-wife vocal duo. McCoo was born on 9/30/1943 in Jersey City, New Jersey. Davis was born on 6/26/1939 in St. Louis, Missouri. Both were members of The 5th Dimension. Married on 7/26/1969. Duo hosted own summer variety TV series in 1977. McCoo co-hosted TV's *Solid Gold* from 1981-84.

McCORMICK, Gayle
Born in 1949 in St. Louis, Missouri. Former lead singer of Smith.

McCOY, Charlie
Born on 3/28/1941 in Oak Hill, West Virginia. Country harmonica player.

McCOY, Freddie
R&B-jazz vibraphonist/songwriter.

McCOY, Neal
Born Hubert Neal McGaughey on 7/30/1958 in Jacksonville, Texas. Country singer.

McCOY, Van
Born on 1/6/1940 in Washington DC. Died of a heart attack on 7/6/1979 (age 39). Disco songwriter/producer.

McCOYS, The
Pop-rock group from Union City, Indiana: brothers Rick (vocals, guitar) and Randy (drums) Zehringer, Randy Hobbs (bass) and Ronnie Brandon (keyboards). Rick later recorded as Rick Derringer. Hobbs died on 8/5/1993 (age 45).

McCRACKLIN, Jimmy
Born James David Walker on 8/13/1921 in Helena, Arkansas. Blues singer/harmonica player/songwriter. Professional boxer in the mid-1940s. First recorded for Globe in 1945. Own band, the Blues Blasters, in 1949.

McCRAE, George
Born on 10/19/1944 in West Palm Beach, Florida. Disco singer. Married to Gwen McCrae from 1967-77.

McCRAE, Gwen
Born on 12/21/1943 in Pensacola, Florida. Disco singer. Married to George McCrae from 1967-77.

McCRARYS, The
R&B vocal group: siblings Linda, Charity, Alfred and Sam McCrary.

McCREADY, Mindy
Born on 11/30/1975 in Fort Myers, Florida. Country singer.

McCURN, George
Born on 1/21/1920 in Chicago, Illinois. Died in April 1985 (age 65). Male singer.

McDANIEL, Donna
Disco singer.

McDANIELS, Gene
Born on 2/12/1935 in Kansas City, Missouri; raised in Omaha, Nebraska. R&B-pop singer. Appeared in the 1962 movie *It's Trad, Dad*. Recorded and "Bubbled Under" as Universal Jones in 1972.

McDEVITT, Chas., Skiffle Group
Born on 12/4/1934 in Glasgow, Scotland. Singer/guitarist. Chas plays guitar and still performs 'skiffle' music today.

McDONALD, Michael
Born on 2/12/1952 in St. Louis, Missouri. Soft-rock singer/songwriter/keyboardist. First recorded for RCA in 1972. Formerly with Steely Dan and The Doobie Brothers. Married Amy Holland in 1983.

McDOWELL, Ronnie
Born on 3/26/1950 in Portland, Tennessee. Country singer/songwriter.

McDUFF, Brother Jack
Born Eugene McDuffy on 9/17/1926 in Champaign, Illinois. Died of a heart attack on 1/23/2001 (age 74). R&B/jazz-styled organist.

McENTIRE, Reba
Born on 3/28/1955 in Chockie, Oklahoma. Country singer/actress. Appeared in several movies and TV shows. Played "Heather Gummer" in the movie *Tremors*. Starred in own TV sitcom *Reba*.

McFADDEN, Bob, & Dor
Born on 1/19/1923 in East Liverpool, Ohio. Died on 1/7/2000 (age 76). Began career in 1950 as a singing emcee for a special Navy show called *The Bob McFadden Show*. Appeared on the comedy albums *The First Family* and *You Don't Have To Be Jewish*. Dor is poet/singer/songwriter/actor Rod McKuen.

McFADDEN & WHITEHEAD
R&B duo from Philadelphia, Pennsylvania: Gene McFadden and John Whitehead. Wrote songs for many Philadelphia soul acts; defined "The Sound Of Philadelphia." Whitehead recorded solo in 1988. John's sons, Kenny & Johnny, charted as the Whitehead Bros. Whitehead was shot to death on 5/11/2004 (age 56). McFadden died of cancer on 1/27/2006 (age 56).

McFERRIN, Bobby
Born on 3/11/1950 in Manhattan, New York. Unaccompanied, jazz-styled improvisation vocalist. Sang the 1987 *Cosby Show* theme and the Levi's 501 Blues jingle. Father was a baritone with the New York Metropolitan Opera.

McGEE, Parker
Born in Mississippi. Pop singer/songwriter. Wrote two Top 10 hits for England Dan & John Ford Coley.

McGHEE, Stick
Born Granville McGhee on 3/23/1918 in Knoxville, Tennessee. Died of cancer on 8/15/1961 (age 43). Singer/guitarist. Brother of Brownie McGhee.

McGILPIN, Bob
Born in Fort Dix, New Jersey. Disco singer/songwriter.

McGOVERN, Maureen
Born on 7/27/1949 in Youngstown, Ohio. Adult Contemporary singer. Sang theme of TV show *Angie*. Cameo roles in *The Towering Inferno* and *Airplane* (as Sister Angelina). Starred in Broadway's *Pirates Of Penzance* for 14 months.

McGRAW, Tim
Born Samuel Timothy Smith on 5/1/1967 in Delhi, Louisiana; raised in Start, Louisiana. Country singer/songwriter/guitarist. Son of former Major League baseball pitcher Tug McGraw. Married Faith Hill on 10/6/1996. Acted in the movies *Friday Night Lights*, *Black Cloud* and *Flicka*.

McGRIFF, Jimmy
Born on 4/3/1936 in Philadelphia, Pennsylvania. Died on 5/24/2008 (age 72). Jazz organist.

McGUFFEY LANE
Country-rock group from Columbus, Ohio: Bob McNelley (vocals), Terry Efaw and John Schwab (guitars), Stephen Douglass (keyboards), Stephen Reis (bass) and Dave Rangeler (drums). Group name taken from a street in Athens, Ohio. Douglass died in a car accident on 1/12/1984 (age 33). McNelley died from a self-inflicted gunshot wound on 1/7/1987 (age 36).

McGUINN, Mark
Born on 8/19/1968 in Greensboro, North Carolina. Country singer/songwriter/guitarist.

McGUINN, CLARK & HILLMAN
Pop-rock trio: Roger McGuinn (vocals, guitar; born on 7/13/1942), Gene Clark (guitar; born on 11/17/1944; died on 5/24/1991, age 46) and Chris Hillman (bass; born on 6/4/1942). All were founding members of The Byrds.

McGUINNESS FLINT
Rock group formed in England: Tom McGuinness (guitar; Manfred Mann), Hughie Flint (drums), Dennis Coulson (vocals), Graham Lyle (guitar) and Benny Gallagher (bass). Also see Gallagher & Lyle.

McGUIRE, Barry
Born on 10/15/1937 in Oklahoma City, Oklahoma. Folk-rock singer. Member of The New Christy Minstrels from 1962-65.

McGUIRE SISTERS, The
Vocal trio from Middletown, Ohio: sisters Phyllis (born on 2/14/1931), Christine (born on 7/30/1929) and Dorothy (born on 2/13/1926) McGuire. Replaced The Chordettes on *Arthur Godfrey And His Friends* show in 1953. Phyllis went solo in 1964. Reunited in 1986.

McIAN, Peter
Born in California. Pop singer/songwriter. Wrote music for TV's *Starsky And Hutch* and *The Love Boat.*

McINTYRE, Joey
Born on 12/31/1972 in Needham, Massachusetts. Former member of New Kids On The Block.

McKENNITT, Loreena
Born on 2/17/1957 in Morden, Manitoba, Canada. Adult Alternative singer/harpist/songwriter.

McKENZIE, Bob & Doug
The McKenzie brothers are actually Canadian comedians Rick "Bob" Moranis (born on 4/18/1954) and Dave "Doug" Thomas (born on 5/20/1949) of *SCTV*. Both featured (as the McKenzie brothers) in the movie *Strange Brew*. Thomas is the brother of Ian Thomas.

McKENZIE, Scott
Born Philip Blondheim on 1/10/1939 in Jacksonville, Florida; raised in Virginia. Sang with John Phillips (The Mamas & The Papas) in the folk group The Journeymen. Co-wrote The Beach Boys' 1988 #1 hit "Kokomo."

McKNIGHT, Brian
Born on 6/5/1969 in Buffalo, New York. R&B singer/composer. His older brother is Claude McKnight of Take 6.

McKUEN, Rod
Born on 4/29/1933 in Oakland, California. Poet/singer/songwriter/actor. Wrote songs for 20th Century-Fox and Universal movies in the 1950s and 1960s. Co-wrote (with Anita Kerr) and narrated a popular late 1960s series of concept albums beginning with *The Sea.*

McLACHLAN, Sarah
Born on 1/28/1968 in Halifax, Nova Scotia, Canada. Adult Alternative folk-pop singer/songwriter/pianist/guitarist.

McLAIN, Tommy
Born on 3/15/1940 in Jonesville, Louisiana. White "swamp-pop" singer/songwriter.

McLEAN, Don
Born on 10/2/1945 in New Rochelle, New York. Adult Contemporary singer/songwriter/guitarist. The hit "Killing Me Softly With His Song" was inspired by a McLean performance.

McLEAN, Penny
Born on 11/4/1948 in Klagenfurt, Austria. Disco singer. Member of Silver Convention.

McLEAN, Phil
Born on 5/4/1923 in Detroit, Michigan. Died on 5/28/1993 (age 70). Popular DJ at WERE radio in Cleveland, Ohio.

McLOLLIE, Oscar, & Jeanette Baker
Black orchestra leader/baritone singer McLollie first recorded for Mercury in 1950. Baker was a member of the female vocal group The Dots on the Caddy label.

McMAHON, Gerard
Born in Wichita, Kansas. Rock singer/songwriter/guitarist. "Bubbled Under" in 1976 as Gerard.

McNALLY, Larry John
Born in Bangor, Maine. Pop singer/songwriter. Wrote "The Motown Song" by Rod Stewart.

McNAMARA, Robin
Born on 5/5/1947 in Newton, Massachusetts. Male pop singer. One of the original cast members of *Hair.*

McNEAL, Lutricia
Born in Oklahoma City, Oklahoma. Female R&B singer.

McNEELY, Big Jay
Born Cecil James McNeely on 4/29/1927 in Los Angeles, California. R&B tenor saxophonist/bandleader. Originator of the acrobatic, wild honking sax style. Active into the 1980s.

McNICHOL, Kristy & Jimmy
TV/movie stars born in Los Angeles, California: Kristy (born on 9/11/1962), a cast member of TV's *Family* and *Empty Nest*, and her brother Jimmy (born on 7/2/1961). Each starred in several movies.

M'COOL, Shamus
Stand-up comedian Richard Doyle; hosted his own cable TV show *Comic Talk* in Los Angeles.

McPHATTER, Clyde
Born on 11/15/1932 in Durham, North Carolina. Died of a heart attack on 6/13/1972 (age 39). Signed by Billy Ward for The Dominoes in 1950. Left The Dominoes in June 1953 to form own group, The Drifters. Drafted in 1954; returned to sing solo. One of the most influential and distinctive male voices of the R&B era.

McPHEE, Katharine
Born on 3/25/1984 in Los Angeles, California. Female singer. Finished in second place on the 2006 season of TV's *American Idol.*

McPHERSON, Wyatt (Earp)
Born on 7/5/1931 in Louisiana. Died on 12/12/1978 (age 47). Male R&B singer/songwriter.

McRAE, Carmen
Born on 4/8/1922 in Harlem, New York. Died of a stroke on 11/10/1994 (age 72). Jazz singer/pianist.

McSHANN, Jay
Born James McShann on 1/12/1916 in Muskogee, Oklahoma. Died on 12/7/2006 (age 90). R&B pianist/bandleader. Nicknamed "Hootie."

McVIE, Christine
Born Christine Perfect on 7/12/1943 in Bouth, Cumbria, England. Vocalist/keyboardist with Fleetwood Mac since 1970. Married to Fleetwood Mac bassist John McVie, 1968-77.

MEAD, Sister Janet
Born in 1938 in Adelaide, Australia. Nun at the Sisters of Mercy convent. Gained prominence through her weekly cathedral rock masses and weekly radio programs.

MEAT LOAF
Born Marvin Lee Aday on 9/27/1947 in Dallas, Texas. Pop-rock singer. Sang lead vocals on Ted Nugent's *Free-For-All* album. Played "Eddie" in the Los Angeles production and movie of *The Rocky Horror Picture Show*. Appeared in several other movies.

MEAT PUPPETS
Rock trio from Phoenix, Arizona: brothers Curt (vocals, guitar) and Cris (bass) Kirkwood with Derrick Bostrom (drums).

MECO
Born Domenico Monardo on 11/29/1939 in Johnsonburg, Pennsylvania. Disco producer. Played trombone in Cadet Band at West Point. Later moved to New York and became a session musician and arranger. Co-produced Gloria Gaynor's hit "Never Can Say Goodbye."

MEDEIROS, Glenn
Born on 6/24/1970 in Lihue, Kauai, Hawaii (of Portugese parents). Pop singer.

MEDLEY, Bill
Born on 9/19/1940 in Santa Ana, California. Baritone of The Righteous Brothers duo. Co-owner of a Las Vegas nightclub named Kicks with Paul Revere of The Raiders.

MEDLIN, Joe
Born on 4/1/1919 in Norfolk, Virginia. Died on 12/12/1995 (age 76). Black vocalist. Sang with Buddy Johnson's band at age 19.

MEGADETH
Thrash-metal band formed in Los Angeles, California: Dave Mustaine (vocals, guitar), Marty Friedman (guitar), Dave Ellefson (bass) and Nick Menza (drums). Mustaine was an early guitarist with Metallica.

MEGATONS, The
Rock and roll band formed in Memphis, Tennessee: Billy Lee Riley (guitar/harmonica), Jimmy Wilson (piano), Martin Willis (sax), Pat O'Neil (bass) and James Van Eaton (drums).

MEGATRONS, The
Rock and roll group of studio musicians led by John Summers.

MEISNER, Randy
Born on 3/8/1946 in Scottsbluff, Nebraska. Pop-rock singer/bassist. Member of Poco (1968-69), Rick Nelson's Stone Canyon Band (1969-71) and the Eagles (1971-77). Wrote the Eagles hit "Take It To The Limit."

MEL & KIM
Dance duo from London, England: sisters Melanie and Kim Appleby. Mel was born on 7/11/1966; died of cancer on 1/19/1990 (age 23). Kim was born on 8/28/1961.

MEL & TIM
R&B vocal duo from Holly Springs, Mississippi: cousins Mel Hardin and Tim McPherson.

MELANIE
Born Melanie Safka on 2/3/1947 in Queens, New York. Folk-pop singer/songwriter. Neighborhood Records formed by Melanie and her husband/producer Peter Schekeryk.

MELENDEZ, Lisette
Born in Harlem, New York. Female dance singer.

MELLENCAMP, John Cougar
Born on 10/7/1951 in Seymour, Indiana. Rock singer/songwriter/guitarist. Worked outside of music until 1975. Given name Johnny Cougar by David Bowie's manager, Tony DeFries. First recorded for MCA in 1976. Directed and starred in the 1992 movie *Falling from Grace*; leader of the Buzzin' Cousins group that appeared in the movie. Married model Elaine Irwin on 9/5/1992.

MELLO-KINGS
White teen doo-wop group from Mount Vernon, New York: Bob Scholl (lead; died on 8/27/1975, age 30), Jerry Scholl and Eddie Quinn (tenors), Neil Arena (baritone) and Larry Esposito (bass). Originally known as The Mellotones; changed their name to the Mello-Kings since another Mello-Tones group recorded on Gee (see next bio).

MELLO-TONES, The
R&B vocal group from Detroit, Michigan, featuring lead singer Jerry Carr (composed "Rosie Lee").

MELLOW MAN ACE
Born Ulpiano Sergio Reyes on 4/12/1967 in Cuba; raised in Southgate, California. Black Hispanic rapper. His brother Senan is a member of Cypress Hill.

MELODEERS, The
White male doo-wop trio from Brooklyn, New York: Robert Rogers, Phil Seminara and Joe Toscano.

MELVIN, Harold, & The Blue Notes
Melvin was born on 6/25/1939 in Philadelphia, Pennsylvania. Died of a stroke on 3/24/1997 (age 57). R&B singer. The Blue Notes in 1960: Melvin, Bernard Williams, Jesse Gillis, Franklin Peaker and Roosevelt Brodie. Numerous personnel changes. Hit lineup from 1972-76: Melvin, Teddy Pendergrass, Lawrence Brown, Lloyd Parks (replaced by Jerry Cummings in 1974) and Bernard Wilson. David Ebo replaced Pendergrass in late 1976. Peaker died on 11/15/2006 (age 71). Brown died on 4/6/2008 (age 63).

MEMPHIS BLEEK
Born Malik Cox on 6/23/1978 in Brooklyn, New York. Male rapper.

MENA, Maria
Born on 2/19/1986 in Oslo, Norway. Female singer/songwriter.

MEN AT LARGE
R&B vocal duo from Cleveland, Ohio: David Tolliver and Jason Champion.

MEN AT WORK
Pop-rock group from Melbourne, Australia: Colin James Hay (lead singer, guitar; born on 6/29/1953), Ron Strykert (lead guitar; born on 8/18/1957), Greg Ham (sax, keyboards; born on 9/27/1953), John Rees (bass) and Jerry Speiser (drums). Speiser and Rees left in 1984.

MENDES, Sergio, & Brasil '66
Born on 2/11/1941 in Niteroi, Brazil. Pianist/bandleader. Brasil '66 consisted of Lani Hall and Janis Hensen (vocals), Joses Soares (percussion), Bob Matthews (bass) and Jao Palma (drums). Hall married Herb Alpert.

MEN OF VIZION
R&B vocal group from Brooklyn, New York: George Spencer, Corley Randolph, Prathan "Spanky" Williams, Brian Deramus and Desmond Greggs.

MENUDO
Teen vocal group from Puerto Rico. The superstar group of Latin America. Many personnel changes due to a rule that members must retire at age 16. Ricky Martin was a member from 1984-89.

MEN WITHOUT HATS
Techno-rock band from Montreal, Quebec, Canada: brothers Ivan Doroschuk (vocals), Stefan Doroschuk (guitar) and Colin Doroschuk (keyboards), with Allan McCarthy (drums; died of AIDS on 8/11/1995, age 38).

ME PHI ME
Born Laron Wilburn in Flint, Michigan. Male rapper. Me Phi Me is Greek for Fraternity Of One.

MERCEDES
Born Raquel Miller in 1978 in Detroit, Michigan. Female rapper.

MERCHANT, Natalie
Born on 10/26/1963 in Jamestown, New York. Alternative-rock singer/songwriter. Lead singer of 10,000 Maniacs from 1981-93.

MERCURY, Freddie
Born Farrokh Bulsara on 9/5/1946 in Zanzibar, Tanzania. Died of AIDS on 11/24/1991 (age 45). Lead singer of Queen. Also recorded as Larry Lurex.

MERCY
Pop group from Florida: James Marvell, Ronnie Caudill, Roger Fuentes, Buddy Good, Debbie Lewis and Brenda McNish.

MERCYME
Christian pop group formed in Oklahoma City, Oklahoma: Bart Millard (vocals), Mike Scheuchzer (guitar), Nathan Cochran (bass) and Robby Shaffer (drums).

MERRY-GO-ROUND, The
Pop-rock group from Hawthorne, California: Emitt Rhodes (vocals), Gary Kato (guitar), Bill Rinehart (bass; The Leaves) and Joel Larson (drums; The Grass Roots).

MESA
Pop group from Los Angeles, California: Ed Rekers (vocals, guitar), Jeff Des Enfants (percussion), Roger Paglia (bass) and Carmine Notaro (drums).

MESSENGERS
Rock group from Milwaukee, Wisconsin: Jeff Taylor (vocals), Pete Barans (guitar), Michael Morgan (organ), Greg Jeresek (bass) and Augie Jurishica (drums).

MESSINA, Jo Dee
Born on 8/25/1970 in Framingham, Massachusetts; raised in Holliston, Massachusetts. Country singer.

METALLICA
Heavy metal band formed in Los Angeles, California: James Hetfield (vocals, guitar; born on 8/3/1963), Kirk Hammett (guitar; born on 11/18/1962), Jason Newsted (bass; born on 3/4/1963) and Lars Ulrich (drums; born on 12/26/1963). Original guitarist Dave Mustaine left in 1982 to form Megadeth. Original bassist Cliff Burton was killed in a bus crash on 9/27/1986 (age 24). Newsted left the group in January 2001; replaced by Rob Trujillo.

METERS, The
R&B instrumental group formed in New Orleans, Louisiana: Arthur Neville (keyboards; brother of Aaron Neville), Leo Nocentelli (guitar), George Porter (bass) and Joseph Modeliste (drums). Group disbanded in 1977, when Art, Aaron, and brothers Charles and Cyril formed The Neville Brothers.

METHOD MAN
Born Clifford Smith on 4/1/1971 in Staten Island, New York. Male rapper. Member of Wu-Tang Clan. Also known as Johnny Blaze or Meth-Tical or The Ticalion Stallion. Starred in the 2001 movie *How High*.

METROS, The
R&B vocal group: James Buckman, Gordon Dunn, Arthur Mitchell, Robert Suttles and Paul Williams.

METRO STATION
Pop band formed in Los Angeles, California: Mason Musso (vocals), Trace Cyrus (guitar), Blake Healy (bass) and Anthony Improgo (drums). Cyrus is the son of Billy Ray Cyrus and the brother of Miley Cyrus (Hannah Montana).

MFSB
Group of studio musicians based at Philadelphia Sigma Sound Studios owned by writer/producers Kenny Gamble and Leon Huff for their own label, Philadelphia International. Recorded earlier as The Music Makers, The James Boys and Family. Name stands for "Mother, Father, Sister, Brother."

M:G
Born Maribel Gonzalez in San Francisco, California. Female dance singer.

M.I.A.
Born Maya Arulpragasam on 7/17/1977 in London, England; raised in India. Female techno artist.

MIA X
Born Mia Young in New Orleans, Louisiana; moved to Queens, New York. Female rapper. Member of Tru.

MICHAEL, George / Wham!
Born Georgios Panayiotou on 6/25/1963 in East Finchley, North London, England; raised in Radlett, Hertfordshire, England (Greek parents). Wham!, formed in early 1980s, centered around Michael's vocals and songwriting, and included Andrew Ridgeley (born on 1/26/1963 in Bushey, England) on guitar. Their association ended in 1986. Ridgeley pursued race car driving, then solo career in 1990.

MICHAELS, Lee
Born on 11/24/1945 in Los Angeles, California. Rock singer/songwriter/keyboardist.

MICHAELSON, Ingrid
Born in 1979 in Staten Island, New York. Female singer/songwriter.

MICHEL, Pras
Born Prakazrel Michel on 10/19/1972 in Harlem, New York. Member of The Fugees.

MICHELE, Yvette
Born in Brooklyn, New York. Female singer/rapper.

MICHEL'LE
Born Michel'le Toussant in Los Angeles, California. R&B-dance singer. Former vocalist with The World Class Wreckin Cru.

MICKEY & SYLVIA
R&B-rock and roll duo: McHouston "Mickey" Baker and Sylvia Vanderpool. Baker (born on 10/15/1925 in Louisville, Kentucky) was a prolific session guitarist. Sylvia (born on 3/6/1936 in Harlem, New York) began solo career in 1973. Their son Joey was leader of West Street Mob.

MIDI MAXI & EFTI
Female pop trio of 16-year-olds (in 1992) formed in Sweden: twin sisters Midi and Maxi (from Ethiopia) with Efti (from the warring Ethiopian province of Eritrea).

MIDLER, Bette
Born on 12/1/1945 in Honolulu, Hawaii (Jewish parents from New Jersey). Adult Contemporary singer/actress. In the Broadway show *Fiddler On The Roof* for three years. Barry Manilow was her arranger/accompanist in early years. Nominated for an Oscar for her performance in *The Rose* (1979). Also in movies *Down And Out In Beverly Hills, Ruthless People, Beaches, For The Boys* and others. Married commodities trader/performance artist Martin von Haselberg on 12/14/1984.

MIDNIGHT OIL
Rock band formed in Sydney, Australia: Peter Garrett (vocals), Martin Rotsey (guitar), James Moginie (keyboards), Dwayne Hillman (bass) and Rob Hirst (drums). Garrett later became involved in politics and was named Australian Arts and Environment Minister in November 2007.

MIDNIGHT STAR
R&B-dance group from Louisville, Kentucky: Belinda Lipscomb (vocals), brothers Reggie and Vince Calloway (horns), Jeff Cooper (guitar), Ken Gant (keyboards), Melvin Gentry (bass) and Bill Simmons (drums). The Calloway brothers later formed Calloway.

MIGHTY CLOUDS OF JOY
Gospel vocal group from Los Angeles, California: Willie Joe Ligon, Johnny Martin, Elmo Franklin, Richard Wallace, Leon Polk and David Walker (Bunker Hill). Martin died in 1987.

MIGHTY DUB KATS, The
Studio dance group assembled by producer Norman "Fatboy Slim" Cook.

MIGHTY MIGHTY BOSSTONES, The
Ska-rock group from Boston, Massachusetts: Dicky Barrett (vocals), Nate Albert (guitar), Ben Carr (dancer), Kevin Lenear, Tim Burton and Dennis Brockenborough (horns), Joe Gittleman (bass) and Joe Sirois (drums).

MIKA
Born Mica Penniman on 8/18/1983 in Beirut, Lebanon; later based in London, England. Male singer/songwriter.

MIKAILA
Born Mikaila Enriquez on 12/15/1986 in Edmond, Oklahoma; raised in Dallas, Texas. Female teen pop singer.

MIKE + THE MECHANICS
Pop-rock group formed in England: Mike Rutherford (bass; Genesis), Paul Carrack and Paul Young (vocals; Sad Café), Adrian Lee (keyboards) and Peter Van Hooke (drums). Young, not to be confused with the same-named solo singer, died of a heart attack on 7/15/2000 (age 53).

MILBURN, Amos
Born on 4/1/1927 in Houston, Texas. Died of a stroke on 1/3/1980 (age 52). Blues/boogie-woogie singer/pianist. Moved to Los Angeles in 1946 and soon started string of hits for the Aladdin label. Highly original style influenced several future stars, including Fats Domino.

MILES, Buddy
Born George Miles on 9/5/1947 in Omaha, Nebraska. Died on 2/26/2008 (age 60). R&B singer/drummer. Prominent session musician. Worked as sideman in the Dick Clark Revue, 1963-64. With Wilson Pickett, 1965-66. In Michael Bloomfield's Electric Flag, 1967. In Jimi Hendrix's Band Of Gypsys, 1969-70. Was the voice of The California Raisins, the claymation TV ad characters.

MILES, Garry
Born James Cason on 11/27/1939 in Nashville, Tennessee. Lead singer of The Statues and Brenda Lee's backing group, The Casuals. Also recorded as Buzz Cason.

MILES, John
Born on 4/23/1949 in Jarrow, England. Rock vocalist/guitarist/keyboardist. Guest vocalist with the Alan Parsons Project.

MILES, Lenny
Born on 12/22/1934 in Fort Worth, Texas. Died of cancer in 1962 (age 27). R&B singer.

MILES, Robert
Born Roberto Concina on 11/3/1969 in Fleurier, Switzerland; raised in Fagagna, Italy. DJ/dance musician.

MILESTONE
All-star R&B group: brothers Kenneth (Babyface), Melvin and Kevon Edmonds (both from After 7), with K-Ci & JoJo.

MILIAN, Christina
Born Christina Flores on 9/26/1981 in Jersey City, New Jersey; raised in Waldorf, Maryland. R&B singer/songwriter.

MILITIA
Duo of rap producers Emanuel Dean and Shawn Billups. Featuring rappers Diz and Devious.

MILLER, Chuck
Born in California. Rock and roll singer/pianist.

MILLER, Clint
Born Isaac Clinton Miller on 5/24/1939 in Ferguson, North Carolina. Teen rockabilly singer.

MILLER, Frankie
Born on 12/17/1931 in Victoria, Texas. Country singer/songwriter. Appeared on *Jubilee USA* on ABC-TV.

MILLER, Frankie
Born on 11/2/1949 in Glasgow, Scotland. Blues-tinged rock singer/songwriter.

MILLER, Jody
Born Myrna Joy Brooks on 11/29/1941 in Phoenix, Arizona; raised in Blanchard, Oklahoma. Country singer.

MILLER, Mitch
Born on 7/4/1911 in Rochester, New York. Producer/conductor/arranger. A&R executive for both Columbia and Mercury Records. Best known for his sing-along albums and TV show (1961-64).

MILLER, Mrs.
Born Elva Miller on 10/5/1907 in Joplin, Missouri. Died on 6/28/1997 (age 89). Tone-deaf singer. As a joke, Capitol released her first album as *Mrs. Miller's Greatest Hits*.

MILLER, Ned
Born Henry Ned Miller on 4/12/1925 in Rains, Utah. Country singer/songwriter. To California in 1956. Signed with Fabor in 1956. Wrote the Gale Storm and Bonnie Guitar hit "Dark Moon."

MILLER, Roger
Born on 1/2/1936 in Fort Worth, Texas; raised in Erick, Oklahoma. Died of cancer on 10/25/1992 (age 56). Country singer/songwriter/guitarist. To Nashville in the mid-1950s, began songwriting career. With Faron Young as writer/drummer in 1962. Own TV show in 1966. Songwriter of 1985's Broadway musical *Big River*.

MILLER, Steve, Band
Born on 10/5/1943 in Milwaukee, Wisconsin; raised in Dallas, Texas. Rock singer/songwriter/guitarist. Formed band in high school, The Marksmen, which included Boz Scaggs. While at the University of Wisconsin-Madison, Miller led the blues-rock band the Ardells, later known as the Fabulous Night Trains, featuring Scaggs. After graduating, studied literature at the University of Copenhagen. To San Francisco in 1966; formed the Steve Miller Band, which featured a fluctuating lineup.

MILLIONS LIKE US
Pop-rock duo from England: John O'Kane (vocals) and Jeep MacNichol (guitar, keyboards).

MILLI VANILLI
Europop act formed in Germany by producer Frank Farian (created Boney M and Far Corporation). Milli Vanilli is Turkish for positive energy. Originally thought to be Rob Pilatus (born on 6/8/1965 in Germany) and Fabrice Morvan (born on 5/14/1966 in France). Duo was stripped of its 1989 Best New Artist Grammy Award when it was revealed that they didn't sing on their debut album. Actual vocalists are Charles Shaw, John Davis and Brad Howe. Pilatus died of a drug overdose on 4/2/1998 (age 32).

MILLS, Frank
Born on 6/27/1942 in Toronto, Ontario, Canada. Pianist/producer/arranger.

MILLS, Garry
Born on 10/13/1941 in West Wickham, Kent, England. Pop singer.

MILLS, Hayley
Born on 4/18/1946 in London, England. Daughter of English actor John Mills. Disney teen movie star of *Pollyanna, The Parent Trap, In Search Of The Castaways* and others. Her son, Crispian Mills, is lead singer of Kula Shaker.

MILLS, Stephanie
Born on 3/22/1957 in Brooklyn, New York. R&B singer/actress. Played "Dorothy" in Broadway's *The Wiz*. Briefly married to Jeffrey Daniels of Shalamar in 1980.

MILLS BROTHERS, The
Legendary black family vocal group from Piqua, Ohio: father John Mills (died on 12/8/1967, age 78), with sons Herbert (died on 4/12/1989, age 67), Harry (died on 6/28/1982, age 68) and Donald (died on 11/13/1999, age 84) Mills.

MILSAP, Ronnie
Born on 1/16/1943 in Robbinsville, North Carolina. Country singer/pianist/guitarist. Blind since birth; multi-instrumentalist by age 12. With J.J. Cale band; own band from 1965. First charted (Bubbling Under) in 1965 on Scepter Records.

MILTON, Roy
Born on 7/31/1907 in Wynnewood, Oklahoma; raised in Tulsa, Oklahoma. Died of a stroke on 9/18/1983 (age 76). R&B singer/drummer/bandleader.

MIMMS, Garnet
Born Garrett Mimms on 11/26/1933 in Ashland, Kentucky. Sang in gospel groups the Evening Stars, Norfolk Four, Harmonizing Four. Formed group The Gainors in 1958.

MIMS
Born Shawn Mims on 3/22/1981 in Manhattan, New York. Male rapper.

MINA
Born Anna Mazzini on 3/25/1940 in Cremona, Italy. Female singer.

MINDBENDERS, The
Rock and roll band from Manchester, England: Wayne Fontana (lead singer; born Glyn Geoffrey Ellis on 10/28/45), Eric Stewart (lead guitar, vocals), Bob Lang (bass) and Ric Rothwell (drums). Fontana left in October 1965. Graham Gouldman joined in 1968. Stewart and Gouldman were later members of Hotlegs and 10cc.

MINEO, Sal
Born Salvatore Mineo on 1/10/1939 in the Bronx, New York. Stabbed to death on 2/12/1976 (age 37). Singer/actor. Starred with James Dean in the 1955 movie classic *Rebel Without A Cause*.

MINIATURE MEN, The
Studio band under the direction of Hank Levine.

MINK DeVILLE
Rock trio formed in San Francisco, California: Willy DeVille (vocals, guitar), Ruben Siguenza (bass) and Thomas Allen (drums).

MINOGUE, Kylie
Born on 5/28/1968 in Melbourne, Australia. Dance singer/actress. Regular on the Australian soap opera *Neighbours*.

MINOR, Shane
Born on 5/3/1968 in Modesto, California. Country singer.

MINOR DETAIL
Pop duo from Ireland: brothers John and Willie Hughes.

MINT CONDITION
R&B group from Minneapolis, Minnesota: Stokley Williams (vocals, drums), Homer O'Dell (guitar), Larry Waddell and Keri Lewis (keyboards), Jeff Allen (sax) and Ricky Kinchen (bass). Lewis married Toni Braxton on 4/21/2001.

MIRACLES, The
R&B vocal group from Detroit, Michigan: Smokey Robinson (born on 2/19/1940), Claudette Rogers (born in 1942), Bobby Rogers (born on 2/19/1940), Ronnie White (born on 4/5/1939) and Warren Moore (born on 11/19/1939). Claudette Rogers retired in 1964; married to Robinson from 1958-86. Bobby Rogers married Wanda Young of The Marvelettes. Robinson wrote many hit songs for the group and other Motown artists. Their first single release was "Got A Job" in 1958 on End 1016. Robinson went solo in 1972; replaced by Billy Griffin. White died of leukemia on 8/26/1995 (age 56).

MIRANDA
Born in 1976 in Burbank, California. Female techno-dance singer/songwriter.

MISSING PERSONS
New-wave group formed in Los Angeles, California: Dale Bozzio (vocals), her then-husband Terry Bozzio (drums), Warren Cuccurullo (guitar), Patrick O'Hearn (bass, synthesizer) and Chuck Wild (keyboards). All but Wild were with Frank Zappa's band. Disbanded in 1986. Terry Bozzio worked with Jeff Beck in 1989. Cuccurullo joined Duran Duran in 1990.

MISSJONES
Born Tarsha Jones in Brooklyn, New York. Female hip-hop singer/songwriter.

MISTA
R&B vocal group: Darryl Allen, Bobby Wilson, Brandon Brown and Byron Reeder.

MISTA GRIMM
Born Rojai Trawick on 8/21/1973 in West Covina, California. Male rapper.

MIS-TEEQ
Female R&B vocal trio from London, England: Alesha Dixon, Sabrina Washington and Su-Elise Nash.

MR. BIG
Pop-disco band from Oxford, England: Jeff Dicken (vocals), Ed Carter (guitar), Robert Hirschman (bass) and Vince Chalk (drums).

MR. BIG
Rock band from San Francisco, California: Eric Martin (vocals), Paul Gilbert (guitar), Billy Sheehan (bass) and Pat Torpey (drums).

MR. CHEEKS
Born Terrance Kelly on 3/28/1971 in Queens, New York. Male rapper. Former member of Lost Boyz.

MR. C THE SLIDE MAN
Born William Perry in Brooklyn, New York. R&B singer/rapper.

MR. MISTER
Pop-rock group formed in Los Angeles, California: Richard Page (vocals, bass), Steve Farris (guitar), Steve George (keyboards) and Pat Mastelotto (drums). Also see Larsen-Feiten Band and Pages.

MR. PRESIDENT
Dance group consisting of German-born singers T-Seven and Lady Danii with British-born rapper DJ Lazy Dee.

MR. VEGAS
Born Clifford Smith in 1975 in St. Andrew, Jamaica. Male reggae singer.

MISTRESS
Rock group from Georgia: Charlie Williams (vocals), Kenny Hopkins (guitar), Danny Chauncey (guitar), David Brown (bass) and Chris Paulsen (drums).

MITCHELL, Chad, Trio
Born on 12/5/1936 in Portland, Oregon. Folk singer. His trio included Mike Koluk and Joe Frazier. Mitchell left in 1965. John Denver joined and group was renamed The Mitchell Trio.

MITCHELL, Guy
Born Al Cernik on 2/27/1927 in Detroit, Michigan. Died on 7/1/1999 (age 72). Sang briefly with Carmen Cavallaro's orchestra in the late 1940s. Appearances in several TV series. In the movies *Those Redheads From Seattle* and *Red Garters*. Married Playboy Playmate Elsa Sorenson (aka Dane Arden).

MITCHELL, Joni
Born Roberta Joan Anderson on 11/7/1943 in Fort McLeod, Alberta, Canada; raised in Saskatoon, Saskatchewan, Canada. Singer/songwriter/guitarist/pianist. Moved to New York in 1966. Wrote the hits "Both Sides Now" and "Woodstock." Married to her producer/bassist, Larry Klein, from 1982-94.

MITCHELL, Kim
Born Joseph Kim Mitchell on 7/10/1952 in Sarnia, Ontario, Canada. Male rock singer/guitarist.

MITCHELL, Willie
Born on 1/3/1928 in Ashland, Mississippi; raised in Memphis, Tennessee. R&B keyboardist/arranger/producer. Led house band and later became president of Hi Records.

MITCHUM, Robert
Born on 8/6/1917 in Bridgeport, Connecticut. Died of cancer on 7/1/1997 (age 79). Legendary actor. Father of actor Chris Mitchum.

MIXTURES, The
Pop group from Melbourne, Australia: Peter Williams (vocals), Fred Wieland (guitar), Chris Spooner (bass) and Don Lebler (drums).

MOB, The
Pop group from Chicago, Illinois: Artie Herrera (vocals), Al Herrera, Jimmy "Ford" Franz, Mike "Paris" Sistak, Tony "Roman" Nedza, Gary "Stevens" Beisber, Bobby Raffino and Jimmy "Soul" Holvay. Holvay and Beisber wrote several hits for The Buckinghams.

MOBB DEEP
Rap duo from Queens, New York: Havoc and Prodigy. Both are members of QB Finest.

MOBY
Born Richard Melville Hall on 9/11/1965 in Harlem, New York; raised in Darien, Connecticut. Techno-dance artist.

MOBY GRAPE
Rock group from San Francisco, California: Alexander "Skip" Spence (vocals, guitar), Jerry Miller and Peter Lewis (guitars), Bob Mosley (bass) and Don Stevenson (drums). Spence, former drummer with Jefferson Airplane, left in 1968. Lewis is the son of actress Loretta Young. Spence died of cancer on 4/16/1999 (age 52).

MOCEDADES
Vocal group from Bilbao, Spain: siblings Amaya, Izaskum and Roberto Amezaga, with Jose Urien, Carlos Uribarri and Javier Barrenechea.

MODELS
Pop-rock group formed in Melbourne, Australia: Sean Kelly (vocals, guitar), Roger Mason (keyboards), James Valentine (saxophone), James Freud (bass) and Barton Price (drums).

MODERNAIRES, The
Vocal group from Buffalo, New York: husband-and-wife Hal Dickinson and Paula Kelly, Chuck Goldstein, Bill Conway and Ralph Brewster. Dickinson died on 11/18/1970 (age 59). Kelly died on 4/2/1992 (age 72).

MODERN ENGLISH
New wave band formed in 1978 in Colchester, England: Robbie Grey (vocals), Gary McDowell (guitar), Stephen Walker (keyboards), Michael Conroy (bass) and Richard Brown (drums).

MODERN JAZZ QUARTET
Highly influential Jazz band: Milt Jackson (vibraphone), John Lewis (piano), Percy Heath (bass) and Kenny Clarke (drums). Connie Kay replaced Clarke in 1955. Known for their improvisational style. Jackson died on 10/9/1999 (age 76). Lewis died on 3/29/2001 (age 80), Heath died on 4/28/2005 (age 81). Clarke died on 1/26/1985 (age 71). Kay died on 11/30/1994 (age 67).

MODERN LOVERS, The
Punk-rock group formed in Boston, Massachusetts: Jonathan Richman (vocals, guitar), Jerry Harrison (keyboards), Ernie Brooks (bass) and David Robinson (drums). Harrison joined Talking Heads. Robinson joined The Cars.

MODEST MOUSE
Alternative-rock trio from Isaaquah, Washington: Isaac Brock (vocals, guitar), Eric Judy (bass) and Jeremiah Green (drums).

MODJO
Dance duo from France: Yann Destagnol and Romain Branchart.

MODUGNO, Domenico
Born on 1/9/1928 in Polignano a Mare, Italy. Died of a heart attack on 8/6/1994 (age 66). Singer/actor.

MOJO MEN, The
Pop-rock band formed in Coral Gables, Florida: Jimmy Alaimo (vocals, guitar), Paul Curcio (guitar), Don Metchick (organ) and Dennis DeCarr (drums). Jimmy, cousin of Steve Alaimo, died of heart failure on 6/30/1992 (age 53).

MOKENSTEF
Black female vocal trio from Los Angeles, California: Monifa, Kenya and Stephanie. All three were cheerleaders at Morningside High School in Inglewood, California.

MOLLY HATCHET
Southern-rock group from Jacksonville, Florida: Danny Joe Brown (vocals), Dave Hlubek, Duane Roland and Steve Holland (guitars), Banner

MOLLY HATCHET — cont'd
Thomas (bass) and Bruce Crump (drums). Jimmy Farrar replaced Brown in 1980; Brown returned and replaced Farrar in 1983. Holland and Thomas left in 1983; John Galvin (keyboards) and Riff West (bass) joined. Brown died of diabetes complications on 3/10/2005 (age 53). Roland died on 6/19/2006 (age 53).

MOMENTS, The
Folk singing group put together by producer Lee Hazlewood.

MOMENTS, The
R&B vocal trio from Hackensack, New Jersey, featuring Mark Greene (falsetto lead). Greene left after first record; replaced by William Brown (lead; born on 6/30/1946) and Al Goodman (born on 3/31/1947). Harry Ray (born on 12/15/1946) joined after "Love On A Two-Way Street" in 1970. Became Ray, Goodman & Brown in 1978. Ray died of a stroke on 10/1/1992 (age 45).

MONACO
Rock duo from England: Peter Hook (of New Order) and David Potts.

MONA LISA
Born on 11/20/1979 in Brooklyn, New York. Female hip-hop singer.

MONARCHS, The
Pop band from Louisville, Kentucky: Mike Gibson (lead vocals), Bob Lange, Lou Lange and Jimmy Wells (backing vocals), Don Leffler (guitar), Leon Middleton (sax), Paul Schuler (trumpet), Dusty Miller (bass) and Butch Snyder (drums). The Langes are cousins. Bob Lange died on 9/26/1994 (age 51).

MONCHY & ALEXANDRA
Male-female Latin vocal duo from the Dominican Republic: Ramon "Monchy" Rijo (born on 9/19/1977) and Alexandra Cabrera (born on 10/19/1978).

MONDAY, Julie
Born in Detroit, Michigan. Pop singer.

MONDO ROCK
Rock group formed in Australia: Ross Wilson (vocals), Eric McCusker (guitar), Duncan Veall (keyboards), Andrew Ross (sax), James Gillard (bass) and J.J. Hackett (drums).

MONEY, Eddie
Born Edward Mahoney on 3/2/1949 in Brooklyn, New York. Rock singer/songwriter. Discovered and subsequently managed by the late West Coast promoter Bill Graham. Formerly an officer with the New York Police Department.

MONEY, JT
Born Jeff Tompkins in Florida. Male rapper. Former leader of the rap duo Poison Clan.

MONICA
Born Monica Arnold on 10/24/1980 in Atlanta, Georgia. Female hip-hop singer. Began singing in church choir as a youth. Discovered by producer Dallas Austin at a local talent showcase in 1993.

MONIFAH
Born Monifah Carter on 1/28/1968 in Harlem, New York. Female R&B singer/actress. Sang backup for Maxi Priest.

MONITORS, The
R&B vocal group: Sandra and John "Maurice" Fagin, Warren Harris and Richard Street. Street, formerly with the Distants, joined The Temptations in 1971. Also recorded as The Majestics.

MONK, T.S.
Born Thelonious Sphere Monk on 12/27/1949 in Harlem, New York. R&B singer/drummer. Son of legendary jazz pianist Thelonious Monk.

MONKEES, The
Pop group formed in 1965 in Los Angeles, California. Members chosen from over 400 applicants for new Columbia TV series. Consisted of Davy Jones (vocals; born on 12/30/1945 in Manchester, England), Michael Nesmith (guitar, vocals; born on 12/30/1942 in Houston, Texas), Peter Tork (bass, vocals; born on 2/13/1944 in Washington DC) and Micky Dolenz (drums, vocals; born on 3/8/1945 in Tarzana, California). Jones had been a racehorse jockey, and appeared in London musicals *Oliver* and *Pickwick*. Nesmith had done session work for Stax/Volt. Tork had been in the Phoenix Singers. Dolenz had appeared in the TV series *Circus Boy*, using the name Mickey Braddock in 1956. Group starred in the movie *Head* (1968) and 58 episodes of *The Monkees* TV show, 1966-68. Tork left in 1968. Group disbanded in 1970. Re-formed (minus Nesmith) in 1986 and again (with Nesmith) in 1996.

MONO
Dance duo from England: Siobahn DeMare (female vocals) and Martin Virgo (instruments).

MONOTONES, The
R&B vocal group from Newark, New Jersey: Charles Patrick (lead), Warren Davis (1st tenor), George Malone (2nd tenor), Warren Ryanes (baritone), Frank Smith (bass) and John Ryanes (bass). John Ryanes died on 5/30/1972 (age 31). Warren Ryanes died in June 1982 (age 45). Smith died of cancer on 11/26/2000 (age 61). Malone died of a stroke on 10/5/2007 (age 67).

MONRO, Matt
Born Terrence Parsons on 12/1/1930 in London, England. Died of liver cancer on 2/7/1985 (age 54). Sang with Cyril Stapleton's Orchestra before going solo.

MONROE, Vaughn
Born on 10/7/1911 in Akron, Ohio. Died on 5/21/1973 (age 61). Big-voiced baritone/trumpeter/bandleader. Very popular on radio, and featured in several movies.

MONROES, The
Pop-rock group from San Diego, California: Jesus Ortiz (vocals), Rusty Jones (guitar), Eric Denton (keyboards), Bob "Monroe" Davis (bass) and Jonnie Gilstrap (drums).

MONTANA, Hannah — see CYRUS, Miley

MONTANAS, The
Pop-rock group from Dudley, England: John Jones (vocals), Will Hayward (guitar), Terry Rowley (keyboards), Jake Elcock (bass) and Graham Hollis (drums).

MONTE, Lou
Born on 4/2/1917 in Lyndhurst, New Jersey. Died on 6/12/1989 (age 72). Italian-styled novelty singer/guitarist.

MONTENEGRO, Hugo
Born on 9/2/1925 in Brooklyn, New York. Died of emphysema on 2/6/1981 (age 55). Conductor/composer/arranger.

MONTENEGRO, Pilar
Born Maria Lopez in Mexico. Latin singer/actress.

MONTEZ, Chris
Born Ezekiel Christopher Montanez on 1/17/1943 in Los Angeles, California. Male Latin singer. Rock and roll style on the Monogram label; Adult Contemporary style on the A&M label.

MONTGOMERY, John Michael
Born on 1/20/1965 in Danville, Kentucky. Country singer/guitarist. Younger brother of Eddie of Montgomery Gentry.

MONTGOMERY, Melba
Born on 10/14/1938 in Iron City, Tennessee; raised in Florence, Alabama. Country singer/guitarist/fiddler.

MONTGOMERY, Wes
Born John Leslie Montgomery on 3/6/1925 in Indianapolis, Indiana. Died on 6/15/1968 (age 43). Jazz guitarist.

MONTGOMERY GENTRY
Country vocal duo of Eddie Montgomery and Troy Gentry. Montgomery was born Gerald Edward Montgomery on 9/30/1963 in Danville, Kentucky; raised in Nicholasville, Kentucky. Older brother of John Michael Montgomery. Gentry was born on 4/5/1967 in Lexington, Kentucky.

MOODY BLUES, The
Art-rock group formed in Birmingham, England: Denny Laine (guitar, vocals; born on 10/29/1944), Ray Thomas (flute, vocals; born on 12/29/1941), Mike Pinder (keyboards, Mellotron, vocals; born on 12/27/1941), Clint Warwick (bass; born on 6/25/1939; died of liver failure on 5/15/2004, age 64) and Graeme Edge (drums; born on 3/30/1941). Laine and Warwick left in the summer of 1966; replaced by Justin Hayward (lead vocals, lead guitar; born on 10/14/1946) & John Lodge (vocals, bass; born on 7/20/1945). Laine joined Paul McCartney's Wings in 1971. Switzerland-born Patrick Moraz (born on 6/24/1948; former keyboardist of Yes) replaced Pinder in 1978; left group in early 1992. Thomas retired in 2003.

MOONEY, Art
Born on 1/26/1913 in Lowell, Massachusetts. Died on 9/9/1993 (age 80). Orchestra leader.

MOONGLOWS, The
R&B vocal group formed in Cleveland, Ohio: Harvey Fuqua, Bobby Lester, Alexander Graves and Prentiss Barnes, with Billy Johnson (guitar). Lester died on 10/15/1980 (age 50). Johnson died on 4/29/1987 (age 63). Barnes died on 9/30/2006 (age 81). Graves died on 10/15/2006 (age 76).

MOONLION
Studio instrumental disco group assembled by producers Rick Bleiweiss and Bill Stahl.

MOORE, Abra
Born on 6/8/1969 in San Diego, California; raised in Puna, Hawaii. Female alternative pop-rock singer/songwriter/guitarist/actress.

MOORE, Bob
Born on 11/30/1932 in Nashville, Tennessee. Top session bass player. Member of the Owen Bradley Quintet. Led the band on Roy Orbison's sessions for Monument Records. Also worked as sideman for Elvis Presley, Brenda Lee, Pat Boone and others.

MOORE, Bobby
R&B-disco singer/bassist. Session work for J.J. Cale, Bob Dylan and Moby Grape.

MOORE, Bobby, & The Rhythm Aces
Born on 7/17/1930 in New Orleans, Louisiana; later based in Montgomery, Alabama. Died of kidney failure on 2/1/2006 (age 75). R&B tenor saxophonist. The Rhythm Aces: Bobby's brother Larry Moore (alto sax), Chico Jenkins (vocals), Marion Sledge (guitar), Clifford Laws (keyboards), Joe Frank (bass) and John Baldwin (drums).

MOORE, Chanté
Born on 2/17/1967 in San Francisco, California. Female R&B-dance singer. Married to actor Kadeem Hardison from 1996-2000. Married Kenny Lattimore on 1/1/2002.

MOORE, Dorothy
Born on 10/13/1947 in Jackson, Mississippi. R&B singer. Lead singer of The Poppies.

MOORE, Gary
Born on 4/4/1952 in Belfast, Ireland. Rock guitarist with Thin Lizzy (1974, 1978-79) and BBM.

MOORE, Johnny
Born on 10/20/1906 in Austin, Texas; raised in Phoenix, Arizona. Died on 1/6/1969 (age 62). Singer/guitarist. Moved to Los Angeles, California; formed his Three Blazers with Charles Brown (piano, vocals) and Eddie Williams (bass). Joined by Moore's younger brother Oscar Moore in 1947, who was formerly with the King Cole Trio. Brown left in January 1949; replaced by Billy Valentine. Frankie Ervin sang lead vocals from 1953-55 (later joined The Shields). Oscar Moore died on 10/8/1981 (age 65). Williams died on 2/18/1995 (age 82). Brown died of heart failure on 1/21/1999 (age 76).

MOORE, Jackie
Born in 1946 in Jacksonville, Florida. Female R&B singer.

MOORE, Mandy
Born Amanda Moore on 4/10/1984 in Nashua, New Hampshire. Pop singer/actress. Starred in the movies *A Walk To Remember*, *Chasing Liberty* and *License To Wed*.

MOORE, Melba
Born Melba Hill on 10/29/1945 in Harlem, New York. R&B-disco singer/actress. Appeared in several movies and Broadway shows.

MOORE, Tim
Born in Manhattan, New York. Pop singer/songwriter/guitarist/keyboardist. Wrote "Rock And Roll Love Letter" by The Bay City Rollers.

MOORE, Wild Bill
Born William Moore on 6/13/1918 in Houston, Texas. Died on 8/8/1983 (age 65). R&B tenor saxophonist.

MORALES, Michael
Born on 4/25/1963 in San Antonio, Texas. Pop singer/songwriter.

MORGAN, Craig
Born Craig Morgan Greer on 7/17/1964 in Kingston Springs, Tennessee. Country singer/songwriter.

MORGAN, Debelah
Born in Detroit, Michigan. Female R&B singer.

MORGAN, George
Born on 6/28/1924 in Waverly, Tennessee; raised in Barberton, Ohio. Died of a heart attack on 7/7/1975 (age 51). Country singer/songwriter/guitarist. Father of singer Lorrie Morgan.

MORGAN, Jane
Born Florence Currier on 12/25/1920 in Newton, Massachusetts; raised in Daytona Beach, Florida. Adult Contemporary singer.

MORGAN, Jaye P.
Born Mary Margaret Morgan on 12/3/1931 in Mancos, Colorado. Sang with Frank DeVol's band from 1950-53. Regular on TV's *The Gong Show*. Sister of recording group The Morgan Brothers.

MORGAN, Lee
Born on 7/10/1938 in Philadelphia, Pennsylvania. Shot to death on 2/19/1972 (age 33). Male jazz trumpeter.

MORGAN, Lorrie
Born Loretta Lynn Morgan on 6/27/1959 in Nashville, Tennessee. Country singer. Married to Keith Whitley from 1986 until his death in 1989. Married to Jon Randall from 1996-99. Married Sammy Kershaw on 9/29/2001 (since separated).

MORGAN, Meli'sa
Born in Queens, New York. Female R&B singer.

MORGAN, Russ
Born on 4/29/1904 in Scranton, Pennsylvania. Died on 8/8/1969 (age 65). Trombonist/pianist/vocalist/bandleader. His trademark: "Music In The Morgan Manner."

MORGAN BROTHERS, The
Vocal trio from Mancos, Colorado: Dick, Duke and Charley Morgan. Brothers of Jaye P. Morgan.

MORISETTE, Johnnie
Born on 7/1/1935 in Montu Island, South Pacific. Died on 8/1/2000 (age 65). Male R&B singer.

MORISSETTE, Alanis
Born on 6/1/1974 in Ottawa, Ontario, Canada. Adult Alternative rock singer/songwriter. At age 12, she acted on the Nickelodeon cable-TV kids series *You Can't Do That On Television*. Played God in the 1999 movie *Dogma*.

MORLEY, Cozy
Born in Philadelphia, Pennsylvania. Teen pop singer. Later became a stand-up comedian.

MORMON TABERNACLE CHOIR, The
Popular 375-voice choir directed by Richard Condie (died on 12/22/1985).

MORODER, Giorgio
Born on 4/26/1940 in Ortisei, Italy; later based in Munich, Germany. Disco-electronica composer/conductor/producer. Produced numerous movie soundtracks; regular producer for Donna Summer.

MORRIS, Marlowe, Quintet
Born on 5/16/1915 in Harlem, New York. Died in May 1978 (age 63). Black jazz pianist.

MORRIS, Nathan
Born on 6/18/1971 in Philadelphia, Pennsylvania. Member of Boyz II Men.

MORRISON, Dorothy
Born in 1945 in Longview, Texas. Former lead vocalist with The Edwin Hawkins' Singers.

MORRISON, Mark
Born on 5/12/1974 in Hanover, Germany; raised in Leicester, England. R&B singer.

MORRISON, Van
Born George Ivan on 8/31/1945 in Belfast, Ireland. "Blue-eyed soul"-rock singer/songwriter. Leader of Them. Wrote the classic rock hit "Gloria."

MORRISSEY
Born Steven Patrick Morrissey on 5/22/1959 in Davyhulme, Manchester, England. Alternative-rock singer/songwriter. Former lead singer/songwriter of The Smiths.

MORROW, Buddy
Born Muni Zudecoff on 2/8/1919 in New Haven, Connecticut. Trombone star for many top big bands. His own swing band was a hit in the early 1950s. Later played with the *Tonight Show* band and conducted the Tommy Dorsey Orchestra.

MOS DEF
Born Dante Smith on 12/11/1973 in Brooklyn, New York. Male rapper/actor. Member of the rap duo Black Star and the rap trios Medina Green and Urban Renewal Program.

MOST, Donny
Born on 8/8/1953 in Brooklyn, New York. Actor/singer. Played "Ralph Malph" on TV's *Happy Days*.

MOTELS, The
Pop-rock group formed in Berkeley, California: Martha Davis (vocals), Guy Perry (guitar), Marty Jourard (keyboards), Michael Goodroe (bass) and Brian Glascock (drums). Guitarist Scott Thurston joined in 1983. Group disbanded in 1987.

MOTEN, Wendy
Born on 11/22/1970 in Memphis, Tennessee. R&B singer/actress. Starred in the musical *Mama I Want To Sing.*

MOTHERLODE
Pop-rock group based in London, Ontario, Canada: William Smith (vocals, keyboards), Ken Marco (guitar), Steve Kennedy (sax) and Wayne Stone (drums). Smith died of a heart attack on 12/1/1997 (age 53).

MOTHER'S FINEST
R&B group formed in Fort Lauderdale, Florida: husband-and-wife Glenn Murdoch and Joyce Kennedy (vocals), Gary Moore (guitar), Michael Keck (keyboards), Jerry Seay (bass) and Barry Borden (drums).

MOTLEY CRUE
Hard-rock band from Los Angeles, California: Vince Neil (vocals; born Vince Wharton on 2/8/1961), Mick Mars (guitar; born Bob Deal on 5/4/1951), Nikki Sixx (bass; born Frank Ferrana on 12/11/1958) and Tommy Lee (drums; born Thomas Bass on 10/3/1962). Sixx married actress Donna D'Errico on 12/23/1996. Lee was married to actress Heather Locklear from 1986-93; married to actress Pamela Anderson from 1995-98. Drummer Randy Castillo joined in early 2000. Castillo died of cancer on 3/26/2002 (age 51).

MOTORS, The
Pop-rock duo from England: Andy McMaster and Nick Garvey. Peter Bramall (later of Bram Tchaikovsky) was an early group member through 1978.

MOTT THE HOOPLE
Glam-rock band formed in England: Ian Hunter (vocals; born on 6/3/1939), Mick Ralphs (guitar), Pete Watts (bass) and Dale Griffin (drums). Group name taken from a Willard Manus novel. Ralphs left in 1973 to join Bad Company; guitarists Morgan Fisher and Ariel Bender joined. Hunter left in 1976; Fisher, Watts and Griffin formed the British Lions.

MOUNTAIN
Power-rock group led by Leslie West (born Leslie Weinstein on 10/22/1945 in New York City, New York) and Felix Pappalardi (born in 1939 in the Bronx, New York; fatally shot on 4/17/1983, age 44). Group formed after Pappalardi produced West's solo album *Mountain.* Numerous personnel changes with regular members Steve Knight (keyboards) and Corky Laing (drums).

MOUTH & MACNEAL
Pop vocal duo from Holland: Willem "Mouth" Duyn and Maggie MacNeal (born Sjoukje Van't Spijker). Duyn died of a heart attack on 12/3/2004 (age 67).

MOVEMENT, The
Techno-dance trio from Los Angeles, California: AJ Mora (synthesizers), Richard "Humpty" Vission (drums) and Hazze (rapper).

MOVING PICTURES
Pop group from Sydney, Australia: Alex Smith (vocals), Garry Frost (guitar), Andrew Thompson (sax), Charlie Cole (keyboards), Ian Lees (bass) and Paul Freeland (drums). Frost later formed 1927.

MOYET, Alison
Born Genevieve Alison-Jane Moyet on 6/18/1961 in Basildon, Essex, England. Female vocalist of synth pop duo Yaz.

M PEOPLE
Dance trio of Michael Pickering (from Manchester, England), Heather Small and Paul Heard (both from London, England).

MRAZ, Jason
Born on 10/20/1977 in Mechanicsville, Virginia. Alternative pop-rock singer/songwriter/guitarist.

MS. ADVENTURES
White dance vocal trio of sisters Charity (age 13 in 1990), Kindra (17) and Amy (20) Morriss from Texas.

MS. JADE
Born Chevon Young on 8/3/1979 in Philadelphia, Pennsylvania. Female rapper.

MTUME
Funk group formed in Philadelphia, Pennsylvania: James Mtume (male vocals, drums), Tawatha Agee (female vocals), Reggie Lucas (guitar), Phil Fields (keyboards) and Ray Johnson (bass).

M2M
Female teen pop vocal duo from Lorenskog, Norway: Marion Ravn and Marit Larsen.

MUDVAYNE
Hard-rock group from Peoria, Illinois: Chad Gray (vocals), Greg Tribbett (guitar), Ryan Martinie (bass) and Matt McDonough (drums).

MUHAMMAD, Idris
Born Leo Morris on 11/13/1939 in New Orleans, Louisiana. R&B drummer.

MULBERRY LANE
Pop vocal group from Omaha, Nebraska: sisters Jaymie, Rachel, Allie and Heather Suiter.

MULDAUR, Maria
Born Maria D'Amato on 9/12/1943 in the Bronx, New York. Female jazz-styled singer.

MULL, Martin
Born on 8/18/1943 in Chicago, Illinois. Comedian/actor. Acted in several movies and TV shows.

MULLINS, Shawn
Born on 3/8/1968 in Atlanta, Georgia. Male Adult Alternative pop-rock singer/songwriter/guitarist.

MUMBA, Samantha
Born on 1/18/1983 in Dublin, Ireland. R&B singer.

MUNGO JERRY
Skiffle group formed in England: Ray Dorset (lead vocals), Colin Earl, Paul King and Mike Cole.

MURDOCK, Shirley
Born in Toledo, Ohio. Female R&B singer.

MURMAIDS, The
Teen "girl group" from Los Angeles, California: sisters Carol and Terry Fischer, with Sally Gordon.

MURMURS, The
Female rock duo from Manhattan, New York: singers/guitarists Heather Grody and Leisha Hailey.

MURPHEY, Michael
Born on 3/14/1945 in Oak Cliff, Texas. Country-pop singer/songwriter. Recorded as Travis Lewis of The Lewis & Clarke Expedition in 1967. Worked as a staff writer for Screen Gems. Appeared in the movies *Take This Job And Shove It* and *Hard Country*. In 1984, changed his artist billing to Michael Martin Murphey.

MURPHY, David Lee
Born on 1/7/1959 in Herrin, Illinois. Country singer/songwriter/guitarist.

MURPHY, Eddie
Born on 4/3/1961 in Brooklyn, New York. Comedian/actor. Former cast member of TV's *Saturday Night Live*. Starred in numerous movies. Married model Nicole Mitchell on 3/18/1993.

MURPHY, Peter
Born on 7/11/1957 in Northampton, England. Rock singer/songwriter. Lead singer of the goth-rock band Bauhaus.

MURPHY, Walter
Born on 12/19/1952 in Manhattan, New York. Studied classical and jazz piano at Manhattan School of Music. Former arranger for Doc Severinsen and *The Tonight Show* orchestra.

MURRAY, Anne
Born Morna Anne Murray on 6/20/1945 in Springhill, Nova Scotia, Canada. High school teacher for one year after college. With CBC-TV show *Sing Along Jubilee*. First recorded for Arc in 1968. Regular on Glen Campbell's *Goodtime Hour* TV series.

MURRAY, Keith
Born on 9/13/1974 in Long Island, New York. Rapper/songwriter.

MURRAY, Mickey
R&B singer/songwriter.

MUSICAL YOUTH
Pop-reggae group from Birmingham, England: Dennis Seaton (vocals), with brothers Kelvin (guitar) and Michael (keyboards) Grant, and Patrick (bass) and Junior Waite (drums). Patrick Waite died on 2/18/1993 (age 24).

MUSIC EXPLOSION, The
Pop-rock group from Mansfield, Ohio: James Lyons (vocals), Don Atkins (guitar), Richard Nesta (guitar), Burton Stahl (bass) and Bob Avery (drums). Avery later joined Owen B. Lyons died on 9/25/2006 (age 57).

MUSIC MACHINE, The
Rock group from Los Angeles, California: Sean Bonniwell (vocals, guitar), Mark Landon (guitar), Doug Rhodes (organ), Keith Olsen (bass) and Ron Edgar (drums). Olsen became a top record producer in the 1980s.

MUSIC MAKERS, The
Studio group. Evolved into MFSB.

MUSIQ
Born Taalib Johnson on 9/16/1977 in Philadelphia, Pennsylvania. Male R&B singer/songwriter. Also recorded as Musiq Soulchild.

MUSIQUE
Disco trio: Christine Wiltshire, Gina Tharps and Mary Seymour.

MUSTANGS, The
Rock and roll instrumental band.

MUSTO & BONES
Dance duo of Tommy Musto and Frankie Bones.

M.V.P. (MOST VALUABLE PLAYAS)
Rap-dance group formed by producer Robert Clivilles (of C & C Music Factory). Members include female singer Jasmine "Mimi" Ray and male singer Victor "Vice Versa" Matos.

MYA
Born Mya Harrison on 10/10/1979 in Washington DC. Female R&B singer/songwriter/dancer.

MY CHEMICAL ROMANCE
Rock band formed in New Jersey: brothers Gerard Way (vocals) and Mikey Way (bass), with Ray Toro (guitar), Frank Iero (guitar) and Matt Pelissier (drums). Bob Bryar replaced Pelissier in early 2005.

MYERS, Billie
Born on 6/14/1970 in Coventry, England. Female Adult Alternative pop-rock singer.

MYLES, Alannah
Born on 12/25/1955 in Toronto, Ontario, Canada; raised in Buckhorn, Ontario, Canada. Female pop-rock singer.

MYLES, Billy
Born William Myles Nobles on 8/29/1924 in Harlem, New York; later based in North Carolina. Died on 10/9/2005 (age 81). R&B singer/songwriter.

MYNT
Dance trio: producers Ken Khaleel and Robert Sutcliffe, with female singer Kim Sozzi.

MYRON
Born Myron Davis in Cleveland, Ohio. R&B singer/songwriter.

MYSTIC MOODS, The
Instrumental studio group produced by Brad Miller. Had a dozen "mood music" charted albums.

MYSTICS, The
White doo-wop group from Brooklyn, New York: Phil Cracolici (lead), Bob Ferrante & George Galfo (tenors), Albee Cracolici (baritone) and Allie Contrera (bass). John Traynor of Jay & The Americans was an early member.

MYSTIKAL
Born Michael Tyler on 9/22/1970 in New Orleans, Louisiana. Male rapper/songwriter/actor. Member of 504 Boyz. Acted in the movies *I Got The Hook Up*, *Makin' Baby* and *13 Dead Men*. Sentenced to six years in prison for sexual battery in January 2004.

NADA SURF
Rock trio formed in New York: Matthew Caws (vocals, guitar), Daniel Lorca (bass) and Ira Elliot (drums).

NAIM, Yael
Born on 2/6/1978 in Paris, France. Female singer/songwriter.

NAJEE
Born Jerome Najee Rasheed in Manhattan, New York; raised in Jamaica, Queens, New York. Contemporary jazz saxophonist. Attended the New England Conservatory of Music.

NAKED BROTHERS BAND, The
Pop band formed in Los Angeles, California: brothers Nat Wolff (vocals) and Alex Wolff (drums), with Qaasim Middleton (guitar), David Levi (keyboards) and Allie DiMeco (bass).

NAKED EYES
Synth-pop duo from England: Pete Byrne (vocals) and Rob Fisher (keyboards, synthesizer). Split in 1984. Fisher later in duo Climie Fisher. Fisher died on 8/25/1999 (age 39).

NALICK, Anna
Born on 3/30/1984 in Glendora, California. Adult Alternative singer/songwriter.

NAPOLEON XIV
Born Jerry Samuels in 1938 in Brooklyn, New York. Novelty singer/songwriter.

NAPPY ROOTS
Rap group formed in Bowling Green, Kentucky: Brian "B. Stille" Scott, Melvin "Scales" Adams, William "Skinny DeVille" Hughes, Vito "Big V" Tisdale, Ryan "R. Prophet" Anthony and Ron "Clutch" Wilson.

NAS
Born Nasir Jones on 9/14/1973 in Brooklyn, New York. Male rapper/songwriter. Member of QB Finest. Married Kelis on 1/8/2005.

NASH, Graham
Born on 2/2/1942 in Blackpool, Lancashire, England. Pop-rock singer/songwriter/guitarist. Former member of The Hollies. Formed Crosby, Stills & Nash in 1968.

NASH, Johnny
Born on 8/19/1940 in Houston, Texas. Black singer/guitarist/actor. Appeared on local TV from age 13. With Arthur Godfrey's TV and radio shows from 1956-63. In the movie *Take A Giant Step* in 1959. Own JoDa label in 1965. Began recording in Jamaica in 1967.

NASHVILLE TEENS, The
Rock group from Weybridge, Surrey, England: Arthur Sharp (vocals), John Allen (guitar), Ramon "Ray" Phillips (harmonica), John Hawkes

(keyboards), Pete Shannon (bass) and Barry Jenkins (drums; joined The Animals in 1966).

NATALIE
Born Natalie Alvarado on 9/2/1979 in Clear Lake, Texas. Female singer/rapper/songwriter. Former cheerleader for the NBA's Houston Rockets.

NATÉ, Ultra
Born in 1968 in Havre de Grace, Maryland. Black female dance singer/songwriter.

NATE DOGG
Born Nathaniel Hale in 1969 in Los Angeles, California. Male rapper. Former partner of Warren G. Cousin of Snoop Dogg.

NATHANSON, Matt
Born on 3/28/1973 in Lexington, Massachusetts. Male singer/songwriter.

NATIONAL LAMPOON
Comedy troupe spawned from the magazine of the same name.

NATURAL FOUR
R&B vocal group from San Francisco, California: Delmos Whitley, Ollan Christopher James, Darryl Cannady and Steve Striplin.

NATURAL SELECTION
Black funk duo from Minneapolis, Minnesota: Elliott Erickson (keyboards) and Frederick Thomas (vocals).

NATURE'S DIVINE
R&B group from Detroit, Michigan: Lynn Smith (female vocals), Robert Carter (male vocals), Duane Mitchell (guitar), Charles Woods and Marvin Jones (keyboards), Charles Green and Opelton Parker (horns), Robert Johnson (percussion), Keith Fondren (bass) and Mark Mitchell (drums).

NAUGHTON, David
Born on 2/13/1952 in Hartford, Connecticut. Pop singer/dancer/actor. Starred in the 1981 movie *An American Werewolf In London* and TV shows *Makin' It* and *My Sister Sam*.

NAUGHTY BY NATURE
Black hip-hop trio from East Orange, New Jersey: Anthony "Treach" Criss (born on 12/2/1970; The Flavor Unit MCs), Vincent Brown and Kier Gist (born on 9/15/1969). Appeared in the movies *The Meteor Man* and *Who's The Man*. Treach was married to Sandra "Pepa" Denton (of Salt-N-Pepa) from 1999-2001.

NAYLOR, Jerry
Born on 3/6/1939 in Stephenville, Texas. Replaced Joe B. Mauldin in The Crickets in 1961.

NAZARETH
Hard-rock band formed in Dunfermline, Fife, Scotland: Dan McCafferty (vocals), Manny Charlton (guitar), Pete Agnew (bass) and Darrell Sweet (drums). Billy Rankin (guitar) and John Locke (keyboards) added in 1981. Sweet died of a heart attack on 4/30/1999 (age 51).

NAZZ
Rock group from Philadelphia, Pennsylvania: Todd Rundgren (guitar), Robert "Stewkey" Antoni (vocals), Carson Van Osten (bass) and Thom Mooney (drums).

NB RIDAZ
Latin hip-hop group from Phoenix, Arizona: Marco "MC Magic" Cardenas and his son Li'l Mischief, with Daniel "Dos" Salas, Ricardo "Zig Zag" Martinez and Sly. First known as Nastyboy Klick. By 2001, pared down to the trio of MC Magic, Dos and Zig Zag (changed group name to NB Ridaz). Group disbanded in early 2006.

NDEGEOCELLO, Me'Shell
Born Michelle Johnson on 8/29/1969 in Berlin, Germany; raised in Oxon Hill, Maryland. Black female R&B-dance singer/bassist. Last name (pronounced: Nuh-DAY-gay-O-CHEL-lo) means "free like a bird" in Swahili.

N'DOUR, Youssou
Born on 10/1/1959 in Dakar, Senegal, Africa. Popular singer in his native country. Often sings in his native language of Wolof. Backing vocalist on Peter Gabriel's "In Your Eyes." Pronounced: YOU-sue en-DURE.

NEELY, Sam
Born on 8/22/1948 in Cuero, Texas. Pop-country singer/songwriter/guitarist.

NEIGHBORHOOD, The
Seven-man, two-woman pop vocal group.

NEKTAR
Art-rock group formed in Hamburg, Germany: Roye Albrighton (vocals, guitar), Allan Freeman (keyboards), Derek Moore (bass) and Ron Howden (drums).

NELLY
Born Cornell Haynes on 11/2/1974 in Austin, Texas; raised in St. Louis, Missouri. Male rapper. Member of St. Lunatics. Acted in the movies *Snipes* and *The Longest Yard*. Started own Vokal clothing line in 2002.

NELSON
Rock duo from Los Angeles, California: Gunnar (vocals, bass) and Matthew (vocals, guitar) Nelson. The identical twin sons (born on 9/20/1967) of Ricky Nelson.

NELSON, Karen, & Billy T
Nelson was born in Kansas City, Kansas; served three years as backup singer/pianist for Paul Anka. Billy T (Tragesser) is from Pittsburgh, Pennsylvania.

NELSON, Marc
Born in Philadelphia, Pennsylvania. R&B singer/songwriter. Son of Phyllis Nelson.

NELSON, Phyllis
Born on 10/3/1950 in Gary, Indiana. Died of breast cancer on 1/12/1998 (age 47). Dance singer. Mother of Marc Nelson.

NELSON, Ricky
Born Eric Hilliard Nelson on 5/8/1940 in Teaneck, New Jersey. Died in a plane crash in DeKalb,

Texas, on 12/31/1985 (age 45). Son of bandleader Ozzie Nelson and vocalist Harriet Hilliard. Rick and brother David appeared on Nelson's radio show from March 1949, later on TV, 1952-66. Formed own Stone Canyon Band in 1969. In movies *Rio Bravo*, *The Wackiest Ship In The Army* and *Love And Kisses*. Married Kristin Harmon (sister of actor Mark Harmon) in 1963; divorced in 1982. Their daughter Tracy is a movie/TV actress. Their twin sons began recording as Nelson in 1990. Ricky was one of the first teen idols of the rock era.

NELSON, Sandy
Born Sander Nelson on 12/1/1938 in Santa Monica, California. Rock and roll drummer. Became prominent studio musician. Heard on "Alley Oop," "To Know Him Is To Love Him," "A Thousand Stars" and many others. Lost portion of right leg in a motorcycle accident in 1963. Returned to performing in 1964.

NELSON, Willie
Born on 4/30/1933 in Abbott, Texas. Prolific country singer/songwriter (writer of the classic "Funny How Time Slips Away," Patsy Cline's "Crazy" and Faron Young's "Hello Walls"). Played bass for Ray Price. Pioneered the "Outlaw" country movement. Appeared in several movies including *The Electric Horseman*, *Honeysuckle Rose* and *Barbarosa*.

NENA
Rock group formed in Berlin, Germany: Gabriele "Nena" Kerner (vocals), Carlo Karges (guitar), Uwe Fahrenkrog-Petersen (keyboards), Jurgen Demel (bass) and Rolf Brendel (drums). Karges died of liver failure on 1/30/2002 (age 50).

NEON PHILHARMONIC, The
Chamber-sized orchestra of Nashville Symphony Orchestra musicians. Project headed by Tupper Saussy (composer) and Don Gant (vocals). Gant died on 3/15/1987 (age 44). Saussy died on 3/16/2007 (age 71).

NERO, Peter
Born Bernard Nierow on 5/22/1934 in Brooklyn, New York. Pop-jazz pianist.

NERVOUS NORVUS
Born James Drake on 5/13/1912 in Memphis, Tennessee. Died of liver failure on 7/24/1968 (age 56). Novelty singer/songwriter.

NESMITH, Michael
Born on 12/30/1942 in Houston, Texas. Pop-rock singer/songwriter/guitarist. Was a professional musician before joining The Monkees; had done session work for Stax/Volt. Wrote Linda Ronstadt's hit "Different Drum." Formed own video production company, Pacific Arts, in 1977; produced movies *Elephant Parts*, *Repo Man* and others.

NETTO, Loz
Former guitarist with Sniff 'N The Tears. From Coventry, England.

NEVIL, Robbie
Born on 10/2/1960 in Los Angeles, California. Pop singer/songwriter/guitarist.

NEVILLE, Aaron

Born on 1/24/1941 in New Orleans, Louisiana. Member of the R&B family group The Neville Brothers. Brother Art was keyboardist of The Meters. Bassist/singer Ivan Neville is Aaron's son.

NEVILLE, Ivan

Born on 7/23/1965 in New Orleans, Louisiana. Rock singer/bassist. Played on The Rolling Stones' *Dirty Work* album. Son of Aaron Neville.

NEWBEATS, The

Pop trio: Larry Henley (lead singer; born on 6/30/1941 in Arp, Texas) with brothers Dean And Marc Mathis (born on 3/17/1939 and on 2/9/1942, respectively, in Hahira, Georgia). Henley co-wrote "Wind Beneath My Wings."

NEW BIRTH, The

R&B group formed in Louisville, Kentucky, by Harvey Fuqua and Tony Churchill as The Nite-Liters. Expanded to 17 members with two vocal groups (The New Birth and Love, Peace & Happiness) and a band (The Nite-Liters). Renamed New Birth, Inc. Band consisted of Churchill, Austin Lander, James Baker, Robert "Lurch" Jackson, Leroy Taylor and Robin Russell. Vocal groups consisted of Ann Bogan, Melvin Wilson, Leslie Wilson, Bobby Downs, Londee Loren, and Alan Frye. Bogan was a former member of The Marvelettes.

NEW BORN

Born Sammy Sanford in Philadelphia, Pennsylvania (age 9 in 1993). Male rapper.

NEWBURY, Mickey

Born Milton Newbury on 5/19/1940 in Houston, Texas. Died on 9/28/2002 (age 62). Pop-country singer/songwriter/guitarist.

NEW CHRISTY MINSTRELS, The

Folk-balladeer troupe named after the Christy Minstrels (formed in 1842 by Edwin "Pop" Christy). Group founded and led by Randy Sparks, and featured Barry McGuire (1963), Kenny Rogers (1966) and Kim Carnes (1968).

NEWCITY ROCKERS

Rock group from Boston, Massachusetts: Ken Kozdra (vocals), Cliff Goodwin (guitar), Mitch Chakour (bass) and Bob Rivers (drums).

NEWCLEUS

Rap-dance group from Brooklyn, New York: brother-and-sister Ben "Cozmo D" and Yvette Cenad, with brother-and-sister Bob "Chilly B" and Monique Crafton.

NEW COLONY SIX, The

Soft-rock group from Chicago, Illinois: Raymond Graffia (vocals), Patrick McBride (harmonica), Gerald Van Kollenburg (guitar), cousins Craig (organ) and Walter (bass) Kemp and Chic James (drums). Craig Kemp left in mid-1966; replaced by Ronnie Rice. Walter Kemp left in mid-1967; replaced by Ellery Temple. Temple left in late 1967; replaced by Les Kummel. James left in 1969; replaced by Billy Herman (vocals, drums). Graffia left in late 1969; replaced by Bruce Gordon (guitar) and Chuck Jobes (keyboards). Kummel and

McBride left in 1970. Kummel died in a car crash on 12/18/1978 (age 33).

NEWCOMERS, The

R&B trio from Memphis, Tennessee: Terry Bartlett, William Somlin and Bertrand Brown. Changed name to Kwick in 1980.

NEW EDITION

R&B teen vocal group from Boston, Massachusetts: Ralph Tresvant (born on 5/16/1968), Ronald DeVoe (born on 11/17/1967), Michael Bivins (born on 8/10/1968), Ricky Bell (born on 9/18/1967) and Bobby Brown (born on 2/5/1969). Formed in 1982 by future New Kids On The Block and Perfect Gentlemen producer, Maurice Starr. Brown left for solo career in 1986; replaced by Johnny Gill in 1988. Bell, Bivins and DeVoe recorded as Bell Biv DeVoe in 1990. Tresvant and Gill recorded solo in the 1990s. All six members reunited in 1996.

NEW ENGLAND

Rock group formed in New York: John Fannon (vocals, guitar), Jimmy Waldo (keyboards), Gary Shea (bass) and Hirsh Gardner (drums).

NEW ESTABLISHMENT, The

Pop vocal group: Vicki Lemon, Arnold Rollins, Rick Ward, Lenny Mathieson, Ron Wilson, Mike Alley and Kenny Johnson. Wilson (of The Surfaris) died of an aneurysm in May 1989.

NEWFIELD, Heidi

Born on 10/4/1970 in Healdsburg, California. Country singer/songwriter/guitarist. Former lead singer of Trick Pony.

NEW FOUND GLORY

Rock group from Coral Springs, Florida: Jordan Pundik (vocals), Chad Gilbert (guitar), Steve Klein (guitar), Ian Grushka (bass) and Cyrus Bolooki (drums).

NEW HOPE, The

Pop group from New Hope, Pennsylvania, led by Carl Hausman. Originally known as The Kit Kats ("Bubbled Under" in 1966 and 1967). Drummer Carson Stewart died on 7/2/2001 (age 61).

NEW KIDS ON THE BLOCK

Teen vocal group from Boston, Massachusetts: Joey McIntyre (born on 12/31/1972), Donnie Wahlberg (born on 8/17/1969), Danny Wood (born on 5/14/1969), and brothers Jon (born on 11/29/1968) and Jordan Knight (born on 5/17/1970). Formed in the summer of 1984 by New Edition's founder/producer, Maurice Starr. Shortened group name to NKOTB in 1991. McIntyre played teacher "Colin Flynn" on TV's *Boston Public*.

NEWLEY, Anthony

Born on 9/24/1931 in London, England. Died of cancer on 4/14/1999 (age 67). Adult Contemporary singer/actor/composer/comedian.

NEWMAN, Jimmy

Born on 8/27/1927 in High Point, Louisiana. Cajun-country singer/guitarist.

NEWMAN, Lionel
Born on 1/4/1916 in New Haven, Connecticut. Died of heart failure on 2/3/1989 (age 73). Top movie composer/conductor with 20th Century Fox for 45 years; responsible for 250+ movie scores. Received 10 Oscar nominations and won an Oscar in 1969 for *Hello Dolly*. Uncle of Randy Newman and brother of composers Alfred and Emil Newman.

NEWMAN, Randy
Born on 11/28/1943 in New Orleans, Louisiana. Singer/composer/pianist. Nephew of composers Alfred, Emil and Lionel Newman. Scored the movies *Ragtime*, *The Natural* and *Avalon*.

NEWMAN, Ted
Born on 5/6/1939 in Custer, South Dakota. Teen pop singer. Later worked as a teacher in Phoenix, Arizona.

NEWMAN, Troy
Born on 10/12/1964 in Perth, Australia. Rock singer/guitarist.

NEW ORDER
Techno-dance group from Manchester, England: Bernard Sumner (vocals, guitar), Gillian Gilbert (keyboards), Peter Hook (bass) and Stephen Morris (drums). Hook also recorded with Monaco. Sumner also recorded with Electronic. Also see Joy Division.

NEW RADICALS
Group is actually solo rock singer/musician Gregg Alexander.

NEW RIDERS OF THE PURPLE SAGE
Country-rock group formed in San Francisco, California: John Dawson (vocals, guitar), David Nelson (guitar), Dave Torbert (bass) and Spencer Dryden (drums; Jefferson Airplane). Dryden died of cancer on 1/11/2005 (age 66).

NEW SEEKERS, The
British-Australian pop group formed by Keith Potger after disbandment of The Seekers in 1969. Consisted of Eve Graham, Lyn Paul, Peter Doyle, Marty Kristian and Paul Layton. Doyle died of cancer on 10/13/2001 (age 52).

NEWSONG
Christian pop group formed in Kennesaw, Georgia: Eddie Carswell (vocals), Billy Goodwin and Leonard Ahlstrom (guitars), Scotty Wilbanks (sax, keyboards), Mark Clay (bass) and Jack Pumphrey (drums).

NEWTON, Juice
Born Judith Kay Cohen on 2/18/1952 in Lakehurst, New Jersey; raised in Virginia Beach, Virginia. Pop-country singer/guitarist. Performed folk music from age 13. Moved to Los Angeles with own Silver Spur band in 1974; recorded for RCA in 1975; group disbanded in 1978.

NEWTON, Wayne
Born on 4/3/1942 in Roanoke, Virginia. Singer/multi-instrumentalist. Top Las Vegas entertainer. Began singing career with regular appearances on Jackie Gleason's TV variety series in 1962. Appeared in the movies *License To Kill*,

The Adventures Of Ford Fairlane and *Vegas Vacation*.

NEWTON-JOHN, Olivia
Born on 9/26/1948 in Cambridge, England; raised in Melbourne, Australia. At age 16, won talent contest trip to England; sang with Pat Carroll as Pat & Olivia. With the group Toomorrow in a British movie of the same name. Granddaughter of Nobel Prize-winning German physicist Max Born. In movies *Grease*, *Xanadu* and *Two Of A Kind*. Married to actor Matt Lattanzi from 1984-95. Opened own chain of clothing boutiques (Koala Blue) in 1984.

NEW VAUDEVILLE BAND, The
Studio creation of British songwriter/record producer Geoff Stephens (born on 10/1/1934 in London, England). Arrangements similar to Rudy Vallee's hits during the 1930s.

NEW YORK CITY
R&B vocal group from Harlem, New York: Tim McQueen, John Brown, Ed Shell and Claude Johnston.

NEW YORK DOLLS
Glam/punk-rock group from New York City: David Johansen (vocals), Johnny "Thunders" Genzale (vocals, guitar), Sylvain Sylvain (guitar), Arthur Harold Kane (bass) and Jerry Nolan (drums). Managed by British entrepeneur Malcolm McLaren who later formed the Sex Pistols. Genzale died of a drug overdose on 4/23/1991 (age 38). Kane died of leukemia on 7/13/2004 (age 55).

NEXT
R&B vocal trio from Minneapolis, Minnesota: Robert Lavelle "RL" Huggar, with brothers Raphael "Tweety" Brown and Terry "T-Low" Brown.

NE-YO
Born Shaffer Smith on 10/18/1979 in Camden, Arkansas; raised in Las Vegas, Nevada. Male R&B singer/songwriter.

NICE & SMOOTH
Rap duo from Brooklyn, New York: Gregg "Nice" Mays and Darryl "Smooth" Barnes.

NICHOLAS, Paul
Born Paul Beuselinck on 12/3/1945 in Peterborough, Cambridgeshire, England. Singer/actor. Played "Dougie Shears" in the 1978 movie *Sgt. Pepper's Lonely Hearts Club Band*.

NICHOLS, Joe
Born on 11/26/1976 in Rogers, Arkansas. Country singer/songwriter.

NICKELBACK
Hard-rock band formed in Hanna, Alberta, Canada: brothers Chad Kroeger (vocals; born on 11/15/1974) and Mike Kroeger (bass; born on 6/25/1972), with Ryan Peake (guitar; born on 3/1/1973) and Ryan Vikedal (drums; born on 5/9/1975). Daniel Adair (of 3 Doors Down) replaced Vikedal in January 2005.

NICKS, Stevie
Born Stephanie Nicks on 5/26/1948 in Phoenix, Arizona; raised in San Francisco, California. Became vocalist of Bay-area group Fritz and subsequently met guitarist Lindsey Buckingham. Teamed up and recorded album *Buckingham-Nicks* in 1973. Joined Fleetwood Mac in January 1975 as vocalist. Quit touring with band after 1990; left in January 1993. Reunited with Fleetwood Mac in 1997.

NICOLE
Born Nicole Wray in 1981 in Salinas, California; raised in Portsmouth, Virginia. R&B-dance singer.

NIELSEN/PEARSON
Pop duo from Sacramento, California: singer/guitarists Reed Nielsen and Mark Pearson.

NIGHT
Pop-rock group: Stevie Lange (female vocals), Chris Thompson (male vocals, guitar; Manfred Mann's Earth Band), Robbie McIntosh (guitar), Nicky Hopkins (piano), Billy Kristian (bass) and Rick Marotta (drums). McIntosh later joined The Pretenders and Paul McCartney's backing band.

NIGHTCRAWLERS
Studio dance project from Glasgow, Scotland; spearheaded by vocalist/DJ Jon Reed.

NIGHTCRAWLERS, The
Garage-rock band from Daytona Beach, Florida: Chuck Conlon (vocals, bass), Robbie Rouse (vocals), Sylvan Wells (guitar), Pete Thomason (guitar) and Tom Ruger (drums).

NIGHTINGALE, Maxine
Born on 11/2/1952 in Wembley, England. R&B-disco singer. First recorded in 1968. In productions of *Hair*, *Jesus Christ Superstar*, *Godspell* and *Savages*.

NIGHT RANGER
Rock group formed in San Francisco, California: Jack Blades (vocals, bass; born on 4/24/1954), Kelly Keagy (vocals, drums; born on 9/15/1952), Jeff Watson (guitar; born on 11/4/1956), Brad Gillis (guitar; born on 6/15/1957), and Alan Fitzgerald (keyboards; born on 6/16/1954). Blades and Gillis were members of Rubicon. Fitzgerald left in 1988; band split up in early 1989. Blades joined supergroup Damn Yankees and formed duo with Tommy Shaw. Night Ranger reunited with original lineup in 1997.

NIKKI
Born Nikki Lee in Okinawa, Japan; raised in Dayton, Ohio. American female singer/multi-instrumentalist. Backing member of the soul-funk group Sun.

NILSSON
Born Harry Nelson on 6/15/1941 in Brooklyn, New York. Died of a heart attack on 1/15/1994 (age 52). Pop singer/songwriter. Wrote Three Dog Night's hit "One"; scored the movie *Skidoo*, the animated TV movie *The Point*, and TV's *The Courtship Of Eddie's Father*.

NINA SKY
Female dancehall reggae vocal duo from New Jersey: twin sisters Nicole and Natalie Albino.

NINE
Born Derrick Keyes on 9/19/1969 in Queens, New York. Male rapper.

NINEDAYS
Rock band from New York: John Hampson (vocals, guitar), Brian Desveaux (vocals, guitar), Jeremy Dean (keyboards), Nick Dimichino (bass) and Vincent Tattanelli (drums).

NINE INCH NAILS
Group is actually industrial rock musician Trent Reznor (born on 5/17/1965 in Mercer, Pennsylvania).

9.9
R&B vocal trio from Boston, Massachusetts: Margo Thunder, Leslie Jones and Wanda Perry.

1910 FRUITGUM CO.
Bubblegum group from New Jersey: Joey Levine (Ohio Express, Crazy Elephant, Reunion; vocals), Mark Gutkowski, Floyd Marcus, Pat Karwan, Steve Mortkowitz and Frank Jeckell. Producers Jerry Kasenetz and Jeff Katz used a revolving-door studio-based membership centered around lead singer Levine.

1927
Soft-rock group from Australia: Eric Weideman (vocals, guitar), brothers Garry (keyboards) and Bill (bass) Frost, and James Barton (drums). Garry Frost was also a member of Moving Pictures.

98°
White teen pop vocal group from Cincinnati, Ohio: brothers Drew (born on 8/8/1976) and Nick Lachey (born on 11/9/1973), with Jeff Timmons (born on 4/30/1973) and Justin Jeffre (born on 2/25/1973). Nick Lachey was married to Jessica Simpson from 2002-06.

95 SOUTH
Hip-hop/bass group from Miami, Florida: Church's, Black, C.C. Lemonhead, Bootyman and K-Knock. Group named after the interstate highway. By 1995, group reduced to a duo of A.B. and Black. Lemonhead later joined the Quad City DJ's.

NINO & the EBB TIDES
White doo-wop group from the Bronx, New York: Antonio "Nino" Aiello (lead), Tony DiBari (tenor), Tony Imbimbo (baritone) and Vinnie Drago (bass).

NIRVANA
Grunge-rock trio from Aberdeen, Washington: Kurt Cobain (vocals, guitar; born on 2/20/1967), Krist "Chris" Novoselic (bass; born on 5/16/1965) and Dave Grohl (drums; born on 1/14/1969). Cobain married Courtney Love (lead singer of Hole) on 2/24/1992. Cobain died of a self-inflicted gunshot wound on 4/5/1994 (age 27). Grohl formed Foo Fighters in 1995.

NITEFLYTE
R&B-disco group led by Howard Johnson and Sandy Torano.

NITTY
Born Frank Ross on 12/23/1977 in the Bronx, New York. Male rapper/songwriter.

NITTY GRITTY DIRT BAND
Country-folk-rock group from Long Beach, California. Led by Jeff Hanna (vocals, guitar; born on 7/11/1947) and John McEuen (banjo, mandolin; born on 12/19/1945). Changed name to Dirt Band in 1976. Resumed using Nitty Gritty Dirt Band name in 1982. Various members included ex-Eagle Bernie Leadon, who replaced McEuen briefly in early 1987. Revamped quartet since late 1987: Hanna, Jimmy Ibbotson, Bob Carpenter and Jimmie Fadden. In the movies *For Singles Only* and *Paint Your Wagon.* Hanna married country singer/songwriter Matraca Berg.

NITZSCHE, Jack
Born Bernard Nitzsche on 4/22/1937 in Chicago, Illinois. Died of heart failure on 8/25/2000 (age 63). Arranger/producer/composer/keyboardist. Arranger for many of Phil Spector's productions. Co-wrote "Needles And Pins" and scored the movies *One Flew Over The Cuckoo's Nest* and *An Officer And A Gentleman.* His wife, Grazia, sang on several of The Blossoms' recordings.

NIVEA
Born Nivea Hamilton on 3/24/1982 in Atlanta, Georgia. Female R&B singer. Married to The Dream from 2004-07.

NIX, Don
Born on 9/27/1941 in Memphis, Tennessee. White soul-rock singer/guitarist/saxophonist. Formerly in the Mar-Keys.

NIXONS, The
Rock group from Dallas, Texas: Zac Maloy (vocals, guitar), Jesse Davis (guitar), Ricky Brooks (bass) and John Humphrey (drums).

NOBLE, Nick
Born Nicholas Valkan on 6/21/1936 in Chicago, Illinois. Adult Contemporary singer.

NOBLES, Cliff, & Co.
Born in 1944 in Mobile, Alabama. R&B bandleader/singer.

NOCERA
Born Maria Nocera in Italy. Female dance singer.

NO DOUBT
New wave-ska band from Orange County, California: Gwen Stefani (vocals), Tom Dumont (guitar), Tony Kanal (bass) and Adrian Young (drums). Stefani married Gavin Rossdale (lead singer of Bush) on 9/14/2002.

NOEL
Born Noel Pagan in the Bronx, New York. Latin-disco singer.

NOGUEZ, Jacky
Born in Paris, France. Male orchestra leader.

NOLAN, Kenny
Born in Los Angeles, California. Pop singer/songwriter. Wrote "My Eyes Adored You,"

"Lady Marmalade" and "Get Dancin'." Fronted studio group The Eleventh Hour and Firefly.

NOMAD
Dance duo from England: Damon Rocheforte and Steve McCutcheon.

NO MERCY
Male techno-dance trio: brothers Ariel and Gabriel Hernandez from Miami, Florida, with Marty Cintron from New York.

NONCHALANT
Born Tanya Pointer in Washington DC. Female singer/rapper/songwriter.

N.O.R.E. (Noreaga)
Born Victor Santiago in Queens, New York. Male rapper. One-half of Capone-N-Noreaga duo.

NORFUL, Smokie
Born William Norful in Little Rock, Arkansas; raised in Muskogee, Oklahoma. Gospel singer/songwriter/organist.

NORMAN, Jimmy
Born on 8/12/1937 in Nashville, Tennessee. R&B singer. Member of The Chargers and The Dyna-Sores.

NORTH, Freddie
Born on 5/28/1939 in Nashville, Tennessee. R&B singer/songwriter/guitarist.

NORTHCOTT, Tom
Born in 1943 in Canada. Folk singer. Hosted own TV show.

NORTHERN LIGHT
Pop-rock group from Minneapolis, Minnesota: Dave Sandler, Spence Peterson, Bud Phillips, Don Beckwith and Steve Hough.

NORTHERN PIKES, The
Rock group from Saskatoon, Saskatchewan, Canada: Jay Semko (vocals, bass), Merl Bryck (vocals, guitar), Bryan Potvin (guitar) and Don Schmid (drums).

NORWOOD, Dorothy
Born in Atlanta, Georgia; later based in Chicago, Illinois. Gospel singer.

NOTORIOUS
Rock duo from England: Robin George (guitar) and Sean Harris (vocals).

NOTORIOUS B.I.G., The
Born Christopher Wallace on 5/21/1972 in Brooklyn, New York. Shot to death on 3/9/1997 (age 24). Male rapper. Also recorded as Biggy Smallz. Married to singer Faith Evans from 1994-97 (his death). Arrested on 6/18/1995 on robbery and assault charges and on 3/23/1996 for assault and weapon offenses. Discovered Junior M.A.F.I.A.

NOVA, Aldo
Born Aldo Caporuscio on 11/13/1956 in Montreal, Quebec, Canada. Rock singer/songwriter/guitarist.

NOVA, Heather
Born on 7/6/1968 on an island in the Bermuda Sound. Adult Alternative pop-rock singer/songwriter. Raised on a 40-foot sailboat in the Caribbean. Later settled in London, England.

NOVAS, The
Garage-rock band from Edina, Minnesota: Bob Nolan (vocals), John Eckley (guitar), Jim Ronald (guitar), Jim Owens (bass) and Jeff Raymond (drums).

NRBQ
Blues-rock group formed in Miami, Florida. Numerous personnel changes. 1974 lineup: brothers Terry (vocals) and Donn (trombone) Adams, Al Anderson (guitar; Clean Living, The Wildweeds), Keith Spring (sax), Joey Spampinato (bass) and Tom Ardolino (drums). Spampinato was married to Skeeter Davis from 1983-96.

*NSYNC
Male teen vocal group formed in Orlando, Florida: Chris Kirkpatrick (born on 10/17/1971), Josh "JC" Chasez (born on 8/8/1976), Joey Fatone (born on 1/28/1977), Justin Timberlake (born on 1/31/1981) and Lance Bass (born on 5/4/1979). Timberlake and Chasez were regulars on TV's *The Mickey Mouse Club*. Fatone appeared in the 2002 movie *My Big Fat Greek Wedding* and was first runner-up on the 2007 season of *Dancing With The Stars*.

N-TRANCE
Electronic dance group from England: Ricardo Da Force (rapper), Gillian Wisdom, Dale Longworth, Lee Limer and Kevin O'Toole.

N2DEEP
White rap duo from Vallejo, California: Jay Trujillo and T.L. Lyon.

NIIU
Male R&B vocal group from New Jersey: Chuckie Howard, Chris Herbert, Don Carlis and Craig Hill.

NU FLAVOR
Teen pop-R&B vocal group from Long Beach, California: Jacob Ceniceros, Anthony Dacosta, Rico Luna and Frank Pangelinan.

NUGENT, Ted
Born on 12/13/1948 in Detroit, Michigan. Hard-rock guitarist/songwriter. Moved to Chicago in 1965 and formed The Amboy Dukes. Moved back to Detroit in 1967. Joined the supergroup Damn Yankees in 1989. An avid game hunter and an active supporter of the National Rifle Association.

NUMAN, Gary
Born Gary Webb on 3/8/1958 in Hammersmith, England. Synth-techno-rock artist.

NU SHOOZ
R&B-dance vocal group from Portland, Oregon, centered around husband-and-wife team of guitarist/songwriter John Smith and lead singer Valerie Day.

NUTMEGS, The
R&B vocal group from New Haven, Connecticut: brothers Leroy Griffin (lead) and James "Sonny" Griffin, with James Tyson, Billy Emery and Leroy McNeil. Leroy Griffin died in a factory accident in September 1966 (age 32). James Griffin died on 12/16/2003 (age 72).

NU TORNADOS, The
String band from Philadelphia, Pennsylvania: Eddie Dono (leader), Phil Dale, Tom Dell, Mike Perno and Louie Mann. Performs in the Philadelphia Mummers New Year's Day parade.

NUTTA BUTTA
Born in 1973 in Harlem, New York. Male rapper.

NUTTIN' NYCE
Female rap-R&B trio from California: Eboni Foster, Onnie Ponder and Teece Wallace.

NUTTY SQUIRRELS, The
Creators and voices: Don Elliot (from Sommerville, New Jersey) and Alexander "Sascha" Burland (from Brooklyn, New York).

N.W.A.
Highly influential rap group from Los Angeles, California: Eric "Eazy-E" Wright, Lorenzo "MC Ren" Patterson, Andre "Dr. Dre" Young, O'Shea "Ice Cube" Jackson and Antoine "Yella" Carraby. Dr. Dre was also a member of World Class Wreckin Cru and is a top record producer. Eazy-E died of AIDS on 3/26/1995 (age 31). N.W.A.: Niggas With Attitude. Members of The West Coast Rap All-Stars.

NYASIA
Born Blanca Iris Battista on 7/31/1967 in Nantana, Florida; raised in Brooklyn, New York. Female dance singer.

NYLONS, The
Acappella group formed in Toronto, Ontario, Canada: Marc Connors, Paul Cooper, Claude Morrison and Arnold Robinson. Connors died on 3/25/1991 (age 41).

NYRO, Laura
Born Laura Nigro on 10/18/1947 in the Bronx, New York. Died of cancer on 4/8/1997 (age 49). White soul-gospel singer/songwriter. Wrote "Stoned Soul Picnic," "Eli's Coming," "Wedding Bell Blues," "And When I Die," "Stoney End" and others.

OAK
Pop-rock group from Maine: Rick Pinette (vocals), Scott Weatherspoon (guitar), David Stone (keyboards), John Foster (bass) and Daniel Caron (drums).

OAKENFOLD
Born Paul Oakenfold on 8/30/1963 in London, England. Dance DJ/remixer.

OAK RIDGE BOYS
Country vocal group formed in Oak Ridge, Tennessee: Duane Allen, Joe Bonsall, Richard Sterban and William Lee Golden.

OAKTOWN'S 3.5.7
Female rap group from Oakland, California: Djuana "Sweet L.D." Johnican, Tabatha "Terrible T" King, Vicious C and Sweet Pea (former Oakland Raiders cheerleader). By 1991, reduced to a duo of

OAKTOWN'S 3.5.7 — cont'd
Johnican and King, who were dancers with M.C.
Hammer's touring posse.

O.A.R.
Pop-rock band from Columbus, Ohio: Marc
Roberage (vocals, guitar), Richard On (guitar), Jerry
DePizzo (sax), Benj Gershman (bass) and Chris
Culos (drums). O.A.R.: Of A Revolution.

OASIS
Rock band from Manchester, England: brothers
Liam (vocals; born on 9/21/1972) and Noel
Gallagher (guitar; born on 5/29/1967), with Paul
Arthurs (guitar; born on 6/23/1965), Paul McGuigan
(bass; born on 5/9/1971) and Tony McCarroll
(drums). Alan White (born on 5/26/1972) replaced
McCarroll in 1995. Liam was married to Patsy
Kensit of Eighth Wonder from 1997-2000.

O'BANION, John
Born on 2/16/1947 in Kokomo, Indiana. Died of
injuries suffered in a fall on 2/14/2007 (age 59). Pop
singer.

O'BRYAN
Born O'Bryan Burnett in 1961 in Sneads Ferry,
North Carolina. Male R&B singer.

O.C.
Born Omar Credle on 5/13/1971 in Brooklyn, New
York. Male rapper.

OCASEK, Ric
Born Richard Otcasek on 3/23/1949 in Baltimore,
Maryland. Lead singer/guitarist/songwriter of The
Cars. Appeared in the 1987 movie *Made In Heaven*.
Married supermodel/actress Paulina Porizkova on
8/23/1989. His son Christopher Otcasek is leader of
Glamour Camp.

OCEAN
Pop group from London, Ontario, Canada: Janice
Morgan (vocals), David Tamblyn (guitar), Greg
Brown (keyboards), Jeff Jones (bass) and Charles
Slater (drums).

OCEAN, Billy
Born Leslie Sebastian Charles on 1/21/1950 in
Trinidad, West Indies; raised in England. R&B-pop
singer.

OCHS, Phil
Born on 12/19/1940 in El Paso, Texas. Committed
suicide on 4/9/1976 (age 35). Folk singer/
songwriter.

O'CONNOR, Carroll, & Jean Stapleton
"Archie and Edith Bunker" of TV's *All In The Family*.
Veteran actors. O'Connor was born on 8/2/1924 in
Manhattan, New York; died of a heart attack on
6/21/2001 (age 76). Stapleton was born Jeanne
Murray on 1/19/1923 in Manhattan, New York.

O'CONNOR, Sinead
Born on 12/8/1966 in Dublin, Ireland. Female
singer/songwriter. Gained notoriety in her various
protests.

O'DAY, Alan
Born on 10/3/1940 in Hollywood, California. Pop
singer/songwriter/pianist.

ODDS & ENDS
R&B vocal trio from Philadelphia, Pennsylvania:
brother-and-sister Larry and Wanda "Doll" Butler,
with friend Jim Grant. The Butler siblings later
formed the trio Three Million.

O'DELL, Brooks
Born in Philadelphia, Pennsylvania. Male R&B
singer.

O'DELL, Kenny
Born Kenneth Gist in 1942 in Oklahoma. Pop
singer/songwriter/guitarist. Worked with Duane
Eddy and own band, Guys And Dolls. Moved to
Nashville in 1969. Wrote Charlie Rich's "Behind
Closed Doors" and The Judd's "Mama He's Crazy."

O'DONIS, Colby
Born Colby O'Donis Colon on 3/14/1989 in Queens,
New York. Latin hip-hop singer/songwriter.

ODYSSEY
Disco vocal trio from the Bronx, New York:
Manila-born Tony Reynolds, and sisters Lillian and
Louise Lopez, originally from the Virgin Islands.

OFARIM, Esther & Abi
Wife and husband from Israel. Esther was born
Esther Zaled on 6/13/1941; Abi was born Abraham
Reichstat on 10/5/1937. Married from 1960-70.

OFF BROADWAY USA
Rock group from Oak Park, Illinois: Cliff Johnson
(vocals), Rob Harding and John Ivan (guitars), John
Pazdan (bass) and Ken Harck (drums).

OFFITT, Lillian
Born on 11/4/1938 in Nashville, Tennessee. Female
R&B singer.

OFFSPRING, The
Punk-rock group from Garden Grove, California:
Bryan "Dexter" Holland (vocals; born on
12/29/1966), Kevin "Noodles" Wasserman (guitar;
born on 2/4/1963), Greg Kriesel (bass; born on
1/20/1965) and Ron Welty (drums; born on
2/1/1971).

O'HENRY, Lenny
Born Daniel Cannon in West Virginia. R&B singer.
Popular "beach music" performer.

OHIO EXPRESS
Bubblegum-rock group from Mansfield, Ohio.
Produced by Jerry Kasenetz and Jeff Katz (worked
with The Music Explosion and 1910 Fruitgum Co.).
Joey Levine (born on 5/29/1947; also with 1910
Fruitgum Co., Reunion and several other
Kasenetz-Katz productions) was lead singer on
most of the hits. Other members: Dale Powers and
Doug Grassel (guitars), Jim Pflayer (keyboards),
Dean Krastan (bass) and Tiim Corwin (drums).

OHIO PLAYERS
R&B-funk group from Dayton, Ohio: Clarence
Satchell (vocals, sax; born on 4/15/1940), Leroy
Bonner (vocals, guitar), Billy Beck (keyboards),
Marvin Pierce and Ralph Middlebrook (trumpets;
born on 8/20/1939), Marshall Jones (bass; born on
10/4/1942) and Jimmy Williams (drums). Jones died
on 8/18/1984 (age 41). Satchell died of a brain

OHIO PLAYERS — cont'd
aneurysm on 12/30/1995 (age 55). Group started as the Ohio Untouchables (backing band for The Falcons).

OINGO BOINGO
New-wave rock group formed in Los Angeles, California: Danny Elfman (vocals), Steve Bartek (guitar), John Avila (bass) and Johnny Hernandez (drums). Group appeared in the 1986 movie *Back To School*. Among several movies, Elfman scored *Beetlejuice*, *Batman*, *Dick Tracy*, and *The Simpsons* TV theme, with Bartek as orchestrator. Band name shortened to Boingo in 1994.

O'JAYS, The
R&B vocal group from Canton, Ohio: Eddie Levert (born on 6/16/1942), Walter Williams (born on 8/25/1942), William Powell (born on 1/20/1942), Bobby Massey and Bill Isles. First known as the Triumphs. Recorded as the Mascots for the King label in 1961. Renamed by Cleveland disc jockey Eddie O'Jay. Isles left in 1965. Massey left to become a record producer in 1971; Levert, Williams and Powell continued as a trio. Powell retired from touring due to illness in late 1975 (died on 5/26/1977, age 35); replaced by Sammy Strain, formerly with Little Anthony & The Imperials. Strain (married to Yvonne Fair) returned to his former group by 1993; replaced by Nathaniel Best. Levert's sons Gerald (died on 11/10/2006) and Sean were members of the trio Levert. Gerald also charted duets with Eddie.

O'KAYSIONS, The
White pop-soul band from Wilson, North Carolina: Donny Weaver (vocals, organ), Wayne Pittman (guitar), Ron Turner (trumpet), Jim Speidel (sax), Jimmy Hennant (bass) and Bruce Joyner (drums).

O'KEEFE, Danny
Born in 1943 in Wenatchee, Washington. Pop singer/songwriter.

OK GO
Pop-rock group formed in Chicago, Illinois: Damian Kulash (vocals), Andy Ross (guitar), Tim Nordwind (bass) and Dan Konopka (drums).

OLA & THE JANGLERS
Male pop-rock band from Sweden: Ola Hakansson (vocals; born on 3/24/1945), Christer Idering (guitar), Johannes Ohlsson (organ), Ake Eldsater (bass) and Leif Johansson (drums).

OLDFIELD, Mike
Born on 5/15/1953 in Reading, England. Classical-rock, multi-instrumentalist/composer.

OL DIRTY BASTARD
Born Russell Jones on 11/15/1968 in Brooklyn, New York. Died of a drug overdose on 11/13/2004 (age 35). Member of Wu-Tang Clan. Also known as Dirt McGirt, Unique Ason, Osirus or Big Baby Jesus.

OLIVE
Electro-pop/dance group from England: Ruth-Ann Boyle (vocals) and producers Robin Taylor-Firth and Tim Kellett.

OLIVER
Born William Oliver Swofford on 2/22/1945 in North Wilkesboro, North Carolina. Died of cancer on 2/12/2000 (age 54). Adult Contemporary singer.

OLIVIA
Born Olivia Longott on 2/15/1981 in Brooklyn, New York; raised in Queens, New York. R&B singer/rapper.

OLIVOR, Jane
Born Linda Cohen on 1/1/1947 in Brooklyn, New York. Adult Contemporary singer.

OLLIE & JERRY
Dance duo of Ollie Brown and Jerry Knight (former member of Raydio).

OLLIE & THE NIGHTINGALES
Formed as the gospel group The Dixie Nightingales in 1950. Consisted of Ollie Nightingale (Ollie Hoskins), Quincy Clifton Billops Jr., Bill Davis, Nelson Lesure and Rochester Neal. Hoskins died on 10/26/1997 (age 61). Also see The Ovations.

OL SKOOL
R&B group from St. Louis, Missouri: Pookie (vocals), Tony Love (guitar), Curtis Jefferson (bass) and Bobby Crawford (drums).

OLSON, Rocky
Rockabilly singer.

OLSSON, Nigel
Born on 2/10/1949 in Merseyside, England. Drummer for Elton John's band from 1971-76.

OLYMPICS, The
R&B vocal group from Compton, California: Walter Ward (lead), Eddie Lewis (tenor), Charles Fizer (baritone) and Walter Hammond (baritone; The 3 Friends). Recorded as The Challengers for Melatone in 1956. Melvin King replaced Fizer in 1958; remained in group as replacement for Hammond when Fizer returned in 1959. Fizer was killed on 8/14/1965 (during the Watts rioting, age 25); replaced by Julian McMichael ("Mack Starr"), former lead of The Paragons. King left in 1966. Kenny Sinclair, formerly of The Six Teens, joined in 1970. McMichael died in a motorcycle accident in June 1981 (age 45). Sinclair died of cancer on 3/16/2003 (age 63). Ward died on 12/11/2006 (age 69).

O'MALLEY, Lenore
Female disco singer.

OMAR, Don
Born William Omar Landrón on 2/10/1978 in Villa Palmeras, Puerto Rico. Latin reggae rapper.

OMARION
Born Omari Grandberry on 11/12/1984 in Los Angeles, California. Male R&B singer/songwriter. Member of B2K.

OMC
Born Pauly Fuemana on 2/8/1969 in Otara, New Zealand. Singer/songwriter. OMC stands for Otara Millionaires Club.

O'NEAL, Alexander
Born on 11/15/1953 in Natchez, Mississippi; raised in Minneapolis, Minnesota. R&B singer. Own band, Alexander, in the late 1970s. Lead singer of Flyte Tyme which included Jimmy "Jam" Harris, Terry Lewis and Monte Moir and later evolved into The Time. Went solo in 1980.

O'NEAL, Jamie
Born Jamie Murphy on 6/3/1968 in Sydney, Australia; raised in Hawaii and Nevada. Female country singer.

O'NEAL, Shaquille
Born on 3/6/1972 in Newark, New Jersey. Male rapper/actor. Professional basketball player with the NBA's Orlando Magic, Los Angeles Lakers and Miami Heat. Starred in the movies *Blue Chips*, *Kazaam* and *Steel*.

ONE HEART AT A TIME
All-star gathering: Garth Brooks, Billy Dean, Faith Hill, Neal McCoy, Michael McDonald, Olivia Newton-John, Victoria Shaw and Bryan White.

100 PROOF AGED IN SOUL
R&B vocal trio from Detroit, Michigan: Clyde Wilson ("Steve Mancha"; see 8th Day), lead; Joe Stubbs and Eddie Anderson ("Eddie Holiday"). Stubbs, brother of Levi Stubbs of the Four Tops, had been in The Contours and The Falcons. Holland-Dozier-Holland's labels, Hot Wax and Invictus, used various musicians on their recordings and put out tracks under any name.

1 OF THE GIRLS
Black female teen vocal group from Cleveland, Ohio: Le'Shawn Sykes, Nina Creque, Ra-Deon Kirkland and Marvelous Ray Miles. Discovered and produced by Gerald Levert.

ONEREPUBLIC
Rock band from Denver, Colorado: Ryan Tedder (vocals), Zach Filkins (guitar), Drew brown (guitar), Brent Kutzle (bass) and Eddie Fisher (drums).

ONE 2 MANY
Pop trio from Norway: Camilla Griehsel (vocals), Jan Gisle Ytterdal (guitar) and Dag Kolsrud (keyboards). Kolsrud was A-Ha's world tour musical director.

ONE TO ONE
Male-female pop duo from Canada: Leslie Howe (keyboards) and Louise Reny (vocals).

112
R&B group from Atlanta, Georgia: Daron Jones (keyboards; born on 12/27/1976), Michael Keith (strings; born on 12/18/1976), Marvin Scandrick (keyboards; born on 9/25/1974) and Quinnes Parker (drums; born on 3/24/1976). All share lead vocals.

ONE WAY
R&B group from Detroit, Michigan: Al Hudson (vocals), Dave Robertson (guitar), Kevin McCord (bass) and Gregory Green (drums). Recorded from 1976-79 as Al Hudson & The Soul Partners. Signed with MCA in 1979; name changed to One Way.

ONYX
Rap group from Jamaica, New York: Sticky Fingaz, Marlon "Big DS" Fletcher, Fredro Star and Suave Sonny Caesar. Big DS left in 1995; died of cancer on 5/22/2003 (age 30). Star acted in the movie *Sunset Park*.

OPUS
Pop-rock group from Austria: Herwig Rudisser (vocals), Ewald Pfleger (guitar), Kurt Rene Plisnier (keyboards), Niki Gruber (bass) and Gunter Grasmuck (drums).

ORBISON, Roy
Born on 4/23/1936 in Vernon, Texas. Died of a heart attack on 12/6/1988 (age 52). Operatic rock and roll-pop singer/songwriter/guitarist. Had own band, the Wink Westerners, in 1952. Attended North Texas State University with Pat Boone. First recorded for Je-Wel in early 1956 as leader of The Teen Kings. Toured with Sun Records shows to 1958. Toured with The Beatles in 1963. Wife Claudette killed in a motorcycle accident on 6/7/1966; two sons died in a fire in 1968. Member of the supergroup Traveling Wilburys in 1988.

ORCHESTRAL MANOEUVRES IN THE DARK
Electro-pop group formed in England: keyboardists/vocalists Andrew McCluskey and Paul Humphreys, multi-instrumentalist Martin Cooper and drummer Malcolm Holmes. Humphreys left in 1989.

ORGY
Electronic alternative-metal rock group from Los Angeles, California: Jay Gordon (vocals), Ryan Shuck (guitar), Amir Derakh (keyboards), Paige Haley (bass) and Bobby Hewitt (drums).

ORIGINAL, The
Born Everett Bradley in Indiana. Dance singer/songwriter/instrumentalist. Directed and performed in the off-Broadway musical *Stomp*.

ORIGINAL CASTE, The
Pop group from Canada: Dixie Lee Innes (lead vocals), Bruce Innes, Graham Bruce, Joseph Cavender and Bliss Mackie.

ORIGINAL CASUALS, The
Rock and roll vocal trio from Dallas, Texas: Frederick "Gary" Mears (lead), Jay Joe Adams and Paul Kearney.

ORIGINALS, The
R&B vocal group from Detroit, Michigan: Freddie Gorman (bass), Crathman Spencer and Henry Dixon (tenors) and Walter Gaines (baritone). Spencer replaced by Ty Hunter (of The Glass House) in 1971. Spencer died of a heart attack on 10/20/2004 (age 66). Gorman died on 6/13/2006 (age 67).

ORIOLES, The
R&B vocal group from Baltimore, Maryland: Sonny Til, Alexander Sharp, George Nelson and Johnny Reed, with Tommy Gaither (guitar). Gaither died in a car crash on 11/5/1950 (age 23). Gregory Carroll, formerly with The Four Buddies, joined in 1954. Nelson died of an asthma attack in 1959 (age 33). Sharp died in January 1970 (age 50). Til died of a heart attack on 12/9/1981 (age 56). Reed died on 6/18/2005 (age 81).

ORION THE HUNTER
Rock group formed in Boston, Massachusetts: Fran Cosmo (vocals), Barry Goudreau (guitar), Bruce Smith (bass) and Michael DeRosier (drums). Goudreau was a member of Boston and later with RTZ. Cosmo joined Boston in 1994.

ORLANDO, Tony (& DAWN)
Born Michael Anthony Orlando Cassavitis on 4/3/1944 in Manhattan, New York (of Greek/Puerto Rican parents). At age 16 was discovered by producer Don Kirshner. In 1967, became manager of April-Blackwood Music publishing company. Lead singer of New York studio group Wind in 1969. In 1970, formed Dawn which featured studio vocalists Toni Wine and Ellie Greenwich; then in 1971, teamed with session singers Telma Hopkins (from Louisville) and Joyce Vincent (from Detroit) to form a permanent Dawn. All of their hits were produced by Hank Medress (The Tokens) and Dave Appell (The Applejacks). Trio hosted weekly TV variety show *Tony Orlando & Dawn* from 1974-76. Group split in 1977. Orlando continued solo career. Hopkins acted on TV's *Bosom Buddies*, *Gimme A Break* and *Family Matters*. Orlando opened the Tony Orlando Yellow Ribbon Music Theater in Branson, Missouri, in the early 1990s.

ORLEANS
Pop-rock band formed in New York: John Hall (vocals, guitar; born on 10/25/1948), brothers Lawrence Hoppen (vocals, guitar) and Lance Hoppen (bass), Jerry Marotta (keyboards), and Wells Kelly (drums). Hall and Marotta left in 1977; replaced by Bob Leinback (keyboards) and R.A. Martin (horns). Kelly died on 10/28/1984 (age 35). Hall was elected to the U.S. House of Representatives (in New York) in 2006.

ORLONS, The
R&B group from Philadelphia, Pennsylvania: Rosetta Hightower (lead; born on 6/23/1944), Marlena Davis (born on 10/4/1944), Steve Caldwell (born on 11/22/1942) and Shirley Brickley (born on 12/9/1944). Davis and Caldwell left in 1964; replaced by Audrey Brickley. Disbanded in 1968. Shirley Brickley was shot to death on 10/13/1977 (age 32). Davis died of lung cancer on 2/27/1993 (age 48).

OR-N-MORE
Dance duo from New York: female singer Orfeh and producer Mike More.

ORPHEUS
Soft-rock group from Boston, Massachusetts: Bruce Arnold (vocals, guitar), Jack McKenes (guitar), John Eric Gulliksen (bass) and Harry Sandler (drums).

ORR, Benjamin
Born Benjamin Orzechowski on 8/9/1947 in Lakewood, Ohio. Died of cancer on 10/3/2000 (age 53). Bassist/vocalist of The Cars.

ORRALL, Robert Ellis
Born on 5/4/1955 in Winthrop, Massachusetts. Country-pop singer/songwriter/pianist.

ORRICO, Stacie
Born on 3/3/1986 in Seattle, Washington. Contemporary Christian-pop singer/songwriter.

ORTEGA, Jeannie
Born on 11/19/1986 in Brooklyn, New York (Puerto Rican parents). Dance singer/songwriter/actress. Appeared in the 2006 movie *Step Up*.

OSBORNE, Jeffrey
Born on 3/9/1948 in Providence, Rhode Island. R&B singer/songwriter/drummer. Lead singer of L.T.D. until 1980.

OSBORNE, Joan
Born on 7/8/1962 in Anchorage, Kentucky. Adult Alternative singer/songwriter/guitarist.

OSBOURNE, Kelly
Born on 10/27/1984 in London, England. Daughter of Ozzy Osbourne.

OSBOURNE, Ozzy
Born John Michael Osbourne on 12/3/1948 in Birmingham, England. Heavy-metal singer; former lead singer of Black Sabbath which he was fired from in 1978. Formed own band featuring guitarist Randy Rhoads who was killed in a plane crash on 3/19/1982 (age 25). Controversial in his concert antics. Married his manager Sharon Arden on 7/4/1982. Appeared in the 1986 movie *Trick Or Treat*. *The Osbournes*, a reality show based on his family's home life, ran on MTV from 2002-05.

OSKAR, Lee
Born on 3/24/1948 in Copenhagen, Denmark. Harmonica player. Studio musician in Los Angeles. Original member of War.

OSMOND, Donny
Born on 12/9/1957 in Ogden, Utah. Seventh son of George and Olive Osmond. Became a member of The Osmonds in 1963. Co-hosted both the musical/variety series *Donny & Marie* with his sister Marie Osmond and later the daytime talk show of the same name. Owned production company Night Star. In the 1990s, starred in the long-running stage production of *Joseph and the Amazing Technicolor Dreamcoat*.

OSMOND, Little Jimmy
Born on 4/16/1963 in Canoga Park, California. Youngest member of The Osmonds.

OSMOND, Marie
Born Olive Marie Osmond on 10/13/1959 in Ogden, Utah. Began performing in concert with her brothers at age 14. Co-hosted both the musical/variety series *Donny & Marie* with her brother Donny Osmond and later the daytime talk show of the same name. Hosted own musical/variety series *Marie*. Co-hosted the TV series *Ripley's Believe It Or Not*. Starred in the 1995 sitcom *Maybe This Time*. Finalist on the 2007 season of TV's *Dancing With The Stars*.

OSMONDS, The
Family group from Ogden, Utah. Alan (born on 6/22/1949), Wayne (born on 8/28/1951), Merrill (born on 4/30/1953), Jay (born on 3/2/1955) and Donny Osmond (born on 12/9/1957). Began as a quartet in 1959, singing religious and

OSMONDS, The — cont'd
barbershop-quartet songs. Regulars on Andy Williams' TV show from 1962-67. Alan, Wayne, Merrill and Jay turned to country music as The Osmond Brothers in the early 1980s.

O'SULLIVAN, Gilbert
Born Raymond O'Sullivan on 12/1/1946 in Waterford, Ireland. Adult Contemporary singer/songwriter.

OTHER ONES, The
Pop-rock group consisting of Australian siblings Jayney (vocals), Alf (vocals) and Johnny (bass) Klimek, and Germans Andreas Schwarz-Ruszczynski (guitar), Stephen Gottwald (keyboards) and Uwe Hoffmann (drums).

OTIS, Johnny, Show
Born John Veliotes on 12/28/1921 in Vallejo, California (of Greek parentage). R&B bandleader/composer. Wrote "Every Beat Of My Heart." Johnny's R&B Caravan featured the top R&B artists of the 1950s.

O-TOWN
Male teen pop vocal group from Orlando, Florida: Trevor Penick, Jacob Underwood, Ashley Parker Angel, Erik-Michael Estrada and Dan Miller. Group was put together while auditioning for the TV series *Making The Band*.

OTTO, James
Born on 7/29/1973 in Fort Lewis, Washington. Country singer/songwriter/guitarist.

OUR LADY PEACE
Rock group from Toronto, Ontario, Canada: Raine Maida (vocals), Mike Turner (guitar), Duncan Coutts (bass) and Jeremy Taggart (drums).

OUTFIELD, The
Pop-rock trio formed in London, England: Tony Lewis (vocals, bass), John Spinks (guitar, songwriter) and Alan Jackman (drums). Jackman left by 1990; Lewis and Spinks continued as a duo.

OUTHERE BROTHERS, The
Male rap-dance duo from Chicago, Illinois: Keith "Malik" Mayberry and Lamar "Hula" Mahone.

OUTKAST
Male hip-hop duo from Atlanta, Georgia: "Andre 3000" Benjamin (born on 5/27/1975) and Antwan "Big Boi" Patton (born on 2/1/1975). Both starred in the 2006 movie *Idlewild*.

OUTLAWS
Southern-rock group formed in Tampa, Florida: Henry Paul (vocals, guitar), Hughie Thomasson and Billy Jones (guitars), Frank O'Keefe (bass) and Monte Yoho (drums). By 1981, Freddie Salem, Rick Cua and David Dix had replaced Paul, O'Keefe and Yoho. Paul was a member of the country trio BlackHawk by 1993. Jones died on 2/7/1995 (age 45). O'Keefe died of a drug overdose on 2/26/1995 (age 44). Thomasson died of a heart attack on 9/9/2007 (age 55).

OUTSIDERS, The
Rock group from Cleveland, Ohio: Sonny Geraci (lead singer), Tom King (guitar), Bill Bruno (lead guitar), Mert Madsen (bass) and Rick Baker (drums). Geraci later led the group Climax.

OVATIONS, The
R&B group led by Louis Williams. Re-formed in 1972 with former members of Ollie & The Nightingales: Rochester Neal, Bill Davis and Quincy Billops (The Mad Lads). Williams died on 10/13/2002 (age 61).

OVERLANDERS, The
Male pop band from England: "Paul Arnold" Friswell (vocals), Pete Bartholomew (guitar), Laurie Mason (piano), Terry Widlake (bass) and David Walsh (drums).

OVERSTREET, Tommy
Born on 9/10/1937 in Oklahoma City, Oklahoma. Country singer/songwriter/guitarist.

OVIS
Born in New Orleans, Louisiana. Male singer/songwriter. As a sound engineer, worked with The B-52s, Green Jelly and Tiffany.

OWEN, Jake
Born Josh Owen on 8/28/1981 in Vero Beach, Florida. Country singer/songwriter.

OWEN, Reg
Born in 1928 in England. Orchestra leader. Also see The Knightsbridge Strings.

OWEN B.
Pop-rock group formed in Mansfield, Ohio: Jim Krause (vocals), Terry Van Auker (guitar), Tom Zinser (bass) and Bob Avery (drums). Avery was a member of The Music Explosion.

OWENS, Buck
Born Alvis Edgar Owens on 8/12/1929 in Sherman, Texas; raised in Mesa, Arizona. Died on 3/25/2006 (age 76). Country singer/guitarist/songwriter. Moved to Bakersfield, California, in 1951. Owens and Roy Clark hosted TV's *Hee Haw*, 1969-86. Backing group: The Buckaroos.

OWENS, Donnie
Born on 10/30/1938 in Pennsylvania. Accidentally shot to death on 10/27/1994 (age 55). Pop singer/guitarist. Played guitar for Duane Eddy's Rebels.

OXO
Pop-rock group from Miami, Florida: Ish "Angel" Ledesma (vocals; Foxy, Company B), Orlando (guitar), Frank Garcia (bass) and Freddy Alwag (drums).

OZARK MOUNTAIN DAREDEVILS
Country-rock group from Springfield, Missouri: Larry Lee (vocals, drums), John Dillon (guitar), Steve Cash (harmonica) and Michael Granda (bass).

OZO
British-based, pop-reggae group (eight members hail from seven different countries).

PABLO, Petey
Born Moses Barrett on 7/22/1973 in Greenville, North Carolina. Male rapper/songwriter.

PABLO CRUISE
Pop-rock group formed in San Francisco, California: Dave Jenkins (vocals, guitar), Bud Cockrell (bass, vocals; It's A Beautiful Day), Cory Lerios (keyboards, vocals) and Stephen Price (drums). Cockrell replaced by Bruce Day in 1977. John Pierce replaced Day, and guitarist Angelo Rossi joined in 1980.

PACIFIC GAS & ELECTRIC
Blues-rock group from California: Charles Allen (vocals), Glenn Schwartz and Tom Marshall (guitars), Brent Block (bass) and Frank Cook (drums). Allen spearheaded a new lineup in 1971; group name shortened to PG&E. Allen died on 5/7/1990 (age 48).

PACK, David
Born on 7/15/1952 in Huntington Park, California. Lead singer of Ambrosia.

PACK, The
Male rap group from Berekeley, California: DaMonte "Lil Uno" Johnson, Brandon "Lil B" McCartney, Lloyd "Young L" Omadhebo and Keith "Young $tunna" Jenkins.

PACKERS, The
R&B band formed by Charles "Packy" Axton (tenor sax). Axton, son of Estelle Axton, co-owner of Stax/Volt, had been in the Mar-Keys. Axton died in January 1974 (age 32).

PAGE, Ellen
Born on 2/21/1987 in Halifax, Nova Scotia, Canada. Female singer/actress. Starred as "Juno MacGuff" in the 2007 movie *Juno*.

PAGE, Martin
Born on 9/23/1959 in Southampton, England. Pop singer/songwriter. Wrote the hits "We Built This City," "These Dreams" and "King Of Wishful Thinking." Former member of the techno-dance duo Q-Feel.

PAGE, Patti
Born Clara Ann Fowler on 11/8/1927 in Muskogee, Oklahoma; raised in Tulsa, Oklahoma. One of 11 children. On radio KTUL with Al Klauser & His Oklahomans, as Ann Fowler, late 1940s. Another singer was billed as "Patti Page" for the Page Milk Company show on KTUL. When she left, Fowler took her place and name. With the Jimmy Joy band in 1947. On *Breakfast Club*, Chicago radio in 1947; signed by Mercury Records. Used multi-voice effect on her recordings. Own TV series *The Patti Page Show*, 1955-58, and *The Big Record*, 1957-58. In the 1960 movie *Elmer Gantry*.

PAGE, Tommy
Born on 5/24/1969 in West Caldwell, New Jersey. Pop singer/songwriter.

PAGES
Rock group from Los Angeles, California: Richard Page, Steve George, Charles Johnson, Jerry

Manfredi and George Lawrence. Page and George later formed Mr. Mister.

PAIGE, Jennifer
Born on 9/3/1973 in Marietta, Georgia. Pop singer.

PAIGE, Kevin
Born on 10/10/1966 in Memphis, Tennessee. Pop singer/songwriter.

PAINTER
Rock group from Canada: Doran Beattie (vocals), Barry Allen and Dan Lowe (guitars), Royden Morice (bass) and Bob Ego (drums).

PAISLEY, Brad
Born on 10/28/1972 in Glen Dale, West Virginia. Country singer/songwriter/guitarist. Married actress Kimberly Williams on 3/15/2003.

PAJAMA PARTY
Female dance-pop vocal trio from New York: Daphne Rubin-Vega, Jennifer McQuilkin and Susan Ranta. Lynn Critelli and Marialisa Costanzo replaced the latter two by 1991. Rubin-Vega acted in the Broadway show *Rent*.

PALMER, Robert
Born on 1/19/1949 in Batley, Yorkshire, England; raised on the Mediterranean island of Malta. Died of a heart attack on 9/26/2003 (age 54). Formed first band Mandrake Paddle Steamer in 1969. Lead singer of short-lived supergroup The Power Station.

PANIC AT THE DISCO
Punk-rock band from Las Vegas, Nevada: Brendan Urie (vocals, guitar), Ryan Ross (guitar), Brent Wilson (bass) and Spencer Smith (drums).

PAN'JABI MC
Born Rajinder Rai in 1975 in Coventry, England (Indian parents). Male DJ. Employs the "Bhangra" style of East Indian chants and beats combined with Western dance music.

PANTERA
Heavy-metal band formed in Arlington, Texas: Philip Anselmo (vocals), "Dimebag" Darrell Abbott (guitar), Rex Brown (bass) and Vinnie Paul Abbott (drums). Darrell and Paul are brothers. Group name is Spanish for Panther. Anselmo also with Down in 1995. Darrell was shot to death on stage on 12/8/2004 (age 38).

PANTHER Soundtrack
Featured on the soundtrack from the movie *Panther* starring Kadeem Hardison.

PAONE, Nicola
Born in 1939 in Spangler, Pennsylvania; raised in Sicily until coming to New York at age 15. Died of pneumonia on 12/25/2003 (age 64). Male vocalist/songwriter.

PAPA ROACH
Hard-rock group from Vacaville, California: Jacoby Shaddix (vocals), Jerry Horton (guitar), Tobin Esperance (bass) and Dave Buckner (drums). Buckner married Mia Tyler (daughter of Aerosmith's Steven Tyler) on 10/25/2003.

PAPERBOY
Born Mitchell Johnson in Los Angeles, California. Male rapper.

PAPER LACE
Pop group formed in England: Phil Wright (vocals, drums), Michael Vaughan and Chris Morris (guitars), and Cliff Fish (bass).

PARADE, The
Pop trio from Los Angeles, California: Jerry Riopelle, Murray MacLeod and Smokey Roberds.

PARADONS, The
R&B vocal group from Bakersfield, California: West Tyler, Chuck Weldon, Billy Myers and William Powers.

PARAGONS, The
R&B vocal group from Brooklyn, New York: Julian McMichael, Ben Frazier, Donald Travis, Ricky Jackson and Al Brown. McMichael later joined The Olympics. McMichael died in a motorcycle accident in June 1981 (age 45).

PARAMORE
Pop-rock band formed in Franklin, Tennessee: Hayley Williams (vocals), brothers Josh Farro (guitar) and Zac Farro (drums), with Jeremy Davis (bass).

PARIS, Mica
Born Michelle Wallen on 4/27/1969 in London, England. R&B-dance singer.

PARIS, Sarina
Born in Canada. Female dance-pop singer.

PARIS SISTERS, The
White "girl group" from San Francisco, California: Albeth, Priscilla and Sherrell Paris. First recorded for Decca in 1954. Priscilla died on 3/5/2004 (age 63).

PARKAYS, The
Instrumental trio from Memphis, Tennessee: Gilbert Caple, Fred "David E." Ford and Walter Maynard.

PARKER, Bobby
Born on 8/31/1937 in Lafayette, Louisiana. Blues singer/guitarist.

PARKER, Fess
Born on 8/16/1927 in Fort Worth, Texas. Actor; starred in the movie *Davy Crockett* and TV's *Daniel Boone* (1964-70).

PARKER, Graham
Born on 11/18/1950 in Camberley, Surrey, England. Pop-rock singer/songwriter/guitarist. The Rumour: Brinsley Schwarz and Martin Belmont (guitars), Bob Andrews (keyboards), Andrew Bodnar (bass) and Stephen Goulding (drums).

PARKER, Little Junior
Born Herman Parker, Jr. on 3/3/1927 in West Memphis, Arkansas. Died of a brain tumor on 11/8/1971 (age 44). Blues singer/harmonica player. Formed own combo, Little Junior's Blue Flames, in 1951. First recorded for Modern Records in 1952. Wrote the Elvis Presley classic "Mystery Train."

PARKER, Ray Jr. / Raydio
Born on 5/1/1954 in Detroit, Michigan. R&B singer/songwriter/guitarist. Prominent session guitarist in California; worked with Stevie Wonder, Barry White and others. Formed and led the band Raydio in 1977 with Arnell Carmichael, Jerry Knight, Larry Tolbert, Darren Carmichael and Charles Fearing. Parker went solo in 1982. Knight later recorded in duo Ollie & Jerry.

PARKER, Robert
Born on 10/14/1930 in New Orleans, Louisiana. R&B singer/saxophonist.

PARKS, Michael
Born on 4/24/1940 in Corona, California. Singer/ actor. Appeared in several movies. Played "Jim Bronson" in the 1969 TV series *Then Came Bronson*.

PARLIAMENT / FUNKADELIC
Highly influential and prolific funk aggregation of nearly 40 musicians spearheaded by George Clinton (born on 7/22/1941; producer/songwriter/lead singer). Clinton founded doo-wop group The Parliaments in 1955 in Newark, New Jersey. First recorded for Hull in 1958. By 1967, evolved into a soul group with lineup of vocalists Clinton, Raymond Davis, Calvin Simon, Clarence "Fuzzy" Haskins and Grady Thomas. In 1967, relocated to Detroit and added rhythm section. In 1968, Clinton formed Funkadelic with rhythm section of The Parliaments, recruited keyboardist Bernie Worrell and changed The Parliaments name to Parliament. Although on different labels, Parliament and Funkadelic shared the same personnel which included former members of The JB's: brothers Phelps "Catfish" (guitar) and William "Bootsy" Collins (bass), Frank "Kash" Waddy (drums) and horn players Maceo Parker (Maceo And The Macks) and Fred Wesley. Known as "A Parliafunkadelicament Thang," this funk corporation included various offshoots: Bootsy's Rubber Band, The Horny Horns, The Brides Of Funkenstein, Parlet and Xavion, among others. Concert tours featured elaborate staging and characters.

PARR, John
Born on 11/18/1954 in Nottingham, Nottingham-shire, England. Pop-rock singer/songwriter.

PARRISH, Dean
Born Phil Anastasi in 1942 in Brooklyn, New York. White R&B-styled singer.

PARSONS, Alan, Project
Born on 12/20/1948 in London, England. Guitarist/keyboardist/producer. Engineered *Abbey Road* by The Beatles and *Dark Side Of The Moon* by Pink Floyd. Project featured various musicians and vocalists. Eric Woolfson (vocals, keyboards) wrote most of the lyrics.

PARSONS, Gram
Born Cecil Connor on 11/5/1946 in Winter Haven, Florida. Died of a drug overdose on 9/19/1973 (age 26). Country-rock singer/guitarist. Member of The Byrds (1968) and the Flying Burrito Brothers (1968-70).

PARTLAND BROTHERS
Pop-rock duo from Colgan, Ontario, Canada: Chris (vocals, guitars) and G.P. (vocals, percussion) Partland.

PARTNERS IN KRYME
Hip-hop duo formed in Syracuse, New York: DJ James Alpern and rapper Richard Usher. KRYME: Keeping Rhythm Your Motivating Energy.

PARTON, Dolly
Born on 1/19/1946 in Locust Ridge, Tennessee. Country singer/songwriter/actress. Regular on Porter Wagoner's TV show (1967-74). Starred in the movies 9 To 5, The Best Little Whorehouse In Texas, Steel Magnolias and Straight Talk. In 1986, opened Dollywood theme park in the Smoky Mountains. Hosted own TV variety show in 1987.

PARTRIDGE FAMILY, The
Popularized through The Partridge Family TV series, broadcast from 1970-74. Recordings by series stars David Cassidy (lead singer) and real-life stepmother Shirley Jones (backing vocals). David, son of actor Jack Cassidy, was born on 4/12/1950 in New York City; raised in California. Shirley, born on 3/31/1934 in Smithton, Pennsylvania, starred in the movie musicals Oklahoma and The Music Man; married David's father in 1956.

PARTY, The
Pop-dance group from Florida: Tiffini Hale, Albert Fields, Chase Hampton, Damon Pampolina and Deedee Magno. All were cast members of TV's The Mickey Mouse Club in 1988.

PASADENAS, The
R&B-dance vocal group from England: brothers Aaron, David and Michael Milliner, with John Banfield and Hammish Seelochan.

PASSIONS, The
White doo-wop group from Brooklyn, New York: Jimmy Gallagher (lead), Tony Armato, Albee Galione and Vinnie Acierno.

PASTELS, The
R&B vocal group formed at the U.S. Air Force base in Narsarssuak, Greenland: Big Dee Irwin (lead), Richard Travis, Tony Thomas and Jimmy Willingham. Irwin died on 8/27/1995 (age 63).

PASTEL SIX, The
Pop group from California: Bob Toten (lead vocals), Tony Stealman, Rick Rodriguez, Erick Fickert, Lynn Hamm, Bill Myers, Dave Cadison. Ages 18-21 in 1962. Headlined at the Cinnamon Cinder club in North Hollywood.

PASTOR TROY
Born Micah LeVar Troy in Augusta, Georgia. Male rapper.

PAT & MICK
DJs Pat Sharp and Mick Brown from London, England. Backing vocals by Mae McKenna, Mirian Stockley and Mike Stock (of the prolific production trio of Stock, Aitken and Waterman).

PAT & the SATELLITES
Rock and roll band of studio musicians featuring Pat Otts (from Olean, New York), King Curtis and Wayne Lips.

PATE, Johnny, Quintet
Born on 12/5/1923 in Chicago Heights, Illinois. Black bassist/bandleader/arranger. Conductor for many of The Impressions hits.

PATIENCE & PRUDENCE
White vocal duo from Los Angeles, California: sisters Patience and Prudence McIntyre (ages 14 & 11 in 1956).

PATRA
Born Dorothy Smith on 11/22/1972 in Kingston, Jamaica. Female dance-reggae singer.

PATTERSON, Kellee
Born in Gary, Indiana. Soul singer/actress. Crowned Miss Indiana in 1971.

PATTON, Robbie
Born in England. Pop-rock singer/songwriter.

PATTY & THE EMBLEMS
R&B vocal group from Camden, New Jersey: Patty Russell (lead), Eddie Watts (1st tenor), Vance Walker (2nd tenor) and Alexander Wilde (baritone). Patty died of leukemia on 9/5/1998 (age 56). Wilde died of kidney failure on 11/13/1998 (age 60).

PAUL, Billy
Born Paul Williams on 12/1/1934 in Philadelphia, Pennsylvania. R&B singer. Also see the Philadelphia International All Stars.

PAUL, Christopher, & Shawn
Brother-and-sister teen pop vocal duo from Salt Lake City, Utah: Christopher and Shawn Engemann. Shawn later known as Shawn Southwick (married TV talk show host Larry King on 9/5/1997). Their father, Carl Engemann, was vice president of A&R for Capitol Records and once managed The Osmonds. Their uncle, Bob Engemann, was a member of The Lettermen.

PAUL, Henry, Band
Born on 8/25/1949 in Kingston, New York. Southern-rock singer/guitarist. Member of the Outlaws and BlackHawk. His band: Dave Fiester and Billy Crain (guitars), Wally Dentz (bass) and Bill Hoffman (drums).

PAUL, Les, & Mary Ford
Paul was born Lester Polsfuss on 6/9/1915 in Waukesha, Wisconsin. Ford was born Colleen Summers on 7/7/1924 in Pasadena, California; died on 9/30/1977 (age 53). Les Paul was an innovator in electric guitar and multi-track recordings. Married to vocalist Mary Ford from 1949-63.

PAUL, Sean
Born Sean Paul Henriques on 1/8/1973 in Kingston, Jamaica. Reggae singer/songwriter. Not to be confused with the member of the YoungBloodz.

PAUL & PAULA
Pop vocal duo. Ray "Paul" Hildebrand was born on 12/21/1940 in Joshua, Texas. Jill "Paula" Jackson was born on 5/20/1942 in McCaney, Texas.

194

PAULETTE SISTERS
Pop vocal group: sisters Barbara, Jane, Gloria and Betty Paulette.

PAVEMENT
Rock group formed in Stockton, California: Stephen Malkmus (vocals, guitar), Scott Kannberg (guitar), Bob Nastanovich (percussion), Mark Ibold (bass) and Steve West (drums).

PAVONE, Rita
Born on 8/23/1945 in Turin, Italy. Pop singer.

PAYCHECK, Johnny
Born Donald Eugene Lytle on 5/31/1938 in Greenfield, Ohio. Died of emphysema on 2/18/2003 (age 64). Country singer/songwriter/guitarist.

PAYNE, Freda
Born on 9/19/1945 in Detroit, Michigan. R&B singer. Sister of Scherrie Payne (of The Supremes). Formerly married to Gregory Abbott.

PC QUEST
Teen pop vocal group from Shawnee, Oklahoma: Kim Whipkey, Drew Nichols, and brothers Chad and Steve Petree.

PEACE CHOIR
All-star choir assembled by Yoko Ono, Sean Ono Lennon and Lenny Kravitz. Comprised of Amina, Adam Ant, Sebastian Bach (Skid Row), Bros, Felix Cavaliere (The Rascals), Terence Trent D'Arby, John Frusciante and Flea (both of The Red Hot Chili Peppers), Peter Gabriel, Kadeem Hardison (TV actor), Ofra Haza, Joe Higgs, Bruce Hornsby, Lee Jaffe, Al Jarreau, Jazzie B (Soul II Soul), Davey Johnstone, Cyndi Lauper, Little Richard, L.L. Cool J, M.C. Hammer, Michael McDonald, Duff McKagan (Guns N' Roses), Alannah Myles, New Voices Of Freedom, Randy Newman, Tom Petty, Iggy Pop, Q-Tip, Bonnie Raitt, Run (Run-DMC), Dave Stewart, Teena Marie, Little Steven Van Zandt, Don Was [Was (Not Was)], Wendy & Lisa, and Ahmet, Dweezil and Moon Zappa.

PEACHES & HERB
R&B vocal duo from Washington DC: Francine "Peaches" Barker (born Francine Hurd on 4/28/1947; died on 8/13/2005, age 58) and Herb Fame (born Herbert Feemster on 10/1/1942). Marlene Mack filled in for Francine from 1968-69. Re-formed with Fame and Linda "Peaches" Green in 1977.

PEACH UNION
Pop trio from England: Lisa Lamb, Pascal Gabriel and Paul Statham.

PEANUT BUTTER CONSPIRACY, The
Psychedelic-rock group from Los Angeles, California: Barbara "Sandi" Robison (vocals), Lance Fent and John Merrill (guitars), Al Brackett (bass) and Jim Voigt (drums). Robison died on 4/22/1988 (age 43). Voigt died on 11/7/2000 (age 54).

PEARL, Leslie
Born on 7/26/1952 in Pennsylvania. Pop singer/songwriter.

PEARLETTES
R&B vocal group from Los Angeles, California: sisters Lynda and Sheila Galloway with Mary Meade and Priscilla Kennedy.

PEARL JAM
Rock group formed in Seattle, Washington: Eddie Vedder (vocals; born on 12/23/1964), Stone Gossard (guitar; born on 7/20/1966), Mike McCready (guitar; born on 4/5/1965), Jeff Ament (bass; born on 3/10/1963) and Dave Krusen (drums; born on 3/10/1966). Dave Abbruzzese (born on 5/17/1968) replaced Krusen in 1993. Gossard and Ament were members of Mother Love Bone. All except Krusen recorded with Temple Of The Dog. Band acted in the movie *Singles* as Matt Dillon's band, Citizen Dick. Abbruzzese left band in August 1994. Drummer Jack Irons (of the Red Hot Chili Peppers; born on 7/18/1962) joined in late 1994. McCready also put together Mad Season in 1994. Matt Cameron (born on 11/28/1962) replaced Irons in 1999.

PEBBLES
Born Perri McKissack on 8/29/1965 in Oakland, California. R&B-dance singer. Nicknamed "Pebbles" by her family for her resemblance to cartoon character Pebbles Flintstone. Formerly married to L.A. Reid (of The Deele). Cousin of Cherrelle. Assembled/managed TLC.

PEDICIN, Mike, Quintet
Born in 1917 in Philadelphia, Pennsylvania. White alto saxophonist. Other members: Al Mauro (vocals, drums), Sam Cocchia (guitar), Buddy LaPlanta (piano) and Lou DeFrancis (bass).

PEEBLES, Ann
Born on 4/27/1947 in Kinloch, Missouri; later based in Memphis, Tennessee. R&B singer/songwriter.

PEEK, Dan
Born on 11/1/1950 in Panama City, Florida. Singer/songwriter. Member of America.

PEEK, Paul
Born on 6/23/1937 in High Point, North Carolina. Died of liver failure on 4/3/2001 (age 63). Rock and roll singer/guitarist. Joined Gene Vincent's Blue Caps as a rhythm guitarist in 1956. Left for a solo career in 1958.

PEELS, The
Novelty-pop studio production by Tash Howard.

PEEPLES, Nia
Born on 12/10/1961 in Hollywood, California. R&B singer/actress. Played "Nicole Chapman" on TV's *Fame*. Hosted *Top Of The Pops* TV show and own syndicated music video dance TV program, *Party Machine*. Married to Howard Hewett from 1989-93.

PENDERGRASS, Teddy
Born on 3/26/1950 in Philadelphia, Pennsylvania. Male R&B singer. Lead singer of Harold Melvin & The Blue Notes from 1970-76. Went solo in 1976. Acted in the 1982 movie *Soup For One*. Auto accident on 3/18/1982 left him partially paralyzed. Also see Philadelphia International All Stars.

PENDULUM
Techno-rock/dance trio: David Barrow, James Paul Kenny and David Quintana. All share vocals.

PENGUINS, The
Doo-wop quartet from Los Angeles, California: Cleveland Duncan (lead), Dexter Tisby (tenor), Bruce Tate (baritone) and Curtis Williams (bass). Tate died on 6/20/1973 (age 36).

PENISTON, Ce Ce
Born on 9/6/1969 in Dayton, Ohio; raised in Phoenix, Arizona. R&B-dance singer/songwriter.

PENN, Dawn
Born in 1952 in Kingston, Jamaica. Reggae singer/songwriter.

PENN, Michael
Born on 8/1/1958 in Manhattan, New York. Pop-rock singer/songwriter/guitarist. Brother of actors Sean and Christopher Penn. Son of actor/director Leo Penn and actress Eileen Ryan. Married Aimee Mann on 12/29/1997.

PENTAGONS, The
R&B vocal group from San Bernardino, California: Josephus Jones (lead), his half-brother Otis Munson and brothers Ken and Ted Goodloe. Herb Reed of The Platters married the Goodloe's sister, Pauline. Ken Goodloe died of a heart attack on 8/4/91.

PEOPLE
Pop-rock group from San Jose, California: Gene Mason and Larry Norman (vocals), Jeoff Levin (guitar), Albert Ribisi (keyboards), Robb Levin (bass) and Denny Friedkin (drums). Norman was inducted into the Gospel Music Hall of Fame in 2001. Norman died of heart failure on 2/24/2008 (age 60).

PEOPLE'S CHOICE
R&B-dance group from Philadelphia, Pennsylvania: Frankie Brunson (vocals), Guy Fiske and Leon Lee (guitars), Roger Andrews (bass) and Dave Thompson (drums). Darnell Jordan replaced Lee in 1973.

PEPPERMINT, Danny
Born Daniel Lamego in Brooklyn, New York. Rock and roll singer. Electrocuted on stage on 1/24/1962 at the Thunderbird Hotel in Las Vegas, Nevada (fully recovered).

PEPPERMINT RAINBOW, The
Pop group from Baltimore, Maryland: sisters Bonnie and Pat Lamdin (vocals), Doug Lewis (guitar), Skip Harris (bass) and Tony Corey (drums). Discovered by producer Paul Leka (Steam).

PEPPERMINT TROLLEY COMPANY, The
Pop band from Redlands, California: brothers Danny Faragher (keyboards) and Jimmy Faragher (bass; later recorded as the Faragher Bros.), Greg Tornquist (guitar) and Casey Cunningham (drums). All share vocals. Group later recorded as Bones.

PEPPERS, The
Pop instrumental studio duo from Paris, France: Mat Camison (synthesizer) and Pierre Dahan (drums).

PEPSI & SHIRLIE
Female R&B-dance vocal duo from England: Lawrie "Pepsi" DeMacque (born on 12/10/1958) and Shirlie Holliman (born on 4/18/1962). Duo worked as backing vocalists for George Michael & Wham!, 1984-86.

PERCELLS, The
Female R&B vocal group formed in Long Island, New York: Gail Jones (lead), Jean Johnson, Betty Lloyd and Joan Paulin.

PEREZ, Amanda
Born in Fort Wayne, Indiana. R&B-dance singer/songwriter.

PERFECT CIRCLE, A
Hard-rock duo from Hollywood, California: Maynard James Keenan (vocals) and Billy Howerdel (guitar). Keenan is also lead singer of Tool.

PERFECT GENTLEMEN
Pre-teen R&B trio from Boston, Massachusetts: Corey Blakely, Tyrone Sutton and Maurice Starr Jr. All were between the ages of 11-12 in 1990. Produced by New Edition and New Kids On The Block producer, Maurice Starr Sr.

PERFECT STRANGER
Country group from Carthage, Texas: Steve Murray (vocals), Richard Raines (guitar), Shayne Morrison (bass) and Andy Ginn (drums).

PERICOLI, Emilio
Born on 1/7/1928 in Cesenatico, Italy. Adult Contemporary singer/actor.

PERKINS, Carl
Born on 4/9/1932 in Ridgely, Tennessee. Died of a stroke on 1/19/1998 (age 65). Rockabilly singer/songwriter/guitarist. Formed family band consisting of Carl (guitar), brothers Jay B. (guitar) and Clayton (bass), and W.B. Holland (drums). Signed with Sam Phillips' Flip label, a subsidiary of Sun Records, in 1954. Member of Johnny Cash's touring troupe from 1965-75. In the movie *Into The Night*.

PERKINS, George, & The Silver Stars
R&B group from Shreveport, Louisiana. Led by singer George Perkins.

PERKINS, Joe
Born in Nashville, Tennessee. R&B singer.

PERKINS, Tony
Born on 4/14/1932 in Manhattan, New York. Died of AIDS on 9/12/1992 (age 60). Actor/singer. Starred in dozens of movies from 1953-92.

PERRY, Katy
Born Katheryn Hudson on 10/25/1984 in Santa Barbara, California. Female singer/songwriter/guitarist.

PERRY, Steve
Born on 1/22/1949 in Hanford, California. Lead singer of Journey.

PERSON, Houston
Born on 11/10/1934 in Florence, South Carolina. Black jazz tenor saxophonist.

PERSUADERS, The
R&B vocal group formed in Harlem, New York:
Doug Scott, Willie Holland, James Barnes and
Charles Stodghill.

PETER & GORDON
Pop vocal duo formed in London, England: Peter
Asher (born on 6/22/1944 in London, England) and
Gordon Waller (born on 6/4/1945 in Braemar,
Scotland). Asher later went into production and
management, including work with Linda Ronstadt,
James Taylor and 10,000 Maniacs.

PETER, PAUL & MARY
Folk trio formed in Greenwich Village, New York:
Peter Yarrow (born on 5/31/1938 in Brooklyn, New
York), Paul Stookey (born on 12/30/1937 in
Baltimore, Maryland) and Mary Travers (born on
11/7/1936 in Louisville, Kentucky). Their first five
albums (1962-65) were all Top 10 hits.

PETERS, Bernadette
Born Bernadette Lazzara on 2/28/1948 in Queens,
New York. Actress/singer. Appeared in several
movies and TV shows.

PETERSEN, Paul
Born on 9/23/45 in Glendale, California. Pop
singer/actor. Member of Disney's "Mouseketeers"
and played teenager "Jeff Stone" on TV's Donna
Reed Show (1958-66).

PETERSON, Bobby, Quintet
R&B-jazz band from Chester, Pennsylvania: Bobby
Peterson (vocals, piano), Joe Pyatt (tenor sax),
Chico Green (bass), David Butler (drums) and Jamo
Thomas (conga drums, bongos).

PETERSON, Michael
Born on 8/7/1959 in Tucson, Arizona. Country
singer/songwriter/guitarist.

PETERSON, Ray
Born on 4/23/1935 in Denton, Texas. Died of cancer
on 1/25/2005 (age 69). Pop singer. Started singing
in his early teens while being treated for polio at a
Texas hospital. Formed own Dunes label in 1960.

PETS, The
Session group formed by Joe Lubin; included Plas
Johnson (sax) and Earl Palmer (drums). Touring
group was put together featuring Richard Podolor
(Richie Allen, The Hondells), who later became a
top producer, working with Three Dog Night and
Steppenwolf, among others.

PET SHOP BOYS
Synth-pop/dance duo formed in England: Neil
Tennant (vocals; born on 7/10/1954) and Chris
Lowe (keyboards; born on 10/4/1959). Tennant was
a writer for the British fan magazine Smash Hits.
Tennant also recorded with the group Electronic.

PETTY, Norman, Trio
Born on 5/25/1927 in Clovis, New Mexico. Died on
8/15/1984 (age 57). His trio: Petty (piano), wife
Violet Ann (piano) and Jack Vaughn (guitar). Later
produced Buddy Holly and The Fireballs.

PETTY, Tom, & The Heartbreakers
Born on 10/20/1950 in Gainesville, Florida. Rock
singer/songwriter/guitarist. Formed The
Heartbreakers in Los Angeles, California: Mike
Campbell (guitar; born on 2/1/1950), Benmont Tench
(keyboards; born on 9/7/1953) Ron Blair (bass; born
on 9/16/1948) and Stan Lynch (drums; born on
5/21/1955). Howie Epstein (born on 7/21/1955; died
of a drug overdose on 2/23/2003, age 47) replaced
Blair in 1982. Blair returned in 2002, replacing
Epstein. Steve Ferrone replaced Lynch in 1995.
Petty appeared in the movies FM and Made In
Heaven. Member of the Traveling Wilburys.

PHAIR, Liz
Born on 4/17/1967 in New Haven, Connecticut.
Rock singer/songwriter.

PHAJJA
R&B vocal trio from Chicago, Illinois: sisters Kena
and Nakia Epps, with Karen Johnson.

PHARCYDE, The
Male rap group from Los Angeles, California:
Trevant Hardson, Imani Wilcox, Romye Robinson
and Derrick Stewart.

PHAROAHE MONCH
Born Troy Jamerson in Queens, New York. Male
rapper. Former member of Organized Konfusion.

PHARRELL
Born Pharrell Williams on 4/5/1973 in Virginia
Beach, Virginia. Male rapper/producer/songwriter.
Member of prolific production trio The Neptunes
(recorded as N*E*R*D).

PHELPS, James
Born in Shreveport, Louisiana. Gospel singer.
Member of The Soul Stirrers from 1964-65.

PHILADELPHIA INTERNATIONAL ALL STARS
Supergroup of Philadelphia International artists: Lou
Rawls, Billy Paul, Teddy Pendergrass, The O'Jays,
Archie Bell and Dee Dee Sharp Gamble.

PHILARMONICS, The
Studio group assembled by British conductor/
arranger Steve Gray.

PHILLIPS, Little Esther
Born Esther Mae Jones on 12/23/1935 in
Galveston, Texas; raised in Los Angeles, California.
Died of liver failure on 8/7/1984 (age 48). R&B
singer. One of the first female superstars of R&B.
Recorded and toured with The Johnny Otis Rhythm
& Blues Caravan, 1948-54. Bouts with drug
addiction frequently interrupted her career and
eventually led to her death.

PHILLIPS, John
Born on 8/30/1935 in Paris Island, South Carolina.
Died of heart failure on 3/18/2001 (age 65).
Co-founder of The Mamas & The Papas. Father of
actress MacKenzie Phillips and singer Chynna
Phillips (of Wilson Phillips). Co-wrote The Beach
Boys' 1988 #1 hit "Kokomo."

PHILLIPS, Phil, With The Twilights
Born John Phillip Baptiste on 3/14/1931 in Lake
Charles, Louisiana. Black singer/guitarist.

PHILLIPS, Shawn
Born on 2/3/1943 in Fort Worth, Texas. Male Adult Contemporary singer/songwriter/guitarist.

PHILLY CREAM
Soul session band from Philadelphia, Pennsylvania. Featured vocalists Valarie Lipford and Samuel Tompkins.

PHILLY DEVOTIONS
R&B-dance group from Philadelphia, Pennsylvania: Ellis "Butch" Hill, Ernest "Chucky" Gibson, Morris Taylor and Matthew Coginton.

PHILLY'S MOST WANTED
Male rap duo from Philadelphia, Pennsylvania: Al "Boobonic" Holly and Joel "Mr. Man" Witherspoon.

PHOTOGLO, Jim
Born on 4/8/1951 in Los Angeles, California. Pop singer/songwriter.

PIAF, Edith
Born Edith Giovanna Gassion on 12/19/1915 in Belleville, Paris, France. Died of cancer on 10/11/1963 (age 47). Legendary French chanteuse. As a teen, sang for pennies in Paris streets; eventually became an international music hall/cabaret star.

PIANO RED
Born William Lee Perryman on 10/19/1911 in Hampton, Georgia; raised in Atlanta, Georgia. Died of cancer on 7/25/1985 (age 73). Boogie woogie singer/pianist.

PICKETT, Bobby "Boris", & The Crypt-Kickers
Born on 2/11/1938 in Somerville, Massachusetts. Died of leukemia on 4/25/2007 (age 69). Novelty singer/songwriter. Began recording career in Hollywood while aspiring to be an actor. A member of The Stompers in early 1962. Leon Russell, Johnny McCrae (Ronny & The Daytonas), Rickie Page (The Bermudas) and Gary Paxton (Hollywood Argyles) were The Crypt-Kickers.

PICKETT, Wilson
Born on 3/18/1941 in Prattville, Alabama; later based in Detroit, Michigan. Died of a heart attack on 1/19/2006 (age 64). Soul singer/songwriter. Nicknamed the "Wicked Pickett." Sang in local gospel groups. To Detroit in 1955. With The Falcons, 1961-63. Career took off after recording in Memphis with guitarist/producer Steve Cropper.

PICKETTYWITCH
Pop group from London, England. Led by female singers Polly Brown and Maggie Farran. Polly later became lead singer of Sweet Dreams.

PICKLER, Kellie
Born on 6/28/1986 in Palestine, North Carolina. Country singer/songwriter. Finalist on the 2006 season of TV's *American Idol*.

PIECES OF A DREAM
Jazz-styled trio from Philadelphia, Pennsylvania: James Lloyd (keyboards), Cedric Napoleon (bass) and Curtis Harmon (drums).

PIECES OF EIGHT
Pop-rock duo: Brent Forston and Steven Caldwell of the Swingin' Medallions. Caldwell died of cancer on 1/28/2002 (age 54).

PIERCE, Webb
Born on 8/8/1921 in West Monroe, Louisiana. Died of heart failure on 2/24/1991 (age 69). Country singer/songwriter/guitarist. Acted in the movies *Buffalo Guns*, *Music City USA* and *Road To Nashville*.

PIGG, Landon
Born on 8/6/1983 in Nashville, Tennessee; raised in Chicago, Illinois. Male singer/songwriter.

PILOT
Pop-rock trio from Edinburgh, Scotland: David Paton (vocals, guitar), Bill Lyall (keyboards) and Stuart Tosh (drums). Lyall died of AIDS in December 1989 (age 36).

PILTDOWN MEN, The
Rock and roll studio band assembeld by Ed Cobb (of The Four Preps): Lincoln Mayorga (piano), Bob Bain (guitar), Scott Gordon (sax), Jackie Kelso (sax), Tommy Tedesco (bass) and Alan Brenmanen (drums). Band named after the infamous "Piltdown Man" hoax of 1912.

PINERA, Mike
Born on 9/29/1948 in Tampa, Florida. Rock singer/songwriter/guitarist. Member of Iron Butterfly and Blues Image.

P!NK
Born Alecia Moore on 9/8/1979 in Doylestown, Pennsylvania; raised in Philadelphia, Pennsylvania. Female pop-dance-rock singer/songwriter.

PINK FLOYD
Progressive-rock band formed in England: David Gilmour (vocals, guitar; born on 3/6/1946; replaced Syd Barrett in 1968), Roger Waters (vocals, bass), Rick Wright (keyboards) and Nick Mason (drums). Wright left in early 1982. Waters went solo in 1984. Band inactive, 1984-86. Gilmour, Mason and Wright regrouped in 1987. Group name taken from Georgia bluesmen Pink Anderson and Floyd Council. Barrett died on 7/9/2006 (age 60). Wright died of cancer on 9/15/2008 (age 65).

PINK LADY
Female disco duo from Shizuoka Prefecture, Japan: Mie Nemoto and Kei Masuda. Hosted own summer TV variety show in U.S., 1979.

PINSON, Bobby
Born in Tulsa, Oklahoma; raised in Texas. Country singer/songwriter/guitarist.

PIPKINS, The
Pop vocal duo formed in England: Roger Greenaway and Tony Burrows (low voice). Worked together in studio group White Plains.

PITBULL
Born Armando Perez on 1/15/1981 in Miami, Florida. Latin male rapper.

PITNEY, Gene
Born on 2/17/1940 in Hartford, Connecticut; raised in Rockville, Connecticut. Died on 4/5/2006 (age 66). Own band at Rockville High School. Recorded for Decca in 1959 with Ginny Arnell as Jamie & Jane. Recorded for Blaze in 1960 as Billy Bryan. First recorded under own name for Festival in 1960. Wrote "Hello Mary Lou," "He's A Rebel" and "Rubber Ball."

PIXIES
Alternative punk-rock group formed in Boston, Massachusetts: Frank Black (vocals), Joey Santiago (guitar), Kim Deal (bass) and David Lovering (drums). Deal was also a member of The Breeders.

PIXIES THREE, The
White teen female trio (ages 14-16 in 1963) from Hanover, Pennsylvania: Midge Bollinger (lead), Debbie Swisher and Kaye McCool. Bonnie Long replaced Bollinger in 1964. Swisher replaced Peggy Santiglia as lead singer of The Angels, 1967-68.

PIZANI, Frank
Born on 1/24/1935 in Chicago, Illinois. Lead singer of The Highlights.

PLACE, Mary Kay
Born on 8/23/1947 in Tulsa, Oklahoma. Singer/composer/comedienne. Script writer for many TV comedy shows. Played "Loretta Haggers" on TV's *Mary Hartman, Mary Hartman*.

PLAIN WHITE T'S
Rock band from Villa Park, Illinois: Tom Higgenson (vocals), Dave Tirio (guitar), Tim Lopez (guitar), Mike Retondo (bass) and De'Mar Hamilton (drums).

PLANET P
Studio group assembled by German producer Peter Hauke. Tony Carey was lead singer.

PLANET SOUL
Dance duo from Miami, Florida: producer George Costa and singer Nadine Renee. Brenda Dee replaced Renee in early 1996.

PLANT, Robert
Born on 8/20/1948 in West Bromwich, England. Hard-rock singer/songwriter. Member of Led Zeppelin and The Honeydrippers. Studied accounting before becoming lead singer of such British blues groups as Black Snake Moan, The Banned and The Crawling King Snakes. Also with the groups Listen and Band Of Joy. Fully recovered from a serious auto accident in Greece on 8/4/1975.

PLATINUM BLONDE
Rock group from Canada: Mark Holmes (vocals), Sergio Galli, Kenny MacLean and Chris Steffler.

PLATT, Eddie
Born Eddie Platakis on 12/8/1921 in Cleveland, Ohio; raised in Rossford, Ohio. Saxophonist/bandleader.

PLATTERS, The
R&B group formed in Los Angeles, California: Tony Williams (lead; born on 4/5/1928; died on 8/14/1992, age 64), David Lynch (tenor; born on 7/3/1929; died on 1/2/1981, age 51), Paul Robi (baritone; born on 8/20/1931; died on 2/1/1989, age 57), Herb Reed (bass; born on 8/7/1931) and Zola Taylor (born on 3/17/1938; died on 4/30/2007, age 69). Group first recorded for Federal in 1954, with Alex Hodge instead of Robi, and without Zola Taylor. Hit "Only You" was written by manager Buck Ram (died on 1/1/1991, age 83) and first recorded for Federal. To Mercury in 1955, re-recorded "Only You." Williams left to go solo; replaced by Sonny Turner in 1959. Taylor replaced by Sandra Dawn; Robi replaced by Nate Nelson (formerly in The Flamingos) in 1966. In 1976, Turner replaced by Monroe Powell. Nelson died of a heart attack on 6/1/1984 (age 52). Reed is the only original member still performing; billed as Herb Reed & The Platters.

PLAY-N-SKILLZ
Male hip-hop duo from Irving, Texas: brothers Juan "Play" Salinas and Oscar "Skillz" Salinas.

PLAYA
R&B vocal trio from Louisville, Kentucky: Ben Bush, John Peacock and Stephen "Static" Garrett. Garrett died on 2/25/2008 (age 33).

PLAYAZ CIRCLE
Male rap duo from College Park, Georgia: Tauheed "Tity Boi" Epps and Earl "Dolla Boy" Conyers.

PLAYBOYS, The
Pop group from Philadelphia, Pennsylvania: Sammy Vale (vocals), Irv Mellman (piano), Ray D'Agostino (saxophone), Joe Franzosa (bass) and Lou Mauro (drums). D'Agostino died on 3/22/1995 (age 64).

PLAYER
Pop-rock group formed in Los Angeles, California: Peter Beckett (vocals, guitar), John Crowley (vocals, guitar), Wayne Cooke (keyboards), Ronn Moss (bass) and John Friesen (drums). Moss played "Ridge Forrester" on the TV soap *The Bold & The Beautiful*.

PLAYMATES, The
Pop vocal trio from Waterbury, Connecticut: Donny Conn, Morey Carr and Chic Hetti.

PLEASURE
R&B group from Portland, Oregon. Core members: Sherman Davis (vocals), Marlon McClain (guitar), brothers Donald and Michael Hepburn (keyboards), Bruce Smith (percussion), Dennis Springer (sax), Nathaniel Phillips (bass) and Bruce Carter (drums).

PLEIS, Jack
Born on 5/11/1917 in Philadelphia, Pennsylvania. Died on 12/5/1990 (age 73). Conducted the studio orchestra and chorus behind many of Decca's pop vocalists during the 1950s.

PLIES
Born Algernod Washington in Fort Myers, Florida. Male rapper.

PLIMSOULS, The
Rock group from Los Angeles, California: Peter Case (vocals), Eddie Munoz (guitar), Dave Pahoa (bass) and Lou Ramirez (drums). Group appeared in the 1983 movie *Valley Girl*. Group name is British slang for gym shoes.

(+44)
Pop-punk band formed in Los Angeles, California:
Blink-182 members Mark Hoppus (vocals, bass)
and Travis Barker (drums), with guitarists Shane
Gallagher and Craig Fairbaugh.

PMD
Born Parrish Smith on 5/13/1968 in Smithtown,
Long Island, New York. Male rapper. One-half of
EPMD duo.

P.M. DAWN
Black dance-rap duo from Jersey City, New Jersey:
brothers Prince Be (Attrell Cordes; born on
5/19/1970) and DJ Minute Mix (Jarrett Cordes; born
on 7/17/1971). P.M. Dawn means "from the darkest
hour comes the light."

P-NUT GALLERY
Studio group featuring lead singer Tommy Nolan.
Early pressings credit artist as: CIRCA '58 and the
Peanut Gallery.

POCKETS
R&B group from Baltimore, Maryland: Larry Jacobs
(vocals), Jacob Sheffer (guitar), Albert McKinney
(keyboards), Charles Williams (trumpet), Irving
Madison (sax), Kevin Barnes (trombone), Gary
Grainger (bass) and George Gray (drums).

POCO
Country-rock band formed in Los Angeles,
California: Rusty Young (pedal steel guitar; born on
2/23/1946) and Buffalo Springfield members Richie
Furay (rhythm guitar; born on 5/9/1944) and Jim
Messina (lead guitar; born on 12/5/1947). Randy
Meisner (born on 3/8/1946; later of the Eagles) left
in 1969; replaced by bassist Timothy B. Schmit
(born on 10/30/1947). As of 1970, group consisted
of Furay, Messina, Young, Schmit and George
Grantham (drums; born on 1/20/1947). Messina left
in 1970; replaced by Paul Cotton. Furay left in 1973.
Grantham and Schmit (joined Eagles) left in 1977;
replacements: Charlie Harrison, Kim Bullard and
Steve Chapman. Disbanded in 1984. In 1989,
Young, Furay, Messina, Grantham and Meisner
reunited.

P.O.D.
Christian hard-rock band from San Diego,
California: Paul "Sonny" Sandoval (vocals), Marcos
Curiel (guitar), Mark "Traa" Daniels (bass) and
Noah "Wuv" Bernardo (drums). Jason Truby
replaced Curiel in early 2003. P.O.D.: Payable On
Death.

POE
Born Annie Danielewski in Manhattan, New York.
Female rock-dance singer/songwriter.

POETS, The
R&B vocal group: Ronnie Lewis, Melvin Bradford,
Paul Fulton and Johnny James.

POINDEXTER, Buster
Born David Johansen on 1/9/1950 in Staten Island,
New York. Founder and lead singer of the pre-punk
group the New York Dolls, 1971-75. Assumed the
Buster Poindexter persona in 1987. Appeared in the
movies *Married To The Mob*, *Let It Ride*, *Tales
From The Darkside*, *Freejack* and others.

POINT BLANK
Rock group from Texas: Bubba Keith (vocals),
Rusty Burns and Kim Davis (guitars), Mike Hamilton
(keyboards), Bill Randolph (bass) and Buzzy Gruen
(drums). Randolph died of a heart attack on
6/19/2001 (age 50).

POINTER, Bonnie
Born on 7/11/1950 in Oakland, California. Member
of the Pointer Sisters from 1971-78.

POINTER SISTERS
R&B vocal group from Oakland, California: sisters
Ruth (born on 3/19/1946), Anita (born on
1/23/1948), June (born on 11/30/1953; died of
cancer on 4/11/2006, age 52) and Bonnie Pointer.
Sang in nostalgic 1940s style from 1973-77.
Appeared as the "Wilson Sisters" in the 1976 movie
Car Wash. Bonnie went solo in 1978; group
continued as a trio in a more contemporary style.

POISON
Glam-metal band formed in Harrisburg,
Pennsylvania: Bret Michaels (vocals; born on
3/15/1963), C.C. DeVille (guitar; born on
5/14/1962), Bobby Dall (bass; born on 11/2/1963)
and Rikki Rockett (drums; born on 8/8/1961). Richie
Kotzen (born on 3/5/1970) replaced DeVille from
1992-97.

POLICE, The
Reggae-inflected rock trio formed in England:
Gordon "Sting" Sumner (vocals, bass; born on
10/2/1951), Andy Summers (guitar; born on
12/31/1942) and Stewart Copeland (drums; born on
7/16/1952). First guitarist was Henri Padovani,
replaced by Summers in 1977. Copeland had been
with Curved Air. Sting began recording solo in 1985.
Copeland formed group Animal Logic in 1989.
Group reunited in 2007.

POLNAREFF, Michel
Born on 7/3/1944 in France. Pop singer/guitarist/
keyboardist.

PONDEROSA TWINS + ONE
Teen R&B group from Cleveland, Ohio: twins Alvin
& Alfred Pelham and twins Keith & Kirk Gardner,
plus Ricky Spencer. Produced by Bobby Massey of
The O'Jays.

PONI-TAILS
Pop female vocal trio from Lyndhurst, Ohio: Toni
Cistone (lead), LaVerne Novak (high harmony) and
Patti McCabe (died of cancer on 1/17/1989, age
49).

POP, Iggy
Born James Osterberg on 4/21/1947 in Muskegon,
Michigan. Punk-rock pioneer. Leader of The
Stooges from 1969-74. Acted in the movies *Cry
Baby*, *Hardware* and *The Crow: City Of Angels*.
Adopted nickname "Iggy" from his first band, The
Iguanas.

POPPIES, The
Female R&B vocal trio formed in Jackson,
Mississippi: Dorothy Moore (lead), Petsye McCune
and Rosemary Taylor.

POPPY FAMILY, The
Pop group from Canada: Susan Jacks (vocals), her husband Terry Jacks (born on 3/29/1944), Craig MacCaw (guitar) and Satwan Singh (percussion). Group and marriage broke up in 1973; Susan and Terry began solo careers.

PORNO FOR PYROS
Rock group formed by former Jane's Addiction members Perry Farrell (vocals) and Stephen Perkins (drums). Includes Peter DiStefano (guitar) and Martyn LeNoble (bass). Mike Watt replaced LeNoble in 1995.

PORTER, Nolan
Born in 1949 in Los Angeles, California. R&B singer. Also recorded as Nolan and N.F. Porter. Produced by Gabriel Mekler.

PORTISHEAD
Modern rock duo from Bristol, England: multi-instrumentalist Geoff Barrow and vocalist Beth Gibbons. Duo named after a coastal shipping town near Bristol.

PORTNOY, Gary
Born on 6/8/1956 in Valley Stream, New York. Pop singer/songwriter.

PORTRAIT
Male R&B vocal group: Eric Kirkland and Michael Angelo Saulsberry (both from Los Angeles, California), Irving Washington III (from Providence, Rhode Island) and Phillip Johnson (from Tulsa, Oklahoma). In 1995, Johnson was replaced by Kurt Jackson (from Aurora, Colorado).

POSEY, Sandy
Born on 6/18/1944 in Jasper, Alabama; raised in West Memphis, Arkansas. Pop singer.

POSITIVE K
Born Darryl Gibson in the Bronx, New York. Male rapper.

POST, Mike
Born on 9/29/1944 in Los Angeles, California. Composer/producer.

POSTAL SERVICE, The
Pop-rock duo from Bellingham, Washington: Benjamin Gibbard and James Tamborello. Gibbard also formed Death Cab For Cutie.

POTLIQUOR
Rock group from Baton Rouge, Louisiana: George Ratzlaff (vocals), Les Wallace (guitar), Guy Schaeffer (bass) and Jerry Amoroso (drums).

POURCEL('S), Franck, French Fiddles
Born on 8/11/1913 in Marseilles, France. Died on 11/12/2000 (age 87). String orchestra leader/composer/arranger/violinist.

POUSETTE-DART BAND
Pop band from Boston, Massachusetts: Jon Pousette-Dart (vocals), John Curtis (guitar), John Troy (bass) and Michael Dawe (drums).

POWELL, Bobby
Born in 1941 in Baton Rouge, Louisiana. R&B singer/pianist. Blind since birth.

POWELL, Cozy
Born Colin Powell on 12/29/1947 in Cirencester, Glouchester, England. Died in a car crash on 4/5/1998 (age 50). Rock drummer. Member of Jeff Beck's group (1971-72), Rainbow (1976-80), Whitesnake (1984), Emerson, Lake & Powell (1986) and Black Sabbath (1990).

POWELL, Jane
Born Suzanne Burce on 4/1/1929 in Portland, Oregon. Star of many movie musicals, 1944-58.

POWELL, Jesse
Born in Gary, Indiana. R&B singer/songwriter. Brother of Trina & Tamara.

POWERS, Joey
Born in 1939 in Canonsburg, Pennsylvania. Pop singer.

POWERS, Tom
Born Joseph Robert Pirollo in 1948 in Washington DC. Pop singer/songwriter.

POWERSOURCE
A 21-member evangelical youth chorus from Bedford, Texas, featuring 6-year-old Sharon Batts.

POWER STATION, The
All-star rock group: Robert Palmer (vocals), Andy Taylor (guitar), John Taylor (bass) and Tony Thompson (drums). The Taylors were members of Duran Duran. Thompson was a member of Chic. Palmer died of a heart attack on 9/26/2003 (age 54). Thompson died of cancer on 11/12/2003 (age 48).

POWTER, Daniel
Born on 2/25/1971 in Vancouver, British Columbia, Canada. Adult Alternative-pop singer/songwriter/pianist.

POZO-SECO SINGERS
Folk-rock trio from Texas: Don Williams, Susan Taylor and Lofton Kline. Williams later became a major country star.

PRADO, Perez
Born Damaso Perez Prado on 12/11/1916 in Mantanzas, Cuba. Died of a stroke on 9/14/1989 (age 72). Bandleader/organist. Known as "The King of The Mambo." Appeared in the movie *Underwater!*

PRATT, Andy
Born on 1/25/1947 in Boston, Massachusetts. Soft-rock singer/songwriter/keyboardist/guitarist.

PRATT & McCLAIN
Pop vocal duo: Truett Pratt (from San Antonio, Texas) and Jerry McClain (from Pasadena, California).

PRECISIONS, The
R&B vocal group from Detroit, Michigan: Bobby Brooks (lead), Dennis Gilmore, Michael Morgan, Billy Prince and Arthur Ashford.

PRELUDE
Folk trio formed in England: husband-and-wife Irene (vocals) and Brian (vocals, guitar) Hume, with Ian Vardy (guitar).

PRELUDES FIVE, The
Black male doo-wop group. Also known as The Chessmen on the Mirasonic label.

PREMIERS, The
Latin-rock band from San Gabriel, California: brothers Larry Perez (guitar) and John Perez (drums), with George Delgado (vocals) and Frank Zuniga (bass).

PRESIDENTS, The
R&B vocal trio from Washington DC: Archie Powell, Bill Shorter and Tony Boyd. Also recorded as Anacostia.

PRESIDENTS OF THE UNITED STATES OF AMERICA, The
Rock trio from Seattle, Washington: Chris Ballew (vocals), Dave Dederer (guitar) and Jason Finn (drums).

PRESLEY, Elvis
"The King of Rock And Roll." Born Elvis Aron Presley on 1/8/1935 in Tupelo, Mississippi. Died of heart failure caused by prescription drug abuse at his Graceland mansion in Memphis on 8/16/1977 (age 42). Moved to Memphis in 1948. First recorded for Sun in 1954. Signed to RCA Records on 11/22/1955. With his good looks, a passionate bluesy voice, a great band (Bill Black, bass; Scotty Moore, guitar; D.J. Fontana, drums), a smooth vocal quartet (The Jordanaires), and managed by Tom Parker (died on 1/21/1997), Presley blazed his way to the #1 star of rock and roll—a position he has not yet relinquished. Made his nationwide TV debut on Tommy and Jimmy Dorsey's *Stage Show* on 1/28/1956. Starred in 31 feature movies (beginning with *Love Me Tender* in 1956). In U.S. Army from 3/24/1958 to 3/5/1960. Married Priscilla Beaulieu on 5/1/1967; divorced on 10/11/1973. Their only child, Lisa Marie (born on 2/1/1968), was married Michael Jackson, 1994-96. Elvis's last live performance was in Indianapolis on 6/26/1977. The first rock and roll artist to be honored by the U.S. Postal Service with his own commemorative stamp on 1/8/1993.

PRESSHA
Born David Jones in Atlanta, Georgia. R&B singer.

PRESTON, Billy
Born on 9/2/1946 in Houston, Texas; raised in Los Angeles, California. Died of kidney failure on 6/6/2006 (age 59). R&B singer/songwriter/keyboardist. With Mahalia Jackson in 1956. Played piano in movie *St. Louis Blues*, 1958. Regular on *Shindig* TV show. Recorded with The Beatles on "Get Back" and "Don't Let Me Down"; worked Concert For Bangladesh in 1969. Prominent session man, played on Sly & The Family Stone hits. With The Rolling Stones U.S. tour in 1975.

PRESTON, Jimmy
Born on 8/18/1913 in Philadelphia, Pennsylvania. Died in December 1984 (age 71). R&B singer/alto saxophonist.

PRESTON, Johnny
Born John Preston Courville on 8/18/1939 in Port Arthur, Texas. Rock and roll singer. Discovered by J.P. "Big Bopper" Richardson at the Twilight Club in Port Neches, Texas.

PRESTON, Mike
Born Jack Davis on 5/14/1934 in London, England. Pop singer.

PRETENDERS, The
New-wave rock band formed in England: Chrissie Hynde (vocals, guitar; born on 9/7/1951 in Akron, Ohio), James Honeyman-Scott (guitar; born on 11/4/1956), Pete Farndon (bass; born on 6/12/1952) and Martin Chambers (drums; born on 9/4/1951). Honeyman-Scott died of a drug overdose on 6/16/1982 (age 25); replaced by Robbie McIntosh (of Night). Farndon died of a drug overdose on 4/14/1983 (age 30); replaced by Malcolm Foster. Hynde was married to Jim Kerr of Simple Minds from 1984-90. Lineup in 1994: Hynde, Chambers, Adam Seymour (guitar) and Andy Hobson (bass).

PRETTY IN PINK
Female teen vocal group: Milini Khan (the 17-year-old daughter of Chaka Khan), Tameika Chaney, Shey Sperry, Maurissa Tancharoen and Taniya Robinson.

PRETTY POISON
Dance group from Philadelphia, Pennsylvania: Jade Starling (vocals), Whey Cooler (keyboards), Louie Franco (guitar) and Bobby Corea (drums).

PRETTY RICKY
R&B-rap group from Miami, Florida: Corey Mathis, Diamond Smith, Spectacular Smith and Marcus Cooper.

PREVIN, Andre
Born on 4/6/1929 in Berlin, Germany. Pianist/conductor/arranger/composer. Became musical director for MGM movies by the age of 21. In the 1970s, served as resident conductor of the London Symphony Orchestra. Married to actress Mia Farrow from 1970-79.

PRICE, Alan, Set
Born on 4/19/1942 in Fatfield, Durham, England. Organist with the original Animals; left in 1965; rejoined group in 1983.

PRICE, Kelly
Born on 4/4/1973 in Queens, New York. Female R&B singer/songwriter. Backing vocalist on several Mariah Carey albums.

PRICE, Kenny
Born James Kenneth Price on 5/27/1931 in Florence, Kentucky. Died of a heart attack on 8/4/1987 (age 56). Country singer. Regular on TV's *Hee-Haw*. Known as "The Round Mound of Sound."

PRICE, Lloyd
Born on 3/9/1933 in Kenner, Louisiana. R&B singer/pianist/composer. First recording was the #1 R&B hit "Lawdy Miss Clawdy" on Specialty. In U.S. Army, 1953-56. Formed own record company, KRC, in 1956; leased "Just Because" to ABC Records. Signed to ABC in 1957. Formed Double-L label in 1963 and Turntable Records in 1969. Continued in music, production, and booking agency work.

PRICE, Ray
Born on 1/12/1926 in Perryville, Texas; raised in Dallas, Texas. Country singer. Known as "The Cherokee Cowboy."

PRIDE, Charley
Born on 3/18/1938 in Sledge, Mississippi. The most successful black country performer. Discovered by Red Sovine in 1963.

PRIEST, Maxi
Born Max Elliott on 6/10/1960 in London, England (Jamaican parents). Dancehall reggae singer.

PRIMA, Louis, & Keely Smith
Prima was born on 12/7/1910 in New Orleans, Louisiana. Died on 8/24/1978 (age 67). Jazz trumpeter/singer/composer/bandleader. Smith was born Dorothy Keely Gambardella on 3/9/1932 in Norfolk, Virginia. They were married from 1953-61.

PRIMITIVE RADIO GODS
Group is actually solo alternative-rock artist Chris O'Connor. Touring group includes Luke McAuliffe (guitar), Jeff Sparks (bass) and Tim Lauteiro (drums).

PRIMUS
Thrash-jazz-rock trio from San Francisco, California: Les Claypool (vocals, bass), Larry LaLonde (guitar) and Tim Alexander (drums).

PRINCE
Born Prince Roger Nelson on 6/7/1958 in Minneapolis, Minnesota. Singer/multi-instrumentalist/composer/producer. Named for the Prince Roger Trio, led by his father. Self-taught musician; own band, Grand Central, in junior high school. Self-produced first album in 1978. Starred in the movies *Purple Rain*, *Under The Cherry Moon*, *Sign 'O' The Times* and *Graffiti Bridge*. Founded own label, Paisley Park. The Revolution featured Lisa Coleman (keyboards), Wendy Melvoin (guitar), Bobby Z (percussion), Matt "Dr." Fink (keyboards), Eric Leeds (saxophone) and Andre Cymone (bass; replaced by Brownmark in 1981). Coleman and Melvoin formed duo Wendy & Lisa in 1987. Sheila E. (drums) joined Prince's band in 1986. Prince formed new band, New Power Generation (named for the oldest Prince fan club in Britain) in 1990, featuring Levi Seacer, Jr. (guitar), Sonny T. (bass), Tommy Barbarella (keyboards), dancer/percussionists Kirk Johnson and Damon Dickson, Michael Bland (drums), rapper Tony M. and Rosie Gaines (keyboards, vocals; replaced by Mayte [pronounced: my-tie] Garcia by 1992). Prince announced that he would no longer record on 4/27/1993. Changed his name on 6/7/1993 to a combination male/female "love symbol." By 1994 referred to as "The Artist Formerly Known As Prince" or "The Artist." Married to Mayte from 1996-99. Announced in May 2000 that he would once again be called "Prince."

PRINCE BE
Born Attrell Cordes on 5/19/1970 in Jersey City, New Jersey. One-half of P.M. Dawn.

PRINCE BUSTER
Born Cecil Bustamente Campbell on 5/24/1938 in Kingston, Jamaica. Reggae singer/producer.

PRINCE MARKIE DEE & The Soul Convention
Born Mark Morales on 2/19/1960 in Brooklyn, New York. Former member of the Fat Boys.

PRISM
Rock group from Canada: Ron Tabak (vocals), Lindsay Mitchell and Tom Lavin (guitars), John Hall (keyboards), Ab Bryant (bass; Chilliwack, Headpins), Rodney Higgs (drums). Bryant and Higgs left in 1978; replaced by Allen Harlow and Rocket Norton. Tabak left by 1982, replaced by Henry Small. Tabak died in a car crash in 1984.

PRISONAIRES, The
Black doo-wop group formed by inmates at the Tennessee State Penitentiary in Nashville: Johnny Bragg (lead), John Drue (first tenor), Ed Thurman (second tenor), Marcel Sanders (bass) and William Stewart (baritone, guitar). Bragg died on 9/1/2004 (age 79). Drue died in December 1977 (age 52). Thurman died in April 1973 (age 56). Sanders died in 1969. Stewart died in 1959.

PROBY, P.J.
Born James Marcus Smith on 11/6/1938 in Houston, Texas. Rock and roll singer/songwriter.

PROCLAIMERS, The
Pop-rock duo from Edinburgh, Scotland: identical twin brothers Craig and Charlie Reid (born on 3/5/1962).

PROCOL HARUM
Rock band formed in England: Gary Brooker (vocals, piano), Keith Reid (lyrics), Ray Royer (guitar), Matthew Fisher (organ), Dave Knights (bass) and Bobby Harrison (drums). Numerous personnel changes. Robin Trower was lead guitarist from 1968-71.

PRODIGY
Techno-rave-dance group from England: Maxim Reality and Keith Flint (vocals), Liam Howlett (instruments) and Leeroy Thornhill (dancer).

PRODUCERS, The
Pop-rock group from Atlanta, Georgia: Van Temple (vocals, guitar), Wayne Famous (keyboards), Kyle Henderson (bass) and Bryan Holmes (drums).

PRODUCT G&B, The
Rap duo from Hempstead, Long Island, New York: David McRae and Marvin Moore-Hough. G&B: Ghetto & Blues.

PROFESSOR LONGHAIR
Born Henry Roeland Byrd on 12/19/1918 in Bogalusa, Louisiana. Died on 1/30/1980 (age 61). Highly influential R&B/blues piano player.

PROFESSOR MORRISON'S LOLLIPOP
Bubblegum-rock group from Lincoln, Nebraska: Jeff Travis (vocals, guitar), Frank Elia (guitar), Kelly Kotera (keyboards), Craig Perkins (bass) and Bruce Watson (drums). Previously recorded as The Coachmen ("Bubbled Under" in 1966). Perkins died on 5/5/2000 (age 52).

PROFYLE
Male R&B vocal group from Shreveport, Louisiana: Baby Boy, Face, Hershey and L Jai.

PROJECT PAT
Born Patrick Houston in 1972 in Memphis, Tennessee. Male rapper. Brother of Three 6 Mafia member Juicy J.

PROTHEROE, Brian
Born in 1944 in Salisbury, Wiltshire, England. Pop-rock singer/composer/actor/guitarist.

PRUETT, Jeanne
Born Norma Jean Bowman on 1/30/1937 in Pell City, Alabama. Country singer/songwriter.

PRUITT, Jordan
Born on 5/19/1991 in Loganville, Georgia. Teen female singer.

PRYSOCK, Arthur
Born on 1/2/1929 in Spartanburg, South Carolina. Died on 6/14/1997 (age 68). R&B singer.

P$C
Male rap group from Atlanta, Georgia: AK, Mac Boney, Big Kuntry and C-Rod. P$C: Pimp Squad Clique.

PSEUDO ECHO
Pop-rock-dance group formed in Melbourne, Australia: Brian Canham (vocals, guitar), James Leigh (keyboards), Pierre Gigliotti (bass) and Vince Leigh (drums).

PSYCHEDELIC FURS
Techno-rock group formed in England: brothers Richard (vocals) and Tim (bass) Butler, John Ashton (guitar), and Vince Ely (drums). Ely left in 1983; returned briefly in 1989. The Butlers formed Love Spit Love in 1994.

PUBLIC ANNOUNCEMENT
R&B vocal group from Chicago, Illinois: Earl Robinson, Felony Davis, Euclid Gray and Glen Wright. Former backing group for R. Kelly.

PUBLIC ENEMY
Highly influential rap group from Long Island, New York: Carlton Ridenhour ("Chuck D"), William Drayton ("Flavor Flav"), Norman Rogers ("Terminator X") and William Griffin ("Professor Griff"). Griffin left in 1989.

PUCKETT, Gary, & The Union Gap
Born on 10/17/1942 in Hibbing, Minnesota; raised in Yakima, Washington. Soft-rock singer/guitarist. Formed The Union Gap in San Diego, California: Gary Withem (keyboards; born on 8/22/1946), Dwight Bement (sax; born on 12/28/1945), Kerry Chater (bass; born on 8/7/1945) and Paul Wheatbread (drums; born on 2/8/1946). Wheatbread was a member of The Hardtimes. Bement and Wheatbread later joined Flash Cadillac & The Continental Kids.

PUDDLE OF MUDD
Hard-rock band formed in Kansas City, Missouri: Wes Scantlin (vocals, guitar), Paul Phillips (guitar), Doug Ardito (bass) and Greg Upchurch (drums).

Group records on Fred Durst's (Limp Bizkit) Flawless record label.

PUFF DADDY / P. DIDDY / DIDDY
Born Sean Combs on 11/4/1969 in Harlem, New York. Rapper/songwriter/producer/entrepreneur. Founder of Bad Boy Entertainment in 1993. Changed performing name to P. Diddy in 2001; shortened to Diddy in 2005. Played "Lawrence Musgrove" in the movie *Monster's Ball*. The most successful hip-hop artist of all time.

PULLINS, Leroy
Born Carl Leroy Pullins on 11/12/1940 in Elgin, Illinois. Died in May 1984 (age 43). Country singer/songwriter.

PUPPIES, The
Pre-teen rap duo from Miami, Florida: brother-and-sister Calvin and Tamara Mills. Produced by their father, Calvin Mills II.

PURDIE, Pretty
Born Bernard Purdie on 6/11/1939 in Elkton, Maryland. Highly regarded R&B session drummer.

PURE PRAIRIE LEAGUE
Country-rock group formed in Cincinnati, Ohio. Core members: Craig Fuller (vocals, guitar; American Flyer), George Ed Powell and Larry Goshorn (guitars), Michael Connor (keyboards), Mike Reilly (bass) and Billy Hinds (drums). Fuller left after "Amie," Powell and Reilly took over lead vocals. Vince Gill joined as lead singer in 1979. Group disbanded in 1983.

PURE SOUL
Female R&B vocal quartet from Washington DC: Shawn Allen, Heather Perkins, Keitha Shepherd and Kirstin Hall.

PURE SUGAR
Dance trio from Los Angeles, California: Jennifer Starr (lead vocals), Pete Lorimer and Richard "Humpty" Vission.

PURIFY, James & Bobby
R&B vocal duo: cousins James Purify (born on 5/12/1944 in Pensacola, Florida) and Robert Lee Dickey (born on 9/2/1939 in Tallahassee, Florida).

PURPLE REIGN
Pop studio group formed in Philadelphia, Pennsylvania. Led by producer Mike Natale.

PURPLE RIBBON ALL-STARS
All-star rap group: Big Boi, Killer Mike, Bubba Sparxxx, Sleepy Brown, Konkrete, Janelle Monae and Scar.

PURSELL, Bill
Born on 6/9/1926 in Oakland, California; raised in Tulare, California. Session pianist.

PUSSYCAT DOLLS, The
Female dance group formed in Los Angeles, California: Nicole Scherzinger, Carmit Bachar, Ashley Roberts, Jessica Sutta, Melody Thornton and Kimberly Wyatt. Scherzinger was a member of Eden's Crush.

PYRAMIDS, The
Surf-rock and roll band from Long Beach, California: Skip Mercer, Willie Glover, Steve Leonard, Ron McMullen and Tom Pittman. Performed with shaved heads. Appeared in the movie *Bikini Beach*.

PYTHON LEE JACKSON
Rock group from Australia: David Bently (keyboards), Mick Liber (guitar), Gary Boyle (guitar), Tony Cahill (bass) and David Montgomery (drums).

Q
Pop group from Beaver Falls, Pennsylvania: Don Garvin (guitar), Robert Peckman (bass), Bill Thomas (keyboards) and Bill Vogel (drums). All share vocals. Garvin and Peckman were members of The Jaggerz.

QB FINEST
All-star rap group: Nas, Capone, Mobb Deep, Tragedy, MC Shan, Marley Marl, Nature, Cormega and Millennium Thug. QB: Queens Bridge.

Q-FEEL
Techno-dance duo from England: Martin Page and Brian Fairweather.

QKUMBA ZOO
Dance group from Johannesburg, South Africa: Levannah (female vocals), Owl (all instruments) and Tziki (dancer).

QT
Born Quentin Bush in Nashville, Tennessee. Male R&B singer.

Q-TIP
Born Jonathan Davis on 11/20/1970 in Harlem, New York. Male rapper. Member of A Tribe Called Quest.

QUAD CITY DJ'S
Studio rap-bass group from Orlando, Florida: Nathaniel "C.C. Lemonhead" Orange, Johnny "Jay Ski" McGowan and Lana. Orange was a member of 95 South.

QUAITE, Christine
Born on 5/11/1948 in Leeds, England. Pop singer.

QUAKER CITY BOYS
String band from Philadelphia, Pennsylvania. Led by Tommy Reilly.

QUARTERFLASH
Pop-rock group from Portland, Oregon: husband-and-wife Marv (guitar) and Rindy (vocals, saxophone) Ross, with Jack Charles (guitar), Rick DiGiallonardo (keyboards), Rich Gooch (bass) and Brian David Willis (drums). Group originally known as Seafood Mama.

QUARTER NOTES, The
Instrumental rock and roll band from Buffalo, New York. Led by orgainst Anthony Sperry (died of throat cancer on 9/19/2000, age 70).

QUATEMAN, Bill
Born on 11/4/1947 in Chicago, Illinois. Pop singer/songwriter/guitarist.

QUATRO, Suzi
Born on 6/3/1950 in Detroit, Michigan. Rock singer/songwriter/guitarist. Played "Leather

Tuscadero" on TV's *Happy Days* in 1977. Her sister Patti was a member of Fanny.

QUEEN
Rock group formed in England: Freddie Mercury (vocals; born Farrokh Bulsara on 9/5/1946 in Zanzibar, Tanzania), Brian May (guitar; born on 7/19/1947), John Deacon (bass; born on 8/19/1951) and Roger Taylor (drums; born on 7/26/1949). May and Taylor had been in the group Smile. Mercury had recorded as Larry Lurex. Wrote soundtrack for the movie *Flash Gordon* in 1980. Mercury died of AIDS on 11/24/1991 (age 45).

QUEEN LATIFAH
Born Dana Owens on 3/18/1970 in Newark, New Jersey. Female rapper/actress. Appeared in the movies *Jungle Fever*, *Set It Off*, *The Bone Collector*, *Chicago* and *Bringing Down The House*. Cast member of Fox TV series *Living Single*. CEO of Flavor Unit Records. Latifah is Arabic for delicate and sensitive.

QUEEN PEN
Born Lynise Walters in Brooklyn, New York. Female rapper.

QUEENS OF THE STONE AGE
Hard-rock duo formed in Palm Desert, California: Josh Homme (vocals, guitar; born on 5/17/1973) and Nick Oliveri (bass; born on 10/21/1971). Touring band includes several different musicians. Oliveri left in early 2004; Homme continued with more musicians.

QUEENSRYCHE
Heavy-metal band from Bellevue, Washington: Geoff Tate (vocals), Chris DeGarmo and Michael WIlton (guitars), Eddie Jackson (bass), and Scott Rockenfield (drums).

? (QUESTION MARK) & THE MYSTERIANS
Hispanic garage-rock band formed in Saginaw, Michigan: Rudy "?" Martinez (vocals), Bobby Balderrama (guitar), Frank Rodriguez (organ), Frank Lugo (bass) and Eddie Serrato (drums).

QUICKSILVER MESSENGER SERVICE
Rock group from San Francisco, California: Gary Duncan (vocals, guitar), John Cipollina (guitar), David Freiberg (bass) and Greg Elmore (drums). Dino Valenti joined as lead singer in 1970. Freiberg left in 1973 to join Jefferson Starship. Cipollina, brother of Huey Lewis & The News' bassist Mario Cipollina, died on 5/29/1989 (age 45). Valenti died on 11/16/1994 (age 57).

QUIET RIOT
Hard-rock band formed in Burbank, California: Kevin DuBrow (vocals), Carlos Cavazo (guitar), Rudy Sarzo (bass) and Frankie Banali (drums). Sarzo later joined Whitesnake. DuBrow died of a drug overdose on 11/25/2007 (age 52).

QUIN-TONES, The
Black doo-wop group from York, Pennsylvania: Roberta Haymon (lead), Phyllis Carr, Carolyn "Sissie" Holmes, Kenny Sexton, Jeannie Crist and Ronnie Scott (pianist). Carr died of cancer on 4/20/2006 (age 66).

RAab
Male R&B singer from Florida.

RABBITT, Eddie
Born Edward Thomas Rabbitt on 11/27/1941 in Brooklyn, New York; raised in East Orange, New Jersey. Died of cancer on 5/7/1998 (age 56). Country singer/songwriter/guitarist. First recorded for 20th Century in 1964. Moved to Nashville in 1968. Became established after Elvis Presley recorded his song "Kentucky Rain" in 1970.

RACONTEURS, The
Rock band formed in Detroit, Michigan: Jack White (vocals, guitar; The White Stripes), Brandon Benson (vocals, guitar), Jack Lawrence (bass) and Patrick Keeler (drums).

RADIANTS, The
R&B vocal group from Chicago, Illinois: Maurice McAlister (lead), Jerome Brookes and Green "Mac" McLaurin (tenors), Wallace Sampson (baritone) and Elzie Butler (bass).

RADIN, Joshua
Born in Shaker Heights, Ohio. Male singer/songwriter/guitarist.

RADIOHEAD
Alternative-rock group from Oxford, England: Thom Yorke (vocals), brothers Jon (guitar) and Colin (bass) Greenwood, Ed O'Brien (guitar) and Phil Selway (drums).

RAEKWON
Born Corey Woods on 1/12/1970 in Staten Island, New York. Male rapper. Member of Wu-Tang Clan. Also known as Chef Raekwon or Lou Diamonds.

RAELETTS, The
Female vocal group formed as a backup group for Ray Charles in 1958. Initial lineup: Margie Hendrix and Ethel "Darlene" McCrea of The Cookies with Pat Moseley and Gwendolyn Berry. Lineup from 1967-69: Berry, Merry Clayton (lead), Alexandra Brown and Clydie King (also recorded as Brown Sugar). Lineup in 1970: Mable John, Susaye Green, Vernita Moss and Estella Yarbrough. Hendrix died of a drug overdose on 7/14/1973 (age 38).

RAES, The
Husband-and-wife disco duo: Robbie Rae (born in Resloven, Wales) and Cherrill Rae (born in Carlisle, Wales).

RAFFERTY, Gerry
Born on 4/16/1947 in Paisley, Scotland. Adult Contemporary singer/songwriter/guitarist. Co-leader of Stealers Wheel.

RAG DOLLS, The
Female vocal trio formed in Philadelphia, Pennsylvania: Jean Thomas, Mikie Harris and Susan Lewis.

RAGE AGAINST THE MACHINE
Alternative hard-rock group formed in Los Angeles, California: Zack DeLa Rocha (vocals), Tom Morello (guitar), Tim Bob (bass) and Brad Wilk (drums). DeLa Rocha left in October 2000; the other three recorded with Chris Cornell as Audioslave.

RAINBOW
Hard-rock band led by British guitarist Ritchie Blackmore and bassist Roger Glover, both members of Deep Purple. Fluctuating lineup included vocalists Ronnie James Dio (Black Sabbath), Graham Bonnet (Michael Schenker Group, Alcatrazz) and Joe Lynn Turner, keyboardist Tony Carey and drummer Cozy Powell (Emerson, Lake & Powell). Group split up upon re-formation of Deep Purple in 1984. In 1990 Turner joined Deep Purple, and Powell joined Black Sabbath. Powell died in a car crash on 4/5/1998 (age 50).

RAINDROPS, The
Songwriting team of Ellie Greenwich (born on 10/23/1940) and husband Jeff Barry (born on 4/3/1938). Divorced in 1965, but continued to work together. Barry wrote "Tell Laura I Love Her"; team wrote "Be My Baby," "Da Doo Ron Ron," "Chapel Of Love," "River Deep-Mountain High," "Hanky Panky," "Leader Of The Pack" and many more. Barry produced such mega-hits as "Sugar Sugar" (The Archies) and "I'm A Believer" (The Monkees). Their song hits were celebrated in the 1985 Broadway musical *Leader Of The Pack*. Ellie also recorded as The Butterflys.

RAINES, Rita
Adult Contemporary singer.

RAINWATER, Marvin
Born Marvin Percy on 7/2/1925 in Wichita, Kansas. Country singer/songwriter/guitarist.

RAINY DAZE, The
Pop-rock band from Denver, Colorado: brothers Tim Gilbert (vocals, guitar) and Kip Gilbert (drums), with Mac Ferris (guitar), Bob Heckendorf (keyboards) and Sam Fuller (bass).

RAITT, Bonnie
Born on 11/8/1949 in Burbank, California. White blues-rock singer/guitarist. Daughter of Broadway actor/singer John Raitt. Married to actor Michael O'Keefe from 1991-99.

RAKIM & KEN-Y
Latin reggae vocal duo from Gurabo, Puerto Rico: Jose "Rakim" Nieves and Kenny "Ken-Y" Vasquez.

RALEIGH, Kevin
Born in Cleveland, Ohio. Rock singer/songwriter/keyboardist. Member of the Michael Stanley Band from 1978-86.

RALKE, Don
Born on 7/13/1920 in Battle Creek, Michigan. Died on 1/26/2000 (age 79). Conductor/composer/arranger.

RAMBEAU, Eddie
Born Edward Fluri on 6/30/1943 in Hazleton, Pennsylvania. Pop singer/songwriter.

RAMBLERS, The
Instrumental rock and roll band from Westport, Connecticut: Kip Martin, Michael Burke, Mike Anthony, Chuck Kenney and Vince Rissolo.

RAMBLERS, The
Pop singer/songwriter/guitar duo from New York:
John Herbert and Sal Nastasi.

RAM JAM
Rock group formed in Long Island, New York: Myke
Scavone (vocals), Bill Bartlett (guitar; The Lemon
Pipers), Howie Blauvelt (bass) and Peter Charles
(drums). Blauvelt died of a heart attack on
10/25/1993 (age 44).

RAMONES
Highly influential punk-rock group formed in
Brooklyn, New York. All members have taken
Ramone as their last name: Joey (Jeffrey Hyman;
vocals), Johnny (John Cummings; guitar), Dee Dee
(Douglas Colvin; bass) and Tommy (Tom Erdelyi;
drums). Group appeared in the 1979 movie *Rock 'n'
Roll High School*. Joey Ramone died of cancer on
4/15/2001 (age 49). Dee Dee Ramone died of a
drug overdose on 6/5/2002 (age 49). Johnny
Ramone died of prostate cancer on 9/15/2004 (age
55).

RAMPAGE
Born Roger McNair in Brooklyn, New York. Male
rapper. Childhood friend of Busta Rhymes. Member
of the Flipmode Squad.

RAMRODS
Instrumental rock and roll band from Connecticut:
Vincent Bell Lee (lead guitar), his cousin Eugene
Moore (guitar), Richard Lane (sax) and his sister
Claire Lane (drums).

RANCID
Punk-rock group from Berkeley, California: Tim
Armstrong (vocals, guitar), Lars Frederiksen
(vocals, guitar), Matt Freeman (bass) and Brett
Reed (drums).

RANDAZZO, Teddy
Born on 5/13/1935 in Brooklyn, New York. Died of a
heart attack on 11/21/2003 (age 68). Member of
The Three Chuckles. Appeared in vintage rock 'n
roll movies *Rock Rock Rock* (1956) and *Mr. Rock &
Roll* (1957). Produced and wrote several hits for
Little Anthony & The Imperials from 1964-68.

RAN-DELLS, The
Rock and roll trio from Villas, New Jersey: cousins
Steve Rappaport, Robert Rappaport and Jon Spirt
(The Sidekicks). Spirt died on 3/19/2003 (age 56).
Steve Rappaport died of a heart attack on 7/4/2007
(age 64).

RANDOLPH, Boots
Born Homer Randolph on 6/3/1927 in Paducah,
Kentucky. Died of a cerebral hemorrhage on
7/3/2007 (age 80). Top session saxophonist.

RANDY & THE RAINBOWS
White doo-wop group from Queens, New York:
Dominick "Randy" Safuto (lead) and brother Frank
Safuto, brothers Mike and Sal Zero, and Ken
Arcipowski. Originally called Jr. And The Counts.

RANKIN, Billy
Born on 4/25/1959 in Glasgow, Scotland. Lead
guitarist with Nazareth from 1981-82.

RANKS, Shabba
Born Rexton Gordon on 1/17/1966 in Sturgetown,
Jamaica. Male reggae singer.

RAPINATION & KYM MAZELLE
Rapination is the Rapino Brothers, two Italian
producers. Mazelle is a London-based dance singer
from Gary, Indiana (childhood neighbor of The
Jacksons). Studied opera at Chicago's Mundelein
College of Music.

RAPPIN' 4-TAY
Born Anthony Forté in 1969 in San Francisco,
California. Male rapper.

RARE EARTH
Rock group from Detroit, Michigan: Pete Rivera
(vocals, drums), Rod Richards (guitar), Kenny
James (keyboards), Gil Bridges (sax), Ed Guzman
(percussion) and John Persh (bass). In 1971, Ray
Monette replaced Richards and Mark Olson
replaced James. Mike Urso replaced Persh in 1972.
Persh died of a staph virus in January 1981 (age
38). Olson died of alcohol-related complications in
1982. Guzman died on 7/29/1993 (age 49). One of
the first white acts signed to a Motown label.

RASCAL FLATTS
Country vocal trio formed in Columbus, Ohio: Gary
LeVox (born on 7/10/1970; lead vocals), Jay
DeMarcus (born on 4/26/1971) and Joe Don
Rooney (born on 9/13/1975).

RASCALS, The
"Blue-eyed soul" pop-rock group formed in New
York: Felix Cavaliere (vocals, organ; born on
11/29/1942), Gene Cornish (vocals, guitar; born on
5/14/1944), Eddie Brigati (vocals, percussion; born
on 10/22/1945) and Dino Danelli (drums; born on
7/23/1944). All except Danelli had been in Joey
Dee's Starliters. Brigati and Cornish left in 1971;
replaced by Robert Popwell (bass), Buzz Feiten
(guitar; Larsen-Feiten Band) and Ann Sutton
(vocals). Group disbanded in 1972. Cavaliere,
Cornish and Danelli reunited in June 1988.

RASPBERRIES
Pop-rock group formed in Mentor, Ohio: Eric
Carmen (vocals, guitar), Wally Bryson (guitar),
David Smalley (bass) and Jim Bonfanti (drums).
Smalley and Bonfanti replaced by Scott McCarl and
Michael McBride in 1974. Carmen went solo in
1975.

RATIONALS, The
Garage-rock band from Ann Arbor, Michigan: Scott
Morgan (vocals, guitar), Steve Correl (guitar), Terry
Trabandt (bass) and Bill Figg (drums).

RATT
Hard-rock group formed in Los Angeles, California:
Stephen Pearcy (vocals), Warren DeMartini and
Robbin Crosby (guitars), Juan Croucier (bass) and
Bobby Blotzer (drums). Crosby died of AIDS on
6/6/2002 (age 42).

RATTLES, The
Rock group from Germany: Edna Bejarano (vocals),
Frank Mille (guitar), Zappo Lüngen (bass) and
Herbert Bornhold (drums).

RAVAN, Genya
Born Genyusha Zelkowitz on 4/19/1940 in Lodz, Poland; raised in Brooklyn, New York. Lead singer of Ten Wheel Drive.

RAVEN, Eddy
Born Edward Garvin Futch on 8/19/1944 in Lafayette, Louisiana. Country singer/songwriter/ guitarist. First recorded for Cosmos label in 1962. Worked as staff writer for Acuff-Rose publishing company.

RAVENS, The
R&B vocal group from Harlem, New York: Maithe Marshall (1st tenor), Leonard "Zeke" Puzey (2nd tenor), Warren Suttles (baritone) and Jimmy Ricks (bass). Suttles was a member of Wini Brown's Boyfriends. Ricks died on 7/2/1974 (age 49). Marshall died in November 1989 (age 65). Puzey died on 10/2/2007 (age 81).

RAVEN-SYMONE
Born Raven-Symoné Pearman on 12/10/1985 in Los Angeles, California. Singer/actress (7 years old in 1993). Played "Olivia Kendall" on TV's *The Cosby Show* and stars as "Raven Baxter" on TV's *That's So Raven*.

RAWLS, Lou
Born on 12/1/1933 in Chicago, Illinois. Died of cancer on 1/6/2006 (age 72). R&B-Adult Contemporary singer known for his very deep voice. Hosted own TV variety show with The Golddiggers in 1969. Appeared in the movies *Angel Angel, Down We Go* and *Believe In Me*. Voice of many Budweiser beer ads and featured singer in the *Garfield* TV specials. Also see Philadelphia International All Stars.

RAY, Diane
Born on 9/1/1942 in Gastonia, North Carolina. Pop singer.

RAY, Don
Born in Germany. Disco producer/arranger/ composer.

RAY, James
Born James Ray Raymond in 1941 in Washington DC. Died of a drug overdose in 1964 (age 23). R&B singer.

RAY, Jimmy
Born on 10/3/1975 in Walthamstow, East London, England. Pop-rock singer.

RAY, Johnnie
Born on 1/10/1927 in Dallas, Oregon. Died of liver failure on 2/25/1990 (age 63). Wore hearing aid since age 14. First recorded for Okeh in 1951. Famous for emotion-packed delivery with R&B influences. Appeared in three movies.

RAY, Ricardo
Born Ricardo Maldonado on 2/15/1945 in Brooklyn, New York (Puerto Rican parents). Latin bandleader. Known as the "King of Salsa."

RAY & BOB
Pop-rock duo from Los Angeles, California: Ray Swayne and Bob Appleberry.

RAYBON BROS.
Country vocal duo from Greenville, Alabama: brothers Tim and Marty Raybon (Shenandoah).

RAYBURN, Margie
Born in 1924 in Madera, California. Died of a heart attack on 6/14/2000 (age 76). Member of The Sunnysiders. Married Norman Milkin of The Sunnysiders.

RAYE, Collin
Born on 8/22/1960 in DeQueen, Arkansas. Country singer.

RAYE, Susan
Born on 10/18/1944 in Eugene, Oregon. Country singer. Regular on TV's *Hee-Haw*.

RAY J
Born Willie Ray Norwood on 1/17/1981 in McComb, Mississippi; raised in Los Angeles, California. R&B singer/actor. Brother of Brandy. Acted on TV's *The Sinbad Show* and in the movie *Steel*.

RAYS, The
Black doo-wop group formed in Harlem, New York: Harold Miller (lead), Walter Ford and David Jones (tenors) and Harry James (baritone). First recorded for Chess in 1955.

RAYVON
Born Bruce Brewster in Barbados. R&B-reggae singer/songwriter.

RAZOR'S EDGE, The
Pop-rock group from West Palm Beach, Florida: Bill Ande (guitar), Tom Condra (rhythm guitar), Vic Gray (bass) and Dave Allen Hieronymus (drums). All shared vocals. Took name from the 1946 movie. Hit "Bubbling Under" chart in 1963 as The Ardells. Recorded as The American Beetles in 1964.

RBD
Latin teen pop vocal group formed in Mexico City, Mexico: Christian Chavez, Anahi Portilla, Alfonso Herrera, Maite Beoriegui, Dulce Maria and Christopher Uckermann. Group stars in the Mexican TV series *Rebelde*.

RCR
Pop vocal trio: sisters Donna and Sandra Rhodes and Charles Chalmers. Backed Frank Sinatra on his 1975 hit "Anytime."

REA, Chris
Born on 3/4/1951 in Middlesborough, Cleveland, England. Soft-rock singer/songwriter/guitarist.

READ, John Dawson
Born in Wokingham, England. Adult Contemporary singer/songwriter/guitarist.

READY FOR THE WORLD
R&B-funk-dance group from Flint, Michigan: Melvin Riley (vocals), Gordon Strozier (guitar), Gregory Potts (keyboards), Willie Triplett (percussion), John Eaton (bass) and Gerald Valentine (drums).

REALITY
Dance duo from Chicago, Illinois: Essential Rudolph and Bad Boy Bill.

REAL LIFE
Pop-rock group from Melbourne, Australia: David Sterry (vocals, guitar), Richard Zatorski (keyboards), Allan Johnson (bass) and Danny Simcic (drums).

REAL McCOY
Techno-dance trio: German rapper/songwriter Olaf "O-Jay" Jeglitza with American singers Vanessa Mason and Lisa Cork.

REAL THING, The
R&B vocal group from Liverpool, England: Chris Amoo, Ray Lake, Dave Smith and Eddie Amoo. Group appeared in the movie *The Stud*.

REBEKAH
Born Rebekah Johnson on 9/3/1976 in Cleveland, Ohio. R&B singer/songwriter.

REBEL PEBBLES, The
Female pop group from Los Angeles, California: Rachel Murray (vocals), Karen Blankfeld (guitar), Robin Fox (bass) and Cheryl Bullock (drums).

REBELS, The
Buffalo DJ Tom Shannon and producer Phil Todaro (Shan-Todd label) produced the Hot-Toddys featuring Bill Pennell on sax, a group from Port Colborne, Canada. In 1960 they brought in the Buffalo group, The Rebels, to record Shannon's theme song, "Wild Weekend." After the song's success in 1963, they re-released the original Hot-Toddys' single as by the Rockin' Rebels.

RECORDS, The
Rock group from England: Huw Gower (vocals), John Wicks (guitar), Phil Brown (bass) and Will Birch (drums). Jude Cole replaced Gower in late 1979; left in 1981.

REDBONE
Native American "swamp-rock" group formed in Los Angeles, California: brothers Lolly (vocals, guitar) and Pat (vocals, bass) Vegas, Anthony Bellamy (guitar) and Peter De Poe (drums). The Vegas brothers had been session musicians and worked the *Shindig* TV show.

REDBONE, Leon
Born Dickran Gobalain on 8/26/1949 in Cyprus; raised in Toronto, Ontario, Canada. White blues singer. Rose to fame in the mid-1970s with appearances on TV's *Saturday Night Live*. Baritone voice of many TV commercials.

REDDING, Gene
Born in 1945 in Anderson, Indiana. R&B singer. No relation to Otis Redding.

REDDING, Otis
Born on 9/9/1941 in Dawson, Georgia. Killed in a plane crash on 12/10/1967 (age 26) in Lake Monona in Madison, Wisconsin. R&B singer/songwriter/producer/pianist. First recorded with Johnny Jenkins & The Pinetoppers on Confederate in 1960. Own label, Jotis. Plane crash also killed four members of the Bar-Kays. Otis's sons formed The Reddings.

REDDINGS, The
R&B trio formed in Atlanta, Georgia: Otis Redding's sons Dexter (vocals, bass) and Otis III (guitar), with cousin Mark Locket (vocals, drums, keyboards).

REDDY, Helen
Born on 10/25/1941 in Melbourne, Australia. Adult Contemporary singer. Family was in show business; Helen made stage debut at age four. Own TV series in the early 1960s. Migrated to U.S. in 1966. Acted in the movies *Airport 1975*, *Pete's Dragon* and *Sgt. Pepper's Lonely Hearts Club Band*.

REDEYE
Rock group formed in Los Angeles, California: Douglas "Red" Mark (vocals), Dave Hodgkins (guitar), Bill Kirkham (bass) and Bob Bereman (drums). Mark was a member of The Sunshine Company.

REDHEAD KINGPIN & THE FBI
Born David Guppy in Englewood, New Jersey. Black rap-dance artist. Members of backing outfit, The FBI, included D.J. Wildstyle, Bo Roc, Lt. Squeak, Buzz and Poochie.

RED HOT CHILI PEPPERS
Rock group formed in Los Angeles, California: Anthony Kiedis (vocals; born on 11/1/1962), Hillel Slovak (guitar; born on 4/13/1962), Michael "Flea" Balzary (bass; born on 10/16/1962) and Jack Irons (drums; born on 7/18/1962). Slovak died of a drug overdose on 6/25/1988 (age 26); replaced by John Frusciante (born on 3/5/1970). Irons left in 1988 and later joined Eleven, then Pearl Jam; replaced by Chad Smith (born on 10/25/1962). Frusciante left in May 1992; replaced by Zander Schloss (Thelonious Monster, The Magnificent Bastards), then by Arik Marshall, then by Jesse Tobias and finally by Dave Navarro (Jane's Addiction) in September 1993. Frusciante returned in 1998, replacing Navarro. Kiedis appeared in the movie *Point Break*. Flea and Kiedes appeared in the movie *The Chase*. Navarro was married to actress Carmen Electra from 2003-07.

REDJACKS, The
Rock and roll group. Led by singer Harold Jackson.

RED JUMPSUIT APPARATUS, The
Pop-punk band from Middleburg, Florida: Ronnie Winter (vocals), Elias Reidy (guitar), Duke Kitchens (guitar), Joey Westwood (bass) and John Wilkes (drums).

REDMAN
Born Reggie Noble on 4/17/1970 in Newark, New Jersey. Male rapper. Discovered by Erick Sermon. Starred in the 2001 movie *How High*.

REDNEX
Euro-dance group from Sweden. Core members: Goran Danielsson, Annika Ljungberg, Cool James and Pat Reiniz (vocals), Bosse Nilsson (fiddle), General Custer (banjo) and Animal (drums).

RED RIDER
Rock group from Canada: Tom Cochrane (vocals), Ken Greer (guitar), Peter Boynton (keyboards), Jeff Jones (bass) and Rob Baker (drums). Steve Sexton replaced Boynton in 1982; left in early 1984.

RED RIVER DAVE
Born David McEnery on 12/15/1914 in San Antonio, Texas. Died on 1/15/2002 (age 87). Singer/actor.

RED ROCKERS
Rock group from Algiers, Louisiana: John Griffith (vocals), James Singletary (guitar), Darren Hill (bass) and Jim Reilly (drums).

REDWAY, Michael
Born in England. Pop singer/songwriter.

REED, Dan, Network
Multi-racial funk-rock group from Portland, Oregon: Dan Reed (vocals), Brion James (guitar), Blake Sakomoto (keyboards), Melvin Brannon (bass) and Daniel Pred (drums).

REED, Dean
Born in 1939 in Denver, Colorado. Pop vocalist/actor. Moved to East Germany in 1972; very popular in the former Soviet Bloc countries. Drowned in an East German lake, under mysterious circumstances, on 6/17/1986.

REED, Denny
Born on 9/25/1941 in East St. Louis, Illinois; raised in Cahokia, Illinois. Teen pop singer.

REED, Jerry
Born Jerry Reed Hubbard on 3/20/1937 in Atlanta, Georgia. Died of emphysema on 9/1/2008 (age 71). Country singer/guitarist/songwriter/actor. Among his many movies, co-starred in *Gator* and *Smokey & The Bandit I & II*. Own TV series *Concrete Cowboys*.

REED, Jimmy
Born Mathis James Reed on 9/6/1925 in Dunleith, Mississippi. Died from an epileptic seizure on 8/29/1976 (age 50). Distinctive, influential blues singer/guitarist/harmonica player/songwriter; active until his death.

REED, Lou
Born on 3/2/1942 in Brooklyn, New York; raised in Freeport, Long Island, New York. Lead singer/songwriter of the New York seminal rock band Velvet Underground; regarded as the godfather of punk rock. Appeared in the movie *One Trick Pony*.

REEL BIG FISH
Ska-punk group from Huntington Beach, California: Aaron Barrett (vocals, guitar), Scott Klopfenstein (vocals, trumpet), Tavis Werts (trumpet), Grant Barry and Dan Regan (trombones), Matt Wong (bass) and Andrew Gonzales (drums).

REEL TIGHT
R&B vocal group from Chattanooga, Tennessee: Reggie Long, Danny Johnson, Bobby Rice and Bobby Torrence.

REEL 2 REAL Featuring The Mad Stuntman
Reggae-rap-dance duo: producer/composer Erick Morillo (born in New York and raised in Union City, New Jersey) and rapper Mark "The Mad Stuntman" Quashie (a native of Trinidad).

REESE, Della
Born Delloreese Patricia Early on 7/6/1931 in Detroit, Michigan. With Mahalia Jackson gospel troupe from 1945-49; with Erskine Hawkins in the early 1950s. First recorded for Great Lakes in 1954. Solo since 1957. Actress/singer on many TV shows. Appeared in the 1958 movie *Let's Rock* and the 1989 movie *Harlem Nights*. Regular on TV's *Della*, *Chico & The Man*, *The Royal Family* and *Touched By An Angel*.

REEVES, Del
Born Franklin Delano Reeves on 7/14/1932 in Sparta, North Carolina. Died on 1/1/2007 (age 74). Country singer/songwriter/guitarist.

REEVES, Jim
Born on 8/20/1923 in Panola County, Texas. Died in a plane crash on 7/31/1964 (age 40). Country singer. Aspirations of a professional baseball career cut short by an ankle injury. DJ at KWKH-Shreveport, Louisiana, home of the *Louisiana Hayride*, early 1950s. First recorded for Macy's in 1950. Joined *Hayride* cast in 1953. In the 1963 movie *Kimberley Jim*.

REFLECTIONS, The
Rock and roll vocal group from Detroit, Michigan: Tony Micale, Danny Bennie, Phil Castrodale, Johnny Dean and Ray Steinberg.

REFLECTIONS, The
R&B vocal group from Harlem, New York: Herman Edwards, Josh Pridgen, Edmund "Butch" Simmons and John Simmons (died on 3/16/1989, age 45). Toured as backup group with Melba Moore in 1972.

RE-FLEX
Techno-rock/dance group formed in London, England: Baxter (vocals, guitar), Paul Fishman (keyboards), Nigel Ross-Scott (bass) and Roland Kerridge (drums).

REFRESHMENTS, The
Rock group from Tempe, Arizona: Roger Clyne (vocals, guitar), Brian Blush (guitar), Buddy Edwards (bass) and P.H. Naffah (drums).

REGAN, Joan
Born on 1/19/1928 in Romford, Essex, England. Adult Contemporary singer.

REGENTS, The
Italian-American doo-wop group from the Bronx, New York: Guy Villari (lead), Sal Cuomo, Chuck Fassert, Don Jacobucci and Tony "Hot Rod" Gravagna. Formed as the Desires in 1958. "Barbara-Ann," written for Fassert's sister, was first recorded as a demo in 1958. Group had disbanded by the time "Barbara-Ann" was released.

REGINA
Born Regina Richards in Brooklyn, New York. Female dance singer.

REHAB
Hip-hop duo from Atlanta, Georgia: James "Brooks" Buford and Danny "Boone" Alexander.

REID, Clarence
Born on 2/14/1945 in Cochran, Georgia. R&B singer/songwriter. Also recorded X-rated party records as Blowfly.

REILLY, Mike
Born in Long Island, New York. Pop singer/ songwriter/bassist. Later joined Pure Prairie League.

REINA
Born in the Bronx, New York. Latin dance singer. Name is Spanish for "Queen."

REISMAN, Joe
Born on 9/16/1924 in Dallas, Texas. Died of a heart attack on 9/25/1987 (age 63). Conductor/composer/ arranger for TV, Broadway and movies. Musical conductor at RCA Victor during the 1950s. Headed RCA's A&R department in Los Angeles from 1962-77.

REISS
Born Michael Reiss in Brooklyn, New York. Pop-rock singer/songwriter.

REJOICE!
Husband-and-wife pop duo from Sausalito, California: Tom and Nancy Brown.

RELIENT K
Christian rock band from Canton, Ohio: Matt Thiessen (vocals, guitar), Matt Hoopes (guitar), Brian Pittman (bass) and Dave Douglas (drums).

RELL
Born Gerrell Gaddis in Harlem, New York. Male rapper.

R.E.M.
Alternative-rock group formed in Athens, Georgia: Michael Stipe (vocals; born on 1/4/1960), Peter Buck (guitar; born on 12/6/1956), Mike Mills (bass; born on 12/17/1958) and Bill Berry (drums; born on 7/31/1958). Developed huge following with college audiences in the early 1980s as one of the first alternative-rock bands. Buck, Mills and Berry also recorded with Warren Zevon as the Hindu Love Gods in 1990. Berry fully recovered from a brain aneurysm suffered on stage in Lausanne, Switzerland, on 3/1/1995; announced he was leaving the group in October 1997. R.E.M. is abbreviation for Rapid Eye Movement, the dream stage of sleep.

REMBRANDTS, The
Pop-rock duo from Los Angeles, California: Danny Wilde and Phil Solem.

REMEDY
Multi-ethnic R&B trio from San Jose, California: Sean Daniel Alaura, Jesse Rodriguez Aguirre and Darryl Lamont Sherman.

RENAY, Diane
Born Renee Diane Kushner on 7/13/1945 in Philadelphia, Pennsylvania. Teen pop singer.

RENE, Googie, Combo
Born Raphael Rene on 3/30/1927 in Los Angeles, California. Bandleader/keyboardist. Son of songwriter/producer Leon Rene.

RENE, Henri
Born on 12/29/1906 in Germany. Died on 4/25/1993 (age 86). Bandleader/arranger/conductor. Began long career with Victor in 1936 as director of their international branch. Arranger/conductor for Perry Como, Dinah Shore, Eartha Kitt, Mindy Carson, and many other singers.

RENE & ANGELA
R&B vocal duo from Los Angeles, California: René Moore and Angela Winbush. Winbush married Ronald Isley on 6/26/1993.

RENE & RAY
Latin vocal duo: Paul Venezuela (René; born in Puerto Rico) and Ray Quinones (born on 1/31/41 in Manhattan, New York); both sang with The Velveteens.

RENE & RENE
Mexican-American duo from Laredo, Texas: Rene Ornelas (born on 8/26/1936) and Rene Herrera (born on 10/2/1935).

RENEE, Nicole
Born in 1975 in Philadelphia, Pennsylvania. R&B singer/songwriter.

RENO, Mike
Born on 1/8/1955 in New Westminster, British Columbia, Canada. Lead singer of Loverboy.

RENTALS, The
Pop-rock group from Los Angeles, California: Matt Sharp (vocals, bass), Cherielynn Westrich (vocals), Petra Haden (violin), Rod Cervera (guitar), Tom Gaimley (synthesizer) and Pat Wilson (drums). Sharp and Wilson are also members of Weezer.

REO SPEEDWAGON
Rock group from Champaign, Illinois: Mike Murphy (vocals), Gary Richrath (guitar; born on 10/18/1949), Neal Doughty (keyboards; born on 7/29/1946), Gregg Philbin (bass) and Alan Gratzer (drums; born on 11/9/1948). Murphy left by 1976; replaced by Kevin Cronin (born on 10/6/1951). Philbin left in 1978; replaced by Bruce Hall (born on 5/3/1953). Gratzer left in 1988; replaced by former Santana drummer Graham Lear. Lineup in 1990: Cronin, Doughty and Hall, joined by new members Dave Amato (guitar), Jesse Harms (keyboards; left by 1991) and Bryan Hitt (drums). Group named after a 1911 fire truck.

REPARATA & THE DELRONS
"Girl group" from Brooklyn, New York: Mary "Reparata" Aiese, Sheila Reillie and Carol Drobnicki. First recorded for Laurie in 1964. Lorraine Mazzola, member from 1966-73, later was leader of Lady Flash under the name "Reparata." Mary Aiese recorded "Shoes" solo as Reparata.

REPLACEMENTS, The
Alternative-rock band from Minneapolis, Minnesota: Paul Westerberg (vocals, guitar, piano), Slim Dunlap (guitar), Tommy Stinson (bass) and Chris Mars (drums).

REPUBLICA
Rock group from London, England: Saffron Sprackling (female vocals), Jonny Male (guitar), Tim Dorney and Andy Todd (keyboards) and Dave Barbarossa (drums).

RESTIVO, Johnny
Born in the Bronx, New York. Pop singer (15 years old in 1959).

RESTLESS HEART
Country group formed in Nashville, Tennessee: Larry Stewart (vocals), Greg Jennings (guitar), David Innis (keyboards), Paul Gregg (bass) and John Dittrich (drums). Stewart went solo in early 1992. Keyboardist Innis left in early 1993. Remaining three continued on with two backing musicians. Group disbanded in 1996.

REUNION
Pop group formed in New York: Joey Levine (lead vocals; Ohio Express), Marc Bellack, Paul DiFranco and Norman Dolph.

REVELATION
R&B-disco group: Phillip Ballou, Benny Diggs, Arthur Freeman and Arnold McCuller.

REVELS, The
Black vocal group from Philadelphia, Pennsylvania: John Kelly, John Grant, Henry Colclough, John Jones and Bill Jackson.

REVERE, Paul, & The Raiders
Born on 1/7/1938 in Harvard, Nebraska. Rock and roll keyboardist. Formed The Raiders in Boise, Idaho. Group had numerous personnel changes through the years. Core members: Mark Lindsay (vocals; born on 3/9/1942), Freddy Weller (guitar), Keith Allison (bass) and Michael Smith (drums). On daily ABC-TV show *Where The Action Is*. Own TV show *Happening* in 1968. Lindsay and Allison recorded with Steve Alaimo as The Unknowns in 1966. Weller went on to become a prolific country singer. Smith died on 3/6/2001 (age 58).

REYNOLDS, Burt
Born on 2/11/1936 in Waycross, Georgia. Became a movie box-office superstar in the mid-1970s.

REYNOLDS, Debbie
Born Mary Reynolds on 4/1/1932 in El Paso, Texas. Actress/singer. Starred in many movies. Married to Eddie Fisher from 1955-59. Mother of actress/author Carrie Fisher.

REYNOLDS, Jody
Born on 12/3/1932 in Denver, Colorado; raised in Oklahoma. Male rockabilly singer/guitarist.

REYNOLDS, Lawrence
Born on 7/13/1914 in St. Stephens, Alabama. Died on 8/15/2000 (age 86). White folk-pop-country singer.

RHINOCEROS
Rock group from Los Angeles, California: John Finley (vocals), Danny Weis and Doug Hastings (guitars), Michael Fonfara (organ), Alan Gerber (piano), Jerry Penrod (bass) and Billy Mundi (drums).

RHODES, Emitt
Born on 2/25/1950 in Hawthorne, California. Pop singer/songwriter. Lead singer of The Merry-Go-Round.

RHYTHM HERITAGE
Studio group assembled by producers Steve Barri and Michael Omartian (keyboards). Vocals by Oren and Luther Waters. Omartian was in the band Gator Creek with Kenny Loggins.

RHYTHM SYNDICATE
R&B group from Connecticut: Evan Rogers (vocals), Carl Sturken (guitar), John Nevin (keyboards), Rob Mingrino (bass) and Kevin Cloud (drums). Rogers and Sturken produced Donny Osmond's "Soldier Of Love" and "Sacred Emotion." Changed spelling of name from Rythm Syndicate to Rhythm Syndicate after first album.

RIBBONS, The
Female R&B vocal group from Los Angeles, California: Vessie Simmons, Aretha Gibson, Evelyn Doty and Lovie.

RIC-A-CHE
Born Steven Rifkind in Detroit, Michigan. Rapper.

RICH, Charlie
Born on 12/14/1932 in Colt, Arkansas. Died of an acute blood clot on 7/25/1995 (age 62). Rockabilly-country singer/pianist/songwriter. First played jazz and blues. Own jazz group, the Velvetones, mid-1950s, while in U.S. Air Force. Session work with Sun Records in 1958. Known as "The Silver Fox."

RICH, Tony, Project
Born Antonio Jeffries on 11/19/1971 in Detroit, Michigan. R&B singer/songwriter/keyboardist.

RICHARD, Cliff
Born Harry Rodger Webb on 10/14/1940 in Lucknow, India (of British parentage). Rock and roll-pop singer/guitarist/actor. To England in 1948. Worked in skiffle groups, mid-1950s. Backing band: The Drifters (later: The Shadows). Richard also recorded Inspirational music since 1967. The Shadows disbanded in 1969. Superstar in England. Knighted by Queen Elizabeth II in 1995.

RICHARD & THE YOUNG LIONS
Psychedelic garage-rock band from Newark, New Jersey: Howie "Richard" Tepp (vocals), Lou Vlahakes (guitar), Bob Freeman (guitar), Freddy Randle (bass) and Mark Greenberg (drums). Previously known as The Emeralds and The Original Kounts. Tepp died on 6/17/2004 (age 57).

RICHARDS, Turley
Born in 1941 in Charleston, West Virginia. White soft-rock singer/guitarist. Went blind at age 28.

RICH BOY
Born Marece Richards in 1985 in Mobile, Alabama. Male rapper/songwriter.

RICHIE, Lionel
Born on 6/20/1949 in Tuskegee, Alabama. R&B-Adult Contemporary singer/songwriter. Grew up on the campus of Tuskegee Institute where his grandfather worked. Former lead singer of the Commodores. Appeared in the movie *Thank God It's Friday*. His adopted daughter, Nicole Richie, starred with Paris Hilton on the reality TV series *The Simple Life*.

RICHIE RICH
Born Richard Serrell on 6/25/1967 in Oakland, California. Male rapper.

RICK & The Keens
Rock and roll band from Wichita Falls, Texas. Led by guitarist John Bland.

RICKS, Jimmy
Born on 8/6/1924 in Jackson, Florida. Died of a heart attack on 7/2/1974 (age 49). R&B singer. Bass vocalist of The Ravens.

RIDDLE, Nelson
Born on 6/1/1921 in Oradell, New Jersey. Died on 10/6/1985 (age 64). Trombonist/arranger with Charlie Spivak and Tommy Dorsey in the 1940s. One of the most in-demand of all arranger/conductors for many top artists, including Frank Sinatra (several classic 1950s albums), Nat King Cole, Ella Mae Morse and Linda Ronstadt; also arranger/musical director for many movies.

RIDGELEY, Andrew
Born on 1/26/1963 in Bushey, England. Former guitarist of Wham! Also pursued race car driving.

RIFF
R&B vocal group from Paterson, New Jersey: Ken Kelly, Steven Capers, Anthony Fuller, Dwayne Jones and Michael Best.

RIGHTEOUS BROTHERS, The
"Blue-eyed soul" vocal duo: Bill Medley (baritone; born on 9/19/1940 in Santa Ana, California) and Bobby Hatfield (tenor; born on 8/10/1940 in Beaver Dam, Wisconsin; died on 11/5/2003, age 63). Formed duo in 1962. First recorded as the Paramours for Smash in 1962. On *Hullabaloo* and *Shindig* TV shows. Split up from 1968-74. Medley went solo; replaced by Jimmy Walker (The Knickerbockers); rejoined Hatfield in 1974.

RIGHT SAID FRED (R*S*F)
Pop-dance-novelty trio from England: brothers Fred (guitar) and Richard (vocals) Fairbrass with Rob Manzoli (guitar).

RIHANNA
Born Robin Rihanna Fenty on 2/20/1988 in St. Michael, Barbados. Female R&B-reggae singer.

RILEY, Billy Lee
Born on 10/5/1933 in Pocahontas, Arkansas. White session musician in Memphis, Tennessee; one of the lesser-known Sun rockabilly artists from 1956-59. Led The Megatons and wrote their 1962 hit "Shimmy, Shimmy Walk."

RILEY, Cheryl Pepsii
Born in Brooklyn, New York. R&B singer. Discovered by the group Full Force.

RILEY, Jeannie C.
Born Jeanne Carolyn Stephenson on 10/19/1945 in Stamford, Texas; raised in Anson, Texas. Country singer.

RILEY, Teddy
Born on 10/8/66 in Harlem, New York. R&B singer/songwriter/producer. Member of Kids At Work, Guy and BLACKstreet. Brother of Markell Riley of Wreckx-N-Effect.

RIMES, LeAnn
Born Margaret LeAnn Rimes on 8/28/1982 in Jackson, Mississippi; raised in Garland, Texas. Country singer. Married actor Dean Sheremet on 2/23/2002.

RINGS, The
Rock group from Boston, Massachusetts: Mark Sutton (vocals, guitar), Mike Baker (keyboards), Bob Gifford (bass) and Matt Thurber (drums).

RIOS, Augie
Child singer/actor. Appeared in the Broadway musical *Jamaica*.

RIOS, Miguel
Born on 6/7/1944 in Granada, Spain. Adult Contemporary singer.

RIOS, Waldo De Los
Born on 9/7/1934 in Buenos Aires, Argentina. Committed suicide on 3/28/1977 (age 42). Composer/conductor.

RIP CHORDS, The
Rock and roll group formed in California: Terry Melcher (Bruce And Terry) and Bruce Johnston (Bruce And Terry, The Beach Boys), Ernie Bringas, Phil Stewart, Richard Rotkin and Arnie Marcus. Touring group included Phil, Richard and Arnie, who also appeared in the Raquel Welch beach movie *A Swingin' Summer*. Melcher died of cancer on 11/19/2004 (age 62).

RIPERTON, Minnie
Born on 11/8/1947 in Chicago, Illinois. Died of cancer on 7/12/1979 (age 31). R&B singer. Member of Rotary Connection from 1967-70. Her daughter Maya Rudolph is a cast member of TV's *Saturday Night Live*.

RIPPLE
Interracial progressive soul group from Kalamazoo, Michigan: Dave Ferguson, Bill Hull, Keith "Doc" Samuels, Curtis Reynolds, Ken Carter, Walter Carter and Brian Sherrer.

RITCHIE FAMILY, The
Female disco trio from Philadelphia, Pennsylvania: Cheryl Jackson, Cassandra Wooten and Gwen Oliver. Named for producer Ritchie Rome.

RITENOUR, Lee
Born on 1/11/1952 in Los Angeles, California. Guitarist/composer/arranger. Top session guitarist. Has appeared on more than 200 albums. Nicknamed "Captain Fingers." Member of jazz outfits Brass Fever and Fourplay.

RITTER, Tex
Born Maurice Ritter on 1/12/1905 in Murvaul, Texas. Died of a heart attack on 1/2/1974 (age 68). Country singer/guitarist/actor. Starred in several western movies. Father of actor John Ritter (died on 9/11/2003, age 54).

RIVERS, Johnny
Born John Ramistella on 11/7/1942 in Brooklyn, New York; raised in Baton Rouge, Louisiana. Rock and roll singer/guitarist/songwriter/producer. Recorded with the Spades for Suede in 1957. Named Johnny Rivers by DJ Alan Freed in 1958. To Los Angeles in 1961. Recorded for 12 different labels (1958-64) before his smash debut on Imperial. Began own Soul City label in 1966. Recorded Christian music in the early 1980s.

RIVIERAS, The
R&B vocal group from New Jersey: Homer Dunn, Charles Allen, Ronald Cook and Andrew Jones.

RIVIERAS, The
Teen rock and roll band from South Bend, Indiana: Bill Dobslaw (vocals), Jim Boal and Willie Gout (guitars), Otto Nuss (organ), Doug Gean (bass) and Paul Dennert (drums). Marty Fortson was lead singer on "California Sun."

RIVINGTONS, The
R&B vocal group from Los Angeles, California: Carl White (lead), Sonny Harris, Rocky Wilson and Al Frazier. Backup on Paul Anka's first recording, Duane Eddy's "Rebel Rouser", and "Little Bitty Pretty One" by Thurston Harris. Known then as The Sharps. White died of acute tonsillitis on 1/7/1980 (age 47).

R.J.'s LATEST ARRIVAL
Funk group from Detroit, Michigan. Led by keyboardist Ralph James Rice.

R.L.
Born Robert Lavelle Huggar on 4/2/1977 in Minneapolis, Minnesota. R&B singer/songwriter. Member of Next.

ROACHFORD
R&B-rock group formed in England: Andrew Roachford (vocals, keyboards; born on 1/22/1965), Hawi Gondwe (guitar), Derrick Taylor (bass) and Chris Taylor (drums; Paul Hyde & The Payolas).

ROAD APPLES, The
Pop group from Boston, Massachusetts. Led by singer/guitarist David Finnerty.

ROBB, AnnaSophia
Born on 12/8/1993 in Denver, Colorado. Teen actress. Appeared in several movies.

ROB BASE & D.J. E-Z ROCK
Rap-dance duo from Harlem, New York: Robert Ginyard with DJ Rodney "Skip" Bryce.

ROBBINS, Marty
Born Martin David Robinson on 9/26/1925 in Glendale, Arizona. Died of a heart attack on 12/8/1982 (age 57). Country singer/guitarist/songwriter. Own radio show with K-Bar Cowboys, late 1940s. Own TV show, *Western Caravan*, KPHO-Phoenix, 1951. First recorded for Columbia in 1952. Regular on the *Grand Ole Opry* since 1953. Own Robbins label in 1958. Raced stock cars. Movies: *Road To Nashville* and *Guns Of A Stranger*.

ROBBINS, Rockie
Born Edward Robbins in Minneapolis, Minnesota. R&B singer/songwriter.

ROBBS, The
Pop-rock band from Oconomowoc, Wisconsin: brothers David "Dee Robb" Donaldson (vocals, guitar), George "Joe Robb" Donaldson (guitar) and Robert "Bruce Robb" Donaldson (keyboards), with friend "Craig Robb" Krampf (drums).

ROBERT & JOHNNY
R&B duo from the Bronx, New York: Robert Carr (died on 5/18/1993) and Johnny Mitchell.

ROBERTS, Austin
Born on 9/19/1945 in Newport News, Virginia. Writer of several country songs. Collaborator on the cartoon series *Scooby Doo* and *Josie & The Pussycats*. Replaced Gene Pistilli in Buchanan Brothers/Cashman, Pistilli & West trio in 1972, and was a member of Arkade.

ROBERTS, John
Born on 11/28/1941 in Houston, Texas. R&B singer/songwriter.

ROBERTS, Julie
Born on 2/1/1979 in Lancaster, South Carolina. Country singer.

ROBERTS, Juliet
Born in London, England (West Indian parents). Black dance singer.

ROBERTS, Kane
Born in Boston, Massachusetts. Rock singer/guitarist. Guitar work with Alice Cooper, Rod Stewart and Berlin.

ROBERTS, Lea
Born Leatha Roberta Hicks on 4/15/1946 in Dayton, Ohio. R&B singer.

ROBERTSON, Don
Born on 12/5/1922 in Peking, China; raised in Chicago, Illinois. Pianist/composer/songwriter. Created the Nashville piano style.

ROBERTSON, Robbie
Born Jaime Robert Klegerman on 7/5/1943 in Toronto, Ontario, Canada. Rock singer/songwriter/guitarist. Member of The Band.

ROBEY
Born Louise Robey on 3/14/1960 in Montreal, Quebec, Canada. Dance singer/actress/model. Played "Micki Foster" on *Friday the 13th - The TV Series* (1987-90).

ROBIC, Ivo
Born on 1/29/1923 in Bjelovar, Yugoslavia. Died of cancer on 3/10/2000 (age 77). Male singer.

ROBIN, Tina
Pop singer. Regular on TV's *Sing Along* in 1958, hosted by Jim Lowe.

ROBIN S
Born Robin Stone in Queens, New York. Female dance singer.

ROBINS, The
R&B vocal group from Los Angeles, California: Ty Terrell, Billy Richards, Roy Richards, and Bobby Nunn. First known as the Four Bluebirds. Carl Gardner and Grady Chapman added in 1954. Gardner and Nunn formed The Coasters in 1955.

ROBINSON, Alvin
Born on 12/22/1937 in New Orleans, Louisiana. Died of a heart attack on 1/24/1989 (age 51). R&B session guitarist/vocalist. Worked with Joe Jones and Dr. John.

ROBINSON, Floyd
Born in 1937 in Nashville, Tennessee. Rock and roll singer/guitarist/composer. Worked on local radio with his high school band, the Eagle Rangers, at age 12. Own programs on WLAC and WSM-Nashville.

ROBINSON, Freddy
Born on 2/24/1939 in Memphis, Tennessee. Black jazz-rock guitarist. With Little Walter's Band, Howling Wolf and John Mayall.

ROBINSON, Rosco
Born on 5/22/1928 in Dumont, Arkansas; raised in Gary, Indiana. Singer/producer.

ROBINSON, Smokey
Born William Robinson on 2/19/1940 in Detroit, Michigan. Formed The Miracles (then called the Matadors) at Northern High School in 1955. First recorded for End in 1958. Married to Miracles' member Claudette Rogers from 1958-86. Left The Miracles on 1/29/1972. Wrote dozens of hit songs for Motown artists. Vice President of Motown Records, 1985-88.

ROBINSON, Stan
Rock and roll singer. Father of Chris and Rich Robinson of The Black Crowes. Member of the folk group The Appalachians.

ROBINSON, Vicki Sue
Born on 5/31/1954 in Harlem, New York (African-American father/white mother); raised in Philadelphia, Pennsylvania. Died of cancer on 4/27/2000 (age 45). Disco singer. Appeared in the original Broadway productions of *Hair* and *Jesus Christ Superstar*.

ROBYN
Born Robyn Carlsson on 6/12/1979 in Stockholm, Sweden. Female dance singer.

ROCHELL & THE CANDLES
R&B vocal group from Los Angeles, California: Johnny Wyatt (1st tenor; born in 1938; died in December 1983, age 45), Rochell Henderson (tenor), Melvin Sasso (baritone) and T.C. Henderson (bass).

ROCK, Pete, & C.L. Smooth
Hip-hop duo from Mt. Vernon, New York: producer/DJ Peter "Pete Rock" Phillips and rapper Corey "C.L. Smooth" Penn.

ROCK & ROLL DUBBLE BUBBLE
Studio creation by producers Bob Feldman and Jerry Goldstein (The Sheep/The Strangeloves).

ROCK-A-TEENS
Rock and roll teen group from Richmond, Virginia: Vic Mizell (leader), Bobby "Boo" Walker, Bill Cook, Paul Evans, Eddie Robertson and Bill Smith.

ROCKELL
Born Rachel Mercaldo on 3/4/1977 in Long Island, New York. Female techno-dance singer.

ROCKETS
Rock group from Detroit, Michigan: David Gilbert (vocals), Jim McCarty and Dennis Robbins (guitars), Donnie Backus (keyboards), Bobby Neil Haralson (bass) and John Badanjek (drums). McCarty and Badanjek were members of Mitch Ryder & The Detroit Wheels. Gilbert died of cancer on 8/1/2001 (age 49).

ROCK FLOWERS
Female pop vocal trio: Rindy Dunn, Ardie Tillman and Debbie Clinger.

ROCK HEROES, The
Band of anonymous studio musicians.

ROCKINGHAM, David, Trio
Born in Chicago, Illinois. R&B organist. His trio also included R.C. "Bobby" Robinson (guitar) and Shante Hamilton (drums).

ROCKIN R'S, The
Instrumental rock and roll trio from Metamora, Illinois: Ron Volz and Ron Wernsman (guitars) and Ted Minar (drums).

ROCKO
Born Rodney Hill in Atlanta, Georgia. Male rapper.

ROCKPILE
Rock and roll group formed in London, England: Dave Edmunds (vocals, guitar), Nick Lowe (vocals, bass), Billy Bremner (guitar) and Terry Williams (drums).

ROCKWELL
Born Kennedy Gordy on 3/15/1964 in Detroit, Michigan. R&B singer/songwriter. Son of Motown chairman, Berry Gordy, Jr.

ROCKY FELLERS, The
Rock and roll family band from Manila, Philippines: father Doroteo "Moro" Maligmat, with his sons Eddie, Albert, Tony and Junior Maligmat. Tony died on 3/4/2007 (age 62).

ROC PROJECT, The
Dance studio production of Ray "Roc" Checo.

RODGERS, Eileen
Born in 1933 in Pittsburgh, Pennsylvania. Adult Contemporary singer. Featured vocalist in Charlie Spivak's band, 1954-56.

RODGERS, Jimmie
Born on 9/18/1933 in Camas, Washington. Pop-folk singer/guitarist. Hosted own TV variety series in 1959. Career hampered following mysterious assault on the San Diego Freeway on 12/1/1967, which left him with a fractured skull. Returned to performing a year later. Starred in movies *The Little Shepherd of Kingdom Come* and *Back Door To*

RODGERS, Jimmie — cont'd
Hell. Not to be confused with the country music pioneer of the same name.

RODGERS, Nile
Born on 9/19/1952 in Brooklyn, New York. R&B guitarist/producer. Member of Chic and The Honeydrippers. Produced Madonna's "Like A Virgin" single.

RODNEY O & JOE COOLEY
Rap trio from Los Angeles, California: Rodney Oliver, Joe Cooley and Jeff Page.

RODRIGUEZ, Daniel
Born in Brooklyn, New York. Operatic tenor. Former member of the New York City Police Department; was on duty during the 9/11 terrorist attacks. Known as "The Singing Policeman."

RODRIGUEZ, Johnny
Born Juan Rodriguez on 12/10/1951 in Sabinal, Texas. Country singer/songwriter/guitarist.

RODWAY
Born Steve Rodway in Kent, England. Electro-pop singer/songwriter.

ROE, Tommy
Born on 5/9/1942 in Atlanta, Georgia. Pop-rock and roll singer/guitarist/composer. Formed band The Satins at Brown High School, worked local dances in the late 1950s. Group recorded for Judd in 1960. Moved to Britain in the mid-1960s; returned in 1969.

ROGER / ZAPP
Born Roger Troutman on 11/29/1951 in Hamilton, Ohio. Shot to death by his brother Larry in a murder-suicide on 4/25/1999. Roger was age 47; Larry was age 54. Roger was the leader of the family electro-funk group Zapp (Roger, Lester, Larry and Tony). Worked with Sly Stone and George Clinton. Father of male singer Lynch.

ROGERS, D.J.
Born DeWayne Julius Rogers in Los Angeles, California. R&B singer/songwriter/keyboardist.

ROGERS, Dann
Adult Contemporary/country singer. Nephew of Kenny Rogers.

ROGERS, David
Born on 3/27/1936 in Atlanta, Georgia. Died on 8/10/1993 (age 57). Country singer/songwriter/ guitarist.

ROGERS, Julie
Born Julie Rolls on 4/6/1943 in London, England. Adult Contemporary singer.

ROGERS, Kenny / First Edition
Born on 8/21/1938 in Houston, Texas. Country singer/songwriter/guitarist/actor. With high school band the Scholars in 1958. Bass player of jazz group the Bobby Doyle Trio, recorded for Columbia. First recorded for Carlton in 1958. In Kirby Stone Four and The New Christy Minstrels, mid-1960s. Formed and fronted The First Edition in 1967. Original lineup included Thelma Camacho, Mike Settle, Terry Williams and Mickey Jones. All but Jones were members of The New Christy Minstrels.

Group hosted own syndicated TV variety show *Rollin* in 1972. Rogers split from group in 1973. Starred in movie *Six Pack* and several TV movies including *The Gambler I, II & III* miniseries, *Coward Of The County*, *Wild Horses* and *Rio Diablo*. Married to actress Marianne Gordon from 1977-93. Later started the Kenny Rogers Roasters restaurant chain.

ROGERS, Roy
Born Leonard Franklin Slye on 11/5/1911 in Cincinnati, Ohio. Died of heart failure on 7/6/1998 (age 86). Popular "singing cowboy." Original member of the famous western group Sons Of The Pioneers. Starred in close to 100 movie Westerns, then in a popular radio and TV series with his wife Dale Evans (died of heart failure on 2/7/2001, age 88).

ROGERS, Timmie "Oh Yeah!"
Born on 7/4/1915 in Detroit, Michigan. Black vaudeville and nightclub comedian.

ROLLERS, The
R&B vocal group from San Bernardino, California: Johnny Torrence (lead), Don Sampson, Willie Willingham, and brothers Eddie and Al Wilson.

ROLLIN, Dana
Born in New York. Female pop singer.

ROLLING STONES, The
Blues-influenced rock group formed in London, England: Mick Jagger (vocals; born on 7/26/1943), Keith Richards (lead guitar; born on 12/18/1943), Brian Jones (guitar; born on 2/28/1942), Bill Wyman (bass; born on 10/24/1936) and Charlie Watts (drums; born on 6/2/1941). Jagger was the lead singer of Blues, Inc. The Stones took its name from the 1950 Muddy Waters song "Rollin' Stone." Promoted as the bad boys in contrast to The Beatles. First U.K. tour with The Ronettes in 1964. Jones left the group on 6/9/1969 and drowned on 7/3/1969 (age 27); replaced by Mick Taylor (born on 1/17/1949). In 1975, Ron Wood (ex-Jeff Beck Group, ex-Faces) replaced Taylor. Movie *Gimme Shelter* is a documentary of the Stones' controversial Altamont concert on 12/6/1969 at which a concertgoer was murdered by a member of the Hell's Angels. Wyman left band in late 1992. Bassist Darryl Jones (billed as a "side musician") played on the 1994 *Voodoo Lounge* album and tour. Considered by many as the world's all-time greatest rock and roll band.

ROMAN, Dick
Born Ricardo DeGiacomo in 1937 in Brooklyn, New York. Died of a heart attack on 10/21/1976 (age 39). Regular on TV's *The Liberace Show*, 1958-59.

ROMAN HOLLIDAY
Pop-rock band formed in Harlow, England: Steve Lambert (vocals), Brian Bonhomme (guitar), Adrian York (keyboards), John Eacott (trumpet), Rob Lambert (saxophone), Jon Durno (bass) and Simon Cohen (drums). Group named after the 1953 movie starring Audrey Hepburn.

ROMANTICS, The
Pop-rock group from Detroit, Michigan: Wally Palmar (vocals, guitar), Coz Canler (guitar), Mike Skill (bass) and Jimmy Marinos (drums). David Petratos replaced Marinos in early 1985.

ROME
Born Jerome Woods on 3/5/1970 in Benton Harbor, Michigan. Male R&B singer.

ROMEO & JULIET SOUNDTRACK
Record contains an actual scene from the 1968 movie. Romeo was played by Leonard Whiting (born on 6/30/1950 in London, England). Juliet was played by Olivia Hussey (born on 4/17/1951 in Buenos Aires, Argentina). Nurse was played by Pat Heywood (born on 1/1/1927 in Gretna Green, Scotland).

ROMEOS, The
R&B group from Philadelphia, Pennsylvania: producers Kenny Gamble, Leon Huff and Thom Bell, with brothers Karl and Roland Chambers, and Winnie Walford. Karl Chambers died of cancer on 2/24/2002 (age 55). Roland Chambers died of heart failure on 5/8/2002 (age 58).

ROMEO'S DAUGHTER
Rock trio from England: Leigh Matty (vocals), Craig Joiner (guitars, vocals) and Tony Mitman (keyboards).

ROMEO VOID
Pop-rock-dance group from San Francisco, California: Debora Iyall (vocals), Peter Woods (guitar), Ben Bossi (sax), Frank Zincavage (bass) and Aaron Smith (drums).

RONALD & RUBY
Teen pop duo: Ronald Gumbs and Beverly "Ruby" Ross (born in 1939). The New Jersey-born Ross wrote "Dim, Dim The Lights," "Lollipop," "Judy's Turn To Cry" and Roy Orbison's "Candy Man."

RON & THE D.C. CREW
Ficticious rap group -- features Miami D.J. Mark Moseley.

RONDELS, The
Rock and roll band from Boston, Massachusetts: Leonard Petze (guitar) and his cousin James Petze (bass), with Ray Pizzi (sax) and Leonard Collins (drums). James Petze died of cancer on 9/12/1993 (age 48).

RON-DELS, The
Pop duo formed in Texas: Delbert McClinton and Ronnie Kelly (died in May 1993, age 49).

RONDO, Don
Born in Springfield, Massachusetts. Adult Contemporary baritone singer. Sang on TV/radio commercials.

RONETTES, The
R&B-rock and roll "girl group" from New York: Veronica Bennett (Ronnie Spector), sister Estelle Bennett Vann and cousin Nedra Talley Ross. Formed as the Darling Sisters in 1958. Sang professionally since junior high school. Backup work

for Phil Spector in 1962. Veronica married to Phil Spector, 1968-74.

RONNIE & THE HI-LITES
Doo-wop group from Jersey City, New Jersey: Ronnie Goodson (lead singer; 12 years old in 1962), Sonny Caldwell and John Whitney (tenors), Stanley Brown (baritone) and Kenny Overby (bass). Originally called The Cascades. Goodson died of a brain tumor on 11/4/1980 (age 31).

RONNY & THE DAYTONAS
Pop-rock group: Ronny is John "Bucky" Wilkin (vocals; born on 4/26/1946 in Tulsa, Oklahoma; son of country songwriter Marijohn Wilkin). Backed on recordings by well-known sessionmen Bobby Russell (wrote "Little Green Apples"), Chips Moman (prolific producer) and Johnny McCrae (member of Bobby "Boris" Pickett And The Crypt-Kickers), among others. The touring group, which featured an entirely different lineup, later charted as The Hombres.

RONSTADT, Linda
Born on 7/15/1946 in Tucson, Arizona. While in high school formed folk trio The Three Ronstadts (with sister and brother). To Los Angeles in 1964. Formed the Stone Poneys with Bobby Kimmel (guitar) and Ken Edwards (keyboards); recorded for Sidewalk in 1966. Went solo in 1968. In 1971 formed backing band with Glenn Frey, Don Henley, Randy Meisner and Bernie Leadon (later became the Eagles). Appeared in the 1978 movie *FM*. In *Pirates Of Penzance* operetta in New York City in 1980, also in the movie version in 1983.

ROOFTOP SINGERS, The
Folk trio from New York: Erik Darling, Willard Svanoe and Lynne Taylor (died in 1982). Disbanded in 1967. Darling was a member of The Tarriers in 1956 and The Weavers, 1958-62. Taylor was a vocalist with Benny Goodman and Buddy Rich. Darling died on 8/2/2008 (age 74).

ROOTS, The
Hip-hop group from Philadelphia, Pennsylvania: Tariq Trotter, Ahmir-Khalib Thompson, Malik Abdul-Basit and Leonard Hubbard.

ROS, Edmundo
Born on 12/7/1910 in Trinidad. Bandleader/drummer based in London, England.

ROSE, Andy
Born in Long Island, New York. Teen pop singer.

ROSE, David
Born on 6/15/1910 in London, England; raised in Chicago, Illinois. Died of heart failure on 8/23/1990 (age 80). Conductor/composer/arranger for numerous movies. Scored many TV series, such as *The Red Skelton Show*, *Bonanza* and *Little House On The Prairie*. Married to Martha Raye (1938-41) and Judy Garland (1941-43).

ROSE COLORED GLASS
Pop vocal group from Dallas, Texas: Mary Owens, Larry Meletio, Bob Caldwell and Bill Tillman (Blood, Sweat & Tears).

ROSE GARDEN, The
Pop band formed in Los Angeles, California: Diana Di Rose (vocals), John Noreen and James Groshong (guitars), William Fleming (bass, piano) and Bruce Boudin (drums).

ROSELLI, Jimmy
Born on 12/26/1925 in Hoboken, New Jersey. Italian-American Adult Contemporary singer.

ROSE ROYCE
R&B-dance group from Los Angeles, California: Gwen "Rose" Dickey (vocals), Kenji Brown (guitar), Kenny Copeland and Freddie Dunn (trumpets), Michael Moore (sax), Terral Santiel (percussion), Victor Nix (keyboards), Lequeint "Duke" Jobe (bass) and Henry Garner (drums). Dickey left after first album, replaced by Rose Norwalt. Dickey then returned from 1978 until she was replaced by Richee McKinney in 1980. Group backed Edwin Starr as Total Concept Unlimited in 1973. Backed The Temptations, became regular band for Undisputed Truth. Name changed to Rose Royce in 1976. Did soundtrack for the movie *Car Wash*.

ROSIE & The Originals
Pop group from San Diego, California. Rosie was born Rosalie Hamlin on 7/21/1945 in Klamath Falls, Oregon; raised in Anchorage, Alaska. The Originals: David Ponci and Noah Tafolla (guitars), Tony Gomez (sax) and Carl Von Goodat (drums).

ROSS, Charlie
Born in Greenville, Mississippi. Pop-country singer. Bassist for Eternity's Children.

ROSS, Diana
Born Diane Ernestine Ross on 3/26/1944 in Detroit, Michigan. R&B singer/actress. In vocal group The Primettes, first recorded for LuPine in 1960. Lead singer of The Supremes from 1961-69. Went solo in late 1969. Oscar nominee for the 1972 movie *Lady Sings The Blues*. Also appeared in the movies *Mahogany* and *The Wiz*. Own Broadway show *An Evening With Diana Ross*, 1976. Married to Norwegian shipping magnate Arne Naess from 1986-2000.

ROSS, Jack
Born on 11/1/1916 in Seattle, Washington. Died on 12/16/1982 (age 66). Comedian.

ROSS, Jackie
Born on 1/30/1946 in St. Louis, Missouri; raised in Chicago, Illinois. Female R&B singer.

ROSS, Rick
Born William Roberts on 2/8/1977 in Miami, Florida. Male rapper/songwriter.

ROSS, Spencer
Born Robert Mersey on 4/7/1917 in Manhattan, New York. Conductor/arranger.

ROSSDALE, Gavin
Born on 10/30/1967 in London, England. Lead singer of Bush. Married Gwen Stefani (of No Doubt) on 9/14/2002.

ROSSINGTON COLLINS BAND
Southern-rock band formed in 1979 in Jacksonville, Florida: Dale Krantz (vocals), Gary Rossington, Allen Collins and Barry Harwood (guitars), Billy Powell (keyboards), Leon Wilkeson (bass) and Derek Hess (drums). Rossington, Collins, Powell and Wilkeson were members of Lynyrd Skynyrd. Disbanded in 1982. Collins (paralyzed in a car accident in 1986) died of pneumonia on 1/23/1990 (age 37). Wilkeson died on 7/27/2001 (age 49).

ROTARY CONNECTION
Multi-racial rock/R&B group formed in Chicago, Illinois: Minnie Riperton, Judy Huff and Sid Barnes (vocals), Bobby Simms (guitar), Charles Stepney (keyboards), Mitch Aliotta (bass) and Kenny Venegas (drums).

ROTH, David Lee
Born on 10/10/1954 in Bloomington, Indiana. Lead singer of Van Halen from 1973-1985. Rejoined Van Halen briefly in 1996 to record two new songs.

ROTHBERG, Patti
Born on 5/4/1972 in Scarsdale, New York. Female singer/songwriter/guitarist/pianist.

ROUGH TRADE
Rock group from Toronto, Ontario, Canada: Carole Pope (vocals), Kevan Staples (guitar), Dave McMorrow (keyboards), Terry Wilkins (bass) and Bucky Berger (drums).

ROULA
Born in Chicago, Illinois. Female dance singer. Produced by 20 Fingers.

ROUND ROBIN
Born in Los Angeles, California. Pop singer.

ROUSSOS, Demis
Born on 6/15/1947 in Alexandria, Egypt (Greek parents). Male singer.

ROUTERS, The
Rock and roll instrumental band formed in Los Angeles, California: Mike Gordon (guitar), Al Kait (guitar), Lynn Frasier (horns), Scott Engel (bass) and Randy Viers (drums).

ROVER BOYS, The
Pop vocal group formed in Toronto, Ontario, Canada: Billy Albert, Doug Wells, Larry Amato and Al Osten.

ROWANS, The
Pop-rock trio from Boston, Massachusetts: brothers Peter (vocals, guitar), Lorin (guitar) and Chris (keyboards) Rowan. Peter was a member of Earth Opera and Seatrain.

ROWLAND, Kelly
Born Kelendria Rowland on 2/11/1981 in Atlanta, Georgia. Female R&B singer/actress. Member of Destiny's Child. Played "Kia" in the movie *Freddy vs. Jason*.

ROWLES, John
Born on 3/26/1947 in Whakatane, New Zealand. Pop singer/songwriter.

ROXANNE
Rock group from Riverside, California: Jamie Brown (vocals), John Butler (guitar), Joey Infante (bass) and Dave Landry (drums).

ROXETTE
Pop-rock duo from Sweden: Marie Fredriksson (born on 5/30/1958 in Ostra Ljungby, Sweden) and Per Gessle (born on 1/12/1959 in Halmstad, Sweden).

ROXY MUSIC
Art-rock group from England: Bryan Ferry (vocals, keyboards), Phil Manzanera (guitar), Andy MacKay (horns) and Paul Thompson (drums).

ROYAL, Billy Joe
Born on 4/3/1942 in Valdosta, Georgia; raised in Marietta, Georgia. Country-pop singer/guitarist.

ROYALETTES, The
R&B vocal group from Baltimore, Maryland: sisters Anita and Sheila Ross, with Terry Jones and Ronnie Brown.

ROYAL GUARDSMEN, The
Novelty-pop group from Ocala, Florida: Barry Winslow (vocals, guitar), Chris Nunley (vocals), Tom Richards (lead guitar), Bill Balough (bass) and Billy Taylor (organ). "Snoopy" songs inspired by Snoopy the Beagle in the "Peanuts" comic strip.

ROYAL JOKERS, The
R&B vocal group from Detroit, Michigan: Norman Thrasher (bass), Noah Howell (tenor), Thearon Hill (tenor), Willie Jones (tenor) and Albert Green (baritone).

ROYAL PHILHARMONIC ORCHESTRA
Orchestra based in London, England. Conducted by Louis Clark. Founded in 1946 by Sir Thomas Beecham.

ROYAL SCOTS DRAGOON GUARDS
The military band of Scotland's armored regiment. Led by bagpipe soloist Major Tony Crease.

ROYAL TEENS
Rock and roll group from Fort Lee, New Jersey: Bob Gaudio (piano), Bill "Buddy Randell" Crandall (sax; The Knickerbockers), Billy Dalton (guitar) and Tom Austin (drums). Crandall was replaced by Larry Qualiano, and Joseph "Joe Villa" Francavilla joined as vocalist in late 1958. Al Kooper joined the group for a short time in 1959. In 1960, Gaudio joined The 4 Seasons. Crandall died in 1998.

ROYALTONES, The
Rock and roll instrumental band from Dearborn, Michigan: David Sanderson (guitar), George Katsakis (sax), brothers Mike (piano) and Greg (drums) Popoff and Kenny Anderson (bass). Sanderson died of a heart attack on 6/25/1994 (age 59).

ROZALLA
Born Rozalla Miller on 3/18/1964 in Ndola, Zambia. Dance singer.

RTZ
Rock group formed in Boston, Massachusetts: Brad Delp (vocals), Barry Goudreau (guitar), Brian Maes (keyboards), Tim Archibald (bass) and David Stefanelli (drums). Delp and Goudreau were members of Boston. Goudreau was also with Orion The Hunter. RTZ: Return To Zero.

RUBBER RODEO
Pop-rock group from Rhode Island: Trish Milliken (vocals), Bob Holmes (guitar), Mark Tomeo (steel guitar), Gary Leib (keyboards), John Doelp (bass) and Barc Holmes (drums).

RUBETTES, The
Pop-rock band from London, England: Alan Williams (vocals), Tony Thorpe (guitar), Peter Arnesen and Bill Hurd (keyboards), Mickey Clarke (bass), and John Richardson (drums).

RUBICON
Pop-rock group from San Francisco, California: Greg Eckler (vocals, drums), Brad Gillis (guitar), Jerry Martini (Sly & The Family Stone), Max Haskett and Dennis Marcellino (horns), Jim Pugh (keyboards), and Jack Blades (bass). Gillis and Blades later formed Night Ranger.

RUBINOOS, The
Pop group formed in Berkeley, California: John Rubin (vocals), Tom Dunbar (guitar), Royse Ader (bass) and Donn Spindt (drums).

RUBIO, Paulina
Born on 6/17/1971 in Mexico City, Mexico. Latin pop-dance singer.

RUBY & THE ROMANTICS
R&B vocal group from Akron, Ohio: Ruby Nash (lead; born on 6/15/1934 in New York), Ed Roberts (died of cancer on 8/10/1993, age 57) and George Lee (tenors), Ronald Mosley (baritone) and Leroy Fann (bass; died in November 1973, age 37).

RUCKER, Darius
Born on 5/13/1966 in Charleston, South Carolina. Former lead singer of Hootie & The Blowfish. Switched to country music.

RUDE BOYS
R&B vocal group from Cleveland, Ohio: Larry Marcus, Melvin Sephus, and brothers Edward Lee "Buddy" Banks and J. Little. Marcus is the cousin of B.B. King. Group discovered by Levert.

RUDOLF, Kevin
Born in New York; later based in Miami, Florida. R&B singer/songwriter/guitarist.

RUFF ENDZ
R&B vocal duo from Baltimore, Maryland: David Chance and Dante Jordan.

RUFFIN, David
Born Davis Eli Ruffin on 1/18/1941 in Whynot, Mississippi. Died of a drug overdose on 6/1/1991 (age 50). R&B singer. Brother of Jimmy Ruffin. Co-lead singer of The Temptations from 1963-68.

RUFFIN, Jimmy
Born on 5/7/1939 in Collinsville, Mississippi. R&B singer. Brother of David Ruffin.

RUFFNECK featuring YAVAHN
Dance group consisting of New Jersey-based producers Dwayne Richardson, Derek Jenkins and Stephen Wilson. Featured vocalist is Joanne "Yavahn" Thomas.

RUGBYS, The
Rock group from Nashville, Tennessee: Steve McNicol (vocals, guitar), Ed Vernon (keyboards), Mike Mornei (bass) and Glenn Howerton (drums).

RUMBLERS, The
Instrumental rock and roll band from Norwalk, California: Bob Jones (sax), Johnny Kirkland (guitar), Mike Kelishes (guitar), Wayne Matteson (bass) and Adrian Lloyd (drums).

RUNDGREN, Todd
Born on 6/22/1948 in Upper Darby, Pennsylvania. Virtuoso rock musician/songwriter/producer/engineer. Leader of groups Nazz and Utopia. Produced Meat Loaf's *Bat Out Of Hell* album and albums for Badfinger, Grand Funk Railroad, The Tubes, XTC, Patti Smith and many others.

RUN-D.M.C.
Highly influential rap trio from Queens, New York: rappers Joseph Simmons (Run) and Darryl McDaniels (DMC) with DJ Jason Mizell (Jam Master Jay). In movies *Krush Groove* and *Tougher Than Leather*. Jam Master Jay was shot to death on 10/30/2002 (age 37).

RuPAUL
Born RuPaul Andre Charles on 11/17/1960 in San Diego, California. Black male dance singer/transvestite. Appeared in the movies *Crooklyn* and *The Brady Bunch Movie*. Hosted own talk show.

RUPEE
Born Rupert Clarke in Germany; raised in England and Barbados. His father was born in Barbados and was a member of the British army stationed in Germany; his mother was born in Germany. Male "soca" (combination of soul-calypso) singer.

RUSH
Hard-rock trio formed in Toronto, Ontario, Canada: Geddy Lee (vocals, bass; born on 7/29/1953), Alex Lifeson (guitar; born on 8/27/1953) and Neil Peart (drums; born on 9/12/1952). Peart writes most of the group's lyrics.

RUSH, Jennifer
Born Heidi Stern on 9/29/1960 in Queens, New York. Pop singer/songwriter.

RUSH, Merrilee
Born on 1/26/1942 in Seattle, Washington. Female pop singer. The Turnabouts: her brother Neil Rush (sax), Karl Wilson (guitar; brother of Nancy and Ann Wilson of Heart), Terry Craig (bass) and Pete Sack (drums).

RUSH, Otis
Born on 4/29/1935 in Philadelphia, Mississippi. Blues singer/guitarist.

RUSHEN, Patrice
Born on 9/30/1954 in Los Angeles, California. Jazz-soul-dance singer/songwriter/keyboardist.

RUSHLOW, Tim
Born on 10/6/1966 in Midwest City, Oklahoma; raised in Arlington, Texas. Former lead singer of Little Texas.

RUSS, Lonnie
Born Gerald Lionel Russ in 1943 in San Francisco, California. R&B singer/songwriter.

RUSSELL, Bobby
Born on 4/19/1941 in Nashville, Tennessee. Died of a heart attack on 11/19/1992 (age 51). Singer/songwriter. Married to Vicki Lawrence from 1972-74.

RUSSELL, Brenda
Born Brenda Gordon on 4/8/1949 in Brooklyn, New York. R&B singer/songwriter/pianist.

RUSSELL, Leon
Born Claude Russell Bridges on 4/2/1942 in Lawton, Oklahoma. Pop-rock singer/songwriter/multi-instrumentalist sessionman. Regular with Phil Spector's "Wall of Sound" session group. Formed Shelter Records with British producer Denny Cordell in 1970. Recorded as Hank Wilson in 1973. Married Mary McCreary (vocalist with Little Sister, part of Sly Stone's "family") in 1976. Formed Paradise label in 1976.

RUSSO, Charlie
Pop-jazz clarinetist/saxophonist.

RUSTED ROOT
Rock group from Pittsburgh, Pennsylvania: Mike Glabicki (vocals, guitar), John Buynak, Liz Berlin, Jenn Wertz and Jim DiSpirito (percussion), Patrick Norman (bass) and Jim Donovan (drums).

RYAN, Barry
Born Barry Sapherson on 10/24/1948 in Leeds, England. Pop singer.

RYAN, Charlie
Born on 12/19/1915 in Graceville, Minnesota; raised in Montana. Died of heart failure on 2/16/2008 (age 92). Country singer/songwriter.

RYDELL, Bobby
Born Robert Ridarelli on 4/26/1942 in Philadelphia, Pennsylvania. Rock and roll teen idol. Regular on Paul Whiteman's amateur TV show, 1951-54. Drummer with Rocco & His Saints, which included Frankie Avalon on trumpet in 1956. First recorded for Veko in 1957. In the movies *Bye Bye Birdie* and *That Lady From Peking*. Rydell, Fabian, Frankie Avalon and Chubby Checker were Philadelphia-based teen idols of the late 1950s-early 1960s.

RYDER, John & Anne
Husband-and-wife Adult Contemporary duo from Sheffield, England.

RYDER, Mitch, & The Detroit Wheels
Born William Levise on 2/26/1945 in Hamtramck, Michigan. White rock and roll/R&B singer. The Detroit Wheels: Jim McCarty and Joe Cubert (guitars), Earl Elliott (bass) and John Badanjek

RYDER, Mitch, & The Detroit Wheels — cont'd
(drums). McCarty and Badanjek later joined the Rockets.

RYLES, John Wesley
Born on 12/2/1950 in Bastrop, Louisiana. Country singer/songwriter/guitarist.

RYSER, Jimmy
Born on 1/31/1965 in Cleveland, Ohio; raised in Columbus, Indiana. Pop-rock singer/guitarist.

RZA
Born Robert Diggs in Staten Island, New York. Rapper/producer. Member of Wu-Tang Clan and Gravediggaz. Pronounced: riz-ah.

SAADIQ, Raphael
Born Raphael Wiggins on 5/14/1966 in Oakland, California. R&B singer. Member of Tony! Toni! Tone! and Lucy Pearl.

SADAT X
Born Derek Murphy on 12/29/1968 in New Rochelle, New York. Male rapper. Former member of the rap group Brand Nubian.

SAD CAFE
Pop-rock group formed in Manchester, England: Paul Young (vocals; Mike + The Mechanics), Ashley Mulford and Ian Wilson (guitars), Vic Emerson (keyboards), John Stimpson (bass) and Dave Irving (drums). Young died of a heart attack on 7/15/2000 (age 53).

SADE
Born Helen Folasade Adu on 1/16/1959 in Ibadan, Nigeria, Africa (of Nigerian/English parents); raised in Clacton-on-Sea, England. Jazz-styled R&B singer/fashion designer/model. Appeared in the 1986 movie *Absolute Beginners*. Her backing band consisted of Andrew Hale (keyboards), Stu Matthewman (guitar, sax) and Paul Denman (bass). Backing band also recorded as Sweetback.

SADLER, SSgt Barry
Born on 11/1/1940 in Carlsbad, New Mexico. Died of heart failure on 11/5/1989 (age 49). Staff Sergeant of U.S. Army Special Forces (a.k.a. the Green Berets). Served in Vietnam until injuring his leg in a booby trap. Shot in the head during a 1988 robbery attempt at his Guatemala home; suffered brain damage.

SAFARIS
White vocal group from Los Angeles, California: Jim Stephens, Richard Clasky, Sheldon Briar and Marvin Rosenberg. Briar died on 12/24/1999 (age 57).

SA-FIRE
Born Wilma Cosme in San Juan, Puerto Rico; raised in East Harlem, New York. Female dance singer.

SAGA
Rock group formed in Toronto, Ontario, Canada: Michael Sadler (vocals), brothers Ian (guitar) and Jim (bass) Crichton, Jim Gilmour (keyboards) and Steve Negus (drums).

SAGAT
Born Faustin Lenon in Baltimore, Maryland. Male club dance singer/rapper. Also produced under the name Chico Jump Slamm. Pronounced: say-GOT.

SAGER, Carole Bayer
Born on 3/8/1946 in Manhattan, New York. Pop singer/prolific songwriter. Married to Burt Bacharach from 1982-91.

SAGITTARIUS
Pop studio band. Included at various times Bruce Johnston and Terry Melcher (Bruce And Terry), Gary Usher (died of cancer on 5/25/1990, age 51), Kurt Boettcher (died of liver failure on 6/14/1987, age 43) and Glen Campbell. The latter three also recorded in The Hondells.

SAIGON KICK
Hard-rock group formed in Miami, Florida: Matt Kramer (vocals), Jason Bieler (guitar), Tom DeFile (bass) and Phil Varone (drums).

SAILCAT
Pop duo from Alabama: Court Pickett (vocals) and John Wyker (vocals, guitar).

SAINTE-MARIE, Buffy
Born on 2/20/1941 in Piapot Reserve, Saskatchewan, Canada. Folk singer/songwriter.

ST. ETIENNE
Dance trio formed in London, England, by keyboardists Bob Stanley and Peter Wiggs. Moira Lambert was vocalist in 1990 for recording "Only Love Can Break Your Heart." Sarah Cracknell joined as permanent vocalist in 1991. Group took its name from a French soccer club. Saint Etienne is also a city in France.

ST. LUNATICS
Rap group from St. Louis, Missouri: Nelly, Ali, City Spud, Kyjuan and Murphy Lee.

ST. PAUL
Born Paul Peterson in Minneapolis, Minnesota. R&B singer/bassist. Member of The Time and The Family.

ST. PETERS, Crispian
Born Robin Peter Smith on 4/5/1939 in Swanley, Kent, England. Pop singer/guitarist.

ST. ROMAIN, Kirby
Born on 10/12/1942 in Alexandria, Louisiana. Pop singer/songwriter.

SAINT TROPEZ
Female disco trio: Teresa Burton, Kathy Deckard and Phyllis Rhodes. Pronounced: san tro-pay.

SAKAMOTO, Kyu
Born on 11/10/1941 in Kawasaki, Japan. Died in a plane crash on 8/12/1985 (age 43). Male singer.

SALES, Soupy
Born Milton Supman on 1/8/1926 in Franklinton, North Carolina. Slapstick comedian. Own ABC-TV series, 1959-60; syndicated show, 1966-68. His sons, Hunt and Tony, were members of the group Tin Machine.

SALIVA
Hard-rock group from Memphis, Tennessee: Josey Scott (vocals), Wayne Swinny (guitar), Dave Novotny (bass) and Paul Crosby (drums).

SALSOUL ORCHESTRA, The
Disco orchestra conducted by Philadelphia producer/arranger Vincent Montana, Jr. Vocalists included Phyllis Rhodes, Ronni Tyson, Carl Helm, Philip Hurt and Jocelyn Brown.

SALTER, Sam
Born on 2/16/1975 in Los Angeles, California. R&B singer/songwriter.

SALT-N-PEPA
Female hip-hop trio from Queens, New York: Cheryl "Salt" James (born on 3/28/1967), Sandra "Pepa" Denton (born on 11/9/1967 in Kingston, Jamaica) and Dee Dee "Spinderella" Roper (born on 8/3/1971). Appeared in the movie *Who's The Man?* Pepa was married to Treach (of Naughty By Nature) from 1999-2001.

SALVAGE
Pop studio group assembled by producers Paul Vance and Lee Pockriss.

SALVO, Sammy
Born on 1/20/1939 in Birmingham, Alabama. Pop singer.

SAM & BILL
R&B vocal duo formed in Newark, New Jersey: Sam Gary (born in Columbus, South Carolina) and Bill Johnson (born on 10/16/1932 in Augusta, Georgia).

SAM & DAVE
R&B vocal duo: Sam Moore (born on 10/12/1935 in Miami, Florida) and Dave Prater (born on 5/9/1937 in Ocilla, Georgia). Prater was killed in a car crash on 4/9/1988 (age 50).

SAMBORA, Richie
Born on 7/11/1959 in Perth Amboy, New Jersey; raised in Woodbridge, New Jersey. Guitarist of Bon Jovi. Married to actress Heather Locklear from 1994-2007.

SAMI JO
Born Jane Jobe on 5/9/1947 in Batesville, Arkansas (later adopted the stage name "Sami Jo Cole"). Female country singer.

SAMMIE
Born Sammie Bush on 3/1/1987 in Boynton Beach, Florida. Male pre-teen R&B singer/songwriter.

SAM THE SHAM & THE PHARAOHS
Born Domingo Samudio on 3/6/1939 in Dallas, Texas. Leader of rock and roll band The Pharaohs: Ray Stinnet (guitar), Butch Gibson (sax), David Martin (bass) and Jerry Patterson (drums). Martin died of a heart attack on 8/2/1987 (age 50).

SANBORN, David
Born on 7/30/1945 in Tampa, Florida; raised in St. Louis, Missouri. Saxophonist/flutist. Stricken with polio as a child. Played with Paul Butterfield from 1967-71; Stevie Wonder from 1972-73. Formed own group in 1975.

SANDEE
Born Sandra Casanas in New York; raised in Florida. Dance singer. Early member of Exposé. Pronounced: sahn-day.

SANDERS, Felicia
Born Felice Schwartz in 1922 in Mount Vernon, New York; raised in California. Died of cancer on 2/7/1975 (age 53). Vocalist on Percy Faith's 1953 #1 hit "Song From Moulin Rouge."

SANDERS, Kim
Female dance singer.

SANDLER, Adam
Born on 9/9/1966 in Brooklyn, New York. Actor/comedian. Cast member of TV's *Saturday Night Live* (1990-95).

SANDPEBBLES, The
R&B vocal trio: Calvin White, Andrea Bolden and Lonzine Wright.

SANDPIPERS, The
Adult Contemporary vocal trio from Los Angeles, California: Jim Brady (born on 8/24/1944), Michael Piano (born on 10/26/1944) and Richard Shoff (born on 4/30/1944). Met while in the Mitchell Boys Choir.

SANDS, Evie
Born in Brooklyn, New York. Female singer.

SANDS, Jodie
Born in Philadelphia, Pennsylvania. Teen pop singer.

SANDS, Tommy
Born on 8/27/1937 in Chicago, Illinois. Teen idol/pop-rock and roll singer/actor. Mother was a vocalist with Art Kassel's band. Married to Nancy Sinatra from 1960-65. In the movies *Sing Boy Sing*, *Mardi Gras*, *Babes In Toyland* and *The Longest Day*.

SANFORD/TOWNSEND BAND, The
Pop-rock duo from Los Angeles, California: singers/keyboardists Ed Sanford and John Townsend.

SANG, Samantha
Born on 8/5/1953 in Melbourne, Australia. Pop singer.

SAN REMO GOLDEN STRINGS
R&B instrumental studio band formed in Detroit, Michigan.

SANS, Billie
Born in Nashville, Tennessee. Male pop singer.

SANTA ESMERALDA
Spanish-flavored disco studio project produced by Nicolas Skorsky and Jean-Manuel de Scarano.

SANTAMARIA, Mongo
Born Ramon Santamaria on 4/7/1917 in Havana, Cuba. Died of a stroke on 2/1/2003 (age 85). Conga player.

SANTANA
Born Carlos Santana on 7/20/1947 in Autlan de Navarro, Mexico. Latin-rock guitarist. Formed his group in San Francisco, California. Various members over the years include Alex Ligertwood (vocals), Gregg Rolie (keyboards, vocals), Neal

SANTANA — cont'd
Schon (guitar), David Brown (bass) and Michael Shrieve (drums). Rolie and Schon formed Journey. Shrieve formed Automatic Man. Santana's brother Jorge was a member of Malo.

SANTANA, Juelz
Born LaRon James on 2/18/1983 in Harlem, New York. Male rapper. Member of The Diplomats.

SANTIAGO, Lina
Born on 9/5/1978 in Los Angeles, California. Female dance singer.

SANTO & JOHNNY
Guitar duo from Brooklyn, New York (of Filipino parents): brothers Santo (steel guitar; born on 10/24/1937) and Johnny (rhythm guitar; born on 4/30/1941) Farina. Mother Ann Farina helped with songwriting.

SANTOS, Larry
Born on 6/2/1941 in Oneonta, New York. Pop singer/songwriter.

SANZ, Alejandro
Born Alejandro Sanchez Pizzaro on 12/18/1968 in Madrid, Spain. Latin singer/guitarist.

SAPP, Marvin
Born in Grand Rapids, Michigan. Contemporary gospel singer. Member of Commissioned.

SAPPHIRES, The
R&B vocal trio from Philadelphia, Pennsylvania: Carol Jackson, George Garner and Joe Livingston.

SARAYA
Rock group from New Jersey: Sandi Saraya (vocals), Tony Rey (guitar), Gregg Munier (keyboards), Gary Taylor (bass) and Chuck Bonfante (drums). Rey, Munier and Taylor left in 1990; Tony Bruno (guitar) and Barry Dunaway (bass) joined.

SARIDIS, Saverio
Born on 6/16/1933 in Brooklyn, New York. Operatic tenor.

SARSTEDT, Peter
Born on 12/10/1941 in New Delhi, India; raised in England. Pop-folk singer/songwriter.

SATISFACTIONS, The
R&B vocal group from Washington DC: James Isom, Lorenzo Hines, Earl Jones and Fletcher Lee.

SATRIANI, Joe
Born on 7/15/1956 in Westbury, New York. Rock guitarist.

SAVAGE
Born Demetrius Savelio on 6/28/1981 in South Auckland, New Zealand (Samoan parents). Hip-hop singer/songwriter.

SAVAGE, Chantay
Born on 7/16/1967 in Chicago, Illinois. Female dance singer/songwriter.

SAVAGE GARDEN
Adult Alternative-pop duo from Brisbane, Queensland, Australia: Darren Hayes (born on 5/8/1972) and Daniel Jones (born on 7/22/1973). Duo split up in 2001.

SAVINA, Carlo
Born on 8/2/1919 in Turin, Italy. Died of heart failure on 6/23/2002 (age 82). Conductor/arranger. The composer of *The Godfather*, Nino Rota, died on 4/10/1979 (age 68).

SAVING ABEL
Rock band from Corinth, Mississippi: Jared Weeks (vocals), Jason Null (guitar), Scott Bartlett (guitar), Eric Taylor (bass) and Blake Dixon (drums).

SAVING JANE
Pop-rock band from Columbus, Ohio: Marti Dodson (vocals), Kris Misevski (guitar), Pat Buzzard (guitar), Joe Cochran (keyboards), Jeremy Martin (bass) and Dak Goodman (drums).

SAVOY, Ronnie
Born Eugene Hamilton on 10/10/1939 in Detroit, Michigan. R&B singer.

SAVOY BROWN
Blues-rock group formed in England: Chris Youlden (vocals), Lonesome Dave Peverett (vocals, guitar), Kim Simmonds (guitar), Tony Stevens (bass) and Roger Earl (drums). Youlden left in mid-1970. Peverett, Stevens and Earl left in 1971 to form Foghat. Many personnel changes thereafter, with Simmonds the only constant member. Peverett died of cancer on 2/7/2000 (age 57).

SAWYER, Ray
Born on 2/1/1937 in Monroeville, Alabama. Male singer/songwriter. Eye-patch wearing member of Dr. Hook.

SAWYER BROWN
Country group formed in Nashville, Tennessee: Mark Miller (vocals), Duncan Cameron (guitar), Gregg Hubbard (keyboards), Jim Scholten (bass) and Joe Smyth (drums). Won "Best Group" on TV's *Star Search* in 1984.

SAYER, Leo
Born Gerard Sayer on 5/21/1948 in Shoreham, Sussex, England. Pop singer/songwriter.

SCAFFOLD, The
Pop-rock vocal trio from England: Mike McGear (Paul McCartney's brother), John Gorman and Roger McGough.

SCAGGS, Boz
Born William Scaggs on 6/8/1944 in Canton, Ohio; raised in Plano, Texas. Eclectic singer/songwriter. Recorded in several different styles (pop, rock, soul and jazz). Played in various groups with Steve Miller during the 1960s. Based in San Francisco since the early 1970s; owned a restaurant there from 1983-87.

SCALES, Harvey, & The Seven Sounds
R&B group from Milwaukee, Wisconsin: Scales (lead; born on 9/27/1941), Monny Smith, Bill Purdie, Rudy Jacobs, Al Vance, Bill Stonewall and Ray Armstead. Scales was formerly with The Esquires. Vance died of a heart attack on 6/15/2003 (age 59).

SCARBURY, Joey
Born on 6/7/1955 in Ontario, California. Adult Contemporary session singer for producer Mike Post.

SCARFACE
Born Brad Jordan on 11/9/1969 in Houston, Texas. Member of the rap group The Geto Boys.

SCARLETT & BLACK
Electro-pop duo from England: Robin Hild and Sue West.

SCATMAN JOHN
Born John Larkin on 3/13/1942 in El Monte, California. Died of cancer on 12/3/1999 (age 57). Dance singer/pianist.

SCHIFRIN, Lalo
Born Boris Schifrin on 6/21/1932 in Buenos Aires, Argentina. Pianist/conductor/composer. Wrote more than 100 scores for movies and television.

SCHILLING, Peter
Born on 1/28/1956 in Stuttgart, Germany. Pop singer/songwriter.

SCHMIT, Timothy B.
Born Timothy Bruce Schmit on 10/30/1947 in Oakland, California; raised in Sacramento, California. Pop-rock singer/songwriter/bassist. Member of Poco and the Eagles.

SCHNEIDER, Fred
Born on 7/1/1951 in Newark, New Jersey. Lead singer of The B-52's.

SCHNEIDER, John
Born on 4/8/1960 in Mount Kisco, New York. Country singer/actor. Played "Bo Duke" on TV's *The Dukes Of Hazzard*. Appeared in numerous TV movies.

SCHOOLBOYS, The
R&B vocal group from Harlem, New York: Leslie Martin (lead), James Edwards (1st tenor), Roger Hayes (2nd tenor), James McKay (baritone) and Renaldo Gamble (bass).

SCHUMANN, Walter, The Voices of
Born on 10/8/1913 in Brooklyn, New York. Died on 8/21/1958 (age 44). Leader of own choral group. Composer of the theme for TV's *Dragnet*.

SCHWARTZ, Eddie
Born on 12/22/1949 in Toronto, Ontario, Canada. Pop-rock singer/songwriter/producer.

S CLUB 7
Teen multi-racial pop vocal group formed in England: Tina Barrett, Paul Cattermole, Jon Lee, Bradley McIntosh, Jo O'Meara, Hannah Spearritt and Rachel Stevens. Group starred in its own TV series on the Fox Family Channel.

SCORPIONS
Hard-rock group from Germany: Klaus Meine (vocals), Rudolf Schenker and Matthias Jabs (guitars), Francis Buchholz (bass) and Herman Rarebell (drums). Schenker is the brother of Michael Schenker (McAuley Schenker Group).

SCOTT, Billy
Born in Philadelphia, Pennsylvania. R&B-Adult Contemporary singer.

SCOTT, Bobby
Born on 1/29/1937 in Mount Pleasant, New York. Died of cancer on 11/5/1990 (age 53). White pop-jazz singer/pianist.

SCOTT, Freddie
Born on 4/24/1933 in Providence, Rhode Island. Died on 6/4/2007 (age 74). R&B singer/songwriter.

SCOTT, Jack
Born Giovanni Scafone Jr. on 1/28/1936 in Windsor, Ontario, Canada. Rock and roll-ballad singer/songwriter/guitarist. Moved to Hazel Park, Michigan, in 1946. First recorded for ABC-Paramount in 1957.

SCOTT, Jill
Born on 4/13/1972 in Philadelphia, Pennsylvania. R&B singer/songwriter.

SCOTT, Judy
Teen pop singer.

SCOTT, Kimberly
Born in 1985 in Baltimore, Maryland. R&B singer.

SCOTT, Linda
Born Linda Joy Sampson on 6/1/1945 in Queens, New York. Moved to Teaneck, New Jersey at age 11. Vocalist on Arthur Godfrey's CBS radio show, late 1950s. Co-host of TV's *Where The Action Is*. Joined the U.S. Army, 1970-72. Later earned a degree in Theology and became a music teacher/director at the Christian Academy in New York.

SCOTT, Marilyn
Born on 12/21/1949 in Alta Dena, California. Adult Contemporary-dance singer.

SCOTT, Neil
Born Neil Bogart on 2/3/1942 in Brooklyn, New York. Died on 5/10/1982 (age 40). Pop singer-turned-producer/promotion man for Cameo/Parkway. President of Buddah; formed Casablanca in 1974; formed Boardwalk in 1980.

SCOTT, Peggy, & Jo Jo Benson
R&B vocal duo. Scott was born Peggy Stoutmeyer on 6/25/1948 in Opp, Alabama; raised in Pensacola, Florida. Benson was born in 1940 in Columbia, Ohio.

SCOTT, Tom
Born on 5/19/1948 in Los Angeles, California. Pop-jazz-fusion saxophonist. Session work for Joni Mitchell, Steely Dan, Carole King and others. Composer of movie and TV scores. Led the house band for TV's *Pat Sajak Show*. Son of Nathan Scott, a composer of TV scores for *Dragnet*, *Wagon Train*, *My Three Sons*, and others.

SCREAMING TREES
Hard-rock group from Ellensburg, Washington: brothers Van (bass) and Gary Lee (guitar) Conner with Mark Lanegan (vocals) and Barrett Martin (drums).

SCRITTI POLITTI
Pop-dance trio formed in England: Green Gartside (vocals), David Gamson (keyboards) and Fred Maher (drums).

SEA, Johnny
Born John Seay on 7/15/1940 in Gulfport, Mississippi. Country singer/songwriter/guitarist.

SEAL
Born Sealhenry Samuel on 2/19/1963 in Paddington, London, England (of Nigerian/Brazilian parents). Male singer/songwriter. Married model Heidi Klum on 5/10/2005.

SEA LEVEL
Blues-rock group: Chuck Leavell (vocals, keyboards), Jimmy Nails and Davis Causey (guitars), Randall Bramblett (piano), Lamar Williams (bass) and Jai Johanny Johanson and George Weaver (drums). Leavell, Williams and Johanson were members of The Allman Brothers Band.

SEALS, Brady
Born on 3/29/1969 in Hamilton, Ohio. Country singer/songwriter/guitarist. Former member of Little Texas. Cousin of Jim (Seals & Crofts) and "England" Dan Seals and nephew of Troy Seals (Jo Ann & Troy).

SEALS, Dan
Born on 2/8/1948 in McCamey, Texas; raised in Iraan and Rankin, Texas. One-half of the duo England Dan & John Ford Coley (both formerly with Southwest F.O.B.). Brother of Jim Seals of Seals & Crofts and cousin of country singers Johnny Duncan, Troy Seals (Jo Ann & Troy) and Brady Seals (Little Texas).

SEALS & CROFTS
Pop duo: Jim Seals (born on 10/17/1941 in Sidney, Texas) and Dash Crofts (born on 8/14/1940 in Cisco, Texas). With The Champs from 1958-65. Own group, the Dawnbreakers, in the late 1960s; entire band converted to Baha'i faith in 1969. Jim is the brother of "England" Dan Seals and the cousin of country singers Troy Seals (Jo Ann & Troy), Brady Seals (Little Texas) and Johnny Duncan.

SEARCHERS, The
Rock and roll band from Liverpool, England: Mike Pender (vocals, guitar; born on 3/3/1942), John McNally (vocals, guitar; born on 8/30/1941), Tony Jackson (vocals, bass; born on 7/16/1940) and Chris Curtis (drums; born on 8/26/1941). Frank Allen replaced Jackson in 1965. John Blunt replaced Curtis in 1966. Billy Adamson replaced Blunt in 1969. Jackson died of liver failure on 8/18/2003 (age 63). Curtis died on 2/28/2005 (age 63).

SEATRAIN
Fusion-rock group from Marin County, California: John Gregory (vocals, guitar), Jim Roberts (lyricist), Richard Greene (violin), Donald Kretmar (sax), Andy Kulberg (bass) and Roy Blumenfeld (drums). Greene, Kulberg and Blumenfeld were members of The Blues Project. Kulberg died of cancer on 1/30/2002 (age 57). Roberts died of cancer on 10/29/2002 (age 59).

SEBASTIAN, John
Born on 3/17/1944 in Greenwich Village, Manhattan, New York. Pop-rock singer/songwriter/guitarist. Lead singer of The Lovin' Spoonful.

SECADA, Jon
Born Juan Secada on 10/4/1961 in Havana, Cuba; raised in Hialeah, Florida. Singer/songwriter.

SECONDHAND SERENADE
Band is actually solo project of singer/songwriter/guitarist John Vesely (born in Menlo Park, California).

2ND II NONE
Male rap duo from Compton, California: cousins Deon "Tha D" Barnett and Kelton "KK" McDonald. Attended high school with their producer DJ Quik.

SECRETS, The
White "girl group" from Cleveland, Ohio: Karen Gray, Jackie Allen, Carole Raymont and Pat Miller.

SECRET TIES
Electro-dance group from San Diego, California: Brian Soares (keyboards, producer, songwriter), with female vocalists Cheryl Ford, Linda Harmon and Christina Veronica.

SEDAKA, Neil
Born on 3/13/1939 in Brooklyn, New York. Pop singer/songwriter/pianist. Studied piano since elementary school. Formed songwriting team with lyricist Howard Greenfield while attending Lincoln High School (partnership lasted over 20 years). Recorded with The Tokens on Melba in 1956. Attended Juilliard School for classical piano. Prolific hit songwriter. Career revived in 1974 after signing with Elton John's new Rocket label.

SEDUCTION
Female dance trio from New York: Idalis Leon (born on 6/15/1966), April Harris (born on 3/25/1967) and Michelle Visage (born on 9/20/1968). Leon left in 1990; replaced by Sinoa Loren (born on 12/6/1966). Leon became a VJ for MTV.

SEEDS, The
Garage-rock band from Los Angeles, California: Richard "Sky Saxon" Marsh (vocals, bass), Jan Savage (guitar), Daryl Hooper (keyboards) and Rick Aldridge (drums).

SEEGER, Pete
Born on 5/3/1919 in Manhattan, New York. Legendary folk singer/songwriter. Formed the Almanac Singers with Woody Guthrie in 1940, and then The Weavers in 1948.

SEEKERS, The
Pop-folk group formed in Australia: Judith Durham (vocals), Keith Potger and Bruce Woodley (guitars), and Athol Guy (bass). Potger formed The New Seekers in 1969.

SEELY, Jeannie
Born Marilyn Jeanne Seely on 7/6/1940 in Titusville, Pennsylvania; raised in Townville, Pennsylvania. Country singer/songwriter. Formerly married to Hank Cochran.

SEETHER
Hard-rock band from South Africa: Shaun Morgan (vocals, guitar), Pat Callahan (guitar), Dale Stewart (bass) and Nick Oshiro (drums). John Humphrey replaced Oshiro in 2003.

SEGER, Bob
Born on 5/6/1945 in Dearborn, Michigan; raised in Detroit, Michigan. Rock singer/songwriter/guitarist. First recorded in 1966, formed the System in 1968. Left music to attend college in 1969; returned in 1970. Formed own backing band, The Silver Bullet Band, in 1976: Alto Reed (horns), Robyn Robbins (keyboards), Drew Abbott (guitar), Chris Campbell (bass) and Charlie Allen Martin (drums). Various personnel changes since then.

SEIKO & DONNIE WAHLBERG
Seiko is a Japanese superstar singer; married to popular Japanese actor Masaki Kanda. Wahlberg, older brother of Mark Wahlberg (Marky Mark), was a member of New Kids On The Block.

SELENA
Born Selena Quintanilla-Perez on 4/16/1971 in Lake Jackson, Texas; raised in Corpus Christi, Texas. Shot to death by Yolanda Saldivar (founder of Selena's fan club) on 3/31/1995 (age 23). Latin singer. Married her guitarist, Chris Perez. Jennifer Lopez starred in the 1997 biographical movie *Selena*.

SELF, Ronnie
Born on 7/5/1938 in Tin Town, Missouri. Died on 8/28/1981 (age 43). Rockabilly singer/songwriter/guitarist. Wrote Brenda Lee's "I'm Sorry" and "Sweet Nothin's."

SELLARS, Marilyn
Born on 12/31/1950 in Northfield, Minnesota. Country singer. Worked as an airline stewardess.

SEMBELLO, Michael
Born on 4/17/1954 in Philadelphia, Pennsylvania. Pop-rock session guitarist/producer/composer/arranger/vocalist. Guitarist on Stevie Wonder's albums from 1974-79.

SEMISONIC
Rock trio from Minneapolis, Minnesota: Dan Wilson (vocals, guitar), John Munson (bass) and Jacob Slichter (drums).

SENATOR BOBBY
Senator Bobby is Bill Minkin of a comedy troupe called The Hardly-Worthit Players. Another of the members is talkshow host Dennis Wholey. Records feature voice impressions of Senator Robert Kennedy and Senator Everett McKinley Dirksen.

SENSATIONS, The
R&B vocal group from Philadelphia, Pennsylvania: Yvonne Mills Baker (lead), Sam Armstrong (baritone), Richard Curtain (tenor) and Alphonso Howell (bass). Howell died on 5/7/1998 (age 61).

SEPTEMBER
Born Petra Marklund on 9/12/1984 in Stockholm, Sweden. Female dance singer.

SERENDIPITY SINGERS, The
Pop-folk group formed in Boulder, Colorado: Jon Arbenz, Mike Brovsky, Diane Decker, Brooks Hatch, John Madden, Bryan Sennett, Tom Tiemann, Lynn Weintraub and Bob Young.

SERMON, Erick
Born on 11/25/1968 in Bay Shore, New York. Male rapper. One-half of EPMD duo.

SETZER, Brian, Orchestra
Born on 4/10/1959 in Massapequa, Long Island, New York. Lead singer/guitarist of the Stray Cats. Played Eddie Cochran in the 1987 movie *La Bamba*. Formed own 16-piece swing orchestra in 1994.

SEVELLE, Taja
Born on 3/18/1962 in Minneapolis, Minnesota. Black female dance singer.

SEVENDUST
Hard-rock band formed in Atlanta, Georgia: Lajon Witherspoon (vocals; born on 10/3/1972), Clint Lowery (guitar; born on 12/15/1971), John Connolly (guitar; born on 10/21/1968), Vinnie Hornsby (bass; born on 10/22/1967) and Morgan Rose (drums; born on 12/13/1968). Sonny Mayo (born on 7/16/1971) replaced Lowery in 2004. Clint is the brother of Corey Lowery (of Stereomud); the Lowery brothers later formed Dark New Day.

SEVEN MARY THREE
Rock group from Virginia: Jason Ross (vocals), Jason Pollock (guitar), Casey Daniel (bass) and Giti Khalsa (drums).

7 MILE
Male R&B vocal group from Detroit, Michigan: Deion Lucas, Seantezz Robinson, Luther Jackson and Glynis Martin.

702
Female R&B vocal trio from Las Vegas, Nevada: Kameelah Williams and sisters Irish and Lemisha Grinstead. Group named after the Las Vegas area code.

707
Rock group from Detroit, Michigan: Kevin Russell (vocals, guitar), Phil Bryant (bass) and Jim McClarty (drums). Kevin Chalfant (vocals) and Tod Howarth (keyboards) added in 1982. Chalfant, a backing singer for Kim Carnes and Night Ranger, co-founded The Storm in 1991.

SEVILLE, David / THE CHIPMUNKS
Born Ross Bagdasarian on 1/27/1919 in Fresno, California. Died of a heart attack on 1/16/1972 (age 52). To Los Angeles in 1950. Appeared in the movies *Viva Zapata*, *Stalag 17* and *Rear Window*. Wrote "Come On-a My House." Creator of The Chipmunks, cartoon characters Seville named Alvin, Simon and Theodore after Liberty executives Alvin Bennett, Simon Waronker and Theodore Keep. The Chipmunks starred in own prime-time animated TV show in the early 1960s and a Saturday morning cartoon series in the mid-1980s. His son, Ross Jr., resurrected the act in 1980.

SEVILLES, The
Male R&B vocal group from Los Angeles, California: Manny Chavez, Ernest Hamilton, James Spencer and Charles Wright.

SEX PISTOLS
Legendary punk-rock group formed in London, England: Johnny "Rotten" Lydon (vocals), Steve Jones (guitar), Sid Vicious (bass) and Paul Cook (drums). Disbanded in January 1978. Lydon formed Public Image Ltd. in 1978. Vicious died of a drug overdose on 2/2/1979 (age 21), while out on bail for the fatal stabbing of girlfriend Nancy Spungen four months earlier. Jones later joined Chequered Past. Movies about group include *The Great Rock 'n' Roll Swindle*, *D.O.A.* and *Sid & Nancy*. Lydon, Jones, Matlock and Cook reunited in 1996.

S-EXPRESS
Dance-pop duo from England: DJ Mark Moore and vocalist Sonique.

SEXTON, Charlie
Born on 8/11/1968 in San Antonio, Texas. Rock singer/guitarist. Lead guitarist for Joe Ely's band. Co-founder of the Arc Angels. Appeared in the movie *Thelma & Louise*.

SEYMOUR, Phil
Born on 5/15/1952 in Tulsa, Oklahoma. Died of cancer on 8/17/1993 (age 41). Pop-rock singer/drummer/bassist. Formerly with the Dwight Twilley Band.

SF SPANISH FLY
Pop vocal duo based in San Francisco, California: John "Milo" Pro and Octaviano Silva.

SGH MOCCA SOUL
Dance project of producer Ron St. Louis, featuring lead vocals by Joy Rose. St. Louis was a staffwriter with Jobette Music. SGH: Soul Goes House.

SHACKLEFORDS, The
Studio creation of producers Lee Hazlewood and Marty Cooper. Named after Hazlewood's wife, Naomi Shackleford.

SHADES
Female R&B vocal group from Boston, Massachusetts: Monique Peoples, Tiffanie Cardwell, Shannon Walker-Williams and Danielle Andrews.

SHADE SHEIST
Born Tramayne Thompson in Los Angeles, California. Male rapper/singer.

SHADES OF BLUE
"Blue-eyed soul" vocal group from Detroit, Michigan: Linda Kerr, Robert Kerr, Ernest Dernai and Nick Marinelli.

SHADOWS OF KNIGHT, The
Garage-rock band from Chicago, Illinois: Jim Sohns (vocals), Joe Kelley and Jerry McGeorge (guitars), Warren Rogers (bass) and Tom Schiffour (drums).

SHAFFER, Paul
Born on 11/28/1949 in Thunder Bay, Ontario, Canada. Keyboardist/arranger. Bandleader for David Letterman's NBC-TV and CBS-TV late night talk shows. Cast member of the 1977 TV sitcom *A

Year At The Top. Piano player on TV's *Saturday Night Live* and for The Blues Brothers during the late 1970s.

SHAFTO, Bobby
Born in London, England. Rock and roll singer.

SHAGGY
Born Orville Richard Burrell on 10/22/1968 in Kingston, Jamaica. Reggae dancehall vocalist. Moved to Brooklyn at age 18. During his four years as a U.S. Marine, served in Kuwait for Operation Desert Storm.

SHAI
R&B vocal group formed in Washington DC: Garfield Bright, Marc Gay, Carl Martin and Darnell Van Rensalier. Pronounced: shy.

SHAKESPEAR'S SISTER
Female pop-rock duo of British native Siobhan Fahey and Detroit native Marcella Detroit. Fahey, wife of Dave Stewart (Eurythmics), was a member of Bananarama. Detroit is Marcy Levy who recorded with Robin Gibb, sang backup for Eric Clapton and co-wrote "Lay Down Sally." Disbanded in 1993.

SHAKIRA
Born Shakira Isabel Mebarak Ripoll on 2/2/1977 in Barranquilla, Colombia. Female Latin-pop singer.

SHALAMAR
R&B-dance vocal trio formed in Los Angeles, California: Jody Watley, Jeffrey Daniels and Howard Hewett.

SHAMEN, The
Techno-rave dance group from Aberdeen, Scotland, formed by Colin "Shamen" Angus and Will "Sin" Sinnott (drowned on 5/23/1991, age 31). Features rapper Mr. C.

SHANA
Born Shana Petrone on 5/8/1972 in Parkridge, Illinois; raised in Ft. Lauderdale, Florida. Dance-disco singer; switched to country in 1998.

SHA NA NA
Rock and roll group specializing in 1950's-style music. Core members: Jon "Bowzer" Bauman, Scott Powell, Johnny Contardo, Fred Greene, Don York and Rich Joffe. Group hosted own TV variety show from 1977-81.

SHAND, Remy
Born in 1978 in Winnipeg, Manitoba, Canada. Male "blue-eyed soul" singer/songwriter/multi-instrumentalist.

SHANGO
Psychedleic-rock group from California: Tommy Reynolds (vocals, keyboards), Richie Hernandez (guitar), Malcolm Evans (bass) and Joe Barile (drums). Reynolds later joined Hamilton, Joe Frank & Reynolds.

SHANGRI-LAS, The
"Girl group" formed in Queens, New York. Consisted of two sets of sisters: Mary (lead singer) and Betty Weiss, and twins Mary Ann and Marge Ganser. Mary Ann Ganser died of a drug overdose

SHANGRI-LAS, The — cont'd
on 3/14/1970 (age 22). Marge Ganser died of breast cancer on 7/28/1996 (age 48).

SHANICE
Born Shanice Wilson on 5/14/1973 in Pittsburgh, Pennsylvania; raised in Los Angeles, California. Female R&B singer.

SHANK, Bud
Born Clifford Shank on 5/27/1926 in Dayton, Ohio. Jazz saxophonist.

SHANNON
Born Brenda Shannon Greene on 5/12/1957 in Washington DC. Female dance singer.

SHANNON, Del
Born Charles Westover on 12/30/1934 in Coopersville, Michigan. Died of a self-inflicted gunshot wound on 2/8/1990 (age 55). With U.S. Army *Get Up And Go* radio show in Germany. Discovered by Ann Arbor DJ/producer Ollie McLaughlin. Formed own Berlee label in 1963. Wrote "I Go To Pieces" for Peter & Gordon. To Los Angeles in 1966; production work.

SHAPIRO, Helen
Born on 9/28/1946 in London, England. Pop-ballad singer.

SHAREEFA
Born Shareefa Cooper on 1/1/1984 in East Orange, New Jersey. Female R&B singer.

SHARISSA
Born Sharissa Dawes on 8/21/1975 in Brooklyn, New York. Female R&B singer/songwriter.

SHARKEY, Feargal
Born on 8/13/1958 in Londonderry, Northern Ireland. Pop-rock singer. Former member of The Undertones.

SHARP, Dee Dee
Born Dione LaRue on 9/9/1945 in Philadelphia, Pennsylvania. R&B singer. Backing vocalist at Cameo Records in 1961. Married record producer Kenny Gamble in 1967, recorded as Dee Dee Sharp Gamble. Also see the Philadelphia International All Stars.

SHARPE, Mike
Born Michael Shapiro on 1/3/1940 in Atlanta, Georgia. Pop-jazz alto saxophonist.

SHARPE, Ray
Born on 2/8/1938 in Fort Worth, Texas. Black rockabilly singer/guitarist.

SHARPEES
R&B vocal group from St. Louis, Missouri: Benny Sharp, Herbert Reeves, Vernon Guy and Horise O'Toole. Guy died in a car crash on 9/10/1998 (age 53).

SHARPLES, Bob
Born on 7/2/1913 in Bury, Lancashire, England. Died on 9/8/1987 (age 74). Bandleader/arranger.

SHAW, Georgie
Born on 1/5/1930 in Philadelphia, Pennsylvania. Died of heart failure on 9/1/2006 (age 76). Male Adult Contemporary singer.

SHAW, Marlena
Born Marlena Burgess on 9/22/1942 in New Rochelle, New York. Jazz-styled singer. Band vocalist with Count Basie, 1967-72.

SHAW, Sandie
Born Sandra Goodrich on 2/26/1947 in Dagenham, England. Pop singer. Discovered by Adam Faith.

SHAW, Timmy
Born Jake Hammonds in Detroit, Michigan. Died of throat cancer on 3/29/1984. Male singer/songwriter.

SHAW, Tommy
Born on 9/11/1953 in Montgomery, Alabama. Rock singer/guitarist. Member of Styx and Damn Yankees.

SHAWNNA
Born Rashawnna Guy on 1/3/1978 in Chicago, Illinois. Female hip-hop singer/rapper. Daughter of blues great Buddy Guy.

SHAWTY LO
Born Carlos Walker in Atlanta, Georgia. Rapper.

SHEAR, Jules
Born on 3/7/1952 in Pittsburgh, Pennsylvania. Leader of Funky Kings, Reckless Sleepers and Jules & The Polar Bears.

SHeDAISY
Country vocal trio from Magna, Utah: sisters Kristyn (born on 8/24/1970), Kelsi (born on 11/21/1974) and Kassidy (born on 10/30/1976) Osborn.

SHEEP, The
Studio band assembled by producers Bob Feldman, Jerry Goldstein and Richard Gottehrer who also charted as The Strangeloves.

SHEIK, Duncan
Born on 11/18/1969 in Montclair, New Jersey; raised in Hilton Head, South Carolina. Alternative pop-rock singer/songwriter/guitarist.

SHEILA
Born Annie Chancel on 8/16/1946 in Creteil, France. White pop singer who also sang disco with a black male trio as Sheila B. Devotion.

SHEILA E.
Born Sheila Escovedo on 12/12/1957 in Oakland, California. R&B singer/percussionist. With father Pete Escovedo in the band Azteca in the mid-1970s. Toured with Lionel Richie; since 1986, toured and recorded with Prince. Member of The Blackout Allstars. Her uncle Coke Escovedo is a noted percussionist.

SHELLEY, Peter
Born Peter Southworth in England. Pop singer/ songwriter/producer. Began career as a talent scout for Decca. Not to be confused with Pete Shelley of The Buzzcocks.

SHELLS, The
R&B vocal group from Brooklyn, New York:
Nathaniel "Little Nate" Bouknight (lead), Gus Geter
(baritone), Bobby Nurse and Shade Alston (tenors)
and Danny Small (bass).

SHELTON, Anne
Born Patricia Sibley on 11/10/1923 in Dulwich,
London, England. Died of a heart attack on
7/31/1994 (age 70). Vocalist with the Ambrose
Orchestra.

SHELTON, Blake
Born on 6/18/1976 in Ada, Oklahoma. Country
singer/songwriter/guitarist.

SHELTON, Ricky Van
Born on 1/12/1952 in Danville, Virginia; raised in
Grit, Virginia. Country singer/songwriter/guitarist.
Van is his middle name. Worked as a pipefitter prior
to his music career.

SHE MOVES
Trio of female singers/dancers: Carla, Danielle and
Diana. Met while performing as dancers at New
York Knicks basketball games.

SHENANDOAH
Country band formed in Muscle Shoals, Alabama:
Marty Raybon (vocals; Raybon Bros.), Jim Seales
(guitar), Stan Thorn (keyboards), Ralph Ezell (bass)
and Mike McGuire (drums). Seales was guitarist for
the R&B group Funkadelic. McGuire was married to
actress Teresa Blake (of TV soap *All My Children*)
from 1994-98. Rocky Thacker replaced Ezell in
1995. Thorn left in 1996.

SHEP & THE LIMELITES
R&B vocal trio from Queens, New York: James
"Shep" Sheppard, lead (formerly with The
Heartbeats) and tenors Clarence Bassett (formerly
in The Five Sharps) and Charles Baskerville
(formerly in The Videos). Group disbanded after
Sheppard's murder on 1/24/1970 (age 34).

SHEPARD, Jean
Born Ollie Imogene Shepard on 11/21/1933 in Pauls
Valley, Oklahoma; raised in Visalia, California.
Country singer. Married to Hawkshaw Hawkins from
1960 until his death on 3/5/1963.

SHEPARD, Vonda
Born on 7/7/1963 in Manhattan, New York; raised in
Los Angeles, California.
Singer/songwriter/keyboardist. Had a recurring role
as a singer on TV's *Ally McBeal*.

SHEPHERD, Kenny Wayne, Band
Born on 6/12/1977 in Shreveport, Louisiana.
Blues-rock guitarist/singer/songwriter.

SHEPHERD SISTERS
Family rock and roll vocal group from Middletown,
Ohio: sisters Martha, Mary Lou, Gayle and Judy
Shepherd.

SHEPPARD, T.G.
Born William Browder on 7/20/1944 in Humbolt,
Tennessee. Country singer.

SHERBS
Pop-rock group from Australia: Daryl Braithwaite
(vocals), Harvey James (guitar), Garth Porter
(keyboards), Tony Mitchell (bass) and Alan Sandow
(drums) Tony Leigh replaced James in early 1981.
Group originally known as Sherbet.

SHERIFF
Pop-rock group from Toronto, Ontario, Canada:
Freddy Curci (vocals), Steve DeMarchi (guitar),
Arnold Lanni (keyboards), Wolf Hassel (bass) and
Rob Elliott (drums). Disbanded in 1983. Hassel and
Lanni formed Frozen Ghost. Curci and DeMarchi
formed Alias.

SHERMAN, Allan
Born Allan Copelon on 11/30/1924 in Chicago,
Illinois. Died on 11/21/1973 (age 48). Novelty
singer/songwriter. Creator/producer of TV's *I've Got
A Secret*. Began recording career in 1962 with 3
consecutive #1 comedy albums.

SHERMAN, Bobby
Born on 7/22/1943 in Santa Monica, California.
Teen idol singer/actor. Regular on TV's *Shindig*;
played "Jeremy Bolt" on TV's *Here Come The
Brides*. First recorded for Starcrest in 1962.
Currently involved in TV production.

SHERMAN, Joe
Born on 9/25/1926 in Manhattan, New York. Prolific
producer/conductor.

SHERRYS, The
R&B "girl group" from Philadelphia, Pennsylvania.
Formed by Joe Cook, included his daughters Dinell
(lead) and Delphine, with Charlotte Butler and
Delores "Honey" Wylie. Cook had own hit in 1957,
"Peanuts," as Little Joe & The Thrillers.

SHERWOOD, Roberta
Born on 7/1/1913 in Long Island, New York. Died of
heart failure on 7/5/1999 (age 86). Jazz-styled
singer.

SHIBLEY, Arkie
Born Arleigh Shibley on 2/26/1915 in Van Buren,
Arkansas. Died on 4/29/1993 (age 78). Country
singer. His Mountain Dew Boys: Leon Kelly, Jack
Hays and Phil Fregon.

SHIELDS, The
R&B group formed by Los Angeles producer
George Motola solely to cover The Slades' original
version of "You Cheated." Frankie Ervin (lead),
Jesse Belvin (falsetto), Johnny "Guitar" Watson, Mel
Williams and Buster Williams.

SHINAS, Sofia
Born in Windsor, Ontario, Canada. Pop-dance
singer/songwriter/actress. Appeared in the movies
The Crow, *Terminal Velocity* and *Hourglass*.

SHINDOGS, The
Rock and roll house band for the ABC-TV show
Shindig: Delaney Bramlett, Joey Cooper, Chuck
Blackwell and James Burton. Bramlett later formed
Delaney & Bonnie.

SHINEDOWN
Rock band from Jacksonville, Florida: Brent Smith (vocals), Jasin Todd (guitar), Brad Stewart (bass) and Barry Kerch (drums).

SHINS, The
Pop-rock group from Albuquerque, New Mexico: James Mercer (vocals, guitar), Marty Crandall (keyboards), Neal Langford (bass) and Jesse Sandoval (drums).

SHIRELLES, The
R&B-rock and roll "girl group" from Passaic, New Jersey: Shirley (Owens) Alston (born on 6/10/1941), Beverly Lee (born on 8/3/1941), Doris (Coley) Kenner (born on 8/2/1941) and Addie "Micki" Harris (born on 1/22/1940). Formed in junior high school as the Poquellos. High school classmates of Joey Dee. First recorded for Tiara in 1958. Kenner left group in 1968; returned in 1975. Alston left for solo career in 1975; recorded as Lady Rose. Harris died on 6/10/1982 (age 42). Kenner died of cancer on 2/4/2000 (age 58). The most successful "girl group" of the rock and roll era.

SHIRLEY, Don
Born on 1/27/1927 in Kingston, Jamaica. Black pop-jazz-classical pianist/organist.

SHIRLEY (& COMPANY)
Disco group: Shirley Goodman (female vocals), Jesus Alvarez (male vocals), Walter Morris (guitar), Bernadette Randle (keyboards), Seldon Powell (sax), Jonathan Williams (bass) and Clarence Oliver (drums). Goodman was one-half of Shirley & Lee duo; she died on 7/5/2005 (age 69).

SHIRLEY & LEE
R&B duo from New Orleans, Louisiana: Shirley Goodman (born on 6/19/1936; died on 7/5/2005, age 69) and Leonard Lee (born on 6/29/1935; died on 10/23/76, age 41). First recorded for Aladdin in 1952. Billed as The Sweethearts Of The Blues; recorded together until 1963.

SHIRLEY & SQUIRRELY
Novelty studio production featuring squirrels instead of chipmunks. Conceived by Bob Milsap.

SHOCKED, Michelle
Born Michelle Johnston on 2/24/1962 in Dallas, Texas. Folk singer/songwriter.

SHOCKING BLUE, The
Rock group from The Hague, Holland: Mariska Veres (vocals), Robbie Leeuwen (guitar), Klaasje Wal (bass) and Cor Beek (drums). Beek died on 4/2/1998 (age 49). Veres died on 12/2/2006 (age 59).

SHOES
Rock group from Zion, Illinois: Gary Klebe (vocals), brothers Jeff (guitar) and John (bass) Murphy, and Skip Meyer (drums).

SHONDELL, Troy
Born Gary Schelton on 5/14/1939 in Fort Wayne, Indiana. Pop-country singer/songwriter.

SHONTELLE
Born Shontelle Layne in Saint James, Barbados. Female singer/rapper.

SHOOTING STAR
Rock group from Kansas City, Missouri: Gary West (vocals), Van McLain (guitar, vocals), Bill Guffey (keyboards), Charles Waltz (violin), Ron Verlin (bass) and Steve Thomas (drums).

SHOP BOYZ
Male rap trio from Atlanta, Georgia: Demetrius "Meanie" Hardin, Richard "Fat" Stevens and Rasheed "Sheed" Hightower.

SHORE, Dinah
Born Frances Rose Shore on 3/1/1917 in Winchester, Tennessee. Died of cancer on 2/24/1994 (age 76). One of the most popular female vocalists of the 1940s. Hostess of the 15-minute, award-winning early evening TV variety *The Dinah Shore Show* from 1951-57; then hosted the very popular *Dinah Shore Chevy Show* from 1956-63. Own morning talk show *Dinah's Place*, 1970-80. Married to actor George Montgomery from 1943-62.

SHORR, Mickey
Born Mickey Moses on 3/16/1926 in Detroit, Michigan. Died on 2/27/1988 (age 61). Detroit DJ and owner of a chain of car-stereo stores.

SHORROCK, Glenn
Born on 6/30/1944 in Rochester, England; raised in Elizabeth, Australia. Lead singer of Little River Band.

SHOT IN THE DARK
Pop-rock group: Krysia Kristianne (vocals), Adam Yurman (guitar), Bryan Savage (sax), Peter White (keyboards) and Robin Lamble (bass). Former backing band for Al Stewart.

SHOWMEN, The
R&B vocal group from Norfolk, Virginia: General Norman Johnson (Chairmen Of The Board), Milton Wells, brothers Gene and Dorsey Knight, and Leslie Felton.

SHOW STOPPERS, The
R&B vocal group from Philadelphia, Pennsylvania: brothers Laddie and Alec Burke (Solomon Burke's brothers), and brothers Earl and Timmy Smith.

SHWAYZE
Born Aaron Smith on 5/29/1986 in Malibu, California. Rapper.

SHYHEIM
Born Shyheim Franklin on 11/14/1979 in Brooklyn, New York. Teen male rapper.

SHYNE
Born Jamal Barrow on 11/8/1978 in Belize City, Belize; raised in Brooklyn, New York. Male rapper. Sentenced to ten years in prison on 6/1/2001 for a shooting incident on 12/27/1999.

SIDEKICKS, The
Pop band from Wildwood, New Jersey: brothers Zack Bocelle (vocals) and Randy Bocelle (bass), with Mike Burke (guitar) and Jon Spirt (drums; The Ran-Dells). Spirt died on 3/19/2003 (age 56).

SIGEL, Beanie
Born Dwight Grant on 3/6/1974 in Philadelphia, Pennsylvania. Male rapper.

SIGLER, Bunny
Born Walter Sigler on 3/27/1941 in Philadelphia, Pennsylvania. R&B-dance singer/songwriter.

SILENCERS, The
Rock group from Pittsburgh, Pennsylvania: Frank Czuri (vocals; Diamond Reo), Warren King (guitar), Dennis Takos (keyboards), Michael Pella (bass) and Ronnie Foster (drums).

SILENCERS, The
Pop-rock group from Scotland: Jimmie O'Neill (vocals, guitar), Cha Burns (guitar), Joe Donnelly (bass) and Martin Hanlin (drums). Burns died of cancer on 3/26/2007 (age 50).

SILHOUETTES, The
R&B vocal group from Philadelphia, Pennsylvania: William Horton (lead), Richard Lewis (tenor), Earl Beal (baritone) and Raymond Edwards (bass). Horton died on 1/23/1995 (age 65). Edwards died of cancer on 3/4/1997 (age 74). Beal died on 3/22/2001 (age 76). Lewis died of kidney failure on 4/19/2005 (age 71).

SILK
R&B vocal group from Atlanta, Georgia: Tim Cameron, Jim Gates, John Rasboro, Gary Jenkins and Gary Glenn.

SILKIE, The
Folk group formed in Hull, England: Silvia Tatler (vocals), Ivor Aylesbury and Mike Ramsden (guitars), and Kevin Cunningham (bass). Ramsden died on 1/17/2004 (age 60).

SILKK THE SHOCKER
Born Vyshonn Miller on 6/18/1975 in New Orleans, Louisiana. Male rapper. Brother of Master P and C-Murder. Member of the group Tru.

SILVA-TONES, The
Rock and roll band from Ayer, Massachusetts. Led by Bob Silva.

SILVER
Pop-rock group formed in Los Angeles, California: John Batdorf (vocals, guitar; Batdorf & Rodney), Greg Collier (guitar), Brent Mydland (keyboards), Tom Leadon (bass) and Harry Stinson (drums). Mydland later joined the Grateful Dead; died of a drug overdose on 7/26/90 (age 37).

SILVERADO
Pop-rock musician/songwriting team from Connecticut: Carl Shillo and Buzz Goodwin.

SILVERCHAIR
Rock trio from Newcastle, Australia: Daniel Johns (vocals, guitar), Chris Joannou (bass) and Ben Gillies (drums). Johns married Natalie Imbruglia on 12/31/2003.

SILVER CONDOR
Rock group from New York: Joe Cerisano (vocals), Earl Slick (guitar), John Corey (keyboards), Jay Davis (bass) and Claude Pepper (drums). Slick joined Phantom, Rocker & Slick in 1985.

SILVER CONVENTION
Disco studio group from Germany assembled by producer Michael Kunze and writer/arranger Silvester Levay. Female vocal trio formed later in 1976 consisting of Penny McLean, Ramona Wolf and Linda Thompson.

SILVERSPOON, Dooley
Born on 10/31/1946 in Lancaster, South Carolina. Male R&B singer.

SILVETTI
Born Juan Silvetti on 3/27/1944 in Argentina. Died of cancer on 7/5/2003 (age 59). Disco producer. Nicknamed "Bebu."

SIMEONE, Harry, Chorale
Born on 5/9/1911 in Newark, New Jersey. Died on 2/22/2005 (age 93). Conductor/arranger.

SIMMONS, Gene
Born on 7/10/1937 in Tupelo, Mississippi. Died on 8/28/2006 (age 69). Pop-rock and roll-country singer/songwriter. First recorded for Sun in 1958.

SIMMONS, Gene
Born Chaim Witz on 8/25/1949 in Haifa, Israel. Bass guitarist of Kiss. Appeared in the movies *Runaway* and *Trick Or Treat*. Own TV reality show *Gene Simmons Family Jewels* since 2006 on A&E.

SIMMONS, Patrick
Born on 10/19/1948 in Aberdeen, Washington; raised in San Jose, California. Vocalist/guitarist. Original member of The Doobie Brothers; wrote their hit "Black Water."

SIMON, Carly
Born on 6/25/1945 in Manhattan, New York. Pop singer/songwriter. Father is co-founder of Simon & Schuster publishing. In folk duo with sister Lucy as The Simon Sisters. Married to James Taylor from 1972-83.

SIMON, Joe
Born on 9/2/1943 in Simmesport, Louisiana. R&B singer/songwriter. Moved to Oakland in 1959. First recorded with the vocal group the Golden Tones for Hush in 1960.

SIMON, Paul
Born on 10/13/1941 in Newark, New Jersey; raised in Queens, New York. Singer/composer/guitarist. Met Art Garfunkel in high school, recorded together as Tom & Jerry in 1957. Recorded as Jerry Landis, Tico And The Triumphs, Paul Kane, Harrison Gregory and True Taylor in the early 1960s. To England from 1963-64. Returned to the U.S. and recorded first album with Garfunkel in 1964. Went solo in 1971. Married to actress/author Carrie Fisher from 1983-85. Married singer Edie Brickell on 5/30/1992. In the movies *Annie Hall* and *One-Trick Pony*.

SIMON & GARFUNKEL
Folk-rock duo from New York: Paul Simon (born on 10/13/1941) and Art Garfunkel (born on 11/5/1941). Recorded as Tom & Jerry in 1957. Duo split in 1964; Simon was working solo in England; Garfunkel was in graduate school. They re-formed in 1965 and stayed together until 1971. Reunited briefly since then.

SIMONE, Nina
Born Eunice Waymon on 2/21/1933 in Tryon, South Carolina. Died of cancer on 4/21/2003 (age 70). Jazz-styled singer.

SIMON F.
Born Simon Fellowes on 5/20/1961 in Kingston, England. Rock singer.

SIMON SISTERS, The
Folk duo from Manhattan, New York: sisters Carly Simon (born on 6/25/1945) and Lucy Simon (born on 5/5/1940). Broke up when Lucy got married.

SIMPLE E
Born Erica Williams in Oakland, California. Female rapper. Produced by Dwayne Wiggins (Tony! Toni! Toné!).

SIMPLE MINDS
Pop-rock group formed in Glasgow, Scotland: Jim Kerr (vocals), Charles Burchill (guitar, keyboards), Michael MacNeil (keyboards), John Giblin (bass) and Mel Gaynor (drums). MacNeil and Giblin left in 1989. Kerr was married to Chrissie Hynde (The Pretenders) (1984-90), then actress Patsy Kensit of Eighth Wonder (1992-96).

SIMPLE PLAN
Punk-rock group from Montreal, Quebec, Canada: Pierre Bouvier (vocals), Jeff Stinco (guitar), Seb Lefebvre (guitar), David Desrosiers (bass) and Chuck Comeau (drums).

SIMPLY RED
Born Mick Hucknall on 6/8/1960 in Denton, Manchester, England. "Blue-eyed soul" singer. Nicknamed "Red" because of his red hair. His backing group included Fritz McIntyre and Tim Kellett (keyboards), Sylvan Richardson (guitar), Tony Bowers (bass) and Chris Joyce (drums).

SIMPSON, Ashlee
Born on 10/3/1984 in Dallas, Texas; raised in Richardson, Texas. Female pop singer/songwriter/actress. Younger sister of Jessica Simpson. Played "Cecilia Smith" on TV's *7th Heaven*. Married Pete Wentz (of Fall Out Boy) on 5/17/2008.

SIMPSON, Jessica
Born on 7/10/1980 in Abilene, Texas; raised in Richardson, Texas. Pop-dance singer. Began career singing on the Christian Youth Conference circuit which included Kirk Franklin and CeCe Winans. Married to Nick Lachey (of 98°) from 2002-06 (they appeared as themselves in the 2003 MTV reality series *Newlyweds*). Played "Daisy Duke" in the 2005 movie *The Dukes Of Hazzard*. Older sister of Ashlee Simpson.

SIMPSON, Valerie
Born on 8/26/1946 in Brooklyn, New York. One-half of husband-and-wife duo Ashford & Simpson. Sang female part on several Marvin Gaye/Tammi Terrell duets due to Terrell's ailing health.

SIMPSONS, The
The voices of the Fox network's animated TV series. Nancy Cartwright is Bart; Dan Castellaneta is Homer; Julie Kavner is Marge; Yeardley Smith is Lisa; and the show's creator Matt Groening is Maggie.

SIMS, Kym
Born on 12/28/1966 in Chicago, Illinois. Dance singer/songwriter. Former commercial jingle singer (Shasta soft drinks).

SIMS TWINS
R&B vocal duo from Los Angeles, California: twin brothers Bobby and Kenneth Sims.

SINATRA, Frank
Born Francis Albert Sinatra on 12/12/1915 in Hoboken, New Jersey. Died of a heart attack on 5/14/1998 (age 82). With Harry James from 1939-40; with Tommy Dorsey, 1940-42. Went solo in late 1942. Appeared in many movies from 1941. Won an Oscar for the movie *From Here To Eternity* in 1953. Own TV show in 1957. Own Reprise record company in 1961; sold to Warner Bros. in 1963. Married to actress Ava Gardner from 1951-57. Married to actress Mia Farrow from 1966-68. Announced his retirement in 1970, but made comeback in 1973. Regarded by many as the greatest popular singer of the 20th century.

SINATRA, Nancy
Born on 6/8/1940 in Jersey City, New Jersey; raised in Los Angeles, California. First child of Nancy and Frank Sinatra. Made national TV debut with father and Elvis Presley in 1960. Married to Tommy Sands, 1960-65. Appeared on *Hullabaloo*, *American Bandstand* and own specials in the mid-1960s. In movies *For Those Who Think Young*, *Get Yourself A College Girl*, *The Oscar* and *Speedway* (with Elvis Presley).

SINCLAIR, Gordon
Born on 6/3/1900 in Toronto, Ontario, Canada. Died on 5/17/1984 (age 83). Broadcaster/author. Oldest person (age 73) to make the Top 40 of the *Hot 100* (not posthumously).

SINGING BELLES, The
Pop duo from Brooklyn, New York: sisters Anne Berry and Angela Berry.

SINGING DOGS, The
Actual recordings of dogs barking, produced by Don Charles in Copenhagen, Denmark.

SINGING NUN, The
Born Jeanine Deckers on 10/17/1933 in Fichermont, Belgium. Committed suicide on 3/31/1985 (age 51). Actual nun; assumed the name Sister Luc-Gabrielle. Recorded under the name Soeur Sourire ("Sister Smile").

SINGLE BULLET THEORY
Pop-rock group from Norfolk, Virginia: Michael Garrett (vocals), Gary Holmes (guitar), Barry Fitzgerald (keyboards), Mick Muller (bass) and Dennis Madigan (drums).

SINGLETARY, Daryle
Born on 3/10/1971 in Cairo, Georgia. Country singer/songwriter.

SINITTA
Born on 10/19/1966 in Seattle, Washington; raised in England (of Native American descent). Female dance singer. Daughter of singer/dancer Miquel Brown. Niece of Amii Stewart. Starred in musicals (*Cats* in London) and TV shows. Appeared in the movies *Shock Treatment* and *Foreign Body*, and a cameo role in *Little Shop of Horrors*.

SIOUXSIE & THE BANSHEES
Avant-punk group formed by singer Siouxsie Sioux (Susan Dallion) and bassist Steve Severin (Steve Havoc). Fluctuating personnel around group's nucleus: Sioux, Severin and Peter "Budgie" Clark (drums). Husband-and-wife, Sioux and Budgie, also recorded as The Creatures.

SIR CHAUNCEY
Sir Chauncey is Ernie Freeman. Also see B. Bumble & The Stingers and Joiner, Arkansas Junior High School Band.

SIR DOUGLAS QUINTET
Rock group formed in San Antonio, Texas: Doug Sahm (vocals, guitar), Augie Myers (organ), Frank Morin (horns), Harvey Regan (bass) and John Perez (drums). Sahm died of heart failure on 11/18/1999 (age 58).

SIR MIX-A-LOT
Born Anthony Ray on 8/12/1963 in Seattle, Washington. Male rapper. Appeared as the host of the anthology TV series *The Watcher*.

SISQO
Born Mark Andrews on 11/9/1978 in Baltimore, Maryland. R&B singer/songwriter. Member of Dru Hill. Appeared as "Dr. Rupert Brooks" in the 2002 movie *Snow Dogs*.

SISTER HAZEL
Pop-rock group formed in Gainesville, Florida: Ken Block (vocals), Ryan Newell and Andrew Copeland (guitars), Jeff Beres (bass) and Mark Trojanowski (drums).

SISTER 7
Rock group from Austin, Texas: Patrice Pike (vocals), Wayne Sutton (guitar), Darrell Phillips (bass) and Sean Phillips (drums).

SISTER SLEDGE
Dance vocal group from Philadelphia, Pennsylvania: sisters Debra, Joni, Kim and Kathy Sledge. First recorded as Sisters Sledge for Money Back label in 1971. Worked as backup vocalists. Began producing their own albums in 1981.

SIXPENCE NONE THE RICHER
Alternative Contemporary Christian group from Austin, Texas: Leigh Nash (vocals), Matt Slocum and Sean Kelly (guitars), Justin Cary (bass) and Dale Baker (drums).

SIX TEENS, The
Black teen R&B vocal group from Los Angeles, California: Trudy Williams, Ken Sinclair, Darrell Lewis, Beverly Pecot, Ed Wells and Louise Williams. In 1956, members ranged in age from 14 to 17. Wells died on 2/18/2001 (age 63). Sinclair died of cancer on 3/16/2003 (age 63).

69 BOYZ
Bass-rap group from Jacksonville, Florida, featuring Albert Bryant and Mike Phillips.

SKAGGS, Ricky
Born on 7/18/1954 in Cordell, Kentucky. Country singer/songwriter/mandolin player. Played mandolin from age five. Member of the Clinch Mountain Boys and The Country Gentlemen. Married Sharon White in 1982.

SKA KINGS, The
Jamaican group led by Byron Lee. Ska is considered by many to be the original music of Jamaica.

SKEE-LO
Born Anthony Roundtree on 3/5/1975 in Riverside, California. Male rapper.

SKELLERN, Peter
Born on 3/14/1947 in Bury, Lancashire, England. Pop singer/songwriter.

SKELTON, Red
Born Richard Skelton on 7/18/1913 in Vincennes, Indiana. Died on 9/17/1997 (age 84). One of America's most loved and enduring comedians. Own TV variety show from 1951-72.

SKID ROW
Heavy-metal band formed in New Jersey: Sebastian Bach (vocals), Dave Sabo and Scott Hill (guitars), Rachel Bolan (bass) and Rob Affuso (drums).

SKINDEEP
Male R&B vocal trio from Brooklyn, New York: Tracy Hester, Rico Desire and Rick Gilsaint.

SKIP & FLIP
Duo of Gary "Flip" Paxton and Clyde "Skip" Battin. Paxton formed the Hollywood Argyles and later started own Garpax record label. Battin died of Alzheimer's disease on 7/6/2003 (age 69).

SKY
Classical-rock group: John Williams and Kevin Peek (guitars), Francis Monkman (keyboards), Herb Flowers (bass) and Tristan Fly (drums).

SKYLARK
Pop group from Vancouver, British Columbia, Canada: Donny Gerrard, Carl Graves and Bonnie Jean Cook (vocals), with David Foster (keyboards) and Duris Maxwell (drums). Foster was later with Attitudes, then a hit producer/songwriter/solo artist.

SKYLINERS, The
White doo-wop group from Pittsburgh, Pennsylvania: Jimmy Beaumont (lead; born on 10/21/1940), Janet Vogel and Wally Lester (tenors), Joe VerScharen (baritone) and Jackie Taylor (bass voice, guitarist). The group that recorded on Jubilee consisted of Jackie Taylor (lead vocals), Thom Davies, Robert Peckman, Jack O'Neil and Elaine Sofocle. Peckman was later a member of The Jaggerz and Q. Vogel committed suicide on 2/21/1980 (age 37). VerScharen died of cancer on 11/3/2007 (age 67).

SKYY
R&B-pop-dance group from Brooklyn, New York: sisters Denise, Delores and Bonnie Dunning (vocals), Solomon Roberts (vocals, guitar), Anibal "Boochie" Sierra (guitar), Wayne Wilentz (keyboards), Gerald LaBon (bass) and Tommy McConnell (drums). Group organized by Randy Muller, former leader of Brass Construction.

SLADE
Hard-rock group formed in Wolverhampton, England: Neville "Noddy" Holder (vocals), David Hill (guitar), Jim Lea (bass, keyboards) and Don Powell (drums).

SLADES, The
White doo-wop trio from Austin, Texas: Don Burch (lead), Jimmy Davis and Tommy Kaspar.

SLATKIN, Felix
Born on 12/22/1915 in St. Louis, Missouri. Died on 2/9/1963 (age 47). Conductor/composer/arranger.

SLAUGHTER
Hard-rock group formed in Las Vegas, Nevada: Mark Slaughter (vocals), Tim Kelly (guitar), Dana Strum (bass) and Blas Elias (drums). Slaughter and Strum were with the Vinnie Vincent Invasion. Kelly died in a car crash on 2/5/1998 (age 35).

SLAVE
R&B-funk band from Dayton, Ohio, formed by Steve Washington (trumpet) in 1975. Longtime members of group included Mark "The Hansolor" Adams (bass), Floyd Miller (vocals, horns) and Danny Webster (vocals, guitar). Washington and members Starleana Young and Curt Jones (vocals) and Tom Lockett, Jr. (sax) left to form Aurra in 1979. Steve Arrington (drums, vocals) was a member from 1979-82. Young and Jones later formed Déja.

SLAY, Frank
Born on 7/8/1930 in Dallas, Texas. Head A&R man for Swan, 1961-63. Produced and wrote the majority of Freddy Cannon's hits. Co-writer of "Silhouettes" and "La Dee Dah."

SLEDGE, Percy
Born on 11/25/1940 in Leighton, Alabama. R&B singer. Worked local clubs with the Esquires Combo until going solo. Cousin of Jimmy Hughes.

SLICK, Grace
Born Grace Wing on 10/30/1939 in Highland Park, Illinois. Female lead singer of Jefferson Airplane/Starship. Prior to joining Jefferson Airplane, she was a member of The Great Society.

SLICK RICK
Born Ricky Walters on 1/14/1965 in South Wimbledon, London, England (to Jamaican parents). Male rapper. To the U.S. at age 14. Attended New York's High School of Music & Art. Teamed with Doug E. Fresh, 1984-85; known as "M.C. Ricky D." In 1991, sentenced to 3-10 years in prison for a shooting incident. Entered a work-release program in June 1993.

SLIM
Born Marvin Scandrick in Atlanta, Georgia. R&B singer/songwriter. Member of 112.

SLOAN, P.F.
Born Phillip Gary Schlein on 9/18/1945 in New York; raised in Los Angeles, California. Pop-rock singer/songwriter/guitarist.

SLUM VILLAGE
Rap trio from Detroit, Michigan: Titus "Baatin" Glover, RL "T3" Altman and Jason "Elzhi" Powers.

SLY & THE FAMILY STONE
Interracial "psychedelic soul" group from San Francisco, California: Sylvester "Sly Stone" Stewart (lead singer, keyboards; born on 3/15/1944 in Dallas, Texas). Sly's brother Freddie Stone (guitar), Cynthia Robinson (trumpet), Jerry Martini (saxophone; Rubicon), Sly's sister Rosie Stone (piano, vocals), Sly's cousin Larry Graham (bass) and Gregg Errico (drums). Sly recorded gospel at age four. Producer and writer for Bobby Freeman, The Mojo Men, and The Beau Brummels. Formed own groups, The Stoners, in 1966 and The Family Stone and Abaco Dream in 1967. Played Woodstock Festival in 1969. Career waned in the mid-1970s. Worked with George Clinton in 1982. Graham formed Graham Central Station in 1973.

SLY FOX
Biracial pop-dance duo: Gary "Mudbone" Cooper (Bootsy's Rubber Band) and Michael Camacho.

SMALL, Millie
Born Millicent Smith on 10/6/1946 in Clarendon, Jamaica. Reggae-ska singer. Nicknamed "The Blue Beat Girl."

SMALL FACES / FACES
Rock group formed in England: Steve Marriott (guitar), Ronnie Lane (bass), Ian McLagan (organ) and Kenney Jones (drums). In 1968, Marriott formed Humble Pie. In 1969, remaining members formed Faces with former Jeff Beck Group members Rod Stewart (vocals) and Ronnie Wood (bass). Lane left in 1973; replaced by Tetsu Yamauchi (Free). Disbanded in late 1975. Wood joined The Rolling Stones in 1976. Jones joined The Who in 1978 and formed The Law in 1991. Marriott died in a fire on 4/20/1991 (age 44). Lane died of multiple sclerosis on 6/4/1997 (age 51).

SMART E'S
Techno-dance trio from Romford, Essex, England: Tom Orton, Chris Howell and Nick Arnold.

SMASHING PUMPKINS, The
Rock group formed in Chicago, Illinois: Billy Corgan (vocals, guitar; born on 3/17/1967), James Iha (guitar; born on 3/26/1968), D'Arcy Wretzky (bass; born on 5/1/1968) and Jimmy Chamberlin (drums; born on 6/10/1964). Touring keyboardist Jonathan Melvoin, brother of Wendy Melvoin (of Prince's Revolution and Wendy & Lisa), died of a drug overdose on 7/12/1996 (age 34). Group disbanded in 2001 and reunited in 2007. Corgan and Chamberlain formed Zwan in 2002.

SMASH MOUTH
Pop-rock group from San Jose, California: Steve Harwell (vocals), Greg Camp (guitar), Paul DeLisle (bass) and Kevin Coleman (drums).

SMIF-N-WESSUN
Rap duo from Brooklyn, New York: Tek and Steele.
Later changed name to Cocoa Brovaz.

SMILEZ & SOUTHSTAR
Male rap duo from Orlando, Florida: Rodney
"Smilez" Bailey and Robert "Southstar" Campman.

SMITH
Pop-rock group from Los Angeles, California: Gayle
McCormick (vocals), Rick Cliburn and Alan Parker
(guitars), Larry Moss (keyboards), Jerry Carter
(bass) and Robert Evans (drums).

SMITH, Betty, Group
British group led by saxophonist Betty Smith.

SMITH, Bro
Born Alan Smith on 4/8/1945 in Brooklyn, New
York. DJ (under the name of "Brother Love") on
WCAO in Baltimore at the time of his hit.

SMITH, Cal
Born Calvin Grant Shofner on 4/7/1932 in Gans,
Oklahoma; raised in Oakland, California. Country
singer/guitarist. Worked with Ernest Tubb from
1961-67.

SMITH, Carl
Born on 3/15/1927 in Maynardville, Tennessee.
Country singer/songwriter/guitarist. Married to June
Carter from 1952-56; their daughter is Carlene
Carter.

SMITH, Connie
Born Constance June Meador on 8/14/1941 in
Elkhart, Indiana; raised in Hinton, West Virginia, and
Warner, Ohio. Country singer/songwriter. Married
singer Marty Stuart on 7/8/1997.

SMITH, Darden
Born on 3/11/1962 in Brenham, Texas. Pop-folk
singer/songwriter/guitarist.

SMITH, Frankie
Born in Philadelphia, Pennsylvania. R&B singer/
songwriter/producer.

SMITH, Huey (Piano)
Born on 1/26/1934 in New Orleans, Louisiana. R&B
and comical rock and roll band leader/songwriter.
With Earl King in the early 1950s. Recorded with
Eddie "Guitar Slim" Jones's band from 1951-54.
Much session work in New Orleans. Own band, The
Clowns, in 1957 with Bobby Marchan (vocals).
Marchan left in 1960, replaced by Curly Smith.

SMITH, Hurricane
Born Norman Smith on 2/22/1923 in London,
England. Died on 3/3/2008 (age 85). Pop
singer/producer.

SMITH, Jerry
Born in Philadelphia, Pennsylvania. Male pianist/
songwriter. Prolific session musician. Also recorded
as Papa Joe's Music Box. Wrote and performed on
The Dixiebelles' "(Down At) Papa Joe's" as
Cornbread & Jerry.

SMITH, Jimmy
Born on 12/8/1925 in Norristown, Pennsylvania.
Died on 2/8/2005 (age 79). Pioneer jazz-blues

organist. Won Major Bowes Amateur Show in 1934.
With father (James Sr.) in song-and-dance team,
1942. With Don Gardner & The Sonotones,
recorded for Bruce in 1953. Smith first recorded with
own trio for Blue Note in 1956.

SMITH, Michael W.
Born Michael Whitaker Smith on 10/7/1957 in
Kenova, West Virginia. Contemporary Christian
singer/songwriter/keyboardist. To Nashville in 1978.
Wrote Amy Grant's hit "Find A Way." Formed own
label, Rocketown, in the mid-1990s.

SMITH, O.C.
Born Ocie Lee Smith on 6/21/1932 in Mansfield,
Louisiana; raised in Los Angeles, California. Died
on 11/23/2001 (age 69). Male R&B singer.

SMITH, Patti
Born on 12/30/1946 in Chicago, Illinois; raised in
New Jersey. Punk-rock singer. Married to Fred
"Sonic" Smith of the MC5 from 1980-94. Her group:
Lenny Kaye (guitar), Richard Sohl (keyboards), Ivan
Kral (bass) and J.D. Daughery (drums). Sohl died
on 6/3/1990 (age 37). Not to be confused with Patty
Smyth of Scandal.

SMITH, Ray
Born on 10/31/1934 in Melber, Kentucky.
Committed suicide on 11/29/1979 (age 45).
Rockabilly singer/guitarist. Recorded for Sun
Records, 1958-62.

SMITH, Rex
Born on 9/19/1956 in Jacksonville, Florida.
Actor/singer. Acted in several movies and Broadway
shows. Brother of Michael Lee Smith of Starz.

SMITH, Roger
Born on 12/18/1932 in South Gate, California.
Played "Jeff Spencer" on the TV series 77 *Sunset
Strip*. Married Ann-Margret on 5/8/1967.

SMITH, Sammi
Born Jewel Fay Smith on 8/5/1943 in Orange,
California; raised in Oklahoma. Died of emphysema
on 2/12/2005 (age 61). Country singer.

SMITH, Somethin', & The Redheads
Adult Contemporary (1930s-styled) trio from Los
Angeles, California: Smith (vocals, guitar), Saul
Striks (piano) and Major Short (violin).

SMITH, Tab
Born Talmadge Smith on 1/11/1909 in Kinston,
North Carolina. Died on 8/17/1971 (age 62). Black
jazz alto saxophonist with the Mills Rhythm Band
(1936-38), Count Basie (1940-42) and Lucky
Millinder (1942-44).

SMITH, Verdelle
Born on 8/28/1930 in St. Petersburg, Florida. Black
female singer.

SMITH, Warren
Born on 2/7/1932 in Humphreys County,
Mississippi. Died of a heart attack on 1/30/1980
(age 47). Rockabilly singer/songwriter.

SMITH, Whistling Jack
Studio session production conceived by songwriters Roger Greenaway and Roger Cook (David & Jonathan) and featuring the Mike Sammes Singers. Billy Moeller (born on 2/2/1946 in Liverpool, England) was later hired to tour as Whistling Jack Smith. Not to be confused with the 1920s singer "Whispering" Jack Smith.

SMITH, Will
Born on 9/25/1968 in Philadelphia, Pennsylvania. Rapper/actor. One-half of D.J. Jazzy Jeff & The Fresh Prince (1986-93). Starred on TV's *Fresh Prince of Bel Air* and in such movies as *Bad Boys*, *Independence Day*, *Men In Black*, *Enemy Of The State*, *Ali* and *The Pursuit Of Happyness*. Married actress Jada Pinkett on 12/31/1997.

SMITHEREENS, The
Power-pop group formed in Carteret, New Jersey: Pat DiNizio (vocals, guitar), Jim Babjak (guitar), Mike Mesaros (bass) and Dennis Diken (drums).

SMITHS, The
Rock group formed in Manchester, England: Morrissey (vocals), Johnny Marr (guitar), Andy Rourke (bass) and Mike Joyce (drums). Marr later joined The The and Electronic.

SMOKE RING, The
Pop band from Norfolk, Nebraska: brothers Bob Hupp (guitar), Joe Hupp (keyboards) and Nick Hupp (bass), with Chuck Asmus (vocals, drums), Jim Casey (guitar) and John Schrad (sax).

SMOKIE
Pop-rock group from Bradford, Yorkshire, England: Chris Norman (vocals), Alan Silson (guitar), Terry Utley (bass) and Pete Spencer (drums).

SMOOTH
Born Juanita Carter in Los Angeles, California. Female R&B singer.

SMOTHERS BROTHERS, The
Comedy team from New York: brothers Tom (guitar; born on 2/2/1937) and Dick (standup bass; born on 11/20/1939) Smothers. Hosted their own TV variety series from 1967-69. Own summer variety series, 1970; 1988-89.

SMYTH, Patty / SCANDAL
Born on 6/26/1957 in New York. Female pop-rock singer. Lead singer of Scandal whose other members include Zack Smith and Keith Mack (guitars), Ivan Elias (bass) and Thommy Price (drums). Smyth was married to punk rocker Richard Hell (Television) in the 1980s; married pro tennis player John McEnroe in 1997. Not to be confused with Patti Smith.

SNAIL
Pop-rock group from Santa Cruz, California: Bob O'Neill (vocals, guitar), Ken Kraft (guitar), Jack Register (bass) and Jim Norris (drums). Jefferson Starship drummer Don Baldwin was a member (1979-82).

SNAP!
Techno-dance duo formed in Pittsburgh, Pennsylvania: Turbo B (rap) and his cousin Jackie

Harris (vocals). By 1992 Turbo B replaced by Niki Harris; Jackie Harris replaced by Pennye Ford.

SNEAKER
Pop-rock group formed in Los Angeles, California: Mitch Crane (vocals, guitar), Michael Carey Schneider (vocals, keyboards), Tim Torrance (guitar), Jim King (keyboards), Michael Cottage (bass) and Mike Hughes (drums).

SNEAKER PIMPS
Dance-rock trio from Reading, England: Kelli Drayton (vocals), Chris Comer (guitar) and Liam Howe (keyboards).

SNIFF 'N' THE TEARS
Rock group formed in London, England: Paul Roberts (vocals), Loz Netto and Mick Dyche (guitars), Alan Fealdman (keyboards), Chris Birkin (bass) and Luigi Salvoni (drums).

SNOOP DOGG
Born Cordozar Calvin Broadus on 10/20/1971 in Long Beach, California. Male rapper/actor. Childhood friend of Dr. Dre and Warren G. Cousin of Nate Dogg and Delmar "Dat Nigga Daz" Armaud (Tha Dogg Pound). Arrested in connection with a drive-by shooting in Los Angeles on 8/25/1993. Acquitted of first-degree murder charges in February 1996.

SNOW
Born Darrin O'Brien on 10/30/1969 in Toronto, Ontario, Canada. White male reggae singer.

SNOW, Hank
Born Clarence Snow on 5/9/1914 in Liverpool, Nova Scotia, Canada. Died of heart failure on 12/20/1999 (age 85). Country singer/songwriter/guitarist. Nicknamed "The Singing Ranger."

SNOW, Phoebe
Born Phoebe Laub on 7/17/1952 in New York; raised in New Jersey. Pop-folk singer/songwriter/guitarist.

SNOW PATROL
Rock band from Dundee, Scotland: Gary Lightbody (vocals, guitar), Nathan Connolly (guitar), Tom Simpson (keyboards), Paul Wilson (bass) and Johnny Quinn (drums).

SNUFF
Country-rock group from Virginia: Jim Bowling (vocals), Robbie House and Chuck Larson (guitars), Cecil Hooker (fiddle), C. Scott Trabue (bass) and Michael Johnson (drums).

SO
Pop-rock duo from London, England: singer/guitarist Mark Long and multi-instrumentalist Marcus Bell.

S.O.A.P.
Euro hip-hop vocal duo from Denmark: sisters Heidi and Line (Lee-nah) Sorensen.

SOBER, Errol
Born in Los Angeles, California. Pop session singer.

SOBULE, Jill
Born on 1/16/1959 in Denver, Colorado. Pop-rock singer/songwriter/guitarist.

SOCCIO, Gino
Born in 1955 in Montreal, Quebec, Canada.
Techno-disco singer/multi-instrumentalist. Producer
of Witch Queen.

SOCIAL DISTORTION
Punk-rock group formed in Los Angeles, California:
Mike Ness (vocals, guitar), Dennis Danell (guitar),
John Maurer (bass) and Christopher Reece
(drums). Danell died of a brain aneurysm on
2/29/2000 (age 38).

SOFFICI, Piero
Born in Italy. Orchestra conductor/composer.

SOFT CELL
Techno-pop duo from London, England: Peter Marc
Almond (vocals; born on 7/9/1957 in Southport,
England) and David Ball (synthesizer). Almond
began solo career in late 1988.

SOHO
Interracial dance trio formed in London, England:
identical twin sisters Jackie and Pauline Cuff
(vocals), with Timothy Brinkhurst (guitar).

SOLÉ
Born Tonya Johnston on 7/17/1973 in Kansas City,
Missouri. Female rapper.

SOLO
R&B vocal group from Brooklyn, New York: Eunique
Mack, Darnell Chavis, Daniele Stokes and Robert
Anderson.

SOLUNA
Female vocal group from Los Angeles, California:
Jessica Castellanos, Christina Lopez, America Olivo
and Aurora Rodriguez. All hail from Latin parentage.

SOME, Belouis
Born Neville Keighley in England. Techno-dance
singer/multi-instrumentalist.

SOMERVILLE, Jimmy
Born on 6/22/1961 in Glasgow, Scotland. Lead
singer/founder of the British dance-pop bands
Bronski Beat and Communards.

SOMETHIN' FOR THE PEOPLE
R&B vocal trio from Oakland, California: Jeff
"Fuzzy" Young, Curtis "Sauce" Wilson and Rochad
"Cat Daddy" Holiday.

SOMMER, Bert
Pop singer/songwriter/actor. Died of liver failure on
7/23/1990 (age 42). Played "Claude" in Broadway's
Hair from 1969-70.

SOMMERS, Joanie
Born Joan Drost on 2/24/1941 in Buffalo, New York;
moved to California in 1954. Sang Pepsi-Cola
jingles in the early and mid-1960s. Appeared in the
movies Everything's Ducky and The Lively Set.

SON BY FOUR
Latin vocal group from Puerto Rico: brothers Javier
and George Montes, with cousin Pedro Quiles and
friend Angel Lopez.

SONGZ, Trey
Born Tremaine Neverson on 11/28/1984 in
Petersburg, Virginia. Male R&B singer/songwriter.

SONIC YOUTH
Post-punk art rock band formed in New York:
husband-and-wife Thurston Moore (guitar; born on
7/25/1958) and Kim Gordon (bass; born on
4/28/1953), with Lee Ranaldo (guitar; born on
2/3/1956) and Steve Shelley (drums; born on
6/23/1963). All share vocals. Moore and Gordon
married in 1984.

SONIQUE
Born Sonia Clarke on 6/21/1968 in London,
England. Black female dance-pop singer. One-half
of the duo S-Express.

SONNY & CHER
Husband-and-wife duo: Sonny Bono (born on
2/16/1935 in Detroit, Michigan) and Cher (born on
5/20/1946). Began career as session singers for
Phil Spector. First recorded as Caesar & Cleo for
Vault in 1963. Married from 1963-75. In the movies
Good Times (1967) and Chastity (1969). Own
CBS-TV variety series from 1971-74, 1976-77.
Sonny was mayor of Palm Springs, California, from
1988-92; elected to Congress in 1994. Sonny died
in a skiing accident on 1/5/1998 (age 62).

SONS OF CHAMPLIN
Rock group from San Francisco, California: Bill
Champlin (vocals, guitar), Terry Haggerty (guitar),
Geoffrey Palmer (keyboards), David Schallock
(bass) and James Preston (drums). Champlin joined
Chicago in 1982.

SONS OF FUNK
R&B vocal group from Richmond, California:
brothers G-Smooth and Dez with their cousins
Renzo and Rico.

SOPWITH "CAMEL", The
Pop group from San Francisco, California: Peter
Kraemer (vocals, sax), Terry MacNeil and William
Sievers (guitars), Martin Beard (bass) and Norman
Mayell (drums). Named after a type of airplane used
in World War I.

S.O.S. BAND, The
Funk-R&B-disco group from Atlanta, Georgia: Mary
Davis (vocals, keyboards), Bruno Speight (guitar),
Willie Killebrew (sax), Bill Ellis (flute), Jason Bryant
(keyboards), John Simpson (bass) and James Earl
Jones III (drums).

SOUL, David
Born David Solberg on 8/28/1943 in Chicago,
Illinois. Actor/singer. Played "Joshua Bolt" on TV's
Here Come The Brides and "Ken Hutchinson" on
TV's Starsky & Hutch. Began career as a folk singer
and appeared several times on The Merv Griffin
Show as "The Covered Man" (wore a ski mask).

SOUL, Jimmy
Born James McCleese on 8/24/1942 in Weldon,
North Carolina. Died of a heart attack on 6/25/1988
(age 45). R&B/calypso-styled singer.

SOUL ASYLUM
Rock group from Minneapolis, Minnesota: Dave
Pirner (vocals, guitar), Daniel Murphy (guitar), Karl
Mueller (bass) and Grant Young (drums). Pirner
appeared in the movie Reality Bites. Sterling

SOUL ASYLUM — cont'd
Campbell (Duran Duran) replaced Young in 1995. Mueller died of throat cancer On 6/17/2005 (age 41).

SOUL BROTHERS SIX
R&B group from Rochester, New York: John Ellison, Von Elle Benjamin, Lester Peleman, Joe Johnson, and brothers Charles and Harry Armstrong.

SOUL CHILDREN, The
R&B vocal group from Memphis, Tennessee: John Colbert, Anita Louis, Shelbra Bennett and Norman West. Colbert later recorded as J. Blackfoot.

SOUL CLAN, The
All-star R&B vocal group: Solomon Burke, Arthur Conley, Don Covay, Ben E. King and Joe Tex.

SOULDECISION
White male vocal trio from Vancouver, British Columbia, Canada: David Bowman, Ken Lewko and Trevor Guthrie.

SOUL FOR REAL
R&B vocal group from Long Island, New York: brothers Chris, Andre, Brian and Jason Dalyrimple.

SOULFUL STRINGS, The
Instrumental studio group from Chicago, Illinois: Lennie Druss (oboe, flute), Bobby Christian (vibes), Philip Upchurch and Ron Steel (guitars). Arranged and conducted by Richard Evans.

SOULJA BOY TELL'EM
Born DeAndre Way on 7/28/1990 in Batesville, Mississippi. Male rapper.

SOULSISTER
Male pop vocal duo from Belgium: Jan Leyers and Paul Michiels.

SOUL SISTERS
R&B vocal duo from Harlem, New York: Thresia Cleveland and Ann Gissendanner.

SOULS OF MISCHIEF
Hip-hop group from Oakland, California: Tajai Massey, Opio Lindsey, Damani Thompson and Adam Carter.

SOUL SURVIVORS
White garage-rock band from New York and Philadelphia, Pennsylvania: vocals by Kenny Jeremiah and brothers Charles and Richard Ingui, with Edward Leonetti (guitar), Paul Venturini (organ) and Joey Forgione (drums).

S.O.U.L. S.Y.S.T.E.M., The
Dance group assembled by Robert Clivilles and David Cole (C & C Music Factory). Featuring vocalist Michelle Visage (of Seduction).

SOUL II SOUL
R&B-dance group from London, England, led by the duo Beresford "DJ Jazzie B." Romeo and Nellee Hooper. Featured female vocalists Caron Wheeler, Do'Reen Waddell and Rose Windross, and musical backing by the Reggae Philharmonic Orchestra. Wheeler left in 1990. Waddell died after being struck by a car on 3/1/2002 (age 36).

SOUL TRAIN GANG
Studio singers from the syndicated TV show *Soul Train*.

SOUND FACTORY
Dance duo from Sweden: St. James (vocals) and Emil Hellman (instruments).

SOUNDGARDEN
Hard-rock group from Seattle, Washington: Chris Cornell (vocals), Kim Thayil (guitar), Ben Shepherd (bass) and Matt Cameron (drums). Cornell and Cameron also recorded with Temple Of The Dog. Group disbanded on 4/9/1997. Cornell later joined Audioslave.

SOUNDS OF BLACKNESS
Gospel group from Minneapolis, Minnesota. Directed by Gary Hines. Featured vocalist is Ann Nesby.

SOUNDS OF SUNSHINE
Adult Contemporary vocal trio from Los Angeles, California: brothers Walt, Warner and George Wilder. Also recorded as the Wilder Brothers.

SOUNDS ORCHESTRAL
Orchestral pop studio trio from England: John Pearson (piano), Tony Reeves (bass) and Ken Clare (drums).

SOUP DRAGONS, The
Rock-dance fusion group from Glasgow, Scotland: Sean Dickson (vocals), Jim McCulloch (guitar), Sushil Dade (bass) and Paul Quinn (drums).

SOUTH, Joe
Born Joe Souter on 2/28/1940 in Atlanta, Georgia. Pop-country singer/songwriter/guitarist. Wrote "Down In The Boondocks," "Hush," "Rose Garden" and "Yo-Yo." Session guitarist for Aretha Franklin, Simon & Garfunkel and Bob Dylan.

SOUTHCOTE
Pop-rock group from Toronto, Ontario, Canada: Beau David (vocals), Charlie White (guitar), Breen LeBoeuf (bass) and Lance Wright (drums).

SOUTHER, J.D.
Born John David Souther on 11/2/1945 in Detroit, Michigan; raised in Amarillo, Texas. Formed Longbranch Pennywhistle with Glenn Frey. Teamed with Chris Hillman and Richie Furay as The Souther, Hillman, Furay Band in 1974.

SOUTHERN, Jeri
Born Genevieve Hering on 8/5/1926 in Royal, Nebraska. Died of pneumonia on 8/4/1991 (one day before her 65th birthday). White jazz singer/pianist.

SOUTH SHORE COMMISSION
R&B-funk group from Washington DC: Frank McCurry (male vocals), Sheryl Henry (female vocals), Sidney Lennear and Eugene Rogers (guitars), David Henderson (bass) and Warren Haygood (drums).

SOUTHSIDE JOHNNY & THE JUKES
Born John Lyon on 12/4/1948 in Neptune, New Jersey. Rock singer/harmonica player. Core members of The Jukes: Billy Rush (guitar), Kevin Kavanaugh (keyboards) and Alan Berger (drums).

SOUTHSIDE JOHNNY & THE JUKES — cont'd
Little Steven Van Zandt was a founding member
(left in 1975).

SOUTH SIDE MOVEMENT, The
R&B-funk group from Chicago, Illinois: Melvin
Moore (vocals), Bobby Pointer (guitar), Morris
Beeks (keyboards), Milton Johnson (sax), Steve
Hawkins (trumpet), Bill McFarland (trombone),
Ronald Simmons (bass) and Willie Hayes (drums).

SOUTHSYDE B.O.I.Z.
R&B group is actually male solo artist Jan Styles
from Phoenix. B.O.I.Z. stands for Beats Originated
In the 'Zon (Arizona).

SOUTHWEST F.O.B.
Psychedelic-pop group formed in Dallas, Texas:
Dan Seals (vocals, sax), John Coley (keyboards),
Larry Stevens (guitar), Mike Woolbright (bass) and
Tony Durrell (drums). Seals and Coley later found
success as England Dan & John Ford Coley.

SOVINE, Red
Born Woodrow Wilson Sovine on 7/17/1918 in
Charleston, West Virginia. Died of a heart attack on
4/4/1980 (age 61). Country singer/songwriter/
guitarist.

SPACE
Disco studio group assembled by French producer
Didier Marouani. Features English session singer
Madeline Bell.

SPACE
Rock group from Liverpool, England: Tommy Scott
(vocals, bass), Jamie Murphy (guitar), Franny
Griffith (keyboards) and Andy Parle (drums).

SPACEHOG
Rock group from Leeds, England: Royston Langdon
(vocals, bass), Richard Steel and Antony Langdon
(guitars), and Jonny Cragg (drums). Langdon
married actress Liv Tyler on 3/25/2003.

SPACEMEN, The
R&B instrumental studio group: Panama Francis
(The Stylers), Haywood Henry, Babe Clark and
Sammy Benskin.

SPACE MONKEYS
Rock group from Manchester, England: Richard
McNevin-Duff (vocals, guitar), Tony Pipes
(keyboards), Dom Morrison (bass) and Chas
Morrison (drums).

SPANDAU BALLET
Pop group formed in London, England: Tony Hadley
(vocals), brothers Gary (guitar) and Martin (bass)
Kemp, Steve Norman (sax) and John Keeble
(drums). The Kemps starred in the 1990 movie *The
Krays*. Gary Kemp was married to actress Sadie
Frost from 1988-97.

SPANIELS, The
R&B doo-wop group from Gary, Indiana; James
"Pookie" Hudson, lead singer. First recorded for
Chance in 1953; then became the first artist to sign
with Vee-Jay Records. Bass singer Gerald Gregory
died on 2/12/1999 (age 64). Hudson died of cancer
on 1/16/2007 (age 72).

SPANKY & OUR GANG
Folk-pop group formed in Chicago, Illinois: Elaine
"Spanky" McFarlane (born on 6/19/1942 in Peoria,
Illinois), Malcolm Hale, Lefty Baker and Nigel
Pickering (guitars), Kenny Hodges (bass) and John
Seiter (drums). Spanky became the new lead singer
of The Mamas & The Papas in the early 1980s.
Named after the *Little Rascals* series. Hale died of
liver failure on 10/31/1968 (age 27). Baker died of
liver failure on 8/11/1971 (age 29).

SPARKLE
Born in Harlem, New York. Female R&B singer.

SPARKS
Pop-rock-dance duo from Los Angeles, California:
brothers Ron (born on 8/12/1948) and Russell (born
on 10/5/1953) Mael. Appeared in the 1977 movie
Rollercoaster.

SPARKS, Jordin
Born on 12/22/1989 in Staten Island, New York;
raised in Glendale, Arizona. Winner on the 2007
season of TV's *American Idol*.

SPARXXX, Bubba
Born Warren Mathis on 3/6/1977 in LaGrange,
Georgia. White rapper. Member of Purple Ribbon
All-Stars.

SPATS, The
Rock band from Garden Grove, California: brothers
Dick Johnson (vocals), Bud Johnson (guitar) and
Ronnie Johnson (bass), with Myron Caprino
(guitar), Bob Dennis (sax), Chuck Scott (piano) and
Mike Sulsona (drums).

SPEARS, Billie Jo
Born Billie Jean Spears on 1/14/1937 in Beaumont,
Texas. Country singer/songwriter.

SPEARS, Britney
Born on 12/2/1981 in Kentwood, Louisiana. Teen
idol singer/actress. Regular on TV's *The Mickey
Mouse Club* (1992-93). Played "Lucy Wagner" in
the 2002 movie *Crossroads*. Married to backing
dancer Kevin Federline from 2004-07. They starred
in their own 2005 reality series *Britney & Kevin:
Chaotic*).

SPECIAL DELIVERY
R&B vocal group from Washington DC: brothers
Terry Huff, Andy Huff and Jimmy Huff, with Al
Johnson (of The Unifics).

SPECIAL GENERATION
R&B vocal group from St. Petersburg, Florida.
Charles Salter, Maurice Dowdell, Maquet Robinson,
Chip Carter and Kendrick Washington are part of
M.C. Hammer's posse.

SPECTOR, Phil
Born on 12/26/1940 in the Bronx, New York. Moved
to Hollywood at age 13. Legendary rock and roll
producer/songwriter/guitarist. His music is often
referred to as the "wall of sound." Owner of Philles
Records. His 1963 album *A Christmas Gift For You*
is the most popular rock and roll Christmas album of
all time. Went to trial in 2007 for the 2003 murder of
40-year-old acress Lana Clarkson.

SPECTOR, Ronnie
Born Veronica Bennett on 8/10/1943 in New York City. Lead singer of The Ronettes. Married to producer Phil Spector, 1968-74.

SPEKTOR, Regina
Born on 2/18/1980 in Moscow, Russia; raised in the Bronx, New York. Female singer/songwriter/pianist.

SPELLBINDERS, The
R&B vocal group from Jersey City, New Jersey: Bob Shivers, Jimmy Wright, Ben Grant, McArthur Munford and Elouise Pennington.

SPELLBOUND
Pop group formed in San Francisco, California: Barry Flast (vocals), Bill Burgess (guitar), David Lenchner (keyboards), Ralph Carter (bass) and Joey Kluchar (drums).

SPELLMAN, Benny
Born on 12/11/1931 in Pensacola, Florida. Worked with Huey "Piano" Smith. Frequent session work as an R&B backup singer. Bass vocalist on Ernie K-Doe's "Mother-In-Law."

SPENCE, Judson
Born on 4/29/1965 in Pascagoula, Mississippi. Pop-rock singer/songwriter/multi-instrumentalist.

SPENCER, Sonny
Born John Berry on 1/3/1938 in Orangeburg, South Carolina. R&B singer/songwriter.

SPENCER, Tracie
Born on 7/12/1976 in Waterloo, Iowa. Female R&B singer. Won the singing competition on TV's *Star Search* in 1986.

SPENCER & SPENCER
Duo of Dickie Goodman and Mickey Shorr.

SPERRY, Steve
Born on 10/3/1941 in Fort Atkinson, Wisconsin. Pop singer/songwriter/jingle writer.

SPICE GIRLS
Female dance-pop vocal group from England: Victoria Adams (Posh Spice; born on 4/17/1974), Melanie Brown (Scary Spice; born on 5/29/1975), Emma Bunton (Baby Spice; born on 1/21/1976), Geri Halliwell (Ginger Spice; born on 8/18/1970) and Melanie Chisholm (Sporty Spice; born on 1/12/1974). Group starred in the movie *Spiceworld*. Halliwell left group in May 1998. Adams married soccer superstar David Beckham on 7/4/1999.

SPIDER
Rock group formed in New York: South African native Amanda Blue (vocals), Keith Lentin (guitar), Holly Knight (keyboards), Jimmy Lowell (bass) and Anton Fig (drums). Knight, a prolific songwriter, later joined Device and then went solo. Fig joined the house band of TV's *Late Night With David Letterman*.

SPIDERS, The
R&B/doo-wop vocal group from New Orleans, Louisiana: brothers Hayward Carbo and Leonard Carbo, with Joe Maxon, Matthew West and Oliver Howard. Leonard Carbo died on 8/18/1998 (age 70). Haywood Carbo died on 7/11/2008 (age 82).

SPIN
Instrumental pop-jazz-rock session band from Holland: Hans Hollestelle (guitar), Rein van der Broek (trumpet), Jan Vennik (reeds), Hans Jansen (keyboards), Jan Hollestelle (bass) and Cees Kranenburg (drums).

SPIN DOCTORS
Rock group formed in New York: Christopher Barron (vocals), Eric Schenkman (guitar), Mark White (bass) and Aaron Comess (drums). Anthony Krizan replaced Schenkman in 1993.

SPINNERS
R&B vocal group formed in Detroit, Michigan. Originally known as the Domingoes. Discovered by producer/lead singer of The Moonglows, Harvey Fuqua, and became the Spinners in 1961. First recorded on Fuqua's Tri-Phi label. Many personnel changes. G.C. Cameron was lead singer from 1968-72. 1972 hit lineup included Philippe Wynne (tenor; born on 4/3/1941), Bobbie Smith (tenor; born on 4/10/1936), Billy Henderson (tenor; born on 8/9/1939), Henry Fambrough (baritone; born on 5/10/1938) and Pervis Jackson (bass; born on 5/16/1938; died of cancer on 8/18/2008, age 70). Wynne left group in 1977 and toured with Parliament/Funkadelic; replaced by John Edwards. Wynne died of a heart attack on 7/13/1984 (age 43). Henderson died of diabetes on 2/2/2007 (age 67).

SPIRAL STARECASE
Pop-rock group from Sacramento, California: Pat Upton (vocals, guitar), Harvey Kaplan (organ), Dick Lopes (sax), Bobby Raymond (bass) and Vinny Parello (drums). Kaplan is the father of Brenda K. Starr.

SPIRIT
Rock group from Los Angeles, California: Jay Ferguson (vocals), Randy California (guitar), John Locke (keyboards), Mark Andes (bass) and Ed Cassidy (drums). Ferguson and Andes left to form Jo Jo Gunne in mid-1971. Andes became an original member of Firefall in 1975; joined Heart in 1983. California drowned in Hawaii on 1/2/1997 (age 45). Locke died on 8/4/2006 (age 62).

SPLENDER
Interracial rock group formed in New York: Waymon Boone (vocals), Jonathan Svec (guitar), James Cruz (bass) and Mark Slutsky (drums).

SPLINTER
Pop-rock vocal duo from England: Bill Elliott and Bob Purvis.

SPLIT ENZ
New-wave pop group from New Zealand: brothers Tim (vocals) and Neil (guitar, vocals) Finn, Eddy Rayner (keyboards), Noel Crombie (percussion), Nigel Griggs (bass) and Malcolm Green (drums). The Finns were later members of Crowded House.

SPOKESMEN, The
Pop-folk trio from Philadelphia, Pennsylvania: Johnny Medora, David White and Roy Gilmore. White was with Danny & The Juniors (Medora wrote "At The Hop").

SPONGE
Rock group from Detroit, Michigan: Vinnie Dombrowski (vocals), Mike Cross and Joe Mazzola (guitars), Tim Cross (bass) and Jimmy Paluzzi (drums). Charlie Grover replaced Paluzzi in early 1996.

SPORTS, The
Rock group formed in Melbourne, Australia: Stephen Cummings (vocals), Andrew Pendlebury and Martin Armiger (guitars), James Niven (keyboards), Robert Glover (bass) and Paul Hitchins (drums).

SPORTY THIEVZ
Rap trio from Brooklyn, New York: Marlon Brando, King Kirk and Big Dubez. Brando died in a car crash on 5/11/2001 (age 22).

SPRINGFIELD, Dusty
Born Mary O'Brien on 4/16/1939 in London, England. Died of cancer on 3/2/1999 (age 59). Blue-eyed soul singer. With brother Tom Springfield and Tim Field in folk trio The Springfields.

SPRINGFIELD, Rick
Born Richard Springthorpe on 8/23/1949 in Sydney, Australia. Pop-rock singer/songwriter/guitarist/actor. Played "Dr. Noah Drake" on the TV soap opera *General Hospital*. Starred in the movie *Hard To Hold*.

SPRINGFIELDS, The
Folk trio from London, England: Dusty Springfield, her brother Tom Springfield and Tim Feild.

SPRINGSTEEN, Bruce
Born on 9/23/1949 in Freehold, New Jersey. Rock and roll singer/songwriter/guitarist. Nicknamed "The Boss." Worked local clubs in New Jersey and Greenwich Village, mid-1960s. Own E-Street Band in 1973, consisted of Clarence Clemons (saxophone), David Sancious (keybaords), Danny Federici (keyboards; died on 4/17/2008, age 58), Gary Tallent (bass) and Vini Lopez (drums). Sancious and Lopez replaced by Roy Bittan and Max Weinberg (became musical director for TV's *Late Night With Conan O'Brien* in 1993). Miami Steve Van Zandt (Little Steven and the Disciples Of Soul; guitar) joined group in 1975. After *Born To Run*, a court injunction prevented the release of any new recordings until 1978. Married to model/actress Julianne Phillips from 1985-89. Appeared in the 1987 movie *Hail! Hail! Rock 'N' Roll*. Split from the E-Street Band in November 1989. Married Patti Scialfa, singer with the E-Street Band, on 6/8/1991. Reunited with the E-Street Band in 1999.

SPRINGWELL
Rock quintet from Detroit, Michigan. Led by David Rule.

SPYRO GYRA
Jazz-pop band formed in Buffalo, New York. Led by saxophonist Jay Beckenstein (born on 5/14/1951). The Brecker Brothers were longtime members.

SPYS
Rock group from New York: John Blanco (vocals), John DiGaudio (guitar), Al Greenwood (keyboards), Ed Gagliardi (bass) and Billy Milne (drums).

Greenwood and Gagliardi were members of Foreigner.

SQUEAK E. CLEAN
Born Samuel Spiegel in Bethesda, Maryland; later based in New York. White DJ/musician/producer. Brother of acclaimed video director Spike Jonze.

SQUEEZE
New wave pop-rock group formed in London, England. Led by vocalists/guitarists Chris Difford and Glenn Tilbrook. Originally known as UK Squeeze due to confusion with American band Tight Squeeze. Paul Carrack (Ace, Mike + The Mechanics) was keyboardist/vocalist in 1981 of fluctuating lineup; re-joined in 1993.

SQUIER, Billy
Born on 5/12/1950 in Wellesley Hills, Massachusetts. Hard-rock singer/songwriter/guitarist.

SQUIRREL NUT ZIPPERS
Eclectic-jazz group from Chapel Hill, North Carolina: Jim Mathus (vocals, guitar, trombone), Katharine Whalen (vocals, banjo), Ken Mosher (guitar, sax), Tom Maxwell (sax, clarinet), Je Widenhouse (trumpet), Don Raleigh (bass) and Chris Phillips (drums). Group name taken from a brand of candy.

S.S.O.
Disco group featuring Douglas Lucas and the Sugar Sisters. S.S.O.: Soul Sensation Orchestra.

STABBING WESTWARD
Rock band from Macomb, Illinois: Christopher Hall (vocals, guitar), Walter Flakus (keyboards), Jim Sellers (bass) and Andy Kubiszewski (drums).

STABILIZERS
Pop-rock duo from Erie, Pennsylvania: Dave Christenson (vocals) and Rich Nevens (keyboards, guitar).

STACEY Q
Born Stacey Swain on 11/30/1958 in Los Angeles, California. Female dance singer.

STACY, Clyde
Born on 8/11/1936 in Eufala, Oklahoma; raised in Lubbock, Texas. Rockabilly singer.

STAFFORD, Jim
Born on 1/16/1944 in Eloise, Florida. Pop-novelty singer/songwriter/guitarist. Hosted own summer variety TV show in 1975 and *Those Amazing Animals* from 1980-81. Married to Bobbie Gentry from 1978-79.

STAFFORD, Jo
Born on 11/12/1917 in Coalinga, California. Died of heart failure on 7/16/2008 (age 90). Female singer. Sang with Tommy Dorsey's band ("Yes Indeed!"), both as a solo artist and with vocal group The Pied Pipers, 1940-43. Married to orchestra leader Paul Weston. Host of own TV musical series, 1954-55.

STAFFORD, Terry
Born on 11/22/1941 in Hollis, Oklahoma; raised in Amarillo, Texas. Died on 3/17/1996 (age 54). Pop-rock and roll singer/songwriter. Elvis Presley sound-alike. Moved to California in 1960. Appeared in the movie *Wild Wheels*.

STAGE DOLLS
Rock trio from Trondheim, Norway: Torstein Flakne (vocals), Terje Storli (bass) and Steinar Krokstad (drums).

STAGGA LEE
Born Eric Newman in the Bronx, New York; raised in Yonkers, New York. White male rapper.

STAIND
Alternative-metal rock group from Boston, Massachusetts: Aaron Lewis (vocals), Mike Mushok (guitar), Johnny April (bass) and Jon Wysocki (drums).

STALLION
Pop-rock group from Denver, Colorado: Buddy Stephens (vocals), Danny O'Neil (guitar), Wally Damrick (keyboards), Jorg Gonzalez (bass) and Larry Thompson (drums).

STALLONE, Frank
Born on 7/30/1950 in Philadelphia, Pennsylvania. Pop singer/songwriter/actor. Brother of actor Sylvester Stallone.

STAMPEDERS
Pop-rock trio from Calgary, Alberta, Canada: Rich Dodson (guitar), Ronnie King (bass) and Kim Berly (drums). All share vocals.

STAMPLEY, Joe
Born on 6/6/1943 in Springhill, Louisiana. Country singer. Leader of The Uniques.

STANDELLS, The
Early punk-rock group from Los Angeles, California: Dick Dodd (vocals, drums), Larry Tamblyn and Tony Valentino (guitars) and Gary Lane (bass). Dodd was an original Mouseketeer of TV's *The Mickey Mouse Club*. Tamblyn is the brother of actor Russ Tamblyn and uncle of actress Amber Tamblyn.

STANLEY, Michael, Band
Born Michael Stanley Gee on 3/25/1948 in Cleveland, Ohio. Rock singer/guitarist. His band: Kevin Raleigh (vocals, keyboards), Bob Pelander (keyboards), Gary Markshay (guitar), Rick Bell (sax), Mike Gismondi (bass) and Tom Dobeck (drums). Don Powers replaced Markshay in 1982.

STANLEY, Paul
Born Paul Stanley Eisen on 1/20/1952 in Queens, New York. Rhythm guitarist of Kiss. Married model Pamela Bowen on 7/26/1992.

STANSFIELD, Lisa
Born on 4/11/1966 in Rochdale, Manchester, England. Dance singer/songwriter. Lead singer of dance trio Blue Zone U.K..

STAPLES, Mavis
Born on 7/10/1939 in Chicago, Illinois. Female R&B singer. Member of The Staple Singers.

STAPLE SINGERS, The
Family R&B group consisting of Roebuck "Pop" Staples (born on 12/28/1915 in Winona, Mississippi; died on 12/19/2000, age 84), with his son Pervis (born on 11/18/1935; left in 1971) and daughters Cleotha (born on 4/11/1934), Yvonne (born on 10/23/1938) and lead singer Mavis Staples (born on

7/10/1939). Roebuck was a blues guitarist in his teens, later with the Golden Trumpets gospel group. Moved to Chicago in 1935. Formed own gospel group in early 1950s. First recorded for United in 1953. Mavis began solo career in 1970.

STAPLETON, Cyril
Born on 12/31/1914 in Nottingham, England. Died on 2/25/1974 (age 59). Orchestra leader.

STARBUCK
Pop-rock group from Atlanta, Georgia: Bruce Blackman (vocals, keyboards), Bo Wagner (marimbas), Sloan Hayes (keyboards), Tommy Strain and Ron Norris (guitars), Jimmy Cobb (bass) and Dave Snavely (drums). Strain, Norris and Snavely left after "Lucky Man," replaced by Darryl Kutz (guitar), David Shaver (keyboards) and Ken Crysler (drums). Also see Eternity's Children and Korona.

STARCHER, Buddy
Born Oby Edgar Starcher on 3/16/1906 in Ripley, West Virginia. Died on 11/2/2001 (age 95). Country singer/songwriter/DJ.

STARDUST
Dance trio from Paris, France: Thomas Bangalter, Alan "Branxe" Queme and Benjamin "Diamond" Cohen. Bangalter was a member of Daft Punk.

STARGARD
Disco trio: Rochelle Runnells, Debra Anderson and Janice Williams. Appeared as "The Diamonds" in the movie *Sgt. Pepper's Lonely Hearts Club Band*.

STARK & McBRIEN
Pop duo: Fred Stark and Rod McBrien.

STARLAND VOCAL BAND
Pop group formed in Washington DC: Bill and wife Taffy Danoff, John Carroll and future wife Margot Chapman. Bill and Taffy had fronted the folk group Fat City (backed John Denver on "Take Me Home, Country Roads"). Group hosted own summer TV variety series in 1977.

STARLETS, The
Female R&B vocal group from Chicago, Illinois: Dynetta Boone, Jane Hall, Maxine Edwards (sister of Earl Edwards of The Dukays), Mickey McKinney, Jeanette Miles and Bernice Williams. While under contract to PAM Records, The Starlets recorded "I Sold My Heart To The Junkman" on the Newtown label. Newtown credited one of its artists, The Blue-Belles (Patti LaBelle's group), on the label.

STARPOINT
Dance group from Maryland: brothers Ernesto, George, Orlando and Gregory Phillips, with Renee Diggs and Kayode Adeyemo.

STARR, Brenda K.
Born Brenda Kaplan on 10/15/1966 in Manhattan, New York. R&B-dance singer/movie actress. Daughter of Harvey Kaplan (of Spiral Starecase).

STARR, Edwin
Born Charles Hatcher on 1/21/1942 in Nashville, Tennessee; raised in Cleveland, Ohio. Died of a heart attack on 4/2/2003 (age 61). R&B singer/

STARR, Edwin — cont'd
songwriter. In the Futuretones vocal group; recorded for Tress in 1957. With Bill Doggett Combo from 1963-65. Recorded duets with Sondra "Blinky" Williams in 1969. Also see The Holidays.

STARR, Kay
Born Katherine Starks on 7/21/1922 in Dougherty, Oklahoma; raised in Dallas, Texas, and Memphis, Tennessee. With Joe Venuti's orchestra at age 15, and sang briefly with Glenn Miller, Charlie Barnet and Bob Crosby before launching solo career in 1945. In the movies *Make Believe Ballroom* and *When You're Smiling.*

STARR, Kenny
Born Kenneth Trebbe on 9/21/1952 in Topeka, Kansas; raised in Burlingame, Kansas. Country singer/guitarist.

STARR, Lucille
Born Lucille Savoie on 5/13/1938 in St. Boniface, Manitoba, Canada. Duo with husband Bob Regan as The Canadian Sweethearts.

STARR, Randy
Born Warren Nadel on 7/2/1930 in the Bronx, New York. Pop singer/songwriter/guitarist. Wrote Elvis Presley's hit "Kissin' Cousins." Formed instrumental duo, The Islanders, with Frank Metis.

STARR, Ringo
Born Richard Starkey on 7/7/1940 in Dingle, Liverpool, England. Drummer with Rory Storm and the Hurricanes before joining The Beatles in 1962. First solo recording in 1970. Acted in several movies, including Paul McCartney's *Give My Regards To Broad Street.* Played "Mr. Conductor" on PBS-TV's *Shining Time Station* from 1989-91. Married actress Barbara Bach on 4/27/1981. Continues to tour with an ever-revolving lineup of top musicians ("The All-Star Band"). Starr's most popular recordings as The Beatles' lead singer included "Yellow Submarine," "Act Naturally," "With A Little Help From My Friends" and "Honey Don't."

STARS on 45
Dutch session vocalists and musicians assembled by producer Jaap Eggermont. John Lennon vocals by Bas Muys, Paul McCartney vocals by Okkie Huysdens and George Harrison vocals by Hans Vermeulen.

STARZ
Hard-rock group formed in New York: Michael Lee Smith (vocals), Rich Ranno and Brendan Harkin (guitars), Piet Sweval (bass; Looking Glass) and Joe Dube (drums). Smith is the brother of Rex Smith. Sweval died on 1/23/1990 (age 41).

STATIC-X
Alternative-metal rock band formed in Los Angeles, California: Wayne "Static" Wells (vocals, guitar), Koichi Fukuda (guitar, keyboards), Tony Campos (bass) and Ken Jay (drums). Fukada left in 2000; Static took over keyboards and Tod "Tripp Eisen" Salvador (guitar) joined. Nick Oshiro (of Seether) replaced Lacey in early 2003. Salvador was fired in 2005; Fukada returned.

STATLER BROTHERS, The
Country vocal group from Staunton, Virginia: brothers Harold (bass) and Don (lead) Reid, Phil Balsley (baritone) and Lew DeWitt (tenor). In 1983, Jimmy Fortune replaced DeWitt, who died from Crohn's disease on 8/15/1990 (age 52). Hosted their own Nashville Network cable TV variety show.

STATON, Candi
Born Canzata Staton on 5/13/1940 in Hanceville, Alabama. R&B singer. Formerly married to Clarence Carter. Own *Candi Staton* show on TBN-TV.

STATUES, The
White vocal trio based in Nashville, Tennessee: James "Buzz" Cason, Hugh Jarrett and Richard Williams. Also see Garry Miles.

STATUS QUO, The
Psychedelic-rock group from London, England: Francis Rossi (vocals), Rick Parfitt (guitar), Roy Lynes (organ), Alan Lancaster (bass) and John Coghlan (drums). Immensely popular in England.

STEALERS WHEEL
Pop-rock duo from Scotland: Gerry Rafferty (vocals, guitar) and Joe Egan (vocals, keyboards).

STEAM
Rock group from Bridgeport, Connecticut. "Na Na Hey Hey Kiss Him Goodbye" was recorded by the trio of Gary DeCarlo, Paul Leka and Dale Frashuer, and released as by Steam. After the song became a hit, Leka assembled an actual Steam group: Bill Steer (vocals), Jay Babins and Tom Zuke (guitars), Hank Schorz (keyboards), Mike Daniels (bass) and Ray Corries (drums).

STEEL BREEZE
Pop-rock group from Sacramento, California: Ric Jacobs (vocals), Ken Goorabian and Waylin Carpenter (guitars), Rod Toner (keyboards), Vinnie Pantleoni (bass) and Barry Lowenthal (drums).

STEELE, Maureen
White pop-dance singer/songwriter.

STEELERS, The
R&B vocal group from Chicago, Illinois: Leonard "Red" Truss, Wales Wallace, Wes "Preach" Wells, Alonzo "Cool" Wells and George "Flue" Wells.

STEELHEART
Hard-rock band from Norwalk, Connecticut: Michael Matijevic (vocals), Chris Risola (guitar), Frank Dicostanzo (guitar), Jimmy Ward (bass) and John Fowler (drums). Fowler died on 3/21/2008 (age 42).

STEELY DAN
Jazz-rock group formed in Los Angeles, California, by Donald Fagen (keyboards, vocals; born on 1/10/1948 in Passaic, New Jersey) and Walter Becker (bass, vocals; born on 2/20/1950 in Queens, New York). Group, primarily known as a studio unit, featured Fagen and Becker with various studio musicians. Duo split from 1981-92.

STEFANI, Gwen
Born on 10/3/1969 in Fullerton, California. Lead singer of No Doubt. Played Jean Harlow in the movie *The Aviator*. Married Gavin Rossdale (lead singer of Bush) on 9/14/2002.

STEIN, Lou
Born on 4/22/1922 in Philadelphia, Pennsylvania. Died on 12/10/2002 (age 80). Session pianist.

STEINER, Tommy Shane
Born on 10/9/1973 in Austin, Texas. Country singer.

STEINMAN, Jim
Born on 11/1/1948 in Brooklyn, New York. Songwriter/pianist/producer. Wrote and produced songs for Meat Loaf, Air Supply and Bonnie Tyler.

STEPHENSON, Van
Born on 11/4/1953 in Hamilton, Ohio. Died of cancer on 4/8/2001 (age 47). Pop-country singer/songwriter. Member of BlackHawk.

STEPPENWOLF
Hard-rock group formed in Los Angeles, California: Joachim "John Kay" Krauledat (vocals, guitar; born on 4/12/1944), Michael Monarch (guitar; born on 7/5/1950), John "Goldy McJohn" Goadsby (keyboards; born on 5/2/1945), John Russell Morgan (bass) and Jerry "Edmonton" McCrohan (drums; born on 10/24/1946). All but Monarch were members of Canadian group Sparrow. Many personnel changes except for Kay. Group named after a 1927 Herman Hesse novel. Edmonton died in a car crash on 11/28/1993 (age 47).

STEREO MC'S
Trio of dance remixers from Gee Street Records based in London, England: Rob Birch, Nick "The Head" Hallam and Owen "If" Rossiter. Features touring/video vocalist Cath Coffey.

STEREOS, The
R&B vocal group from Steubenville, Ohio: Bruce Robinson, Nathaniel Hicks, Sam Profit, George Otis and Ronnie Collins.

STEVENS, Cat
Born Steven Georgiou on 7/21/1948 in London, England. Pop-folk singer/songwriter/guitarist. Began career playing folk music at Hammersmith College in 1966. Contracted tuberculosis in 1968 and spent over a year recuperating. Adopted new style when he re-emerged. Lived in Brazil in the mid-1970s. Converted to Muslim religion in 1979; took name Yusuf Islam.

STEVENS, Connie
Born Concetta Ingolia on 8/8/1938 in Brooklyn, New York. Pop singer/actress. Played "Cricket Blake" on TV's *Hawaiian Eye* from 1959-63. Appeared in many movies. Married to Eddie Fisher from 1967-69; singer Tricia Leigh Fisher is their daughter.

STEVENS, Dodie
Born Geraldine Ann Pasquale on 2/17/1946 in Chicago, Illinois; raised in Temple City, California. Female pop singer. Discovered while singing on Art Linkletter's *House Party* TV show at age 8. First

recorded as Geri Pace on Gold Star in 1954; also recorded as Geraldine Stevens ("Bubbled Under").

STEVENS, Ray
Born Harold Ray Ragsdale on 1/24/1939 in Clarksdale, Georgia. Country-novelty singer/songwriter. Proficient on several instruments. Production work in the mid-1960s. Numerous appearances on the Andy Williams TV show in the late 1960s. Hosted own TV variety show in 1970. Also recorded as Henhouse Five Plus Too.

STEVENS, Shakin'
Born Michael Barratt on 3/4/1948 in Cardiff, Wales. Rockabilly singer/songwriter.

STEVENSON, B.W.
Born Louis Stevenson on 10/5/1949 in Dallas, Texas. Died of heart failure on 4/28/1988 (age 38). Soft-rock singer/guitarist.

STEVIE B
Born Steven Hill in Miami, Florida. Dance-pop singer/multi-instrumentalist.

STEWART, Al
Born on 9/5/1945 in Glasgow, Scotland. Pop singer/songwriter/guitarist. Also see Shot In The Dark.

STEWART, Amii
Born on 1/29/1956 in Washington DC. Disco singer/dancer/actress. In the Broadway musical *Bubbling Brown Sugar*. Aunt of singer Sinitta.

STEWART, Andy
Born on 12/20/1933 in Glasgow, Scotland. Died of a heart attack on 10/11/1993 (age 59). Pop singer/actor/comedian.

STEWART, Baron
Born in Los Angeles, California. Male singer/songwriter.

STEWART, Billy
Born on 3/24/1937 in Washington DC. Died in a car crash on 1/17/1970 (age 32). R&B singer/composer/keyboardist. Discovered by Bo Diddley in 1956. First recorded for Chess/Argo in 1956. Did not record from 1957-61. Nicknamed "Fat Boy." First cousin of Grace Ruffin of The Jewels.

STEWART, Dave, & Barbara Gaskin
Duo from London, England: singer Gaskin and keyboardist Stewart (not to be confused with David A. Stewart of Eurythmics).

STEWART, David A.
Born on 9/9/1952 in Sunderland, England. Multi-instrumentalist/composer/producer. In The Tourists. One-half of the Eurythmics duo. Married Siobhan Fahey (Bananarama, Shakespear's Sister) on 8/1/1987.

STEWART, Gary
Born on 5/28/1944 in Jenkins, Kentucky; raised in Fort Pierce, Florida. Committed suicide on 12/16/2003 (age 59). Country singer/songwriter/guitarist. Member of rock groups the Tomcats and the Amps in the early 1960s.

STEWART, Jermaine
Born on 9/7/1957 in Columbus, Ohio. Died of cancer on 3/17/1997 (age 39). R&B-dance singer.

STEWART, John
Born on 9/5/1939 in San Diego, California. Died of a stroke on 1/19/2008 (age 68). Folk-pop singer/songwriter. Member of The Kingston Trio from 1961-67. Brother of Mike Stewart (drummer for We Five).

STEWART, Rod
Born Roderick Stewart on 1/10/1945 in Highgate, London, England. Pop-rock singer/songwriter. Worked as a folk singer in Europe in the early 1960s. Recorded for English Decca, 1964. With the Hoochie Coochie Men, Steampacket and Shotgun Express. Joined Jeff Beck Group, 1967-69. With Faces from 1969-75; also recorded solo during this time. Left Faces in December 1975. Married to actress Alana Hamilton from 1979-84. Married to supermodel Rachel Hunter from 1990-2003. One of the rock era's leading performers for over 35 years. Also see Small Faces.

STEWART, Sandy
Born Sandra Galitz on 7/10/1937 in Philadelphia, Pennsylvania. Regular on the Eddie Fisher and Perry Como musical/variety TV shows.

STEWART, Wynn
Born Wynnford Stewart on 6/7/1934 in Morrisville, Missouri. Died of a heart attack on 7/17/1985 (age 51). Country singer/songwriter/guitarist. Own club and TV series in Las Vegas in the late 1950s.

STIGERS, Curtis
Born on 10/18/1965 in Hollywood, California; raised in Boise, Idaho. Pop-jazz singer/saxophonist/songwriter.

STILLS, Stephen
Born on 1/3/1945 in Dallas, Texas. Singer/songwriter with Buffalo Springfield and Crosby, Stills & Nash. Manassas included Chris Hillman (guitar; The Byrds), Dallas Taylor (drums), Fuzzy Samuels (bass), Paul Harris (organ), Al Perkins (guitar) and Joe Lala (percussion).

STILLWATER
Rock group from Warner Robins, Georgia: Jimmy Hall (vocals; not to be confused with leader of Wet Willie), Bobby Golden, Michael Causey and Rob Walker (guitars), Bob Spearman (keyboards), Allison Scarborough (bass) and Sebie Lacey (drums).

STING
Born Gordon Sumner on 10/2/1951 in Wallsend, England. Pop-rock singer/songwriter/bassist. Lead singer of The Police. In the movies *Quadrophenia*, *Dune*, *The Bride*, *Plenty* and others. Married actress/producer Trudie Styler on 8/20/1992. Nicknamed "Sting" because of a yellow and black jersey he liked to wear.

STIPE, Michael
Born on 1/4/1960 in Decatur, Georgia. Lead singer of R.E.M.

STITES, Gary
Born on 7/23/1940 in Denver, Colorado. Pop singer/songwriter/guitarist.

STOCKMAN, Shawn
Born on 9/26/1972 in Philadelphia, Pennsylvania. Member of Boyz II Men.

STOKES, Simon
Born on 4/3/1945 in Reading, Massachusetts. R&B singer/songwriter.

STOLOFF, Morris
Born on 8/1/1898 in Philadelphia, Pennsylvania. Died on 4/16/1980 (age 81). Composer/conductor/violinist. Became musical director for Columbia Pictures in 1936. Winner of three Academy Awards.

STOMPERS, The
White rock and roll band from Medford, Massachusetts: Leonard Capizzi, Bill Capizzi (aka Chesley Uxbridge), Ron Deltorto, Lou Toscano and Bobby "Boris" Pickett (left for his own solo career; replaced by Don Squire). Formed as The Cordials.

STOMPERS, The
Pop-rock group from Boston, Massachusetts: Sal Baglio (vocals, guitar), Dave Friedman (keyboards), Stephen Gilligan (bass) and Mark Cuccinello (drums).

STONE, Angie
Born on 1/30/1961 in Columbia, South Carolina. R&B singer. Former member of groups Sequence and Vertical Hold.

STONE, Cliffie
Born Clifford Snyder on 3/1/1917 in Stockton, California; raised in Burbank, California. Died of a heart attack on 1/17/1998 (age 80). Square-dance bandleader/bassist/songwriter/DJ/record company executive. Radio/TV personality in Los Angeles, from the 1940s-60s, hosting several programs. An A&R executive for Capitol Records.

STONE, Doug
Born Douglas Brooks on 6/19/1956 in Marietta, Georgia. Country singer/guitarist. Changed name to avoid confusion with Garth Brooks. At age seven, opened on guitar for a Loretta Lynn concert. Starred in the 1995 movie *Gordy*.

STONE, Joss
Born Joscelyn Stoker on 4/11/1987 in Dover, Kent, England. White female soul-styled singer.

STONE, Kirby, Four
Born on 4/27/1918 in Manhattan, New York. Died in July 1981 (age 63). His vocal group included Eddie Hall, Larry Foster and Mike Gardner.

STONEBOLT
Pop group from Vancouver, British Columbia, Canada: David Willis (vocals), Ray Roper (guitar), John Webster (keyboards), Dan Atchison (bass) and Brian Lousley (drums).

STONE ROSES, The
Alternative pop-rock group from Manchester, England: Ian Brown (vocal), John Squire (guitar), Gary Mournfield (bass) and Alan Wren (drums).

STONE SOUR
Rock group formed by Slipknot members Corey Taylor (vocals), Jim Root (guitar) and Sid Wilson (bass), with Josh Rand (guitar) and Joel Eckman (drums). By 2006, Shawn Economaki replaced Wilson and Roy Mayorga replaced Eckman.

STONE TEMPLE PILOTS
Rock group formed in San Diego, California: Scott Weiland (vocals), brothers Dean (guitar) and Robert (bass) DeLeo, and Eric Kretz (drums). Group originally known as Mighty Joe Young, then Shirley Temple's Pussy. Weiland also formed side project The Magnificent Bastards in 1995. The DeLeo brothers and Kretz formed side project Talk Show in 1997.

STOOKEY, Paul
Born on 12/30/1937 in Baltimore, Maryland. Folk singer/songwriter/guitarist. Member of Peter, Paul & Mary.

STOREY SISTERS, The
Rock and roll duo from Philadelphia, Pennsylvania: Ann and Lillian Storey.

STORIES
Rock group from Brooklyn, New York: Ian Lloyd (vocals, bass), Michael Brown (keyboards; founding member of The Left Banke), Steve Love (guitar) and Bryan Madey (drums). Brown left group in 1973; replaced by Ken Aaronson (bass; later charted with Sammy Hagar) and Ken Bichel (keyboards).

STORM, The
Rock group formed in San Francisco, California: Kevin Chalfant (vocals), Gregg Rolie (vocals, keyboards), Josh Ramos (guitar), Ross Valory (bass) and Steve Smith (drums). Rolie was a member of Santana. Rolie, Valory and Smith were members of Journey. Chalfant was a member of 707.

STORM, Billy
Born William Jones on 6/29/1938 in Dayton, Ohio. Lead singer of the R&B vocal group The Valiants.

STORM, Gale
Born Josephine Cottle on 4/5/1922 in Bloomington, Texas. Pop singer/actress. Starred in several movie musicals. Star of TV's *My Little Margie* (1952-55) and *The Gale Storm Show* (1956-62).

STORM, Warren
Born Warren Schexnider on 2/18/1937 in Abbeville, Louisiana. Swamp-pop singer/drummer.

STOTT, Lally
Born Harold Stott in Liverpool, England. Died in a bike accident in 1977. Pop singer/songwriter.

STRAIT, George
Born on 5/18/1952 in Poteet, Texas; raised in Pearsall, Texas. Country singer. Starred in the movie *Pure Country*.

STRANGE, Billy
Born on 9/29/1930 in Long Beach, California. Session guitarist.

STRANGELOVES, The
Writers/producers Bob Feldman, Jerry Goldstein and Richard Gottehrer. Team wrote/produced The Angels' "My Boyfriend's Back," produced The McCoys' "Hang On Sloopy" and The Sheep. Gottehrer became a partner in Sire Records and produced the Go-Go's' first two albums and Blondie's debut album.

STRANGERS, The
Rock and roll instrumental group from San Diego, California: Joel Scott Hill (lead guitar), Harold Kirby, Ron Lynch and John Collard. Hill joined Canned Heat in 1972.

STRAWBERRY ALARM CLOCK
Psychedelic-rock band formed in Glendale, California: Ed King (lead guitar), Mark Weitz (keyboards), Lee Freeman (guitar), Gary Lovetro (bass), George Bunnel (bass) and Randy Seol (drums). King joined Lynyrd Skynyrd, 1973-75. Originally known as Thee Sixpence.

STRAY CATS
Rockabilly trio from Long Island, New York: Brian Setzer (vocals, guitar; born on 4/10/1959), Lee Rocker (string bass; born Leon Drucher) and Slim Jim Phantom (drums; born Jim McDonnell). Recorded two albums in Britain in 1981 and 1982. Disbanded in 1984. Phantom and Rocker formed trio Phantom, Rocker & Slick in 1985. Setzer portrayed Eddie Cochran in the movie *La Bamba*. Phantom portrayed Charlie Parker's drummer in the movie *Bird*, 1984-93. Band reunited in 1988. Setzer formed own "jump" orchestra in 1998.

STREEK
Pop group from Los Angeles, California: Ron Abrams (guitar), Billy DeMartines (keyboards), Daniel Ricciardelli (sax), Randy Oviedo (bass) and Guivanni Bartoletto (drums).

STREET, Janey
Born in Manhattan, New York. Pop-rock singer/songwriter.

STREET PEOPLE
Studio group featuring Rupert Holmes.

STREETS
Rock group formed in Atlanta, Georgia: Steve Walsh (vocals, keyboards), Mike Slamer (guitar), Billy Greer (bass) and Tim Gehrt (drums). Walsh was co-founder of Kansas.

STREISAND, Barbra
Born Barbara Joan Streisand on 4/24/1942 in Brooklyn, New York. Made Broadway debut in *I Can Get It For You Wholesale*, 1962. Lead role in Broadway's *Funny Girl*, 1964. Movie debut in *Funny Girl* in 1968 (tied with Katharine Hepburn for Best Actress Oscar); also starred in *A Star Is Born*, *Hello Dolly*, *Funny Lady*, *The Way We Were* and many others. Produced/directed/starred in the movies *Yentl* and *Prince Of Tides*. Married to actor Elliott Gould from 1963-71. Married actor James Brolin on 7/2/1998.

STRING-A-LONGS, The
Guitar rock and roll instrumental group from Plainview, Texas: Keith McCormack, Aubrey Lee de Cordova, Richard Stephens and Jimmy Torres (guitars) and Don Allen (drums).

STROKES, The
Rock band from Manhattan, New York: Julian Casablancas (vocals), Albert Hammond Jr. (son of Albert Hammond) and Nick Valensi (guitars), Nikolai Fraiture (bass) and Fab Moretti (drums).

STROLLERS, The
R&B vocal group.

STRONG, Barrett
Born on 2/5/1941 in Mississippi. R&B singer/songwriter. Wrote many of The Temptations' hits with Norman Whitfield. Also wrote Marvin Gaye's "I Heard It Through The Grapevine."

STRUNK, Jud
Born Justin Strunk on 6/11/1936 in Jamestown, New York; raised in Farmington, Maine. Killed in a plane crash on 10/15/1981 (age 45). Regular on TV's *Laugh In*.

STRYPER
Christian heavy-metal band from Orange County, California: brothers Michael (vocals) and Robert (drums) Sweet, with Oz Fox (guitar; born Richard Martinez) and Tim Gaines (bass; born Tim Hagelganz). Michael Sweet left in mid-1992.

STUART, Marty
Born John Marty Stuart on 9/30/1958 in Philadelphia, Mississippi. Country singer/songwriter/guitarist. Toured with Lester Flatt (Flatt & Scruggs) and Nashville Grass from age 13. Toured with the Johnny Cash Band from 1979-85. Once married to Cash's daughter Cindy. Married Connie Smith on 7/8/1997.

STUCKEY, Nat
Born Nathan Stuckey on 12/17/1933 in Cass County, Texas. Died of cancer on 8/24/1988 (age 54). Country singer/songwriter/guitarist.

STUDDARD, Ruben
Born on 7/14/1978 in Frankfurt, Germany (U.S. Army base); raised in Birmingham, Alabama. Black male vocalist. Winner on the 2003 season of TV's *American Idol*.

STUDIO ALL-STARS
Band of anonymous studio musicians.

STYLE COUNCIL, The
Techno-pop duo from England: Paul Weller (vocals) and Mick Talbot (keyboards).

STYLERS, The
White pop vocal trio from Brooklyn, New York: Harry Boorows, brothers Tony (died of a heart attack in 1975) and Louis Colombo.

STYLES
Born David Styles on 11/28/1974 in Corona, Queens, New York. Male rapper. Former member of The Lox.

STYLISTICS, The
R&B vocal group from Philadelphia, Pennsylvania: Russell Thompkins, Jr. (lead; born on 3/21/1951), Airrion Love (born on 8/8/1949), James Smith (born on 6/16/1950), James Dunn (born on 2/4/1950) and Herbie Murrell (born on 4/27/1949). Thompkins, Love and Smith sang with the Percussions; Murrell and Dunn with the Monarchs from 1965-68. First recorded for Sebring in 1969.

STYX
Pop-rock group from Chicago, Illinois: Dennis DeYoung (vocals, keyboards; born on 2/18/1947), Tommy Shaw (lead guitar; born on 9/11/1953), James Young (guitar; born on 11/14/1949), and twin brothers John (drums) and Chuck (bass) Panozzo (born on 9/20/1948). Band earlier known as TW4. Shaw replaced John Curulewski in 1976. Most songs written by Dennis DeYoung and/or Tommy Shaw. Band broke up when DeYoung and Shaw went solo in 1984. Reunited in 1990 with guitarist Glen Burtnick replacing Shaw, who joined Damn Yankees. John Panozzo died on 7/16/1996 (age 47). In Greek mythology, Styx is a river in Hades.

SUAVE'
Born Waymond Anderson Jr. on 2/22/1966 in Los Angeles, California. R&B singer. Son of Waymond Anderson (of GQ).

SUBLIME
Ska-rock trio from Long Beach, California: Brad Nowell (vocals, guitar), Eric Wilson (bass) and Bud Gaugh (drums). Nowell died of a drug overdose on 5/25/96 (age 28).

SUBWAY
Black teen vocal group from Chicago, Illinois: Eric McNeal, Roy Jones, Keith Thomas and Trerail Puckett.

SUDDEN CHANGE
Female R&B trio from New Jersey: Linne Mondestin, Jessie Mondestin and Katia Pinard.

SUGABABES
Female pop vocal trio from England: Keisha Buchanan, Mutya "Rosa" Buena and Heidi Range.

SUGA FREE
Born in Oakland, California; raised in Compton, California. Male rapper.

SUGAR BEARS
Pop studio production by Jimmy Bowen. Kim Carnes wrote and performed vocals for the group. Based on General Foods' "Sugar Crisp" cereal character.

SUGARHILL GANG
Rap trio from Harlem, New York: Michael "Wonder Mike" Wright, Guy "Master Gee" O'Brien and Henry "Big Bank Hank" Jackson. The first commercially successful hip-hop/rap group.

SUGARLAND
Country trio from Atlanta, Georgia: Jennifer Nettles (vocals), Kristen Hall (guitar) and Kristian Bush (mandolin). Hall left trio in early 2006.

SUGARLOAF
Rock group from Denver, Colorado: Jerry Corbetta (vocals, keyboards), Bob Webber (guitar), Bob Raymond (bass) and Bob MacVittie (drums). Robert Yeazel (guitar, vocals) joined in 1971. By 1974, Myron Pollock replaced MacVittie, and Yeazel had left.

SUGAR RAY
Rock group from Los Angeles, California: Mark McGrath (vocals; born on 3/15/1968), Craig Bullock (DJ; born on 12/17/1970), Rodney Sheppard (guitar; born on 11/25/1967), Murphy Karges (bass; born on 6/20/1967) and Stan Frazier (drums; born on 4/23/1968). McGrath became anchor of TV entertainment magazine *Extra* in 2004.

SULLIVAN, Jazmine
Born on 4/9/1987 in Philadelphia, Pennsylvania. R&B singer/songwriter.

SUM 41
Punk-rock group from Ajax, Ontario, Canada: Deryck Whibley (vocals, guitar), Dave Baksh (guitar), Cone McCaslin (bass) and Steve Jocz (drums). Whibley married Avril Lavigne on 7/15/2006.

SUMMER, Donna
Born LaDonna Andrea Gaines on 12/31/1948 in Boston, Massachusetts. "The Queen of Disco." With group Crow, played local clubs. In German production of *Hair*, European productions of *Godspell*, *The Me Nobody Knows* and *Porgy And Bess*. Settled in Germany, where she recorded "Love To Love You Baby." In the movie *Thank God It's Friday* in 1978. Married Bruce Sudano (Alive And Kicking, Brooklyn Dreams) on 7/16/1980.

SUMMER, Henry Lee
Born on 7/5/1955 in Brazil, Indiana. Rock singer/songwriter/guitarist.

SUMMERS, Bill
Born in Detroit, Michigan. R&B singer/songwriter/percussionist. Plays several different percussion instruments. Member of Herbie Hancock's group. Also did session work for Quincy Jones.

SUN
Soul-funk group from Dayton, Ohio: Byron Byrd (vocals), Sheldon Reynolds and Anthony Thompson (guitars), Dean Francis (keyboards), Ernie Knisley (percussion), Robert Arnold, Gary King and Larry Hatchet (horns), Don Taylor (bass), and Robert "Mitch" Kinney (drums).

SUN, Joe
Born James Joseph Paulson on 9/25/1943 in Rochester, Minnesota. Country singer. Began as a DJ. Later became promo man for Ovation Records, which led to recording career.

SUNDAY
Female R&B vocal group from Newark, New Jersey: sisters Tawanda, Notasha and Tiffany, with cousins Shakira and Stacey.

SUNDAYS, The
Pop-rock group from London, England: Harriet Wheeler (vocals), David Gavurin (guitar), Paul Brindley (bass) and Patrick Hannan (drums).

SUNDOWN COMPANY
Male-female studio group produced by Joe Beck.

SUNNY & THE SUNGLOWS
Latin group from San Antonio, Texas: Sunny Ozuna, with brothers Jesse, Oscar and Ray Villanueva, Tony Tostado, Gilbert Fernandez and Alfred Luna.

SUNNYSIDERS, The
Vocal group formed in New York: Freddy Morgan (banjo), Norman Milkin, Jad Paul and Margie Rayburn. Morgan and Paul were members of Spike Jones & The City Slickers from 1947-58. Morgan died of a heart attack on 12/21/1970 (age 60). Rayburn died of a heart attack on 6/14/2000 (age 76).

SUNRAYS, The
Rock and roll band from California: Rick Henn, Marty DiGiovanni, Byron Case, Eddy Medora and Vince Hozier. Produced by Murry Wilson (father and producer of The Beach Boys). Medora died on 10/27/2006 (age 60). Hozier died on 3/18/2007 (age 61).

SUNSCREEM
Techno-pop group from Essex, England: Lucia Holm (vocals), Darren Woodford (guitar), Paul Carnell (keyboards), Rob Fricker (bass) and Sean Wright (drums).

SUNSHINE COMPANY, The
Pop group formed in Los Angeles, California: Mary Nance (vocals), Douglas "Red" Mark and Maury Manseau (guitars), Larry Sims (bass) and Merle Brigante (drums). Mark later formed Redeye.

SUPERBS, The
R&B vocal group from Los Angeles, California: Eleanor Green, Bobby Swayne, Ronnie Cook, Gordy Harmon and Walter White. Harmon later joined The Whispers. Eleanor later married pro baseball player Rudy May.

SUPER CAT
Born William Maragh on 6/25/1963 in Kingston, Jamaica (of East Indian heritage). Dance-hall/hip-hop/reggae singer.

SUPERDRAG
Rock group from Knoxville, Tennessee: John Davis (vocals), Brandon Fisher (guitar), Tom Pappas (bass) and Don Coffey Jr. (drums).

SUPERTRAMP
Rock group formed in England: Roger Hodgson (vocals, guitar; born on 3/21/1950), Rick Davies (vocals, keyboards; born on 7/22/1944), John Helliwell (sax; born on 2/15/1945), Dougie Thomson (bass; born on 3/24/1951; older brother of Ali Thomson) and Bob Siebenberg (drums). Hodgson went solo in 1983. Band formed in 1969 and took band name from a 1938 book by W.H. Davies, *The Autobiography Of A Supertramp*.

SUPREMES, The
R&B vocal group from Detroit, Michigan: lead singer Diana Ross (born on 3/26/1944), Mary Wilson (born on 3/6/1944), Florence Ballard (born on 6/30/1943; died of cardiac arrest on 2/22/1976, age 32) and Barbara Martin. Formed as the Primettes in 1959. Recorded for LuPine in 1960. Signed to Motown's Tamla label in 1960. Changed name to The Supremes in 1961; Martin left shortly thereafter. Worked as backing vocalists for Motown until 1964. Backed Marvin Gaye on "Can I Get A Witness" and "You're A Wonderful One." Ballard discharged from group in 1967; replaced by Cindy Birdsong, formerly with Patti LaBelle's Blue Belles. Ross left in 1969 for solo career; replaced by Jean Terrell. Birdsong left in 1972; replaced by Lynda Laurence. Terrell and Laurence left in 1973. Mary Wilson re-formed group with Scherrie Payne (sister of Freda Payne) and Cindy Birdsong. Birdsong left again in 1976; replaced by Susaye Greene. In 1978, Wilson toured England with Karen Ragland and Karen Jackson, but lost rights to the name "Supremes" thereafter. Diana Ross, Scherrie Payne and Lynda Laurence reunited in 2000 for a concert tour.

SURFACE
R&B trio from New Jersey: Bernard Jackson (vocals), David Townsend (guitar, keyboards; son of producer/songwriter Ed Townsend) and Dave Conley (bass, sax; former horn player with Mandrill). Townsend died on 10/26/2005 (age 50).

SURFARIS, The
Teen rock and roll-surf band from Glendora, California: Ron Wilson (drummer), Jim Fuller (lead guitar), Bob Berryhill (rhythm guitar), Pat Connolly (bass) and Jim Pash (sax, clarinet). Wilson was with The New Establishment in 1969. Wilson died of a brain aneurysm on 5/19/1989 (age 44).

SURVIVOR
Pop-rock group formed in Chicago, Illinois: Dave Bickler (vocals; former lead singer of Jamestown Massacre), Frankie Sullivan (guitar), Jim Peterik (keyboards; born on 11/11/1950; former lead singer of Ides Of March), Stephan Ellis (bass) and Marc Droubay (drums). Bickler replaced by Jimi Jamison in early 1984. Droubay and Ellis left in early 1988.

SUTHERLAND BROTHERS & QUIVER
Rock and roll group formed in England: brothers Iain (vocals, guitar) and Gavin (vocals, bass) Sutherland, with their four-piece group Quiver: Tim Renwick (guitar), Pete Wood (keyboards), Bruce Thomas (bass) and Willie Wilson (drums; Cochise). Quiver disbanded in 1977 and Thomas joined Elvis Costello's Attractions.

SUTTON, Glenn
Born Royce Glenn Sutton on 9/28/1937 in Hodge, Louisiana; raised in Henderson, Texas. Died of a heart attack on 4/17/2007 (age 69). Country singer/songwriter. Married to Lynn Anderson from 1968-77.

SWALLOWS, The
R&B group from Baltimore, Maryland. Signed to King Records in 1951. Members in 1958: Calvin Rowlette (lead singer), Eddie Rich, Money Johnson,

Earl Hurley, "Buddy" Crawford and Buddy Bailey. Bobby Hendricks (The Drifters) was briefly a member in 1956.

SWAN, Billy
Born on 5/12/1942 in Cape Girardeau, Missouri. Pop-country singer/songwriter/keyboardist/guitarist. Wrote "Lover Please" for Clyde McPhatter. Produced Tony Joe White's first three albums. Toured with Kris Kristofferson from the early 1970s. Formed band Black Tie with Randy Meisner in 1986.

SWANN, Bettye
Born Betty Champion on 10/24/1944 in Shreveport, Louisiana. R&B singer.

SWANS, The
"Girl group." Backing vocalists for The Sapphires.

SWAYZE, Patrick
Born on 8/18/1952 in Houston, Texas. Movie actor. Starred in *Red Dawn*, *Dirty Dancing*, *Road House*, *Ghost* and many others.

SWEAT, Keith
Born on 7/22/1961 in Harlem, New York. R&B singer/songwriter. Worked as a brokerage assistant on Wall Street. Also see LSG.

SWEATHOG
Rock group: Lenny Goldsmith (vocals, keyboards), Bob Morris (guitar), Dave Johnson (bass) and Barry Frost (drums).

SWEENEY TODD
Canadian rock band founded by James McCulloch (guitar) and Nick Gilder (vocal), who was replaced by Bryan Adams in mid-1976. Gilder and Adams later scored as solo artists. Group named after the 19th century "Demon Barber of Fleet Street."

SWEET
Rock and roll band formed in England: Brian Connolly (vocals; born on 10/5/1945), Andy Scott (guitar, keyboards; born on 7/30/1949), Steve Priest (bass; born on 2/23/1950) and Mick Tucker (drums; born on 7/17/1947). Connolly died of liver failure on 2/9/1997 (age 51). Tucker died of leukemia on 2/14/2002 (age 54).

SWEET, Matthew
Born on 10/6/1964 in Lincoln, Nebraska. Pop-rock bassist/drummer/singer. Toured as guitarist with Lloyd Cole.

SWEET, Rachel
Born on 7/28/1962 in Akron, Ohio. Pop singer/actress.

SWEETBOX
Dance duo: German producer Geo and Maryland-born singer Tina Harris.

SWEET DREAMS
Soul-reggae duo from England: Polly Brown and Tony Jackson. Brown was lead singer of Pickettywitch.

SWEET INSPIRATIONS, The
R&B vocal group: Cissy Houston, Estelle Brown, Sylvia Shemwell and Myrna Smith. Spent nearly six years as a studio group, primarily for Atlantic. Work included backing Aretha Franklin and Elvis Presley. Houston, mother of Whitney Houston and aunt of Dionne Warwick, recorded solo in 1970.

SWEET SABLE
Born Ceybil Jeffries in Brooklyn, New York. Female R&B singer.

SWEET SENSATION
Soul group from Manchester, England: Marcel King (lead vocals), St. Clair Palmer, Vincent James and Junior Daye (backing vocals), Garry Shaughnessy (guitar), Leroy Smith (keyboards), Barry Johnson (bass) and Roy Flowers (drums).

SWEET SENSATION
Female dance trio from the Bronx, New York: Betty LeBron, and sisters Margie and Mari Fernandez. Sheila Bega replaced Mari in 1989.

SWIFT, Taylor
Born on 12/13/1989 in Reading, Pennsylvania. Female teen country singer/songwriter/guitarist.

SWINGING BLUE JEANS, The
Rock and roll group from Liverpool, England: Ray Ennis (vocals, guitar), Ralph Ellis (guitar), Les Braid (bass) and Norman Kuhlke (drums). Braid died of cancer on 7/31/2005 (age 64).

SWINGIN' MEDALLIONS
Rock and roll group from Greenwood, South Carolina: John McElrath (vocals), Jimbo Dores (guitar), Brent Fortson (organ), Carroll Bledsoe, Charlie Webber and Steven Caldwell (horns), Jim Perkins (bass) and Joe Morris (drums). Fortson and Caldwell formed Pieces Of Eight. Caldwell died of cancer on 1/28/2002 (age 54). Webber died of cancer on 1/17/2003 (age 57).

SWING OUT SISTER
Pop-dance trio formed in England: Corinne Drewery (vocals), Andy Connell and Martin Jackson. Drewery was a fashion designer. Reduced to a duo in 1989 with the departure of Jackson.

SWIRL 360
Rock duo of twin brothers from Jacksonville, Florida: Denny and Kenny Scott.

SWITCH
Soul-funk group from Mansfield, Ohio: Philip Ingram (vocals), brothers Bobby (keyboards) and Tommy (bass) DeBarge, Greg Williams and Eddie Fluellen (horns), and Jody Sims (drums). Discovered by Jermaine Jackson. The DeBarges are brothers to the family group DeBarge. Bobby DeBarge died of AIDS on 8/16/1995 (age 36).

SWITCHFOOT
Christian rock group from San Diego, California: brothers Jon Foreman (vocals, guitar) and Tim Foreman (bass), with Jerome Fontamillas (keyboards) and Chad Butler (drums).

SWIZZ BEATZ
Born Kasseem Dean in the Bronx, New York; raised in Atlanta, Georgia. Male rap producer. Member of Ruff Ryders.

SWV (Sisters With Voices)
Female R&B vocal trio from Brooklyn, New York: Cheryl "Coko" Gamble, Tamara "Taj" Johnson and Leanne "Lelee" Lyons.

SYBIL
Born Sybil Lynch in Paterson, New Jersey. R&B singer/songwriter.

SYLK-E. FYNE
Born in Los Angeles, California. Female rapper.

SYLVERS, Foster
Born on 2/25/1962 in Memphis, Tennessee. R&B singer. Member of The Sylvers.

SYLVERS, The
Family group of 9 brothers and sisters from Memphis, Tennessee: Olympia-Ann, Leon, Charmaine, James, Edmund, Ricky, Angelia, Pat and Foster Sylvers. Leon formed the group Dynasty in 1979. Edmund died of lung cancer on 3/11/2004 (age 47).

SYLVESTER
Born Sylvester James on 9/6/1947 in Los Angeles, California. Died of AIDS on 12/16/1988 (age 41). Male disco singer/songwriter. To San Francisco in 1967. With vocal group the Cockettes. In movie *The Rose*. Backing vocals by Martha Wash and Izora Rhodes (later known as Two Tons O' Fun and The Weather Girls) and Jeanie Tracy.

SYLVIA
Born Sylvia Vanderpool on 3/6/1936 in Harlem, New York. R&B-disco singer/songwriter/producer. First recorded with Hot Lips Page for Columbia in 1950 as Little Sylvia. One-half of Mickey & Sylvia duo. Married Joe Robinson, owner of All-Platinum/ Vibration Records (later known as Sugar Hill). Their son Joey was leader of West Street Mob.

SYLVIA
Born Sylvia Kirby on 12/9/1956 in Kokomo, Indiana. Country singer/songwriter.

SYMS, Sylvia
Born on 12/2/1917 in Brooklyn, New York. Died of a heart attack on 5/10/1992 (age 74). Singer/actress. Dubbed the "world's greatest saloon singer" by Frank Sinatra. Discovered by actress Mae West in 1948. Star of several musical comedies.

SYNCH
Pop-rock group from Wilkes-Barre, Pennsylvania: Jimmy Harnen (vocals), brothers Bill (keyboards) and Rich (drums) Kossuth, Jon Lorance (guitar), Chuck Yarmey (keyboards) and Mike Warner (bass).

SYNDICATE OF SOUND
Garage-rock band from San Jose, California: Don Baskin (vocals), Jim Sawyers and John Sharkey (guitars), Bob Gonzalez (bass) and John Duckworth (drums).

SYSTEM, The
Techno-funk-dance duo based in New York: Mic Murphy (vocals, guitar; born in Raleigh, North Carolina) and David Frank (synthesizer; born in Dayton, Ohio).

SYSTEM OF A DOWN
Alternative-metal rock band from Los Angeles, California: Serj Tankian (vocals; born on 8/21/1967), Daron Malakian (guitar; born on 7/18/1975), Shavo Odadjian (bass; born on 4/22/1974) and John Dolmayan (drums; born on 7/15/1973).

TACO
Born Taco Ockerse on 7/21/1955 in Jakarta, Indonesia (to Dutch parents). German-based techno-pop singer.

TAG
Pop duo from Penzance, England: Treana Morris (lead singer) and Gareth Young. Tag is an acronym of Treana And Gareth.

TAG TEAM
Hip-hop duo from Atlanta, Georgia: Cecil Glenn ("DC, The Brain Supreme") and Steve Gibson ("Steve Roll'n"). High school classmates in Denver, Colorado.

TAKE THAT
"Boy band" from England: Gary Barlow (lead; born on 1/20/1971), Howard Donald, Jason Orange, Mark Owen and Robbie Williams (left in early 1995). Disbanded in February 1996.

TAKING BACK SUNDAY
Rock band from Amityville, Long Island, New York: Adam Lazzara (vocals), Eddie Reyes (guitar), Fred Mascherino (guitar), Matt Rubano (bass) and Mark O'Connell (drums).

TALKING HEADS
New-wave/rock band formed in New York: David Byrne (vocals, guitar), Jerry Harrison (keyboards, guitar), Tina Weymouth (bass) and Chris Frantz (drums). Formed as a trio of Byrne, Weymouth and Frantz at the Rhode Island School of Design in 1974. Harrison, earlier of The Modern Lovers, joined in 1977; Weymouth and Frantz married on 6/18/1977. Weymouth and Frantz also formed Tom Tom Club. Much production work of other artists by each member. Disbanded in late 1991. Harrison, Weymouth and Frantz reunited in 1996.

TALK TALK
Techno-rock/dance group from England: Mark Hollis (vocals), Simon Brenner (keyboards), Paul Webb (bass) and Lee Harris (drums). Brenner left in 1983.

TAMAR
Born Tamar (pronounced tay-mar) Braxton in Severn, Maryland. Female R&B singer. Sister of Toni Braxton.

TA MARA & THE SEEN
Dance group from Minneapolis, Minnesota: Margaret "Ta Mara" Cox (vocals), Oliver Leiber (guitar), Gina Fellicetta (keyboards), Keith Woodson (bass) and Jamie Chez (drums). Leiber is the son of songwriter Jerry Leiber (of Leiber & Stoller).

TAMIA
Born Tamia Washington on 5/9/1975 in Windsor, Ontario, Canada. Female R&B singer.

TAMI SHOW
Pop group formed in Chicago, Illinois: sisters Cathy and Claire Massey (vocals), Tommy Gawenda (guitar), George McCrae (keyboards), Mark Jiaras (bass) and Ken Harck (drums). The *T.A.M.I. Show* is a 1964 movie of a superstar concert in Santa Monica, California.

TAMS, The
R&B "beach music" group from Atlanta, Georgia: brothers Charles and Joseph (lead singer) Pope, with Robert Smith, Floyd Ashton and Horace Key. First recorded for Swan in 1960. Joseph Pope died on 3/16/1996 (age 63).

TANEGA, Norma
Born on 1/30/1939 in Vallejo, California. White pop-folk singer/songwriter/pianist/guitarist.

TANGIER
Hard-rock group from Philadelphia, Pennsylvania: Bill Mattson (vocals), Doug Gordon and Gari Saint (guitars), Garry Nutt (bass) and Bobby Bender (drums).

TANK
Born Durrell Babbs in Milwaukee, Wisconsin. Male R&B singer/songwriter.

TANKIAN, Serj
Born on 8/21/1967 in Beirut, Lebanon; later based in Los Angeles, California. Lead singer of System Of A Down.

TANNER, Gary
Born in New York. Pop singer/songwriter.

TANNER, Marc, Band
Born on 8/20/1952 in Hollywood, California. Pop-rock singer/songwriter/guitarist.

TANTO METRO & DEVONTE
Reggae duo: DJ Tanto Metro was born Mark Wolfe in Kingston, Jamaica; Devonte is a male singer from Jamaica.

TARNEY/SPENCER BAND, The
Pop-rock duo from Australia: Alan Tarney (vocals, guitar, keyboards) and Trevor Spencer (drums).

TARRIERS, The
Folk trio: Erik Darling (tenor, banjo), Bob Carey (bass, guitar) and future movie actor Alan Arkin (baritone, guitar). Darling replaced Pete Seeger in The Weavers, 1958-62, then formed The Rooftop Singers. Darling died on 8/2/2008 (age 74).

TASSELS, The
White doo-wop group from New Jersey: John and sister Rochelle Gaudet (lead singer), Leo Joyce and Joe Intelisano.

TASTE OF HONEY, A
Disco group from Los Angeles, California: Janice Johnson (vocals, guitar), Hazel Payne (vocals, bass), Perry Kibble (keyboards) and Donald Johnson (drums). Re-formed in 1980 as a duo:

TASTE OF HONEY, A — cont'd
Janice Johnson and Payne. Kibble died of heart failure in February 1999 (age 49).

TATE, Howard
Born on 8/14/1939 in Macon, Georgia; raised in Philadelphia, Pennsylvania. R&B singer. Before going solo, sang with The Bill Doggett Band and The Gainors (founded by Garnet Mimms).

t.A.T.u.
Female teen dance-rock duo from Moscow, Russia: Julia Volkova and Lena Katina.

TAVARES
Family R&B-disco vocal group from New Bedford, Massachusetts. Consisted of brothers Ralph (born on 12/10/1941), Antone "Chubby" (born on 6/2/1945), Feliciano "Butch" (born on 5/18/1948), Arthur "Pooch" (born on 11/12/1943) and Perry Lee "Tiny" (born on 10/24/1949) Tavares. Worked as Chubby & The Turnpikes from 1964-69. Butch was married to actress/singer Lola Falana.

TAYLOR, Andy
Born on 2/16/1961 in Cullercoats, England; raised in Wolverhampton, England. Lead guitarist of Duran Duran and The Power Station.

TAYLOR, B.E., Group
Born William (Bill) Edward Taylor in 1954 in Aliquippa, Pennsylvania. Rock singer/songwriter/guitarist.

TAYLOR, Bobby, & The Vancouvers
Interracial R&B band based in Vancouver, British Columbia, Canada: Bobby Taylor (vocals), Thomas Chong (guitar; of Cheech & Chong), Edward Patterson (guitar), Robbie King (keyboards), Wes Henderson (bass) and Ted Lewis (drums). Jimi Hendrix played guitar for the group in 1963. Bobby Taylor discovered The Jackson 5. King died of cancer on 9/17/2003 (age 56).

TAYLOR, Debbie
Born in Memphis, Tennessee. Female R&B singer.

TAYLOR, Felice
Born on 1/29/1948 in Richmond, California. Female R&B singer.

TAYLOR, Gloria
R&B singer/songwriter.

TAYLOR, James
Born on 3/12/1948 in Boston, Massachusetts. Soft-rock singer/songwriter/guitarist. With older brother Alex in the Fabulous Corsairs in 1964. In New York group The Flying Machine in 1967, with friend Danny Kortchmar. Moved to England in 1968, recorded for Peter Asher. Married to Carly Simon from 1972-83. In movie *Two Lane Blacktop* with Dennis Wilson in 1973. Sister Kate Taylor and brothers Alex (died on 3/12/1993) and Livingston Taylor also recorded. Their father, Isaac, was the dean of the University of North Carolina medical school until 1971.

TAYLOR, John
Born on 6/20/1960 in Birmingham, England. Bass guitarist of Duran Duran and The Power Station.

TAYLOR, Johnnie
Born on 5/5/1938 in Crawfordsville, Arkansas. Died of a heart attack on 5/31/2000 (age 62). Soul singer. With gospel group the Highway QC's in Chicago, early 1950s. In vocal group The Five Echoes, recorded for Sabre in 1954. In the Soul Stirrers gospel group before going solo. First solo recording for SAR in 1961. Known as The Soul Philosopher.

TAYLOR, Kate
Born on 8/15/1949 in Boston, Massachusetts. Singer/songwriter/guitarist. Younger sister of James Taylor.

TAYLOR, Ko Ko
Born Cora Walton on 9/28/1935 in Memphis, Tennessee. Female blues singer.

TAYLOR, Little Johnny
Born Johnny Merrett on 2/11/1943 in Gregory, Arkansas; raised in Memphis, Tennessee and Los Angeles, California. Died of diabetes on 5/17/2002 (age 59). Blues singer/songwriter/harmonica player. With Mighty Clouds Of Joy and Stars Of Bethel gospel groups. Duets with Ted Taylor (no relation) in the 1970s.

TAYLOR, Livingston
Born on 11/21/1950 in Boston, Massachusetts. Singer/songwriter/guitarist. Younger brother of James Taylor. Hosted TV's *This Week's Music* in 1984.

TAYLOR, R. Dean
Born in 1939 in Toronto, Ontario, Canada. Pop singer/songwriter. First recorded for Barry in 1960. Co-wrote The Supremes' hit "Love Child" and The Temptations' hit "All I Need."

TAYLOR, Ted
Born Austin Taylor on 2/16/1934 in Okmulgee, Oklahoma. Died in a car accident on 11/22/1987 (age 53). R&B singer/songwriter. Formerly with Glory Bound Travellers and Mighty Clouds Of Joy gospel groups, and with The Cadets/The Jacks.

T-BONES, The
A Joe Saraceno studio production. Also see Current; Hamilton, Joe Frank & Reynolds; The Routers and Tony And Joe.

T-BOZ
Born Tionne Watkins on 4/26/1970 in Des Moines, Iowa; raised in Atlanta. Member of TLC. Married Mack 10 on 8/19/2000.

T-CONNECTION
Black disco group from Nassau, Bahamas: brothers Theo (vocals, keyboards) and Kirk (bass) Coakley, Dave Mackey (guitar) and Tony Flowers (drums).

TEARS FOR FEARS
Synth-pop duo from England: Roland Orzabal (vocals, guitar, keyboards; born on 8/22/1961) and Curt Smith (vocals, bass; born on 6/24/1961). Adopted name from Arthur Janov's book *Prisoners Of Pain* in 1981. Smith left duo by 1992.

TECHNIQUES
White pop vocal group from Georgia: Jim Tinney, Jim Moore, Jim Falin and Buddy Funk. All were students at Georgia Tech University.

TECHNOTRONIC
Techno-dance studio group created by Belgian DJ/producer Thomas DeQuincey (born Jo Bogaert) featuring England-born rapper MC Eric and Zairean rapper Ya Kid K (Hi Tek 3; born Manuela Barbara Kamosi). Non-vocalist Felly, a model from Zaire, fronted the group for videos.

TEDDY & The Twilights
R&B group from Philadelphia, Pennsylvania. Lead vocals by Fred Cohen.

TEDDY BEARS, The
White doo-wop trio from Los Angeles, California: Phil Spector (born on 12/26/1940 in the Bronx, New York), Carol Connors (lead singer; born Annette Kleinbard) and Marshall Leib (born on 1/26/1939). Spector became a superstar writer and producer; owner of Philles Records. He was inducted into the Rock and Roll Hall of Fame in 1989. Connors co-wrote "Gonna Fly Now" (theme from the movie *Rocky*). Leib died of a heart attack on 3/15/2002 (age 63).

TEE, Willie
Born Wilson Turbinton on 2/6/1944 in New Orleans, Louisiana. Died of colon cancer on 9/11/2007 (age 63). R&B singer/pianist.

TEEGARDEN & VAN WINKLE
Rock and roll duo from Tulsa, Oklahoma: David Teegarden (drums) and Skip "Van Winkle" Knape (keyboards). Teegarden was a member of Bob Seger's Silver Bullet Band from 1978-81.

TEEN QUEENS, The
Black teen doo-wop duo from Los Angeles, California: sisters Betty and Rosie Collins. Sisters of Aaron Collins of The Cadets/The Jacks.

TEE SET, The
Pop group from Delft, Netherlands: Peter Tetteroo (vocals), Hans Van Eijck (organ), Dill Bennink (guitar), Franklin Madjid (bass) and Joop Blom (drums). Tetteroo died of cancer on 9/5/2002 (age 55).

TELA
Born Winston Rogers in Memphis, Tennessee. Male rapper.

TELEPOPMUSIK
Dance trio of DJ/producers from France: Fabrice Dumont, Stephan Haeri and Christopher Hetier.

TELEVISION
Punk-rock group from New York: Tom Verlaine (vocals, guitar), Richard Lloyd (guitar), Fred Smith (bass) and Billy Ficca (drums). Ficca later joined The Waitresses. Early member Richard Hell was once married to Patty Smyth.

TEMPO, Nino, & April Stevens
Brother-and-sister duo from Niagara Falls, New York: Nino Tempo (born Antonio Lo Tempio on 1/6/1935) and April Stevens (born Carol Lo Tempio

on 4/29/1936). Prior to teaming up, Nino was a session saxophonist and April had recorded solo.

TEMPOS, The
Pop vocal group from Pittsburgh, Pennsylvania: Mike Lazo, Gene Schachter, Jim Drake and Tom Minoto.

TEMPREES, The
R&B vocal trio: Del Juan Calvin, Harold "Scottie" Scott and Jasper "Jabbo" Phillips. Calvin replaced by William Norvell Johnson in 1972. In the movie *Wattstax* in 1972.

TEMPTATIONS, The
White doo-wop group from Flushing, New York: Neil Stevens, Larry Curtis, Artie Sands and Artie Marin.

TEMPTATIONS, The
R&B vocal group from Detroit, Michigan: Eddie Kendricks (born on 12/17/1939), Paul Williams (born on 7/2/1939), Melvin Franklin (born on 10/12/1942), Otis Williams (born on 10/30/1941; not to be confused with the same-named member of the Charms) and Elbridge Bryant (who was replaced by David Ruffin [born on 1/18/1941] in 1963. Originally called the Primes and Elgins; first recorded for Miracle in 1961. Ruffin (cousin of Billy Stewart) replaced by Dennis Edwards (ex-Contours) in 1968. Kendricks and Paul Williams left in 1971; replaced by Ricky Owens (ex-Vibrations) and Richard Street (The Monitors). Owens was replaced by Damon Harris. Harris left in 1975 to join Impact; replaced by Glenn Leonard. Edwards left group, 1977-79; replaced by Louis Price. Ali Ollie Woodson replaced Edwards from 1984-87. 1988 lineup: Otis Williams, Franklin, Street, Edwards and Ron Tyson. Recognized as America's all-time favorite R&B group. Paul Williams died of a self-inflicted gunshot on 8/17/1973 (age 34). Ruffin died of a drug overdose on 6/1/1991 (age 50). Kendricks died of cancer on 10/5/1992 (age 52). Franklin died of heart failure on 2/23/1995 (age 53). Original member, Otis Williams, still recording with a lineup consisting of Ron Tyson, G.C. Cameron, Terry Weeks and Joe Herndon.

TENACIOUS D
Comedic rock duo: Jack Black (actor; born on 8/28/1969) and Kyle Gass (born on 7/14/1961).

10cc
Art-rock group formed in Manchester, England, that evolved from Hotlegs: Eric Stewart (guitar), Graham Gouldman (bass), Lol Creme (guitar, keyboards; born on 9/19/1947) and Kevin Godley (drums; born on 10/7/1945). Stewart and Gouldman were members of The Mindbenders. Godley & Creme left in 1976; replaced by drummer Paul Burgess. Added members Rick Fenn, Stuart Tosh and Duncan MacKay in 1978. Gouldman later in duo Wax.

TENDER SLIM
Studio project produced and directed by Teddy Vann.

10,000 MANIACS
Alternative-rock group formed in Jamestown, New York: Natalie Merchant (vocals), Robert Buck (guitar), Dennis Drew (keyboards), Steven

10,000 MANIACS — cont'd
Gustafson (bass) and Jerome Augustyniak (drums). Merchant left in August of 1993; replaced by Mary Ramsey. Original member John Lombardo left in 1986; returned in 1996. Buck died of liver failure on 12/19/2000 (age 42).

TEN WHEEL DRIVE With Genya Ravan
Jazz-rock group: Genya Ravan (vocals), Michael Zager (keyboards), Aram Schefrin (guitar), Steve Satten, John Gatchell, Dave Liebman, John Eckert and Dennis Parisi (horns), Bob Piazza (bass) and Allen Herman (drums).

10 YEARS
Hard-rock band from Knoxville, Tennessee: Jesse Hasek (vocals), Ryan "Tater" Johnson (guitar), Matt Wantland (guitar), Lewis "Big Lew" Cosby (bass) and Brian Vodinh (drums).

TEN YEARS AFTER
Blues-rock group formed in Nottingham, England: Alvin Lee (vocals, guitar), Chick Churchill (keyboards), Leo Lyons (bass) and Ric Lee (drums). Alvin Lee was also a top session guitarist.

TEPPER, Robert
Born Antoine Roberto Teppardo in Bayonne, New Jersey. Rock singer/songwriter.

TERRELL, Tammi
Born Thomasina Montgomery on 4/29/1945 in Philadelphia, Pennsylvania. Died of a brain tumor on 3/16/1970 (age 24). R&B singer. First recorded for Wand in 1961. Worked with the James Brown Revue. Tumor diagnosed after collapsing on stage in 1967.

TERROR FABULOUS
Born Cecil Campbell in Kingston, Jamaica. Reggae rapper.

TERROR SQUAD
Rap group formed in the Bronx, New York: Fat Joe, Prospect, Armageddon, Remy Ma and Tony Sunshine.

TERRY, Tony
Born on 3/12/1964 in Pinehurst, North Carolina; raised in Washington DC. R&B-funk singer/songwriter. Former backing vocalist for Sweet Sensation and The Boogie Boys.

TESH, John
Born on 7/9/1952 in Garden City, New York. New Age/Contemporary Christian multi-instrumentalist. Former host of TV's *Entertainment Tonight*. Appeared in the movie *Shocker*. Married actress Connie Sellecca on 4/4/1992.

TESLA
Hard-rock group formed in Sacramento, California: Jeff Keith (vocals), Frank Hannon and Tommy Skeoch (guitars), Brian Wheat (bass) and Troy Luccetta (drums). Band named after the inventor of the alternating current generator, Nikola Tesla.

TEX, Joe
Born Joseph Arrington Jr. on 8/8/1933 in Rogers, Texas. Died of a heart attack on 8/13/1982 (age 49). R&B singer/songwriter. Sang with local gospel groups. Won recording contract during Apollo Theater talent contest in 1954. First recorded for King in 1955. Converted to the Muslim faith; changed name to "Joseph Hazziez" in July 1972. Also see The Soul Clan.

TEXANS, The
Duo is actually brothers Johnny Burnette (guitar) and Dorsey Burnette (upright bass, guitar).

TEXAS
Pop-rock group from Glasgow, Scotland: Sharleen Spiteri (vocals, guitar), Ally McErlaine (guitar), John McElhone (bass) and Stuart Kerr (drums). McElhone was a member of Hipsway and Altered Images. Kerr was an early member of Love And Money.

THALIA
Born Ariadna Thalia Sodi Miranda on 8/26/1971 in Mexico City, Mexico. Female Latin singer. Married record executive Tommy Mottola (former husband of Mariah Carey) on 12/2/2000.

THEE MIDNITERS
Mexican-American rock group from Los Angeles, California: Willie Garcia (vocals), Roy Marquez and George Dominguez (guitars), Ronnie Figueroa (organ), Romeo Prado (trombone), Larry Rendon (sax), Jimmy Espinoza (bass) and George Salazar (drums).

THEE PROPHETS
Pop-rock group from Milwaukee, Wisconsin: Brian Lake (vocals, keyboards), Jim Anderson (guitar), Dave Leslie (bass) and Chris Michaels (drums).

THEM
Rock band from Belfast, Northern Ireland: Van Morrison (vocals), brothers Jackie McAuley (piano) and Pat McAuley (drums), Billy Harrison (guitar), Alan Henderson (bass) and Pete Bardens (keyboards). Disbanded in late 1966.

THEORY OF A DEADMAN
Rock band from Delta, British Columbia, Canada: Tyler Connolly (vocals, guitar), David Brenner (guitar), Dean Back (bass) and Tim Hart (drums).

THEY MIGHT BE GIANTS
Alternative-rock duo from Boston, Massachusetts: John Flansburgh (guitar; born on 5/6/1960) and John Linnell (accordian; born on 6/12/1959). Supported by various musicians. Group named after the 1971 movie starring George C. Scott.

THICKE, Robin
Born on 3/10/1977 in Los Angeles, California. "Blue-eyed soul" singer/songwriter. Son of actress Gloria Loring and actor Alan Thicke.

THINK
Studio group assembled by producers Lou Stallman and Bobby Susser.

THIN LIZZY
Rock group formed in Dublin, Ireland: Phil Lynott (vocals, bass; born on 8/20/1951), Brian Robertson and Scott Gorham (guitars), and Brian Downey (drums). Lynott died on 1/4/1986 (age 34).

3RD BASS
White rappers from Queens, New York: Prime Minister Pete Nice (Pete Nash) and MC Serch (Michael Berrin). Supported by black DJ Richie Rich (Richard Lawson). Disbanded in early 1992. Nash and Lawson continued as the duo Prime Minister Pete Nice and DJ Daddy Rich; Berrin went solo.

THIRD EYE BLIND
Rock group from San Francisco, California: Stephan Jenkins (vocals), Kevin Cadogan (guitar), Arion Salazar (bass) and Brad Hargreaves (drums).

3RD PARTY
Female techno-dance trio: Karmine, Maria Christensen and Elaine Borja.

THIRD RAIL, The
Studio project featuring lead singer Joey Levine (Ohio Express and Reunion).

THIRD WORLD
Reggae fusion band from Jamaica: William "Bunny Rugs" Clarke (vocals), Stephen "Cat" Coore (guitar), Michael "Ibo" Cooper (keyboards), Richard Daley (bass), Willie Stewart (drums) and Irvin "Carrot" Jarrett (percussion). To England and the U.S. from 1975-76. Toured with Stevie Wonder in 1982.

THIRTEENTH FLOOR ELEVATORS, The
Garage-rock band from Austin, Texas: Roky Erickson (vocals), Stacy Sutherland and Tommy Hall (guitars), Dan Galindo (bass) and Danny Thomas (drums). Sutherland was murdered on 8/24/1978 (age 32). Galindo died of liver failure on 5/17/2001 (age 51).

38 SPECIAL
Southern-rock group formed in Jacksonville, Florida: Donnie Van Zant (vocals; born on 6/11/1952; younger brother of Lynyrd Skynyrd's Ronnie Van Zant), Don Barnes (guitar; born on 12/3/1952), Jeff Carlisi (guitar; born on 7/15/1952), Larry Junstrom (bass; born on 6/22/1949), Steve Brookins (drums; born on 6/2/1951) and Jack Grondin (drums; born on 10/3/1951). By 1988, Barnes and Brookins replaced by Danny Chauncey (guitar) and Max Carl (keyboards). Barnes returned in 1992 to replace Carl.

30 SECONDS TO MARS
Rock band formed in Los Angeles, California: brothers Jared Leto (vocals, guitar) and Shannon Leto (drums), with Tomo Milicevic (guitar) and Matt Wachter (bass). Jared Leto is also a popular actor (played "Jordan Catalano" on TV's *My So-Called Life*).

THOMAS, B.J.
Born Billy Joe Thomas on 8/7/1942 in Hugo, Oklahoma; raised in Rosenberg, Texas. Pop-country singer. Joined band, The Triumphs, while in high school. Also recorded gospel music since 1976.

THOMAS, Carl
Born on 6/15/1970 in Aurora, Illinois. R&B singer/ songwriter.

THOMAS, Carla
Born on 12/21/1942 in Memphis, Tennessee. "The Queen of Memphis Soul." Daughter of Rufus Thomas; sister of R&B singer Vaneese Thomas. Sang with the Teentown Singers at age 10. First recorded for Satellite in 1960. Recorded duets with her father, Rufus, and with Otis Redding.

THOMAS, Dante
Born on 1/7/1978 in Salt Lake City, Utah. Pop-R&B singer. Discovered by Pras Michel of The Fugees.

THOMAS, Evelyn
Born on 8/22/1953 in Chicago, Illinois. Disco singer.

THOMAS, Gene
Born on 12/4/1938 in Palestine, Texas. Gene of Gene & Debbe. Writer for Acuff-Rose Music from 1967-72.

THOMAS, Ian
Born in Hamilton, Ontario, Canada. Pop singer/ songwriter. Brother of comedian Dave Thomas ("Doug McKenzie").

THOMAS, Irma
Born Irma Lee on 2/18/1941 in Ponchatoula, Louisiana. R&B singer. Nicknamed "The Soul Queen of New Orleans."

THOMAS, Jamo
Born in Chicago, Illinois. Soul singer/percussionist. Member of the Bobby Peterson Quintet from 1958-62.

THOMAS, Jon
Born on 2/21/1918 in Cincinnati, Ohio. Died on 10/28/1994 (age 76). Blues singer/keyboardist. Staff musician at King Records from 1956-60.

THOMAS, Lillo
Born in Brooklyn, New York. Male R&B singer/ songwriter. World class sprinter. Qualified for the 1984 Olympics but a car crash kept him from competing. Became a popular session singer.

THOMAS, Nolan
Born Mark Kalfa on 8/24/1966 in Jersey City, New Jersey; raised in Edison, New Jersey. R&B singer/ songwriter.

THOMAS, Pat
Born in Chicago, Illinois. Black female pop-jazz vocalist.

THOMAS, Rob
Born on 2/14/1972 in Landstuhl, Germany (U.S. military base); raised in Daytona, Florida. Lead singer of pop-rock group Matchbox Twenty.

THOMAS, Rufus
Born on 3/26/1917 in Cayce, Mississippi; raised in Memphis, Tennessee. Died on 12/15/2001 (age 84). R&B singer/songwriter/choreographer. Father of singers Vaneese and Carla Thomas. First recorded for Star Talent in 1943. DJ at WDIA-Memphis from 1953-74. Recorded for Alligator Records in the late 1980s.

THOMAS, Tasha
Born in 1950 in Jeutyn, Alaska. Died of cancer on 11/8/1984 (age 34). Black disco singer. Moved to New York in 1970. Played "Auntie Em" in Broadway's *The Wiz*. Session singer for Kiss, Cat Stevens, Diana Ross and others.

THOMAS, Timmy
Born on 11/13/1944 in Evansville, Indiana. R&B-disco singer/songwriter/keyboardist. Studio musician at Gold Wax Records in Memphis. Moved to Miami in 1970. Session work for Betty Wright and KC & The Sunshine Band.

THOMPSON, Gina
Born in 1974 in Vineland, New Jersey. R&B singer.

THOMPSON, Hank
Born on 9/3/1925 in Waco, Texas. Died of lung cancer on 11/6/2007 (age 82). Country singer/songwriter.

THOMPSON, Kay
Born on 11/9/1913 in St. Louis, Missouri. Died on 7/2/1998 (age 84). Wrote *Eloise* series of children's books. In the movie musical *Funny Face*, 1957.

THOMPSON, Robbin, Band
Pop-rock group from Virginia: Robbin Thompson (vocals, guitar), Velpo Robertson (guitar), Eric Heiberg (keyboards), Michael Lanning (bass) and Bob Antonelli (drums). Thompson played in Bruce Springsteen's early Steel Mill band.

THOMPSON, Sue
Born Eva Sue McKee on 7/19/1926 in Nevada, Missouri; raised in San Jose, California. Became a popular Country singer in the 1970s.

THOMPSON, Tony
Born on 9/2/1975 in Waco, Texas; raised in Oklahoma City, Oklahoma. Died of a drug overdose on 6/1/2007 (age 31). Lead singer of Hi-Five.

THOMPSON TWINS
Synth-rock/dance trio from England: Tom Bailey (lead singer, synthesizer; born on 1/18/1957), Alannah Currie (xylophone, percussion; born on 9/28/1957; native of New Zealand) and Joe Leeway (conga, synthesizer; born on 11/15/1957). Leeway left in 1986. Bailey and Currie recorded in 1993 as Babble.

THOMSON, Ali
Born in Glasgow, Scotland. Pop singer/songwriter. Younger brother of Supertramp's Dougie Thomson.

THOMSON, Cyndi
Born on 10/19/1976 in Tifton, Georgia. Country singer/songwriter.

THORNE, David
Black Adult Contemporary vocalist.

THORNTON, Willie Mae "Big Mama"
Born on 12/11/1926 in Montgomery, Alabama. Died of a heart attack on 7/25/1984 (age 57). Legendary blues singer.

THOROGOOD, George, & The Destroyers
Born on 12/31/1952 in Wilmington, Delaware. Blues-rock singer/guitarist. The Destroyers: Hank

Carter (sax), Billy Blough (bass) and Jeff Simon (drums).

THORPE, Billy
Born on 3/29/1946 in Manchester, England; raised in Australia. Died of a heart attack on 2/28/2007 (age 60). Rock singer/guitarist. Superstar artist in Australia. Member of Mick Fleetwood's (of Fleetwood Mac) Zoo.

THREE CHUCKLES, The
Pop vocal trio from Brooklyn, New York: Teddy Randazzo (accordion), Tom Romano (guitar) and Russ Gilberto (bass). Appeared in the movies *Rock Rock Rock* and *The Girl Can't Help It*. Randazzo died of a heart attack on 11/21/2003 (age 68).

THREE DAYS GRACE
Hard-rock band from Norwood, Ontario, Canada: Adam Gontier (vocals), Barry Stock (guitar), Brad Walst (bass) and Neil Sanderson (drums).

THREE DEGREES, The
Female R&B vocal trio from Philadelphia, Pennsylvania: Fayette Pinkney, Linda Turner and Shirley Porter. Turner and Porter replaced by Sheila Ferguson and Valerie Holiday in 1966. Discovered by Richard Barrett. Group appeared in the 1971 movie *The French Connection*.

THREE DOG NIGHT
Pop-rock vocal trio formed in Los Angeles, California: Danny Hutton (born on 9/10/1942), Cory Wells (born on 2/5/1942) and Chuck Negron (born on 6/8/1942). Named for the coldest night in the Australian outback. Disbanded in the mid-1970s. Re-formed in the mid-1980s.

3 DOORS DOWN
Rock band from Escatawpa, Mississippi: Brad Arnold (vocals; born on 9/27/1978), Matt Roberts (guitar; born on 1/10/1978), Chris Henderson (guitar; born on 4/30/1971), Todd Harrell (bass; born on 2/13/1972) and Daniel Adair (drums; born on 2/19/1975). Adair left in January 2005 to join Nickelback; replaced by Greg Upchurch (born on 12/1/1971).

311
Rock-funk group from Omaha, Nebraska: Nicholas Hexum and Doug Martinez (vocals), Tim Mahoney (guitar), P-Nut (bass) and Chad Sexton (drums). 311 is the police code for indecent exposure. Pronounced: three eleven.

3 FRIENDS, The
Black doo-wop trio from Compton, California: Julius Brown and brothers Clay and Walter Hammond (The Olympics).

THREE G'S, The
Pop vocal trio from the Los Angeles, California: brothers Ted, Robert and Jerry Glasser.

3LW
Female R&B vocal trio from New Jersey: Naturi Naughton, Kiely Williams and Adrienne Bailon. Williams and Bailon later joined The Cheetah Girls. 3LW: 3 Little Women.

3 MAN ISLAND
Dance trio based in London, England: Tim Cox,
Nigel Swanston and Mike Whitford.

THREE PLAYMATES, The
Female R&B doo-wop trio from Newark, New
Jersey: sisters Lucille and Alma Beatty with Gwen
Brooks. Label credit similar to The Playmates
(Donny-Morey-Chic): The Three Playmates
(Lucille-Alma-Gwen).

THREE 6 MAFIA
Male hip-hop trio from Memphis, Tennessee:
Jordan "Juicy J" Houston, "DJ Paul" Beauregarde
and Ricky "Lord Infamous" Dunigan.

3T
R&B teen vocal trio from Los Angeles, California:
brothers Taryll, T.J. and Taj Jackson. Sons of Tito
Jackson (The Jacksons).

THUNDER
Hard-rock group from England: Daniel Bowes
(vocals), Luke Morley (guitar), Ben Matthews
(keyboards), Mark Luckhurst (bass) and Gary
James (drums).

THUNDER, Johnny
Born Gil Hamilton on 8/15/1941 in Leesburg,
Florida. R&B singer.

THUNDERCLAP NEWMAN
Rock trio formed in England: Andy Newman
(keyboards), John "Speedy" Keene (vocals, drums)
and Jimmy McCulloch (guitarist with Wings,
1975-77). McCulloch died of heart failure on
9/27/1979 (age 26). Keene died on 3/21/2002 (age
56). Group assembled by Pete Townshend.

THUNDERKLOUD, Billy, & The Chieftones
Country group of Native American musicians from
British Columbia, Canada: Vincent "Billy
Thunderkloud" Clifford, Jack Wolf, Barry Littlestar
and Richard Grayowl.

T.I.
Born Clifford Harris on 9/25/1980 in Atlanta,
Georgia. Male rapper/record producer/songwriter/
actor. Starred in the 2006 movie ATL. Co-owner of
the record label Grand Hustle.

TIA
Born in Lynbrook, Long Island, New York. Female
disco singer. Discovered by producer Roy Be
(Ecstasy, Passion & Pain).

TIANA
Born on 5/2/1967 in Vermont. Female dance singer.

TIERRA
Latin group formed in Los Angeles, California:
brothers Steve (trombone, timbales) and Rudy
(guitar) Salas, Joey Guerra (keyboards), Bobby
Navarrete (reeds), Andre Baeza (congas), Steve
Falomir (bass) and Phil Madayag (drums). The
Salas brothers and Baeza were formerly with El
Chicano.

TIFFANY
Born Tiffany Darwish on 10/2/1971 in Norwalk,
California. Teen idol/pop singer.

TIGGI CLAY
Black trio: Debravon "Fizzy Qwick" Lewis (lead
singer), Romeo McCall and Billy Peaches. Fizzy
Qwick hit the R&B charts in 1986.

TIGHT FIT
Studio group assembled by British producer Ken
Gold: Steve Grant, Denise Gyngell, Julie Harris,
Vicki Pemberton, Carol Stevens and Roy Ward.

TILLIS, Mel
Born Lonnie Melvin Tillis on 8/8/1932 in Tampa,
Florida; raised in Pahokee, Florida. Country singer/
songwriter/guitarist/actor. Acted in several movie.
Owned several music publishing companies.
Backing band: The Statesiders. Father of country
singer Pam Tillis. Known for his stuttering speech.

TILLMAN, Bertha
Born in San Diego, California. R&B singer.

TILLOTSON, Johnny
Born on 4/20/1939 in Jacksonville, Florida; raised in
Palatka, Florida. Teen idol pop singer/songwriter.
On local radio Young Folks Revue from age nine.
DJ on WWPF. Appeared on the Toby Dowdy TV
show in Jacksonville, then own show. Signed by
Cadence Records in 1958. In the movie Just For
Fun.

'TIL TUESDAY
Pop-rock group formed in Boston, Massachusetts:
Aimee Mann (vocals, bass), Robert Holmes (guitar),
Joey Pesce (keyboards) and Michael Hausman
(drums). Michael Montes replaced Pesce in 1988.

TIMBALAND & MAGOO
Male hip-hop duo from Norfolk, Virginia. Timbaland
was born Timothy Mosley on 3/10/1971. One of
rap's top producers since the late 1990s. Magoo
was born Melvin Barcliff on 7/12/1973.

TIMBERLAKE, Justin
Born on 1/31/1981 in Memphis, Tennessee.
Member of *NSYNC. Regular on TV's The Mickey
Mouse Club (1992-93). Leader of the teen pop
explosion of the 1990s and 2000s.

TIMBUK 3
Husband-and-wife alternative pop-rock duo from
Austin, Texas: Patrick and Barbara MacDonald. Met
while Barbara was attending the University of
Wisconsin in 1978.

TIME, The
R&B-funk-dance group from Minneapolis,
Minnesota: Morris Day (vocals), Jesse Johnson
(guitar), Jimmy "Jam" Harris and Monte Moir
(keyboards), Terry Lewis (bass) and Jellybean
Johnson (drums). Lewis, Harris and Moir left before
band's featured role in movie Purple Rain. Paul "St.
Paul" Peterson (The Family) and Lewis's
half-brother, Jerome Benton, joined in 1984; group
disbanded later that year. Day and Jesse Johnson
went solo; Lewis and Harris became highly
successful songwriting/producing team. Lewis
married Karyn White. Original lineup plus Benton
regrouped in 1990.

TIMES TWO
White male electro-pop duo of vocalists/keyboardists from Pt. Reyes, California: Shanti Jones and John Dollar.

TIMETONES, The
Interracial doo-wop group from Glen Cove, Long Island, New York: Rodgers LaRue (lead), Glenn Williams, Claude "Sonny" Smith, Tom DeGeorge and Tom Glozek.

TIMEX SOCIAL CLUB
R&B-funk-dance trio from Berkeley, California: Michael Marshall, Marcus Thompson and Alex Hill. Produced by Jay King, who later formed and fronted Club Nouveau.

TIMMY -T-
Born Timmy Torres on 9/21/1967 in Fresno, California. Dance-pop singer/songwriter.

TIM TAM & The Turn-Ons
Doo-wop/rock and roll group formed at Allen Park High in Allen Park, Michigan: Rick "Tim Tam" Wiesend and his brother Dan Wiesend with John Ogen, Don Gunderson, Earl Rennie and Nick Butsicaris. Tim Tam died of leukemia on 10/22/2003 (age 60).

TING TINGS, The
Alternative pop-rock duo from Manchester, England: Katie White and Jules DeMartino.

TIN TIN
Pop duo from Australia: Steve Kipner (keyboards) and Steve Groves (guitar). Disbanded in 1973. Kipner later co-wrote Chicago's "Hard Habit To Break" and Olivia Newton-John's "Physical" and "Twist Of Fate."

TINY TIM
Born Herbert Khaury on 4/12/1930 in Brooklyn, New York. Died of heart failure on 11/30/1996 (age 66). Novelty singer/ukulele player. Shot to national attention with appearances on TV's *Rowan & Martin's Laugh-In*. Married "Miss Vicki" on Johnny Carson's *Tonight Show* on 12/18/1969; divorced in 1977.

TIPPIN, Aaron
Born on 7/3/1958 in Pensacola, Florida; raised in Travelers Rest, South Carolina. Country singer/songwriter.

TISDALE, Ashley
Born on 7/2/1985 in West Deal, New Jersey. Female singer/actress. Played "Sharpay Evans" in the popular TV movie series *High School Musical*.

TITIYO
Born in 1967 in Stockholm, Sweden. Female dance singer. Daughter of percussionist Ahmadu Jah. Pronounced: tee-tee-o.

TJADER, Cal
Born Callen Tjader on 7/16/1925 in St. Louis, Missouri. Died on 5/5/1982 (age 56). Latin jazz vibraphonist.

TKA
Latin disco trio from Harlem, New York: Tony Ortiz, Louis "K7" Sharpe and Ralph Cruz.

TLC
Female R&B trio from Atlanta, Georgia: Tionne "T-Boz" Watkins (born on 4/26/1970), Lisa "Left Eye" Lopes (born on 5/27/1971) and Rozonda "Chilli" Thomas (born on 2/27/1971). Founded and managed by Pebbles. Lopes was sentenced to five years probation for setting fire to the house of her boyfriend Andre Rison, an NFL football player, on 6/9/1994. Group filed for Chapter 11 bankruptcy in 1995. T-Boz married Mack 10 on 8/19/2000. Lopes died in a car crash on 4/25/2002 (age 30).

T.M.G.
Pop-rock group: Ted Mulry (vocals), Gary Dixon (guitar), Les Hall (bass) and Herm Kovac (drums). T.M.G.: Ted Mulry Group.

TOADIES
Rock group from Fort Worth, Texas: Todd Lewis (vocals, guitar), Darrel Herbert (guitar), Lisa Umbarger (bass) and Mark Reznicek (drums).

TOAD THE WET SPROCKET
Alternative-rock group from Santa Barbara, California: Glen Phillips (vocals), Todd Nichols (guitar), Dean Dinning (bass) and Randy Guss (drums). Name taken from a Monty Python skit: "Rock Notes."

TO BE CONTINUED...
Black funk trio from California: M&M Sweet, Spunky D and Wayne-Wayne.

TOBY BEAU
Pop group from Texas: Balde Silva (vocals, harmonica), Danny McKenna (guitar), Ron Rose (banjo), Steve Zipper (bass) and Rob Young (drums). McKenna committed suicide on 4/26/2006 (age 54).

TODAY'S PEOPLE
Pop vocal group from France.

TODD, Art & Dotty
Pop vocal duo from Elizabeth, New Jersey. Art Todd was born on 3/11/1920. Doris "Dotty" Todd was born on 6/22/1913; died on 12/12/2000 (age 87). Married in 1941.

TODD, Nick
Born Nicholas Boone on 6/1/1935 in Jacksonville, Florida. Pop singer. Younger brother of Pat Boone.

T.O.K.
Reggae vocal group from Kingston, Jamaica: Craig Thompson, Alistaire McCalla, Roshaun Clarke and Xavier Davidson. T.O.K.: Touch Of Klass.

TOKENS, The
Vocal group formed in Brooklyn, New York: Hank Medress (born on 11/19/1938; died of lung cancer on 6/18/2007, age 68), Neil Sedaka (born on 3/13/1939), Eddie Rabkin and Cynthia Zolitin. First recorded for Melba in 1956. Rabkin replaced in 1956 by Jay Siegel (born on 10/20/1939). Zolitin and Sedaka left in 1958. Medress then formed Darrell & The Oxfords, 1958-59; then re-formed The Tokens with brothers Phil (born on 4/1/1942) and Mitch (born on 5/25/1947) Margo and recorded for Warwick in 1960. Formed own label, B.T. Puppy, in 1964 and produced The Happenings. Medress

TOKENS, The — cont'd
produced Tony Orlando & Dawn, then left The Tokens, who continued as a trio (Siegel and the Margos) and recorded as Cross Country in 1973.

TOLBERT, Israel "Popper Stopper"
Born on 10/29/1934 in Memphis, Tennessee. Died on 4/26/2007 (age 72). R&B singer/songwriter/pianist. Blind since birth.

TOM & JERRIO
R&B dance duo: Robert "Tommy Dark" Tharp and Jerry "Jerryo" Murray. Tharp was a baritone in The Ideals vocal group from 1952-65.

TOMLINSON, Trent
Born on 7/3/1975 in Blytheville, Arkansas; raised in Kennett, Missouri. Country singer/songwriter/guitarist.

TOMMY TUTONE
Rock group formed in San Francisco, California: Tommy Heath (vocals), Jim Keller (guitar), Jon Lyons (bass) and Victor Carberry (drums).

TOMS, Gary, Empire
Disco group formed in New York: Gary Toms (keyboards), Helen Jacobs (vocals), Rick Kenny (guitar), Eric Oliver (trumpet), Les Rose (sax), Warren Tesoro (percussion), John Freeman (bass) and Rick Murray (drums).

TOM TOM CLUB
Studio project formed by Talking Heads members/husband-and-wife Chris Frantz and Tina Weymouth. Production work for Ziggy Marley & The Melody Makers, Happy Mondays and others.

TONE LOC
Born Anthony Smith on 3/3/1966 in Los Angeles, California. Male rapper/actor. Appeared in several movies. Stage name, pronounced: tone loke, derived from his Spanish nickname "Antonio Loco."

TONEY, Oscar Jr.
Born on 5/26/1939 in Selma, Alabama; raised in Columbus, Georgia. R&B singer.

TONIC
Rock group from Los Angeles, California: Emerson Hart (vocals, guitar), Jeff Russo (guitar), Dan Rothchild (bass) and Kevin Shepard (drums).

TONY & JOE
Rock and roll vocal duo: Tony Savonne and Joe Saraceno.

TONY! TONI! TONÉ!
R&B-funk trio from Oakland, California: brothers Dwayne (born on 2/14/1963) and Raphael (born on 5/14/1966) Wiggins, with cousin Timothy Christian (born on 12/10/1965). Raphael recorded as Raphael Saadiq. Appeared in the movie *House Party 2*. Dwayne produced Simple E.

TOOL
Hard-rock group from Los Angeles, California: Maynard James Keenan (vocals), Adam Jones (guitar), Justin Chancellor (bass) and Danny Carey (drums). Keenan also formed duo A Perfect Circle.

TOO $HORT
Born Todd Shaw on 4/28/1966 in Los Angeles, California. The first West Coast rap star.

TOOTS & THE MAYTALS
Reggae trio from Jamaica: Fred "Toots" Hibbert, Nate Matthias and Henry Gordon.

TORA TORA
Hard-rock group from Memphis, Tennessee: Anthony Corder (vocals), Keith Douglas (guitar), Patrick Francis (bass) and John Patterson (drums). Band name taken from a Van Halen song.

TORME, Mel
Born on 9/13/1925 in Chicago, Illinois. Died of a stroke on 6/5/1999 (age 73). Jazz singer/songwriter/pianist/drummer/actor. Wrote "The Christmas Song." Frequently appeared as himself on TV's *Night Court*. Nicknamed "The Velvet Fog."

TORNADOES, The
Surf-rock instrumental group formed in England: Alan Caddy (lead guitar), George Bellamy (rhythm guitar), Roger Jackson (keyboards), Heinz Burt (bass) and Clem Cattini (drums). Burt died of muscular dystrophy on 4/7/2000 (age 57).

TOROK, Mitchell
Born on 10/28/1929 in Houston, Texas. Pop-country singer/songwriter/guitarist.

TORONTO
Rock group from Toronto, Ontario, Canada: Holly Woods (vocals), Sheron Alton and Brian Allen (guitars), Scott Kreyer (keyboards) and Jim Fox (drums).

TORRENCE, George, & The Naturals
Born in New York. Funk-R&B singer/songwriter.

TOSH, Peter
Born Winston Hubert MacIntosh on 10/9/1944 in Jamaica. Reggae singer/songwriter. Fatally shot during a robbery at his home in Kingston on 9/11/1987 (age 42). Former member of Bob Marley's Wailers.

TOTAL
Female R&B vocal trio from Harlem, New York: JaKima Raynor, Keisha Spivey and Pam Long.

TOTAL COELO
Female dance group from England: Ros Holness, Anita Mahadervan, Lindsey Danvers, Lacey Bond and Sheen Doran.

TOTO
Pop-rock group formed in Los Angeles, California: Bobby Kimball (vocals; born on 3/29/1947), Steve Lukather (guitar; born on 10/21/1957), David Paich (keyboards; born on 6/21/1954), Steve Porcaro (keyboards; born on 9/2/1957), David Hungate (bass) and Jeff Porcaro (drums; born on 4/1/1954). Prominent session musicians, most notably behind Boz Scaggs in the late 1970s. Hungate was replaced by Mike Porcaro in 1983. (The Porcaros are brothers.) Kimball replaced by Fergie Fredericksen in 1984; Fredericksen replaced by Joseph Williams (conductor John Williams's son) in 1986. Steve Porcaro left in 1988. Paich and his

TOTO — cont'd
father, Marty, won an Emmy for writing the theme for the TV series *Ironside*. Kimball, Lukather and Paich with Far Corporation in 1986. Jeff Porcaro died of a heart attack on 8/5/1992 (age 38).

TOUCH
Rock group from Long Island, New York: Mark Mangold (vocals), Craig Brooks (guitar), Doug Howard (bass) and Glenn Kitchcart (drums).

TOURISTS, The
Rock group from London, England: Annie Lennox (vocals, keyboards), David A. Stewart and Peet Coombes (guitars), Eddie Chinn (bass) and Jim Toomey (drums). Lennox and Stewart formed Eurythmics in December 1980.

TOWER OF POWER
Interracial R&B-funk group from Oakland, California: Lenny Williams (vocals), Willie Fulton (guitar), Greg Adams, Mic Gillette, Steve Kupka, Emilio Castillo and Lenny Pickett (horns), Chester Thompson (keyboards), Francis Prestia (bass) and David Garibaldi (drums).

TOWNES, Carol Lynn
Born in Brooklyn, New York. Disco singer.

TOWNSELL, Lidell, & M.T.F.
Born in Chicago, Illinois. Black dance DJ/mixer. M.T.F. (More Than Friends): singer Martell and rapper Silk E.

TOWNSEND, Ed
Born on 4/16/1929 in Fayetteville, Tennessee. Died of heart failure on 8/13/2003 (age 74). R&B singer/songwriter. Son David is a member of Surface. Wrote Marvin Gaye's "Let's Get It On" and Theola Kilgore's "The Love Of My Man."

TOWNSHEND, Pete
Born on 5/19/1945 in London, England. Rock singer/songwriter/guitarist. Member of The Who. First solo album *Who Came First*, 1972. Own publishing house, Eel Pie Press, mid-1970s. Currently plagued by a significant hearing loss.

TOYA
Born Toya Rodriguez in St. Louis, Missouri. Female R&B singer/rapper.

TOY DOLLS, The
Female pre-teen pop duo from Los Angeles, California: Susan Leslie and Libby Redwine.

TOYS, The
Female R&B vocal trio from Jamaica, Queens, New York: Barbara Harris, June Montiero and Barbara Parritt. Appearances on *Shindig* TV show in 1965. In the movie *The Girl In Daddy's Bikini*.

T-PAIN
Born Faheem Najm on 9/30/1985 in Tallahassee, Florida. Male rapper/songwriter.

T'PAU
Pop-rock-dance group from Shrewsbury, England: Carol Decker (vocals), Dean Howard and Ronnie Rogers (guitars), Mick Chetwood (keyboards), Paul Jackson (bass) and Tim Burgess (drums). Band

named after a Vulcan princess in an episode of the TV series *Star Trek*.

T.P.E.
A creation of producer Adam Marano, who later created Collage. T.P.E. stands for The Philadelphia Experiment.

TQ
Born Terrance Quaites in Mobile, Alabama; raised in Los Angeles, California. R&B singer/songwriter.

TRACTORS, The
Country-rock group formed in Tulsa, Oklahoma: Casey Van Beek (vocals), Steve Ripley (guitar), Walt Richmond (keyboards), Ron Getman (bass) and Jamie Oldaker (drums).

TRADEWINDS, The
Pop group from New Jersey: Ralph Rizzoll, Phil Mehill, Sal Capriglione and Angel Cifelli.

TRADE WINDS, The / INNOCENCE, The
Pop singing/songwriting/production duo from New York: Pete Anders (Andreoli) and Vinnie Poncia. First recorded with group The Videls. Also recorded as The Innocence. Poncia produced several albums for Ringo Starr and Melissa Manchester.

TRAFFIC
Rock group formed in England. Original lineup: Steve Winwood (keyboards, guitar), Dave Mason (guitar), Jim Capaldi (drums) and Chris Wood (flute, sax). Many personnel changes until the group disbanded in 1974. Winwood and Capaldi reunited in 1994. Wood died on 7/12/1983. Capaldi died of cancer on 1/28/2005 (age 60).

TRAGEDY • CAPONE • INFINITE
Male rap trio from New York.

TRAIN
Rock group from San Francisco, California: Patrick Monahan (vocals), Rob Hotchkiss and Jimmy Stafford (guitars), Charlie Colin (bass) and Scott Underwood (drums).

TRAMMPS, The
Disco group from Philadelphia, Pennsylvania: Jimmy Ellis (lead tenor), Earl Young (lead bass), Harold and Stanley Wade (tenors) and Robert Upchurch (baritone). Own Golden Fleece label in 1973.

TRANS-SIBERIAN ORCHESTRA
Rock opera-styled project formed and produced by Paul O'Neill in Florida. "Christmas Eve (Sarajevo 12/24)" was originally released as by the hard-rock band Savatage in 1995. O'Neill then produced a Christmas rock opera album in 1996 under the name Trans-Siberian Orchestra and included the original Savatage recording on it.

TRANSVISION VAMP
Pop-rock group from England: Wendy James (vocals), Nick Christian Sayer (guitar), Tex Axile (keyboards), Dave Parsons (bass) and Pol Burton (drums).

TRANS-X
Born Pascal Languirand in Montreal, Quebec, Canada. Techno-rock singer/songwriter.

TRAPP
Trapp is male rapper John Parker. Founder of the Atlanta-based Deff Trapp record label.

TRAPT
Hard-rock band from Los Gatos, California: Chris Brown (vocals, guitar), Simon Ormandy (guitar), Peter Charell (bass) and Aaron Montgomery (drums).

TRASHMEN, The
Garage-rock band from Minneapolis, Minnesota: Tony Andreason, Dal Winslow and Bob Reed (guitars), with Steve Wahrer (drums). Wahrer died of cancer on 1/21/1989 (age 47).

TRAVELING WILBURYS
Supergroup masquerading as a band of brothers. Spearheaded by Nelson (George Harrison), with Lucky (Bob Dylan), Otis (Jeff Lynne of ELO), Lefty (Roy Orbison) and Charlie T. Junior (Tom Petty) Wilbury. Orbison died of a heart attack on 12/6/1988 (age 52). Harrison died of cancer on 11/29/2001 (age 58).

TRAVERS, Mary
Born on 11/7/1936 in Louisville, Kentucky. Folk singer. Member of Peter, Paul & Mary.

TRAVERS, Pat
Born on 4/12/1954 in Toronto, Ontario, Canada. Rock singer/guitarist.

TRAVIS, McKinley
Born on 2/2/1945 in Los Angeles, California. R&B singer.

TRAVIS, Randy
Born Randy Traywick on 5/4/1959 in Marshville, North Carolina. Country singer/songwriter/guitarist/actor. Appeared in several movies and TV shows.

TRAVIS & BOB
Pop-country duo from Jackson, Alabama: Travis Pritchett and Bob Weaver.

TRAVOLTA, Joey
Born on 10/14/1950 in Englewood, New Jersey. Pop singer/actor/director/producer/screenwriter. Older brother of John Travolta.

TRAVOLTA, John
Born on 2/18/1954 in Englewood, New Jersey. Actor/singer. Played "Vinnie Barbarino" on the TV series *Welcome Back Kotter*. Starred in many movies. Married actress Kelly Preston on 9/12/1991.

TRÉ
Female R&B vocal trio from Cleveland, Ohio: Rebecca Forsha, Kimberly Cromartie and Niko Williams.

TREE SWINGERS, The
Pop-novelty duo from Asbury Park, New Jersey: Art Polhemus (born on 8/16/1940) and Terry Byrnes (born on 5/6/1940).

TREMELOES, The
Pop-rock group from England: Len "Chip" Hawkes (vocals, bass), Alan Blakely and Ricky West (guitars), and Dave Munden (drums). Formed as backing band for British vocalist Brian Poole (born on 11/3/1941 in England). Blakely is the brother of Mike Blakely of Christie. Hawkes is the father of singer Chesney Hawkes. Blakely died of cancer on 6/10/1996 (age 54).

TRENIERS, The
R&B vocal group from Mobile, Alabama: identical twin brothers Claude and Cliff, with other brothers Buddy and Milt Trenier. Appeared in the movies *Don't Knock The Rock*, *The Girl Can't Help It* and *Calypso Heat Wave*. Stunning, raucous stage show anticipated rock 'n' roll in the early 1950s. Cliff died of cancer in March 1983 (age 63). Claude died of cancer on 11/17/2003 (age 84).

TRESVANT, Ralph
Born on 5/16/1968 in Roxbury, Massachusetts. R&B singer. Member of New Edition. Appeared in the movie *House Party 2*.

T. REX
Glam-rock band from England: Marc Bolan (vocals, guitar; born Marc Feld on 7/30/1947), Mickey Finn (guitar; born on 6/3/1947), Steve Currie (bass) and Bill Legend (drums). Bolan died in a car crash on 9/16/1977 (age 30). Currie died in a car crash on 4/28/1981 (age 33). Finn died of liver failure on 1/11/2003 (age 55).

TRIBE CALLED QUEST, A
Rap trio from Queens, New York: Jonathan "Q-Tip" Davis, Ali Shaheed Muhammad (Lucy Pearl) and Malik "Phife Dawg" Taylor.

TRICE, Obie
Born on 11/14/1979 in Detroit, Michigan. Male rapper.

TRICK DADDY
Born Maurice Young in Miami, Florida. Male "thug" rapper/producer.

TRICK PONY
Country trio formed in Nashville, Tennessee: Heidi Newfield (vocals), Keith Burns (guitar) and Ira Dean (bass).

TRICK-TRICK
Born Christian Mathis in Detroit, Michigan. Male rapper/songwriter.

TRILLVILLE
Male rap trio from Atlanta, Georgia: Jamal "Dirty Mouth" Glaze, Donnell "Don P" Prince and Lawrence "Lil LA" Edwards.

TRILOGY
Dance trio from the Bronx, New York: Duran Ramos, Angel DeLeon and Darrin Dewitt Henson. Choreography work for New Kids On The Block. Henson replaced by Joey Kid.

TRINA
Born Katrina Taylor on 12/3/1978 in Miami, Florida. Female hardcore rapper. Discovered by Trick Daddy.

TRINA & TAMARA
R&B vocal duo from Gary, Indiana: Trina and Tamara Powell. Sisters of Jesse Powell.

TRIPLETS, The
Triplet sisters Diana, Sylvia and Vicky Villegas. Born on 4/18/1965, seven minutes apart. Raised in Mexico by their American mother and Mexican father. Gained recognition after winning an *MTV Basement Tapes* competition in 1986.

TRIPPING DAISY
Pop-rock group from Dallas, Texas: Tim DeLaughter (vocals), Wes Berggren (guitar), Mark Pirro (bass) and Bryan Wakeland (drums). Berggren died on 10/27/1999 (age 28).

TRITT, Travis
Born James Travis Tritt on 2/9/1963 in Marietta, Georgia. Country singer/songwriter/guitarist.

TRIUMPH
Hard-rock trio formed in Toronto, Ontario, Canada: Rik Emmett (guitar, vocals), Mike Levine (keyboards, bass) and Gil Moore (drums).

TRIXTER
Hard-rock group from Paramus, New Jersey: Peter Loran (vocals), Steve Brown (guitar), P.J. Farley (bass) and Mark Scott (drums).

TROCCOLI, Kathy
Born on 6/24/1958 in Brooklyn, New York. Christian singer/songwriter.

TROGGS, The
Rock group from Andover, England: Reg Presley (vocals; born Reg Ball), Chris Britton (guitar), Pete Staples (bass) and Ronnie Bullis (drums). Bullis died on 11/13/1992 (age 51).

TROLLS, The
Rock band from Lake Bluff, Illinois: Richard Clark (vocals, organ), Richard Gallagher (guitar), Max Jordan (bass) and Kenny "Apples" Cortese (drums). Cortese later became Jim Croce's publicist (died in the same plane crash that killed Croce on 9/20/1973).

TROOP
R&B vocal group from Pasadena, California: Steve Russell, Allen McNeil, Rodney Benford, John Harreld and Reggie Warren. Troop stands for Total Respect Of Other People. Group discovered by Gerald Levert.

TROOPER
Rock group from Vancouver, British Columbia, Canada: Ra McGuire (vocals, guitar), Brian Smith (guitar), Frank Ludwig (keyboards), Doni Underhill (bass) and Tommy Stewart (drums).

TROWER, Robin
Born on 3/9/1945 in London, England. Rock guitarist/songwriter. Original member of Procol Harum.

TROY, Doris
Born Doris Higgensen on 1/6/1937 in Harlem, New York. Died of emphysema on 2/16/2004 (age 67). R&B singer/songwriter. Used Doris Payne as her pen name. The off-Broadway musical *Mama, I Want To Sing* is based on her life. Backing vocalist on Pink Floyd's album *Dark Side Of The Moon*.

TROYER, Eric
Born in Brooklyn, New York. Pop singer/songwriter.

TRU
Rap group from New Orleans, Louisiana: brothers Master P, Silkk the Shocker and C-Murder, with Mia X and Mo B Dick. TRU stands for The Real Untouchables.

TRUE, Andrea, Connection
Born on 7/26/1943 in Nashville, Tennessee. White female disco singer/actress. Appeared in several X-rated movies in the 1970s.

TRUMPETEERS, The
Big-band styled group directed by Billy Mure (guitarist with Leo Addeo's orchestra).

TRUSTCOMPANY
Rock group from Montgomery, Alabama: Kevin Palmer (vocals, guitar), James Fukai (guitar), Josh Moates (bass) and Jason Singleton (drums).

TRUTH, The
Rock duo from England: Dennis Greaves (lead vocals, guitar) and Mick Lister (vocals, guitar).

TRUTH HURTS
Born Shari Watson in Los Angeles, California. Female hip-hop singer.

TRYNIN, Jennifer
Born on 12/27/1963 in New Jersey. Rock singer/songwriter/guitarist.

T.S.U. TORONADOES, The
R&B band from Texas Southern University: Cal Thomas and Will Thomas (guitars), Robert Sanders (organ), Clarence Harper, Nelson Mills and Leroy Lewis (horns), Jerry Jenkins (bass) and Dwight Burns (drums). Similar in sound to Archie Bell & The Drells.

TUBB, Ernest
Born on 2/9/1914 in Crisp, Texas. Died of emphysema on 9/6/1984 (age 70). Country singer/songwriter/guitarist. Known as "The Texas Trouba-dour." Acted in several movies. Broadcast from his own Ernest Tubb Record Shop in Nashville begin-ning in 1947. Father of country singer Justin Tubb.

TUBES, The
Pop-rock group from San Francisco, California: Fee Waybill (vocals), Bill Spooner and Roger Steen (guitars), Michael Cotton and Vince Welnick (keyboards), Rick Anderson (bass) and Prairie Prince (drums). Welnick joined Grateful Dead in 1990. Group appeared in the 1980 movie *Xanadu*. Welnick died on 6/2/2006 (age 55).

TUCKER, Louise
Born in Bristol, England. Classical-styled vocalist.

TUCKER, Tanya
Born on 10/10/1958 in Seminole, Texas; raised in Wilcox, Arizona. Country singer. Had her first chart hit at age 13. Bit part in the movie *Jeremiah Johnson* in 1972.

TUCKER, Tommy
Born Robert Higginbotham on 3/5/1939 in Springfield, Ohio. Died of poisoning on 1/22/1982 (age 42). R&B singer/songwriter/pianist.

TUESDAYS, The
Female pop group from Norway: Laila Samuels (vocals), Hege Solli (guitar), Kristin Werner (keyboards), Veslemoy Hole (bass) and Linda Gustafsson (drums).

TUFANO & GIAMMARESE
Duo from Chicago, Illinois: Denny Tufano and Carl Giammarese (members of The Buckinghams).

TUNE ROCKERS, The
Instrumental rock and roll band from Buffalo, New York: Gene Strong (lead guitar), Fred Patton (guitar), Johnny Capello (sax), Tim Nolan (bass) and Mickey Vanderlip (drums).

TUNE WEAVERS, The
R&B vocal group from Boston, Massachusetts: Margo Sylvia (lead), husband John Sylvia (bass), Gilbert Lopez (Margo's brother; tenor) and Charlotte Davis (Margo's cousin). Margo died of a heart attack on 10/25/1991 (age 55).

TUNSTALL, KT
Born Kate Tunstall on 6/23/1975 in Edinburgh, Scotland; raised in St. Andrews, Scotland. Female singer/songwriter/guitarist.

TURBANS, The
R&B vocal group from Philadelphia, Pennsylvania: Al Banks, Matthew Platt, Charles Williams and Andrew Jones. Banks died in 1980 (age 43).

TURNER, "Big Joe"
Born on 5/18/1911 in Kansas City, Missouri. Died of a heart attack on 11/24/1985 (age 74). Blues-R&B vocalist. Early in career teamed with boogie-woogie pianist Pete Johnson. Appeared in the movie *Shake, Rattle And Rock!* in 1957.

TURNER, Ike & Tina
Husband-and-wife R&B duo: guitarist Ike Turner (born on 11/5/1931 in Clarksdale, Mississippi; died on 12/12/2007, age 76) and vocalist Tina Turner (born Anna Mae Bullock on 11/26/1938 in Brownsville, Tennessee). Married from 1958-76. At age 11, Ike was backing pianist for bluesmen Sonny Boy Williamson (Aleck Ford) and Robert Nighthawk (of the Nighthawks). Formed own band, the Kings of Rhythm, while in high school; backed Jackie Brenston's hit "Rocket '88'." Prolific session, production and guitar work during the 1950s. In 1960 developed a dynamic stage show around Tina; "The Ike & Tina Turner Revue" featuring her backing vocalists, The Ikettes, and Ike's Kings of Rhythm. Disbanded in 1974. In the mid-1980s, Tina emerged as a successful solo artist.

TURNER, Jesse Lee
Born in Bowling, Texas. Male rockabilly singer.

TURNER, Josh
Born on 11/20/1977 in Florence, South Carolina; raised in Hannah, South Carolina. Country singer/songwriter/guitarist.

TURNER, Sammy
Born Samuel Black on 6/2/1932 in Paterson, New Jersey. Tommy Edwards-styled vocalist.

TURNER, Spyder
Born Dwight Turner on 2/4/1947 in Beckley, West Virginia; raised in Detroit, Michigan. R&B singer.

TURNER, Tina
Born Anna Mae Bullock on 11/26/1938 in Brownsville, Tennessee. R&B-rock singer/actress. One-half of Ike & Tina Turner duo, when married to Ike from 1958-76. In movies *Tommy* and *Mad Max-Beyond Thunderdome*. With Ike, inducted into the Rock and Roll Hall of Fame in 1991. Her autobiography, *What's Love Got To Do With It*, was made into a movie in 1993.

TURNER, Titus
Born on 5/11/1933 in Atlanta, Georgia. Died on 9/13/1984 (age 51). R&B singer/songwriter.

TURTLES, The
Pop-rock group formed in Los Angeles, California: Mark Volman (vocals; born on 4/19/1947), Howard Kaylan (vocals; born on 6/22/1947), Jim Tucker (guitar; born on 10/17/1946), Al Nichol (keyboards; born on 3/31/1945), Chuck Portz (bass; born on 3/28/1945) and Don Murray (drums; born on 11/8/1945). Volman and Kaylan (under the names Flo and Eddie) later joined Frank Zappa's Mothers of Invention. Murray died on 3/22/1996 (age 50).

TUXEDO JUNCTION
Female disco group: Jamie Edlin, Marilyn Jackson, Sue Allen and Marti McCall.

TWAIN, Shania
Born Eileen Regina Edwards on 8/28/1965 in Windsor, Ontario, Canada; raised in Timmins, Ontario, Canada. Country singer/songwriter. Adopted the name Shania which means "I'm on my way" in the Ojibwa Indian language. Married Robert John "Mutt" Lange (producer of Def Leppard, The Cars, Foreigner and many others) on 12/28/1993.

T.W.D.Y.
Rap production presented by Ant Banks. T.W.D.Y.: The Who Damn Yey.

TWEET
Born Charlene Keys on 3/4/1971 in Rochester, New York. Female R&B singer/songwriter.

12 GAUGE
Born Isiah Pinkney in Augusta, Georgia. Male hardcore rapper.

TWENNYNINE FEATURING LENNY WHITE
R&B-funk band from New York: Donald Blackmon (vocals), Eddie Martinez and Nick Moroch (guitars), Denzil Miller (keyboards), Barry Johnson (bass) and Lenny White (drums).

20 FINGERS featuring GILLETTE
Duo of Chicago-based dance producers Charles Babie and Manfred Mohr, with female rapper Sandra Gillette.

21st CENTURY, The
R&B vocal group from Chicago, Illinois: Fred Williams, Alphonso Smith, Tyrone Moores, Pierre Johnson and Alonzo Martin.

TWILIGHT 22
An electro-dance-rap production led by New York synthesizer player Gordon Bahary (born in 1960). Worked with Harry Chapin in 1975, and with Stevie Wonder from 1976.

TWILLEY, Dwight
Born on 6/6/1951 in Tulsa, Oklahoma. Rock singer/songwriter/pianist. Formed the Dwight Twilley Band with Phil Seymour (bass, drums) in 1974.

TWINZ
Rap duo from Long Beach, California: identical twin brothers Deon ("Trip Locc") and DeWayne ("Wayniac") Williams.

TWISTA
Born Carl Mitchell on 11/27/1973 in Chicago, Illinois. Male rapper/songwriter. Known as Tung Twista in 1992 when he was recognized as the world's fastest rapper by the Guinness Book of World Records.

TWISTED SISTER
Hard-rock group from Long Island, New York: Dee Snider (vocals), Jay French and Eddie Ojeda (guitars), Mark Mendosa (bass), and A.J. Pero (drums).

TWITTY, Conway
Born Harold Jenkins on 9/1/1933 in Friars Point, Mississippi; raised in Helena, Arkansas. Died of an abdominal aneurysm on 6/5/1993 (age 59). From rock and roll teen idol to superstar country singer. Formed own group, the Phillips County Ramblers, at age 10. Offered a professional baseball contract with the Philadelphia Phillies when drafted. With service band, Cimmarons, in Japan, early 1950s. Changed his name in 1957 (borrowed from Conway, Arkansas and Twitty, Texas) and first recorded for Sun (unissued recordings). In the movies *Sexpot Goes To College* and *College Confidential*. Switched from rock and roll to country music in 1965. Moved to Nashville in 1968.

II D EXTREME
R&B trio from Washington DC: D'Extra Wiley, Randy Gill (brother of Johnny Gill) and his cousin Jermaine Mickey.

2GE+HER
Male vocal group formed for the same-named MTV series: Evan Farmer ("Jerry O'Keefe"), Michael Cuccione ("Jason McKnight"), Alex Solovitz ("Mickey Parke"), Noah Bastian ("Chad Linus") and Kevin Farley ("Doug Linus"). Farley is the younger brother of the late comedian Chris Farley. Cuccione died of respiratory failure on 1/13/2001 (age 16).

2 HYPED BROTHERS & A DOG
2 Hyped Brothers are Frank "Doo Doo Brown" Ski (a DJ at Baltimore's V-103 FM) and Stanley Evans, Jr. Dog is Rhondo V. Haus Fokwulfe, Frank's German Shepherd.

2 IN A ROOM
Dance duo from Washington Heights, New York: rapper Rafael "Dose" Vargas and remixer Roger "Rog Nice" Pauletta.

2 LIVE CREW / LUKE
Rap group from Miami, Florida: David "Mr. Mixx" Hobbs, Chris "Kid-Ice" Wong Won, Mark "Brother Marquis" Ross and leader, Luther "Luke Skyywalker" Campbell (owner of Luke Records). Group's obscenity arrests sparked national censorship controversy in 1990. By 1994, group consisted of Campbell, Won and Larry "Verb" Dobson, with special appearances by Rudy Ray "Dolomite" Moore; changed name to The New 2 Live Crew. By 1996, Campbell split from group to record as Luke; group now a trio of Hobbs, Won and Ross.

2nu
Pop-novelty group from Seattle, Washington: Jock Blaney (vocals, production director of KPLZ-Seattle at time of hit), Mike Nealy, Tom Martin and Phil DeVault.

2 OF CLUBS
Female pop duo: Patti Valantine and Linda Parrish (former wife of Carl Edmonson, leader of The Dolphins).

2PAC
Born Tupac Amaru Shakur on 6/16/1971 in Brooklyn, New York (the son of 2 Black Panther members); raised in Oakland, California. Died on 9/13/1996 (age 25) of wounds suffered on 9/7/1996 in a shooting in Las Vegas, Nevada. Gangsta rapper/actor. Member of Digital Underground in 1991. Also recorded in 1996 as Makaveli. Appeared in the movies *Nothing But Trouble*, *Juice*, *Poetic Justice* and *Above The Rim*. Numerous run-ins with the law. Found guilty on 2/10/1994 of the 1993 assault and battery of *Menace II Society* co-director Allen Hughes. Survived after being shot five times during a robbery in Manhattan on 11/29/1994. Sentenced for up to four years in prison on 2/7/1995 for a 1993 sexual assault; paroled in late 1995.

2 PISTOLS
Born Jeremy Saunders in Tarpon Springs, Florida. Male rapper.

2 UNLIMITED
Techno-house dance duo from Amsterdam, Netherlands: Ray "Kid Ray" Slijngaard (born on 6/28/1971) and Anita Doth (born on 12/25/1971).

TYCOON
Pop-rock group from New York: Norman Mershon (vocals), Jon Gordon (guitar), Mark Rivera (sax), Michael Fonfara (keyboards), Mark Kreider (bass) and Richard Steinberg (drums).

TYGA
Born Michael Stevenson in Compton, California. Male rapper.

TYLER, Bonnie
Born Gaynor Hopkins on 6/8/1953 in Swansea, Wales. Pop-rock singer. Worked local clubs until the mid-1970s. Distinctive raspy vocals caused by operation to remove throat nodules in 1976.

TYMES, The
R&B vocal group from Philadelphia, Pennsylvania:
George Williams (lead), George Hilliard, Donald
Banks, Albert Berry and Norman Burnett. First
called the Latineers. Berry and Hilliard were
replaced by female singers Terri Gonzalez and
Melanie Moore in the early 1970s.

TYRESE
Born Tyrese Gibson on 12/30/1978 in Watts,
California. Male R&B singer/songwriter/actor.
Starred in the movies *Baby Boy*, *2 Fast 2 Furious*,
Flight Of The Phoenix and others.

UB40
Interracial reggae group formed in Birmingham,
England: brothers Ali (vocals, guitar; born on
2/15/1959) and Robin (guitar, vocals; born on
12/25/1954) Campbell, Terence "Astro" Wilson
(vocals; born on 6/24/1957), Earl Falconer (bass;
born on 1/223/1959), Michael Virtue (keyboards;
born on 1/19/1957), Norman Hassan (percussion;
born on 1/26/1958), Brian Travers (sax; born on
2/7/1959) and James Brown (drums; born on
11/20/1957). Name taken from a British
unemployment form.

UGGAMS, Leslie
Born on 5/25/1943 in Harlem, New York. Black
actress/singer. Played "Kizzy" in the TV mini-series
Roots. Regular on TV's *Sing Along With Mitch*.
Hosted own TV variety series in 1969.

UGK
Male rap duo from Port Arthur, Texas: Chad "Pimp
C" Butler and Bernard "Bun B" Freeman. Also
recorded as Underground Kingz. Butler died on
12/4/2007 (age 33).

UGLY KID JOE
Rock group from Isla Vista, California: Whitfield
Crane (vocals), Klaus Eichstadt and Dave Fortman
(guitars), Cordell Crockett (bass), and Mark Davis
(drums).

U-KREW, The
Rap group from Portland, Oregon: Kevin Morse,
Larry Bell, Lavell Alexander, James McClendon and
Hakim Muhammad.

ULLMAN, Tracey
Born on 12/30/1959 in Burnham, Buckinghamshire,
England. Actress/singer/comedienne. Hosted own
TV show from 1987-90.

ULTIMATE
Disco studio group assembled by producers Juliano
Salerni and Bruce Weeden.

ULTRAVOX
Electronic-rock group formed in London, England:
Midge Ure (vocals, guitar; born James Ure on
10/10/1953 in Glasgow, Scotland), Billy Currie
(synthesizer, piano), Chris Cross (bass) and Warren
Cann (drums).

UMILIANI, Piero
Born on 7/17/1926 in Florence, Italy. Died on
2/14/2001 (age 75). Composer/conductor.

UNCLE DOG
Rock group from England featuring vocalists Carol
Grimes and David Skinner with Phil Crooks, John
Porter, Sam Mitchell and Terry Stannard.

UNCLE KRACKER
Born Matthew Shafer on 6/6/1974 in Mount
Clemens, Michigan. White pop-rock singer/DJ.
Member of Kid Rock's posse.

UNCLE SAM
Born Sam Turner in Detroit, Michigan. R&B singer.

UNDERGROUND SUNSHINE
Rock group from Montello, Wisconsin: brothers
Egbert "Berty" (vocals, bass) and Frank (drums)
Kohl, Chris Connors (guitar; born John Dahlberg)
and Jane Little (keyboards). Actual last name of the
German-born brothers is Koelbl.

UNDERWOOD, Carrie
Born on 3/10/1983 in Muskogee, Oklahoma; raised
in Checotah, Oklahoma. Country singer. Winner on
the 2005 season of TV's *American Idol*.

UNDERWORLD
Rock group from England: Karl Hyde (vocals,
guitar), Alfie Thomas (guitar), Rick Smith
(keyboards), Baz Allen (bass) and Pascal Console
(drums).

UNDISPUTED TRUTH, The
R&B-disco vocal trio from Detroit, Michigan: Joe
Harris, Billie Calvin and Brenda Evans.

UNIFICS, The
R&B vocal group from Washington DC: Al Johnson
(lead), Michel Ward and Greg Cook (tenors), and
Hal Worthington (baritone). Johnson later joined
Special Delivery. Worthington was shot to death on
2/20/1990 (age 42).

UNIPOP
Husband-and-wife pop duo from New York: Manny
and Phyllis Loiacono.

UNIQUES, The
Pop-rock band from Shreveport, Louisiana: brothers
Joe Stampley (vocals, keyboards) and Bobby
Stampley (bass), with Ray Mills (guitar), Bobby
Sims (guitar) and Michael Love (drums). Joe
Stampley later became a country music star.

UNIT FOUR PLUS TWO
Pop-rock group from Hertfordshire, England: Peter
Moules (vocals), David Meikle and Howard Lubin
(guitars), Thomas Moeller (keyboards), Rod
Garwood (bass) and Hugh Halliday (drums).

UNIVERSAL ROBOT BAND
Interracial disco group from New York.

UNK
Born Anthony Platt in 1982 in Atlanta, Georgia.
Male DJ/rapper.

UNKNOWNS, The
All-star trio formed in Los Angeles, California: Steve
Alaimo, Mark Lindsay and Keith Allison. Lindsay
and Allison were also members of Paul Revere &
The Raiders.

UNV
R&B vocal group from Detroit, Michigan: brothers John and Shawn Powe, John Clay and Demetrius Peete. Clay also plays keyboards. UNV stands for Universal Nubian Voices. John and Shawn later charted as The Poww Bros.

UPBEATS, The
Male Adult Contemporary vocal group.

UPCHURCH, Philip, Combo
Born on 7/19/1941 in Chicago, Illinois. R&B guitarist. Session player for George Benson, Quincy Jones, The Jacksons and many others.

UPTOWN
Female dance-disco trio from New York City, New York.

URBAN, Keith
Born on 10/26/1967 in Whangarei, New Zealand; raised in Caboolture, Queensland, Australia. Country singer/songwriter. Former member of The Ranch. Married actress Nicole Kidman on 6/25/2006.

URBAN DANCE SQUAD
Rap-dance group from Amsterdam, Netherlands: Patrick "Rude Boy" Remington, Magic Stick, DNA, Silly Sil and Tres Manos.

URE, Midge
Born James Ure on 10/10/1953 in Glasgow, Scotland. Former lead guitarist/vocalist of Ultravox. Co-writer of "Do They Know It's Christmas?" Musical director of the Prince's Trust charity concerts.

URGENT
Rock quintet — Michael Kehr, lead singer.

URGE OVERKILL
Male pop-rock trio formed in 1986 in Chicago, Illinois: Nash Kato (guitar), "Eddie" King Roeser (bass) and Blackie Onassis (drums).

URIAH HEEP
Hard-rock group from England. Core members: David Byron (vocals), Mick Box (guitar), Ken Hensley (keyboards; later with Blackfoot), Gary Thain (bass) and Keith Baker (drums). Thain died of a drug overdose on 3/19/1976 (age 27). Byron died on 2/28/1985 (age 38).

USA FOR AFRICA
USA: United Support of Artists. Collection of top artists formed to help suffering people of Africa.

USED, The
Rock group from Orem, Utah: Bert McCracken (vocals), Quinn Allman (guitar), Jeph Howard (bass) and Branden Steineckert (drums).

USHER
Born Usher Raymond on 10/14/1978 in Chattanooga, Tennessee. Male R&B singer/actor. Age 15 at the time of his chart debut. Played "Jeremy" on TV's *Moesha*. Acted in several movies.

U.S. 1
Bubblegum pop-rock studio creation of Joey Levine (Ohio Express).

US3
Jazz-rap collaboration by London producers Mel Simpson (keyboards) and Geoff Wilkinson (samples). Samples of recordings from the Blue Note jazz record label serve as the backdrop for new rap solos and jazz playing by some of Britain's top players. Pronounced: us three.

UTAH SAINTS
Techno-rave duo from England: Jez Willis and Tim Garbutt.

UTFO
Rap group from Brooklyn, New York: Shawn Fequiere, Fred Reeves, Jeff Campbell and Maurice Bailey. UTFO: Untouchable Force Organization.

UTOPIA
Pop-rock group: Todd Rundgren (vocals, guitar), Roger Powell (keyboards), Kasim Sulton (bass) and John Wilcox (drums).

U2
Rock group formed in Dublin, Ireland: Paul "Bono" Hewson (vocals; born on 5/10/1960), Dave "The Edge" Evans (guitar; born on 8/8/1961), Adam Clayton (bass; born on 3/13/1960) and Larry Mullen (drums; born on 10/31/1961). Met while students at Dublin's Mount Temple High School. Emerged in 1987 as one of the world's leading rock acts. Released a concert tour documentary movie *Rattle And Hum* in 1988.

VACELS, The
Rock band from Long Island, New York: Ricky Racano, Harvey Cooper, Vinnie Cappola, and brothers Vinnie and Peter Gutowski.

VALADIERS
R&B vocal group formed in Detroit, Michigan: Stuart Avig (lead), Martin Coleman, Art Glasser and Jerry Light.

VALE, Jerry
Born Genaro Vitaliano on 7/8/1932 in the Bronx, New York. Adult Contemporary-ballad singer.

VALENS, Ritchie
Born Richard Valenzuela on 5/13/1941 in Pacoima, California. Killed in the plane crash that also took the lives of Buddy Holly and the Big Bopper on 2/3/1959 (age 17). Latin rock and roll singer/songwriter/guitarist. In the movie *Go Johnny Go*. The 1987 movie *La Bamba* was based on his life.

VALENTE, Caterina
Born on 1/14/1931 in Paris, France (of Italian parentage). Singer/dancer/actress. Sings in six languages.

VALENTI, John
Born John LaVigni in Chicago, Illinois. "Blue-eyed soul" singer/songwriter/drummer. Member of the group Puzzle in the early 1970s.

VALENTINE, Brooke
Born on 10/5/1985 in Houston, Texas. Female R&B singer/songwriter.

VALENTINO, Bobby
Born on 2/27/1982 in Jackson, Mississippi; raised in Atlanta, Georgia. R&B singer/songwriter.

VALENTINO, Danny
Born on 2/19/1941 in Flushing, New York. Teen pop singer.

VALENTINO, Mark
Born Anthony Busillo on 3/12/1942 in Philadelphia, Pennsylvania. Rock and roll singer.

VALENTINOS, The
Family R&B group from Cleveland, Ohio: Bobby Womack and his brothers Cecil, Curtis, Friendly Jr. and Harris. Originated as the Womack Brothers gospel group. Also recorded as The Lovers. Signed to Sam Cooke's SAR Records in 1962. Cecil married for a time to Mary Wells.

VALERY, Dana
Born in Milan, Italy; raised in Johannesburg, South Africa. Pop session singer/actress. Sister of Sergio Franchi.

VALIANTS, The
R&B vocal group from Los Angeles, California: Billy Storm, Brice Coefield, Sheridan Spencer and Chester Pipkin.

VALINO, Joe
Born Joseph Paolino on 3/9/1929 in South Philadelphia, Pennsylvania. Died of a heart attack on 12/26/1996 (age 67). Big band-styled singer.

VALJEAN
Born Valjean Johns on 11/19/1934 in Shattuck, Oklahoma. Male pianist.

VALLI, Frankie
Born Francis Castellucio on 5/3/1937 in Newark, New Jersey. Recorded his first solo single in 1953 as Frank Valley on the Corona label. Formed own group, the Variatones, in 1955 and changed its name to The Four Lovers in 1956, which evolved into The 4 Seasons by 1961. Began solo work in 1965. Suffered from a disease that caused hearing loss in the late 1970s; corrected by surgery.

VALLI, June
Born on 6/30/1930 in the Bronx, New York. Died on 3/12/1993 (age 62). Co-star of *Lucky Strike Hit Parade* for three years in the 1950s. Voice for Chiquita Banana commercials. Married Chicago DJ Howard Miller.

VANCE, Paul
Born on 11/4/1929 in Brooklyn, New York. Paul of Lee and Paul. Prolific songwriter with partner Lee Pockriss.

VANDENBERG
Born Adrian Vandenberg on 1/31/1954 in the Netherlands. Hard-rock guitarist. His group: Bert Heerink (vocals), Dick Kemper (bass) and Jos Zoomer (drums). Vandenberg later joined Whitesnake.

VANDROSS, Luther
Born on 4/20/1951 in the Bronx, New York. Died on 7/1/2005 (age 54). R&B singer/songwriter/producer. Commercial jingle singer, then a prolific session vocalist/arranger. Sang lead on a few of Change's early albums. Appeared in the movie *The Meteor Man*. Much songwriting and production work for other artists. One of the all-time greatest love ballad singers. His older sister Patricia was a member of The Crests.

VAN DYKE, Leroy
Born on 10/4/1929 in Spring Fork, Missouri. Worked as a newspaper reporter. Served in U.S. Army in the early 1950s. Former livestock auctioneer. In the movie *What Am I Bid?* in 1967.

VAN DYKES, The
Male R&B vocal group from New York.

VAN DYKES, The
R&B vocal trio from Fort Worth, Texas: Rondalis Tandy (lead), Wenzon Mosley (tenor) and James May (baritone).

VANGELIS
Born Evangelos Papathanassiou on 3/29/1943 in Valos, Greece. Keyboardist/composer. Also see Jon & Vangelis.

VAN HALEN
Hard-rock group formed in Pasadena, California: David Lee Roth (vocals; born on 10/10/1955), Eddie Van Halen (guitar; born on 1/26/1955), Michael Anthony (bass; born on 6/20/1954) and Alex Van Halen (drums; born on 5/8/1953). The Van Halen brothers were born in Nijmegen, Netherlands; moved to Pasadena in 1968. Sammy Hagar replaced Roth as lead singer in 1985. Eddie married actress Valerie Bertinelli on 4/11/1981 (since separated). Hagar left in June 1996. Roth rejoined group in 2007. Gary Cherone (Extreme) joined as lead singer in September 1996.

VANILLA FUDGE
Psychedelic-rock group formed in New York: Mark Stein (vocals, keyboards), Vinnie Martell (guitar), Tim Bogert (bass) and Carmine Appice (drums). Both Bogert and Appice also played with Jeff Beck and Rod Stewart's backing bands.

VANILLA ICE
Born Robert Van Winkle on 10/31/1968 in Miami Lakes, Florida. White rapper. Starred in the movie *Cool As Ice*.

VANITY
Born Denise Matthews on 1/4/1959 in Niagara Falls, Ontario, Canada. Lead singer of Vanity 6 (assembled by Prince). Model/actress. Acted in the movies *The Last Dragon*, *52 Pick-Up*, *Action Jackson* and *Highlander II*. Married to pro football player Anthony Smith from 1995-96.

VANITY FARE
Pop group from England: Trevor Brice (vocals), Tony Goulden (guitar), Barry Landeman (piano), Tony Jarrett (bass) and Dick Allix (drums).

VANN, Teddy
Born in Brooklyn, New York. Black singer/songwriter/producer. Also recorded as The Wheels. Also see Tender Slim.

VANNELLI, Gino
Born on 6/16/1952 in Montreal, Quebec, Canada. Pop singer/songwriter. His brother Ross produced Earth, Wind & Fire, Howard Hewett and The California Raisins.

VANWARMER, Randy
Born Randall VanWormer on 3/30/1955 in Indian Hills, Colorado. Died of leukemia on 1/12/2004 (age 48). Pop singer/songwriter/guitarist.

VAN ZANT
Country duo from Jacksonville, Florida: brothers Donnie Van Zant and Johnny Van Zant. Donnie was lead singer of the rock group 38 Special. Both are the younger brothers of former Lynyrd Skynyrd leader Ronnie Van Zant.

VAPORS, The
Pub-rock group from Guildford, Surrey, England: David Fenton (vocals), Ed Bazalgette (guitar), Steve Smith (bass) and Howard Smith (drums).

VARIOUS ARTISTS
All-star gathering: soloists (in order): Bono (U2), Stevie Wonder, Norah Jones, Brian Wilson (Beach Boys), Alicia Keys, Scott Weiland (Stone Temple Pilots), Billie Joe Armstrong (Green Day), Tim McGraw and Steven Tyler (Aerosmith). Backing band includes Alison Krauss and Velvet Revolver.

VASEL, Marianne, & Erich Storz
German yodeling duo.

VASSAR, Phil
Born on 5/28/1965 in Lynchburg, Virginia. Country singer/songwriter.

VAUGHAN, Frankie
Born Frank Abelson on 2/3/1928 in Liverpool, England. Died of heart failure on 9/17/1999 (age 71). Popular entertainer in England. In movie *Let's Make Love* (1960). In London cast of *42nd Street* in 1985.

VAUGHAN, Sarah
Born on 3/27/1924 in Newark, New Jersey. Died of cancer on 4/3/1990 (age 66). Jazz singer. Dubbed "The Divine One." Studied piano from 1931-39. Won amateur contest at the Apollo Theater in 1942, which led to her joining Earl Hines's band as vocalist/second pianist. First recorded solo for Continental in 1944. With Billy Eckstine from 1944-45. Married manager/trumpeter George Treadwell in 1947. Later husbands included pro football player Clyde Atkins and trumpeter Waymon Reed.

VAUGHAN, Stevie Ray
Born on 10/3/1954 in Dallas, Texas. Died in a helicopter crash on 8/27/1990 (age 35). Blues-rock singer/guitarist. Brother of Jimmie Vaughan (of The Fabulous Thunderbirds). Stevie and Jimmie recorded together as The Vaughan Brothers. Double Trouble: Reese Wynans (keyboards), Tommy Shannon (bass) and Chris Layton (drums).

VAUGHN, Billy
Born Richard Vaughn on 4/12/1919 in Glasgow, Kentucky. Died of cancer on 9/26/1991 (age 72). Organized The Hilltoppers vocal group in 1952.

Music director for Dot Records. Arranger/conductor for Pat Boone, Gale Storm, The Fontane Sisters and many other Dot artists. Vaughn had more pop hits than any other orchestra leader during the rock era.

VAUGHN, Denny
Born Charles Dennis Vaughn on 12/21/1921 in Toronto, Ontario, Canada. Died of cancer on 10/2/1972 (age 50). Adult Contemporary singer/songwriter/orchestra leader.

VAZQUEZ, Mario
Born on 6/15/1977 in the Bronx, New York (Puerto Rican parents). Pop singer. Dropped out of the *American Idol* talent competition before the finals in 2005.

VEE, Bobby
Born Robert Velline on 4/30/1943 in Fargo, North Dakota. Pop singer. Formed The Shadows (not Cliff Richard's group) with his brother and a friend in 1959. After Buddy Holly's death in a plane crash on 2/3/1959, The Shadows filled in for Buddy's next scheduled show in Fargo. First recorded for Soma in 1959. In the movies *Swingin' Along, It's Trad Dad, Play It Cool, C'mon Let's Live A Little* and *Just For Fun*.

VEGA, Suzanne
Born on 7/11/1959 in Sacramento, California. Folk-pop singer/songwriter/guitarist. Attended the New York High School of Performing Arts. Married to record producer Mitchell Froom (ex-Gamma) from 1995-98.

VEJTABLES, The
Rock group from San Francisco, California: Bob Bailey (vocals), Bob Cole (guitar), Ned Hollis (organ), Rick Dey (bass) and Jan Ashton (drums). One of the few rock groups with a female drummer.

VELAIRES, The
Rock and roll band from Sioux City, Iowa: Dan Matousek (vocals, guitar), Bob Dawdy (guitar), Jerry DeMers (bass) and Don Bourret (drums).

VELOURS, The
R&B vocal group from Brooklyn, New York: Jerome Ramos (lead), John Cheetom, Don Haywood, John Pearson and Charles Moffett. Also see The Fantastics.

VELS, The
Techno-rock/dance trio: Alice DeSoto, Chris Larkin and Charles Hanson.

VELVELETTES, The
Female R&B vocal group formed in Kalamazoo, Michigan: sisters Millie and Carol "Cal" Gill, cousins Bertha and Norma Barbee, and Betty Kelly (member of Martha & The Vandellas, 1964-67).

VELVET, Jimmy
Born James Tennant in Memphis, Tennessee. Pop singer.

VELVET REVOLVER
All-star rock group: Scott Weiland (vocals; Stone Temple Pilots) and Dave Kushner (guitar), with former Guns N' Roses members Saul "Slash"

VELVET REVOLVER — cont'd
Hudson (guitar), Michael "Duff" McKagen (bass) and Matt Sorum (drums).

VELVETS, The
Black doo-wop group from Odessa, Texas: Virgil Johnson, Will Soloman, Mark Prince, Clarence Rigby and Bob Thursby. Rigby died in a car crash in 1978.

VELVET UNDERGROUND, The
Highly influential rock band formed in New York City, despite little commercial success: Lou Reed (vocals, guitar), John Cale (keyboards), Sterling Morrison (bass) and Maureen Tucker (percussion). Andy Warhol managed the group from 1965-67. Recorded first album with female singer Nico (born Christa Paffgen on 10/16/1939 in Cologne, Germany; died of a brain hemorrhage on 7/18/1988, age 48). Morrison died of cancer on 8/30/1995 (age 53).

VENETIANS, The
Rock group from Australia: Rick Swinn (vocals), Dave Skeet (guitar), Matt Hughes (keyboards), Pete Watson (bass) and Tim Powles (drums).

VENGABOYS
Dance group assembled by Spanish producers Danski and DJ Delmundo: Kim, Robin, Deniece and Roy. Pronounced: bengaboys.

VENTURES, The
Instrumental rock and roll band from Seattle, Washington: guitarists Nokie Edwards (bass; born on 5/9/1935), Bob Bogle (lead; born on 1/16/1934) and Don Wilson (rhythm; born on 2/10/1933), with drummer Howie Johnson. First recorded for own Blue Horizon label in 1959. Johnson suffered serious injuries in a 1961 car accident; replaced by Mel Taylor (born on 9/24/1933). Taylor formed Mel Taylor & The Dynamics in 1973; returned in 1978. Edwards left in 1967; replaced by Gerry McGee. Edwards returned in 1972 and then left again in 1985. Added keyboardist John Durrill in 1969. Latest recordings featured Bogle, Wilson, Taylor and McGee. Group still active into the 2000s; extremely popular in Japan. Johnson died in January 1988 (age 50). Taylor died of cancer and heart failure on 8/11/1996 (age 62); his son, Leon Taylor, is now the drummer with the group.

VENUS, Vik
Born Jack Spector on 9/15/1928 in Brooklyn, New York. Died of a heart attack on 3/8/1994 (age 65). Popular New York radio personality.

VERA, Billy
Born William McCord on 5/28/1944 in Riverside, California; raised in Westchester County, New York. Pop singer/songwriter. In the movies *Buckaroo Banzai* and *The Doors*, and the HBO movie *Baja Oklahoma*. Formed The Beaters (an R&B-based, 10-piece band) in Los Angeles in 1979.

VERNE, Larry
Born Larry Vern Erickson on 2/8/1936 in Minneapolis, Minnesota. Photo studio worker-turned-singer by coincidence. A trio of California songwriters who worked in Verne's building selected him to record "Mr. Custer" because of his Southern drawl.

VERONICA
Born Veronica Vazquez in 1975 in the Bronx, New York (Puerto Rican parents). Female R&B-dance singer.

VERTICAL HOLD
R&B vocal trio: Willie Bruno, David Bright and Angie Stone (former member of Sequence).

VERTICAL HORIZON
Rock group from Boston, Massachusetts: Matt Scannell (vocals), Keith Kane (guitar), Sean Hurley (bass) and Ed Toth (drums).

VERUCA SALT
Rock group from Chicago, Illinois: Nina Gordon and Louise Post (vocals, guitar), with Steven Lack (bass) and Jim Shapiro (drums). Name taken from a character in the children's book *Charlie and The Chocolate Factory*.

VERVE, The
Rock group from Wigan, England: Richard Ashcroft (vocals), Nick McCabe (guitar), Simon Jones (bass) and Peter Salisbury (drums).

VERVE PIPE, The
Rock group from East Lansing, Michigan: brothers Brian (vocals) and Brad (bass) Vander Ark, A.J. Dunning (guitar), Doug Corella (keyboards) and Donny Brown (drums).

VESTA
Born Vesta Williams in 1963 in Coshocton, Ohio; raised in Los Angeles, California. Female R&B singer.

VIBRATIONS, The
R&B vocal group from Los Angeles, California: James Johnson, Carlton Fisher, Richard Owens, Dave Govan and Don Bradley. Originally recorded as The Jayhawks (Johnson, Fisher, Govan and Carver Bunkum). Also recorded the hit "Peanut Butter" as The Marathons. Owens joined The Temptations for a short time in 1971.

V.I.C.
Born Victor Owusu on 4/27/1987 in Queens, New York. Male rapper.

VICIOUS
Born in Brooklyn, New York. Pre-teen male black rapper/dancehall singer.

VIDAL, Maria
Dance singer. Formerly with Desmond Child & Rouge.

VIDELS, The
Pop vocal group from Providence, Rhode Island, featuring Pete Anders and Vinnie Poncia. Also see The Trade Winds.

VIGRASS & OSBORNE
Folk-rock duo from England: Paul Vigrass and Gary Osborne.

VILLAGE PEOPLE
Disco vocal group formed in New York: Victor Willis (policeman), Randy Jones (cowboy), David Hodo (construction worker), Felipe Rose (Indian chief), Glenn Hughes (biker) and Alexander Briley (G.I.). Willis replaced by Ray Simpson (brother of Valerie Simpson of Ashford & Simpson) in late 1979. Formed by French producer Jacques Morali (died of AIDS on 11/15/91, age 44). Appeared in the movie *Can't Stop The Music* (1980). Hughes died of cancer on 3/4/2001 (age 50).

VILLAGE SOUL CHOIR, The
Ten-member, interracial group from Jamaica, Queens, New York. Managed by former opera singer Charles Matthews.

VILLAGE STOMPERS, The
Dixieland-styled band from Greenwich Village, New York: Dick Brady, Ralph Casale, Don Coates, Frank Hubbell, Mitchell May, Joe Muranyi, Al McManus and Lenny Pogan.

VINCENT, Gene
Born Vincent Eugene Craddock on 2/11/1935 in Norfolk, Virginia. Died of a bleeding ulcer on 10/12/1971 (age 36). Legendary rock and roll singer/songwriter/guitarist. Injured left leg in motorcycle accident in 1953; had to wear steel brace thereafter. Formed the Blue Caps in Norfolk in 1956. Appeared in the movies *The Girl Can't Help It* and *Hot Rod Gang*. To England from 1960-67. Injured in car crash that killed Eddie Cochran in England in 1960.

VINTON, Bobby
Born Stanley Robert Vinton on 4/16/1935 in Canonsburg, Pennsylvania. Father was a bandleader. Formed own band while in high school; toured as leader of the backing band for Dick Clark's "Caravan of Stars" in 1960. Left band for a singing career in 1962. Own musical variety TV series from 1975-78. Dubbed "The Polish Prince."

VIOLATOR
Rap production duo from Brooklyn, New York: Chris Lighty and Eric Nicks.

VIOLENT FEMMES
Punk-rock trio from Milwaukee, Wisconsin: Gordon Gano (vocals, guitar), Brian Ritchie (bass) and Victor DeLorenzo (drums). Guy Hoffman replaced DeLorenzo in 1992.

VIRTUES, The
Rock and roll instrumental band from Philadelphia, Pennsylvania: Frank Virtue (guitar), Jimmy Bruno (guitar), Ralph Frederico (piano), Sonny Ferns (sax) and Barry Smith (drums).

VISCOUNTS, The
Rock and roll instrumental group from New Jersey: Harry Haller (tenor sax), brothers Bobby (guitar) and Joe (bass) Spievak, Larry Vecchio (organ) and Clark Smith (drums).

VITAMIN C
Born Colleen Fitzpatrick on 7/20/1972 in Old Bridge, New Jersey. Former lead singer of Eve's Plum. Portrayed "Amber Von Tussle" in the 1988 movie *Hairspray*. Named for her orange hair.

VITAMIN Z
Pop group from Sheffield, Yorkshire, England: Geoff Barradale (vocals), Neil Hubbard and David Rhodes (guitars), Nick Lockwood (keyboards, bass) and Jerry Marotta (drums).

VITO & THE SALUTATIONS
Male doo-wop group from Brooklyn, New York: Vito Balsamo (lead), Randy Silverman, Shelly Buchansky, Frankie Fox and Lenny Citrin.

VIXEN
Female hard-rock group formed in Los Angeles, California: Janet Gardner (vocals, guitar), Jan Kuehnemund (guitar), Share Pedersen (bass) and Roxy Petrucci (drums).

VOEGELE, Kate
Born on 12/8/1986 in Bay Village, Ohio. Singer/songwriter.

VOGUES, The
Pop-Adult Contemporary vocal group formed in Turtle Creek, Pennsylvania: Bill Burkette (lead), Hugh Geyer and Chuck Blasko (tenors), and Don Miller (baritone). Met in high school.

VOICE OF THE BEEHIVE
Rock band formed in London, England, by California-born sisters Melissa (vocals) and Tracey (vocals, guitar) Belland. British personnel include Mike Jones (guitar), Martin Brett (bass) and former Madness member Dan Woodgate (drums). The Bellands are the daughters of Bruce Belland of The Four Preps.

VOICES
Pre-teen R&B girl group from Los Angeles, California: Monique Wilson (age 12 in 1992), Arike Rice (age 10), and sisters LaToya (age 11) and LaPetra (age 10) McMoore. Rice went on to join Before Dark.

VOICES OF AMERICA
A project of the USA for Africa foundation.

VOICES OF THEORY
Male Latino R&B vocal group from Philadelphia, Pennsylvania: James Cartagena, Mechi Cebollero, David Cordoba, Hector Ramos and Eric Serrano.

VOICES THAT CARE
Benefit spearheaded by David Foster and his fiancee Linda Thompson Jenner (ex-wife of Olympian Bruce Jenner) supporting the Persian Gulf allied troops and their families. Among superstar choir: Kevin Costner, Meryl Streep, Billy Crystal, Richard Gere, Gloria Estefan, Wayne Gretzky and many others.

VOLUME'S, The
R&B doo-wop group from Detroit, Michigan: Ed Union (lead), Elijah Davis, Larry Wright, Joe Truvillion and Ernest Newson.

VONTASTICS, The
R&B group from Chicago, Illinois: Bobby Newsome, Kenneth Golar, Jose Holmes and Raymond Penn.

VOUDOURIS, Roger
Born on 12/29/1954 in Sacramento, California. Died on 8/3/2003 (age 48). Pop singer/songwriter/guitarist.

VOXPOPPERS, The
Pop-rock and roll group from Brooklyn, New York, featuring brothers Freddie, Sal and Harry Tamburo.

VOYAGE
Disco group from Europe: Sylvia Mason (vocals), Slim Pezin (guitar), Marc Chantereau (keyboards), Sauver Mallin (bass) and Pierre-Alain Dahan (drums).

VOYCE
Dance trio of cousins from Brooklyn, New York: Carlos Colon (lead vocals), Danny Madera and Miguel Cordero.

VYBE
Female R&B vocal group from Los Angeles, California: Pam Olivia, Tanya Robinson, Debbie Mitchell and Stacey Dove-Daniels.

WACKERS, The
Pop-rock group formed in Montreal, Quebec, Canada: Randy Bishop (vocals), Robert Segarini (guitar), J.P. Lauzon (keyboards), Bill "Kootch" Trochim (bass) and Spencer "Ernie" Earnshaw (drums).

WACKO
Born in New Orleans, Louisiana. Male rapper.

WADE, Adam
Born on 3/17/1937 in Pittsburgh, Pennsylvania. Black Adult Contemporary singer. Attended Virginia State College and worked as lab assistant with Dr. Jonas Salk team. TV actor/host of the 1975 game show *Musical Chairs*. Worked in *Guys & Dolls* musical in Las Vegas in 1978. TV talkshow host in Los Angeles in the 1980s.

WADSWORTH MANSION
Pop-rock group formed in Los Angeles, California: brothers Steve (vocals) and Mike (drums) Jablecki, Wayne Gagnon (guitar) and John Poole (bass).

WAGNER, Jack
Born on 10/3/1959 in Washington, Missouri. TV actor/singer. Played "Frisco Jones" on the TV soap opera *General Hospital* (1983-87). Also acted on several other TV soaps.

WAGONER, Porter
Born on 8/12/1927 in West Plains, Missouri. Died of lung cancer on 10/28/2007 (age 80). Country singer Host of his own TV variety series, 1960-79.

WAIKIKIS, The
Instrumental studio group from Belgium.

WAILERS, The
Teen rock and roll instrumental group from Tacoma, Washington: John Greek and Rich Dangel (guitars), Mark Marush (sax), Kent Morrill (piano) and Mike Burk (drums). Dangel died on 12/2/2002 (age 60).

WAINWRIGHT, Loudon III
Born on 9/5/1946 in Chapel Hill, North Carolina. Satirical folk singer/songwriter. His father was the

longtime editor of *Life* magazine. Played "Capt. Calvin Spaulding" in three episodes of TV's *M*A*S*H*. Appeared in the movies *The Slugger's Wife* and *Jacknife*. Married briefly to Kate McGarrigle (McGarrigle Sisters) in the mid-1970s, and Suzzy Roche (The Roches) in the 1980s.

WAITE, John
Born on 7/4/1955 in Lancaster, Lancashire, England. Lead singer of the rock groups The Babys and Bad English.

WAITRESSES, The
Rock group from Akron, Ohio: Patty Donahue (vocals; died of cancer on 12/9/1996, age 40), Chris Butler (guitar), Dan Klayman (keyboards), Mars Williams (sax), Tracy Wormworth (bass) and Billy Ficca (drums; Television).

WAITS, Tom
Born on 12/7/1949 in Pomona, California. Gravelly-voiced song stylist/actor.

WAKELIN, Johnny
Born in 1939 in Brighton, Sussex, England. White reggae-styled singer/songwriter.

WALDEN, Narada Michael
Born Michael Walden on 4/23/1952 in Kalamazoo, Michigan. R&B singer/songwriter/drummer/producer. With John McLaughlin's Mahavishnu Orchestra from 1974-76. With Jeff Beck in 1975. Solo artist and much session work since 1976. Producer for Whitney Houston.

WALDMAN, Wendy
Born on 11/29/1950 in Los Angeles, California. Folk-pop singer/songwriter/producer.

WALKER, Billy
Born on 1/14/1929 in Ralls, Texas. Died in a car crash on 5/21/2006 (age 77). Country singer.

WALKER, Boots
Born on 3/24/1938 in Marshall, Texas. Pop-novelty singer.

WALKER, Chris
Born in Houston, Texas. Male R&B singer/jazz bassist.

WALKER, Clay
Born Ernest Clayton Walker on 8/19/1969 in Beaumont, Texas. Country singer/songwriter/guitarist.

WALKER, Gloria
Born in Detroit, Michigan. R&B singer.

WALKER, Jerry Jeff
Born Ronald Clyde Crosby on 3/16/1942 in Oneonta, New York. Country-folk-rock singer/songwriter. Wrote "Mr. Bojangles."

WALKER, Jr., & The All Stars
Born Autry DeWalt-Mixom on 6/14/1931 in Blytheville, Arkansas. Died of cancer on 11/23/1995 (age 64). R&B singer/saxophonist. The All Stars: Willie Woods (guitar), Vic Thomas (keyboards) and James Graves (drums). Woods died on 5/27/1997 (age 60). First recorded for Harvey in 1962. Walker contributed sax solo to

WALKER, Jr., & The All Stars — cont'd
Foreigner's 1981 hit "Urgent"; appeared in 1988 movie *Tapeheads*. His son Autry DeWalt, Jr. (drums) joined band in 1983.

WALKER, T-Bone
Born Aaron Thibeaux Walker on 5/28/1910 in Linden, Texas. Died of pneumonia on 3/16/1975 (age 64). Highly influential blues singer/guitarist. Stage antics with guitar closely followed by early Elvis Presley.

WALKER BROS., The
"Blue-eyed soul" trio from Los Angeles, California: Scott Engel, Gary Leeds and John Maus. More popular in England than the U.S.

WALL, Paul
Born Paul Slayton on 3/30/1980 in Houston, Texas. Male rapper/songwriter.

WALLACE, Jerry
Born on 12/15/1928 in Guilford, Missouri; raised in Glendale, Arizona. Died of heart failure on 5/5/2008 (age 79). Pop-country singer/guitarist. First recorded for Allied in 1951.

WALLACE BROTHERS
R&B vocal duo: brothers Ernest Wallace and Johnny Wallace.

WALLFLOWERS, The
Rock group formed in Los Angeles, California: Jakob Dylan (vocals), Michael Ward (guitar), Rami Jaffe (keyboards), Greg Richling (bass) and Mario Calire (drums). Dylan is the son of Bob Dylan.

WALL OF VOODOO
Alternative-rock group formed in Los Angeles, California: Stan Ridgway (vocals), Marc Moreland (guitar), Chas T. Gray (bass) and Joe Nanini (drums). Moreland died of kidney failure on 3/13/2002 (age 44).

WALSH, Joe
Born on 11/20/1947 in Wichita, Kansas; raised in Cleveland, Ohio. Rock singer/songwriter/guitarist. Member of The James Gang (1969-71) and the Eagles (1975-82, 1994). Own band (1972-75), Barnstorm, featured drummer Joe Vitale and bassist Kenny Passarelli.

WALTERS, Jamie
Born on 6/13/1969 in Boston, Massachusetts. Male singer/actor. Former lead singer of The Heights.

WAMMACK, Travis
Born in 1946 in Walnut, Mississippi; raised in Memphis, Tennessee. Prolific session guitarist of the FAME studios in Muscle Shoals, Alabama.

WANDERERS, The
R&B vocal group: Ray Pollard, Frank Joyner, Robert Yarborough and Sheppard Grant.

WANDERLEY, Walter
Born on 5/12/1932 in Recife, Brazil. Died of cancer on 9/4/1986 (age 54). Samba organist.

WANG CHUNG
Pop-rock trio from London, England: Jack Hues (vocals, guitar, keyboards), Nick Feldman (bass,

keyboards) and Darren Costin (drums). Costin left in 1985.

WAR
Latin funk-rock band from Long Beach, California: Lonnie Jordan (keyboards; born on 11/21/1948), Howard Scott (guitar; born on 3/15/1946), Charles Miller (sax; born on 6/2/1939), Morris "B.B." Dickerson (bass; born on 8/3/1949), Harold Brown (drums; born on 3/17/1946) and Thomas "Papa Dee" Allen (percussion; born on 7/19/1931), and Lee Oskar (harmonica; born on 3/24/1948). Eric Burdon's backup band until 1971. Alice Tweed Smyth (vocals) added in 1978. By 1979, Luther Rabb replaced Dickerson; Pat Rizzo (horns) and Ronnie Hammond (percussion; of R&B band Aalon) joined. Rabb and Hammond were members of Ballin' Jack. Miller was shot to death in June 1980 (age 41). Allen died of an aneurysm on 8/30/1988 (age 57). Smyth left group in 1982. Lineup by 1994: Jordan, Scott, Brown and Hammond with Rae Valentine, Charles Green, Kerry Campbell, Tetsuya Nakamura and Sal Rodriguez.

WARD, Anita
Born on 12/20/1956 in Memphis, Tennessee. Disco singer.

WARD, Billy
Born on 9/19/1921 in Los Angeles, California. Died on 2/16/2002 (age 80). R&B pianist. His vocal group, The Dominoes: Charlie White (tenor), Joe Lamont (baritone) and Bill Brown (bass). Signed by King/Federal in 1950. Lead singers, at various times: Clyde McPhatter (1950-53), Jackie Wilson (1953-57) and Eugene Mumford.

WARD, Dale
Born in Florida. Pop-country singer. Was not a member of The Crescendos, as rumored.

WARD, Joe
Born in 1947 in Brooklyn, New York. Discovered by Steve Allen. On NBC-TV's *Juvenile Jury* from age five to nine. Prolific commercial songwriter/producer/arranger/singer as an adult.

WARD, Robin
Born Jacqueline Eloise McDonnell in Hawaii; raised in Nebraska. Pop singer.

WARINER, Steve
Born on 12/25/1954 in Noblesville, Indiana. Country singer/songwriter/guitarist.

WARNES, Jennifer
Born on 3/3/1947 in Seattle, Washington; raised in Orange County, California. Adult Contemporary singer/actress. Lead actress in the Los Angeles production of *Hair*. Also recorded as Jennifer Warren and simply as Jennifer.

WARRANT
Male hard-rock group from Los Angeles, California: Jani Lane (vocals), Erik Turner and Joey Allen (guitars), Jerry Dixon (bass) and Steven Sweet (drums).

WARREN G
Born Warren Griffin on 11/10/1970 in Long Beach, California. Male rapper.

WARWICK, Dee Dee
Born on 9/25/1945 in East Orange, New Jersey. Died on 10/18/2008 (age 66). R&B singer. Younger sister of Dionne Warwick; cousin of Whitney Houston. Sang in the gospel group the Drinkard Singers. Backup work for many artists.

WARWICK, Dionne
Born Marie Dionne Warwick on 12/12/1940 in East Orange, New Jersey. In church choir from age six. With the Drinkard Singers gospel group. Formed the Gospelaires trio with sister Dee Dee Warwick and their aunt Cissy Houston. Dionne is a cousin of Whitney Houston. Attended Hartt College Of Music, Hartford, Connecticut. Much backup studio work in New York during the late 1950s. Added an "e" to her last name for a time in the early 1970s. Dionne was Burt Bacharach's and Hal David's main "voice" for the songs they composed. Co-hosted TV's *Solid Gold* 1980-81, 1985-86. Beginning in the early 1990s, hosted TV infomercials for the Psychic Friends Network.

WASH, Martha
Born on 12/28/1953 in San Francisco, California. Former backing singer for Sylvester. One-half of Two Tons O' Fun duo, later known as The Weather Girls. Uncredited lead vocalist of "Everybody Everybody" by Black Box, "Gonna Make You Sweat" by C & C Music Factory and "You're My One And Only (True Love)" by Seduction.

WASHINGTON, Baby
Born Justine Washington (aka: Jeanette Washington) on 11/13/1940 in Bamberg, South Carolina; raised in Harlem, New York. R&B singer/pianist. Sang in vocal group The Hearts. First recorded solo for J&S in 1957.

WASHINGTON, Dinah
Born Ruth Lee Jones on 8/29/1924 in Tuscaloosa, Alabama. Died of an alcohol/pill overdose on 12/14/1963 (age 39). All-time great jazz-blues vocalist/pianist. Moved to Chicago in 1927. With Sallie Martin Gospel Singers, 1940-41; local club work in Chicago, 1941-43. With Lionel Hampton, 1943-46. First recorded for Keynote in 1943. Solo touring from 1946. Married seven times, once to singer Eddie Chamblee.

WASHINGTON, Ella
Born in Miami, Florida. R&B singer. First recorded for Octavia in 1965. Turned to gospel singing in 1973.

WASHINGTON, Grover Jr.
Born on 12/12/1943 in Buffalo, New York. Died on 12/17/1999 (age 56). Jazz-R&B saxophonist.

WASHINGTON, Keith
Born in Detroit, Michigan. R&B singer/songwriter.

WAS (NOT WAS)
Interracial pop-dance-R&B group from Detroit, Michigan. Fronted by composer/bassist Don Fagenson ("Don Was") and lyricist/flutist David Weiss ("David Was"). Includes vocalists Sweet Pea Atkinson and Sir Harry Bowens. Group appeared in the movie *The Freshman*.

WATERFRONT
Male pop-rock duo from Cardiff, Wales: Chris Duffy (vocals) and Phil Cillia (guitar).

WATERS, Crystal
Born in 1964 in Philadelphia, Pennsylvania. Black dance singer/songwriter.

WATERS, Muddy
Born McKinley Morganfield on 4/4/1915 in Rolling Fork, Mississippi. Died of a heart attack on 4/30/1983 (age 68). Highly influential and legendary blues singer/guitarist/harmonica player.

WATLEY, Jody
Born on 1/30/1959 in Chicago, Illinois. Female singer for the R&B-dance trio Shalamar (1977-84) and former dancer on TV's *Soul Train*. Goddaughter of Jackie Wilson.

WATSON, Gene
Born Gary Gene Watson on 10/11/1943 in Palestine, Texas; raised in Paris, Texas. Country singer/guitarist. Own band, Gene Watson & The Other Four. First recorded for Tonka in 1965. Played for many years at the Dynasty Club in Houston.

WATSON, Johnny "Guitar"
Born on 2/3/1935 in Houston, Texas. Died of a heart attack on 5/17/1996 (age 61) while performing at the Yokohama Blues Cafe in Japan. R&B singer/songwriter/guitarist. First recorded for Federal in 1952. Member of the R&B group The Shields.

WATTS, Noble "Thin Man"
Born on 2/16/1926 in DeLand, Florida. Died of emphysema on 8/24/2004 (age 78). R&B saxophonist/songwriter.

WA WA NEE
Pop group from Australia: brothers Paul (vocals, keyboards) and Mark (bass) Gray, with Steve Williams (guitar) and Chris Sweeney (drums).

WAX
Pop duo: Andrew Gold and Graham Gouldman (10cc). Credited later as Wax U.K.

WAYNE, Jimmy
Born Jimmy Wayne Barber on 10/23/1972 in Bessemer City, North Carolina; raised in Gastonia, North Carolina. Country singer/songwriter.

WAYNE, Thomas
Born Thomas Wayne Perkins on 7/22/1940 in Battsville, Mississippi. Died in a car accident on 8/15/1971 (age 31). Brother of guitarist Luther Perkins of Johnny Cash's band. Backing vocals by the female group The DeLons.

WC
Born William Calhoun in Los Angeles, California. Male rapper. Member of Westside Connection.

WEATHER GIRLS, The
R&B-disco duo from San Francisco, California: Martha Wash and Izora Redman. Formerly "Two Tons O' Fun." Backup singers for Sylvester in the late 1970s. Wash was the uncredited lead vocalist of "You're My One And Only (True Love)" by

WEATHER GIRLS, The — cont'd
Seduction, "Everybody Everybody" by Black Box and "Gonna Make You Sweat" by C & C Music Factory. Redman died of heart failure on 9/16/2004.

WEATHERLY, Jim
Born on 3/17/1943 in Pontotoc, Mississippi. Pop-country singer/songwriter. Wrote Gladys Knight's hits "Neither One Of Us," "Midnight Train To Georgia" and "Best Thing That Ever Happened To Me." Played quarterback for the University of Mississippi.

WEBB, Paula
Born in Ypsilanti, Michigan. Age 10 in 1975.

WEBBIE
Born Webster Gradney on 9/6/1985 in Baton Rouge, Louisiana. Male rapper/songwriter.

WEBER, Joan
Born on 12/12/1935 in Paulsboro, New Jersey. Died on 5/13/1981 (age 45). Pop singer (19 years old in 1954).

WEBSTAR & YOUNG B
Hip-hop trio from Harlem, New York: Troy "Webstar" Ryan, Bianca "Young B" Dupree and Anthony "The Voice Of Harlem" Glover.

WEDNESDAY
Pop group from Oshawa, Ontario, Canada: Mike O'Neil (vocals), Paul Andrew-Smith, John Dufek and Randy Begg.

WEEZER
Rock group from Los Angeles, California: Rivers Cuomo (vocals, guitar), Brian Bell (guitar), Matt Sharp (bass) and Pat Wilson (drums). Also see The Rentals.

WE FIVE
Pop group from San Francisco, California: Beverly Bivens (vocals), Bob Jones and Jerry Burgan (guitars), Pete Fullerton (bass) and Mike Stewart (drums). Stewart (brother of John Stewart) died on 11/13/2002 (age 57).

WEIR, Bob
Born Robert Hall on 10/16/1947 in San Francisco, California. Co-founder of the Grateful Dead. Later formed Kingfish and Bobby & The Midnites.

WEISSBERG, Eric, & Steve Mandell
Prominent session musicians. Both had worked with Judy Collins and John Denver. Weissberg was a member of The Tarriers in the 1960s.

WELCH, Bob
Born on 7/31/1946 in Los Angeles, California. Pop-rock singer/guitarist. Member of Fleetwood Mac from 1971-74.

WELCH, Lenny
Born on 5/15/1938 in Asbury Park, New Jersey. Black Adult Contemporary singer.

WELK, Lawrence
Born on 3/11/1903 in Strasburg, North Dakota. Died of pneumonia on 5/17/1992 (age 89). Accordion player and sweet band leader since the mid-1920s. Band's style labeled as "champagne music." Own

national TV musical variety show began on 7/2/1955 and ran on ABC until 9/4/1971. New episodes in syndication from 1971 to 1982. Reruns still enjoy immense popularity.

WELLER, Freddy
Born on 9/9/1947 in Atlanta, Georgia. Pop-country singer/guitarist. Member of Paul Revere & The Raiders (1967-71).

WELLS, Kitty
Born Ellen Muriel Deason on 8/30/1919 in Nashville, Tennessee. Singer/songwriter/guitarist. Known as "The Queen of Country Music". Married Johnny Wright (of Johnnie & Jack) on 10/30/1937.

WELLS, Mary
Born on 5/13/1943 in Detroit, Michigan. Died of cancer on 7/26/1992 (age 49). R&B singer. At age 17, presented "Bye Bye Baby," a tune she had written for Jackie Wilson, to Wilson's producer, Berry Gordy, Jr. Gordy signed her to his newly formed label, Motown. Wells was the first artist to have a Top 10 and #1 single for that label. Married for a time to Cecil Womack (brother of Bobby Womack).

WENDY & LISA
Pop duo from Los Angeles, California: Wendy Melvoin (born on 1/26/1964) and Lisa Coleman (born on 6/8/1960). Formerly with Prince's band, The Revolution. Wendy is daughter of Mike Melvoin (The Plastic Cow); twin sister of Susannah Melvoin (The Family); sister of the late Jonathan Melvoin (touring keyboardist with Smashing Pumpkins).

WERNER, Max
Born in Holland. Lead singer of Kayak.

WESLEY, Fred, & The J.B.'s
Born on 7/4/1943 in Mobile, Alabama. Trombonist/arranger/musical director for James Brown. Member of The First Family. Core members of his band: Hearlon "Cheese" Martin (guitar), Maceo Parker (sax), Fred Thomas (bass) and John "Jabo" Starks (drums).

WEST, Dottie
Born Dorothy Marsh on 10/11/1932 in McMinnville, Tennessee. Died on 9/4/1991 (age 58) from injuries suffered in a car accident on 8/30/1991. Country singer.

WEST, Kanye
Born on 6/8/1977 in Atlanta, Georgia; raised in Chicago, Illinois. Male rapper/songwriter/producer. Produced hit songs for Eminem, Jay-Z, Janet Jackson, Alicia Keys, The Game, John Legend and Common.

WEST COAST RAP ALL-STARS, The
Rap benefit for inner city youth: Above The Law, Body & Soul, Def Jef, Digital Underground, Eazy-E, Ice-T, J.J. Fad, King Tee, M.C. Hammer, Michel'le, N.W.A., Oaktown's 3-5-7, Tone Loc and Young MC

WESTLIFE
"Boy band" from Dublin, Ireland: Nicky Byrne, Shane Filan, Kian Egan, Mark Feehily and Bryan McFadden.

WESTON, Kim
Born Agatha Natalie Weston on 12/30/39 in Detroit, Michigan. R&B singer; previously sang in gospel groups.

WESTSIDE CONNECTION
Collaboration of rap stars Ice Cube, Mack 10 and WC.

WEST STREET MOB
Dance trio from Englewood, New Jersey: Joey Robinson, Warren Moore and Sebrina Gillison. Robinson is the son of Sylvia.

WE THE KINGS
Pop-rock band from Bradenton, Florida: brothers Hunter Thomsen (guitar) and Drew Thomsen (bass), with Travis Clark (vocals) and Danny Duncan (drums).

WET WET WET
Pop-rock group from Glasgow, Scotland: Marti Pellow (vocals), Neil Mitchell (keyboards), Graeme Clark (bass) and Tom Cunningham (drums). Band name inspired from a line in the Scritti Politti song "Getting, Having, and Holding."

WET WILLIE
Southern-rock band from Mobile, Alabama: brothers Jack (bass) and Jimmy Hall (vocals), Rick Hirsch (guitar), John Anthony (keyboards) and Lewis Ross (drums). Michael Duke (keyboards, vocals) joined in late 1975.

WHAT IS THIS
Pop-rock trio: Alain Johannes (vocals, guitar), Chris Hutchinson (bass) and Jack Irons (drums; Red Hot Chili Peppers, Pearl Jam).

WHATNAUTS
R&B vocal trio from Baltimore, Maryland: Billy Herndon (lead), Garnet Jones (tenor) and Gerald Pinkney (baritone).

WHEELER, Billy Edd
Born on 12/9/1932 in Whitesville, West Virginia. Folk singer/songwriter/guitarist. Wrote "Reverend Mr. Black" for The Kingston Trio and "Coward Of The County" for Kenny Rogers. Co-owner of Sleepy Hollow Music.

WHEELER, Caron
Born on 1/19/1963 in London, England (of Jamaican parents). Female R&B singer. Featured vocalist on Soul II Soul's hits "Keep On Movin'" and "Back To Life." Backup singer for Elvis Costello in 1983.

WHEN IN ROME
Electro-dance trio from England: Clive Farrington and Andrew Mann (vocals), with Michael Floreale (keyboards).

WHIRLWIND
R&B-disco trio: Sandie Ancrum and her brothers Charles and Eddie Ancrum.

WHISPERS, The
R&B-dance vocal group formed in Los Angeles, California: twin brothers Walter and Wallace "Scotty" Scott, Gordy Harmon (The Superbs),

Marcus Hutson and Nicholas Caldwell. First recorded for Dore in 1964. Harmon replaced in 1973 by Leaveil Degree, who was briefly a member of The Friends Of Distinction. Group founded the Black Tie record label.

WHISTLE
R&B vocal group from Brooklyn, New York: Brian Faust, Rickford Bennett, Kerry Hodge and Tarek Stevens.

WHITCOMB, Ian
Born on 7/10/1941 in Woking, Surrey, England. Pop singer/songwriter/author.

WHITE, Barry
Born on 9/12/1944 in Galveston, Texas; raised in Los Angeles, California. Died of kidney failure on 7/4/2003 (age 58). Deep-voiced smooth soul singer/songwriter/keyboardist/producer/ arranger. With Upfronts vocal group, recorded for Lummtone in 1960. A&R man for Mustang/Bronco, 1966-67. Formed Love Unlimited in 1969, which included future wife Glodean James. Leader of 40-piece Love Unlimited Orchestra.

WHITE, Danny
Born in New Jersey. Pop-disco singer.

WHITE, Karyn
Born on 10/14/1965 in Los Angeles, California. R&B-dance singer. Touring vocalist with O'Bryan in 1984. Recorded with jazz-fusion keyboardist Jeff Lorber in 1986. Married to superproducer Terry Lewis (member of The Time).

WHITE, Kitty
Adult Contemporary singer.

WHITE, Lari
Born on 5/13/1965 in Dunedin, Florida. Country singer. Pronounced: Laurie.

WHITE, Maurice
Born on 12/19/1941 in Memphis, Tennessee. Percussionist with Ramsey Lewis from 1966-71. Founder and co-lead vocalist of Earth, Wind & Fire.

WHITE, Tony Joe
Born on 7/23/1943 in Goodwill, Louisiana. Bayou-rock singer/songwriter. Wrote Brook Benton's hit "Rainy Night In Georgia."

WHITEHEAD BROS.
Duo of Kenny and Johnny Whitehead; sons of prolific songwriter John Whitehead of McFadden & Whitehead. Charted, while teens, in 1986 on the R&B singles chart as Kenny & Johnny Whitehead.

WHITE LION
Hair-metal band formed in Brooklyn, New York: Mike Tramp (vocals), Vito Bratta (guitar), James Lomenzo (bass) and Greg D'Angelo (drums).

WHITE PLAINS
Studio group from England. Featuring Tony Burrows (vocals), who was also with The Brotherhood Of Man, Edison Lighthouse, First Class and The Pipkins.

WHITESNAKE

Former Deep Purple vocalist David Coverdale, who recorded solo as Whitesnake in 1977, formed British heavy-metal band in 1978. Coverdale fronted everchanging lineup. Early members included his Deep Purple bandmates, keyboardist Jon Lord (1978-84) and drummer Ian Paice (1979-81). Players in 1987 included John Sykes (guitar), Neil Murray (bass) and Aynsley Dunbar (former Jefferson Starship drummer). Sykes left in 1988 to form Blue Murder. Ex-Dio guitarist Vivian Campbell was a member from 1987-88, later with Riverdogs, Shadow King and Def Leppard. 1989 lineup included Steve Vai (David Lee Roth's former guitarist), Adrian Vandenberg (former guitarist of Vandenberg), Rudy Sarzo (bass; Quiet Riot) and Tommy Aldridge (drums). Lineup in 1994: Coverdale, Vandenberg, Sarzo, Warren De Martini (guitar; Ratt), Paul Mirkovich (keyboards) and Denny Carmassi (drums; Heart). Coverdale married to actress Tawny Kitaen from 1989-92.

WHITE STRIPES, The

Rock duo from Detroit, Michigan: Jack White (vocals, guitar; born John Gillis) and Meg White (drums). Married from 1996-2000. Jack played "Georgia" in the movie Cold Mountain. Jack also formed The Raconteurs.

WHITE TOWN

Born Jyoti Mishra on 7/30/1966 in Rourkela, India; raised in England. Male synth-pop singer/multi-instrumentalist.

WHITE ZOMBIE

Hard-rock group formed in New York: Rob Zombie (vocals), Jay Yuenger (guitar), Sean Yseult (bass) and John Tempesta (drums). Band named after a 1932 Bela Lugosi movie.

WHITFIELD, David

Born on 2/2/1926 in Hull, Yorkshire, England. Classical-styled tenor.

WHITING, Margaret

Born on 7/22/1924 in Detroit, Michigan; raised in Hollywood, California. Daughter of popular composer Richard Whiting ("Till We Meet Again"). One of the top female vocalists of the 1940s.

WHITMAN, Slim

Born Otis Whitman on 1/20/1924 in Tampa, Florida. Country balladeer/yodeller. Gained greatest fame with best-selling compilation albums sold exclusively over TV.

WHITNEY, Marva

Born Marva Manning on 5/1/1944 in Kansas City, Kansas. Female R&B singer.

WHITTAKER, Roger

Born on 3/22/1936 in Nairobi, Kenya, Africa (of British parents). Adult Contemporary singer.

WHO, The

Rock group formed in London, England: Roger Daltrey (vocals; born on 3/1/1944), Pete Townshend (guitar, vocals; born on 5/19/1945), John Entwistle (bass; born on 10/9/1944) and Keith Moon (drums; born on 8/23/1947). Originally known as the High Numbers in 1964. All but Moon had been in The Detours. Developed stage antics of destroying their instruments. 1969 rock opera album Tommy became a movie in 1975. Solo work by members began in 1972. Moon died of a drug overdose on 9/7/1978 (age 31); replaced by Kenney Jones (formerly with Small Faces). 1973 rock opera album Quadrophenia became a movie in 1979. The Who's biographical movie, The Kids Are Alright, was released in 1979. Eleven fans trampled to death at their concert in Cincinnati on 12/3/1979. Disbanded in 1982. Regrouped at "Live Aid" in 1986. Daltrey, Townshend and Entwistle reunited with an ensemble of 15 for a U.S. tour in 1989 and again in 2000. Jones formed The Law with Paul Rodgers in 1991. Entwistle died of a heart attack on 6/27/2002 (age 57).

WHODINI

Rap trio from Brooklyn, New York: Jalil Hutchins, John Fletcher and Drew Carter.

WICKS, Chuck

Born on 6/20/1979 in Smyrna, Delaware. Country singer/songwriter. Featured performer on the 2007 TV reality series Nashville.

WIEDLIN, Jane

Born on 5/20/1958 in Oconomowoc, Wisconsin; raised in California. Pop-rock singer/guitarist. Member of the Go-Go's.

WIER, Rusty

Born in Austin, Texas. Country-rock singer/songwriter/guitarist.

WILBURN BROTHERS

Counrty duo from Hardy, Arkansas: brothers Virgil "Doyle" Wilburn (born on 7/7/1930; died on 10/16/1982, age 52) and Thurman "Teddy" Wilburn (born on 11/30/1931; died on 11/24/2003, age 71). Regulars on the Louisiana Hayride from 1948-51. Duo hosted own syndicated TV show from 1963-74. Doyle was once married to singer Margie Bowes.

WILCOX, Harlow

Born on 1/28/1943 in Norman, Oklahoma. Session guitarist.

WILD, Jack

Born on 9/30/1952 in Rayton, Manchester, England. Died of cancer on 3/1/2006 (age 53). Child actor. Played "The Artful Dodger" in the movie Oliver! and "Jimmy" on TV's H.R. Pufnstuf.

WILD BLUE

Pop group from Chicago, Illinois: Renee Varo (vocals), Mike Gorman, Ken Harck, Frank Barbalace and Joe Zanona.

WILD-CATS, The

Rock and roll instrumental trio from New Jersey: Dennis Gorgas (guitar), Frank Rainey (organ) and Pat Piccininno (drums). Discovered by guitarist Billy Mure.

WILD CHERRY

White funk group from Steubenville, Ohio: Robert Parissi (vocals, guitar), Bryan Bassett (guitar), Mark Avsec (keyboards; Cellarful Of Noise), Allen Wentz (bass) and Ron Beitle (drums).

WILDE, Eugene
Born Ron Broomfield in Miami, Florida. R&B singer/
songwriter. Member of the family group Life.

WILDE, Kim
Born Kim Smith on 11/18/1960 in Chiswick, London,
England. Pop-rock-dance singer. Daughter of Marty
Wilde.

WILDE, Marty
Born Reginald Smith on 4/15/1936 in London,
England. Pop singer/songwriter. Father of Kim
Wilde. Also recorded as Shannon.

WILDER, Matthew
Born on 1/24/1953 in Manhattan, New York. White
singer/songwriter/keyboardist. Session singer for
Rickie Lee Jones and Bette Midler. Later produced
group No Doubt.

WILDFIRE
Pop vocal group formed in Atlanta, Georgia: Jack
"Stack-A-Track" Grochmal, Scott Shannon, Ralph
Penguinn and Herman Penguinn. Grochmal is a
noted session musician. Shannon is a popular radio
personality.

WILD ORCHID
Teen female vocal trio from Los Angeles, California:
Stacy "Fergie" Ferguson, Stefanie Ridel and Renee
Sandstrom. Both Ferguson (1984-89) and
Sandstrom (1984-87) were regulars on the TV show
Kids Incorporated. Ferguson later joined Black Eyed
Peas.

WILDWEEDS, The
Garage-rock band from Connecticut: Al Anderson
(guitar; Clean Living, NRBQ), Ray Zeiner
(keyboards), Skip Yakitis (percussion), Bob Dudek
(bass) and Andy Lepak (drums). Dudek died of
heart failure on 6/2/2002 (age 57).

WILKINSONS, The
Country vocal trio from Belleville, Ontario, Canada:
father Steve with children Amanda and Tyler
Wilkinson.

WILLIAMS, Andre
Born in 1936 in Chicago, Illinois. R&B singer/
songwriter/producer.

WILLIAMS, Andy
Born Howard Andrew Williams on 12/3/1927 in Wall
Lake, Iowa. Formed quartet with his brothers and
eventually moved to Los Angeles. With Bing Crosby
on hit "Swingin' On A Star," 1944. With comedienne
Kay Thompson in the mid-1940s. Went solo in
1952. On Steve Allen's *Tonight Show* from 1952-55.
Own NBC-TV variety series from 1962-67, 1969-71.
Appeared in the movie *I'd Rather Be Rich* in 1964.
Married to singer/actress Claudine Longet from
1962-67. One of America's greatest Adult
Contemporary singers.

WILLIAMS, Anson
Born Anson William Heimlick on 9/25/1952 in Los
Angeles, California. Actor/singer. Played "Potsie
Weber" on TV's *Happy Days*.

WILLIAMS, Billy
Born on 12/28/1910 in Waco, Texas. Died on
10/17/1972 (age 61). Lead singer of The
Charioteers from 1930-50. Formed own Billy
Williams Quartet with Eugene Dixon, Claude
Riddick and John Ball in 1950. Many appearances
on TV, especially *Your Show Of Shows* with Sid
Caesar. By the early 1960s, had lost voice due to
diabetes. Moved to Chicago and worked as a social
worker until his death.

WILLIAMS, Christopher
Born in Harlem, New York. R&B singer/songwriter.
Nephew of jazz great Ella Fitzgerald.

WILLIAMS, Danny
Born on 1/7/1942 in Port Elizabeth, South Africa.
Died on 12/6/2005 (age 63). Black ballad singer.

WILLIAMS, Deniece
Born Deniece Chandler on 6/3/1951 in Gary,
Indiana. R&B singer/songwriter. Recorded for
Toddlin' Town, early 1960s. Member of
Wonderlove, Stevie Wonder's backup group, from
1972-75. Also a popular Inspirational artist.

WILLIAMS, Diana
Born on 8/9/1959 in Nashville, Tennessee. Country
singer.

WILLIAMS, Don
Born on 5/27/1939 in Floydada, Texas. Country
singer/songwriter/guitarist. Leader of the Pozo-Seco
Singers. In movies *W.W. & The Dixie Dancekings*
and *Smokey & The Bandit II*.

WILLIAMS, Geoffrey
Born in 1965 in London, England (of West Indian
parentage). R&B-dance singer/songwriter.

WILLIAMS, Hank
Born Hiram King Williams on 9/17/1923 in Mount
Olive, Alabama. Died of alcohol/drug abuse on
1/1/1953 (age 29). Legendary Country singer/
songwriter/guitarist. Father of Hank Williams, Jr.
and grandfather of Hank Williams III. George
Hamilton portrayed Hank in the movie biography
Your Cheatin' Heart.

WILLIAMS, Hank Jr.
Born Randall Hank Williams on 5/26/1949 in
Shreveport, Louisiana; raised in Nashville,
Tennessee. Country singer/songwriter/guitarist. Son
of country music's first superstar, Hank Williams.
Nicknamed "Bocephus" by his father. Injured in a
climbing accident on 8/8/1975 in Montana; returned
to performing in 1977. Richard Thomas starred as
Hank in his 1983 biographical TV movie *Living
Proof: The Hank Williams, Jr. Story*. Sings the
opening song for TV's *Monday Night Football*.

WILLIAMS, John
Born on 2/8/1932 in Flushing, Long Island, New
York. Noted composer/conductor of many top
box-office movie hits. Succeeded Arthur Fiedler as
conductor of the Boston Pops Orchestra in 1980;
resigned in 1993 but continued as music adviser.
His son, Joseph, became a member of Toto in
1986.

WILLIAMS, Johnny
Born on 1/15/1942 in Tyler, Alabama. Died in December 1986 (age 44). R&B singer.

WILLIAMS, Larry
Born on 5/10/1935 in New Orleans, Louisiana. Committed suicide on 1/2/1980 (age 44). R&B-rock and roll singer/songwriter/pianist. With Lloyd Price in the early 1950s. Convicted of narcotics dealing in 1960; jail term interrupted his career. The Beatles recorded his songs "Slow Down," "Dizzy Miss Lizzy" and "Bad Boy."

WILLIAMS, Lenny
Born on 2/6/1945 in Little Rock, Arkansas; raised in Oakland, California. R&B singer. Member of Tower Of Power from 1972-75.

WILLIAMS, Mason
Born on 8/24/1938 in Abilene, Texas. Folk guitarist/songwriter/author/photographer/TV comedy writer (*The Smothers Brothers Comedy Hour*, 1967-69; *Saturday Night Live*, 1980).

WILLIAMS, Maurice, & The Zodiacs
Born on 4/26/1938 in Lancaster, South Carolina. R&B singer. His group originally recorded as The Gladiolas; became The Zodiacs in 1959. Williams re-formed group with Wiley Bennett, Henry Gaston, Charles Thomas, Albert Hill and Little Willie Morrow in 1960.

WILLIAMS, Mike
Soul singer/songwriter.

WILLIAMS, Paul
Born on 9/19/1940 in Omaha, Nebraska. Singer/songwriter/actor. Wrote "We've Only Just Begun" and "Rainy Days & Mondays" with partner Roger Nichols, and co-wrote "Evergreen" with Barbra Streisand. Acted in several movies.

WILLIAMS, Paul
Born on 7/13/1915 in Lewisburg, Tennessee. Died of heart failure on 9/14/2002 (age 87). R&B saxophonist/bandleader.

WILLIAMS, Robbie
Born on 2/13/1974 in Port Vale, England. Pop-rock singer/songwriter. Former member of Take That.

WILLIAMS, Roger
Born Louis Weertz on 10/1/1924 in Omaha, Nebraska. Pianist. Learned to play piano by age three. Educated at Drake University, Idaho State University, and Juilliard School of Music. Took lessons from Lenny Tristano and Teddy Wilson. Win on the TV show *Arthur Godfrey's Talent Scouts* led to recording contract.

WILLIAMS, Tené
Born in Harlem, New York. Female R&B-dance singer.

WILLIAMS, Vanessa
Born on 3/18/1963 in the Bronx, New York; raised in Millwood, New York. R&B singer/actress. In 1983, became the first black woman to win the Miss America pageant; relinquished crown after *Penthouse* magazine scandal. Married to Ramon Hervey (manager of Babyface) from 1987-97.

Began hosting *Soul of VH-1* on the video music TV channel in 1991. Acted in several movies and Broadway shows. Married NBA player Rick Fox on 9/26/1999.

WILLIAMS BROTHERS, The
Twin nephews of Andy Williams: Andrew and David Williams. Born on 2/22/1959 in Henderson, Nevada.

WILLIAMSON, Sonny Boy
Born John Lee Williamson on 3/30/1914 in Jackson, Tennessee. Murdered during a robbery attempt on 6/1/1948 (age 34) in Chicago, Illinois. Blues singer/harmonica player. Not to be confused with next artist below.

WILLIAMSON, "Sonny Boy"
Born Aleck Ford on 12/5/1899 in Glendora, Mississippi. Died of tuberculosis on 5/25/1965 (age 65). Also known as Alex "Rice" Miller. Blues guitarist/harmonica player. Not to be confused with artist above.

WILLIE MAX
Female R&B vocal trio from Detroit, Michigan: sisters Rose, Sky and Lyric Smith.

WILLI ONE BLOOD
Born in Brooklyn, New York. White dancehall/reggae singer.

WILLIS, Bruce
Born Walter Bruce Willis on 3/19/1955 in Idar-Oberstein, West Germany; raised in Penns Grove, New Jersey. Played "David Addison" on TV's *Moonlighting*. Starred in the *Die Hard* movies and many others. Married to actress Demi Moore from 1987-2000.

WILLIS, Chuck
Born Harold Willis on 1/31/1928 in Atlanta, Georgia. Died of a bleeding ulcer on 4/10/1958 (age 30). R&B singer/songwriter. Billed as the "King of the Stroll" and known as the "Sheik of The Blues" for the turban he wore while performing.

WILL-O-BEES, The
Pop trio from New York: Janet Blossom, Steven Porter and Robert Merchanthouse.

WILLOWS
R&B doo-wop group formed in Harlem, New York: Tony Middleton (lead), Richard Davis, Ralph Martin, Joseph Martin (died on 2/19/2005, age 70) and Freddie Donovan (died on 5/13/1997).

WILLS, Mark
Born Daryl Mark Williams on 8/8/1973 in Cleveland, Tennessee; raised in Blue Ridge, Georgia. Country singer.

WILL TO POWER
Pop-dance trio from Florida: Bob Rosenberg, Dr. J. and Maria Mendez. Rosenberg is the son of singer Gloria Mann. By 1990, reduced to a duo of Rosenberg and Elin Michaels. Group name taken from the work of 19th-century German philosopher Friedrich Nietzsche.

WILMER & THE DUKES
R&B-soul group from Rochester, New York. Led by Wilmer Alexander Jr.

WILSON, Al
Born on 6/19/1939 in Meridian, Mississippi. Died of kindey failure on 4/21/2008 (age 68). R&B singer/drummer. Member of The Rollers from 1960-62.

WILSON, Ann
Born on 6/19/1951 in San Diego, California. Lead singer of the rock group Heart.

WILSON, Carl
Born on 12/21/1946 in Hawthorne, California. Died of cancer on 2/6/1998 (age 51). Guitarist of The Beach Boys. Married Dean Martin's daughter, Gina, on 11/8/1987.

WILSON, Charlie
Born in Tulsa, Oklahoma. R&B singer/songwriter. Member of The Gap Band. Nicknamed "Uncle Charlie" by Snoop Dogg.

WILSON, Gretchen
Born on 6/26/1973 in Granite City, Illinois; raised in Pocahontas, Illinois. Country singer/songwriter/guitarist.

WILSON, J. Frank
Born on 12/11/1941 in Lufkin, Texas. Died on 10/4/1991 (age 49). The Cavaliers: Sid Holmes (guitar), Lewis Elliott (bass) and Ray Smith (drums).

WILSON, Jackie
Born on 6/9/1934 in Detroit, Michigan. Died on 1/21/1984 (age 49). One of the all-time great soul singers; dubbed "Mr. Excitement." Sang with local gospel groups; became an amateur boxer. Worked as a solo singer until 1953, then joined Billy Ward And His Dominoes as Clyde McPhatter's replacement. Solo since 1957. Godfather of Jody Watley. Cousin of Hubert Johnson of The Contours. Wilson collapsed after suffering a stroke on stage at the Latin Casino in Cherry Hill, New Jersey on 9/29/1975; spent the rest of his life in nursing homes.

WILSON, Meri
Born on 6/15/1949 in Japan (father was a U.S. Air Force officer); raised in Marietta, Georgia. Died in a car crash on 12/28/2002 (age 53). Was the director of elementary education for Georgia.

WILSON, Nancy
Born on 2/20/1937 in Chillicothe, Ohio; raised in Columbus, Ohio. R&B/jazz-styled singer. Not to be confused with Nancy Wilson of Heart.

WILSON, Phill
Born on 6/19/1940 in Sidney, Ohio. Pop singer/songwriter/actor/playwright. Acted in the movies *Mischief, Teachers* and *The Unseen Force*.

WILSON BROS.
Pop duo: Steve and Kelly Wilson.

WILSON PHILLIPS
Pop-Adult Contemporary vocal trio formed in Los Angeles, California: sisters Carnie (born on 4/29/1968) and Wendy (born on 10/16/1969) Wilson, with Chynna Phillips (born on 2/12/1968). Carnie and Wendy's father is Brian Wilson (The Beach Boys). Chynna, the daughter of Michelle and

John Phillips (The Mamas & The Papas), acted in the movie *Caddyshack II*. Carnie became host of own TV talk show in 1995.

WILTON PLACE STREET BAND
Studio disco group assembled in Los Angeles, California, by producer Trevor Lawrence (who resided on Wilton Place in L.A.).

WINANS, BeBe & CeCe
Younger brother and sister of the Detroit gospel-singing family, The Winans: Benjamin "BeBe" and Priscilla "CeCe." They are the seventh and eighth children in a 10-sibling family.

WINANS, Mario
Born on 3/6/1979 in Orangeburg, South Carolina; raised in Detroit, Michigan. R&B singer/songwriter/keyboardist. Nephew of BeBe & CeCe Winans.

WINBUSH, Angela
Born in 1954 in St. Louis, Missouri. R&B singer/songwriter. One-half of Rene & Angela duo. Married Ronald Isley of The Isley Brothers on 6/26/1993.

WINCHESTER, Jesse
Born on 5/17/1944 in Shreveport, Louisiana. Pop singer/songwriter/guitarist.

WINDING, Kai
Born on 5/18/1922 in Aarhus, Denmark. Died on 5/6/1983 (age 60). Jazz trombonist. Moved to U.S. in 1934. With Benny Goodman and Stan Kenton in the mid-1940s.

WINEHOUSE, Amy
Born on 9/14/1983 in Southgate, London, England. Female R&B singer.

WING & A PRAYER FIFE & DRUM CORPS.
Disco studio group assembled by producer Harold Wheeler. Vocals by Linda November, Vivian Cherry, Arlene Martell and Helen Miles.

WINGER
Hair-metal band formed in New York: Kip Winger (vocals, bass), Reb Beach (guitar), Paul Taylor (keyboards; left in 1992) and Rod Morgenstein (drums). Kip was a member of Alice Cooper's band. Morgenstein was a member of Dixie Dregs.

WINGFIELD, Pete
Born on 5/7/1948 in Kiphook, Hampshire, England. Pop singer/keyboardist/producer. Also see Band Of Gold.

WINSTONS, The
R&B group from Washington DC: Richard Spencer (vocals), Ray Maritano (sax), Quincy Mattison (guitar), Phil Tolotta (organ), Sonny Peckrol (bass) and G.C. Coleman (drums). Toured as backup band for The Impressions.

WINTER, Edgar, Group
Born on 12/28/1946 in Beaumont, Texas. Rock singer/keyboardist/saxophonist. Younger brother of Johnny Winter. Group included Dan Hartman (1972-76), Ronnie Montrose (1972-74) and Rick Derringer (1974-76).

WINTER, Johnny
Born on 2/23/1944 in Leland, Mississippi.
Blues-rock singer/guitarist. Both Johnny and brother
Edgar Winter are albinos. A prominent 1960s
sessionman, Johnny toured with Muddy Waters and
was a member of The Traits.

WINTERHALTER, Hugo
Born on 8/15/1909 in Wilkes-Barre, Pennsylvania.
Died of cancer on 9/17/1973 (age 64). Conductor/
arranger for RCA Records from 1950-63. His
orchestra backed more artists (17), who had chart
hits, than any other conductor from 1940-54.

WINTERS, Ruby
Born in Louisville, Kentucky; raised in Cincinnati,
Ohio. R&B singer.

WINWOOD, Steve
Born on 5/12/1948 in Birmingham, England. Rock
singer/keyboardist/guitarist. Lead singer of Spencer
Davis Group, Blind Faith and Traffic.

WISEGUYS, The
Techno-rock duo from England: Regal and Touché.

WISIN & YANDEL
Latin reggae duo from Puerto Rico: Juan "Wisin"
Luna and Llandel "Yandel" Malavé.

WITCH QUEEN
Studio disco group produced by Peter Alves and
Gino Soccio.

WITHERS, Bill
Born on 7/4/1938 in Slab Fork, West Virginia. R&B
singer/songwriter/guitarist. Married to actress
Denise Nicholas.

WITHERSPOON, Jimmy
Born on 8/8/1923 in Gurdon, Arkansas. Died of
throat cancer on 9/18/1997 (age 74). Blues singer/
bassist. First recorded for Philo/Aladdin in 1945; has
recorded for over two dozen labels.

WITTER, Jimmy
Born on 1/5/1940 in Tampa, Florida. Died in
December 1974 (age 34). Pop singer.

WOLCOTT, Charles
Born on 9/29/1906 in Flint, Michigan. Died on
1/26/1987 (age 80). Pianist/composer/arranger.

WOLF
Born William Wolfer in Cheyenne, Wyoming.
Keyboardist/synthesizer/vocorder player.

WOLF, Peter
Born Peter Blankfield on 3/7/1946 in the Bronx, New
York. Lead singer of the J. Geils Band. Married to
actress Faye Dunaway from 1974-79. Not to be
confused with the producer of the same name.

WOMACK, Bobby
Born on 3/4/1944 in Cleveland, Ohio. R&B
singer/guitarist/songwriter. Sang in family gospel
group, the Womack Brothers. Group recorded for
SAR as The Valentinos and The Lovers, 1962-64.
Toured as guitarist with Sam Cooke. Backup
guitarist on many sessions, including Wilson Pickett,
The Box Tops, Joe Tex, Aretha Franklin and Janis
Joplin. Nicknamed "The Preacher." Married for a

time to Sam Cooke's widow, Barbara. Bobby's
brother, Cecil, married Sam Cooke's daughter,
Linda (recorded as Womack & Womack).

WOMACK, Lee Ann
Born on 8/19/1966 in Jacksonville, Texas. Country
singer.

WOMBLES, The
Pop studio group from England. Creation of
writer/producer/arranger Mike Batt. The Wombles
were furry characters seen on British TV.

WOMENFOLK, The
Female folk group from Pasadena, California:
Elaine Gealer, Joyce James, Leni Ashmore,
Barbara Cooper and Judy Fine. James died on
4/3/2001 (age 69).

WONDER, Stevie
Born Steveland Morris on 5/13/1950 in Saginaw,
Michigan. R&B singer/songwriter/multi-
instrumentalist/producer. Age 13 at the time of his
first hit. Blind since birth. Signed to Motown in 1960,
did backup work. First recorded in 1962, named
"Little Stevie Wonder" by Berry Gordy, Jr. Married
to Syreeta Wright from 1970-72. Near-fatal auto
accident on 8/16/1973. In the movies *Bikini Beach*
and *Muscle Beach Party*.

WONDER, Wayne
Born VonWayne Charles in Jamaica. Reggae
singer.

WONDER BAND, The
Disco studio group assembled by producers Silvio
Tancredi and Armando Noriega.

WONDERS, The
Fictitious band created for the movie *That Thing
You Do!* Jonathan Schaech is "Jimmy" (vocals),
Steve Zahn is "Lenny" (guitar), Ethan Embry is the
nameless bass-player and Tom Everett Scott is
"Guy" (drums). The actual recording is performed by
studio musicians, including lead singer Mike Viola.

WOOD, Bobby
Born on 1/25/1941 in Memphis, Tennessee.
Pop-country singer/songwriter/pianist.

WOOD, Brenton
Born Alfred Smith on 7/26/1941 in Shreveport,
Louisiana; raised in San Pedro, California. R&B
singer/songwriter/pianist.

WOOD, Lauren
Born in Pittsburgh, Pennsylvania. Pop singer/
songwriter/keyboardist.

WOODS, Stevie
Born in Columbus, Ohio. Male R&B singer/
songwriter. Son of jazz great Rusty Bryant.

WOOLEY, Sheb
Born Shelby Wooley on 4/10/1921 in Erick,
Oklahoma. Died of leukemia on 9/16/2003 (age 82).
Country singer/songwriter/actor. Played "Pete
Nolan" on the TV series *Rawhide*. Appeared in
several movies. Also made comical recordings
under pseudonym Ben Colder.

WOOLIES, The
Garage-rock band from East Lansing, Michigan: Stormy Rice (vocals), brothers "Boogie" Bob Baldori (piano, harmonica) and Jeff Baldori (guitar), with Ron English (bass) and Bill "Bee" Metros (drums).

WORLD CLASS WRECKIN CRU, The
Rap-funk group from Los Angeles, California: Alonzo Williams, Andre "Dr. Dre" Young, Antoine "Yella" Carraby, Shakespeare and Michelle "Michel'le" Toussant.

WORLD PARTY
Group is actually rock singer/keyboardist Karl Wallinger (born on 10/19/1957 in Prestatyn, Wales).

WORLEY, Darryl
Born on 10/31/1964 in Pyburn, Tennessee; raised in Savannah, Tennessee. Country singer/songwriter/guitarist.

WORTH, Marion
Born Mary Ann Ward on 7/4/1930 in Birmingham, Alabama. Died of emphysema on 12/19/1999 (age 69). Country singer.

WRAY, Bill
Born in Louisiana. Rock singer/songwriter.

WRAY, Link, & His Ray Men
Born Frederick Lincoln Wray on 5/2/1929 in Dunn, North Carolina. Died of a heart attack on 11/5/2005 (age 76). Rock and roll guitarist. The Ray Men: Link's brothers Doug (drums) and Vernon Wray (rhythm guitar), and Shorty Horton (bass).

WRECKERS, The
Country duo: Michelle Branch and Jessica Harp.

WRECKX-N-EFFECT
Male rap duo: Aquil Davidson and Markell Riley (brother of Teddy Riley of Guy).

WRIGHT, Betty
Born on 12/21/1953 in Miami, Florida. R&B singer. In family gospel group, Echoes Of Joy, from 1956. First recorded for Deep City in 1966. Hosted own local TV talk show in Miami.

WRIGHT, Charles
Born in 1942 in Clarksdale, Mississippi. R&B singer/songwriter/pianist/guitarist/producer. Leader of an eight-man R&B-funk band from the Watts section of Los Angeles, California. Evolved from the Soul Runners. Big break came through assistance by comedian Bill Cosby.

WRIGHT, Chely
Born Richelle Wright on 10/25/1970 in Kansas City, Missouri. Country singer/guitarist.

WRIGHT, Dale
Born Harlan Dale Riffe on 2/4/1938 in Middletown, Ohio. Rock and roll singer/songwriter. Worked as a DJ in the Midwest.

WRIGHT, Gary
Born on 4/26/1943 in Creskill, New Jersey. Pop-rock singer/songwriter/keyboardist. Appeared in *Captain Video* TV series at age seven. In the Broadway play *Fanny*. Co-leader of the rock group Spooky Tooth.

WRIGHT, O.V.
Born Overton Vertis Wright on 10/9/1939 in Leno, Tennessee. Died of heart failure on 11/16/1980 (age 41). Blues singer.

WRIGHT, Priscilla
Born in 1941 in London, Ontario, Canada. Teen pop singer.

WRIGHT, Ruby
Born on 1/8/1914 in Anderson, Indiana. Died on 3/9/2004 (age 90). Adult Contemporary singer. Sang on the *50-50 Club*.

WRIGHT, Samuel E.
Born on 11/20/1946 in Camden, South Carolina. Black actor/singer/voice-over artist. Appeared in several TV shows, movies and Broadway productions.

WU-TANG CLAN
Rap group from Staten Island, New York: Gary Grice (GZA/Genius), Clifford Smith (Method Man), Russell Jones (Ol Dirty Bastard; died of a drug overdose on 11/13/2004, age 35), Corey Woods (Raekwon), Jason Hunter (Inspektah Deck), Dennis Coles (Ghostface Killah), Lamont Hawkins (U-God), Robert Diggs (RZA) and Elgin Turner (Masta Killa). Diggs was also a member of Gravediggaz.

WYATT, Keke
Born Ketara Wyatt in Indianapolis, Indiana. Female R&B singer.

WYMAN, Bill
Born William Perks on 10/24/1936 in London, England. Bass guitarist of The Rolling Stones from 1962-92.

WYNETTE, Tammy
Born Virginia Wynette Pugh on 5/5/1942 in Itawamba County, Mississippi. Died of a blood clot on 4/6/1998 (age 55). Dubbed "The First Lady of Country Music." Married to George Jones from 1969-75.

WYNONNA
Born Christina Ciminella (her biological father was Charlie Jordan) on 5/30/1964 in Ashland, Kentucky. Country singer. One-half of The Judds duo with her mother, Naomi. Moved to Hollywood in 1968. Appeared in *More American Graffiti*. To Nashville in 1979. Naomi's chronic hepatitis forced duo to split at the end of 1991. Wynonna's half-sister is actress Ashley Judd.

X
Punk rock group formed in Los Angeles, California: Exene Cervenka (vocals), Billy Zoom (guitar), John Doe (bass) and Don Bonebrake (drums).

X-ECUTIONERS, The
Rap-DJ production group from Brooklyn, New York: Mista Sinista, Rob Swift, Total Eclipse and Roc Raida.

XSCAPE
Female R&B vocal group formed in Atlanta, Georgia: sisters Tamika (born on 8/5/1975) and LaTocha Scott (born on 10/2/1972), with Kandi Burruss (born on 5/17/1976) and Tameka Cottle (born on 7/14/1975).

XTC
Alternative-rock trio formed in Wiltshire, England: Andy Partridge (guitar), Dave Gregory (keyboards) and Colin Moulding (bass). All share vocals.

XYMOX
Techno-rock/dance trio formed in Amsterdam, Netherlands: Ronny Moorings (vocals, guitar, keyboards), Pieter Nooten (keyboards) and Anka Wolbert (bass, vocals, keyboards).

XZIBIT
Born Alvin Joiner on 9/18/1974 in Detroit, Michigan; raised in New Mexico. Male rapper.

YAKI-DA
Female pop-dance duo from Sweden: Linda Schonberg and Marie Knutsen.

YAMIN, Elliott
Born on 7/20/1978 in Los Angeles, California; raised in Richmond, Virginia. "Blue-eyed soul" singer/songwriter. Finalist on the fifth season of TV's *American Idol* in 2006.

Y&T
Hard-rock group from San Francisco, California: Dave Meniketti (vocals, guitar), Joey Alves (guitar), Philip Kennemore (bass) and Leonard Haze (drums). Band name stands for Yesterday & Today.

YANKEE GREY
Country group from Cincinnati, Ohio: Tim Hunt (vocals, guitar), Matt Basford (guitar), Joe Caverlee (fiddle), Jerry Hughes (keyboards), Dave Buchanan (bass) and Kevin Griffin (drums).

YANKOVIC, "Weird Al"
Born on 10/23/1959 in Lynwood, California. Novelty singer/accordionist. Specializes in song parodies. Starred in the movie *UHF*.

YARBROUGH, Glenn
Born on 1/12/1930 in Milwaukee, Wisconsin. Folk singer. Lead singer of The Limeliters (1959-63).

YARBROUGH & PEOPLES
Male-female R&B-funk duo from Dallas, Texas: Cavin Yarbrough and Alisa Peoples. Discovered by The Gap Band.

YARDBIRDS, The
Legendary rock group formed in Surrey, England: Keith Relf (vocals, harmonica; electrocuted on 5/14/1976, age 33), Anthony "Top" Topham and Chris Dreja (guitars), Paul "Sam" Samwell-Smith (bass, keyboards) and Jim McCarty (drums). Formed as the Metropolitan Blues Quartet at Kingston Art School. Topham replaced by Eric Clapton (10/'63 - 3/'65). Clapton replaced by Jeff Beck (3/'65-10/'66). Samwell-Smith left in 1966; Dreja switched to bass and Jimmy Page (guitar) was added (6/'66-7/'68). Group disbanded in July 1968. Page formed the New Yardbirds in October

1968, which evolved into Led Zeppelin. Relf and McCarty formed Renaissance in 1969. Relf later in Armageddon, 1975; McCarty in Illusion, 1977.

YARROW, Peter
Born on 5/31/1938 in Brooklyn, New York. Folk singer/songwriter/guitarist. Peter of Peter, Paul & Mary. Wrote Mary MacGregor's "Torn Between Two Lovers."

YASMEEN
Born in Los Angeles, California. Female R&B singer.

YASMIN
Born Yasmin Jacobsen on 6/6/1969 in Copenhagen, Denmark. Her mother is from the Faeroe Islands, and father is from Turkey.

YAYO, Tony
Born Marvin Bernard on 3/31/1978 in Queens, New York. Male rapper. Spent time in prison on weapons charges.

YAZ
Synth-dance duo from England: Genevieve Alison Moyet (vocals) and Vince Clarke (formerly of Depeche Mode; keyboards, synthesizers). Duo formerly named Yazoo. Clarke later formed Erasure, and Moyet went solo.

YAZZ & THE PLASTIC POPULATION
Male/female techno-dance vocal duo. Yazz is U.K. female singer Yasmin Evans (of Jamaican descent).

YEAH YEAH YEAHS
Punk-rock trio from Long Island, New York: Karen Orzolek (vocals), Nick Zinner (guitar) and Brian Chase (drums).

YEARWOOD, Trisha
Born Patricia Lynn Yearwood on 9/19/1964 in Monticello, Georgia. Country singer. Married to Robert Reynolds of The Mavericks from 1994-99. Married Garth Brooks on 12/10/2005.

YELLO
Computer/synthesizer-dance duo from Zurich, Switzerland: Dieter Meier and Boris Blank.

YELLOW BALLOON, The
Pop group formed in Los Angeles, California: Alex Valdez (vocals), Paul Canella (guitar), Frosty Green (keyboards), Don Braught (bass) and Don Grady (drums). Grady played "Robbie Douglas" on TV's *My Three Sons*.

YELLOWCARD
Punk-rock band from Jacksonville, Florida: Ryan Key (vocals, guitar), Sean Mackin (violin, vocals), Benjamin Harper (guitar), Alex Lewis (bass) and Longineu Parsons (drums). By 2006, Ryan Mendez replaced Harper and Peter Mosely replaced Lewis.

YELLOW MAGIC ORCHESTRA
Electronic instrumental trio from Japan: Ryuichi Sakamoto, Yukihiro Takahashi and Haruomi Hosono.

YES
Progressive-rock group formed in London, England: Jon Anderson (vocals; born on 10/25/1944; Jon & Vangelis), Peter Banks (guitar), Tony Kaye (keyboards; born on 1/11/1945), Chris Squire (bass; born on 3/4/1948) and Bill Bruford (drums; born on 5/17/1949). Banks, who went on to form Flash and After The Fire, was replaced by Steve Howe in 1971. Kaye (joined Badfinger in 1979) was replaced in 1971 by Rick Wakeman (born on 5/18/1949). Bruford left to join King Crimson; replaced by Alan White in late 1972. Wakeman replaced by Patrick Moraz in 1974; re-joined in 1976 when Moraz left. Wakeman and Anderson left in 1980; replaced by The Buggles' Trevor Horn (guitar) and Geoff Downes (keyboards). Group disbanded in 1980. Howe and Downes joined Asia. Re-formed in 1983 with Anderson, Kaye, Squire, White and South African guitarist Trevor Rabin. Anderson left group in 1988. Anderson, Bruford, Wakeman and Howe formed self-named group in early 1989.

YING YANG TWINS
Hip-hop duo from Atlanta, Georgia: Deongelo "D-Roc" Holmes (born on 2/13/1979) and Eric "Kaine" Jackson (born on 12/16/1978). They are not related.

YIPES!!
Rock group from Milwaukee, Wisconsin: Pat McCurdy (vocals), Andy Bartel and Mike Hoffmann (guitars), Pete Strand (bass) and Teddy Freese (drums).

YOAKAM, Dwight
Born on 10/23/1956 in Pikeville, Kentucky. Country singer/songwriter/actor. Appeared in several movies.

YORK, Bird
Born Kathleen York in New York. White female singer/songwriter/actress. Played "Andrea Wyatt" on TV's The West Wing.

YORK, Dave
Born David Kinzie on 7/22/1937 in Hammond, Indiana. The Beachcombers on "Beach Party" were Glen Campbell (guitar), Gary Paxton (piano), Steve Douglas (sax), Ray Polman (bass) and Jerry Reaple (drums).

YORK, Rusty
Born Charles Edward York on 5/24/1935 in Harlan, Kentucky. Rock and roll singer.

"YOU KNOW WHO" GROUP!, The
Studio band assembled by producer Bob Gallo.

YOUNG, Barry
Born in California. Male singer.

YOUNG, Faron
Born on 2/25/1932 in Shreveport, Louisiana. Died of a self-inflicted gunshot wound on 12/10/1996 (age 64). Country singer/guitarist. In movies The Young Sheriff, Daniel Boone and Hidden Guns. Founder and one-time publisher of the Music City News magazine in Nashville.

YOUNG, Georgie, & The Rockin' Bocs
Rock and roll backing band on Bobby Rydell's "Kissin' Time": Young (sax), Bob DeNardo (guitar), Bob McGraw (bass), Fred Bender (organ) and Pete Cozzi (drums).

YOUNG, John Paul
Born on 6/21/1950 in Glasgow, Scotland; raised in Sydney, Australia. Pop singer/songwriter/pianist.

YOUNG, Karen
Born on 3/23/1951 in Philadelphia, Pennsylvania. Died of a bleeding ulcer on 1/26/1991 (age 39). Disco singer.

YOUNG, Kathy, with The Innocents
Born on 10/21/1945 in Santa Ana, California. Teen pop singer. Married for a time to a member of The Walker Bros.

YOUNG, Neil
Born on 11/12/1945 in Toronto, Ontario, Canada. Rock singer/songwriter/guitarist. Joined Detroit rock band the Mynah Birds, featuring lead singer Rick James in 1965. To Los Angeles in 1966 and formed Buffalo Springfield. Went solo in 1969 with backing band Crazy Horse. Joined with Crosby, Stills & Nash, 1970-71. Appeared in the 1987 movie Made In Heaven. Reunited with Crosby, Stills & Nash in 1988 and again in 1999.

YOUNG, Paul
Born on 1/17/1956 in Bedfordshire, England. Pop-rock singer/songwriter/guitarist.

YOUNG, Victor
Born on 8/8/1900 in Chicago, Illinois. Died on 11/11/1956 (age 56). Conductor/composer/violinist. Wrote "Stella By Starlight," "My Foolish Heart," "Blue Star," and many others. Composed the movie score for Around The World In 80 Days.

YOUNG & RESTLESS
Rap duo from Miami, Florida: Charles Trahan (born on 8/24/1971) and Leon Johnson (born on 10/14/1971).

YOUNG BLACK TEENAGERS
White rap group from New York: Firstborn, Kamron, A.T.A. and DJ Skribble.

YOUNGBLOOD, Sydney
Born Sydney Ford in San Antonio, Texas. R&B singer.

YOUNGBLOODS, The
Folk-rock group formed in Boston, Massachusetts: Jesse Colin Young (born Perry Miller; vocals, bass), Lowell Levinger and Jerry Corbitt (guitars), and Joe Bauer (drums; died in 1982).

YOUNGBLOODZ
Rap duo from Atlanta, Georgia: "Sean Paul" Joseph (not to be confused with the same-named solo artist) and Jeffrey "J-Bo" Grigsby.

YOUNG BUCK
Born David Brown on 3/3/1981 in Nashville, Tennessee. Male rapper. Member of G-Unit.

YOUNG DRO
Born D'Juan Hart on 1/15/1979 in Atlanta, Georgia. Male rapper/songwriter.

YOUNG GUNZ
Male rap duo from Philadelphia, Pennsylvania: Chris "Young Chris" Ries and Hanif "Neef" Mohammad.

YOUNG HEARTS
R&B vocal group from Los Angeles, California: Ronald Preyer, Charles Ingersoll, Earl Carter and James Moore.

YOUNG-HOLT UNLIMITED
Soul-jazz instrumental group from Chicago, Illinois: Eldee Young (bass), Isaac "Red" Holt (drums; both of the Ramsey Lewis Trio) and Don Walker (piano). Walker left by 1968. Young died on 2/12/2007 (age 71).

YOUNG JEEZY
Born Jay Jenkins on 10/12/1977 in South Carolina; raised in Macon, Georgia. Male rapper/songwriter.

YOUNG M.C.
Born Marvin Young on 5/10/1967 in London, England; raised in Queens, New York. Rapper. Co-writer of Tone Loc's "Wild Thing" and "Funky Cold Medina." Graduated with economics degree from University of Southern California.

YOUNGSTOWN
"Boy band" from Youngstown, Ohio: Sammy Lopez, James Dallas and David Yeager.

YO-YO
Born Yolanda Whitaker on 8/4/1971 in Los Angeles, California. Female rapper.

YUNG BERG
Born Christopher Ward on 9/29/1985 in Chicago, Illinois. Male rapper.

YUNG JOC
Born Jasiel Robinson on 4/2/1983 in Atlanta, Georgia. Male rapper/songwriter.

YUNG WUN
Born James Anderson in Brooklyn, New York. Rapper.

YURO, Timi
Born Rosemarie Timotea Aurro on 8/4/1940 in Chicago, Illinois; raised in Los Angeles, California. Died on 3/30/2004 (age 63). White female soul singer.

YUTAKA
Born Yutaka Yokokura in Tokyo, Japan. Male jazz-pop keyboardist/singer.

YVONNE
Born Yvonne Garcia in the Bronx, New York; raised in Miami, Florida. Dance singer.

ZABACH, Florian
Born on 8/15/1921 in Chicago, Illinois. Violinist/ composer. Host of his own TV variety series in 1956.

ZACHARIAS, Helmut
Born on 1/27/1920 in Germany. Died of lung failure on 2/28/2002 (age 82). Violinist.

ZACHERLE, John, "The Cool Ghoul"
Born on 9/26/1918 in Philadelphia, Pennsylvania. Hosted horror movies on WCAU-TV in Philadelphia during the late 1950s.

ZADORA, Pia
Born Pia Schipani on 5/4/1954 in Hoboken, New Jersey. Singer/actress. Appeared in several movies.

ZAGER, Michael, Band
Born on 1/3/1943 in Passaic, New Jersey. Disco keyboardist/producer. Member of Ten Wheel Drive from 1968-73.

ZAGER & EVANS
Pop-folk duo from Lincoln, Nebraska: Denny Zager and Rick Evans (both sing and play guitar).

ZAHND, Ricky, & The Blue Jeaners
Born on 7/22/1946 in Manhattan, New York. Lawyer since 1972. From 1979-86, was vice president of the New York Knicks basketball team and the New York Rangers hockey team.

ZAPPA, Frank
Born on 12/21/1940 in Baltimore, Maryland; raised in California. Died of prostate cancer on 12/4/1993 (age 52). Rock music's leading satirist. Singer/ songwriter/guitarist/activist. Formed The Mothers Of Invention in 1965. In the movies *200 Motels* and *Baby Snakes*. Father of Dweezil and Moon Unit Zappa (both performed on the 1991 Peace Choir, "Give Peace A Chance"). Also see Missing Persons.

ZAVARONI, Lena
Born on 11/4/1963 in Rothesay, Scotland. Died of complications from anorexia nervosa on 10/1/1999 (age 35). Pre-teen singer.

ZEBRA
Rock trio from New Orleans, Louisiana: Randy Jackson (vocals, guitar), Felix Hanemann (bass) and Guy Gelso (drums).

ZELLA, Danny
Born on 7/31/1938 in Detroit, Michigan. Died on 1/27/2003 (age 64). Rock and roll singer/ saxophonist.

ZENTNER, Si
Born Simon Zentner on 6/13/1917 in Manhattan, New York. Died of leukemia on 1/31/2000 (age 82). Jazz trombonist.

ZEVON, Warren
Born on 1/24/1947 in Chicago, Illinois. Died of cancer on 9/7/2003 (age 56). Rock singer/ songwriter/pianist. Parents were Russian immigrants. Recorded with female vocalist Tule Livingston as the duo Lyme & Cybelle in 1966. Worked as the keyboardist/bandleader for The Everly Brothers, shortly before their breakup. Wrote Linda Ronstadt's "Poor Poor Pitiful Me." Recorded with three R.E.M. members as the Hindu Love Gods in 1990.

ZHANE
Female R&B-dance vocal duo from Philadelphia, Pennsylvania: Reneé Neufville and Jean Norris. Pronounced: jah-nay.

ZILL, Pat
Born in Columbus, Ohio. Male singer.

ZOMBIE, Rob
Born Robert Cummings on 1/12/1966 in Haverhill, Massachusetts. Founder of White Zombie. Wrote and directed the movies *House Of 1000 Corpses* and *The Devil's Rejects*. Older brother of Michael "Spider One" Cummings of Powerman 5000.

ZOMBIE NATION
Techno-rock/rave/dance group is actually German dance producer Gnork Zomb (aka Splank).

ZOMBIES, The
Rock group from Hertfordshire, England: Rod Argent (keyboards), Colin Blunstone (vocals), Paul Atkinson (guitar), Chris White (bass) and Hugh Grundy (drums). Disbanded in late 1967. Rod formed Argent in 1969. Atkinson died of liver failure on 4/1/2004 (age 58).

ZWOL
Born Walter Zwol in Canada. Pop-rock singer/songwriter.

ZZ TOP
Boogie-rock trio formed in Houston, Texas: Billy Gibbons (vocals, guitar; born on 12/16/1949), Dusty Hill (vocals, bass; born on 5/19/1949) and Frank Beard (drums; born on 6/11/1949). Gibbons had been lead guitarist in Moving Sidewalks, a Houston psychedelic-rock band. Hill and Beard had played in American Blues, based in Dallas. Group appeared in the movie *Back To The Future III*. Gibbons and Hill are the long-bearded members.